FLAVIUS JOSEPHUS

VOLUME 4

JUDEAN ANTIQUITIES BOOKS 5-7

FLAVIUS JOSEPHUS

TRANSLATION AND COMMENTARY

EDITED BY

STEVE MASON

VOLUME 4

JUDEAN ANTIQUITIES BOOKS 5-7

TRANSLATION AND COMMENTARY

BY

CHRISTOPHER BEGG

BRILL
LEIDEN · BOSTON
2005

This book is printed on acid-free paper.

Library of Congress Cataloging-in-Publication Data

Josephus, Flavius.
    [Antiquitates Judaicae. Liber 5-7. English]
    Flavius Josephus ; Judean antiquities books 5-7 / translation and commentary by
Christopher Begg.
        p. cm.
    Originally published as v. 4 of Flavius Josephus, translation and commentary
(Leiden ; Boston : Brill, 2001)
    Includes bibliographical references and index.
    ISBN 90-04-11785-7 (alk. paper)
    1. Jews—History—1200-953 B.C. 2. Bible. O.T. Joshua—History of Biblical
events—Early works to 1800. 3. Bible. O.T. Judges—History of Biblical events—Early
works to 1800. 4. Bible. O.T. Samuel—History of Biblical events—Early works to 1800. 5.
Josephus, Flavius. Antiquitates Judaicae. Liber 5-7. I. Begg, Christopher. II. Title.

DS121.55. J6713 2004
933—dc22

                                                                2004056640

ISBN   90 04 11785 7

PRINTED IN THE NETHERLANDS

To the memory of my beloved stepmother
Catherine Beck Fantom Begg (1923-2002)

CONTENTS

SERIES PREFACE

THE BRILL JOSEPHUS PROJECT

Titus (?) Flavius Josephus (37–ca. 100 CE) was born Joseph son of Mattathyahu, a priestly aristocrat in Judea. During the early stages of the war against Rome (66-74 CE), he found himself leading a part of the defense in Galilee, but by the spring of 67, his territory overrun, he had surrendered under circumstances that would furnish grounds for endless accusation. Taken to Rome by the Flavian conquerors, he spent the balance of his life writing about the war, Judean history and culture, and his own career. He composed four works in thirty volumes.

If Josephus boasts about the unique importance of his work (*War* 1.1-3; *Ant.* 1.1-4) in the fashion of ancient historians, few of his modern readers could disagree with him. By the accidents of history, his narratives have become the indispensable source for all scholarly study of Judea from about 200 BCE to 75 CE. Our analysis of other texts and of the physical remains unearthed by archaeology must occur in dialogue with Josephus' story, for it is the only comprehensive and connected account of the period.

Although Josephus' name has been known continuously through nearly two millennia, and he has been cited extensively in support of any number of agendas, his writings have not always been valued as compositions. Readers have tended to look beyond them to the underlying historical facts or to Josephus' sources. Concentrated study in the standard academic forms—journals, scholarly seminars, or indeed commentaries devoted to Josephus—were lacking. The past two decades, however, have witnessed the birth and rapid growth of "Josephus studies" in the proper sense. Signs of the new environment include all of the vehicles and tools that were absent before, as well as K. H. Rengstorf's *Complete Concordance* (1983), Louis Feldman's annotated bibliographies, and now a proliferation of Josephus-related dissertations. The time is right, therefore, for the first comprehensive English commentary to Josephus.

The commentary format is ancient, and even in antiquity commentators differed in their aims and methods. Philo's goals were not those of the author of Qumran's *Commentary on Nahum* or of the Church Father Origen. In order to assist the reader of this series, the Brill Project team would like to explain our general aims and principles. Our most basic premise is that we do not intend to provide the last word: an exhaustive exegesis of this rich corpus. Rather, since no commentary yet exists in English, we hope simply to provide a resource that will serve as an invitation to further exploration.

Although we began with the mandate to prepare a commentary alone, we soon realized that a new translation would also be helpful. Keeping another existing translation at hand would have been cumbersome for the reader. And since we must comment on particular Greek words and phrases, we would have been implicitly challenging such existing translations at every turn. Given that we needed to prepare a working translation for the commentary in any case, it seemed wisest to include it with the commentary as an efficient point of reference. A few words about the translation, then, are in order.

Granted that every translation is an interpretation, one can still imagine a spectrum of options. For example, the translator may set out to follow the contours of the original language more expressly or to place greater emphasis on idiomatic phrasing in the target language. There is much to be said for both of these options and for each interim stop in the spectrum. Accuracy is not necessarily a criterion in such choices, for one might gain precision in one respect (e.g., for a single word or form) only at the cost of accuracy elsewhere (e.g., in the sentence). Homer's epic poems provide a famous example of the problem: Does one render them in English dactylic hexameter, in looser verse, or even in prose to better convey the sense? One simply needs to make choices.

In our case, the course was suggested by the constraints of the commentary. If we were preparing a stand-alone translation for independent reading, we might have made other choices. And certainly if Josephus had been an Athenian poet, other considerations might have weighed more heavily. But Greek was his second or third language. His narratives are not great literature, and they vary in quality considerably from one part to another. Since the commentary bases itself upon his particular Greek words and phrases, it seemed necessary in this case that we produce a translation to reflect the patterns of the Greek as closely as possible. We can perhaps tolerate somewhat less clarity in the translation itself, where the Greek is ambiguous, because we intend it to be read with the commentary.

We happily confess our admiration for the Loeb translation, which has been the standard for some time, begun by Henry St. John Thackeray in the 1920s and completed by our colleague on the Brill Project (responsible for *Ant.* 1-4) Louis H. Feldman in 1965. For us to undertake a new translation implies no criticism of the Loeb in its context. The older sections of it are somewhat dated now but it still reads well, often brilliantly.

The chief problem with the Loeb for our purpose is only that it does not suit the needs of the commentator. Like most translations, it makes idiomatic English the highest virtue. It renders terms that Josephus frequently uses by different English equivalents for variety's sake; it often injects explanatory items to enhance the narrative flow; it collapses two or more Greek clauses into a single English clause; it alters the parts of speech with considerable freedom; and it tends to homogenize Josephus' changing style to a single, elevated English level. Since we have undertaken to annotate words and phrases, however, we have required a different sort of foundation. Our goal has been to render individual Greek words with as much consistency as the context will allow, to preserve the parts of speech, letting adjectives be adjectives and participles be participles, to preserve phrases and clauses intact, and thus to reflect something of the particular stylistic level and tone of each section.

Needless to say, even a determined literalness must yield to the ultimate commandment of basic readability in English. Cases in which we have relinquished any effort to represent the Greek precisely include Josephus' preference for serial aorist-participle clauses. Given the frequency of complicated sentences in Josephus, as among most of his contemporaries, we have dealt quite freely with such clauses. We have often broken a series

into separate sentences and also varied the translation of the form, thus: "After X had done Y," "When [or Once] X had occurred," and so on. Again, although in a very few cases Josephus' "historical present" may find a passable parallel in colloquial English, we have generally substituted a past tense. Thus we have not pursued literalness at all costs, but have sought it where it seemed feasible.

In the case of Josephus' personal names, we have used the familiar English equivalent where it is close to his Greek form. Where his version differs significantly from the one familiar to Western readers, or where he varies his form within the same narrative, we have represented his Greek spelling in Roman characters. That is because his unusual forms may be of interest to some readers. In such cases we have supplied the familiar English equivalent in square brackets within the text or in a footnote. Similarly, we keep Josephus' units of measurement and titles, giving modern equivalents in the notes.

We do not pretend that this effort at literalness is always more accurate than an ostensibly freer rendering, since translation is such a complex phenomenon. Further, we have not always been able to realize our aims. Ultimately, the reader who cares deeply about the Greek text will want to study Greek. But we have endeavored to provide a translation that permits us to discuss what is happening in the Greek with all of its problems.

The commentary aims at a balance between what one might, for convenience, call historical and literary issues. "Literary" here would include matters most pertinent to the interpretation of the text itself. "Historical" would cover matters related to the hypothetical reconstruction of a reality outside the text. For example: How Josephus presented the causes of the war against Rome is a literary problem, whereas recovering the actual causes of the war is the task of historical reconstruction. Or, understanding Josephus' Essenes is a matter for the interpreter, whereas reconstructing the real Essenes and their possible relationship to Qumran is for the historian—perhaps the same person, but wearing a different hat. These are not hermetically sealed operations, of course, but some such classification helps us to remain aware of the various interests of our readers.

To assist the reader who is interested in recovering some sense of what Josephus might have expected his first audience to understand, we have tried to observe some ways in which each part of his narrative relates to the whole. We point out apparently charged words and phrases in the narratives, which may also occur in such significant contexts as the prologues, speeches, and editorial asides. We look for parallels in some of the famous texts of the time, whether philosophical, historical, or dramatic, and whether Greco-Roman, Jewish, or Christian. We observe set pieces (*topoi*) and other rhetorical effects. Even apparently mundane but habitual features of Josephus' language and style are noted. Where puzzling language appears, we discuss possible explanations: rhetorical artifice, multiple editions, unassimilated vestiges of sources, the influence of a literary collaborator, and manuscript corruption.

A basic literary problem is the content of the text itself. Although we decided against preparing a new Greek edition as part of the project, we have paid close attention to textual problems in translation and commentary. The translation renders, essentially, Benedictus Niese's *editio maior*, since it remains the standard complete text with apparatus. But we have tried to take note of both the significant variants in Niese's own critical apparatus and other modern reconstructions where they are available. These include: the Loeb Greek text, the Michel-Bauernfeind edition of the *Judean War*, the current Münster project directed by Folker Siegert for Josephus's later works, and the ongoing French project led by Étienne Nodet. Niese's reconstructed text in the *editio maior* is famously conservative, and we have felt no particular loyalty to it where these others have proposed better readings.

Under the "historical" rubric fall a variety of subcategories. Most important perhaps are the impressive archaeological finds of recent decades in places mentioned by Josephus: building sites, coins, pottery, implements, inscriptions, and other items of material culture. Reading his stories of Masada or Herodium or Gamala is greatly enriched by observation of these newly identified sites, while in return, his narrative throws light on the history of those places. The commentary attempts to include systematic reference to the relevant archaeology. Other major historical categories include the problems of Josephus' own biography, his social context in Rome, and the historical reconstruction of persons, places, events, and social conditions mentioned by him. These issues can

only be explored by reference to outside texts and physical evidence. Alongside questions of interpretation, therefore, we routinely discuss such problems as they appear in particular passages.

In preparing a commentary on such a vast corpus, it is a challenge to achieve proportion. Some stretches of narrative naturally call for more comment than others, and yet the aesthetics of publication requires a measure of balance. We have attempted to maintain both flexibility and a broad consistency by aiming at a ratio between 4:1 and 8:1 of commentary to primary text. This commitment to a degree of symmetry (cf. *Ant.* 1.7!) has required us to avoid too-lengthy discussion of famous passages, such as those on Jesus or the Essenes, while giving due attention to easily neglected sections.

A different kind of challenge is posed by the coming together of ten independent scholars for such a collegial enterprise. To balance individual vision with the shared mission, we have employed several mechanisms. First is simply our common mandate: Having joined together to produce a balanced commentary, we must each extend ourselves to consider questions that we might not have pursued in other publishing contexts. Second, each completed assignment is carefully read by two experts who are not part of the core team, but who assist us in maintaining overall compliance with our goals. Third, each assignment is examined by the same general editor, who encourages overall consistency. Finally, for the *War* and *Antiquities* we use a system of double introductions: the general editor introduces each of Josephus' major works, to provide a coherent context for each segment; then each principal contributor also introduces his own assignment, highlighting the particular issues arising in that section. The *Life* and *Against Apion* have only one introduction each, however, because in those cases the individual assignment corresponds to the entire work.

Thus uniformity is not among our goals. Committees do not create good translations or commentaries. We have striven rather for an appropriate balance between overall coherence and individual scholarly insight—the animating principle of humanistic scholarship. The simple Greek word *Ioudaios* affords an example of the diversity among us. Scholars in general differ as to whether the English "Judean" or "Jew" comes closest to what an ancient Greek or Roman heard in this word, and our team members reflect that difference. Some of us have opted for "Judean" as a standard; some use both terms, depending upon the immediate context; and others use "Jew" almost exclusively. For the modern translator, as for Josephus himself, any particular phrase is part of an integrated world of discourse; to coerce agreement on any such point would violate that world. We hope that our readers will benefit from the range of expertise and perspective represented in these volumes.

It remains for the team members to thank some central players in the creation of this work, *amici* in scholarship whose names do not otherwise appear. First, many scholars in Josephan studies and related fields have offered encouragement at every step. Though we cannot name them all, we must express our debt to those who are reading our work in progress, without thereby implicating them in its faults: Honora Howell Chapman, David M. Goldenberg, Erich Gruen, Gohei Hata, Donna Runnalls, and Pieter van der Horst.

Second, we are grateful to the editorial staff at Brill for initiating this project and seeing it through so professionally. Elisabeth Erdman, Elisabeth Venekamp, Job Lisman, and Sam Bruinsma have proven extremely flexible and supportive as the project has evolved into something much larger than originally anticipated. They have raised even our enthusiasm with their energetic attention.

In addition to expressing the group's thanks to these fine representatives of a distinguished publishing house—not least in Josephan studies— I wish to record my personal gratitude to the Social Sciences and Humanities Research Council of Canada for its generous funding through a research grant (1998-2001), and to the Faculty of Arts at York University for a research-leave fellowship (1999-2000) to facilitate my involvement with the project.

Steve Mason, York University
General Editor, Brill Josephus Project

INTRODUCTION

This brief introduction will cover the entire segment of *Antiquities* that I have prepared, namely 5.1-10.185. The segment comprises the second fourth of Josephus' 20-book *opus*. It likewise covers a historical span of some 650 years (*ca.* 1240-585 BCE), during which time the Israelites lived as an independent nation on their land, from the occupation under Joshua through the deportations under Nebuchadnezzar that temporarily ended the people's life in the land. Within the lengthy period treated by 5.1-10.185 one can distinguish five major epochs, each with its distinctive form of government: 1) the entry into the land under the collective leadership of Joshua, Eleazar and the "senate" (5.1-119); 2) the age of the Judges (5.120-6.85); 3) the united monarchy of Saul, David, and Solomon (6.86-8.211); 4) the divided monarchy, ending with the demise of the northern kingdom (8.212-9.291); and 5) the later history and eventual destruction of the remnant southern kingdom (10.1-185). Of these five epochs it is the third, a period of about 100 years, in which Josephus displays the greatest interest; to it he assigns three fourths of Book 6, the whole of Book 7, and half of Book 8. Within his narrative of the united monarchy, in turn, it is the reign of David that receives the most attention, occupying the entire Book 7 with its 394 paragraphs.

In recounting his history in *Ant.* 5.1-10.185 Josephus had available and made greater or lesser use of three distinct blocs of biblical source material. Of these, he took as his primary source the so-called "Former Prophets" (the books Joshua through 2 Kings), which provided him with a continuous account of the entire period to be treated. In second place, he supplemented the narrative of the Former Prophets with additional material drawn from the Books of Chronicles, whose presentation in 1 Chronicles 10-2 Chronicles 36 runs parallel to that of 1 Samuel 31-2 Kings 25 for the period from the death of Saul to the fall of Jerusalem. Finally, Josephus also drew, albeit very selectively, on several books of the "Latter Prophets" (Isaiah-Malachi) set in the pre-exilic period— Jonah, Nahum, Isaiah, Jeremiah, and Ezekiel—even while making no mention of several other such books, namely, Hosea, Amos, Micah, Habakkuk, and Zephaniah.

In composing *Ant.* 5.1-10.185 Josephus did not, however, limit himself to the relatively extensive biblical material available to him. In eight different contexts of this segment one finds him either explicitly citing or alluding to an array of Gentile historians who provided corroboration of and/or supplementation to his Bible-based account.[1]

Still another source—though one more difficult to characterize with assurance—was the mass of traditions about biblical figures, events, laws, etc. that developed in turn-of-the-era Judaism and is now preserved in documents either contemporary with Josephus (e.g., the *Biblical Antiquities* of Pseudo-Philo) or later than his time (e.g., Rabbinic literature). All these varied sources are the raw materials for Josephus' new version of Israel's pre-exilic history in its land; he treats them all with considerable freedom in accordance with his own overarching interests and purposes.[2]

My translation of 5.1-10.185 is based, with minor exceptions, on the Greek text established well over a century ago by Benedict Niese.[3] In accord with the plan of the series, the translation aims to

---

[1] For a list of these references, see Bowley 1994: 205. They are: *Ant.* 7.101-103 (Nicolas of Damascus on Adads, kings of Damascus); 8.144-149 (Menander and Dios on the riddles of Solomon and Hiram); 8.157 (Herodotus on the Egyptian kings); 8.253,260 (Herodotus on Pharaoh Isok/Shishak); 8.324 (Menander on the Levantine drought); 9.283-287 (Menander on Shalmaneser's invasion of Phoenicia); 10.18-20 (Herodotus and Berosus on Sennacherib's invasion of Egypt); and

10.34 (Berosus on Balad, king of Babylon).

[2] On these, see Mason 2000: xxii-xxviv.

[3] Niese's text is itself based on a group of medieval manuscripts, of which he regards five as of particular significance, i.e. P (Codex Parisinus Gr 1419, 11th cent.); S (Codex Vindobenensis Historicus Graecus 20, 11th cent.) M (Codex Marcianus 381, 13th cent.); L (Codex Laurentianus 69.20, 14th century [I use the

provide a rather literalistic, straightforward rendering of Josephus' Greek. It likewise aims to translate Josephan key words, such as εὐδαιμονία ("well-being") and πρόνοια ("providence, providential
care"), in a consistent way so as highlight their occurrences also for readers without knowledge of
Greek. Given these aims, my translation lacks the verbal variety of that by R. Marcus in the relevant volumes (1934, 1937) of the Loeb Classical Library, even while it is greatly indebted to that
scholar's efforts.

In line with my previous publications, my commentary focuses on two overarching and interre-
lated questions. First, which text(s) of his biblical sources did Josephus use? In pursuing this question, I systematically point out instances of Josephus' agreement with distinctive readings of one
or other of the major biblical textual witnesses, i.e. the Masoretic Text (MT), the Septuagint or Old
Greek (LXX), and the Targum (Tg). Where (as happens, for example, with the codices Alexan-
drinus [A] and Vaticanus [B] in the Book of Judges[4] and with Vaticanus [B] and the Lucianic [L]
manuscripts in the Books of Samuel[5]) the LXX witnesses differ significantly among themselves,
I take note of this in my textual comparison as well.[6]

The second overarching question addressed in my commentary concerns the range of rewriting
techniques Josephus brings to bear on the biblical data. Under this head I call attention to the
numerous expansions, deletions, modifications, and re-arrangements that mark his presentation in
comparison with the Bible's own account. I further attempt to elucidate the reasons for and the
effect of these types of changes. With these two questions as its focus, the commentary also offers,
on a more limited basis, observations on Josephus' vocabulary, the similarities and differences
between his treatment of the biblical material and that found in the wider Jewish tradition (the
contemporary *Biblical Antiquities* of Pseudo-Philo, in particular), and Greco-Roman parallels.

It should be emphasized that my commentary is essentially a series of annotations on particular
points in Josephus' text. Given that character, the commentary does not claim to provide a sustained, comprehensive discussion of, for example, Josephus' portrayal of individual biblical figures or the line of thought in given passages. For such discussion, I constantly refer readers to the
two volumes of collected essays by Louis H. Feldman (1998, 1998a) on the Josephan portraits of
scriptural personages and my own monographs (1993, 2000) and articles (see bibliography) dealing with various portions of *Ant.* 5.1-10.185.

---

siglum Lau for this manuscript, given that I employ the
siglum L to designate the Lucianic manuscripts of the
LXX]); and O (Oxoniensis Bodleianus 186, 15th cent.).
In addition, Niese took into account the readings of 7
further manuscripts, the Latin translation (siglum: Lat)
originating in the 5th/6th centuries, several collections
of excerpts drawn from the *Antiquities* (i.e. the *Excerpta
Peiresciana* [Exc, 10th cent.], the Epitome [E, 10/11th
cents.] and the *Chronicon* of Zonaras [Zon, 12th cent.])
and the *Editio princeps* (*Ed. pr.*, printed in Basel in
1544). For more details on these witnesses, see Feldman
2000: xxvvii-xxviii; cf. also the siglum list in this volume, p. xix.

[4] On the differences between these two major LXX
witnesses for the Book of Judges, see Harlé 1999: 25-
27.

[5] On the distinctive text of the group of Greek witnesses to the Books of Samuel designated collectively
as the Lucianic [L] manuscripts given their traditional
association with a recension of the LXX developed by

the Christian martyr Lucian of Samosata (d. 311/312),
see Fernández Marcos and Busto Saiz 1989: xv-lxxxix.
The Lucianic manuscripts in Samuel are of particular
interest in that Josephus often agrees with their readings as against those of MT and/or LXX B; see ibid,
xxxv-xxviii.

[6] Mention should be made here of several terms/
indications used in my textual comparison between
Josephus and the biblical witnesses. I use the term
"plus" to refer to an element that is present in one witness (e.g., the MT), but absent in another (e.g., the
LXX). The > sign indicates that a particular textual element is absent in a given witness. An asterisk following a siglum (e.g., L*) calls attention to the fact that
only some representatives of the text designated by that
siglum exhibit the reading in question. Finally, I employ Roman (i.e. "a" and "b") and Greek (α and β) letters to indicate the component sense units and sub-units
of biblical verses, thus Josh 1:1aα.

It remains to offer a word of thanks to those persons most directly involved in the evolution and final appearance of this work: my editor Steve Mason (whose constructive criticism greatly improved both the translation and commentary), Joseph E. Jensen (who assisted with computer issues and the indexes), and the staff of Brill Academic Press (whom I kept waiting for a long time).

ACKNOWLEDGEMENTS

Revised Standard Version of the Bible, copyright 1952 by the Division of Christian Education of the National Council of the Churches of Christ in the United States of America. Used by permission. All rights reserved.

The text and translation of Pseudo-Philo, *Biblical Antiquities* is taken from Howard Jacobson, *A Commentary on Pseudo-Philo's* Liber Antiquitatum Biblicarum *with Latin Text and English Translation*, Vol. 1. Leiden: Brill, 1996. Used by permission.

All texts and translations of Greco-Roman works are taken from the LCL edition.

SIGLA[1]

[1] The sigla used for journals and monograph series, etc. are those prescribed in Alexander et al.: 1999.

I. *Biblical Sigla*

A	Codex Alexandrinus of the LXX
B	Codex Vaticanus of the LXX
L	The Lucianic Manuscripts of the LXX
LXX	The (original) Greek Translation of the Hebrew Bible
MT	The Massoretic Text of the Hebrew Bible
OL	The Old Latin Translation of the Bible
Tg.	The Targum (Aramaic Translation of the Bible)
Vulg.	The Vulgate (Latin) Translation of the Bible
4QSam[a]	A Samuel Manuscript from Qumran, cave 4

II. *Josephan Sigla*

E	Epitome (10th-11th cents.)
Ed. pr.	*Editio princeps* (first printed edition, 1544)
Exc	Excerpta Peiresciana (10th cent.)
Lat	Latin translation (original, 6th cent.)
Lau	Codex Laurentianus (14th cent.)
M	Codex Marcianus (Venetus) (13th cent.)
O	Codex Oxoniensis (15th cent.)
P	Codex Parisinus G 1419 (11th cent.)
R	Codex Regius Parisinus (14th cent.)
S	Codex Vindobonensis (11th cent.)
V	Codex Vaticanus (13th-14th cents.)
Zon	Zonaras' *Chronicon* (12th cent.)

JOSEPHUS, *JUDEAN ANTIQUITIES*

BOOK FIVE

(1.1) 1. When Moyses had departed from humanity in the manner told above and all the prescribed [rites] for him had come to an end and the mourning had been concluded,[1] Iesous[2] instructed the crowd to be ready for a campaign.[3]

Transition: Moses to Joshua

2. He sent spies[4] into Jericho[5] to ascertain its strength and state of mind, while he himself was mustering the army so that afterwards he might lead it over the Jordan.[6]

Spies dispatched

3. Having called up the rulers of the tribe of Roubel and the chiefs of those of Gad and Manassitis (for half of this tribe had been allowed to settle in Amoria, this being a seventh part of the land of the Chananaians[7]), he reminded them of what they had promised Moyses.[8] **4.** He further appealed to them, out of regard for that man's care for them that had not waned even as he was dying[9] and of the common advantage, to do with eagerness what they had been instructed.[10] With them following,[11] he set out with 50,000[12] troops from Abele[13] to the Jordan,[14] a distance of 60 *stadia*.[15] **(1.2) 5.** Immediately upon his pitching camp, the spies arrived, not at all ignorant about how things stood with the Chananaians.[16] For, initially undetected,

Transjordanians exhorted

Spies in Jericho

---

[1] This transitional notice elaborates on the opening words of Josh 1:1 ("after the death of Moses the servant of the Lord...") and recapitulates the account of Moses' end given in *Ant.* 4.323-331.

[2] On Josephus' portrait of Joshua overall see Feldman 1998: 443-60; Spilsbury 1998: 147-50.

[3] In proceeding directly from his notice on the death of Moses (// Josh 1:1a) to Joshua's address to the people (// 1:10-11), Josephus passes over God's extended opening speech to him of Josh 1:1b-9. On the phenomenon of "detheologizing" throughout Josephus' version of the Book of Joshua, see Feldman 1998: 453-57.

[4] Josh 2:1 specifies that there were 2 spies. Rabbinic tradition identifies the pair as Caleb and Phineas, or alternatively, as Perez and Zerah; see Ginzberg 1913: 4-5; 1928: 171, n. 10. Pseudo-Philo (*Bib. Ant.* 20.6) makes them Caleb's sons Cenaz and Naam.

[5] In the Book of Joshua the dispatch of the spies (2:1) follows the exchange between the leader and the Transjordanian tribes (1:12-18). Josephus reverses this sequence.

[6] The above indications concerning the purpose of Joshua' dispatching the spies and what he himself will do during their absence are Josephus' additions to Josh 2:1.

[7] This parenthetical notice recalls Josephus' account of Moses' awarding "Amoritis" to the 2 and 1/2 tribes in *Ant.* 4.166-171 (see Numbers 32). Marcus (*ad loc.*) follows Weill in suggesting that Josephus derives his qualification of "Amoria" as constituting a 7th part of the Canaanite country from the mention of the Amorites in the list of 7 peoples living in the land before the Israelites' arrival in Josh 3:10, etc.

[8] In Josh 1:13 Joshua reminds the Transjordanians rather of Moses' own word to them. On the Transjordanians' promise to Moses; see *Ant.* 4.170.

[9] This proposed motivation for the Transjordanians' acting on their promise to Moses is Josephus' addition to Joshua's words in Josh 1:14-15. The chronological indication in *Ant.* 4.165 dates Moses' granting their lands to the Transjordanians (4.166-171) to the time when he "was already an old man."

[10] The above exhortation represents a generalization of the more specific directives Joshua gives the Transjordanians in Josh 1:14-15.

[11] This allusion to the Transjordanians' "following" Joshua is a narrative transposition of their words pledging support for him in Josh 1:16-18.

[12] According to Josh 4:13 *40,000* armed Israelites crossed the Jordan.

[13] In Josh 3:1 the Israelites depart from "Shittim." Josephus' name for the departure site corresponds to the opening component of its full biblical designation, i.e. "Abel-shittim" (see Num 33:49). In *Ant.* 4.176 the site is called "Abile"; see Feldman 2000 *ad loc.*

[14] In mentioning Israel's advance at this point, Josephus reverses the sequence of Josh 3:1 and 2:2-24 where the spy story precedes the Israelites' move to the Jordan.

[15] This indication has no biblical equivalent. The *stadion* equals 606 3/4 English feet; see LSJ *s.v.*

[16] This notice on the spies' return (see Josh 2:23) picks up on the mention of their dispatch in 5.2, following the account of Joshua's initiatives during their time away in 5.3-4 (see Josh 1:12-18; 3:1). It employs the literary device of the *litotes*, in which a positive

they had inspected their entire city at their ease, noting which of the walls were strong and which did not have this capacity for security, as well as which of the small gates would be suitable, given their weakness, for entry by the army. **6.** Those who encountered them ignored their looking about, attributing their careful examination of everything in the city to that curiosity natural to foreigners, rather than to a hostile mindset.[17]

Spies endangered   **7.** When evening came they repaired to a certain inn[18] near the wall,[19] which they entered for supper. Then when their sole thought was for their departure,[20] **8.** the king was informed during supper[21] that certain men who had come from the camp of the Hebrews[22] in order to spy out the city were now in the inn of Raabe,[23] greatly concerned about being discovered.[24] He immediately sent [men] to them, directing these to arrest them and bring them up to him,[25] so that, by subjecting them to torture, he might find out why they had come and what they wanted.[26]

Rahab saves   **9.** Now since she was drying armfuls of flax on the wall, Raabe, when she learned
spies   of their approach, hid the spies in these,[27] while to those sent by the king she said that some unknown strangers had come and, after having supper at her place a little before sunset,[28] had departed.[29] If, however, they seemed a source of fear for the city or if their coming brought danger for the king,[30] they could easily capture them by pursuing them.

("they knew all about") is expressed by means of a negative.

[17] The whole above sequence lacks a counterpart in Joshua 2 where, immediately upon entering the city, the spies repair (v. 1b) to Rahab's house. The insertion makes clear that the spies did indeed carry out Joshua's directive (see 5.2) that they reconnoiter the city, and provides an explanation of how they were able to do this without impediment, i.e. the inhabitants did not realize they were spies, taking them rather for curious tourists.

[18] In Josh 2:1b (MT and LXX) the spies go to the house of the "harlot" Rahab. Josephus' designation of her establishment corresponds to one meaning ("inn-keeper") of the Aramaic term פונרקיתא used of Rahab's profession in the Tg. of Josh 2:1b (the term also, however, may have the sense of "harlot"; see Levy *s.v.*) In *Ant.* 3.276 Josephus states that priests may not marry "inn-keepers," a prohibition not otherwise paralleled in Jewish tradition; see Feldman 2000 *ad loc.*

[19] Josephus anticipates this specification about the location of Rahab's residence from Josh 2:15.

[20] Josh 2:1b speaks of the spies' "lodging" at Rahab's house, thus seeming to envisage a longer stay for them.

[21] This indication about what the king was doing when he received the report about the spies lacks a counterpart in Josh 2:2; it recalls the mention of the spies themselves entering Rahab's place "for supper" in 5.7.

[22] On Josephus' use of the designation "Hebrews," see Harvey 1996: 124-29; Spilsbury 1998: 36-42.

[23] MT (Josh 2:1, etc.) רהב (Eng.: "Rahab"); LXX Ῥαάβ; Josephus Ῥαάβη.

[24] In Josh 2:2 the king is told only that men have come to spy out "the land," not their actual whereabouts within the city. In having him supplied with this additional information, Josephus accounts for the king's knowing where to send those who are to arrest the spies in what follows.

[25] In Josh 2:3a the king, through his messengers, commands Rahab herself to bring forth the spies.

[26] The above statement by the king concerning his intentions in having the interlopers brought before him replaces the declaration he instructs his men to make to Rahab in Josh 2:3b, i.e. the Israelites have come to spy out the land.

[27] In Josh 2:4a and 6 there is a double reference to Rahab's concealing the spies, separated by her words to the king's men in 2:4b-5. Josephus first conflates the data of 2:4a and 6, and then has "Raabe" address the royal messengers. Niese reads "wall" here with the majority of the witnesses, whereas Marcus (*ad loc.*) follows the reading "roof" of E, which itself corresponds to the mention of the "roof" in Josh 2:6.

[28] This reference, echoing the wording of 5.7, lacks a basis in Rahab's report to the royal messengers in Josh 2:4b.

[29] Josephus omits Rahab's further statement (Josh 2:5a) that the spies had left at dusk when the city gate was about to be shut.

[30] These suggested motivations for a pursuit of the spies are an addition to Rahab's "pursuit command" in Josh 2:5b.

10. Now they, hoodwinked by the woman in this way and suspecting no deception, went away without searching the inn.[31] They then rushed over those roads they supposed them especially likely to have taken[32] and those leading to the river. But finding no trace of them, they ceased their effort.[33]

11. When the uproar had subsided, Raabe brought the men down[34] and told them of the danger that she had undergone for the sake of their safety; for, if she had been caught hiding them, she would not have escaped punishment by the king, but, along with all her household, would have been harshly executed.[35] **12.** She appealed to them, when they had subjugated and were ruling over the land of the Chananaians[36] to remember to repay her, once they would be able, for their present safety. She directed them to go back to their fellows,[37] after they had sworn to save her and her household when, having taken the city by storm, they would annihilate all those within it in accordance with the decision they had taken.[38] For she knew of these matters, having been instructed by signs from God.[39]

13. [The spies] declared their thanks to her for her present help[40] and swore that they would repay her by their deeds in the future.[41] They advised, however,[42] that, when she perceived that the city was about to be captured, to place her possessions and all her household inside the inn and shut them in; she was also to extend red cloths[43] before the doors, so that knowing the house, the general[44] might keep from harming it.[45] **14.** "For we will inform him," they said, "that we were saved due to

Rahab—spies exchange

---

[31] This notice on the effect of Rahab's words on the king's men and their non-search of her establishment is Josephus' amplification of Josh 2:7.

[32] This specification about the pursuers' route is Josephus' insertion.

[33] Josephus anticipates this notice on the unsuccessful outcome of the pursuit from Josh 2:22b. Conversely, he omits the mention of the shutting of the city gate following the pursuers' exit in 2:7b.

[34] In Josh 2:8 Rahab speaks to the spies on the roof itself. In having her first bring the men down into her house, Josephus makes her exchange with them occur in a more secure setting.

[35] This opening component of Rahab's speech in Josephus' version is an anticipation (and amplification) of her subsequent allusion (see Josh 2:12) to her having "dealt kindly" with the spies.

[36] Josephus derives this item from the opening words ("I know that the Lord has given you the land") of Rahab's extended "theological confession" in Josh 2:9-11, the rest of which he leaves aside, likely finding it implausible in the mouth of a pagan (see, however, the note to "God" at 5.12).

[37] Josephus anticipates this item from Rahab's subsequent, 2nd speech to the spies; cf. Josh 2:16.

[38] Josephus here amplifies Rahab's plea at the end of Josh 2:13: "deliver our lives from death." Her mention of the Israelites' prior "decision" to annihilate Jericho's inhabitants recalls Moses' instruction in *Ant.* 4.300 that the "race of the Chananaians"— to which the people of Jericho belonged—were to

be "obliterated utterly."

[39] This concluding statement by Josephus' Rahab picks up on her opening affirmation (Josh 2:9) about her "knowing" of the Lord's intentions. It also provides a suggestion as to how the pagan foreigner Rahab obtained such knowledge. As to the nature of the "signs" to which Rahab alludes here, Marcus (*ad loc.*) suggests that these might be the miracles God had done for the Israelites as cited by Rahab in 2:10. On the word "sign" (Greek: σημεῖον) and related terms for "miracles" in Josephus, see Remus 1982: 543-44.

[40] This opening word of recognition for Rahab's services is Josephus' amplification of the spies' word to her in Josh 2:14.

[41] Joshua 2 does not explicitly recount the spies' act of "swearing" to Rahab; cf., however, the allusions to this in vv. 12, 17, 20. Josephus omits the spies' warning to Rahab about betraying their secret in 2:14b (and its recapitulation in 2:20).

[42] Josephus anticipates the spies' "advice" to Rahab from their subsequent, 2nd exchange with her in Josh 2:18.

[43] In Josh 2:18 the spies propose the use of a scarlet "cord" by Rahab. "Cloths" would be more visible to the attackers.

[44] On Josephus' characteristic (and non-biblical) title of στρατηγός ("general") for Joshua, see Feldman 1998: 448.

[45] This indication about the intended purpose of the prescribed signal is Josephus' amplification of the spies' words in Josh 2:18.

your eagerness. If, however, anyone of yours should fall in the battle, you will have no cause to reproach us,[46] and we ask the God by whom we have sworn not to be displeased, as if with transgressors of their oaths."[47]

Spies return   **15.** Once they had agreed to these things, they went off by way of the wall, letting themselves down by a rope.[48] When they had safely reached their fellows,[49] they disclosed to them what they had done when they came to the city.[50] Iesous related to the high priest Eleazar[51] and the senate what the spies had sworn to Raabe, and they approved the oath.[52]

Jordan crossed   **(1.3) 16.** Now, although the army was anxious about the crossing because the river had a powerful current and was not passable by bridges—for it had not been spanned in the past, and if they wanted to lay bridges now, they assumed that they would not enjoy the leisure to do so from their enemies, and they happened to have no ferries—,[53] God promised them that he would make the river crossable by diminishing its magnitude.[54]

17. After waiting two days,[55] Iesous led the army and the entire crowd across in this way: the priests with the ark went first,[56] then the Levites bringing the tent and the implements used in the sacrificial service. The whole populace followed the Levites[57] according to their tribes; they had the children and women in the middle,

---

[46] Josephus spells out the meaning of the figurative phrase "his [i.e. the member of Rahab's household who fails to remain inside] blood shall be upon his head" used by the spies in their address to Rahab in Josh 2:19a.

[47] This appeal to God replaces the spies' acknowledgement (Josh 2:19b) that they will indeed be liable, should anyone of Rahab's relatives who remains in her house be harmed.

[48] In Josh 2:15 it is Rahab who lets the spies down. As they are on the point of descending a second exchange between her and them occurs (2:16-21a), which Josephus omits, having incorporated elements of it into his version of their preceding conversation.

[49] Josephus leaves aside the spies' preliminary wait in the hills (Josh 2:22) until the Jericho pursuers have abandoned the search for them (as also Rahab's instruction about this in 2:16), since, in his presentation, the pursuers have come back empty-handed even before the spies exit Jericho; see 5.10. Josephus has already anticipated mention of the spies' own return in 5.5.

[50] In Josh 2:23 the spies report to Joshua alone. Josephus leaves aside the returned spies' statement about the Lord's having given Israel the land and the inhabitants' faintheartedness of Josh 2:24, which itself alludes back to Rahab's word about the inhabitants "melting away" before the Israelites in 2:9, likewise omitted by him. On Josephus' down-playing of the biblical promises of the land as a response to the contemporary Zealots' efforts to regain the land, see Amaru: 1980-1981; 1994: 95-115.

[51] Josephus has reported the succession of Eleazar

as high priest in place of his dying father Aaron in *Ant.* 4.83 (// Num 20:28).

[52] Joshua's submitting matters to these other organs of governance for their ratification is Josephus' addition; similar such additions elsewhere serve to accentuate Joshua's piety; see Feldman 1998: 452-53. On the "senate" (Greek: γερουσία; alternative translation: "council of the elders") as the retrojection by Josephus of a much later institution into the time of Moses and Joshua, see Goodblatt 1994: 30-43, 90-99 and Mason 2003: 573-81.

[53] The whole above sequence has no biblical basis. It functions to explain why a supernatural intervention, as spoken of in what follows, was needed to get the people across the Jordan.

[54] In Josh 3:13b it is Joshua—speaking in God's name (see 3:9)—who assures the people that the Jordan's waters will "stand in a heap."

[55] Cf. Josh 3:2, "at the end of *three* days." In proceeding directly to the actual crossing here, Josephus passes over the various preliminary directives issued by the "officers" (3:2-3), Joshua (3:5-6), God (3:7-8), and Joshua speaking for God (3:9-13).

[56] See Josh 3:14.

[57] This mention of the Levites—as distinct from the priests—and the sacral objects they carry is Josephus' addition. The insertion harks back to *Ant.* 3.258 (cf. Num 3:8), where Moses entrusts "the Tent and the sacred vessels" to the Levites. The insertion is noteworthy given Josephus' overall tendency to downplay the Levites' role in his retelling of biblical history (on which see Glessmer 1994: 139, 148-51).

anxious that they not to be carried away by the current.[58]

18. Now when the river seemed passable to the priests, who had entered first—for its depth had been lowered and the river-gravel, which the current was not strong or swift enough to carry off by force from beneath them, lay like solid ground—[59] all now confidently entered the river, recognizing that it was just as God had predicted he would make it.[60] **19.** The priests remained standing in the middle of it until the crowd had crossed and securely reached dry ground. When all had crossed,[61] the priests came out, leaving the current now free to flow as usual. As soon as the Hebrews had left it behind them, the river swelled and regained its normal size.[62]

(1.4) 20. When they had advanced fifty *stadia*, they pitched camp ten *stadia* from Jericho.[63] Iesous, having erected an altar from the stones that each of the tribal rulers had picked up from the river-bed in accordance with the prophet's directions[64] as a future memorial of the stoppage of the current, sacrificed to God on it.[65] They also celebrated the *Phaska* in that region,[66] **21.** being now well and readily provided for with all those things they had earlier lacked.[67] For they harvested the grain of the Chananaians that was already ripe[68] and, in addition, carried off plunder.[69] For at that time the manna food that they had used for forty years likewise ceased.[70]

Initial events in land

---

[58] This specific mention of the women and children and of the people's fear for their safety is Josephus' addition.

[59] Josephus here downplays the marvelous character of the event as described in Josh 3:15-16a, in which the waters above the transit site are heaped up at "Zamah," while those below the site cease to flow.

[60] The people's confidence—in contrast to their earlier anxiety (see 5.16-17)—and the allusion to God's promise as cited in 5.16 are Josephus' additions to Josh 3:16b.

[61] See Josh 3:17.

[62] See Josh 4:18. In thus combining his version of 3:17 (see previous note) and 4:18, Josephus passes over the whole intervening sequence, 4:1-17: erection of 12 memorial stones in the Jordan itself (4:1-10); the Transjordanians' leading the crossing (4:12-13), the Lord's exaltation of Joshua (4:14), and Joshua's directing the priests, in the Lord's name, to come out of the Jordan (4:15-17).

[63] Josephus supplies the 2 distance specifications in his version of Josh 4:19, from which, conversely, he omits—for the moment (but see 5.34)—the name of Israel's initial campsite, i.e. "Gilgal."

[64] See Josh 4:20-24 (the erection of the stones and their significance). Josephus derives his mention of Joshua's "directions" about the picking up of the stones from the Jordan from Josh 4:5 (earlier passed over by him), where Joshua, speaking for the Lord (cf. 4:3), enjoins the tribal leaders to do this. Elsewhere too Josephus gives Joshua the "unbiblical" title "prophet"; see *Ant.* 3.165, 311, and cf. Feldman 1998: 447.

[65] Josh 4:20-24 does not qualify the erected stones

as an "altar" or speak of sacrifice on them. Josephus' addition of these items might reflect the influence of Deut 27:1-8 (cf. *Ant.* 4.305), where Moses prescribes (27:2) the erecting of stones, the building of an altar, and sacrifice on Mt. Ebal on the day (see 27:1) that Israel crosses the Jordan.

[66] See Josh 5:10, from which Josephus omits the specification that the feast was celebrated on the 14th day of the month. In combining mention of the memorial stones (Josh 4:20-24) and the Passover celebration (5:10), Josephus passes over the biblical notices on the fear of the Canaanite kings (5:1) and Joshua's circumcision of the Israelites (5:2-9). His reason for omitting the latter passage might be that, in its tacit admission that the younger Israelite generation had not been circumcised during the desert wanderings (see vv. 5, 7), it reflects badly on his people and their adherence to a central requirement of the Law; see Spilsbury 1998: 149, n. 14. For his possible subsequent use of the notice of 5:1, see 5.22.

[67] This notice on the advantages that the Israelites finally acquired upon entering the land is a Josephan insertion. It represents an implicit fulfillment of the biblical Moses' promises about the good things awaiting the people in the promised land as cited in such passages as Deut 8:7-9; 11:8-12.

[68] See Josh 5:11, 12b.

[69] The Book of Joshua does not mention the Israelites' acquiring "plunder" already at this point.

[70] See Josh 5:12a, which does not mention the length of time the manna was given to the people. Josephus supplies the same figure for the duration of the manna in *Ant.* 3.32 (// Exod 16:35).

(1.5) 22. Since while the Israelites were doing these things[71] the Chananaians did not march out, but, protected by their walls, remained inactive,[72] Iesous decided to besiege them.[73] On the first day of the feast,[74] as the priests were carrying the ark, a certain contingent of troops was in a circle around it, guarding it.[75] **23.** Seven [other priests] went ahead, blowing their horns[76] and appealing to the army's prowess.[77] They walked around the walls with the senate following.[78] The priests merely blew the horns; having done no more than this, they returned to the camp.[79]

24. After they had done this for six days,[80] on the seventh day, Iesous assembled the body of troops and the entire people and announced the good news of the capture of the city to them. On that very day, God would bring this about for them: the walls would collapse of themselves, without any exertion on their part.[81] **25.** He appealed to them, however, to kill everyone whom they might take, and neither give up the slaughter of their enemies because they were tired, nor by yielding to pity, nor, in their concern for plunder, to overlook their fleeing foes. **26.** They were rather to destroy all living things,[82] not taking these for their own benefit.[83] Whatever silver or gold there might be, he directed them to gather this together as a choice first-fruits [offering] of the spoils to keep for God from the capture of the city as the one they had first taken by storm.[84] They were to save only Raabe and her family be-

---

[71] This transition to the story of the fall of Jericho (Joshua 6) replaces the episode of Joshua's encounter with the "commander of the army of the Lord" (Josh 5:13-15) that Josephus simply omits, perhaps because it has no further function in the subsequent story, ending as it does with Joshua merely being told to remove his shoes (see 5:15).

[72] In Josh 6:1 the reference is to Jericho's being "shut up from within and without." Josephus' more general allusion to the Canaanites' inactivity may reflect the reference to the "melting of the hearts" of the Canaanite kings and to their lack of "spirit" in Josh 5:1 (earlier passed over by him).

[73] This notice has in view the instructions issued by Joshua in Josh 6:6-7. Josephus leaves aside the initial divine directives about how Jericho is to be taken in 6:2-5; compare his omission of the Lord's speech to Joshua in Josh 1:1b-9 (see 5.1).

[74] This mention of "the feast," apparently the *Phaska* cited in 5.20, is Josephus' addition. According to *S.ʿOlam Rab.* 11.7 the siege of Jericho began only after the celebration of Passover had concluded.

[75] See Josh 6:8-9.

[76] This translation follows that of Marcus (*ad loc.*) and is based on the reading of Lat (*aliique sacerdotes*). According to the Greek codices it is (the same) priests mentioned in 5.22 as carrying the ark who go on ahead, blowing their 7 horns—2 activities that would have been very difficult to perform simultaneously. Josh 6:8 designates the priests' instruments as "trumpets of rams' horns."

[77] Josephus appends this reference to the purpose of the horn-blowing by the priests.

[78] Joshua 6 does not make specific mention of this

group. See note to "oath" at 5.15.

[79] See Josh 6:11. Josephus omits Joshua's prohibition of the people's shouting until he gives them the order to do so, 6:10.

[80] See Josh 6:14b. Josephus leaves aside the repetitive description of the proceedings on the 2nd day in 6:12-14a.

[81] Compare Joshua's telling the people "the Lord has given you the city" in Josh 6:16b. On the verb εὐαγγελίζομαι ("announce good news") used by Josephus to designate Joshua's declaration to the people and its cognates, see Spicq 1982 (III): 296-306. Josephus repositions the 7-fold march of the Israelites around the city on the 7th day as related in Josh 6:15 to a point after the conclusion of Joshua's instructions (6:16b-19), where it seems more chronologically appropriate.

[82] With the above formulations Josephus spells out the meaning of Joshua's instruction (Josh 6:17a) that the people "devote to the Lord for destruction" the city and everything in it. The language used (partially) echoes that of Moses' instructions concerning the extermination of the inhabitants of the land in Deut 7:2; on the handling of this problematic text by Philo, Pseudo-Philo and Josephus, see Feldman 2003.

[83] See Josh 6:18a. Josephus omits the biblical Joshua's warning (6:18b) about the violation of this prohibition bringing "trouble" on Israel.

[84] See Josh 6:19, where "vessels of bronze and iron" are specified as well, and it is prescribed that all metal items captured are to be put in the "treasury of the Lord." Josephus appends a motivation for such handling of the plunder of Jericho, i.e. its status as the first city to be captured by the Israelites west of the Jordan.

cause of the oaths given to her by the spies.[85]

(1.6) 27. When he had said these things and organized the army, he advanced *Fall of Jericho* towards the city. They went around the city again with the ark leading, and the priests with their horns stirring up the force for its task.[86] Once they had gone round it seven times and then remained quiet for a short while, the wall fell down without any machine or other violence having been brought to bear on it by the Hebrews.[87]

(1.7) 28. Once they entered Jericho, they killed everyone, those who were in it being dismayed by the unexpected collapse of the wall and their minds having become incapable of resistance. And so they were dispatched, slaughtered in the streets, and caught unawares in their houses. **29.** Nothing served them as an appeal; all were executed, even women and children; the city was full of corpses and nothing escaped.[88] They set fire to the entire city and its hinterland.[89]

30. The spies did save Raabe and her household who had fled together to the *Sequels to Jeri-* inn.[90] In addition, Iesous, once she was brought before him, promised that she would *cho's fall* be shown favor for her saving of the spies and stated that his repayment of her good deed would not appear inferior to this. And, in fact, he immediately gave her fields and held her in all honor.[91]

(1.8) 31. As for the city, if the fire had spared anything, he demolished this. Against those who would inhabit it, should anyone wish to reerect what had been devastated,[92] he pronounced curses: the one laying the foundation of the walls would be deprived of his eldest son, while the one completing it would forfeit the youngest of his sons to death.[93] The Deity, for his part, did not neglect this curse. We shall, however, report the suffering this involved at a later point.[94]

(1.9) 32. A quite vast amount of silver and gold as well as bronze was assembled from the [city's] capture. No one disobeyed what had been decreed or appropriated these things for his own benefit, but [everyone] refrained, as from things already consecrated to God. Iesous, for his part, handed these things over to the priests to

---

[85] Josephus' motivation of Joshua's command concerning the sparing of Rahab in terms of the "oaths" given to her (see 5.12, 13, 15) replaces mention of her having hid the spies in Josh 6:17b (whose directive concerning Rahab Josephus likewise shifts to the end of his version of Joshua's instructions, just prior to the fall of Jericho).

[86] See Josh 6:15-16a. The purpose of the horn-blowing (v. 16a; cf. 5.23) is Josephus' addition.

[87] See Josh 6:20a, where, however, the people "shout" (cf. Josh 6:10, 16) just prior to the collapse of the wall, and there is no allusion to the (non-) use of "machines," etc.

[88] Josephus elaborates on Josh 6:20b-21 with, e.g., mention of the inhabitants' dismay which prevented them from resisting. From the list of the slain (6:21) he omits the various groups of animals.

[89] See Josh 6:24a, which speaks only of a burning of the city itself.

[90] In Josh 6:22 the spies' sparing of the family (6:23a) is preceded by Joshua's directive that they are to bring out Rahab and her relatives. Josephus also omits the notice of 6:23b that the family was placed

"outside the Israelite camp" once they had been removed from their refuge in Rahab's house.

[91] Josephus elaborates on the summary statement of Josh 6:25a about Joshua's "saving alive" all Rahab's kin, while omitting the etiological notice of 6:25b that Rahab dwelt in Israel "to this day." According to Rabbinic tradition, Rahab became a proselyte and married Joshua himself; various prophets and priests (e.g., Jeremiah) were descendants of this union. See Ginzberg 1913: 5; 1928: 171, n. 12.

[92] These background notices to Joshua's adjuring the Israelites not to rebuild Jericho (Josh 6:26) are Josephus' insertions.

[93] See Josh 6:26.

[94] This Josephan appendix to Joshua's curse (Josh 6:26) has in view the account of its fulfillment in the time of King Ahab as cited in 1 Kgs 16:34, a passage to which Josephus, curiously, has no equivalent in the context of his own account of Ahab. See Begg 1993: 154-55 for a discussion of the possible reasons for this omission. He leaves aside the appended statement about the Lord's being with Joshua and the latter's fame of 6:27.

Achan's theft

deposit in the treasuries. In this way Jericho was annihilated.[95]

(1.10) 33. But a certain Achar,[96] son of Zebedai[97] of the tribe of Judah, found a royal mantle woven all of gold and a loaf-shaped lump of gold weighing 200 shekels.[98] He thought it a terrible thing to forego a gain he had acquired with danger to himself, and to bring and give this to God—who did not need it.[99] Making a deep hole in his tent, he buried [these things] in it, thinking in this way to conceal [them] from his fellow-soldiers and from God.[100]

Camp at Gilgal

(1.11) 34. The place where Iesous pitched camp was called Galgala. This name means "Freedom." For, having crossed the river, they recognized that they themselves were now free both from the Egyptians and from their miseries in the desert.[101]

Defeat at Ai

(1.12) 35. A few days after the misfortune of Jericho, Iesous sent 3,000 troops to Naia,[102] a city situated above Jericho,[103] to take it by storm.[104] When the Naietans joined battle with them and they fled, they lost thirty-six men.[105]

Israelites' reaction

36. When this was announced to the Israelites, it caused them great grief and terrible dejection, not only because of their kinship with those who had been slain—although all of those who had been destroyed were good men[106] and deserving of

---

[95] Josephus elaborates on Josh 6:24b, underscoring the people's obedience to Joshua's commands and interjecting mention of the priests' role. In repositioning mention of the disposition of the plunder to the very end of his account of Jericho's fall, Josephus makes this the immediate transition to the following story of Achar's (Achan's) misdeed involving that plunder.

[96] Josephus' form of the culprit's name corresponds to that of LXX; compare MT "Achan." In focusing immediately on him, Josephus leaves aside the general editorial notice of Josh 7:1aα about a transgression having been committed by the entire people of Israel. On Josephus' version of the "Achan-Ai story" (Josh 7:1-8:29) in 5.33-48, see Begg 2001.

[97] In Josh 7:1b, where a 3-member genealogy is given, "Zabdi" (LXX Ζαμβρεί) is Achan's *grandfather*, "Carmi," his father.

[98] Josephus anticipates the list of specific items taken by "Achar" from his confession of his theft in Josh 7:21 (where the "mantle" is qualified as "from Shinar" [MT])/ "variegated" [LXX]). He likewise conflates the biblical list's mention of "200 shekels of silver" and "a bar of gold weighing 50 shekels" taken by Achan into a single metal object appropriated by him.

[99] In this editorial notice concerning the thief's psychology, Josephus anticipates and elaborates on Achan's confession in Josh 7:21 ("I coveted them [the dedicated objects] and took them"), adding the self-justifying allusion to God's not "needing" such things.

[100] Josephus turns into a narrative notice about what Achan did at this point his subsequent confession ("they [the pilfered objects] are hidden in the earth inside my tent") of Josh 7:21bβ, likewise supplying a

motivation for his action. Having thus reworked the summary notice of 7:1aβ about Achan's theft in light of the later 7:21, Josephus leaves aside the foreshadowing allusion to the Lord's "anger" against all Israel of 7:1b.

[101] This parenthetical notice about Israel's campsite represents Josephus' "delayed" use of Josh 4:19; 5:8-9. In Josh 5:9a God himself supplies a etymology for the name "Gilgal" (LXX Γάλγαλα, so Josephus), stating "on this day I have rolled away (Hebrew גלל [LXX: removed]) the reproach of Egypt from you." Josephus recasts the divine affirmation into a "realization" by the people that they are now "free." On "freedom" (Greek: ἐλευθερία) as a leitmotif of Josephus' presentation of Jewish history, see Feldman 1998: 148. On the background of the concept in the Bible, Jewish tradition, and Greco-Roman literature, see Nestle 1972: 269-306; Heiligenthal 1983: 498-502; Jones 1992: 855-59.

[102] MT (Josh 7:2) העי (Eng.: "Ai"); LXX Γαί; Josephus Ναιά (Schalit *s.v.* reads ᾿Αιά with E).

[103] Josh 7:2 situates Ai "near Beth-aven, east of Bethel."

[104] Josephus simplifies the presentation of Josh 7:2-4a, where Joshua initially sends spies against Ai (v. 2) who, in turn, report to him that he need dispatch only 2,000 or 3,000 against it, given the fewness of its people (v. 3), whereupon 3,000 Israelites do proceed against the city (v. 4a).

[105] See Josh 7:5aα. Josephus compresses, omitting mention of the inhabitants' pursuit of the Israelites (7:5aβ).

[106] This (unbiblical) characterization of the fallen is paralleled in *S. Eli. Rab.* 18, p. 102.

their solicitude—but rather out of despair.¹⁰⁷ **37.** For believing that they were already masters of the land and that their army would suffer no casualties in their battles, as God had previously promised, they now found that the enemy had unexpectedly taken courage.¹⁰⁸ Putting sackcloth over their clothing, they spent the whole day in tears and mourning; having no desire for food, they were excessively distraught over what had happened.¹⁰⁹

(1.13) 38. Seeing the army so dismayed and already assuming negative expectations about everything, Iesous adopted frank speech¹¹⁰ with God. **39.** "For," he said, "we were not carried away by pride so as to subjugate this land by means of weapons. Rather, it was your slave¹¹¹ Moyses who urged us on to this, to whom, through many proofs, you kept promising that you would enable us to inherit this land and that you would make our army always superior to the weapons of the enemy.¹¹² **40.** And indeed, some things have happened according to your promises to us;¹¹³ now, however, we have unexpectedly suffered defeat and lost some of our force as well. We are distraught at these things, as though those [promises] of yours and those things that Moyses predicted are not reliable. Even worse, our hope for the future is in distress, now that we met this first experience.¹¹⁴

41. But since you, O Master,¹¹⁵ have the power to find a remedy for these things by furnishing victory in our present pain, eradicate from our minds the hopelessness we feel about the future."¹¹⁶ **(1.14) 42.** Falling on his face,¹¹⁷ Iesous asked these

Joshua's prayer

---

¹⁰⁷ Josephus here elaborates on the laconic imagery used of the Israelites' reaction in Josh 7:5b: "the hearts of the people melted, and became as water."

¹⁰⁸ This motivation for the people's despairing reaction is a further Josephan elaboration of Josh 7:5b; see 5.36. The divine "promise" to which Josephus alludes here has a counterpart in God's words to Joshua cited in Josh 1:1b-9 (previously omitted by him); see "no man shall be able to stand before you all the days of your life..." (v. 2) and "be strong and of good courage; be not frightened, neither be dismayed; for the Lord your God is with you wherever you go" (v. 9b). The allusion is an example of Josephus' habit of making use also of those biblical passages that he does not reproduce as such.

¹⁰⁹ In Josh 7:6 it is Joshua himself who (together with the elders) engages in various mourning practices.

¹¹⁰ Greek: παρρησία; on the word, see Spicq 1982 (III): 526-33. Josephus' (inserted) characterization of Joshua's following prayer (Josh 7:7-9) has a counterpart in, e.g., b. Sanh. 43b. On the prayers of Antiquities 1-11 overall, see Harding 1994.

¹¹¹ Greek: δοῦλος. Elsewhere Josephus uses this term in reference to "slaves/servants" of God in Ant. 11.90 (Zerubbabel and Jeshua), 101 (the Jews and their leaders); cf. 9.135, where the reference is to the "slaves" of foreign gods. The designation corresponds to the frequent biblical honorific title "servant (LXX: δοῦλος) of the Lord" used of Moses (see, e.g., Josh 1:1), David (see e.g., 1 Kgs 11:13), etc.

¹¹² This opening, more positive affirmation by Joshua about the source of the Israelites' confidence in

advancing into the land takes the place of his initial accusatory question to the Lord about his intentions in leading the people to their destruction and his (Joshua's) own wish that Israel had remained beyond the Jordan in Josh 7:7. On the divine "promises" which Joshua invokes here see note to "courage" at 5.37.

¹¹³ This prefatory acknowledgement on Joshua's part—which serves as a captatio benevolentiae—lacks a counterpart in Josh 7:8, where Joshua proceeds forthwith to deplore Israel's ignominious defeat.

¹¹⁴ This statement concerning the effect of the people's defeat on them—which echoes Josephus' own account of the matter in 5.36-38—lacks a counterpart in the biblical Joshua's prayer.

¹¹⁵ This form of address (Greek: δεσπότης) replaces the double title "O Lord God" (Hebrew אדני יהוה; LXX has simple Κύριε) used by Joshua in Josh 7:7; on Josephus' use of the term δεσπότης overall, see Fischer 1958-1959. On his virtually complete avoidance of the title "Lord" (Greek: Κύριος) as a divine title—due, it would seem, to the absence of such a usage in secular Greek—see Schlatter 1932: 25-26; Begg 1993: 45, n. 219. Moses uses the same title as does Joshua here in addressing God at the moment of his commissioning in Ant. 2.270 (cf. Exod 3:11).

¹¹⁶ This confident, concluding appeal replaces Joshua's pointed question about what the Lord will "do for his great name" in the face of the anticipated Canaanite assault upon his people in Josh 7:9.

¹¹⁷ In Joshua 7 mention of Joshua's prostration (7:6) proceeds his prayer (7:7-9) to God.

God's response things of God. God responded [by telling him] to get up and purify the army from the pollution that had occurred in it, namely: a theft, brazenly undertaken, of the objects dedicated to him, for it was on account of these that they had just now met defeat. But should the culprit be sought out and punished, victory would always be given them over their enemies.[118]

Achan punished Iesous related these things to the people,[119] **43.** and having called Eleazar the high priest and those in authority,[120] he cast the lot by tribe. When this disclosed that the brazen act [came] from the tribe of Iouda, he had the lot cast again according to its clans. Then the true [source] of the crime was found [to lie] with Achar's relatives. **44.** And when the investigation proceeded man by man, they took Achar.[121] He, being unable to deny it, since God had compelled him in this terrible way, admitted his theft[122] and brought out the stolen goods in public.[123] He was immediately done away with,[124] and at nightfall got the ignominious burial suitable for a condemned criminal.[125]

Victory at Ai **(1.15) 45.** After purifying the army,[126] Iesous led them out against Naia. Having previously set ambushes around the city by night,[127] he engaged the enemy at day-

---

[118] Josephus condenses the lengthy divine reply of Josh 7:10-15. He, e.g., omits the Deity's opening question (v. 10) about the reason for Joshua's prostration and his specific instructions about how the culprit is to be found out (vv. 14-15). He likewise turns the Lord's negative warning that he will not be with the people (v. 12b) unless the devoted things are removed from their midst into a positive promise of their perpetual victory should this be done.

[119] Joshua's informing the people of God's response is not mentioned explicitly in Joshua 7.

[120] The presence of these figures for the lot-casting procedure initiated by Joshua is not mentioned in Josh 7:16. See 5.15 for Josephus' recurrent insertions concerning Joshua's cooperation with Israel's other authorities. According to *Pirqe R. El.* 38 it was by examining the stones on the breast-plate of an (unnamed) high priest that Joshua determined that the culprit belonged to the tribe of Judah.

[121] Josephus' account of a 3-stage lot-casting procedure corresponds to the LXX (B) and OL versions of Josh 7:16-18, which lack the 2nd of the 4 stages recounted in MT, i.e. the "taking" of the Zerhaite clan within the tribe of Judah (7:17).

[122] In Josh 7:20-21 Achan makes his confession in response to a summons by Joshua (7:19). Josephus has his admission prompted rather by a divine "compulsion." He here limits Achan's confession to the mere acknowledgement of his deed (= 7:20), having anticipated the details concerning this (see 7:21) in his introductory account of the crime in 5.33.

[123] Josephus continues to compress and simplify the biblical account where, not Achan himself, but rather messengers dispatched by Joshua (Josh 7:22), bring out the stolen items (7:23).

[124] With this summary notice Josephus compresses the elaborate biblical account of Josh 7:24-25. In particular, he omits the (theologically problematic) source reference to Achan's household sharing his fate. In so doing, he goes further in the line of LXX (B) and OL, which, while they do speak of the household's being taken to the place of execution (7:24a), have no equivalent to the mention of their being "burned" and "stoned" together with Achan of MT 7:25bβ. Thereby, Josephus avoids the appearance of a contradiction between the procedure used in Joshua 7 and the prohibition of Deut 24:16 (= *Ant.* 4.289) of a culprit's family members being punished along with him.

[125] This concluding notice takes the place of the complex of items making up Josh 7:26: the raising of a stone heap over Achan's remains, the Lord's turning from his anger, and the naming of the spot the "Valley of Achor" (Josephus also omits the previous references to this name and its etymology in Josh 7:24b-25a). In speaking of Achar's "ignominious" (Greek ἀτίμως) burial, Josephus echoes his combined version of the laws of Lev 24:16 and Deut 21:22-23 in *Ant.* 4.202, according to which the blasphemer is to "buried ignominiously (Greek: ἀτίμως)." The specification that Achar was buried "at nightfall" echoes the wording of Deut 21:23, which states that the corpse of a executed person is not to "remain *all night* upon the tree."

[126] This transitional phrase, echoing God's demand for such "purification" in 5.42, takes the place of the divine speech that precedes Joshua's move against Ai (Josh 8:3a) in Josh 8:1-2.

[127] This phrase summarizes the extended segment (Josh 8:3b-8) devoted to Joshua's instructions to the 3,000 "men of valor" whom he sets in ambush, prior to his own spending the night with the people (8:9).

break.[128] When they[129] self-confidently approached them because of their previous victory, he, by pretending to give ground, lured them in this way far from the city, with thoughts of pursuit and contemptuous assurance of victory.[130]

46. Then wheeling about, he made his force face them; giving the signs he had previously prescribed for those in ambush, he sent them out into battle.[131] They burst into the city, whose inhabitants were on the walls, some of them busy observing the plan of those outside.[132] **47.** They seized the city and killed all whom they met,[133] while Iesous did violence to those coming against him for combat and caused them to turn to flight. When they, being pushed back together towards the city they thought remained intact, looked and discovered that it had been seized and burnt to the ground along with their wives and children, they were scattered through the fields, unable to resist due to their separation.[134]

48. Such was the misfortune that happened to the Naietans: a mob of children, women and servants, as well as a countless amount of other material was captured.[135] The Hebrews likewise took herds of livestock and a lot of money, for the region was wealthy.[136] And Iesous, who was at Galgala,[137] divided all these things among the soldiers.[138]

(1.16) 49. Now the Gabaonites[139] who lived near Hierosolyma,[140] seeing the suf- *Gibeonites' scheme*

---

[128] See Josh 8:10. Josephus passes over Joshua's additional pre-battle measures (including a 2nd ambuscade of 5,000 men) cited in Josh 8:11-12.

[129] In Josh 8:14 there is specific mention of the "king of Ai" leading the sortie. Josephus nowhere mentions this figure in his version of Joshua 8.

[130] The reference to the pursuers' state of mind and the grounds for this is Josephus' embellishment of Josh 8:14. Josephus omits the notices on the total emptying of the city of its population in 8:16-17, which seem inherently implausible and which are not in accordance with his own subsequent presentation (or with Josh 8:24, which presupposes the continued presence of persons in the city); cf. note to "outside" at 5.46.

[131] In Josh 8:18 Joshua's signalling to those in ambush is done by means of his javelin (later, Josephus omits the notice of 8:26 about Joshua's keeping his javelin extended until Ai has been destroyed as well) and at the command of the Lord; compare Josephus' omission of the divine speech in 8:1-2.

[132] In light of Josh 8:16-17, the Israelites would be entering an empty city in 8:18. On Josephus' divergent presentation, see note to "victory" at 5.45.

[133] Josephus anticipates this notice on the slaughter of those in the city from Josh 8:24b, where it follows mention of the rout of the pursuers outside (8:20-24a).

[134] This is Josephus' condensed account of the rout of the pursuers as described in Josh 8:20-24a. From this sequence, he omits, e.g., the notice on the capture of the king of Ai in 8:23 (accordingly, he likewise passes over the killing and burial of the king related in 8:29) as well as the entrapment (8:22) of the pursuers between the Israelite forces on their front and

their rear (i.e. those coming out of the just destroyed city).

[135] Josh 8:25 speaks of the women of Ai being killed—rather than captured—along with the males for a total of 12,000. Joshua 8 makes no mention of the city's "children" or "servants."

[136] See Josh 8:27a. Josephus substitutes mention of the area's "wealth" for the indication of 8:27b that, in taking the cattle for themselves, the Israelites acted in accord with the Lord's "command" to Joshua, i.e. the one given in 8:2b, a passage also not cited by him.

[137] Josephus interjects this site-name from 5.34, where he notes that Israel was camped at "Galgala" just prior to its advance against "Naia" (5.35). The 2 uses of the place-name "Galgala" form an inclusion around his version of the Ai episode in 5.35-48a.

[138] In Josh 8:26 the Israelites simply "take" the plunder of Ai on their own. Josephus' formulation underscores both the authority of their leader Joshua and his astuteness as a general who knows how to keep his troops satisfied.

[139] In attaching his version of Israel's treaty with the Gibeonites (Josh 9:3-27) directly to his account of the capture of Ai (8:1-29), Josephus passes over 2 intervening biblical text-units, i.e. MT Josh 8:30-35 (the ceremonies at Mts. Ebal and Gerizim) and 9:1-2 (the coalition of the Canaanite kings against Israel (in LXX the 2 units appear in reverse order, while 4QJosª's fragmentary version of MT Josh 8:30-35 comes at a still different point, i.e. prior to the circumcision report of MT Josh 5:2-7; see Noort 1998). Josephus reproduces the former text subsequently in 5.69-70; he has no equivalent to the latter passage. On Josephus' version of the

ferings that had happened to the Jerichonites and the Naietans, and suspecting that
this terrible thing would come upon themselves, nonetheless decided not to appeal
to Iesous. For they did not suppose that they would get any moderate [terms], seeing that their opponent was bent on the extermination of the whole nation of the
Chananaians.[141] **50.** Instead, they appealed to the Kepherites and Kariathiarimites,
their neighbors, for an alliance, saying that they would not escape danger if they
themselves were overcome and taken by the Israelites, whereas by joining them in
arms they might contrive to elude their force.[142]

*Gibeonite-Isra-
elite exchange*

51. Once their words had been accepted, they send as messengers to Iesous to
conclude a friendship [treaty] those of the citizens whom they supposed especially
capable of acting in the interests of the crowd.[143]

52. Now these men, thinking it dangerous to declare themselves Chananaians,
while supposing that they would escape danger if they said that they had nothing in
common with the Chananaians but lived very far from them,[144] asserted that the
report of his valor had reached [them] and that they had made a long forced march.
In proof of this word, they showed their dress.[145] **53.** For their clothes had been new
when they set out, but due to the length of time of their journey they wore out—for
to make this credible to them they had deliberately donned rags.[146]

54. Standing therefore among them, they said they had been sent by the
Gabaonites and the surrounding cities that were very far away from this land to
make a friendship [treaty] with them by the agreements that were ancestral among
them.[147] For having learned that the land of the Chananaians had been given them

---

story of the Gibeonites (Joshua 9) in 5.49-57, see Begg
1997.

[140] This localization of the Gibeonites' territory is
unparalleled in Joshua 9-10. Josephus likely drew it
from his own knowledge of Palestinian topography
(Gibeon is located some 8 miles NW of Jerusalem). In
Ant. 7.283 and *War* 2.516 Josephus cites the distance
between "Gabao(n)" and Jersualem as being 40 and 50
stadia, respectively.

[141] The above remarks on the Gibeonites' thought
process in response to their hearing of the fate of Jericho and Ai are Josephus' amplification of Josh 9:3. The
allusion to Joshua's being bent on the extermination of
the Canaanite race echoes Moses' directive on the matter as cited in *Ant.* 4.300.

[142] This whole paragraph is an anticipated elaboration of Josh 9:17, where the Israelites discover that the
Gibeonites' cities comprise, in addition to Gibeon itself, "Chephirah, Beeroth, and Kiriathjearim" (MT;
LXX Ἰαρείν). Josephus' notice serves to explain, in advance, how 2 of these 3 sites (he does not mention
"Beeroth") came to be aligned with the Gibeonites.

[143] This reference to the Gibeonites' constituting a
select embassy to send to the Israelites seems inspired
by a later moment in the source account, namely Josh
9:11, where the Gibeonite envoys, in their exchange
with Joshua, refer to their having been instructed by
"our elders and all the inhabitants of our country" to
"make a covenant" with the Israelites.

[144] The envoys' "thoughts" here are Josephus' creation. They take the place of the enumeration of the cam-
ouflage measures adopted by them as cited in Josh
9:4-5.

[145] Josephus here both compresses and modifies the
source's double exchange, first between the Gibeonites
and the Israelites (Josh 9:7-8a) and then between them
and Joshua (9:8b-13). Leaving aside the former sequence entirely, he restricts himself to a few select items
from the latter, amplifying these with an initial reference by the envoys to Joshua's "valor" designed to win
a favorable hearing from the general. In particular, the
Gibeonites' statement about being from "far off" echoes 9:9a, while their displaying the state of their garments in proof of this parallels 9:13b (9:12-13a cite
additional such "proofs," namely the state of their
bread, wineskins, and shoes).

[146] Josephus here makes delayed use of Josh 9:5's
mention of the worn-out clothes donned by the
Gibeonites, using this to explain the reason for their
approaching Joshua dressed in this odd fashion.

[147] See the Gibeonites' words about the purpose of
their mission in Josh 9:11b, already anticipated by
Josephus in 5.51. In 9:11b the Gibeonites request a
"covenant" (Hebrew: ברית); Josephus invariably substitutes alternative wording (here: φιλία, "friendship
[treaty]"; συνθῆκαι, "agreements") for the standard LXX
rendering of this term, namely, διαθήκη, a word that was
not current in the meaning "covenant" in secular

to possess by the favor and gift of God,[148] they said that they were pleased by these things and requested to become their fellow-citizens.[149] **55.** When they had said these things and displayed the proofs of their journey, they kept appealing to the Hebrews for agreements and a friendship [treaty].[150] Iesous, believing what they were saying, namely that they were not of the Chananaian nation, made a friendship [treaty] with them.[151] Eleazar the high priest together with the senate swore that they would regard them as friends and allies and would inflict no wrong upon them, while the crowd gave its assent to these oaths.[152]

56. Having obtained what they wished by deceit, they went off to their own homes.[153] Iesous, however, campaigning into the lowland of Chananaia and learning that the Gabaonites lived not far the Hierosolymites and were of the race of the Chananaians,[154] summoned those in authority among them and denounced them for their deceit.[155] **57.** When they alleged that they had no other possibility of safety than this and therefore had had recourse to it by necessity,[156] he called together Eleazar the high priest and the senate.[157] When they decided to make them servants of the people so as not to transgress the oath, he appointed them to these [tasks].[158]

Gibeonites' deceit discovered

Greek; see Begg 1993: 100-101, n. 609.

[148] This formulation recalls Rahab's statement about her "knowing" of the Israelites' future domination of Canaan, via "signs given her by God" in 5.12. Compare Josh 9:9b-10, where the Gibeonites simply claim to have heard of God's dealings with Egypt and the 2 Transjordanian kings. The phrase "favor and gift (Greek: χάρις καὶ δωρεά) of God" used by the Gibeonites here echoes the same combination of terms—there in the plural—in Moses' address to the people distressed by their lack of water in *Ant.* 3.14. On the word χάρις, see Spicq 1978 (II): 960-66.

[149] The envoys' words to Joshua cited in Josh 9:8b-13 lack an equivalent to this double statement with its patent intention of currying favor with the hearers.

[150] The words ("agreements," "friendship [treaty]") Josephus attributes to the Gibeonites here echo those of their earlier plea in 5.54.

[151] See Josh 9:15a. Josephus interjects the reference to Joshua's "belief"; on "belief/faith language" (Greek: πίστις; πιστεύειν) in Josephus' writings generally, see Lindsey 1993. He leaves aside the preceding mention (9:14) of the Israelites' eating of the Gibeonites' provisions (the earlier allusions to which [9:4, 12] were also passed over by him) without consulting the Lord.

[152] In Josh 9:15b it is the "leaders of the congregation" who swear and there is no mention of an assent by the people as a whole. On the combined role of Eleazar and the "senate," there too in connection with an oath of protection, see 5.15.

[153] This notice on the envoys' return home lacks an equivalent in Joshua 9. The reference to the Gibeonites' "deceit" is anticipated from Josh 9:22, where Joshua asks them "why did you deceive us?"

[154] In Josh 9:16 the Israelites as a whole hear, 3 days later, that the Gibeonites are in fact their "neighbors." On the Gibeonites' proximity to Jerusalem, see 5.49.

[155] See Josh 9:22. Josephus passes over the intervening sequence of 9:17-21, which features (9:18-21) a conflict between the leaders of the congregation and the people regarding the former's (wrongful) swearing to the Gibeonites. Josephus' omission of this item is understandable given that, in his version of 9:15, he has recorded the people's assent to the oaths made by their leaders; see 5.55. For the source portrayal of intra-Jewish recriminations Josephus thus substitutes an idealized picture of the entire community acting in harmony. He likewise does not reproduce Joshua's cursing of the Gibeonites and his imposition of menial tasks in the temple upon them as cited in 9:23, already prior to their attempt at self-exculpation in 9:24.

[156] Cf. the Gibeonites' words as cited in Josh 9:24. Josephus leaves aside their further statement, submitting themselves to whatever Joshua may decide concerning them of 9:25.

[157] See 5.55 for the role of these authorities earlier in the proceedings.

[158] In Josh 9:24 and 27 it is Joshua, acting alone, who imposes their future service upon the Gibeonites, while in 9:21 the leaders of the congregation take this initiative without reference to Joshua. Josephus' portrayal of the Israelite leadership figures making a joint decision here recalls his similar presentations in 5.15 and 43. In his version of Joshua 9 harmony prevails, not only among the leaders, but also between them and the people (contrast Josh 9:18-20). In Joshua 9 there is likewise ambiguity as to whom/what the Gibeonites are to serve (see the divergent indications in vv. 21, 23, 27); Josephus clarifies the matter by specifying that they are to be "servants of the people."

And so they, although a misfortune came upon them, found defense and security.[159]

(1.17) 58. The king of the Hierosolymites resented the Gabaonites' going over to Iesous,[160] and appealed to the kings of the neighboring nations to jointly undertake war against them.[161] When the Gabaonites saw that these kings had come with him—there were four of them—and were encamped at a certain spring not far from their city preparing for a siege,[162] they called upon Iesous as their ally.[163] **59.** For, in these [conditions], the circumstances were such that, whereas they expected that they would be annihilated by these [compatriots] of theirs, they supposed that they would be saved—on account of the existing friendship [treaty]—by those who were campaigning for the extermination of the Chananaian race.[164]

60. After hastening to their aid with his whole army and making a forced march by day and night,[165] Iesous assaulted the enemy at daybreak and put them to flight.[166] He followed in pursuit down a sloping area called Bethor.[167] There he learned as well the cooperation[168] of God, signified to him by thunder, the discharge of lightning bolts[169] and a greater than usual torrent of hail. **61.** In also happened that the day was increased further so that nightfall would not check the Hebrews' eagerness.[170] The result was that Iesous took the kings hidden in a certain cave at Makchida[171] and punished them all.[172] That the duration of the day was prolonged and exceeded the usual on that occasion is disclosed in the writings present in the temple.[173]

---

[159] This transition to his following account of the Israelites' rescue of the Gibeonites from assault by the Canaanites is Josephus' own creation.

[160] In Josh 10:1-2 Adonizedek, king of Jersualem, "fears" because even the mighty Gibeonites have made their peace with the Israelites.

[161] See Josh 10:3-4; in v. 3 the names of the kings and their domains are cited.

[162] Josh 10:5 mentions the encampment of the 5 Canaanite kings near Gibeon, but not the Gibeonites' sighting of them or a "spring" in the vicinity of the city.

[163] See Josh 10:6, where the content of the Gibeonites' "appeal" to Joshua is spelled out.

[164] This motivation for the Gibeonites' appeal (5.58) is Josephus' appendix to their making that appeal as cited in Josh 10:6. Its closing words concerning the aim of the Israelites' campaign echoes the Gibeonites' earlier perception concerning Joshua's hostile intentions as reported in 5.49.

[165] See Josh 10:7-9, from which Josephus omits the divine word of assurance to Joshua as he is setting out to battle (v. 8).

[166] In Josh 10:10a it is God who initiates matters by throwing the enemy coalition "into a panic."

[167] Compare Josh 10:10b: "... and chased them by way of the ascent of Bethoron (LXX: Θρωνείν), and smote them as far as Azekah and Makkedah." In *War* 2.521 "Bet-horon" is the site of the defeat of Cestius Gallus by the Jews in 66 CE. that precipitated full-scale war between them and the Romans.

[168] Greek: συνεργία. Josephus uses this term of God's "cooperation" with humans also in *War* 4.26; 6.39 (plural); and *Ant.* 5.301.

[169] Josephus dramatizes the happening by adding thunder and lightning to the God-sent "hailstones" mentioned in Josh 10:11.

[170] Josh 10:12-14 tells the miracle of the stopping of the sun in greater detail, citing the poetic words Joshua addresses to both sun and moon (v. 12b-13). On Josephus' tendency to play down the miracles associated with the conquest, see Feldman 1998: 453-56.

[171] MT (Josh 10:16, etc.) מקדה (Eng.: "Makkedah"); LXX Μακηδά; Josephus Μακχίδα.

[172] Josephus here reduces to a minimum the circumstantial account of the fate of the 5 kings given in Josh 10:16-27.

[173] Compare Josh 10:13bα (LXX B lacks an equivalent): "Is this [the words of Joshua in 10:12b-13a] not written in the Book of Jashar?" Josephus' invocation of "temple writings" as his source for the "fantastic" events associated with Joshua's victory serves to give an heightened credibility to his summary account of those events. Elsewhere as well, Josephus interjects similar allusions to documents housed in the temple concerning events related by him; see *Ant.* 3.38 ("a writing lying in the temple reveals that God foretold to Moyses that water would thus issue forth from the rock") and 4.303 (Moses left behind a hexameter poem [the Song of Moses, Deuteronomy 32] "in a book in the temple"), and the notes of Feldman 2000 *ad loc.*

(1.18) 62. The affair of the kings who had made war on and campaigned against the Gabaonites being thus concluded, Iesous returned again to the hill country of Chananaia and, having perpetrated great slaughter on those in it and taken plunder,[174] came to the camp in Galgala.[175]

63. When much talk concerning the valor of the Hebrews circulated among the neighboring peoples, dismay took hold of those who heard of the number of the slain.[176] The Chananaian kings around Mt. Liban and those in the Chananaian plains campaigned against them; joining forces with the Palestinoi,[177] they encamped at Beroth, a city of upper Galilee not far from Kedesa. This too is in the country of the Galileans.[178]

Israel's north-ern victory

64. Their entire army comprised 300,000 troops, 10,000 horsemen, and 20,000 chariots.[179] The number of the enemy dismayed both Iesous himself and the Israelites who, due to their overwhelming anxiety, became apprehensive about their hope of superiority.[180] **65.** But God, rebuking their fear and their desiring anything other than help from him, promised that they would be victorious over their enemies and directed them to disable their horses and burn their chariots.[181] Emboldened by God's promises, he [Iesous] marched out against the enemy.[182]

66. Coming upon them on the fifth day, he engaged; there ensued a violent battle and a slaughter that was almost beyond belief to those who heard of it.[183] He went out in pursuit of them for a long distance and destroyed the enemy's entire army, except for a few; all their kings fell too.[184]

67. Then, when there were no more people left to kill, Iesous did away with their horses[185] and burned the chariots. He passed through the country at his ease, with

---

[174] This notice sums up Josh 10:28-42, which relates Joshua's destruction of a whole series of named sites in the south of the land.

[175] See Josh 10:43 (MT; LXX B lacks an equivalent).

[176] This transitional notice between Joshua's southern (Joshua 10) and northern (Joshua 11) campaigns lacks a biblical equivalent at this juncture (cf., however, 10:2 with its reference to King Adonizedek's "great fear"); it underscores the impression made by Israel's military prowess upon all who heard of it.

[177] Josh 11:1-3 provides a much more detailed listing of the components of the enemy coalition assembled by Jabin, king of Hazor. That list does not, however, mention the "Philistines" (Josephus' "Palestinoi") explicitly; note, however, the reference to the kings "in the lowland," the Philistine homebase, in 11:2. Josephus makes an initial mention of this people and their "hostile attitude" towards the Israelites, "due to an ancient enmity with them" in *Ant.* 2.322.

[178] Josh 11:5 (MT) locates the enemy encampment at "the waters of Merom" (LXX Μαρρών; Schalit *s.v.* proposes Μήρωθ for the form Βηρώθη read by Niese and Marcus here in 5.63); this site is generally localized in the same Galilean region where Josephus places their camp. He anticipates the name of his other Galilean city, Kedesh, from Josh 20:7. Josephus provides a description of the Upper and Lower Galilee of his time in

War 3.35-43.

[179] These "precise" figures replace, as often in Josephus, the Bible's indeterminate ones; compare Josh 11:4: "... a great host, in number like the sand that is upon the seashore, with very many horses and chariots."

[180] This interjected remark about Joshua and the Israelites' emotional state is Josephus' inference from God's telling Joshua "do not be afraid of them [the enemy coalition]" in Josh 11:6 (// 5.65), which seems to presuppose that he (and they) have, in fact, entertained such fear.

[181] See Josh 11:6.

[182] This notice concerning the effect of God's word upon Joshua lacks a counterpart in Joshua 11.

[183] See Josh 11:7. Josephus adds the specification concerning the duration of Israel's march and dramatizes the violence of the battle.

[184] See Josh 11:8, from which Josephus omits the place names and the opening reference to the Lord's giving the enemy into Israel's hand. The explicit mention of the death of the enemy kings is his addition, paralleling their fate with that of the southern kings in 5.61.

[185] In Josh 11:9bα Joshua hamstrings the enemy horses, as God had commanded him in 11:6. Josephus varies the wording between command ("disable," 5.65) and execution ("do away with," 5.67).

Tent erected at Shiloh

no one venturing to come out for battle. Capturing the cities by siege, he slaughtered all whom he took.[186]

(1.19) 68. Five years[187] had now already passed and none of the Chananaians remained any longer,[188] except for some who escaped due to the solidity of their walls.[189] Iesous, having moved his camp from Galgala[190] into the hill country, erected the holy tent at the city of Silo,[191] for he thought the site suitable—given its beauty—until the situation would allow them to build a sanctuary.[192]

Shechem rites

69. Proceeding from there to Sikima with all the people, he erected an altar where Moyses had foretold.[193] Then dividing the army, he stationed one half on Mt. Garizeis,[194] and the other half on Mt. Hebel[195] (on which the altar was as well), together with the Levitical tribe and the priests.[196] **70.** Having sacrificed[197] and pronounced curses[198] that they left behind inscribed on the altar,[199] they returned to Silo.[200]

Joshua's Shiloh address

(1.20) 71. Iesous, who was now already old, saw that the cities of the Chana-

---

[186] This notice sums up the account of Joshua's subsequent conquests and massacres in Josh 11:10-23 (12:1-24). Compare Josephus' summary of Josh 10:28-42 in 5.62.

[187] Josephus derives this figure for the duration of the conquest from Josh 14:10, where, with the conquest process (essentially) complete, Caleb states that 45 years have now elapsed since Moses promised him (14:9) him that he would enter the promised land. Of these, 40 were spent in the desert (see *Ant.* 3.32), this leaving the remaining 5 years for the occupation of the land.

[188] This statement picks up the extermination notices of, e.g., Josh 11:14, 17, 21.

[189] Cf. Josh 13:2-6, which specifies those portions of the country that remained unsubjugated. Josephus' remark about the survivors' finding safety behind their walls is his own.

[190] See 5.62, where Joshua returns to camp at "Galgala" following his victory on behalf of the Gibeonites.

[191] MT (Josh 18:1) שלה (Eng.: "Shiloh"); LXX Σηλώ; Josephus Σιλοῦς.

[192] See Josh 18:1, to which Josephus appends his remark about the rationale for Joshua's choice of this particular site for the erection of the tent and the temporary nature of its placement there. Josephus describes the tent in detail *Ant.* 3.115-133 and inserts mention of its transport across the Jordan by the Levites in 5.17.

[193] See Josh 8:30-31a (MT), where the site "Shechem" is not mentioned explicitly; Josephus' naming of it reflects Moses' prescription as cited in *Ant.* 4.305 (= Deut 27:5) that the altar be built "not far from the city of the Sikimites." On the divergent placing of the MT segment Josh 8:30-35 in the various witnesses, see note to "Gabaonites" at 5.49. For more details on Josephus' rendering of this passage in 5.69-70, see Begg 1997a; on the version of Pseudo-Philo in *Bib. Ant.* 21.7-10, see Begg 1997b.

[194] MT (Josh 8:33) גרזים (Eng.: "Gerizim"); LXX (Josh 9:6) Γαριζείν; Josephus Γαριζεῖς.

[195] MT (Josh 8:33) עיבל (Eng.: "Ebal"); LXX (Josh 9:6) Γαιβάλ; Josephus Ἥβηλος.

[196] In Josh 8:33 the people are lined up on either side of the ark facing the Levitical priests with half of them standing in front of Mt. Gerizim, the other half in front of Mt. Ebal. Josephus' presentation, with its distinction between the "priests" and "Levites" and non-mention of the ark, corresponds more closely to his own rendering of Moses' prescription on the matter in *Ant.* 4.305 (cf. Deut 27:11-14). The parenthetical reference to the presence of the altar on Mt. Ebal parallels the notice on Joshua's building an altar on that site in 8:30.

[197] In Josh 8:31b the sacrifices are mentioned prior to the dividing up of the assembly (8:32). Josephus omits the cross-reference to Moses' command (see Deut 27:5-6a) about the way in which the altar is to be built of Josh 8:31a.

[198] Compare Josh 8:34, where Joshua (alone) reads "all the words of the law, the blessing and the curse." In *Ant.* 4.306-307 (see Deut 27:11-13) the 2 divisions of the people (4.305) are designated to pronounce blessings and curses, respectively. Here in 5.70 Josephus speaks only of the latter (compare Josh 8:33, where blessings alone are mentioned).

[199] Compare Josh 8:32, where, in accordance with Moses' injunction in Deut 27:8, what is written on the altar stones is rather a "copy of the law of Moses" (so also *Bib. Ant.* 21.7, while *m. Soṭah* 7.5 avers that the law was inscribed in the 70 languages of humanity). Josephus' formulation on the point (partially) reflects his version of Deut 27:8 in *Ant.* 4.308, where Moses (proleptically) inscribes "them," i.e. the blessings and the curses spoken of in 4.307, on both sides of the altar.

[200] This return to Shiloh (see 5.68) has no biblical basis.

naians would not be easy to capture on account of the ruggedness of the sites where they were and the strength of their walls. Having added these to the natural advantages of their cities, [the inhabitants] were expecting that the enemy would desist from the siege out of despair of taking them. **72.** For, having learned that the Israelites had made their journey from Egypt for the purpose of exterminating themselves, the Chananaians spent all that time in strengthening their cities.[201] Bringing the people together at Silo, Iesous convened the assembly.[202]

73. When they had come together in haste, he said that their past successes and the deeds they had accomplished were outstanding and worthy both of the Deity who had granted them and of the excellence of the laws they observed.[203] He further disclosed that the thirty-one kings who had ventured to enter into conflict with them had been conquered,[204] and an entire army, which was once so confident of its force as to join battle with them, had been destroyed, such that not a family of them survived.[205]

74. But now, since, although some of their cities had been taken by storm, for the others time and a great siege would be necessary on account of the solidity of their walls and the confidence of the inhabitants in this,[206] he thought it appropriate to now dismiss to their homes those from beyond the Jordan, who had joined with them and shared the dangers as their relatives, once they had thanked them for their help.[207] **75.** [He further proposed] to send one man from each tribe of outstanding and attested virtue. "These men should measure the land in a trustworthy way, doing nothing underhandedly, and disclose its extent to us without deception."[208]

(1.21) 76. When Iesous had finished these words, the crowd gave its assent, and he sent off men to measure out their country, associating with them some knowledgeable surveyors from whom the truth would not be concealed, on account of their skill.[209] He gave them commands about appraising separately the extent of the fruitful land and that which was less good. **77.** For the nature of the land of the Chananaians is such that one sees wide plains that are highly suitable for producing crops and that, when compared with other land, would be thought altogether fruitful. In comparison, however, with the regions of the Jerichonites and the Hierosolymites,

Character of land

---

[201] Josephus derives the datum about Joshua's age at the opening of 5.71 from Josh 13:1a. The appended considerations, which he attributes to the leader about the situation facing his people, are his own, taking the place of the divine speech to Joshua concerning the yet unconquered land and its division in 13:1b-7. Mention of the Canaanites' awareness of the Israelites' intention of "exterminating" them recalls the knowledge of Joshua's purpose that Josephus attributes to the Gibeonites in 5.49.

[202] Josephus derives his reference to the assembly at Shiloh, which will establish the procedure for the division of the land west of the Jordan, from Josh 18:1.

[203] This opening *captatio benevolentiae* takes the place of Joshua's initial accusatory question to the people in Josh 18:3 ("how long will you be slack to go in and take possession of the land...?").

[204] Josephus here has Joshua allude to the catalogue of 31 conquered kings whose cities are cited in Josh 12:(7-8)9-24.

[205] Joshua's reference here is apparently to the Israelite rout of the northern coalition as described in 5.66 (where, however, it is stated that some few of the enemy did survive). In any case, neither this reference nor the preceding one to the 31 conquered kings has an equivalent in Joshua's speech at Shiloh in Josh 18:3-7.

[206] Joshua here articulates to the people those reflections which Josephus had previously attributed to him in 5.71-72.

[207] See 5.3-4 (// Josh 1:12-18). The above sequence elaborates on Joshua's recalling the fact that the Transjordanians had already received their inheritance in Josh 18:7b.

[208] In Josh 18:4 Joshua simply calls for the selection of 3 men from each tribe, and says nothing about ethical requirements for them and their task.

[209] Compare Josh 18:8abα, where there is no mention of the people's assent to Joshua's proposal, nor a distinction between the tribal representatives and the professional "surveyors" who accompany them.

these would prove to be nothing. **78.** Indeed, whereas their land happens to be quite small in size and mostly hilly, as regards its abundant crop-production and beauty, it is not inferior to any other. Therefore Iesous supposed that the portions should be assessed by value rather than by size, one *plethron*[210] often being worth 1,000.[211]

Land apportioned
79. Now the men sent out were ten.[212] After traveling around and assessing the land according to its value, they came in the seventh month to him [Iesous] at the city of Silo, where the tent had been put up.[213]

(1.22) 80. Iesous, consulting Eleazar and the senate, along with the tribal rulers, then divided up [the land] for the nine tribes and half of the Manasseites, apportioning it according to the size of each of the tribes.[214]

81. When he cast the lot, Iouda[215] received as its allotted share all of upper Idumea,[216] [its length] extending as far as the Hierosolymites and its breadth reaching down to the sea of the Sodomites.[217] In this portion were the cities of Askalon and Gaza.[218]

82. Semeon—for it came second[219]—received by lot that part of Idumea that adjoins Egypt and Arabia.[220] The length of that which the Benjamites obtained by lot extended from the Jordan river to the sea, while its breadth was bounded by the Hierosolymites and Bethelites.[221] This portion was very narrow because of the excellence of the land,[222] for they received Jericho and the city of the Hierosolymites.[223]

---

[210] The *plethron* is equivalent to 10,000 square feet; see Rengstorf 1979 *s.v.*

[211] The above disquisition (5.76b-79) on the varying quality of the land that is to be kept in mind in its allotment is Josephus' creation, no doubt drawn from his own knowledge of Palestinian topography. It recalls his comparative description of the various components of the land of Palestine in *War* 3.35-58.

[212] This figure corresponds to the notice of 5.74 on Joshua's dispatching "one man from each tribe" (i.e. other than the Transjordanian ones [who have already received their allotment] and the Levites [who will not be given a territory of their own]; cf. Josh 18:7). Josh 18:8 does not specify the number of those who set out on the surveying task; Joshua's directive in 18:4 that 3 men from each of the (Cisjordanian) tribes are to be sent suggests that there were 30.

[213] Compare Josh 18:9, which does not indicate the duration of the surveyors' tour, but speaks rather of their generating a description of the land according to its 7 divisions. On Joshua's previous erection of the tent at Shiloh, see 5.68.

[214] In Josh 18:10 itself Joshua allots the land on his own (cf., however, the summary statement of 19:51, where Eleazar and the "heads of the fathers' houses" divide up the land along with him). 18:10 likewise makes no mention of the relative size of the tribes being taken into account in the allotment.

[215] In the Book of Joshua Judah's boundaries are described in 15:1-63, i.e. prior to the determination of the allotment procedure in 18:2-7. Josephus repositions

the former segment to a more logical place, i.e. after the procedure has been fixed, likewise drastically compressing it.

[216] Josephus follows LXX Josh 15:1 in its name for the region which MT calls "Edom." He notes the difference between the 2 names in *Ant.* 2.3, where he states that the Greeks "with greater dignity" designate as "Idumea" the land known in Hebrew as "Adomos" ("redness").

[217] Josh 15:5 designates Judah's eastern border as the "Salt Sea." In *War* 4.476-485 Josephus gives an extended description of this body of water (which he there calls "Lake Asphaltitis") and its surroundings in his own time.

[218] Whereas Josh 15:45-47 assigns Judah 3 Philistine towns i.e., Ekron, Ashdod, and Gaza, it does not mention "Ashkelon."

[219] In Josh 19:1 Simeon does receive the 2nd lot, not, however, after Judah (as in Josephus), but following Benjamin (18:11-28).

[220] Josephus generalizes the boundary indications for Simeon found in Josh 19:1-11, omitting, e.g., the Bible's mention (see vv. 2, 9) that Simeon's inheritance was in the midst of that of Judah.

[221] For his delimitation of Benjamin's inheritance Josephus makes selective use of data found in Josh 18:12, 13, 16, 19. In Josh 18:11-28 Benjamin is the first of the tribes to be awarded its territory by lot at Shiloh, rather than the 3rd, i.e. after Judah and Simeon, as in Josephus.

[222] This statement, which picks up on Josephus' (in-

83. The tribe of Ephran[224] received by lot a territory extending (in length) from the Jordan river as far as Gazara, while its width extended from Bethel to its termination in the great plain.[225] The allotment of half the Manasseites was from the Jordan to the city of Dor and its breadth was as far as Bethesan that is now called Scythopolis.[226]

84. After these [came] Isachar, with Mt. Karmel and the river marking the limits of its length, and Mt. Itabyrion those of its breadth.[227] The Zeboulonites received an allotted portion extending up to [the (lake of] Genesar, sloping down towards Karmel and the sea.[228]

85. The Aserites occupied the territory beginning at Karmel, called the "Valley," due to its being such—all of it that faces Sidon.[229] In that region the city of Arke, also called Edkeipa, was assigned to them.[230]

86. The Nephthalites received those regions situated to the east as far as the city of Damascus and the upper Galilee up till Mt. Liban and the sources of the Jordan that have their starting point at that mountain, from which it descends through the northern regions surrounding the city of Arke.[231]

87. The Danites had allotted to them those parts of the valley that are oriented westward and bounded by Azotos and Dor. Their portion was all Iamneia and Gitta and Akkaron as far as the mountain where the tribe of Iouda took its beginning.[232]

---

serted) remarks in 5.76-79 about the fertility of the land, has no biblical counterpart.

[223] Josh 18:22 and 28, respectively, list Jericho and Jebus/Jerusalem among the Benjamite cities.

[224] This is the form of the tribe's name found in R and adopted by Niese. Marcus (*ad loc.*) reads the more biblical form Ἐφραίμ with SPLau.

[225] The Book of Joshua treats the inheritance of "Ephraim" in 16:5-10 as part of an extended segment (16:1-17:18) dealing with the allotments of the 2 descendants of "Joseph," prior to presenting the allotment procedure itself in 18:1-10. As he did in the case of Judah (5.81), Josephus repositions the former text to a point after his version of the latter. Josh 16:10 avers that the Canaanites were not in fact driven out of "Gezer." The "great plain" mentioned by Josephus is the "plain of Jezreel" or "Valley of Megiddo."

[226] Josephus' statement on the allotment of Cisjordanian Manasseh summarizes Josh 17:7-13, which mentions "Bethshean" and "Dor" as part of that allotment in v. 11. Josephus supplies the contemporary Greek name for the former city 3 further times, i.e. in *Ant.* 6.374; 12.348; 13.188. Photos of the site appear in Mason 2001: Appendix A, 207.

[227] Josephus reverses the biblical sequence concerning the inheritances of Zebulun (Josh 19:10-16) and Issachar (19:17-23). The latter text does not mention Mt. Carmel as belonging to Issachar. Josephus' Mt. "Itabyrion" is his equivalent for the "Tabor" (LXX B Γαιθβόρ) of Josh 19:22; see Marcus *ad loc*. The name occurs also in *War* 1.177; 2.573; 4.1, 54, 61; *Ant.* 5.203; 8.37; 13.306; 14.102; *Life* 188.

[228] See Josh 19:10-16, whose many proper place names Josephus leaves aside. The 2 bodies of water marking the boundaries of Zebulon according to Josephus are the contemporary sea of Galilee and the Mediterranean, respectively.

[229] See Josh 19:24-31, which mentions (v. 28) "Sidon the Great" as a boundary for the territory of "Asher." The "valley" mentioned by Josephus as making up the territory of Asher is the coastal plain along the Mediterranean south of Sidon, where the tribe was settled.

[230] Schalit (*s.v.*) views the reading "Arke" here (and in 5.86) as a mistake for "Ake," the later Ptolemais. For "Ekdeipa" he conjectures (*s.v.*) "Ekdippa," identifying this with the city of "Achzib" cited in Josh 19:29. "Ekdippa" is mentioned also in *War* 1.257.

[231] Compare Josh 19:32-39, which, e.g., does not speak of Naphtali's territory extending as far as Damascus. Marcus (*ad. loc.*) brackets the words "whence it descends through the northern regions as far as the city of Arke," noting that the sequence is absent in Lat and calling it "unintelligible."

[232] Compare Josh 19:40-48. Of Josephus' 5 place names, only 2, i.e. "Akkaron" (= Ekron, 19:43) and "Gitta" (= Gath-rimmon, 19:45) have a clear equivalent in the source. Of the remainder, "Iamneia" is Hebrew "Jabneh," while "Azotos" is the LXX's rendering of Hebrew "Ashdod"; see Schalit *s.v.* Josephus does not reproduce the notice of Josh 19:47 on Dan's later change of territory, a development he will treat in some detail in 5.175-178.

(1.23) 88. Iesous thus divided up six nations of the sons of Chananaios who bore his surname and gave their land to the nine and a half tribes to possess.[233] **89.** For we have earlier disclosed how Moyses had already occupied Amoritis (also so-called after one of the children of Chananaios) and divided it up among the two and a half tribes.[234] However, the [areas] around Sidon, as well as those of the Aroukaians,[235] Amathians[236] and the Aridaians[237] remained unallotted.[238]

Joshua's admonition

(1.24) 90. Since by this time he was already impeded by old age from doing the things he had in mind and since those who received the leadership after him were careless about the public advantage,[239] Iesous instructed each of the tribes not to leave any of the race of the Chananaians in the land they had acquired by lot.[240] For their security and the preservation of their ancestral customs[241] depended on this alone, as Moyses had foretold to them and as he himself was convinced.[242]

Levites receive cities

91. To the Levites they were to hand over thirty-eight cities (for they had already received the [remaining] ten throughout Amoraia).[243] Of these he [Iesous] designated

---

[233] With this summarizing notice compare Josh 19:51, which does not, however, allude to the nations descended from Canaan. In *Ant.* 1.139 Josephus, following Gen 10:15-17, lists *7* eponymous descendants of Chananaios who were later exterminated by the Hebrews. (Of these, the 3rd, "Amorraios," appears in 5.89 under the country-name "Amoritis," this bringing the total number of Chananaios' descendants in 5.89-90 up to that enumerated in 1.139; see also 5.3, where Josephus calls "Amoria" the "*7th* part of country of the Chananaians"). Cf. Feldman 2000 *ad loc.*

[234] See *Ant.* 4.166-171 (= Numbers 32) and the allusion to this in 5.3. In the Book of Joshua itself there is a detailed recapitulation of Moses' awarding the Transjordanians their territories in 13:8-33. Josephus cites the name of the son of Chananaios who gave his name to "Amoritis" as "Amorraios" (the LXX's equivalent for Hebrew "Amori") in *Ant.* 1.139 (= Gen 10:16); see previous note.

[235] In *Ant.* 1.138 "Aroukaios" appears as a son of Chananaios who occupies "Arke" in Lebanon. Josephus' form here corresponds to LXX's rendering of MT "Arki" in Gen 10:17.

[236] See *Ant.* 1.138, which mentions "Amathous," son of Chananaios, who founded a city with the same name (Hebrew: "Hamath," cf. Gen 10:18).

[237] Cf. *Ant.* 1.138, where "Aroudaios," son of Chananaios, is said to have occupied the island of Arados. In MT Gen 10:18 the name appears as ארודי (LXX Ἀράδαιος).

[238] With the above list of 4 unassigned sites, compare the enumeration of the unconquered territories in Josh 13:2-6, which mentions the "Sidonians" (vv. 4, 6) and the "entrance of Hamath" (v. 5).

[239] In Josh 23:1 Joshua's age (mentioned already in 13:1a= 5.71), but not his awareness of his successors' dereliction of duty, is cited as the occasion for his following farewell discourse. Josephus' additional motiva-

tion both underscores the urgency of Joshua's admonition at this juncture, and serves to prepare his subsequent presentation, where, following Joshua's death, Israel's polity falls precipitously into disarray; see 5.132-135. By anticipating his version of Joshua 23 to this point, Josephus avoids having him deliver 2 farewell discourses back to back—as happens in Joshua 23-24.

[240] Whereas Joshua's speech in Joshua 23 features urgent warnings against mixing with the indigenous nations (v. 7) and intermarrying with them (v. 12), it does not call for their actual extermination. The annihilation of the Canaanites as the goal of Israel's entry into the land is a recurrent theme throughout Josephus' account of the period of Joshua; see 5.12, 49, 59, 72.

[241] Greek: τὰ πάτρια ἔθη. On the word πάτριος ("ancestral") as a key positive item of Josephus' vocabulary and the various terms it modifies ("laws," "customs," etc.), see Schröder 1996.

[242] This "motivation," itself harking back to Moses' directive as cited in *Ant.* 4.300 (// Deut 20:17), for Joshua's preceding admonition about exterminating the Canaanites has no clear equivalent in the speech of Joshua 23. Compare, however, v. 13, where Joshua warns that, should the Israelites intermarry with the Canaanites, the latter will become a "snare and a trap" to them, this eventuating in Israel's loss of its land.

[243] Josh 21:41 (see also Num 35:7 and *Ant.* 4.67) speaks of a total of *48* Levitical cities. As the above parenthesis indicates, Josephus' figure here in 5.91 reflects his earlier mention of Moses' establishing 10 such cities in Transjordania in *Ant.* 4.172. At this point, Josephus shifts from his version of Joshua's farewell discourse (// Joshua 23), to an earlier initiative by him, i.e. the distribution of the Levitical cities west of the Jordan (// 21:1-42).

three for fugitives to live in—for he took great care not to neglect anything Moyses had laid down—[244] these were Hebron in the tribe of Iouda, Sikima in Ephraim, and Kedesa in Nephthalia (this was in the region of upper Galilee[245]).[246]

92. He also divided up what remained of the plunder, of which there was a great deal. All together and each one individually received possession of great wealth, gold and silver and clothing and other possessions, as well as such a crowd of beasts that their number could not be learned.[247]

Plunder distributed

(1.25) 93. Then, bringing the army together in an assembly, Iesous spoke thus to those settled beyond the Jordan throughout Amoraia, these consisting of 50,000[248] troops who had been their fellow soldiers: "Since God, the father and master of the Hebrew race, gave us this land to possess and promised to preserve it as our possession for all time,[249] **94.** since too you willingly gave your cooperation in everything when we asked this of you in accordance with his command,[250] it is just[251] that you, now that no further difficulties remain, should obtain your rest. Maintain your eagerness, so that, should we again need it, we might have it available if necessary, rather than being so worn out by present [matters] as to be somewhat listless in the future.[252]

Joshua dismisses Trans-jordanians

95. We are therefore grateful to you and will be so not only now but for all time, for having shared in our dangers. We do well to remember our friends and to keep in mind what we have due to them. For you postponed your enjoyment of the good things available to you for our sakes, and you decided to exert yourselves for that

---

[244] This positive characterization of Joshua echoes that used of him in Josh 11:15: "he left nothing undone that the Lord had commanded Moses."

[245] In 5.63 Josephus situated "Kedesa" in "the country of the Galileans."

[246] See Josh 20:7. Josephus passes over the 3 Transjordanian refuge cities cited in Josh 20:8, having already alluded to Moses' establishment of these in *Ant.* 4.172. He likewise leaves aside the extended preceding divine instruction to Joshua concerning the refuge cities and their functioning in Josh 20:1-6 that itself duplicates the Lord's words about these in Num 35:9-34 (and summarized by Josephus in *Ant.* 4.172).

[247] On Joshua's earlier, general distribution of the plunder captured from Ai at Gilgal, see 5.48. In Josh 22:8 (// 5.96) it is to the Transjordanian troops alone that Joshua awards the various items of plunder (including also bronze and iron) at the moment he dismisses them to their homes.

[248] Josh 22:1 does not mention a figure for the Transjordanians addressed by Joshua in 22:2-7. Compare the "precise" figures for the Canaanite forces introduced by Josephus in 5.64. Josephus reverses the order of Joshua 22 (// 5.93-114, the dismissal of the Transjordanians and its sequel) and 23 (// 5.90, Joshua's farewell discourse many years after this; see v. 1), thus making also the Transjordanians recipients of that discourse.

[249] Compare Josh 22:4a: "... the Lord your God has given rest to your brethren, as he promised them...." Josephus' specification concerning the everlasting validity of God's land promise here is noteworthy, given his tendency to downplay this particular biblical promise; see note to "city" at 5.15. The same combination of divine titles, namely, "father" (Greek: πατήρ) and "master" (Greek: δεσπότης), appears in the prologue of *Ant.* in 1.20, there, however, with the universalizing qualification of God as "father and lord of all." On Josephus' use of the title "father" for God, see Schlatter 1910: 14-16; on this usage in turn of the era Jewish writings generally, see Strotmann: 1991.

[250] On the Transjordanians' committing themselves to participate in the conquest of the land west of the Jordan at Moses' urging, see *Ant.* 4.169-171; cf. Joshua's reminding them of this commitment in 5.3-4.

[251] Greek: δίκαιος. On this Josephan key word and its cognates and the background to his usage, see Mason 1991: 86-87, 142-49, 219-21; Feldman 1998: 113-16.

[252] Josephus here expatiates considerably on Joshua's words of appreciation for the Transjordanians' assistance and their obedience to him (and Moses) as cited in Josh 22:2-3. Thereby, he depicts the Transjordanians as exemplars of that sense of intra-Jewish solidarity he wishes to inculcate in *Antiquities*.

which now, by God's loyalty,[253] we have attained, and only then to participate in those things.[254] **96.** To those good things you possess there has now been added the abundant wealth you have won by your exertions with us; you will take with you much plunder and gold and silver and, what is still more than these things, our loyalty and eagerness to recompense you in whatever way you desire.[255] For you have not failed in anything of what Moyses predicted,[256] or despised him once he departed from humanity[257]; nor is there anything for which we do not give you thanks.

97. Therefore we dismiss you, rejoicing, to your allotments,[258] and appeal to you to realize that there is no boundary to your kinship with us. Likewise do not, because this river is between us, think of us as aliens, rather than as Hebrews. For we are all, whether living on this side or that, [descendants] of Abraham; there is one God[259] who brought our ancestors and yours to life.[260] **98.** Pay attention to his worship[261] and keep full watch over the constitution[262] he established through Moyses[263] in order that, with you adhering to these things, God will show himself loyal[264] and an ally,[265] whereas if you turn aside to the imitation of other nations, he will be alienated from your race."[266]

99. When he had said these things and greeted those in authority one by one and the crowd in common, he himself remained behind.[267] The people saw them off; not

---

[253] Greek: εὔνοια; the term recurs in 5.96, where the Israelites speak of their "loyalty" towards the Cisjordanians. On the word, see Spicq 1982 (III): 316-21.

[254] This further expression of gratitude in the name of the whole people lacks a parallel in Joshua's words to the Transjordanians as cited in Josh 22:2-6.

[255] This invitation to the Transjordanians to take some of the plunder acquired in the Cisjordanian campaign corresponds to that issued by Joshua in Josh 22:8. It echoes as well Josephus' earlier notice on Joshua's awarding the plunder to the whole people in 5.92.

[256] Compare Joshua's opening words to the Transjordanians in Josh 22:2: "you have kept all that Moses... commanded you...." Joshua has already touched on the Transjordanians' fidelity to what was asked of them in 5.94. His praise of them here echoes Josephus' accolade for Joshua himself in 5.91.

[257] The circumstances of Moses' death are described in *Ant.* 4.324-327. In 5.1 there is an allusion to this event, using a phrase similar to the one employed here in 5.96.

[258] Joshua 22 twice cites Joshua's dismissal of the Transjordanians, first in v. 4b, and then at the opening of v. 8.

[259] Greek: θεός εἷς. See the listing of similar formulas, inspired by the *Shema'* of Deut 6:4, concerning the oneness/unicity of God elsewhere in Josephus in Schlatter 1910: 16. Compare the formula εἷς θεός in Eph 4:6; 1 Tim 2:5.

[260] This extended affirmation of the solidarity between the Transjordanians and Cisjordanians is Josephus' own amplification of the biblical Joshua's words to the former. Joshua's statement about his hear-

ers' common status as "descendants of Abraham" is paralleled in John 8:33, where the Jews make this claim for themselves (compare Matt 3:9// Luke 3:8, where John the Baptist warns them against complacent invocation of Abraham as their "father"). On Abraham's "paternity" in Josephus overall, see Spilsbury 1998: 55-56; for references to Abraham as ancestor of the Jews in Greco-Roman authors, see Siker 1987: 197-201.

[261] Greek: θρησκεία. On the word and its cognates, see Schlatter 1910: 77; 1932: 98, 242, 247.

[262] Greek: πολιτεία. On Josephus' use of this term as a comprehensive designation for Israel's God-given system of laws and form of government, see Troiani 1994; Schröder 1996: *passim*.

[263] On Moses as the mediator of Israel's constitution, see, e.g., *Ant.* 3.213; 4.196, 302.

[264] This adjective (Greek: εὔνους) for God echoes the cognate noun εὔνοια ("loyalty") used of him in 5.95; see note to "loyalty" at 5.95.

[265] On Josephus' use of the term "ally" (Greek: σύμμαχος) as a title for God, see Attridge 1976: 79-80.

[266] In Josh 22:5a Joshua urges the Transjordanians to "observe the commandment and law" given them by Moses, while in v. 5b he specifies that this entails whole-hearted attachment to the Lord. Josephus replaces the latter element with a reference to the respective consequences of the Transjordanians' heeding or not heeding his foregoing exhortation regarding the Mosaic "constitution."

[267] Compare Josh 22:6, where Joshua "blesses" the departing Transjordanians. Josephus eliminates this action on the part of the non-priest Joshua.

without tears and reluctance did they separate from each other.[268]

(1.26) 100. Once they had crossed the river, the tribe of Roubel and that of Gad and as many of the Manasseites as were joined to them erected an altar on the banks of the Jordan, that this might be a memorial to those who would later be, [a symbol][269] of their relationship with those living on the other side.[270]

Transjordanians erect altar

101. When, however, those on the other side heard that those whom they had just dismissed had erected an altar, not for the purpose for which they had set it up, but rather with revolutionary intent[271] and as an introduction of strange gods, they were not unwilling to disbelieve this. Rather, thinking this slander about their divine worship convincing, they took up arms, doing so in order to inflict vengeance on those who had erected the altar by crossing the river and punishing them for their deviation from the ancestral customs.[272] **102.** For it seemed good to them to give no thought to their kinship with them or to the status of those accused, but rather to the will of God and the manner in which he rejoices to be honored.[273] **103.** But as they were about to undertake the campaign under the sway of their wrath, Iesous and Eleazar, the high priest, and the senate restrained them by their words, advising them to first test their intentions. Then, should they learn that their mind was evil, they might proceed to arms against them.[274]

Reaction of Cisjordanians

104. They therefore sent ambassadors to them, Phinees,[275] the son of Eleazar, and with him ten of those held in honor by the Hebrews. They were to learn what they were thinking when, having crossed over, they set up the altar on the banks of the river.[276]

105. Once they forded the river and reached them, an assembly was called. Phinees[277] standing among them, said that their offense was too great[278] for a repri-

Phineas addresses Transjordanians

---

[268] The "parting notice" of Josh 22:9 identifies Shiloh as the site of the farewells, but makes no mention of the participants' emotional state.

[269] This word (Greek: σύμβυλον) is absent in E and Lat; both Niese and Marcus view it as a likely later addition.

[270] Josephus here expands the altar-building notice of Josh 22:10 with an editorial comment, inspired by the Transjordanians' subsequent affirmation about what they have done in Josh 22:27, which makes clear, from the start, the (legitimate) nature of their construction. Contrast *Bib. Ant.* 22.1, where, right at the beginning of Pseudo-Philo's version of the story, the Israelites are (correctly) informed that the Transjordanians are offering sacrifices on their altar and have instituted priests for their sanctuary. On Josephus' and Pseudo-Philo's versions of the Transjordanian altar story of Josh 22:10-34, see Begg 1997c and Spilsbury 1998: 150-53.

[271] Greek: νεωτερισμός. On Josephus' pejorative use of this term and its cognates in relation to the "revolutionaries" of his time and their "spiritual ancestors" of earlier periods (e.g., Jeroboam), see Feldman 1998a: 238; 2000: 397, n. 573; Mason 2001: 28, n. 122.

[272] Josephus elaborates Josh 22:12 (the Cisjordanians' recourse to arms) with mention both of the (mistaken) thinking that prompts this and the purpose of their intended initiative. On the phrase "ancestral cus-

toms," see 5.90. Related phrases will recur throughout Josephus' altar story; see "ancestral laws" in 5.108 and 5.112 (here literally "the ancestrals").

[273] These indications concerning the Cisjordanians' state of mind are a further elaboration of Josh 22:12. On the "will of God" concept in Josephus and the terms of the βουλ-stem (here: τὸ τοῦ θεοῦ βουλητόν) used by him in reference to this, see Attridge 1976: 74-76.

[274] This intervention by the leadership has no counterpart in Josh 22:13-14, where, on their own, the people proceed to send a delegation to the Transjordanians. On Josephus' tendency to denigrate "the crowd" as an entity in constant need of the moderating guidance of its leaders, see Feldman 1998: 145-47.

[275] Josephus introduced this figure, the biblical "Phineas," in *Ant.* 4.152. On the portrayal of him in Josephus and Pseudo-Philo, see Feldman 2002.

[276] See Josh 22:13-14, to which Josephus appends mention of the charge given the delegation. In *Bib. Ant.* 22.2 Pseudo-Philo eliminates the sending of a delegation and has Joshua and the elders address the culprits directly.

[277] In Josh 22:15-20 the delegation as a whole addresses the Transjordanians. Josephus' version consistently highlights the role of the priest Phineas in the proceedings.

[278] This statement by Phineas takes the place of the

mand in words and an admonition for the future. Nonetheless, rather than requiting them according to the magnitude of the transgression by immediately rushing to arms and punishment through combat, they, looking to their kinship and the possibility that they might become prudent[279] from their words, had first initiated an embassy.[280]

106. "It is our purpose to learn what led you[281] to construct the altar, so that we not appear rash in chastising you by force of arms, should you have made the altar for some holy reason.[282] Nonetheless, we shall take just vengeance, should the charge prove true.[283] **107.** For we did not think that you, given your experience of God's intention and your having been obedient hearers of the laws that he has given us, once you separated from us and came to your own portion that, by the favor of God and his providential care[284] for us, you received by lot, forgetting him, deserting the tent, the ark, and our ancestral altar, and going over to the evils of the Chananaians, have introduced strange gods.[285]

108. But you will be thought to have done nothing wrong if, changing your mind,[286] and being insane no longer, you respect and stay mindful of the ancestral laws.[287] If, however, you persist in your offenses, we shall not shrink from any exertion on behalf of the laws. Rather, fording the Jordan, we shall give them—and God still more—our help, considering you no different from the Chananaians, but destroying you just like them.[288] **109.** For do not think that, having crossed the river, you are also beyond God's power. Everywhere, rather, you are [encompassed by] what is his, and are unable to escape his authority and the judgment [that derives] from this.[289]

110. If, however, you see your presence here as an obstacle to prudent thinking,

---

delegation's opening question in Josh 22:16 ("what is this treachery which you have committed against the God of Israel...?"), which *Bib. Ant.* 22.2 expands into a series of accusatory questions.

[279] Greek: σωφρονέω. On Josephus' use of this verb and its cognates in reference to the cardinal virtue of "prudence," see Feldman 1998: 110-11, and, more generally, Spicq 1978 (II): 867-74. The word recurs twice subsequently in Phineas' speech (5.109, 110), as well as in the Transjordanians' response (5.112).

[280] These statements informing the Transjordanians of what has just transpired among their fellows (see 5.101-104) are unparalleled in the delegation's speech in Josh 22:17-18 (+ 20), which itself features a series of further accusations against the culprits.

[281] Such switches from indirect (see 5.105) to direct discourse in the course of a single speech are not infrequent in Josephus; see Begg 1993: 123-24, n. 772.

[282] This Josephan addition echoes the charge—likewise inserted by him—given the delegation in 5.104.

[283] Compare the leaders' concluding words to the people, holding open such a possibility, in 5.103.

[284] On God's "providence"/ "providential care" (Greek: πρόνοια) as a key theme of *Antiquities*, see Attridge 1976: 71-106; Spilsbury 1998: 72-74.

[285] This expression of confidence by Phineas as to

what he and those for whom he is speaking ("we") do not think the Transjordanians have done stands in contrast to the consistently accusatory tone of the delegation's speech in Josh 22:16-20. The statement's reference to "strange gods" echoes the same phrase in the notice on the Cisjordanians' hearing that the Transjordanians had built their altar as a "introduction of strange gods" in 5.101.

[286] Greek: μετανοέω. On Josephus' various "repentance terms," see Schlatter 1932: 146-47; Dietrich 1936: 306-15.

[287] Compare the delegation's appeal in Josh 22:19b: "only do not rebel against the Lord...," which Josephus expands with a word of promise by Phineas. The phrase "ancestral laws" (Greek: νόμοι πάτριοι) here is a variant of the expression "ancestral customs" in 5.90, 101. See note to "ancestral customs" at 5.90.

[288] This threat, balancing Phineas' preceding (conditional) promise, is a further Josephan elaboration of the biblical delegation's speech. On the Israelites' task of exterminating the Canaanites, see 5.49, 59, 72, 90.

[289] Also this reminder of God's inescapability lacks a counterpart in the delegation's speech in Josh 22:16-20. Similar statements concerning God's omnipresence and omniscience are found in, e.g., *Ant.* 2.129; 8.108; *Apion* 2.160; see Schlatter 1932: 26.

nothing prevents our redistributing the land once again and abandoning this region to sheep-grazing.[290] But in any case, you would do well to be prudent and think better of your recent offenses. We appeal to you as well for the sake of your children and wives not to make us use compulsion. Conduct your deliberations therefore as if your own safety and that of those you love depends on this assembly, considering it preferable to be overcome by words than to await the test of deeds and war."[291]

(1.27) 111. When Phinees had said these things, the heads of the assembly and the entire crowd itself began to make a defense regarding the things alleged against them. They said that they would neither deviate from their kinship with them, nor had they set up their altar with revolutionary intent.[292] *Transjordanians respond*

112. They knew that there is one God, common to all the Hebrews, and that sacrifices were to be made to him on the bronze altar in front of the tent.[293] They had erected the one they had set up and on account of which they had become suspect, not for worship,[294] "but that it might be a symbol and a token of our everlasting relationship with you and of the necessity of thinking prudently and abiding by the ancestral [laws],[295] rather than as a beginning of transgression, as you surmise.

113. May God be a credible witness for us that we constructed the altar for this very purpose. May you then have a better opinion of us and not condemn us for these things, for which all those belonging to the race of Abraham who adopt revolutionary[296] ways, contrary to customary practice, would justly be wiped out."[297]

(1.28) 114. After commending them for saying these things,[298] Phinees came to *Altar issue resolved*

---

[290] Compare the invitation ("but now, if your land is unclean, pass over to the Lord's land... and take for yourself a possession among us") issued to the Transjordanians in Josh 22:19a. Josephus appends an indication as to what would become of their present holdings in that eventuality.

[291] This concluding admonition takes the place of the warning reference to Achan's sin and its consequences for Israel with which the delegation terminates its speech in Josh 22:20.

[292] This opening statement replaces the invocation of the Lord with which the Transjordanians begin their defense in Josh 22:22-24. A version of the later segment does, however, occur at the conclusion of Josephus' version of the altar-builders' defense; see 5.113. The term "revolutionary intent" (Greek: νεωτερισμός) echoes the same expression in 5.101 (where Josephus himself states that the Transjordanians had not built their altar for such a purpose); see note to "intent" at 5.101. The related adjective νεώτερος ("revolutionary") occurs at the end of the Transjordanians' reply in 5.113.

[293] This affirmation draws on the Transjordanians' assurances of their commitment to the sacrificial service at the one legitimate altar in Josh 22:27, 29b. Their acknowledgement of the Hebrews' "one, common God" picks up on Joshua's reminder to them (5.97) "that there is one God who brought our ancestors and yours to life." Likewise their references to the tent and the

altar echo Phineas' statement that their fellows could not think that they had abandoned these in 5.107. On the erection of the "bronze altar in front of the tent" in Moses' time, see *Ant.* 3.149.

[294] See the Transjordanians' double denial of the sacrificial character of their altar in Josh 22:26, 28b. Compare *Bib. Ant.* 22.3-4, where the Transjordanians assert that whereas their altar was indeed intended for sacrificial purposes, their motivation in constructing it was legitimate, i.e. that their descendants might be kept from turning to other gods as a result of their not having an altar of their own on which to sacrifice to the Lord.

[295] In Josh 22:27 the Transjordanians state that their altar is intended as a "witness" to their participation in the one legitimate sacrificial cult.

[296] Greek: νεώτερος. See note to "intent" at 5.111.

[297] These concluding words of Josephus' Transjordanians reflect those with which their biblical counterparts open their defense: appeal to what the Lord "knows" about them (Josh 22:22) and admission that they may rightly be punished by their fellows if they are, in fact, guilty of the charges made against them (22:23). The assembly's reference to the "race of Abraham" echoes Joshua's affirmation that all Jews are "descendants of Abraham" in 5.97.

[298] See Josh 22:30-31, where Phineas acknowledges that the Transjordanians have not "committed treachery against the Lord" and thereby "saved" Israel. Com-

Iesous and reported these [words] of theirs to the people.[299] Iesous rejoiced that there was no necessity at present to muster them or lead them out for armed warfare against men who were their kin.[300] He offered thanksgiving sacrifices to God because of these things.[301] Thereafter, dismissing the crowd, each one to his own allotment, Iesous himself remained in Sikima.[302]

Joshua's fare-well discourse

115. Twenty years later, being extremely old, he summoned the notables of the cities, the rulers and the senate, and assembled to himself whoever of the crowd that might readily do so.[303] When they arrived, he reminded them of all God's benefits,[304] there being many who had advanced from a humble state to one of glory and abundance.[305] **116.** He appealed to them to preserve the outlook God had towards them, since it was by piety alone[306] that the Deity would remain a friend[307] to them.[308] For it was fitting for him who was about to depart this life to bequeath this admonition to them, and he requested them to remember his appeal.[309]

Deaths of Joshua and Eleazar

(1.29) 117. When he had said such things to those present, he died, after living 110 years.[310] Of these, he lived together with Moyses for forty years for purposes of

---

pare the response made by Joshua to the Transjordanians' self-defense in *Bib. Ant.* 22.5-6, in which he reproves them for failing to teach their sons God's law and commands them to destroy their altar (as they proceed to do, 22.7).

[299] Compare Josh 22:32, where the entire delegation, rather than Phineas alone, reports back to Israel. In contrast to Josephus, who accentuates Phineas' role in the affair, Pseudo-Philo's version never mentions him.

[300] Josh 22:33 speaks of the entire people's being "pleased" by the delegation's report and foregoing their projected campaign. In contrast to MT Josh 22:10-34, which never mentions Joshua (in LXX 22:34 he gives a name to the Transjordanian altar), Josephus makes recurrent reference to his involvement in the affair. See already 5.103, where, along with the other leaders, he intervenes to restrain the crowd.

[301] Joshua 22 does not mention such an offering of sacrifices. In *Bib. Ant.* 22.7 sacrifices are offered by the Cisjordanians, but these are in expiation of their fellows' sin.

[302] This concluding notice, alluding back to 5.93, where Joshua convenes—at an unspecified site—the assembly in order to dismiss the Transjordanians, takes the place of Josh 22:34 with its mention of the name ("Witness") which the Transjordanians (MT; in LXX Joshua confers the name) give their altar. Josephus likely derives the site "Sikima" (Shechem) from Josh 24:1, where this is the place to which Joshua summons the Israelites for his final words to them (of which Josephus' summary parallel appears in the immediately following 5.115).

[303] Compare Josh 24:1, which does not mention the passage of 20 years, Joshua's extreme old age (see, however, 13:1a= 23:1b; cf. 5.71, 90), or his calling together, not merely the various leadership groups, but (a portion of) the people as well.

[304] Greek: εὐεργεσία. On this term and its word-field, see Spicq 1978 (I): 307-13.

[305] This summary "reminder" takes the place of Joshua's extended review of God's benefits extending from Abraham down to the divine gifts to the current generation in Josh 24:2-13. In contrast to Josephus' compression, Pseudo-Philo expatiates on the retrospective of Josh 24:2-13 in *Bib. Ant.* 23.4-11.

[306] The text is uncertain here. SP's reading runs "by showing him [God] every honor and that piety...." On "piety" (Greek: εὐσέβεια) as the fundamental requirement of the God-human relationship in Josephus, see Schlatter 1932: 37-38, 96-97; Feldman 1998: 126-29.

[307] Josephus uses the term φίλος ("friend") of God in relation to humans rather infrequently; another such usage is in *Ant.* 6.20. Somewhat more often he speaks of individuals or the people as a whole as God's "friend(s)"; see *War* 7.327 (the Jewish race); *Ant.* 5.213 (Gideon); 6.294 (Samuel); cf. Schlatter 1932: 39.

[308] Josephus here eliminates the "choice" between serving the Lord or other gods which Joshua offers the people in Josh 24:14-15; his Joshua does not even raise the latter possibility.

[309] This conclusion to Joshua's final speech replaces the extended exchange between him and the people (Josh 24:16-24) on the possibility of their serving the Lord, which is itself followed by a renewal of the covenant (24:25), erection of a witness stone (24:26-27), and dismissal of the people (24:28). Pseudo-Philo does present a parallel to Josh 24:24 (the people's pledge to serve the Lord) and 25 (the renewal of the covenant) in *Bib. Ant.* 23.14.

[310] See Josh 24:29.

useful instruction, while after the latter's death he was a general for twenty-five years.[311] **118.** He was a man not lacking in sagacity, nor unskilled in explaining his thoughts clearly to the many;[312] rather, he was extraordinary in both these respects.[313] He was great-souled and most daring in the face of tasks and dangers, most competent too in guiding the affairs of peacetime, and being at all times in conformity with virtue.[314]

119. He was buried in the city of Thamna of the tribe of Ephraim.[315] At about the same time Eleazar the high priest also died, leaving the high priesthood behind to his son Phinees.[316] There is a memorial to him and a tomb in the city of Gabatha.[317]

(2.1) 120. After their deaths, Phinees, in accordance with the will of God, prophesied[318] that the tribe of Iouda was being awarded the leadership in the extermination of the Chananaian race.[319] For the people was solicitous to learn what was pleasing to God.[320] Having secured the aid of Semeon on the understanding that, once they had exterminated those subject to themselves, they would do the same to those living in Semeon's allotment, [they went out to battle].[321]

Phineas' directive

(2.2) 121. At that time the Chananaians were at the height of their power.[322] They

Judah and Simeon's initiatives

---

[311] This "breakdown" for the 2 key periods of Joshua's life lacks an equivalent in Joshua 24. Josephus obtains the 25-year figure for Joshua's time as leader by combining the indications given by him in 5.68 (the conquest under Joshua lasted 5 years) and 5.115 (20 years intervened between Joshua's post-conquest initiatives and his final address to the people). In *Bib. Ant.* 24.6 the people speak of Joshua's having led them, like Moses, for 40 years, while *S. 'Olam Rab.* 12.1 assigns him a term of 28 years.

[312] Josephus begins his eulogy of Joshua with a double *litotes*.

[313] On such ability in public speaking as a key element of the cardinal virtue of "wisdom" that Josephus regularly ascribes to his heroes, see Feldman 1998: 104-5.

[314] The Book of Joshua itself lacks such an eulogy for Joshua; Josephus' encomium for him itself echoes the words with which he introduces the hero in *Ant.* 3.49: "a most courageous man and excellent in enduring toil, and most capable in understanding, and in speech, one who worshipped God outstandingly...." Such eulogies are a recurrent feature in Josephus' presentation of the heroes of his history. They serve to drive home the point that the Jews did indeed have their great men, possessing all the key virtues prized by his Greco-Roman readers.

[315] Josh 24:30 supplies further details concerning Joshua's burial place: "Timnath-serah" was Joshua's own inheritance (see Josh 19:50) and situated "north of the mountain of Gaash" (MT; LXX B ἀπὸ Βορρᾶ τοῦ ὄρους τοῦ Γαλαάδ). Josephus leaves aside Josh 24:31 (Israel serves the Lord during the lifetimes of Joshua and the elders who survived him) and 32 (the bones of Joseph that had been brought up from Egypt are buried

in Shechem). The latter omission is surprising in that Josephus does reproduce (*Ant.* 2.319) the notice of Exod 13:19 about Joseph's bones being removed from Egypt by the departing Israelites, as well as Joseph's own command about the matter (Gen 50:25= *Ant.* 2.200).

[316] Josephus' notice about Phineas' succeeding Eleazar his father has a certain parallel in the LXX plus at the end of Josh 24:33, which speaks of the former serving as priest in place of Eleazar until his own death. MT Josh 24:33 simply mentions Eleazar's burial in Gibeah, "the town of Phineas his son."

[317] MT Josh 24:33 calls Eleazar's burial place "Gibeah," LXX Γαβαάρ, this being then specified as a site belonging to his son Phineas that had been given him in the hill country of Ephraim. Josephus' mention of a "monument" and a "tomb" for Eleazar are his own elaboration of the source burial notice.

[318] On Josephus' recurrent linkage of the priestly (here represented by Phineas) and prophetic functions, see Blenkinsopp 1974; Feldman 1990: 419-21.

[319] In Judg 1:1-2 the Israelites take the initiative in "inquiring," in some unspecified manner, of the Lord about who should advance first against the Canaanites. Thereupon, the Lord responds to them directly, announcing that Judah, to whom he has awarded its land, is to go up first.

[320] This appended remark reflects the mention of the people's "inquiring of the Lord" in Judg 1:1.

[321] See Judg 1:3. The words "they went out to battle" have been supplied, following Marcus (*ad loc.*), to fill an obvious lacuna in Josephus' text.

[322] This remark has no equivalent in Judges 1. Its insertion serves to heighten the magnitude of Judah's subsequent victory.

took their stand for battle with a large army at Zebeke,[323] having entrusted the leadership to the king of the Zebekenoi, Adonizebek (whose name means "lord of the Zebekenoi," for *adoni* is "lord" in the Hebrew language).[324] They were hoping to conquer the Israelites on account of the death of Iesous.[325] **122.** But when the Israelites joined battle with them, the two tribes I just mentioned fought splendidly and killed some 10,000 of them;[326] putting the rest to flight and pursuing them, they captured Adonizebek.

123. After being mutilated by them[327] he stated: "I could not be hidden from God for ever; what I just suffered is that which I earlier did not hesitate to do to seventy-two kings."[328] **124.** They brought him still living to Hierosolyma, and buried him once he died.[329] As they passed through, they stormed the cities; having taken many,[330] they besieged Hierosolyma. Eventually taking its lower part, they killed all the inhabitants. The upper part was, however, too difficult for them to storm given the solidity of the walls and the nature of the site.[331]

(2.3) 125. From there they moved their camp to Hebron;[332] taking this by storm, they killed everyone.[333] There yet survived the race of the giants. In the size of their bodies and appearance they were unlike other people; they were astonishing to see and terrible to hear of. Even now their bones, which are unlike those that have come to our knowledge, are displayed.[334]

126. They then gave this [Hebron] as a special gift of honor to the Levites along

---

[323] Judg 1:4-5 (MT and LXX) designates the battle site as "Bezek."

[324] Judg 1:5 (MT and LXX) calls the enemy leader "Adonibezek." Josephus supplies both the title of "king" for him and the explanation of the meaning of his name in Hebrew.

[325] Josephus adds this remark, harking back to the opening of 5.120, about the enemy's state of mind as the hostilities commence.

[326] Conflating the duplicate battle notices of Judg 1:4 and 5, Josephus draws his casualty figure from the former verse. His reference to the tribes' fighting "splendidly" is an embellishment. He leaves aside the source's double designation of the enemy as "the Canaanites and the Perizzites."

[327] Judg 1:6b specifies that the victors cut off Adonibezek's "thumbs and great toes."

[328] In Judg 1:7a Adonibezek's "confession" ends with his affirming that God has "requited" him in accordance with his own treatment of the *70* kings who, having been deprived of their thumbs and great toes, ate scraps under his table. On the divine "inescapability" to which Josephus' Adonibezek here alludes, see 5.109.

[329] Judg 1:7b does not mention Adonibezek's burial.

[330] Judges 1 does not refer to such a capture of other cities prior to Judah's assault on Jerusalem itself (see v. 8).

[331] Josephus' distinction between Jerusalem's "lower" and "upper" parts, of which Judah captured the

former, but not the latter, represents a reworking of Judg 1:8, where the entire city appears to fall to the besiegers. He introduces the distinction with an eye to the account of 2 Sam 5:6-10 (= *Ant.* 7.60-64), where Jerusalem is still not under Israelite control at the beginning of David's reign (see also Josh 15:63, which states that the Judeans could not drive the Jebusites out of Jerusalem).

[332] This reading of the site name follows that given in Judg 1:10a, MSPELat, and Marcus's text; Niese reads "Nebron" with RO. Josephus leaves aside the city's earlier name ("Kiriatharba"), just as he passes over the notice of Judg 1:9 about Judah moving against the Canaanites living in the hill country, the Negeb, and the Shephelah.

[333] Judges 1 does not explicitly mention Judah's capture of Hebron or massacre of its population.

[334] Josephus elaborates on the reference to the expulsion of "the descendants of Anak" from Hebron by Caleb in Judg 1:20b (= Josh 15:14), taking the source's phrase "descendants of Anak" in the sense of "giants" in light of Num 13:32-33, just as he does in his version of the latter text in *Ant.* 3.305, where he cites the spies' report that "in Hebron... they had encountered the descendants of giants." His appended mention of the giants' bones still being available for viewing serves to confirm the reliability of the biblical references to these fantastic beings; compare his notice on the remains of Noah's ark being displayed by the Armenians in his own time in *Ant.* 1.92; 20.25.

with 2,000 cubits,[335] while in accordance with Moyses' commandments they gave the [remaining] land as a gift to Chaleb, one of the spies whom Moyses sent into Chananaia.[336]

127. They also gave land to the descendants of Iothor[337] the Madianite[338] (for he was the father-in-law of Moyses) to live in it.[339] For they had left behind their ancestral land and followed them, accompanying them through the desert.[340]

(2.4) 128. The tribes of Iouda and Semeon captured the cities in the hill-country of Chananaia,[341] as well as Askalon and Azotus in the plain near the sea. Gaza and Akkaron eluded them,[342] however, for these, being in the plain and having a large supply of chariots, inflicted harm on the invaders.[343] Having done very well for themselves in war, the [two] tribes returned to their own cities and laid down their weapons.[344]

(2.5) 129. Now the Benjamites, since Hierosolyma belonged to them,[345] permitted

Benjamites spare Canaanites

---

[335] This award is not mentioned in the context of Judges 1. For the datum Josephus draws on Josh 21:11 (cf. his general summary of Joshua 21 in 5.91), where the Kohathite Levites are given "Kiriath-arba, that is Hebron." The 2,000 cubits conferred on the Levites in addition to the city itself derive from LXX Num 35:4 (= *Ant.* 4.67), where this (MT has 1,000) is the prescribed extent of the pasture lands surrounding the Levitical cities.

[336] See Judg 1:20a. Earlier, Josephus passed over the fuller account of Caleb's receiving his inheritance, Josh 14:6-15, where it is Joshua who awards Hebron to him (v. 13), just as he does not reproduce the divine directives of Num 14:24; Deut 1:36—to which he is alluding here—promising a portion of land to the faithful Caleb. In the present context, Josephus omits the sequence Judg 1:11-15 (= Josh 15:15-19, also omitted by him), featuring the capture of Debir (v. 11), and Caleb's awarding his daughter Achsah to Othniel (vv. 12-13) and water-springs to her (vv. 14-15). He further passes over the reference to Caleb's exclusion of the three sons of Anak (Judg 1:20b), given that in 5.125 he has already anticipated its content; see note to "displayed" there.

[337] MT Judg 1:16 does not give the name of Moses' father-in-law; LXX A⁺ calls him "Ioab," LXX B "Iothar," and LXX L etc. "Iobab." In *Ant.* 2.258; 3.63-74 Josephus designates him as "Ragouel," in line with the "Reuel" of Exod 2:18. On Josephus' portrayal of the figure, see Feldman 1998a: 38-54.

[338] Judg 1:16 calls Moses' father-in-law "the Kenite." Josephus' designation harmonizes with Exod 2:16 (cf. *Ant.* 2.257-258), where he is called "the priest of Midian."

[339] Such an allotment of land to Jethro's descendants by Judah is not explicitly mentioned in Judg 1:16, where the former simply "settle" with the latter after accompanying them on their migration.

[340] In Judg 1:16 the Kenites accompany Judah

"from the city of palms into the wilderness of Judah which lies in the Negeb near Arad...."

[341] Josephus conflates Judg 1:17 (the 2 tribes defeat the Canaanites) and 1:19a (Judah takes possession of "the hill country"). From the former verse he omits the mention of "Zephath" as the Canaanite site which was destroyed and so received the name "Hormath" ("ruin"), while from the latter he leaves aside its reference to God's being with Judah.

[342] Josephus' notice here has similarities and differences with both MT and LXX Judg 1:18. According to MT, the 2 tribes did capture the 3 Philistine cities of Gaza, Ashkelon, and Ekron (compare Josephus where they capture only the 2nd of these). In common with LXX, he mentions a 4th city, Azotus (= Hebrew Ashdod); whereas, however, LXX avers that none of the 4 cities were taken, Josephus differentiates between Ashkelon and Azotus, which were captured, and Gaza and Ekron, which were not. In 5.81 Judah was allotted the cities of Askalon and Gaza; at this point, the tribe gains actual possession of the former, but not the latter.

[343] Josephus' reference to the "chariots" that impeded the capture of the 2 Philistine cities reflects MT Judg 1:19b (Judah "could not drive out the inhabitants of the plain, because they had chariots [רכב] of iron"). In LXX the Hebrew word is read as the proper name, i.e. "Rekhab" (see Jeremiah 35), who forbade the dispossession of the plains-dwellers. The Targum prefaces its rendering of Judg 1:19b with the statement "because they [the Judeans] sinned...."

[344] This concluding notice to the segment 5.120-128 (// Judg 1:8-20), focusing on the successes of Judah and Simeon, lacks a biblical counterpart.

[345] This parenthetical comment harks back to 5.82 (cf. Josh 11:16) where the "Hierosolymites" are said to mark the boundary of Benjamin's territory. It likewise anticipates the notice on Benjamin's dealings with the Jebusites in Judg 1:21, which Josephus will elaborate in what follows. Both Judges 1 and Josephus' own presen-

the inhabitants to pay tribute. Thus everyone was at rest; the former ceasing to kill, the latter to be in danger, they had leisure to cultivate the land. The other tribes did the same; imitating the Benjamites, they were content with payment of tribute and allowed the Chananaians to live in peace.[346]

Bethel captured

(2.6) 130. Ephran besieged Bethel, but did not find a result commensurate with the time and exertions of the siege; though frustrated by the delay, they kept at it.[347] **131.** Then, having seized one of citizens who had gone out to attend to necessities, they gave him pledges that they would save him and his relatives, should he hand over the city.[348] He then swore that he would deliver up the city to them on these conditions. And when he had handed it over, he was saved along with his household, while they killed all the [other] inhabitants and got hold of the city.[349]

Israelites neglect their constitution

(2.7) 132. After these things the Israelites became inactive with regard to the enemy; they devoted themselves to the land and the toils involved in this. As their wealth increased, surrendering themselves to comfort and pleasure, they thought little of the order of their constitution and no longer paid careful attention to the laws.[350]

133. Angered at these things, the Deity announced through an oracle[351] that, just as they had earlier spared the Chananaians in opposition to his intent, so the latter would have the opportunity of employing much cruelty against them.[352]

134. They, for their part, while despondent at these [messages] from God, were nonetheless indisposed for war, having taken much from the Chananaians, and being already weary of exertion due to their comforts.[353] **135.** Now it happened that

---

tation in 5.124, 129 leave uncertain which tribe—Judah or Benjamin—was the intended master of Jerusalem.

[346] Josephus here explicates the statement of Judg 1:21 that the Benjamites did not expel the Jebusites from Jerusalem, the latter continuing to live among the former "to this day": in their desire to devote themselves to farming, the Benjamites (whose example the other tribes follow), limited themselves to taxing the inhabitants, rather than exterminating them, as Joshua had enjoined; see 5.90.

[347] This is an elaboration of Judg 1:22a, where it is the "house of Joseph" (of which "Ephraim" [Ephran] was a component) that goes up against Bethel; Josephus omits the remark of 1:22b about the Lord (so MT LXX B; LXX A has Judah) "being with" them.

[348] In Judg 1:23-24 spies are dispatched against Bethel by "the house of Joseph" and it is they who address the man who has exited the city (whose earlier name, i.e. "Luz," cited in 1:23b, Josephus omits).

[349] See Judg 1:25, which does not mention the Bethelite's "swearing." Josephus omits 1:26 (the spared man founds a new city to which he gives Bethel's earlier name of "Luz"; see 1:23b).

[350] This generalizing notice takes the place of Judg 1:27-36, which enumerates the failures of various tribes to expel the inhabitants from their respective territories (as well as their imposition of forced labor on them). The notice's language echoes Josephus' comment about Benjamin in 5.129, as well as his remark in 5.90

on Joshua's perceiving the carelessness of those who would succeed him concerning "the public advantage." The passage further serves to introduce an extended reflective insertion (5.132-135) on the causes and consequences of Israel's fall into political degeneracy in the time after Joshua's death. On this segment, see Attridge 1976: 135-36; Feldman 1998: 143-44.

[351] In Judg 2:1 it is an "angel of the Lord" (the Targum substitutes "the prophet") who addresses the people in the Lord's name, having traveled from Gilgal to Bochim to do this. On this and other instances of Josephus' replacing biblical mentions of "angels" with alternative formulations, see Mach 1992: 300-322 and Feldman 1998: 212-13.

[352] Josephus' condensed version of the angelic word in Judg 2:1b-3 confines itself to adapting the statements of its vv. 2* (the Israelites have transgressed the prohibition of making covenants with the inhabitants) and 3bα (the inhabitants will become "adversaries" to them). He leaves aside the content of vv. 1b (the Lord has led the people from Egypt into the promised land and pledged not to break his covenant with them), 2* (Israel is to break down the inhabitants' altars [LXX adds a prohibition of their bowing down to the gods of the natives and the call to break their statues], and the concluding rhetorical question, "what is this you have done?"), and 3abβ (the Lord's resolve not to expel the inhabitants whose gods will be a "snare" to Israel).

[353] This notice, preparing Josephus' following char-

the aristocratic form of government was already destroyed.[354] They no longer appointed senates[355] nor any other type of rulership that had earlier been customary, but were on their farms, addicted to the pleasure of profit-making.[356] Due to their grave enervation, terrible civil strife came upon them once again, and they were induced to make war upon one another for the following cause:[357]

(2.8) 136. A Levite,[358] a man of the lower ranks,[359] from the tribal territory of Ephran where he lived, married a woman[360] from Bethlema (this site is in the tribe of Iouda). He greatly loved the woman and was captivated by her beauty, but failed in his attempt to win a like response from her.[361] **137.** She was ill-disposed [towards him],[362] and therefore inflamed his passion all the more. There were continual quar-

The Levite and his wife reconciled

---

acterization of the period of the Judges (see 5.135), elaborates on the reference to the people's "weeping" in response to the angel's words in Judg 2:4. Josephus leaves aside the etymological notice on the origin of the place name "Bochim" (meaning "weepers" in Hebrew) and the reference to the people's sacrificing at this site (2:5). He likewise passes over the complex of notices Judg 2:6-10, (partially) paralleling those of Josh 24:28-31, concerning the death and burial of Joshua, etc., the latter segment having already been utilized by him in 5.117-119.

[354] In 4.223 Josephus, when making his first use of the term in *Antiquities*, has Moses aver that "aristocracy (Greek: ἀριστοκρατία) and life therein is best." On Josephus' (positive) view of the aristocratic form of government and his identification of this with "theocracy," see Feldman 1998: 145; 2000: 414, n. 696; Mason 2000: xxvi-xxvii.

[355] On the prominence of the *gerousia* ("senate") in the period of Joshua, see note to "oath" at 5.15. The disappearance of the institution at this point is indicative of the marked difference between that period and the post-Joshua epoch that is now beginning. Deprived of the leadership provided by this body, the Israelites are bound to go astray, as Josephus will show them doing again and again throughout the period of the Judges.

[356] As Feldman (1998: 144) points out, the connection between obsession with money-making and political degeneracy is a *topos* of Greco-Roman writers as well; see, e.g., the preface to Livy's history (#12), where he states: "of late, riches have brought in avarice, and excessive pleasures the longing to carry wantonness and licence to the point of ruin for oneself and of universal destruction."

[357] This segment, with its focus on the political abuses into which the Israelites now fell, takes the place of the long introduction to the Book of Judges (Judg 2:6-3:6) where the emphasis is rather on Israel's defection from the Lord, the former stress being one that would be more congenial to Josephus' politically-minded Gentile readers; see Feldman 2000a: 264-65. The concluding reference to the "civil strife" (Greek:

στάσις) which engulfed the people at this point and the "cause" of this serves to prepare the story of the "Benjamite War," itself occasioned by the "Gibeah outrage" (Judges 19-21), which in Josephus will follow immediately (5.136-174). On "civil strife" as a key, negatively-charged category in Josephus' portrayal of the course of Jewish history in both *War* and *Antiquities*, see Feldman 1998: 140-42.

[358] In Judges itself the story (Judges 19) of the Levite and his concubine (together with its sequel, the Benjamite War, Judges 20-21) stands as the book's final episode. Josephus shifts his version of the biblical complex (5.136-178) to this early point in his retelling of the Judges period in order to provide a dramatic illustration of Israel's (political) decline as presented by him in 5.132-135 (Josephus' "antedating" of the above 2 episodes has a counterpart in *S. Olam Rab.* 12.4-5, which assigns them to the time of "Cusahan-rishathaim," Israel's first oppressor during the period of the Judges [see Judg 3:7-11]). In thus repositioning Judges 19, Josephus leaves aside the chronological note of 19:1a ("in those days, when there was no king in Israel...") with its pro-monarchical implications, given his own anti-kingship stance, for which, see Feldman 1998: 502-504. On the retellings of Judges 19 by Josephus and Pseudo-Philo (*Bib. Ant.* 45-47), see Spilsbury 1998: 154-56; Begg 2000; and Feldman 2000a: 267-76.

[359] In Judg 19:1b the reference is to the "recesses" of the Ephraimite hill country where the Levite dwells. Josephus re-interprets the allusion in a (somewhat derogatory) socio-political sense, this reflective of his ambiguous stance towards the Levites overall. See Feldman 2000a: 267-69.

[360] In all witnesses for Judg 19:1b the Levite takes a "concubine." Josephus enhances the status of both parties by speaking of a regular marriage between them.

[361] Judges 19 says nothing about the Levite's feelings towards the woman. Josephus' insertion on the matter is part of his sustained effort to accentuate the romantic dimensions of the episode; see Feldman 2000a: 269-73 and, more generally, Moehring 1957.

rels between them, and finally the woman, feeling oppressed by these, left her husband and went to her parents in the fourth month.[363] Given his love for her, the man took this badly and went to his parents-in-law;[364] resolving their quarrels, he was reconciled to her.[365]

Journey to Gibeah

138. He spend four days there, with her parents treating him kindly.[366] On the fifth day, he decided to leave for his own home. He set out towards evening; for the parents dismissed their daughter reluctantly and so wasted the day.[367] A single attendant followed them; they also had a donkey on which the woman was riding.[368]

139. When they were near Hierosolyma, having come thirty *stadia* already,[369] the attendant advised them to lodge somewhere, so that nothing unpleasant happen to them, who were travelling by night and were not far from the enemy, seeing that an opportune time often makes even friends dangerous and suspect.[370]

140. But the Levite did not favor the plan of taking shelter among alien men, for the city was Chananaian.[371] Instead, he preferred that they advance twenty *stadia* further on to a city of their own people to lodge there.[372] His plan prevailing, he arrived at Gaba, in the tribe of the Benjamites, when it was already evening.[373]

Events in Gibeah

141. When none of those in the market-place offered him hospitality,[374] an old man, who was of the tribe of Ephraim but living in Gaba, met him, as he was com-

---

[362] Josephus' formulation here seems inspired by LXX AL (ὠργίσθη αὐτῷ) and OL Judg 19:2, which speak of the woman being "angry at" the Levite, as opposed to both MT, where she "plays the harlot against him" and LXX B, where "she goes from him." Josephus' subsequent references to the troubled course of their relationship are his elaboration of this item.

[363] In Judg 19:2 the "4 months" are the duration of the woman's stay at her family home prior to the Levite's coming to retrieve her. Josephus' modification eliminates the "unromantic" suggestion that the Levite managed to live an extended period without his beloved (see 5.136) wife.

[364] Throughout Judg 19:2-9 only the woman's father is mentioned.

[365] See Judg 19:3a, from which Josephus omits—for the moment—the appended parenthetical notice about the Levite's having his servant and a couple of asses with him. He will make (modified) use of this notice subsequently; see 5.138.

[366] Compare Judg 19:3b-4, where the Levite is entertained for *3* days by the woman's father (alone; see note to "parents-in-law" at 5.137).

[367] Josephus here compresses the segment Judg 19:5-10aα, where the Levite is persuaded to remain the 4th day (vv. 5-7), but then insists on setting out, his father-in-law's objections notwithstanding, on the evening of the 5th day (vv. 8-10aα).

[368] Josephus draws the figure of the Levite's attendant from Judg 19:3aβ (earlier passed over by him; see 5.137). Judg 19:10b (like 19:3aβ) speaks of "a couple of asses" and of the woman's simply "being with" the Levite.

[369] Josephus supplies this indication concerning the distance between Bethlehem (the woman's home according to 5.136) and Jerusalem. In *Ant.* 7.312 he cites a different figure for the same distance, i.e. 20 *stadia*.

[370] Compare Judg 19:11, where the servant proposes that they stop for the night specifically in "this city of the Jebusites." The rationale appended to the servant's proposal about stopping is Josephus' own. In *Bib. Ant.* 45.1 (whose retelling of Judges 19 opens with a version of its v. 11), the party arrives first at Gibeah, i.e. their final destination in the Bible and Josephus.

[371] See Judg 19:12a, where the Levite responds that they will not enter "the city of foreigners, who do not belong to the people of Israel." On Jerusalem's earlier avoiding full capture and/or extermination by the Israelites, see 5.124, 129. In *Ant.* 7.61 Josephus likewise identifies the Jebusites as being "of the race of the Chananaians."

[372] In Judg 19:13 the Levite proposes to "draw near to one of these places, and spend the night at Gibeah or at Ramah." The figure for the proposed distance still to be travelled is, like that given in 5.139, Josephus' own. Josephus' formulation here points up the irony of the situation: the party passes up a Canaanite city in favor of one belonging to "their own people" where, however, they will meet with unimaginable horrors. He highlights a similar irony in *War* (see 1.10, 27) where the Jews are treated better by the Roman enemy than by the fanatic rebel leaders.

[373] MT Judg 19:15 calls the site "Gibeah," LXX Γαβαά. In *Bib. Ant.* 45.1 the party, having already passed by "Gibeah," ends up stopping at "Nob."

[374] See Judg 19:15b. On "hospitality" (Greek ξενία;

ing in from the fields.[375] He asked who he was and why he was travelling when it was already dark, having taken the makings of the evening meal with him.[376] **142.** He stated that he was a Levite who was conducting his wife from her parents to his own home; he further disclosed that his residence was in the tribal territory of Ephraim.[377]

143. Then the old man, on account of their kinship and their belonging to the same tribe, as well as their chance meeting, brought him to his house to give him hospitality.[378] Some young men of the Gabaenes, however, who had observed the woman in the market-place and admired her beauty, once they learned that she was lodging with the old man, despising their weakness and fewness, came to the doors.[379] When the old man appealed to them to depart and not inflict violence or outrage,[380] they demanded that he hand over his woman guest[381] so as to be done with the matter.

144. The old man said that he was a relative and a Levite and that they would be doing a terrible thing by offending against the laws for the sake of pleasure.[382] They, however, thought little of and ridiculed what was just and threatened to kill him, should he impede their desires.[383]

---

words of the ξεν- root permeate Josephus' story of the Gibeah outrage) as a value whose practice on the part of the Jews—also towards non-Jews—Josephus highlights throughout *Antiquities*, see Feldman 1998: 122-23. The inhabitants of Gibeah thus appear as non-typical Jews in their lack of hospitality to the travelers.

[375] See Judg 19:16. *Bib. Ant.* 45.2 introduces the old man as "a certain Levite whose name was Bethac."

[376] In Judg 19:17b the old man asks where the Levite is going and whence he has come; in *Bib. Ant.* 45.2b he asks simply "Are you Beel from my tribe?" In having the man note the provisions the Levite has in hand, Josephus anticipates the latter's statement in Judg 19:19 about the "bread and wine" he has available.

[377] The Levite's response as cited in Judg 19:18 does not mention his status or the woman, but adds that no one had taken him in (see 19:15b). In having the Levite state that he is proceeding to "his own home" Josephus aligns himself with LXX ABL, where he speaks of going to "my home" as against MT, where his destination is rather "the house of the Lord." In *Bib. Ant.* 45.2c the Levite simply acknowledges that he is indeed "Beel"; see 45.2b and see note on "fields" at 5.141.

[378] See Judg 19:21, which Josephus amplifies with mention of the motivations behind the old man's taking them in (he leaves aside the man's preceding invitation, v. 20, which Pseudo-Philo [*Bib. Ant.* 45.2dg] turns into an ominous warning with, e.g., an allusion to the Sodomites' assault on Lot and his guests [Gen 19:4-11]). See note on "hospitality" at 5.141.

[379] Josephus amplifies Judg 19:22 with mention of

what prompted the assailants to come to the old man's house and the state of mind in which they approach.

[380] This reference to the old man's initial attempt to dissuade the assailants lacks a biblical parallel.

[381] In Judg 19:22 the assailants demand that the old man hand over his male visitor; Josephus' modification reflects his embarrassment over the biblical picture of an anticipated homosexual rape on the part of Jews; see Feldman 2000a: 274-75. In *Ant.* 1.200 Josephus does reproduce the biblical (see Gen 19:5) notice on the Sodomites' intention of forcing sexual relations on Lot's male (angelic) visitors, but there the (would-be) perpetrators are not Jews. According to *Bib. Ant.* 45.3ab the men demand both of "Bethac's" visitors, threatening to burn both him and them if he refuses.

[382] In Judg 19:23 the old man invokes the Levite's status as a visitor to his home in attempting to dissuade the assailants. *Bib. Ant.* 45.3cd represents "Bethac" as reminding those at the door that his visitors are "brothers" of them all and urging them to refrain from evil so as not to "multiply sins."

[383] With this response by the assailants Josephus drastically intensifies the notice of Judg 19:25a ("the men would not listen to him"), which itself follows upon the host's offering them his own virgin daughter and the Levite's concubine in 19:24. By delaying his version of the old man's "offer" to a later point in the exchange (see 5.145) and by highlighting the danger faced by him, Josephus depicts him as putting up more resistance to the assailants' reprobate demands than does the Bible. In *Bib. Ant.* 45.3e the assailants' response is the assertion that "strangers" have never hitherto given orders to local residents—as "Bethac" has just attempted to do.

145. Being forced into a difficult situation and not wanting quietly to allow his guests to suffer outrage,[384] he offered them his own daughter,[385] saying that it was more legitimate for them to thus satisfy their lusts than by an outrage upon his guests.[386] In this way he thought that he would not wrong those whom he had received.[387]

146. They, however, did not slacken in their craving for his woman guest, but kept demanding that she be handed over. Although he begged them not to venture on such a transgression,[388] they snatched her away[389] and, poised to abandon themselves to the compulsion of pleasure, brought the woman to their homes. Having satiated their outrageous desire throughout the night, they dismissed her at daybreak.[390]

147. She, exhausted by what had happened, came to the house of her host and from grief over what she had been through and in her shame not daring to come into her husband's presence—for she reasoned that he especially would be irremediably hurt by these events[391]—breathing out her soul, died.[392]

148. Her husband, thinking his wife to be lying in a deep sleep, and suspecting nothing horrible, tried to rouse her, intending to comfort her by saying that she had not voluntarily handed herself over to those who had committed the outrage. It was rather they who, coming to the house of their host, had snatched her away.[393]

Tribes informed of Gibeah outrage

149. When, however, he learned that she was dead, made prudent by the immensity of the calamities,[394] he placed his dead wife on his beast and brought it to his own home.[395] Cutting her up piece by piece into twelve parts, he sent these round to

---

[384] This inserted remark on the old man's hopeless situation continues Josephus' endeavor to portray him in a more favorable light; see previous note.

[385] In Judg 19:24 the old man offers the assailants not only his daughter but also the Levite's concubine.

[386] The host's words here echo those of Lot facing the Sodomites' demand that he hand over his (angelic) visitors to them in *Ant.* 1.201: "... he would offer his own daughters for their lust in place of them...."

[387] In Judg 19:24 the old man concludes his words to the assailants by calling on them not to violate the Levite. Josephus' rendition of his words shows him evidencing equal concern for the security of both his guests, neither of whom he is willing to hand over to them. Going further in the same direction, Pseudo-Philo omits the old man's "offer" completely.

[388] This mention of a final attempt by the old man to dissuade the assailants, paralleling that introduced by him in 5.143, is Josephus' insertion, designed to cast the figure in a more favorable light.

[389] Josephus here notably reworks the biblical presentation (Judg 19:25bα) according to which the Levite himself, at this point, takes the initiative in handing his concubine over to them. The modification is in line with Josephus' previous emphasis on the Levite's love for his wife—with which his biblical action at this point would hardly accord. Pseudo-Philo modifies similarly: in *Bib. Ant.* 45.3ef the assailants break in, carry off both the Levite and his concubine, but then release the former.

[390] Judg 19:25bβ does not mention the assailants' lustful urges or their taking the woman to their houses.

[391] Judg 19:26 makes no mention of the woman's sentiments as she positions herself before the door of her host's house. Compare Josephus' earlier, also inserted reference to the woman's being "ill-disposed" towards the Levite in 5.137.

[392] MT Judges 19 nowhere explicitly mentions the woman's "death." Josephus' statement on the point here anticipates the LXX plus at the end of Judg 19:28a ("but she was dead"). Pseudo-Philo likewise anticipates mention of the woman's death, further supplying a reason why she came to so bad an end, i.e. as divine punishment for her having once committed adultery with the Amalekites (*Bib. Ant.* 45.3f).

[393] Judg 19:27 says nothing concerning the Levite's state of mind as he encounters the woman's body. Josephus' extended insertion on the matter accentuates, once again, his attachment to his wife; see note to "from her" at 5.136.

[394] Compare Judg 19:28a: "He said to her, 'Get up, let us be going.' But there was no answer (+ but she was dead, LXX)." In place of the biblical Levite's brusque, heartless command, Josephus depicts him "coming to his senses" about the reality of what has happened.

[395] See Judg 19:28b. *Bib. Ant.* 45.4 has the man proceed to "Kadesh."

each tribe,[396] ordering the bearers to tell the causes of the woman's death and the disgraceful deed of the [Benjamite] tribe.[397]

(2.9) 150. They for their part, were angered at the sight and the report of deeds of violence wickedly perpetrated, of which no one previously had had experience. In their intense and just wrath,[398] they gathered at Silo;[399] mustering before the tent, they were rushing into immediate recourse to weapons and treating the Gabaenes as enemies.

Israelites' response

151. The senate, however, restrained them, persuading them that they ought not thus precipitously launch a war upon their compatriots before they had spoken to them about the charges. For the law did not permit them to lead their army even against aliens without an embassy and other such attempts to make the purported wrong-doers change their minds.[400] **152.** It would be good therefore for them to obey the law by sending off to the Gabaenes to demand the surrender of those responsible,[401] and if they were handed over, to be satisfied with their punishment. If, however, they despised [their demands], they would take vengeance on them by means of weapons.

---

[396] Josephus' specification of "each tribe" as the recipient of the pieces corresponds to the LXX AL reading in Judg 19:29 ("to all the tribes of Israel") against MT LXX B, where the pieces are sent "throughout all the territory of Israel."

[397] Josephus' mention of the instruction given to the bearers by the Levite corresponds to the LXX AL reading in Judg 19:30, where the words—which in MT and LXX B are placed on the lips of those beholding the body parts—are formulated rather as a command by the Levite concerning what the bearers are to say to the Israelites. Josephus likewise reformulates the content of the words in question, which in 19:30 involve an exclamation concerning the unprecedented character of the happening and a call to a joint consultation about this. *Bib. Ant.* 45.4 too cites the "message" of the Levite that is to accompany the pieces (here he claims to have been "locked up" at the moment his concubine was seized, whereas 45.3 states that he was removed from the house along with her).

[398] Josephus' reference to the people's emotional reaction to seeing the woman's remains is an amplification of the notices on their words (Judg 19:30, MT LXX B; see previous note) and their assembling (20:1). His allusion to no one's ever having experienced such a thing echoes the opening words ascribed to the people (MT LXX B)/messengers (LXX AL) in 19:30, minus the appended chronological indication "from the day the people of Israel came out of Egypt until this day." *Bib. Ant.* 45.5 introduces its version of Judg 20:1 with mention of the tribes' being "disturbed." On Josephus' account of the Benjamite War episode (Judges 20-21) in 5.150-174, see Begg 1998 and Feldman 2000a: 276-90.

[399] In Judg 20:1 the assembly takes place at Mizpah; Josephus' relocalization agrees with that of *Bib. Ant.* 45.5. Feldman (2000a: 289-90) suggests positively

that "Shiloh" would be a more appropriate site for the assembly given the presence of the Tent of Meeting there (see Josh 18:1= *Ant.* 5.68; cf. the mention of the tent in the continuation of 5.150), while negatively Josephus may not have wished to place the Israelites' "vengeful assembly" at the same locale where Saul (towards whom Josephus has a more positive stance than the Bible) would one day be chosen king, i.e. Mizpah (see 1 Sam 10:27= *Ant.* 6.60).

[400] Judg 20:2 mentions the "chiefs of all the people of the tribes of Israel." There, however, they simply "present themselves" in the assembly. Josephus' attributing an active, restraining role to them here is highly reminiscent of his introducing "Iesous, Eleazar and the senate" in the exercise of a like role when the aroused people are ready to march against the Transjordanian altar-builders in 5.103. The "law" to which the senate alludes here is that of Deut 20:16, cited by Josephus in *Ant.* 4.296, which enjoins that before going to war with (foreign, but non-Canaanite) cities, Israel is to offer them terms. *A fortiori* then, this procedure must be used in dealings with a fellow Israelite city.

[401] In Judg 20:12-13 the "tribes of Israel" dispatch a delegation on their own, without being urged to do so by their leaders. Josephus' insertion continues to accentuate the role of the latter vis-à-vis the people as a whole; see previous note. In moving from Israel's assembly (20:1) to its embassy to the Benjamites (20:12), Josephus passes over the intervening segment, 20:2-11, this consisting (mostly) of words spoken at the assembly, i.e. the Levite's report of what had happened (20:4-7, a matter already known to readers from what precedes) and the Israelites' resolutions concerning their response to this (20:8-11). In *Bib. Ant.* 45.5b the assembled people ask a rhetorical question about whether they should keep quiet in face of the crime. To

Failure of ne-
gotiations

153. They therefore sent to the Gabaenes,[402] accusing the young men regarding the affair of the woman and demanding for punishment those who had done what was not lawful and who deserved to die for those [deeds] of theirs.[403]

154. The Gabaenes[404] however, did not surrender the young men, thinking it a terrible thing to obey the orders of aliens[405] out of fear of war; nor did they suppose themselves inferior in weapons, numbers, or greatness of soul.[406] They made great preparations, as did the other members of the same [Benjamite] tribe, for they sided with them, as if they were driving off doers of violence.[407]

(2.10) 155. When these [words] of the Gabaenes were announced to the Israelites, they swore that none of them would give his daughter to a Benjamite man in marriage,[408] and that they would campaign against them. For their wrath towards them was still greater than that which we are told our ancestors felt against the Chananaians.[409] **156.** They immediately brought out against them an army of 400,000[410] troops, while the Benjamites' contingent numbered 25,600,[411] of whom 500 were outstanding left-handed slingers.[412]

Double defeat
of Israelites

157. When battle was joined at Gaba[413] the Benjamites put the Israelite men to

---

this 45.6 attaches a divine word addressed to "the adversary," wherein God announces his intention of frustrating the people's projected initiative, given that they had failed to show a like indignation over Micah's idol-making (see Judges 17-18= *Bib. Ant.* 44). Thereafter, one finds a certain parallel to Josephus' insertion concerning the senate's suggestion that the Gabaenes first be confronted concerning the charges against them; see 46.1a, where the Israelites propose that they go "and investigate the sin that has been committed."

[402] In Judg 20:12 the Israelites sent their emissaries "through all the tribe of Benjamin," rather than specifically to Gibeah. Josephus modifies in light of the senate's proposal in 5.152 that the people send to the Gabaenes.

[403] In Judg 20:13a the embassy's demand concludes rather with a reference to the anticipated "putting away of evil from Israel" that would be effected through the execution of the culprits.

[404] As the recipients of the envoys' message (see 5.152, 153) the Gabaenes likewise are the ones to respond to this, whereas in Judg 20:13b the Benjamites as a whole reject what has been demanded of them all (20:12-13a).

[405] In 5.151 this same term (Greek: ἀλλότριος) was used to refer to non-Israelites; its utilization for fellow Israelites by the Gabaenes here underscores the depth of their estrangement from their own people.

[406] Josephus supplies the reasoning behind the Gabaenes' rejection of the embassy's demand.

[407] Josephus accentuates the Benjamites' sense of solidarity with the "Gabaenes," whom they perceive to be facing injury by the other Israelites. Compare Judg 20:14, where the Benjamites simply proceed to Gibeah

to fight with Israel, with no mention of the thinking behind their initiative.

[408] Josephus anticipates this item from Judg 21:1, where it appears as a kind of afterthought.

[409] This appended statement about the Israelites' emotions as they pledge to make war upon the Benjamites (cf. Judg 20:8-11) echoes the (likewise inserted) reference to their "intense and just wrath" in 5.150.

[410] This figure agrees with that given in Judg 20:17.

[411] Josephus here conflates the separate figures given for the (rest of the) Benjamites (MT 26,000; LXX AL 25,000; LXX B 23,000) and for those from Gibeah itself (700 in all witnesses) in Judg 20:15. His figure for the former group thus agrees with that of LXX AL.

[412] MT Judg 20:16a (LXX AB lack a number) gives a figure of *700* for the Benjamite/Gibeah slingers (i.e. the same total for the Gibeah warriors cited in 20:15). Josephus leaves aside the qualification of them (20:16b) as able to "sling a stone at a hair, and not miss." His qualification of the archers as "left-handed" agrees with MT's description of them, whereas LXX AB call them "ambidextrous."

[413] Josephus passes over the preliminaries to the first battle (Judg 20:18-20). In particular, he does not reproduce the preceding "consultation" of the Lord at Bethel by the Israelites cited in 20:18, to which the Lord responds by directing Judah to go up first. Thereby, Josephus eliminates the theological problem of the Lord's seeming to encourage Israel to go into a battle that will end in its defeat (20:21). By contrast, Pseudo-Philo (*Bib. Ant.* 46.1) has the Lord unambiguously promise his support for Israel, doing this, as he comments, in order to fulfill his words (i.e. those announcing his intention of punishing Israel cited in

flight; 22,000 of them fell.[414] More would probably have perished if night had not restrained them and separated the combatants.[415]

158. The Benjamites returned rejoicing to the city,[416] the Israelites, dismayed at their defeat, to their camp.[417] The next day, when they again engaged, the Benjamites prevailed and killed 18,000 of the Israelites who, in their anxiety over the slaughter, abandoned their camp.[418]

Israelites' appeal to God

159. Proceeding to Bethel, a city situated nearby,[419] and having fasted,[420] the next day they begged God, through Phinees the high priest,[421] to cease from his wrath against them and, satisfied with their two defeats, to give them victory and triumph over their enemies.[422] And God promised these things through Phinees' prophesying.[423]

Israelites' victory

(2.11) 160. Forming then their army into two divisions, they set one half in ambush around the city by night;[424] the other half engaged the Benjamites and retreating as they advanced. The Benjamites pursued the Hebrews, who fell back slowly and for a great distance, wanting them all to come out. The former followed as the latter withdrew.[425]

45.6; see note to "responsible" at 5.152). Cf. Feldman 2000a: 279-80.

[414] See Judg 20:22. *Bib. Ant.* 46.2d gives a figure of 45,000 for Israel's casualties in the first battle.

[415] As Feldman (2000a: 279) points out, this appended remark has a close parallel in Josephus' (also inserted) notice concerning the outcome of the battle between Israel and the Amalekites in *Ant.* 3.54.

[416] This reference to the victors' emotions is biblically unparalleled.

[417] Josephus here modifies the wording of Judg 20:23, where the Israelites first weep before and then inquire of the Lord who directs them to proceed again against the enemy. The modification reflects the same theological sensitivity evidenced in his omission of the first such consultation (20:18; see note to "Gaba" at 5.157), since here too the Lord seems to be misleading Israel, which in fact will suffer another defeat. Josephus further leaves aside the notice about the Israelites' "taking courage" and reforming their battle lines in 20:22, which does not seem to cohere very well with the immediately following portrayal of their emotional state subsequent to their first defeat in 20:23a. By contrast, Pseudo-Philo not only reproduces, but elaborates the consultation scene of 20:23 in *Bib. Ant.* 46.3ac.

[418] See Judg 20:25, which does not mention an abandonment of the Israelite camp. In *Bib. Ant.* 46.3d the figure for the Israelite casualties is much higher than that in either the Bible or Josephus, i.e. 46,000.

[419] This indication about Bethel's proximity to the battle site at Gibeah is Josephus' own.

[420] Compare Judg 20:26, which mentions the Israelites' weeping before the Lord and offering sacrifices to him at Bethel as well. *Bib. Ant.* 46.4a cites the words of the people's post-defeat lament, along with their prostration before the ark (cf. Judg 20:27), rending their

garments, and putting ashes on their heads.

[421] It is the people as a whole who "inquire of" God in Judg 20:27a. In making Phineas their mouthpiece (compare his similar procedure in 5.120 vis-à-vis Judg 1:1), Josephus is likely inspired by the parenthetical notice of Judg 20:27b-28a about Phineas' officiating before the ark at Bethel "in those days." Likewise Pseudo-Philo depicts Phineas (*Bib. Ant.* 46.4-47.1) as the one who voices the people's distress on this occasion (which, however, he does not locate at Bethel, as in the Bible and Josephus, but at Shiloh; see 46.3).

[422] In Judg 20:28bα the people simply ask whether they should go to battle yet again or desist. In *Bib. Ant.* 47.2 Phineas' prayer culminates in the plea that the Lord make known why he has twice deceived the people regarding the outcome of the battles.

[423] Josephus continues to underscore the role of Phineas, now as the "prophet" through whom God speaks (compare 5.20); in Judg 20:28bβ God addresses the people directly, telling them to "go up" and announcing that he will give the enemy into their hand. Pseudo-Philo develops the Bible's summary divine response into an extended discourse (*Bib. Ant.* 47.3-8) in which God, picking up his earlier word to "the adversary" (45.6), discloses that he "deceived" the people in punishment for their failure to respond as vigorously to Micah's idolatry as they did to the violation of the Levite's concubine.

[424] See Judg 20:29, to which Josephus adds the further details about the division of the army into 2 divisions, of which one is placed in ambush at night.

[425] See Judg 20:31-32(39); Josephus appends the motivation behind the Israelites' (pretended) flight. During the Galilean campaign, Josephus himself employed a similar tactic; see *Life* 399-400.

161. Thus even the old men and the boys in the city, who had been left behind due to weakness, all rushed out together after them, wishing to overpower the enemy.[426] But when they were at a considerable distance from the city, the fleeing Hebrews halted, and turning round, took their stand for battle and raised the agreed-upon sign for those in ambush.[427]

162. These rose up with a shout and went against the enemy,[428] who, from the moment they perceived that they had been deceived, were placed in a desperate situation.[429] Driven together into a certain hollow, narrow site, they were shot down by those who surrounded them. The result was that all but 600 were destroyed.[430]

163. These [600 survivors], massing together and closing ranks, forced their way through the midst of the enemy and fled to the nearby hills, which they occupied and settled.[431] All the rest, about 25,000,[432] died.

Destruction of Gibeah and Jabesh-Gilead

164. The Israelites, for their part, set fire to Gaba and cut down the women and the under-age males, doing the same to the other cities of the Benjamites.[433] They were likewise so enraged that they sent 12,000 from their ranks, directing them to do away with Iabes in the Galadite country because it had not fought alongside them against the Benjamites.[434] **165.** Those who had been sent slaughtered the city's fighting men, along with the children and the women, except for 400 virgins.[435] They were prompted to do this by their wrath at their suffering on account both of the woman and the massacre of their troops.[436]

Return of 400 surviving Benjamites

(2.12) 166. Now, however, they had a change of heart at the Benjamites' misfortune and decreed a fast for them.[437] Nevertheless, they considered that they had suffered justly for their offenses against the laws.[438] Through messengers they

---

[426] This notice on the complete emptying of the city of its defenders lacks a counterpart in Judges 20.

[427] Cf. Judg 20:33-34, 37-41a, whose confusingly repetitive description of the course of the battle Josephus simplifies and synthesizes; compare his similar treatment of the complicated battle account of Josh 8:1-29 in 5.45-48; and cf. Feldman 2000a: 278. Pseudo-Philo (*Bib. Ant.* 47.9) does likewise.

[428] Josephus combines the 2 separate notices about the Israelites' emerging from ambush of Judg 20:33b, 37 into a single one.

[429] See Judg 20:41b.

[430] See Judg 20:47. In Judg 20:43, 45 the Benjamites are killed on the roads as they flee.

[431] Judg 20:47 specifies that the site in question was called the "rock of Rimmon" (a datum utilized by Josephus only subsequently; see 5.166) and that the escapees spent 4 months there. Josephus dramatizes their struggle to reach the place.

[432] This figure for the total Benjamite casualties agrees with that given in Judg 20:46 (itself a combination of the partial totals cited in 20:44-45: 18,000+ 5,000 + 2,000); compare 20:35 (25,100). According to *Bib. Ant.* 47.10, 85,000 inhabitants of Nob (i.e. the site of the outrage to the Levite's concubine according to 45.1) were killed.

[433] Josephus here combines (and modifies) data from Judg 20:37 (burning of Gibeah, killing of its inhabit-

ants) and 20:48 (slaughter of the Benjamite persons and beasts and burning of all their towns).

[434] In the biblical presentation (see Judg 21:8-12) the dispatch of the 12,000 against non-cooperative Jabesh-gilead comes at a later point, i.e. after the end of Israel's climactic battle with the Benjamites and in the context of the victorious Israelites' post-battle assembly. As Feldman (2000a: 282) points out, Josephus' having the Israelites undertake their violent initiative against Jabesh while still in the heat of battle, serves to exculpate their deed (of which Pseudo-Philo makes no mention).

[435] See Judg 21:10b-12a. Josephus does not mention the expedition's return to the Israelites at Shiloh (21:12b).

[436] Also this editorial comment about their motivation aims to exculpate the Israelites' deed; see note on "Benjamites" at 5.164.

[437] The account of the Israelites' post-battle measures at Bethel in Judg 21:2-7 does not mention their "fasting" (see 5.159), but rather, weeping, questioning of the Lord (21:3), building of an altar, and sacrifices (21:4). On the people's changed stance towards the Benjamites, see 21:6a ("the people of Israel had compassion for Benjamin their brother...").

[438] This comment on the Israelites' continued conviction of the rightness of their previous dealings with the Benjamites has no biblical counterpart.

also called their 600 fugitives, for these had settled down on a certain rock called "Roas," situated in the desert.[439]

167. Now these messengers, having lamented a misfortune that was not only theirs [the Benjamites'], but also their own, since the slain were their relatives too, persuaded them to bear matters with resignation, make common cause with them, and insofar as this was in their power, not to impose total extermination upon the Benjamite tribe. "We grant to you," they said, "the land of [your] entire tribe and as much plunder as you are able to carry."[440]

168. The survivors, acknowledging that what had happened to them was by the sentence of God and in accordance with their wrong-doing, went down to the ancestral [territory] of the tribe, having been persuaded by those who had issued the invitation.[441] The Israelites gave them as wives the 400 virgins of Iabes, while likewise considering how the remaining 200 might be provided with wives with whom to procreate children.[442]

Finding wives for the 400 Benjamite survivors

169. There still remained, however, their oaths from before the war that they would not marry their daughters to any Benjamite.[443] Some were advising that they disregard the oaths as having been sworn in wrath rather than with deliberate judgment. If, they said, one were able to save a whole tribe in danger of annihilation, one would not be acting in opposition to God. Perjuries are not serious or dangerous when they occurred under necessity, but only when they were ventured upon with evil intent.[444]

170. Although the senate was incensed by the very mention of perjury,[445] someone said to them that he had something to say about supplying wives and keeping their oaths. When he was asked for his idea,[446] he replied: "when we assemble three times a year at Silo for a popular festival, our wives and daughters join us.[447]

171. Let us allow the Benjamites to take in marriage as spoil those of them whom they can, we ourselves neither encouraging nor preventing them.[448] Should their

---

[439] See Judg 21:13. "Roas" is Josephus' Greek translation of the Hebrew name ("Rimmon," i.e. "pomegranate" that LXX simply transliterates) for the survivors' place of refuge. In his earlier mention of the 600's escape (see 5.163) Josephus avoided naming the site (contrast Judg 20:47).

[440] This speech of the messengers, expressive of the Israelites' new-found sense of solidarity with the surviving Benjamites, is a Josephan invention.

[441] See Judg 21:14a, to which Josephus appends the remark concerning the Benjamites' "acknowledgement" (itself echoing the conviction he attributes to the Israelites themselves in 5.166).

[442] Cf. Judg 21:14, 16. Josephus inserts mention of "procreation" as the purpose for which wives are to be obtained for the remaining Benjamites. The addition echoes Josephus' other statements about procreation as the end of marriage; see *War* 2.160-161; *Apion* 2.199; cf. Mayer-Schärtel 1995: 229-30.

[443] See 5.155, where Josephus anticipates his reference to the Israelites' pre-battle oath from Judg 21:1.

[444] In Judg 21:16-22 it is "the elders of the congregation" (v. 16) who alone speak regarding the problem of the wifeless Benjamites. Josephus enlivens the pro-

ceedings by having the problem addressed by 3 different sets of speakers (on this literary device, known as "trichotomy", which Josephus introduces also in other biblical contexts, see Begg 1998: 295, n. 97). The first group of speakers, featured here in 5.169, posits the "thesis" (the abrogation of the oaths taken) to which the following speakers will propose, respectively, an "antithesis" and finally a "synthesis."

[445] Compare Judg 21:18, where the "elders" (see v. 16) point up the problem posed by the people's earlier oath which prohibits them from now awarding their daughters to the remaining Benjamites. On Josephus' recurring emphasis on the sanctity of the oaths taken by biblical characters and its apologetic import, see Feldman 2000a: 283-84.

[446] Josephus' extended introduction of the 3rd and final speaker serves to arouse curiosity about how he will resolve Israel's dilemma.

[447] See Judg 21:19. Josephus omits the verse's extended indications concerning the location of "Shiloh." Pseudo-Philo (*Bib. Ant.* 48.3) identifies the feast in question as "Passover."

[448] Cf. the command on the matter issued the Benjamites by the elders in Judg 21:20; Josephus'

Wife-knapping at Shiloh

fathers complain and demand that they be punished, we will say to them that they were responsible for failing to watch over their daughters, and that we need to moderate our excessive wrath against the Benjamites, which even earlier we displayed to excess."[449]

172. Convinced by his words, they awarded the Benjamites marriage as a spoil. When the festival came round, the 200 in their twos and threes awaited the coming of the virgins in ambush before the city, in the vineyards, and the places where they would be hidden.

Benjamin's restoration

173. The virgins, suspecting nothing of what was about to happen, were strolling about, playfully and unguardedly; rising up, the 200 took hold of them as they scattered.[450] Having married in this way, they devoted themselves to agricultural work;[451] making this their care, they again recovered their former well-being.[452] **174.** The tribe of the Benjamites, after having thus been in danger of total extermination as related above, was saved through the wisdom of the Israelites and immediately made rapid progress in population and in all other ways. Thus this war ended.[453]

Danites gain a new territory

(3.1) 175. But it happened that the tribe of Dan suffered similar things to these, as a result of the following cause.[454] **176.** Now that the Israelites had already abandoned their training for warfare and were involved in agricultural work, the Chananaians grew contemptuous of them and assembled a force. Expecting no loss themselves, but rather harboring the firm hope that they would inflict harm on the Hebrews, they supposed that they would live in their cities in security in the future.[455]

177. They therefore outfitted chariots and drafted a body of troops. Their cities shared a common purpose, and they seized Askalon and Akaron and many other cities in the plain from the tribe of Iouda.[456] They likewise compelled the Danites to

---

speaker appends the reference to the Israelites' own proposed non-involvement in the proceedings. In *Bib. Ant.* 48.3 the Israelites as a whole, without previous discussion, issue the command of 21:20 to the Benjamites.

[449] Compare Judg 21:22, where the elders' proposed statement to the women's male relatives is formulated in less "judgmental" terms, i.e. without mention of a failure on the part of the women's fathers or reference to the people's own excessive anger against the Benjamites.

[450] Josephus dramatically elaborates the scene as described in Judg 21:23a. On the similarities and differences between Josephus' account of the Benjamites' wife-stealing and Livy's story (1.9) of the Romans' carrying off the Sabine women, see Feldman 2000a: 285-87.

[451] Josephus' wording here echoes that used by him in 5.135, his introduction to the Gibeah Outrage/Benjamite War complex (5.136-174), where it is the people's preoccupation with agricultural pursuits to the exclusion of their civic responsibilities that leads to those calamities.

[452] Greek: εὐδαιμονία. On Josephus' use of this key term of Greek moral philosophy, see Weiss 1979: 427-28; Feldman 1984-85: 241, n. 79; Mason 1991: 185. The term nowhere occurs in the LXX.

[453] This concluding notice to Josephus' version of

Judges 19-21 (5.136-174) takes the place of the closing statements of Judg 21:24-25 (the Israelites depart to their inheritances; everyone does what was right in his own eyes due to Israel's lack of king—cf. Judg 19:1, also omitted by Josephus).

[454] In Judges 17-18 the story of the resettlement of the tribe of Dan is interwoven with that of Micah's idol that ends up at the sanctuary of Dan. Josephus, apparently for apologetic reasons, completely omits the latter component of the story; see Feldman: 2000a: 257-58. Concentrating exclusively on the political aspect of Dan's relocation, Josephus presents this happening in 5.175-178 by conflating the 2 biblical versions of the event, i.e. Judg 1:34 (earlier passed over by him) and 18*. (Conversely, Pseudo-Philo omits Dan's move, while expatiating on Micah's idol-making [Judges 17] in *Bib. Ant.* 44). In addition, Josephus reverses the sequence of Judges 17-18 and 19-21, making the latter—which he relates in highly compressed form—a mere appendix to the former—which he recounts in much greater detail (Pseudo-Philo retains the biblical order in *Bib. Ant.* 44-48).

[455] This inserted editorial notice serves to prepare the Canaanite initiative in what follows; its wording picks up that used in 5.132, 135.

[456] This event is not recorded in Judges. In 5.128 (cf. Judg 1:18) Josephus relates that whereas Judah cap-

flee together to the hill-country, thus leaving them without even a little access to the plain.[457]

178. The Danites, incapable of making war and lacking sufficient land, sent five of their men into the interior to spy out the land on which they might resettle.[458] Advancing almost as far as Mt. Liban and the sources of the lesser Jordan opposite the great plain, one day's journey from the city of Sidon, the spies discovered a good and very fruitful land and informed their own people.[459] They, rushing out with their army, founded at that very spot a city called "Dan," named for the son of Jacob after whom their tribe was called.[460]

(3.2) 179. Because of their incapacity for exertion and their disregard of the Deity,[461] calamities now arose for the Hebrews. For, once they deviated from the order of their constitution, they turned to living in accordance with pleasure and their own will. The result was that they became entangled in the vices customary among the Chananaians.[462]

Renewed defection of Israelites

180. Therefore God became wrathful at them and they forfeited through luxury the well-being they had acquired by multiple exertions.[463] For when Chousarsath,[464] the king of the Assyrians,[465] campaigned against them, they lost many of those drawn up for battle and were besieged and taken by storm.[466]

Assyrian oppression

181. Out of fear, some of them voluntarily submitted to him; they paid the tribute

---

tured "Askalon," it failed to take "Akkaron."

[457] See Judg 1:34.

[458] Cf. Judg 18:1-2a, from which Josephus omits the ("pro-monarchical") notice on there being no king of Israel in that time (v. 1a) and whose motivation for Dan's initiative ("... for until then no inheritance had fallen to them," v. 1bβ) he modifies, given that in 5.87 (cf. Josh 19:40-48) he has related Dan's reception of its (initial) territory in the time of Joshua.

[459] Josephus conflates (elements of) Judg 18:7 (the spies' arrival at Laish, "not far from the Sidonians") and 8-10 (their report to the Danites), while passing over their visit to Micah's idol sanctuary (18:2b-6). In eliminating the source reference (v. 7) to a city ("Laish") that the spies come upon, Josephus prepares his own subsequent presentation, in which there will be no destruction of that city and its inhabitants (compare Judg 18:27). He mentions the proximity of Dan to "the sources of the lesser Jordan" again in *Ant.* 8.226; see also *War* 4.3.

[460] Cf. Judg 18:28b-29. Josephus here drastically abridges the biblical account, passing over the entire sequence Judg 18:11-28a, which tells of the Danites' march towards Laish, including their stop at Micah's shrine (vv. 13-26) and their slaughter of the inhabitants of Laish (vv. 27-28a). In omitting the latter segment, Josephus bypasses the apologetical problem posed by the Danites' unprovoked assault on "a quiet and unsuspecting" people (Judg 18:27); in his version, the entire operation is a peaceful process in which the Danites simply move into unoccupied land. Finally, Josephus,

in line with his overall apologetic tendency (see note to "cause" at 5.175), also omits the concluding verses (30-31) of Judges 18 with their mention of several unedifying religious developments, i.e. the setting up of Micah's image at Dan and the extended functioning of a Mosaic priesthood there.

[461] Greek: ἡ περὶ τὸ θεῖον ὀλιγωρία. Closely related formulations occur in *Ant.* 3.19 (subject: the people) and 9.204 (King Amaziah).

[462] This concluding note to Josephus' account of Dan's migration (5.175-178) creates an inclusion with his remarks concerning the background to that development in 5.176, just as it recalls his earlier remarks on the people's fall into degeneracy after Joshua's death in 5.132, 135. The segment has a certain biblical parallel in Judg 3:1-6, which highlights Israel's fatal involvement with the earlier inhabitants.

[463] Compare Judg 3:7-8aα, where God's wrath is motivated rather by the people's turning to the worship of "Baal and the Asheroth." On the word "well-being" (Greek: εὐδαιμονία), see note to "well-being" at 5.173.

[464] Compare Cushanrishathaim (MT Judg 3:8); Χουσαρσαθωμ (LXX A); Χουσαρσαθάιμ (LXX B); "Cushan the sinner" (Tg.).

[465] MT Judg 3:8 calls him king of "Aram Naharayim," LXX AB of "Syria of the rivers," and Tg. of "Aram."

[466] This is Josephus' replacement for/ elaboration of the theological notice of Judg 3:8aβ: "(the Lord) sold them into the hand of Cushanrishathaim."

imposed on them, which was beyond their means. For eight years they endured outrages of every sort, after which they were freed from their calamities in the following way.[467]

Israel liberated by Keniaz

(3.3) 182. There was a certain Keniaz of the tribe of Iouda, an enterprising and high-minded man.[468] It was revealed to him by an oracle that he ought not to overlook the Israelites who lay under necessity, but should venture to rescue them for freedom.[469] He appealed to certain men to share the dangers with him, there being only a few who were ashamed of their present state and eager for change.[470] **183.** First, he destroyed the garrison of Chousarsath that was among them; when more fellow-soldiers joined him, seeing that his first initiative had not failed, they engaged the Assyrians in battle and, having put them all to flight, compelled them to cross the Euphrates.[471] **184.** Having thus provided proof of his manliness, Keniaz received the rulership as a reward for this by the crowd that he might judge the people.[472] He died after ruling for forty years.[473]

Fall into anarchy

(4.1) 185. After his death the Israelites' affairs were again ruined by anarchy. Due to their failure to pay honor to God and obey the laws, they fell into a still worse calamity.[474]

Oppression by Eglon

186. It thus happened that Eglon,[475] king of the Moabites, contemptuous of the disorder of their constitution,[476] made war upon them. Having defeated them in many battles and subdued those who showed greater spirit than the others, he completely humbled their force and imposed tribute on them.[477]

187. After erecting a palace for himself in Jericho, he refrained from nothing

---

[467] Josephus elaborates on the simple mention of Israel's 8-year servitude found in Judg 3:8b. Conversely, he leaves aside the Israelites' "cry" to the Lord (3:9a), which prompts his intervention on their behalf (3:9b).

[468] In Judg 3:9 Israel's deliverer is rather "Othniel, *the son of Kenaz*, Caleb's younger brother." Previously, Josephus left aside the biblical mention of Othniel as the conqueror of Debir, Judg 1:13. Likewise Pseudo-Philo attributes Israel's initial deliverance from its foes in the period of the Judges, not to Othniel, but rather to "Cenaz"; see *Bib. Ant.* 27, where the enemy whom he overcomes are the Amorites. The reference to Keniaz' qualities is Josephus' own.

[469] In Judg 3:10aα "the spirit of the Lord comes upon" Othniel, and there is no report of a message given him. On Josephus' tendency to avoid biblical references to the (divine) "spirit," see Best 1959; Levison 1996. On the "freedom theme" in his history, see note to "freedom" at 5.34.

[470] Judg 3:10bα simply mentions Othniel's going "out to war." Josephus highlights the paucity of those who support him in this initiative.

[471] Josephus expatiates on Judg 3:10bβ: "the Lord gave Cushanrishathaim... into his [Othniel's] hand, and his hand prevailed over Cushanrishathaim," even while eliminating its theological indication, just as he did that of 3:8a; see note on "Chousarsath" at 5.180.

[472] Judg 3:10aβ speaks of Othniel's "judging" Israel, already prior to his engaging Cushanrishathaim (3:10b), and does not mention his being given office by the people in recognition of his victory.

[473] Compare Judg 3:11: "So the land had rest for forty [MT LXX B; LXX AL: 50] years. Then Othniel the son of Kenaz died."

[474] Compare Judg 3:12a: "And the people of Israel again did what was evil in the sight of the Lord." Josephus adds a political dimension to the Bible's theological statement concerning Israel's regression. On "anarchy" (Greek: ἀναρχία) in Josephus, see Feldman 1998a: 145; the term is used by him only once elsewhere, i.e. in *Ant.* 6.84 (there in reference to the people's political state during the 18 years that followed the death of Joshua).

[475] Josephus' form of the name corresponds to that of MT Judg 3:12; LXX calls him "Eglom."

[476] Greek: ἡ ἀκοσμία ἡ κατὰ τὴν πολιτείαν. This phrase represents a play on words with the expression ὁ κόσμος τῆς πολιτείας ("the order of their constitution") of 5.179. Josephus' two remaining uses of the word ἀκοσμία ("disorder") are in *Ant.* 5.255 and 6.369.

[477] Cf. Judg 3:12b-13a, from which Josephus omits mention of the help given King Eglon both by the Lord (v.12b) and the Ammonites and the Amalekites (v. 13a), thereby accentuating the success of Eglon personally.

that would bring calamity on the crowd; for eighteen years he reduced them to poverty.[478] Then God, taking pity[479] on the Israelites for what they were suffering and moved by their supplications, delivered them from the outrage of the Moabites; they were freed in the following manner.[480]

God relents

(4.2) 188. There was a young man of the tribe of the Benjamites,[481] Ioud,[482] whose father was Gera.[483] He was very courageous, acting audaciously and most competent in using his body.[484] His left hand was the stronger of the two; it was there that he had all his strength.[485] **189.** He too lived in Jericho, and became acquainted with Eglon by obsequiously attending to him with gifts; for this reason he was beloved by those around the king as well.[486]

Ehud (Ioud) introduced

190. Once, along with two[487] servants he brought gifts to the king. Having secretly attached a dagger[488] to his right thigh,[489] he went in to him. Since it was summer and already the middle of the day, the guards were relaxing because of the heat and engaged in their midday meal.[490] **191.** Once then the youth had given his gifts to Eglon,[491] who was residing in a certain chamber well-adapted to the summer heat, they engaged in a private conversation.[492] They were alone, since the king had di-

Eglon assassinated

---

[478] See Judg 3:13b-14. In 3:13b the reference is to the enemy coalition's (see 3:13a) getting possession of "the city of palms" (so MT and LXX; the Tg., like Josephus, identifies the site as "Jericho"). Josephus goes beyond the Bible in accentuating the severity of the 18-year servitude (3:14) Eglon imposed on Israel.

[479] Greek: λαβὼν οἶκτον. With God as subject this phrase occurs also in *Ant.* 1.188; 2.211; 5.201; cf. 4.40 (with the verb "to do").

[480] In Judg 3:15aβ the Lord's "raising up a deliverer" for the people comes in response to their "crying" to him. Josephus interjects the reference to the divine "pity" that prompts God to respond favorably to the people's appeals.

[481] So MT 3:15; in LXX MT's בן־הימיני is rendered "son of Iemeni," "Iemeni" being taken as the grandfather of the hero "Aod" (= MT "Ehud").

[482] MT "Ehud"; LXX Αώδ; Josephus Ἰούδης. On Josephus' treatment of this figure, see Feldman 1998a: 137-52. It is unclear whether or not the judge "Zebul" of *Bib. Ant.* 29 is to be identified with the biblical "Ehud" (see Feldman [1998a: 137-38, n. 2]); in any case, what Pseudo-Philo tells of the former figure bears no resemblance to the story of Ehud in Judg 3:12-30.

[483] This is the name of Ehud's father according to both MT and LXX Judg 3:15.

[484] Josephus attributes these qualities to "Ioud" without explicit biblical basis; compare his appended characterization of "Keniaz" (biblical Othniel) in 5.182.

[485] With this wording, Josephus seems to take into account the divergent readings of both MT 3:15 (Ehud's "right hand was restricted," which RSV takes as a circumlocution for "left-handed") and LXX which designates "Aod" as "ambidextrous." See Feldman

1998a: 139-40, and cf. note on "left-handed slingers" at 5.156 on Josephus' handling of the similarly divergent readings of MT and LXX Judg 20:16 in 5.156.

[486] Josephus here modifies the statement of Judg 3:15bβ: "the people of Israel sent tribute (MT מנחה, LXX δῶρα) by him [Ehud] to Eglon...." In his presentation, the "gifts" seem to come from Ehud personally, who thereby obtains for himself the easy access to the king presupposed in the biblical story.

[487] Judg 3:18 does not specify the number of the tribute-carriers who accompany Ehud to Eglon.

[488] MT Judg 3:16 designates Ehud's weapon as a "sword"; LXX calls it a μάχαιρα which may denote either a "sword" or a "dagger, knife." Josephus' term for the object is ξιφίδιον ("little sword, dagger").

[489] Josephus leaves aside the additional details of Judg 3:16 concerning Ehud's weapon, i.e. its being "two-edged," the obscure specification of its length (RSV: "a cubit"), and his girding it "under his clothes."

[490] This mention of the reasons for the guards' negligence has no biblical counterpart; it explains, e.g., why Ehud was not—as might have been expected—thoroughly searched before approaching the king.

[491] Judg 3:17 (MT) appends to its mention of Ehud's presenting the tribute a characterization of Eglon as "a very fat man" (LXX calls him rather ἀστεῖος, "handsome"). As part of his overall endeavor to ameliorate the image of Eglon, Josephus omits the remark; see Feldman 1998a: 144-46.

[492] In Judg 3:19 Ehud appears to make an unmotivated trip to Gilgal once he has delivered the tribute, thereafter returning to Eglon. Josephus more plausibly represents him as continuing in attendance on Eglon, prolonging their interview by engaging the king in conversation. On Josephus' attempt to dispose of the

rected those attendants who had come in to go away so that he could converse with Ioud.[493]

192. Now as the king sat on his throne, anxiety came over Ioud[494] that he might fail to deliver a deadly blow. He therefore caused him to get up, saying that he had a dream to disclose to him by order of God.[495]

193. The king, in his joy over the dream, leapt up from his throne.[496] Ioud struck him in the heart;[497] then leaving the dagger behind, he went out, closing the door.[498] The attendants remained inactive, thinking that the king had fallen asleep.

Moabites over-thrown

(4.4) 194. Secretly giving a signal to the Jerichonites, Ioud appealed to them to take an initiative for freedom's sake.[499] They themselves heard this with delight, took up arms, and sent around the country those who would give the signal by means of rams' horns (for it was by these that the crowd was assembled according to ancestral [custom]).[500]

195. Eglon's entourage was for a long time ignorant of the suffering that had happened to him. But since it was now about evening, anxious that something strange had occurred to him, they entered the room, and finding him dead, stood around in utter consternation.[501] Before the garrison could assemble, the crowd of Israelites had come against them.[502]

196. Some were done away with immediately; the others—of whom there were some 10,000—turned to flight that they might find safety in the Moabite country. The Israelites, who had previously occupied the Jordan ford, pursued and killed them, dispatching many at the ford. Not one escaped their hands.[503]

---

many such obscurities of the biblical story, see Feldman 1998a: 146-49. He derives his reference to the site of the exchange from Judg 3:20, which speaks of their meeting in Eglon's "cool roof chamber."

[493] Compare Judg 3:19b (Eglon commands "silence" [so MT LXX B; LXX A: "from the midst"], whereupon all the servants retire).

[494] This reference to Ehud's "anxiety" at the story's climactic moment is a Josephan dramatization.

[495] See Judg 3:20bα. Josephus' formulation spells out the (intended) purpose of Ehud's announcement and of the king's rising, while its designation of the divine message as a "dream" heightens the message's interest for Eglon. In this connection Josephus also takes care to eliminate the duplication of Ehud's announcement to the king as found in Judg 3:19aβ and 20b. On the topic of dreams in Josephus overall, see Gnuse 1996.

[496] In Judg 3:20bβ Eglon simply "rises"; Josephus dramatizes, likewise providing a motivation for the king's alacrity.

[497] Josephus here compresses the gory, degrading details of the assassination as related in Judg 3:21-22, these including the king's excrement coming out, once he is run through (so MT 3:22; LXX lacks the item).

[498] See Judg 3:23. Josephus adds the notice on Ehud's leaving the murder weapon behind, likely on the consideration that, should he be searched when ex-

iting, the fact of his carrying of a weapon would undoubtedly cause his arrest.

[499] The noun "freedom" (Greek: ἐλευθερία) here echoes the cognate verb ἐλευθερόω ("to free") with which Josephus introduces his story of Ehud's deed in 5.187.

[500] Josephus here modifies the account of Judg 3:26-28a, where the fugitive Ehud reaches "Seirah" (v. 26), whereupon he himself sounds the trumpet (v. 27) and summons those who gather to follow him, affirming that the Lord has given the Moabites into their hand (v. 28). By contrast, Josephus has Ehud giving a signal in Jericho itself to the inhabitants who then undertake to alert their compatriots on his behalf. He likewise replaces the theological statement of 3:28a with a call by Ehud that his hearers do something for the sake of "freedom"; see previous note.

[501] Cf. Judg 3:24-25, from which Josephus omits the vulgar detail about the servants' supposing Eglon to be "relieving himself" (v. 24b), and to which he adds mention of their reaction to their discovery of the king's body.

[502] This notice, underscoring the speed of the Israelite assault that does not allow the Moabites to take counter measures, is an Josephan insertion.

[503] See Judg 3:28b-29, the sequence of which Josephus rearranges, mentioning, e.g., the seizure of the Jordan ford (3:28bα) as a kind of afterthought.

197. In this way the Hebrews were delivered from their slavery to the Moabites.[504] Honored for this reason with the leadership of the whole crowd,[505] Ioud died, having exercised his rulership for eighty years.[506] He was a man deserving of praise, even apart from the above-mentioned action.[507] After him Sanagar,[508] son of Anath,[509] having been chosen to rule, died in his first year of rule.[510]

Rule of Ehud (Ioud) and Shamgar

(5.1) 198. But once again the Israelites, drawing no lesson for their betterment from what they had previously undergone, neither worshipping God nor obeying the laws prior to their brief respite from slavery under the Moabites,[511] were enslaved by Abito, king of the Chananaians.[512] **199.** He, marching from the city of Asor[513]— this is situated above the Semachonidian lake[514]—was backed by an army of 300,000 troops and 10,000 horsemen, and outfitted with 3,000 chariots.[515] The general of this force was Sisares, who enjoyed the highest honor from the king.[516] He brought such terrible calamity upon the Israelites who joined battle with him that he imposed the payment of tribute on them.

Israel oppressed by Canaanite King

(5.2) 200. Suffering these things then for twenty years,[517] they themselves made no progress in the thought of being good from their bad luck. God, for his part, wished to chastise their arrogance[518] on account of their obstinacy towards him, in order that, changing their ways, they might become prudent for the future.[519] Taught

---

[504] Compare Judg 3:30a: "So Moab was subdued that day under the hand of Israel."

[505] Judges 3 does not mention such an "appointment" of Ehud by the people; compare Josephus' similar insertion concerning "Keniaz" in 5.184.

[506] Josephus' notice here reflects the LXX plus at the end of Judg 3:30b which adds to MT's statement "the land had rest for 80 years" the notice "and Aod judged them until his death." Compare 5.184, where Josephus similarly replaces Judg 3:11's figurative reference to the land's "having rest" for 40 years with mention of Keniaz' "exercising his rule" for that period.

[507] This "eulogy" for Ehud has no biblical parallel; compare Josephus' (also inserted) opening mention of his qualities in 5.188.

[508] MT (Judg 3:31) "Shamgar"; LXX B⁺ Σαμαγάρ; LXX BA Σαμεγάρ.

[509] Josephus' name for Shamgar's father corresponds to that ("Anath") given by MT and LXX A Judg 3:31 (LXX B has the corrupt form "Deinach").

[510] Josephus' reference to Shamgar's 1-year rule— the Bible does not mention the duration of his leadership—takes the place of the exploit attributed to him by Judg 3:31, i.e. killing 600 Philistines with an oxgoad that he might have found too implausible.

[511] Josephus expatiates on Judg 4:1: "and the people of Israel again did what was evil in the sight of the Lord." The reference to "their slavery under the Moabites" harks back to the wording of 5.197.

[512] Compare Judg 4:2a: "Jabin king of Canaan." Schalit (*s.v.* Ιάβινος) holds that the phrase Ἀβίτου τοῦ Χαναναῖων of the codices is a corruption of an original [Ι]αβι[ν]ου τοῦ τῶν Χαναναῖων. In 5.209 the codices do read a form of the name ("Joabin") more in line with

the biblical one. Just as he did in the case of Judg 3:8 (see note to "storm" at 5.180), Josephus avoids the reference to the Lord's "selling Israel into the hand of" of Judg 4:2.

[513] Judg 4:2a speaks of Jabin's "reigning in Hazor." This is Josephus' first (and only) mention of a king (called "Abito" by him in 5.198) of Hazor. Thereby, he eliminates the problem posed by the Bible itself, where, after the mention of the killing of a King Jabin and the destruction of his city Hazor by Joshua in Josh 11:1, 10, Judg 4:2a now speaks of Jabin and Hazor as currently existing, with no indication that the reference is to a different king of that name or that Hazor had been rebuilt in the meantime.

[514] Josephus supplies this localization of Hazor. The body of water in question, mentioned also in *War* 3.515; 4.2, is the contemporary Lake Huleh.

[515] Judg 4:3bα mentions only the enemy's "900 chariots of iron." Pseudo-Philo (*Bib. Ant.* 30.3) supplies an even higher figure for their chariots, i.e. 8,000.

[516] Josephus' characterization of "Sisares" here takes the place of the reference to "Haroseth-ha-goyim" as the residence of "Sisera" in Judg 4:2b.

[517] Compare Judg 4:3bβ: "he (Jabin/Sisera) oppressed the people of Israel cruelly for twenty years."

[518] Greek: ὕβρις. On Josephus' use of this key term of Greek tragedy, see Feldman 1998: 180-81.

[519] The reference to God's punishment being designed to make the people "become prudent" (Greek: σωφρονέω) here echoes the leaders' urging that a delegation be sent to the Transjordanians that they might "become prudent" from their words in 5.105. See also 5.110; and see note on "prudent" at 5.105.

*Deborah's in-
tercession*
in this way that these misfortunes had occurred to them because of their scorning the laws,[520] **201.** they kept begging a certain prophetess[521] named Dabora (in Hebrew her name means "bee")[522] to pray to God to take pity[523] on them and not overlook those who were being slain by the Chananaians.[524] God, for his part, assured them of safety, and chose Barak (which means "lightning" in Hebrew) of the Nephthalite tribe as general.[525]

*Deborah-Barak
exchange*
(5.3) 202. Dabora summoned Barak and directed him to recruit 10,000 young men and advance against the enemy; for that many would suffice, since God had spoken beforehand and announced victory.[526] **203.** When Barak said that he would not act as general unless she were his co-general,[527] she became indignant:[528] "You," she said, "are yielding to a woman a dignity that God has given you; nevertheless, I do not decline it."[529] Once the 10,000 were mustered, they encamped on Mt. Itabyrion.[530]

*Canaanites de-
feated*
204. At the direction of the king[531] Sisares went to meet them, and they encamped not far from the enemy. The numbers of the enemy dismayed the Israelites and Barak and they decided to retreat.[532] Dabora, however, restrained them, directing them to

---

[520] The extended editorial comment of 5.200 has no counterpart in Judges 4. It recalls the wording of the moral of Josephus' entire history as set out by him in *Ant.* 1.20.

[521] Josephus, concentrating on Deborah's role as "prophetess," leaves aside the further personal details given in Judg 4:4-5: her husband Lappidoth and her "judging" Israel under the "palm of Deborah." On Josephus' treatment of this figure (whose role he, in contrast to Pseudo-Philo, tends to downplay), see Brown 1992: 38-92; Feldman 1998a: 153-62; 2001: 200-206; and Roncace 2000: 249-59. The only other figure of whom Josephus uses the feminine form προφῆτις ("prophetess") is Huldah; see *Ant.* 10.50, 60.

[522] Josephus supplies this etymology for the Hebrew name "Deborah."

[523] This same expression is used of God in 5.187; see note on "taking pity" at 5.187.

[524] In Judg 4:3a the Israelites appeal to God directly, simply "crying" to him "for help." Josephus has them go through Deborah, intercession being one the key activities of the biblical prophets/ prophetesses in his presentation; compare his inserted reference to Josiah's directing his delegation to ask the prophetess Huldah to intercede with God for the people in *Ant.* 10.59.

[525] Josephus draws his designation of Barak as Israel's divinely appointed general from Judg 4:6, where Deborah informs him of God's command that he assemble his men on Mt. Tabor. Josephus omits the name of Barak's father (MT: Abinoam) and home-town (MT: Kedesh), while supplying an etymology for his name, just as he did for that of Deborah herself in 5.201.

[526] See Deborah's words to Barak as reported in Judg 4:6-7, from which Josephus omits, e.g., the name

of the site (Mt. Tabor), where the Israelites are to assemble, the 2 tribes (Naphtali and Zebulon) from which Barak is to draw his army, and the place ("by the river Kishon") where the battle will occur. Conversely, he introduces a "theological" explanation as to how the relatively small Israelite force (10,000 men) could have any hope of defeating the vastly larger enemy force (see 5.199).

[527] In Judg 4:8 (MT) Barak does not, as does his Josephan counterpart, make Deborah's sharing his command the condition for his accepting his commission, but only that she "go with him." LXX amplifies his words with its attached explanation of his demand: "for I do not know the day when the Lord will place the messenger/angel on the good way with me." Pseudo-Philo does not report a (verbal) response by Barak to Deborah's instructions to him in *Bib. Ant.* 31.1.

[528] Josephus inserts this reference to Deborah's emotional reaction to Barak's response.

[529] Josephus' formulation of Deborah's answer picks up on his modification of Barak's previous response to her. In Judg 4:9a Deborah simply states that she will accompany Barak, but then goes on to inform him that the campaign will not redound to his own glory in that the Lord intends "to sell Sisera into the hand of a woman." Josephus will allude to Deborah's statement subsequently, however; see 5.209.

[530] Josephus here conflates the data of Judg 4:10, 12, leaving aside the parenthetical reference to Heber the Kenite (4:11). On Mt. "Itabyrion" as Josephus' rendering of the biblical "Mt. Tabor" (4:12), see note on "its breadth" at 5.84.

[531] In Judg 4:13 the general Sisera acts on his own initiative in countering Israel's movement.

[532] Judges 4 has no counterpart to this notice on the

join battle on that day, for they would be victorious and God would assist them.[533]

(5.4) 205. When therefore they engaged and attacked, there was a great storm with much precipitation and hail. The wind drove the rain into the faces of the Chananaians, impairing their vision, so that their bows and slings were useless to them. On account of the cold, their troops likewise could not use their swords. **206.** The bad weather impeded the Israelites less since it was to their backs. Taking courage at the thought of God's help, they pressed forward into the midst of the enemy and killed many of them. These fell, some beneath the Israelites, others panicked by their own cavalry, so that many of them died beneath their chariots.[534]

207. Now Sisares had jumped down from his chariot when he saw how things were going; in his flight he reached a certain woman of the Kenelides, whose name was Iale.[535] When he requested to be hidden, she welcomed him,[536] and when he asked for a drink, she gave him milk that was already curdled.[537]

Jael kills Sisera

208. After he had drunk deeply from the cup, he fell asleep.[538] But as he slept, Iale brought an iron tent-peg that she wielded like a hammer on his mouth and jaw, driving it into the ground.[539] To Barak's entourage, which arrived a little later, she showed him nailed to the ground.[540]

209. Thus, this victory redounded to the credit of a woman, as Dabora had said.[541]

---

emotional state of Barak and his army in the face of the vastly superior enemy force. Compare Josephus' (also inserted) reference to the dismay of Joshua and the Israelites prompted by the size of the enemy army in his rendition of Josh 11:4 in 5.64.

[533] Compare Deborah's encouraging address to Barak in Judg 4:14a: "Up! For this is the day in which the Lord has given Sisera into your hand. Does not the Lord go up before you [Tg.: Is not the angel of the Lord going forth to insure success before you]?"

[534] The entire sequence 5.205-206 represents Josephus' dramatization of the rather jejune battle account of Judg 4:14b-15a, 16, in which once the Lord routs the enemy army (v. 15), Barak pursues and annihilates them (v. 16). Pseudo-Philo embellishes still more, affirming (*Bib. Ant.* 31.2; cf. Judg 5:20) that, at God's command, the stars burned up 8,730,000 of the enemy in a single hour.

[535] See Judg 4:15b, 17. In 4:17 "Jael" is called the wife of Heber the *Kenite* (cf. 4:11), and Sisera's going to her is explained in terms of the existing "peace" between King Jabin and her husband.

[536] In Judg 4:18 it is Jael who takes the initiative in offering hospitality/protection to Sisera and who further covers him with a rug. Pseudo-Philo (*Bib. Ant.* 31.3) follows the Bible in this regard, likewise mentioning Jael's beauty, her adorning herself for her meeting with Sisera, and the roses that Sisera sees scattered on her bed.

[537] See Judg 4:19, which does not mention the "curdled" state of the milk Jael gives Sisera, but adds that, once he had drunk, Jael "covered him" (so MT LXX B; LXX AL specify his face). Pseudo-Philo (*Bib. Ant.* 31.5-

7) greatly embellishes the biblical "drinking motif," citing, e.g., Jael's extended prayer as she milks her flock to get the milk for Sisera (31.5).

[538] In Judges 4, Sisera's falling asleep is mentioned, not immediately after his drinking (4:19b), but rather at a later point (4:21bα, with his directive to Jael that she not betray his presence with her (v. 20) and her stealthy approach to him (v.21a) supervening. Like Josephus, Pseudo-Philo (*Bib. Ant.* 31.6) directly links Sisera's drinking with his falling asleep.

[539] See Judg 4:21a, which distinguishes 2 different implements used by Jael in killing Sisera, i.e. a tent-peg and a hammer, and which further has her drive the peg through his "temple" (so MT LXX BL; LXX A reads "cheek" and adds that Sisera, before dying, "had a convulsion between Jael's knees and emitted a sigh"). Pseudo-Philo embellishes the murder scene with mention of Jael's reflection and prayer prior to perpetrating the deed, as well as of an exchange between her and the dying Sisera (*Bib. Ant.* 31.7).

[540] In Judg 4:22 Jael displays Sisera's corpse to Barak himself. This is the case also in *Bib. Ant.* 31.9, where Barak responds with a word of benediction to what he is shown and then, having decapitated Sisera, dispatches the head to his (Sisera's) mother (cf. Judg 5:28-30) with a mocking message.

[541] This notice—to which Judges 4 lacks an equivalent—alludes back to Deborah's announcement to Barak in Judg 4:9b, previously passed over by Josephus; see note to "it" at 5.203. Pseudo-Philo has something comparable at this point in his narration; see Barak's statement upon viewing Sisera's corpse in *Bib. Ant.* 31.9: "Blessed be the Lord who sent his spirit and

Barak's gener-
alship

As Barak was campaigning against Asor, he killed Ioabin[542] who had come to meet him; once its general fell, he razed the city to the ground.[543] [Barak] functioned as general of the Israelites for forty years.[544]

Midianite op-
pression

(6.1) 210. After Barak and Dabora both died at the same time,[545] the Madianites appealed to the Amalekites and the Arabs, and campaigned against the Israelites.[546] They were victorious over those whom they engaged in battle, devastated their crops and carried away plunder.[547]

211. When they had done this for seven years,[548] the majority of the Israelites retired to the hill-country, abandoning the plains. They made underground tunnels and caves and kept in these whatever had eluded the enemy.[549] **212.** For the Madianites, campaigning during midsummer, allowed the Israelites to till the soil in the rainy winter season, so that they might have some [product] of their labors to which they could do damage.[550] There was a famine and scarcity of food, and they [the Israelites] had recourse to supplication, appealing to God to save them.[551]

Gideon's vision

(6.2) 213. Now Gedeon,[552] son of Ias,[553] who was among the most distinguished

---

said, 'Into the hand of a woman Sisera will be delivered'." (Like Josephus, Pseudo-Philo did not previously reproduce Deborah's announcement of Judg 4:9b.)

[542] Compare this form of the king's name (Greek: Ἰοαβινός) with the form found in 5.198, i.e. "Abito."

[543] The above notice represents a reworking of Judg 4:23-24, highlighting the figure of Barak (unmentioned in the biblical sequence, which attributes the ultimate "destruction" of Jabin to the people of Israel as a whole), and adding explicit mention of the "razing" of Hazor (likewise unmentioned in 4:23-24).

[544] Josephus derives this round figure from Judg 5:31b, where however, it refers to the period of "rest" enjoyed by the land. Josephus, in line with his general tendency not to reproduce the poetic interludes of his biblical narrative sources, leaves aside the "Song of Deborah and Barak" (Judg 5:1-31a) that supervenes between the source components of 5.209, i.e. 4:23-24 and 5:31b, respectively; see Feldman 1998a: 160-161. By contrast, Pseudo-Philo (*Bib. Ant.* 32) elaborates on the Song's content.

[545] The Bible does not make explicit mention of the deaths of Barak and Deborah. Pseudo-Philo (*Bib. Ant.* 33) precedes his account of the latter's demise with an extended farewell discourse by her.

[546] See Judg 6:3, where the 3rd group that assaults the Israelites is designated as "the people of the East." Josephus omits the theological background statement of 6:1 about the Israelites "doing evil in the Lord's sight" and the Lord in turn "giving them into the hand of the Midianites."

[547] See Judg 6:4, to which Josephus adds mention of the enemy's defeating the Israelites as a prelude to despoiling them, while omitting its specification of the extent of the Midianite penetration ("as far as Gaza").

[548] Josephus derives this chronological indication

from the end of Judg 6:1, which is otherwise omitted by him; see note to "Israelites" at 5.210.

[549] Josephus elaborates on Judg 6:2b, which simply mentions the Israelites' making themselves "dens in the mountains, caves and strongholds."

[550] Josephus elaborates on the reference to the enemy coalition coming up "whenever the Israelites put in seed" at the beginning of Judg 6:3, spelling out why they invaders showed up precisely when they did in Israel. On winter as the season of rains in Palestine, see, e.g., Song of Songs 2:11.

[551] In Judg 6:6 the Israelites, having been brought very low, "cry for help to the Lord." Josephus omits the implausibly high figures for the enemy forces intimated by Judg 6:5 (they "come like locusts for number"; they and their camels are "innumerable"). Like the Qumran MSS 4QJudg[a], Josephus has no equivalent to the speech by a nameless prophet (6:7-10) replying to the people's appeal to the Lord (6:6) denouncing them for their lack of fidelity to the Lord despite his benefactions to him. This speech has no effect on the subsequent course of events, while its negative tone seems out of line with God's positive initiative on Israel's behalf that he will thereafter set in motion through Gideon.

[552] Greek: Γεδεών, the LXX form of the hero's name (Hebrew: Gideon). On the portrayal of Gideon by Josephus, who (like Pseudo-Philo, *Bib. Ant.* 35-36) drastically abridges the Bible's 3-chapter account of him (Judges 6-8), see Feldman 1998a: 163-76; 2001: 207-18; Roncace 2000: 257-74. On the treatment of Gideon in ancient Jewish and early Christian tradition overall, see Legasse 2000.

[553] Greek: Ἴασος. Judg 6:11 designates Gideon's father as "Joash" (LXX: Ἰωάς). Josephus leaves aside the father's clan affiliation (MT: "the Abiezrite").

men of the Manassite tribe,[554] used to carry his sheaves of grain and secretly thresh them in a wine press, for he was too anxious about the enemy to do this openly on the threshing floor.[555] There appeared standing beside him a vision in the form of a young man[556] who called him happy and a friend of God.[557] In reply he said, "it is indeed a great token of his benevolence[558] that I am using a wine press rather than the threshing floor."[559] **214.** When he appealed to him to be of good cheer and make an effort to recover their freedom,[560] he said that this was impossible. For the tribe to which he belonged was few in number. Moreover, he himself was a youth, too weak for such great matters.[561] But God[562] promised that he himself would supply the rest and, with him as their general, would grant victory to the Israelites.[563]

---

[554] Josephus derives Gideon's tribal affiliation from Judg 6:15, where the hero alludes to his belonging to this tribe. His further characterization of Gideon as part of the tribe's elite may have been inspired by the angel's address to him in Judg 6:12, "you mighty man of valor" (compare Pseudo-Philo's opening qualification of him as "a valiant man among all his brothers" in *Bib. Ant.* 35.1). By contrast, Gideon, in Judg 6:15b (= 5.214) calls himself the "least" in a family whose clan is itself the "weakest" in Manasseh; see note to "matters" at 5.214.

[555] The reference to the "threshing floor," the regular place for beating out grain, takes the place of the "oak at Ophrah" owned by Gideon's father, where Gideon is threshing according to Judg 6:11b. The modification serves to prepare Gideon's retort to the angel at the conclusion of the paragraph.

[556] In Judg 6:12, as in *Bib. Ant.* 35.1, "an/the angel of the Lord" appears to Gideon. Of Josephus' 2 alternative designations for the being here in 5.213, he uses the first, i.e. "vision" (Greek: φάντασμα) in place of (or alongside) biblical references to an "angel" in *Ant.* 1.325 (// Gen 32:1-2), 133 (// Gen 32:24-32); 3.62 (Exod 3:2); and 5.277 (// Judges 13); see Mach 1992: 308, n. 82. His other such term, i.e. "young man" (Greek: νεανίσκος/ νεανίας) is used by him in contexts where the Bible mentions angel(s) in *Ant.* 1.200 (// Genesis 19); and 5.279 (compare 5.277, where Josephus' initial designation of 5.213, i.e. "vision" is employed of the figure who appears to Manoah's wife). On the designation of angels as "young men" elsewhere in ancient literature, both Greco-Roman and Judeo-Christian, see Mach 1992: 307-8, n. 81. Josephus leaves aside the odd detail about the angel "sitting" beneath the oak of Gideon's father (6:11), prior to his speaking to Gideon (6:12).

[557] Compare Judg 6:12b: "The Lord is with you, you mighty man of valor." As Feldman (1998a: 169) points out, Josephus' phrase "friend of God" (Greek: φίλος τῷ θεῷ) serves to underscore Gideon's piety, being likewise applied by him to the great prophet Samuel in *Ant.* 6.294. On the term φίλος ("friend") as a designation for God in relation to humans, see note on

"friend" at 5.116.

[558] Greek: εὐμένεια. The cognate adjective εὐμενής is used some 40 times by Josephus in reference to God. According to Schlatter (1910: 62) these words are Josephus' most frequent terms for expressing God's positive disposition towards humans.

[559] Gideon's sarcastic reply here takes the place of the series of accusatory questions/assertions about what the Lord has (not) done for Israel made by him in Judg 6:13. Its wording harks back to the reference to Gideon's fearing to thresh on the threshing floor at the beginning of the paragraph; see note on "floor" at 5.213. In *Bib. Ant.* 35.3 the angel responds to Gideon's complaints with a speech justifying God's ways in terms of Israel's own sinfulness.

[560] In Judg 6:14a there is a shift from "the angel of the Lord" (6:11) to the Lord himself as speaker. Josephus will introduce a like shift of speaker at a later point in his version; see 5.214b. The apparition's summons to Gideon to act on behalf of Israel's "freedom" here echoes similar language introduced by Josephus in his version of several of the preceding Judge stories (see 5.182, 187, 194). This summons replaces the Lord's commission to Gideon of 6:14b: "go in this might of yours and deliver Israel from the hand of Midian; do not I send you?"

[561] In comparison with Judg 6:15, Josephus accentuates the modesty implicit in Gideon's response; see Feldman 1998a: 167. Gideon's reported remarks about himself here stand in contrast with Josephus' earlier description of him as "among the most distinguished men of the Manassite tribe"; see note to "Manassite tribe" at 5.213.

[562] At this point (compare 5.213-214a) Josephus follows the source (Judg 6:16) in making the Deity address Gideon directly. Pseudo-Philo (*Bib. Ant.* 35) retains the angel as Gideon's conversation partner throughout.

[563] At this point, Josephus omits 2 extended segments of the biblical Gideon story, i.e. the "fire miracle" by which the angel demonstrates his identity to Gideon (Judg 6:17-24) and Gideon's own initiative against the pagan cult artifacts (Judg 6:25-32). The

(6.3) 215. Gedeon was believed upon his relating these things to some of the young men. They immediately made ready for the struggle, their camp consisting of 10,000 men.[564] God, however, showed himself to Gedeon in a dream[565] and disclosed to him that human nature is self-loving[566] and hostile to those of outstanding virtue.[567] Hence, rather than ascribing the victory to God, they would think it their own, seeing that they were a large army and were the enemy's equal militarily.[568] **216.** In order then that they might learn the reality of his help,[569] he advised him, around the middle of the day, when the noonday heat was at its height,[570] to lead the army to the river.[571] He was to consider those who knelt down to drink as men of high spirits, but to think of those who did their drinking in haste and fright as cowards who had been dismayed by the enemy.[572]

---

former omission is reflective of Josephus' tendency to downplay the Bible's miraculous element (see Feldman 1998a: 170-171), while the latter is in line with his endeavor to soft-peddle biblical instances of Jewish religious intolerance (see Feldman 1998a: 168). Pseudo-Philo does offer a—quite different—version of the fire-miracle (*Bib. Ant.* 35.5-6), but does not reproduce Gideon's iconoclastic deed (cf., however, the allusion to this in the subsequent divine word of 36.4).

[564] Josephus here drastically compresses the notices on Gideon's initial assembling of the Israelite forces found in Judg 6:33-7:3. From that sequence he eliminates the reference to the divine Spirit's "possessing" Gideon and so prompting his initiative (Judg 6:34; cf. note to "freedom" at 5.18a). He likewise passes over the "fleece miracle," which Gideon is granted by the angel prior to proceeding further (6:36-40; Pseudo-Philo does likewise), just as he leaves aside the first, divinely ordered reduction of Gideon's force, according to which the cowards are all to be sent home, this leaving 10,000 men remaining (7:2-3). Finally, Josephus omits Gideon's alternative name, i.e., "Jerubbaal," used of him in Judg 7:1 and occasionally elsewhere in Judges 6-8. The reason for this omission is Josephus' dropping (see note to "Israelites" at 5.214) of the iconoclastic episode of Judg 6:25-32 which culminates in Gideon's being given that name (v. 32) which itself recalls his father's statement "let Baal contend (Hebrew: ירב) for himself" (v. 31).

[565] In Judg 7:4 the Lord simply "speaks" to Gideon, the circumstances being left indeterminate. Compare 5.192-193, where in his account of the exchange between Ehud and Eglon (// Judg 3:20), Josephus interjects mention of the former's (purported) dream.

[566] Josephus attributes a similar observation on human "self-love" to Moses in *Ant.* 3.190, the only other passage in his writings where he uses the word φίλαυτος ("loving oneself").

[567] On the theme of envy, to which he has God allude here, as a leading factor in human affairs (and in his own personal experience) in Josephus' writings, see

Feldman 1998: 198-203.

[568] Josephus combines this characteristic reflection about human nature with his version of God's expression of concern in Judg 7:2 that the Israelites are "still too many" and so will "vaunt themselves against me, saying, 'My own hand has delivered me'." Whereas, however, in Judges 7 this divine reflection is the basis for God's directive ordering an initial reduction of the army via a dismissal of the cowards among them (7:3), which will then be followed by a 2nd such reduction in 7:4-7, Josephus omits the first reduction (see note to "men" at 5.215) and makes his rendering of 7:2 the grounds for the single reduction, corresponding to that of 7:4-7, which he will subsequently relate.

[569] This indication of the purpose of the procedure that God is about to prescribe represents a Josephan expansion of the divine word in Judg 7:4.

[570] In Judg 7:4 God does not specify when the prescribed procedure is to be performed.

[571] Josephus derives this divine directive to Gideon from Judg 7:4a. He omits God's appended general injunction (7:4b) that Gideon is to take with him those men whom he (God) will indicate, while those whom he tells him not to take along are to remain behind.

[572] With this formulation Josephus attempts to clarify the nature of the distinction between the 2 groups of "drinkers" spoken of by God in Judg 7:5b, i.e. those who lap the water "as a dog laps" and those who "kneel down to drink." In his understanding the latter group is courageous, the former cowardly. In fact, however, this does not seem to be the sense of the source distinction in that the cowards have already been sent home by Gideon (7:3, omitted by Josephus; see note to "militarily" at 5.215). Some commentators suggest that the distinction is rather between alert soldiers (the "lappers") and careless ones (those who kneel to drink), while others aver that no such qualitative distinction is intended and the procedure is a purely arbitrary way of dividing up the army into 2 groups, one of which will be retained, the other dismissed.

217. When Gedeon acted in accordance with God's injunctions,[573] 300 men were found drinking the water with their hands, confused by their fear.[574] God said to lead these out to engage the enemy.[575] They made camp above the Jordan that they were set to ford on the following day.[576]

(6.4) 218. Gedeon fell into fear, for God told him in advance to engage during the night.[577] Wishing to rid him of this anxiety, God directed him to take one of the soldiers[578] and to advance close to the tents of the Madianites, since it was from them that he would obtain confidence of mind.

Gideon in the Midianite camp

219. Obeying, Gedeon went, taking with him his own attendant, named Phroura.[579] Drawing near to a certain tent, he found those inside it awake, one of them telling a dream[580] to his tent-mate such that Gedeon heard it.[581] The dream was as follows: a barley-cake, so worthless as to be scarcely edible by humans,[582] seemed to roll through the camp and knocked down the king's tent and those of all the soldiers.[583]

220. His companion judged that the vision signified the extermination of the army,[584] likewise saying how he came to realize this: just as every seed called "barley" is universally regarded as totally worthless, "so of all the Asians, the Israelites are now seen as the most disreputable and most similar in kind to barley.[585]

---

[573] Josephus reverses the sequence of Judg 7:5, where Gideon first leads the army to the river (v. 5a) and then receives God's more specific directive about what is to be done there (v. 5b).

[574] In describing the 300 as drinking "with their hands," Josephus follows the reading of MT LXX B and Tg. Judg 7:6, as opposed to LXX AL, where they lap the water "with their tongues." Josephus omits the further specification of 7:6 that the remainder of the army "knelt down to drink," keeping all attention focussed on the group that will remain with Gideon.

[575] See Judg 7:7, from which Josephus omits God's additional directive that the rest of the army return home. Going further than Josephus, Pseudo-Philo leaves aside, not just the first (Judg 7:3), but also the 2nd (7:4-7) divinely-prescribed reduction of the Israelite army.

[576] In Judg 7:8b the reference is rather to Midian's camp. Josephus omits Gideon's dismissal (7:8a; see 7:7b, God's order that Gideon do this, also omitted by him) of the rest of his army, whose jars and "horns" (MT LXX AB)/ "trumpets" (LXX L) he, however, retains for subsequent use.

[577] Josephus' inserted reference to Gideon's "fear" seems inspired by God's word to him in Judg 7:10 ("but if you fear..."), while his motivation for that fear reflects the initial divine directive cited in 7:9, instructing Gideon to go down against the Midianite camp.

[578] In Judg 7:10 God directs Gideon to take with him "Purah your servant"; subsequently (see 5.219), Josephus will utilize this biblical designation for Gideon's companion.

[579] Here, Josephus aligns himself with Judg 7:11b in having Gideon accompanied, not by a "soldier" (see note on "soldiers" at 5.218), but by his "attendant" (whom MT calls "Purah"). Schalit (*s.v.* Φαρά), following J. Hudson, sees the form of the servant's name read by the MSS (Θρουρά) as a corruption of the original one, which would have corresponded to LXX's form, i.e. Φαρά.

[580] On Josephus' version of the Midianite's dream in relation to its biblical parallel in Judg 7:13-15, see Gnuse 1996: 167-68.

[581] See Judg 7:13a. Josephus "delays" the parenthetical notice of 7:12 on the size of the Midianite encampment; see note on "circle" at 5.224.

[582] This negative characterization of the "barley-cake" is Josephus' addition to the Midianite's narrative of his dream in Judg 7:13.

[583] In Judg 7:13 the barley-cake overthrows a single tent, which is designated as "the tent" without further specification (so MT LXX B; LXX A qualifies it as "the tent of Madiam").

[584] This initial "non-theological" interpretation of the dream without mention of Gideon has no counterpart in Judg 7:14, where the interpreter immediately identifies the rolling barley cake with the "sword of Gideon" into whose hand God has given "Midian and all the host." Subsequently however, Josephus will have the speaker employ the language of 7:14; see 5.221.

[585] The above explanation, itself pointing back to Josephus' inserted negative characterization of the barley cake in 5.219, as to how the Midianite came to his interpretation of his fellow's dream lacks a biblical basis. As Feldman (1998a: 173) observes, the explanation

221. Moreover, it is Gedeon and the army with him who are, at present, the ones with confidence among the Israelites. Because therefore you say that you saw the barley-cake overturning our tents, I am afraid that God has granted victory to Gedeon over us."[586]

(6.5) 222. Good hope and confidence took hold of Gedeon when he heard the dream, and he ordered his fellows to arm themselves, also telling them of the enemies' vision.[587] They were receptive to his instructions, being encouraged by what had been disclosed.[588]

Gideon defeats Midianites

223. Around the fourth watch Gedeon led out his army, dividing it into three parts, each of which consisted of 100 men.[589] All were carrying empty jars and lighted torches inside these so that their approach would not be detected by the enemy.[590] In their right hands they had a ram's horn which they were using in place of a trumpet.[591] **224.** The enemy camp occupied a lot of ground, for they happened to have many camels and were all grouped by nation within a single circle.[592] **225.** The Hebrews, having been told beforehand that they, once they were near the enemy and once the trumpets[593] had been sounded as a signal and the jars smashed, were to rush forward with the torches while raising the battle-cry, "victory for Gedeon with God's help," did these things.[594]

226. Consternation and terror took hold of the persons who were still sleeping. For it was night and God wished it thus.[595] A few were killed by the enemy, but most by their own allies on account of their differences of language. **227.** Once they had fallen into consternation, they did away with everyone they encountered, thinking them to be enemies; great was the slaughter.[596] When a report of Gedeon's vic-

---

elucidates a point which the Bible leaves unresolved, namely the nature of the connection between the barley cake and Israel, which would prompt the Midianite to think of the latter when hearing of the former. This is Josephus' only use of the adjective "Asian" (Greek Ἀσιανός).

[586] For this conclusion to the interpreter's response, Josephus makes delayed use of his statement in Judg 7:14, where the speaker identifies the barley cake with the "sword of Gideon" into whose hand "God has given Midian and all the host." See note to "army" at 5.220.

[587] Cf. Judg 7:15, to which Josephus adds mention of Gideon's emotional state at this juncture—contrast his "fear" in 5.218—and his telling his troops of what he had overheard in the Midianite camp.

[588] Also this reference to the effect of Gideon's report on his men is a Josephan insertion. Pseudo-Philo replaces the sequence of Judg 7:7-18 with an account (*Bib. Ant.* 36.1-2) in which Gideon and his 300 hear the Midianites speaking to each other about their impending destruction by God, whereupon the spirit of the Lord "clothes" Gideon (cf. Judg 6:34, omitted by Josephus), who then urges his men to join battle.

[589] Josephus combines Judg 7:16a (the division of the 300 into 3 groups) and 7:19a (their advance to the enemy camp at the start of the "middle watch").

[590] Josephus provides an explanation for Gideon's directive to his men in Judg 7:16b that they are to place

their torches inside the empty jars.

[591] With this formulation Josephus combines the designations used for the musical instruments carried by the 300 in MT LXX AL ("horns") and LXX L ("trumpets") Judg 7:16.

[592] This is Josephus' delayed equivalent (see note to "heard it" at 5.219) to the notice of Judg 7:12 on the size of the Midianite camp, whose implausible figures (an army "like locusts for multitude," camels like "the sand upon the seashore") he does not, however, reproduce, just as he omits the similar indications of 6:5; see note to "save them" at 5.212.

[593] See note on "trumpet" at 5.223.

[594] Josephus here conflates the instructions Gideon gives his men (Judg 7:18) and their execution of these (7:20).

[595] The reference to the enemy's being asleep because it is still night is Josephus' embellishment of the battle account of Judg 7:21-23.

[596] Josephus expatiates on the notice of Judg 7:22aβ about the Lord's "setting every man's sword against his fellow and against all the army," specifying that God, in turning the coalition partners against each other, made use of the difference of languages among them; cf. the reference to the enemy camp being "grouped by nation" in 5.224. He omits the specifications of 7:22b concerning the end points of the enemy's flight.

tory was brought to the Israelites, they too armed themselves; in their pursuit, they overtook the enemy at a certain hollow site surrounded by impassable ravines.[597] Standing around them, the Israelites killed them all, along with the two kings Oreb and Zeb.[598]

228. The remaining leaders urged on the surviving soldiers—there were some 18,000 of them—and they made camp at a great distance from the Israelites.[599] Gedeon, however, did not slacken in his exertions; rather, pursuing with his entire army[600] and joining battle,[601] he destroyed the enemy, and carried off the remaining leaders, Zebe[602] and Zarmoune,[603] whom he had taken captive.

229. There had perished in the [earlier] battle about 120,000 of the Madianites and their fellow-soldiers, the Arabs.[604] Much plunder was taken by the Hebrews: gold, silver, woven stuff, camels, and beasts of burden.[605] Arriving at Ephra, his ancestral town,[606] Gedeon killed the kings of the Midianites.[607]

(6.6) 230. The Ephraimite tribe took Gedeon's success amiss, however, and decided to campaign against him, complaining that he had not given them prior notice of his undertaking against the enemy.[608] Gedeon, who was a man of moderation and

Gideon-Ephraim confrontation

---

[597] Josephus embellishes the pursuit notice of Judg 7:23 with mention of the site at which the fleeing enemy forces become entrapped. Feldman (1998a: 175, n. 6) points out that in 5.162 Josephus gives a rather similar picture of the locality in which the Benjamites end up trapped as they flee from the Israelites.

[598] In Judg 7:24-25 it is specifically the Ephraimites who, in separate actions, kill the 2 Midianite "princes/ chiefs," slaying "Oreb" at the "rock of Oreb" (MT; LXX A "at Sourin," LXX B "at Sour") and "Zeeb" at "the wine press of Zeeb" (MT; LXX AB transliterate "at Iakephzeb"). Pseudo-Philo does not mention the pair's execution.

[599] In Judg 8:10 the figure given for the surviving enemy forces is "about 15,000."

[600] Josephus leaves aside, at this juncture, the confrontational exchanges between Gideon and first the Ephraimites (Judg 7:24-8:3) and then the men of Succoth and Penuel (8:4-9), which occur during his pursuit of the Midianites. He will, however, make a delayed use of the former episode in 5.230-231. His omission of the latter incident (likewise passed over by Pseudo-Philo) likely has do with its exemplification of those intra-Jewish animosities Josephus is concerned to attenuate throughout his *Antiquities*; see Feldman 1998a: 172.

[601] See Judg 8:11aβ. Josephus leaves aside the topographical indications concerning the battle site of 8:10-11aα as well as the notice of 8:11b about the Midianite army being "off guard."

[602] Compare Zebah (MT); Zebee (LXX).

[603] Compare Zalmuna (MT); Salmana (LXX A); Selmana (LXX B). Schalit (*s.v.*) attributes Josephus' form (Ζαρμούνης) to a confusion between the consonants λ and ρ.

[604] See Judg 8:10 (the "earlier battle" here is the one described by Josephus in 5.227// Judg 7:22). For Josephus' replacement of "the people of the East" (so 8:10) by "Arabs," see note to "Israelites" at 5.210.

[605] Josephus anticipates this notice on the plunder taken from Judg 8:25-26, which cites earrings, crescents, pendants, royal purple garments, and camel collars.

[606] MT Judg 8:27 calls Gideon's hometown "Ophrah," while LXX reads "Ephrata." Having earlier omitted Gideon's threats against the inhabitants of Succoth and Penuel (Judg 8:4-9; see note to "army" at 5.228), Josephus naturally also leaves aside his execution of those threats as described in 8:13-17, prior to Gideon's dealing with the Midianite kings in 8:18-21.

[607] Josephus reduces the narrative of Judg 8:18-21 to its core content, i.e. Gideon's killing the kings with his own hands (8:21bα), even while introducing the specification that their execution took place in the hero's hometown. In particular, he leaves aside the double exchange between the pair and Gideon (vv. 18-19, 21a), Gideon's intervening command to his son Jether to slay the kings and the latter's non-compliance out of fear (v. 20), and Gideon's taking of the crescents on the necks of the kings' camels (v. 21bβ). These 2 kings are nowhere mentioned by Pseudo-Philo.

[608] In Judges 7-8 the Ephraimites' complaint about not having been called on to join the fight against Midian (Judg 8:1-3) occurs in the midst of Gideon's pursuit of the Midianites and its sequels (7:23-25; 8:4-21); see note to "army" at 5.228. Josephus' placement of the complaint seems to make better sense, here at a point where the Midianite campaign has been definitively concluded and so there is no opportunity for the Ephraimites to participate. Josephus likewise eliminates

pre-eminent in every virtue,[609] said, however, that it was not on his own, using his [own] reasoning, but rather in accordance with God's directive that he had attacked the enemy without them. The victory, he declared, was no less theirs than of those who had participated in the campaign.[610] **231.** By mollifying their wrath with these words,[611] he proved of greater benefit to the Hebrews than by his success against their enemies; for he preserved them from the civil strife they were about to begin.[612] That tribe, however, paid the penalty for its arrogance, as we shall disclose at the proper time.[613]

Gideon's end

232. Gedeon, though wishing to lay aside his rulership,[614] was compelled to exercise it for forty years,[615] deciding cases for them and the disputes that were brought to him. All such matters were regulated in accordance with what he said.[616] Dying as an old man, he was buried at Ephra, his ancestral city.[617]

---

the seeming discrepancy between the Ephramites' complaint about not having been called out (8:1) and Gideon's prior summons to them in 7:24, by leaving the latter passage aside. Pseudo-Philo makes no mention of the Ephraimites in his version of the Gideon story.

[609] This characterization of Gideon is a Josephan insertion. Its high praise of him reflects the importance Josephus attaches to maintaining peace among his people—as Gideon will do in what follows. See also his appended comment concerning Gideon's initiative in 5.231. The designation of Gideon as "pre-eminent in every virtue (Greek: ἀρετή)" recalls God's warning to him about human nature being hostile to those of "outstanding virtue (Greek: ἀρετή)" in 5.215. The truth of this divine observation is now being demonstrated in Gideon's own experience with the Ephraimites.

[610] In Judg 8:2-3a Gideon responds to the Ephraimites' complaint by exalting that tribe's own achievement in capturing the Midianite princes Oreb and Zeeb (see 7:25) above his own. Josephus' reformulation of Gideon's response was necessitated by the fact that in 5.227 he has attributed the capture of the Midianite "kings," not to the Ephraimites specifically, but rather to Gideon personally.

[611] Cf. Judg 8:3b: "and their anger was abated, when he had said this."

[612] This inserted evaluation of Gideon's "pacification" of the Ephraimites reflects Josephus' recurrent emphasis on the importance of intra-Jewish solidarity and the horrors of its opposite; see Feldman 1998a: 171-72.

[613] With this insertion Josephus foreshadows the massacre of the Ephraimites that Jephthah will perpetrate in Judges 12 (= 5.267-269).

[614] This statement about Gideon's desire to relinquish his military command takes the place of Judg 8:22-23, where Gideon refuses the people's request that he and his descendants rule over them, declaring that God is to be their ruler, a passage which Pseudo-Philo

omits entirely. One might have expected Josephus to reproduce the biblical sequence as he found it since this would seem to accord well with his own anti-monarchical outlook (on this see Feldman 1998: 502-4). Perhaps, however, he wishes the people's similar proposal about a hereditary kingship in the time of Samuel (see 1 Samuel 8) to appear as a unique first in their history, and accordingly all the more reprehensible.

[615] Josephus derives this figure from Judg 8:28b, which speaks of the land having rest for 40 years in Gideon's time.

[616] Here Josephus spells out the nature of Gideon's reluctant "rule," likely under the influence of the presentation of the "minor judges" in Judg 10:1-5; 12:7-13. In the interest of upholding Gideon's standing as a model figure (see his inserted characterization of him in 5.230), Josephus leaves aside the following biblical incident (Judg 8:24-27), where Gideon fashions an idolatrous "ephod" from the various items the people give him at his request (on this see Feldman 1998a: 169-70). Pseudo-Philo (who offers a much less positive portrayal of Gideon than does Josephus) reproduces this episode in *Bib. Ant.* 36.3, where he speaks of Gideon's making "idols" from what was given him and worshipping these himself (compare Judg 8:27, where Israel "plays the harlot" after Gideon's ephod).

[617] See Judg 8:32, which further specifies that Gideon was buried in the tomb of his father Joash. Unlike the Bible, Pseudo-Philo addresses the question of why the idol-making Gideon should have lived to a "good old age" (so Judg 8:32). He has (*Bib. Ant.* 36.4) God answer the question with the statement that if Gideon were to die early, people would suppose that he had been struck down by Baal, just as Gideon's father had challenged Baal to do to his son who had torn down that god's altar (cf. Judg 6:31). The problem does not arise for Josephus given his omission of Gideon's making of the idolatrous ephod; see note to "his rulership" at 5.232.

(7.1) 233. He had seventy legitimate sons, for he married many wives;[618] there was also an illegitimate one, Abimelech[619] by name, whom he had by his concubine Drouma.[620] He, after the death of his father, returned to Sikima,[621] to his mother's relatives (for she was from there).[622] He took money from them, [and hired certain miscreants],[623] who were notorious for the number of their misdeeds.[624]

Abimelech seizes power in Shechem

234. He came with them to his father's house and killed all his brothers except Iotham; for he was saved by fleeing successfully.[625] Abimelech transformed the government into a tyranny;[626] appointing himself lord, he did whatever he pleased instead of what was lawful and was terribly scornful of those who upheld what was just.[627]

(7.2) 235. Then, when there was a public festival of the Sikimites and the whole crowd was assembled there,[628] his brother Iotham, who had escaped, as we mentioned, ascended Mt. Garizin (which is situated above the city of Sikimites).[629] Crying out for a hearing, he asked the crowd to give him their attention so that they might learn what he had to say.[630]

Jotham's warning about Abimelech

---

[618] In Judg 8:30 Gideon's sons and wives are mentioned prior to the notice on his death (8:32).

[619] On Josephus' portrayal of Abimelech, see Begg 1996.

[620] Judg 8:31 leaves the mother of Abimelech unnamed. On the possible derivation of her name from the place-name "Arumah" of Judg 9:41, see Begg 1996: 147, n. 11.

[621] This is the form of the city's name (MT: Shechem), read by LXX A Judg 9:1 (LXX B has Συχέμ).

[622] Josephus here combines elements of Judg 8:32 (Gideon's death); 9:1 (Abimelech's going to Shechem to his mother's kin) and 8:31 (Shechem as his mother's residence). He leaves aside the parenthetical notices concerning the general apostasy of the Israelites and their failure to duly requite Gideon's family following his death of 8:33-35.

[623] The bracketed phrase above is adopted from Marcus (*ad loc.*) who, with reference to Judg 9:4 ([with the money given him] Abimelech "hired worthless and reckless fellows who followed him"), posits a lacuna in Josephus' text at this point.

[624] In Judg 9:4a the Shechemites *en bloc*, at the urging of Abimelech's kinsmen (9:3)—who themselves had been previously prompted by him (9:1-2)—give Abimelech "seventy pieces of silver out of the house of Baal-berith." Josephus simplifies this whole presentation, having Abimelech deal exclusively with his natural supporters, i.e. his mother's relations at this point, just as he leaves aside the mention (9:4) of "the house of Baal-berith" as the source for the money given Abimelech.

[625] Josephus leaves aside several details from Judg 9:5 concerning Abimelech's deed: the site of Gideon's house (Ophrah, MT), the killing of the brothers "upon one stone," and the status of "Jotham" (LXX A "Ioatham," LXX B "Ioathan") as the youngest son of

Gideon. He likewise replaces the biblical explanation of Jotham's escape ("for he hid himself") with a reference to his "flight." Pseudo-Philo (*Bib. Ant.* 37.1) motivates Abimelech's fratricide by his desire "to be the leader of the people."

[626] Josephus transfers the initiative behind Abimelech's assumption of rule from the people of Shechem (who "make him king by the oak of the pillar at Shechem" in Judg 9:6) to Abimelech himself. On "tyranny" (Greek: τυραννίς) which Josephus, following Plato (*Resp.* 8.544D) and Aristotle (*Pol.* 4.8.1295 A), views as the worst possible form of government, see Feldman 1998: 147-48; Mason 2001: 118, n. 1102. Josephus' application of the term to Abimelech's rulership, establishes an implicit parallelism between him and his own arch-enemy, John of Gischala, whom he accuses of aspiring to "tyranny" (*War* 4.208) and designates as "the tyrant" (*War* 6.98, 129).

[627] With this appendix to his version of Judg 9:6, Josephus underscores the oppressive character of Abimelech's rule.

[628] This indication concerning the context in which Jotham addresses the people lacks a parallel in Judg 9:7 itself, but may be inspired by the reference to a (later) Shechemite festival in 9:27. In any case, the allusion helps explain the presence of a large audience for his words.

[629] Josephus inserts this parenthetical notation concerning the location of the mountain from which Jotham speaks. In 5.69 he mentions Mt. Garizin as the site where half the Israelite army took its place for the ceremony of sacrifice and imprecation that Joshua conducted on the facing Mt. Hebel.

[630] From Jotham's opening words to the assembly in Judg 9:7 Josephus omits the (presumptuous) assurance that God will listen to them if they listen to him.

236. When silence had been obtained, he said that once, when trees were endowed with a human voice, they held a meeting[631] and the fig-tree was asked to rule over them.[632] It refused in view of the innate honor that it already enjoyed because of its fruits and that was not conferred on it from outside by others.[633] The trees did not, however, give up their endeavor regarding the rulership; rather, they resolved to award the honor to the vine.[634]

237. But upon being elected, the vine declined the rulership, using the same words as the fig-tree.[635] When the olive-tree also did the same,[636] the bramble—for the trees asked it to assume the kingship, **238.** since it is good in providing wood for kindling[637]—promised to take on the rulership and exercise it energetically.[638] They, for their part, ought to sit down beneath its shade, if, however, they were thinking of its extermination, they would be destroyed by the fire that was within it.[639]

239. "I do not," he [Iotham] said, "say these things for the sake of amusement,[640] but because, after having experienced many good things from Gedeon, they were now overlooking [the fact] that Abimelech, who was in charge of all public affairs and with whom they had killed his brothers, would be no different from a fire."[641]

---

[631] Josephus' references to the trees' past possession of the human capacity to speak and their meeting together are elaborations of the background for their opening initiative given in Judg 9:8.

[632] In Judg 9:8 the first tree to be asked is the olive, with the fig being approached only in 3rd place. Also Pseudo-Philo (*Bib. Ant.* 37.2) makes the fig the first tree to be offered rulership.

[633] In his version of the fig tree's response (compare Judg 9:11), Josephus inserts both its explicit refusal and its appeal to the "innate honor" with which its fruits endow it.

[634] Like Pseudo-Philo (*Bib. Ant.* 37.2), Josephus has the vine approached in 2nd rather than 3rd place (so Judg 9:12). He inserts the transitional reference to the trees' persistence in their quest to find a ruler.

[635] In Judg 9:13 the vine is given a distinctive response of its own, i.e. an evocation of the wine it produces which gratifies both god(s) and men (so MT; the versions turn this into a reference to wine prompting humans' praise of God [so LXX B] or being the source of libations for God [Targum]).

[636] Josephus both compresses the exchange between the olive and the other trees and makes the former the 3rd plant to turn them down (compare Judg 9:8-9, where the olive-tree is the first to be asked). Pseudo-Philo (*Bib. Ant.* 37.2) designates the trees' 3rd candidate as the "apple tree" (*malus*). In contrast to both Josephus and the Bible, he likewise has each of the 3 plants that reject the offer of kingship relate a "prophecy" of what awaits Abimelech and the Shechemites, this inspired by the further course of the story in Judges 9.

[637] Josephus inserts this motivation for the trees' finally turning to the bramble (Judg 9:14).

[638] This explicit acceptance of the trees' offer by the bramble is a Josephan addition to its words in Judg 9:15.

[639] In Judg 9:15 the bramble offers the trees both a positive (if they have acted in good faith they may take shelter in its shade) and negative (otherwise the "cedars of Lebanon" face destruction by its fire) outcomes for their initiative in offering it the rulership. Josephus' rendition omits the source reference both to the trees' possible good faith in choosing the bramble and to the cedars of Lebanon (that have not previously been mentioned in Jotham's fable). Pseudo-Philo (*Bib. Ant.* 37.3-4a) greatly elaborates on the bramble's answer, having it, e.g., invoke the role of the thorn in past biblical history and the symbolic significance of the 3 plants that had previously rejected the rulership; thereafter (37.4b), the bramble's fire actually does consume the trees, this taking the place of the application given his parable by Jotham in Judg 9:16-20.

[640] This negative statement of purpose is Josephus' opening addition to Jotham's "application" of his parable in Judg 9:16-20.

[641] Jotham's concluding word in Judg 9:16-20 comprises a double conditional statement, vv. 16-19 and 20, of which the first contains an extended parenthesis (vv. 17-18), followed by a resumption of the protasis of v. 16 in v. 19. Josephus reduces the content of this conclusion to its 2 main elements: Gideon's benefits to the hearers (cf. 9:17) and the comparison of the murderer Abimelech with "fire" (in 9:20 Jotham calls for "fire" to consume the Shechemites if they have acted dishonorably.) Moreover, whereas in Judg 9:18 Jotham charges the Shechemites alone with the murder of Gideon's sons, Josephus' formulation adds a reference to Abimelech's own involvement in their deaths, in line

Having said these things, he withdrew and stayed concealed three years[642] in the mountains,[643] in his anxiety over Abimelech.

(7.3) 240. Not long after the festival,[644] the Sikimites, because they changed their minds about having murdered the sons of Gedeon,[645] expelled Abimelech from their city and tribe,[646] while he, for his part, had it in mind to bring calamity on the city.[647] When it was time to glean the grapes, they were anxious about going out to gather the produce, lest Abimelech cause them some calamity.[648]

Abimelech expelled

241. Now there was sojourning among them a certain Gual, one of the rulers, together with his troops and relatives.[649] The Sikimites asked that he provide a guard for them until they gleaned the grapes.[650] When he agreed to their request, they set out; Gual [went] with them, leading his own body of troops.[651] **242.** Thus, the produce was gathered in securely. As they were having supper in their groups, they now ventured to openly denigrate Abimelech.[652] Likewise the rulers, having set ambushes around the city, arrested and did away with many of Abimelech's [supporters].[653]

Gaal (Gual) protects the Shechemites

(7.4) 243. A certain Zaboul,[654] however, one of the Sikimite rulers and a close

Zebul's intervention

---

with his account of their deaths in 5.234 (// Judg 9:5), where their murder is attributed solely to Abimelech.

[642] Judg 9:22 mentions "3 years" as the period during which Abimelech "ruled over Israel." Pseudo-Philo (*Bib. Ant.* 37.5) gives him a reign of a year and a half.

[643] Josephus substitutes this general indication concerning Jotham's hiding place for the proper place name cited in Judg 9:21, i.e. "Beer" (MT), "Baier" (LXX B), "Rara" (LXX AL).

[644] This chronological indication refers back to Josephus' (also inserted) mention of the "public festival" in 5.235.

[645] Josephus substitutes this alternative explanation (which picks up on Jotham's accusation of them as co-murderers of Gideon's sons in 5.239) for the Shechemites' turning against Abimelech for the one cited in Judg 9:23, i.e. God's sending an "evil spirit" between the 2 parties. Thereby he contrives to exculpate God from the responsibility for having set in motion the resultant chain of violence; indeed, throughout his version of Judges 9, Josephus omits any mention of the Deity's involvement.

[646] In Judg 9:25a the Shechemites set ambushes against Abimelech on the mountain tops (and rob all passersby). Josephus' having them rather expel Abimelech from the city looks to the continuation of the story (see 9:30, 34, 41), where Abimelech is consistently portrayed as being outside Shechem (where he had installed himself in Judg 9:1// 5.233). Subsequently, however, Josephus will make use of the content of Judg 9:25a; see 5.242a.

[647] In Judg 9:25b Abimelech is simply informed of the Shechemites' initiatives against him; Josephus highlights the former's resolve to requite their treatment of him.

[648] This notice combines an anticipation of the mention of the people's going forth to harvest the grapes (// Judg 9:27) with an allusion to the effect on them of Abimelech's hostile intentions; see previous note. The notice, in turn, will generate a whole series of additional Josephan expansions/modifications of the biblical account.

[649] Judg 9:26a neither specifies the status of "Gaal" nor mentions his having not only relatives, but also "troops" around him.

[650] Josephus concretizes the general statement of Judg 9:26b ("the men of Shechem put their confidence in him [Gaal]") in light of his previous mention of the Shechemites' "anxiety" about going out to glean the grapes (5.240).

[651] In Judg 9:27a the Shechemites proceed into the field unescorted, with no mention of Gaal accompanying them.

[652] See Judg 9:27, from which Josephus leaves aside a series of details: the treading of the grapes by the Shechemites, their holding a festival, and their going to "the house of their god" (cf. the "house of Baalberith" in 9:4, which Josephus previously left unmentioned as well).

[653] This notice represents Josephus' delayed use of the content of Judg 9:25a; see note to "tribe" at 5.240. It takes the place, at this juncture, of the "anti-Abimelech" speech by Gaal cited in 9:28-29 (to which Josephus will have Zebul allude in his version of the latter's subsequent speech [9:38] in 5.245; cf. note to "evil" at 5.245).

[654] Compare Zebul (MT Judg 9:30); Zeboul (LXX AB).

friend of Abimelech,[655] sent messengers to inform him of how Gual had stirred up the populace; he also urged him to wait in ambush before the city.[656] For he would convince Gual to come out against him; for the rest, it was up to him to avenge himself. Once this had happened, he would endeavor to reconcile him with the populace.[657]

244. Abimelech therefore sat in ambush,[658] while Gual remained without a care in the suburbs along with Zaboul.[659] But then, seeing troops being brought up, Gual said to Zaboul that armed men were approaching them.[660] **245.** The latter stated that they were shadows on the rocks,[661] but as they were already near, Gual recognized the true state of affairs, and said that they were not shadows, but a human ambush.[662] Zaboul replied, "Did you not accuse Abimelech of evil?[663] Why then do you not display the greatness of your valor by engaging him in battle?"[664]

246. Thrown into confusion,[665] Gual attacked Abimelech's men; some of those with him fell, while he himself fled to the city, leading the others.[666] Accusing him of having put up only a weak struggle against Abimelech's soldiers, Zaboul caused Gual to be expelled from the city.[667]

247. When Abimelech found out that the Sikimites were about to come out to glean grapes, he set ambushes around the city.[668] Once they had advanced out, the third part of his army occupied the gates, thus depriving the citizens of access. The remainder chased the fugitives, and there was an all-round slaughter.[669]

---

[655] Judg 9:30a does not mention Zebul's relationship to Abimelech; Josephus' insertion on the matter serves to explain how it is that the former, though one of the "rulers" of the Shechemites who are said to have turned against Abimelech as a body in Judg 9:23, 25a (see 5.240), should now be ready to assist him. Conversely, Josephus leaves aside the mention (9:30b) of Zebul's "anger" at Gaal's words against Abimelech (cf. 9:28-29).

[656] See Judg 9:31. In his report of Zebul's "mission" Josephus has no equivalent to a problematic item of the source verse. In MT Zebul sends to Abimelech בתרמה ("in Tarmah"?, a mistake for "Arimah," 9:41, so RSV), while LXX B and Tg. have him sending "secretly," and LXX AL "with gifts."

[657] Zebul's statements about what he himself intends to do on behalf of Abimelech are Josephus' amplifications of the former's message as reported in Judg 9:31-33, which speaks only of what Zebul is urging Abimelech himself to do. The Josephan Zebul's readiness to take an active role on Abimelech's behalf accords with Josephus' earlier (unbiblical) designation of him as the latter's "close friend."

[658] Judg 9:34 mentions that Abimelech set the ambushes by night, dividing his forces into 4 companies.

[659] Judg 9:35 mentions Gaal alone standing at the city gate; Josephus' joining Zebul to him has in view the continuation of the story in 9:36ff., where the pair will converse.

[660] In Judg 9:36a Gaal speaks of men "coming down from the mountain tops."

[661] In Judg 9:36b Zebul responds that Gaal has mistaken the "shadow of the mountains" for men.

[662] Josephus leaves aside Gaal's mention (Judg 9:37) of the various directions from which those in ambush are advancing.

[663] With this initial question (see Judg 9:38), Zebul harks back to Gaal's denunciation of Abimelech as cited in 9:28-29, which Josephus had previously passed over; see note to "supporters" at 5.242.

[664] Josephus accentuates the sarcasm of Zebul's closing word to Gaal as cited at the end of Judg 9:38 ("go out now and fight with them").

[665] This (inserted) reference to Gaal's emotional state contrasts effectively with the mention of his being "without a care" just previously in 5.244.

[666] See the battle account in Judg 9:39-40. Josephus introduces an ironic contrast between Zebul's (sarcastic) reference to the "greatness of your [Gaal's] valor" (5.245) and the latter's leading the retreat before Abimelech here in 5.246.

[667] With this notice Josephus provides an answer to the question of what became of Gaal subsequent to his rout before Abimelech. Once again, he underscores Zebul's active role as the "intimate" of Abimelech (see 5.243). Gaal's expulsion from the city recalls that of Abimelech himself in 5.240.

[668] Cf. Judg 9:42-43a, the sequence of which Josephus rearranges.

[669] Josephus here compresses the circumstantial battle account of Judg 9:43b-44.

248. When [Abimelech] had razed the city to the ground—for it did not resist his siege—he sowed the ruins with salt and then set out.[670] Thus all the Sikimites were annihilated. Those who by scattering throughout the country escaped the danger gathered at a certain solid rock on which they settled, making preparations to fortify this with a wall.[671]

249. Abimelech beat them to it, however; once he learned of their plan, he came against them with his force and surrounded the spot with bundles of dry wood that he carried himself, appealing to his army to do likewise.[672] When the rock had been thus quickly encircled, they set fire to the wood with whatever was most flammable by nature, and raised a great flame.[673]

250. No one escaped from the rock; about 1,500 men were annihilated together with their wives and children, as well as a considerable number of others.[674] This misfortune that happened to the Sikimites would have been beyond grief, were it not for the fact that [it came] as judgment for their having contrived so great a calamity against a man who had been their benefactor.[675]

(7.5) 251. Having dismayed the Israelites with the calamities of the Sikimites, Abimelech now made clear that he was aiming for something more and would not make an end of his violence until he had annihilated them all.[676] He therefore marched against Thebas[677] and took it by assault; in it there was, however, a great tower in which the whole crowd took refuge together and that he prepared to besiege.[678]

Abimelech attacks Thebez (Thebas)

252. As he was rushing about near the gates,[679] it happened that a woman tossed down a piece of a millstone on his head.[680] As he fell, Abimelech appealed to his armor-bearer to kill him, so that his death would not be thought the work of a woman. And he did as he was ordered.[681] **253.** This was the penalty he paid for his transgression against his brothers and for what he dared to do to the Sikimites,[682]

Abimelech killed

---

[670] See Judg 9:45.

[671] Compare Judg 9:46, where, subsequent to the destruction of Shechem itself (9:45), the "people of the Tower of Shechem" repair to "the stronghold (LXX A τὸ ὀχύρωμα) of the house of El-berith (cf. 9:4, 27)." Josephus' reference to a "solid rock" as the group's place of refuge here is reminiscent of "the rock of Rimmon" to which the surviving Benjamites flee in Judg 20:47 (cf. 5.166).

[672] Josephus abbreviates the detailed description of Abimelech's measures given in Judg 9:47-49a, leaving aside, e.g., his initial ascent of the (otherwise unknown) Mt. Zalmon at the beginning of v. 48.

[673] Josephus elaborates on the "firing" of the refuge site as mentioned in Judg 9:49aβ. Abimelech's arson here recalls Jotham's statement that he would turn out to be "no different from a fire" in 5.239.

[674] Judg 9:49b mentions 1,000 as the approximate total for the men and women killed at the stronghold.

[675] This editorial remark might be seen as Josephus' (anticipated) version of the theological commentary of Judg 9:57a: "God also made all the wickedness of the men of Shechem fall back upon their heads...." Its language echoes Jotham's reference to the "many good things" the Shechemites had experienced from Gideon

in 5.239. On the word "benefactor" (Greek: εὐεργέτης) and its cognates, see Spicq 1978 (I): 307-13.

[676] This transitional notice is a Josephan insertion; it underscores the thirst for blood that animates all Abimelech's initiatives.

[677] Compare Thebez (MT); Thebes (LXX A); Thēbēs (LXX B).

[678] See Judg 9:50-52a. Josephus omits the detail about the people mounting to the roof of the tower (v. 51b).

[679] Judg 9:52b speaks of Abimelech drawing near to the tower door to set fire to it.

[680] In Judg 9:53 the "upper millstone" crushes Abimelech's skull. Pseudo-Philo, having passed over the whole narrative of Judges 9 subsequent to Jotham's parable (vv. 7-20= *Bib. Ant.* 37.2-4), does reproduce (37.5b) this notice on Abimelech's death, joining it directly with mention of his one and a half year reign (37.5a; cf. Judg 9:22).

[681] See Judg 9:54 (MT LXX A), which specifies that the armor-bearer killed Abimelech with his (the armor-bearer's) sword, which the latter had directed him to draw.

[682] In Judg 9:56 Abimelech's punishment is attributed explicitly to God. Josephus makes his punishment

whose misfortune came upon them in accordance with the prediction of Iotham.[683] Now when Abimelech fell, the army that was with him scattered and returned to their homes.[684]

Judge Jair (Iar)

(7.6) 254. Iar the Galadenite of the Manassean tribe[685] now assumed the leadership over the Israelites. A fortunate man in other respects, he fathered thirty good sons who were outstanding horsemen and who obtained rulership of the cities throughout Galadene.[686] He exercised his rulership for twenty-two years and died as an old man;[687] he was honored with burial in the city of Kamon in Galadene.[688]

Ammonite oppression

(7.7) 255. Now, however, all the Hebrews' [affairs] degenerated into disorder and arrogance against God and the laws.[689] In their contempt for them, the Ammanites and the Palestinoi plundered the country with a large army and took possession of all Peraia;[690] moreover, they were already venturing to cross [the river] so as to get possession of what was left.[691]

Israel's appeal and God's response

256. The Hebrews, made prudent by their calamities, turned to supplication of God; they offered sacrifices[692] and appealed to him to be indulgent and, paying at-

---

a requital also for his offenses against the Shechemites.

[683] Judg 9:57b speaks of the Shechemites undergoing "the curse" of Jotham. The "prediction" to which Josephus alludes here is Jotham's concluding warning that Abimelech will prove "no different from a fire" in 5.239. As he did with Abimelech's bad end (see previous note), Josephus avoids the attribution of this to God as found in 9:57a. Cf., however, 5.250, where he characterizes the Shechemites' overthrow as their "judgment" for having repaid Gideon's benefactions with evil; see note to "benefactor" at 5.250.

[684] In the sequence of Judges 9 the dispersal of the Israelites (v. 55) is mentioned prior to the theological commentary upon the punishment of both Abimelech (v. 56) and the Shechemites (v. 57).

[685] The minor judge cited in Judg 10:3 is there called "Jair the Gileadite (LXX Galaadite)"; Josephus adds the further specification about his tribal affiliation (on Gilead as part of the tribal territory of "Manasseh," see Josh 17:1). Like Pseudo-Philo, Josephus skips over the minor judge "Tola" of Judg 10:1-2, passing directly from Abimelech to Jair.

[686] Josephus' figure for Jair's sons agrees with that of MT Judg 10:4, whereas LXX AB read 32. He leaves aside the etymological indication of 10:4 about the cities obtained by Jair's sons being called "Havoth-jair (LXX AB Ἐπαύλεις Ιαίρ) to this day."

[687] Josephus derives his figure for Jair's term of office from Judg 10:3b, adding the mention of his being an old man at death.

[688] See Judg 10:5, where Jair's burial site is called "Kamon" (= Josephus) in MT, Ραμμω in LXX A, and Ραμνών in LXX B. Josephus, on the basis of the mentions of "Gilead" in the context, specifies that it was in "Gadalene." Unlike both the Bible and Josephus with their positive, albeit very brief portrayal of the judge Jair, Pseudo-Philo (*Bib. Ant.* 38) presents both a more

extended and altogether negative picture of him as an instigator of idolatry who ends up being burned alive by the angel of the Lord.

[689] Josephus generalizes Judg 10:6 with its lengthy catalogue of the other deities to which Israel now turned. He omits the divine reaction of anger and "selling" the people into the hand of their enemies from 10:7 (although he will utilize its names of the 2 oppressor peoples in what follows).

[690] "Peraia" is Josephus' "updated" replacement for the localization given in Judg 10:8b, i.e. "beyond the Jordan in the land of the Amorites, which is in Gilead." Josephus draws the names of Israel's 2 oppressors from 10:7, where the Lord "sells them into the hand" of the Philistines and the Ammonites. In Judges 10-14, LXX AL mostly (i.e. 27 out of a total of 33 times) designate the Philistines with the general term ἀλλόφυλοι ("aliens"), whereas LXX B consistently calls them Φυλιστιιμ ("Philistines") in accord with the MT designation; Josephus invariably uses the corresponding term "Palestinoi" (Παλαιστῖνοι) to denote the people in question. See Harlé 1999: 58-60.

[691] Josephus here synthesizes the data of Judg 10:7b-9 on the oppression of Israel by the Philistines and Ammonites. From that sequence he omits, e.g., the duration of the oppression (18 years, 10:8b; cf., however, his subsequent use of the figure in 5.263) and the mention of the various Cisjordanian tribes that the Ammonites are preparing to attack (v. 9). Conversely, he adds mention of the enemies' "contempt" for Israel (this taking the place of the divine handing of Israel over to them [10:7a; cf. note to "laws" at 5.255] as the impetus for their assault). Pseudo-Philo (*Bib. Ant.* 39.1) offers no motivation for the Ammonites' invasion of Israel.

[692] Such sacrifices are not mentioned as part of the people's appeal in Judg 10:10, which likewise does not

tention to their prayer, to cease from his wrath.[693] God, being prompted to a greater moderation, was now about to help them.[694]

(7.8) 257. When the Ammanites made a campaign against Galadene, the inhabitants met them in the hill-country, but needed a general.[695] Now there was a certain man named Iaphthas,[696] who was powerful both in virtue of his ancestral valor and his maintenance of a personal force of mercenaries.[697] **258.** Accordingly, they sent to him, requesting him to be their ally and promising to award him the leadership over themselves in perpetuity.[698] He, however, did not assent to their appeal, complaining that they had not helped him when he was obviously being wronged by his brothers.[699] **259.** (For he was not of the same mother as they, but of a different mother, having been imposed upon them by their father as the outcome of erotic desire;[700] his brothers, contemptuous of his weakness, expelled him.)[701]

260. He lived in the region called Galaditis and welcomed all who came to him

Jephthah (Iaphthas) assumes command

---

refer to their being "made prudent" (Greek: σωφρονέω; see note to "prudent" at 5.105) by their afflictions.

[693] In Judg 10:10-16 there is an initial confession of sin by the people (10:10b), to which the Lord responds with a refusal to deliver them any longer (10:11-14), whereupon the people reply with a renewed confession and urgent appeal for help (10:15), which in turn prompts a change of heart on God's part (10:16). Josephus leaves aside the first 2 elements of this sequence in order to concentrate on the people's appeal. Thereby, he eliminates as well the Bible's portrayal of a seemingly vacillating, indecisive Deity, who, having sharply rejected the people's first appeal, then suddenly becomes solicitous for them when they renew their appeal.

[694] Compare Judg 10:16b: "(God) became indignant over the misery of Israel." Josephus omits the preceding notice of 10:16a about the people's putting aside their foreign gods (i.e. those catalogued in 10:6, a listing previously left aside by him) and serving the Lord. Pseudo-Philo, for his part, completely omits the sequence Judg 10:10-16.

[695] Cf. Judg 10:17-18, from which Josephus omits, e.g., the specification that Israel camped at Mizpah in the face of the Ammonite threat (v. 17b) and the leaders' affirmation (v.18b) that the one who assumes command against the Ammonites "will be head over all the inhabitants of Gilead." In contrast to Josephus, Pseudo-Philo (*Bib. Ant.* 39.1) elaborates upon the words of those assembled at Mizpah.

[696] MT (Judg 11:1) יפתה (Eng.: "Jephthah"); LXX Ἰεφθάε; Josephus Ἰαφθᾶς. On Josephus' ambivalent depiction of Jephthah, see Feldman 1998a: 177-92.

[697] Josephus derives Jephthah's 2 qualifications from Judg 11:1a (Jephthah is called "a mighty warrior") and 11:3b ("worthless fellows collected around Jephthah, and went raiding with him"). In the case of the latter verse, he eliminates its negative qualification of

Jephthah's associates, which might call into question his own suitability as a leader.

[698] In Judges 11 the invitation to Jephthah (v. 6) is extended in the face of the new (or renewed) Ammonite threat cited in v. 4, after that mentioned in 10:17, prior to the introduction of Jephthah in 11:1-3. Josephus has the invitation come in response to the single Ammonite incursion of which he speaks; see 5.257 and the note to "raid" at 5.261.

[699] Josephus here conflates elements of Judg 11:7 (Jephthah's refusal of the offer of leadership) and 11:2 (the notice on his brothers' expulsion of him, which he will reproduce parenthetically in 5.259). At the same time, he also "harmonizes" the divergent biblical indications concerning those responsible for Jephthah's expulsion: compare Judg 11:2 (the brothers thrust him out) and 7 (Jephthah accuses the elders of having driven him out). In Josephus' presentation, the Gileadites were complicit in the injustice done Jephthah in that they failed to aid him when he was being expelled by his brothers; see Feldman 1998a: 188, n. 21.

[700] Out of concern for Jephthah's image, Josephus substitutes a circumlocution for the straightforward statement of Judg 11:2 that he was "the son of a harlot" (MT אשה זונה; LXX γυνή πόρνη); see Feldman 1998a: 179-80. In the same line the Tg. employs the term פונדקיתא for Jephthah's mother, a term that may mean "innkeeper" and that it also uses of Rahab in Josh 2:1 (see note to "inn" at 5.7). Pseudo-Philo, going still further, omits any reference to Jephthah's parentage.

[701] Cf. Judg 11:2, where is no mention of the brothers' contempt for Jephthah (in *Bib. Ant.* 39.2 it is Jephthah himself who "envies" [Latin: *zelo*] his brothers). Josephus does not reproduce the name of Jephthah's father, cited in Judg 11:1-2 as "Gilead," perhaps because in the context (see 10:17-18; 11:4) this appears rather as a place name.

from whatever place with a salary.[702] But when [the Israelites] earnestly entreated him and swore that they would award him the leadership for ever, he undertook the campaign.[703]

Failed negotia-
tions

(7.9) 261. Quickly taking matters in hand,[704] he stationed his army in the city of Masphatha,[705] and sent a delegation to the Ammanite [king] to object to the raid.[706] He, dispatching a counter-embassy, reproached the Israelites for their exodus from Egypt and demanded that they withdraw from Amoraia, as originally being their [the Ammanites'] ancestral [land.][707]

262. Iaphthas, however, answered[708] that it was not reasonable to accuse their forebears regarding Amoraia;[709] rather, they themselves owed them gratitude for their having bypassed the land of the Ammanites, for Moyses had been capable of taking this too.[710] Telling him [the Ammanite king] therefore to withdraw from their own

---

[702] See Judg 11:3a, where Jephthah retires to "the land of Tob"; Pseudo-Philo retains this biblical place name in *Bib. Ant.* 39.2-3. Josephus has already mentioned (see 5.257) the associates who assemble around Jephthah according to 11:3b.

[703] Josephus here concludes his account of the (ultimately successful) negotiations between Gilead and Jephthah (11:9-11) that he introduced in 5.258 (// 11:6-8), but then broke off to supply background information, drawn from 11:1-3a, concerning Jephthah in 5.259-260a. As Feldman (1998a: 187) points out, Josephus eliminates the invocations of the Deity by both parties (see 11:9, 10), thereby downplaying the piety of the biblical hero. By contrast, Pseudo-Philo has Jephthah thrice mention God in his lengthy (single) reply to the Israelites in *Bib. Ant.* 39.4-5a.

[704] This inserted transitional note underscores Jephthah's enterprising character.

[705] Josephus conflates the double mention of "Mizpah" in the biblical Jephthah account; see Judg 10:17 (the people of Israel encamp at Mizpah prior to the introduction of Jephthah in 11:1-3) and 11:11b (the new general Jephthah speaks "all his words before the Lord at Mizpah").

[706] Unlike Judg 11:12, Josephus does not explicitly designate Jephthah's addressee as the Ammonite "king"; by contrast, *Ant. Bib.* 39.8 gives the king a name, i.e. "Getal." The Ammonite "raid" of which Jephthah complains here is that mentioned in 5.257, the single such incursion cited by Josephus; compare 10:17 and 11:4, and see note to "perpetuity" at 5.258.

[707] In Judg 11:13 the Ammonite king asserts that, upon its departure from Egypt, Israel had appropriated his land and demands that this be restored peacefully (MT LXX A; LXX B adds "and I will go [away]"). Josephus' designation "Amoraia" for the country the Ammonite king is telling the Israelites to vacate could be inspired by the mention of the "Amorites" in Jephthah's subsequent reply to the king (see Judg 11:19, 20,

23). In any case, Josephus leaves aside the source verse's specifications concerning the boundaries of the contested land ("from the Arnon to the Jabbok and to the Jordan").

[708] In this paragraph Josephus presents a drastically abridged and rearranged version of Jephthah's reply as cited in Judg 11:14-27 (like MT and LXX B 11:14, he has no equivalent to the LXX AL plus at the end of the verse, i.e. "and the messengers returned to Jephthah"). Among the items from Jephthah's discourse omitted by Josephus is the theologically problematic question of 11:24a: ("Will you not possess what Chemosh gives you to possess?") with its seeming recognition of the existence and power of a deity other than the Lord; see Feldman 1998a: 188. Pseudo-Philo (*Bib. Ant.* 39.9) makes Jephthah affirm that the "gods" whom the Ammonite king claims gave him the disputed territory are, in fact, "no gods."

[709] With this phrase Josephus alludes to Jephthah's extended reminiscence of Israel's conquest of Sihon, king of the Amorites, in Judg 11:19-23, which itself harks back to the account of this event found in Num 21:21-32 (cf. Deut 2:26-37) that Josephus reproduces in *Ant.* 4.86-95. Josephus' reference to the Ammonite "accusation regarding Amoraia" has a counterpart in *Bib. Ant.* 39.9, where the Ammonite king threatens to "avenge the Amorites whom you have harmed."

[710] Cf. Judg 11:15, where Jephthah reminds the Ammonite king: "Israel did not take away the land of Moab or the land of the Ammonites." Josephus' omission of the source reference to "the land of Moab" likely has in view the seeming irrelevance of this allusion, given that the dispute is between Ammon and Israel, not Israel and Moab. In the same line Josephus leaves aside Jephthah's further statements concerning Israel's march route (11:16-18), which in fact make no mention of Ammon itself, featuring rather its circumvention of Moab and Edom.

land, that God had obtained for them and that they still possessed after 300 years,[711] he stated that he would fight against them.[712]

(7.10) 263. Having said these things to the emissaries, he dismissed them.[713] He himself prayed for victory and promised[714] that, if he returned safe and sound to his house, he would sacrifice and offer up whatever[715] would first come to meet him. Then joining battle, he won a great victory;[716] slaughtering, he pursued as far as the city of Maniath.[717] Crossing over into Ammanitis,[718] he obliterated many[719] cities, carried off plunder,[720] and delivered his fellows from the slavery they had endured for eighteen years.[721]

264. Upon his return, however, he underwent a misfortune that was not at all like his achievements.[722] For his daughter[723] met him; she was his only[724] child and still a virgin.[725] He, lamenting the magnitude of his suffering,[726] blamed his daughter for

Jephthah's vow and victory

Jephthah sacrifices his daughter

---

[711] Josephus here combines 2 distinct elements of the biblical Jephthah's speech, i.e. his affirmation (Judg 11:24b) that Israel will possess "all that the Lord has dispossessed before us" and his reference to the 300 years during which Israel had been left undisturbed by the Ammonites in its possession of the now suddenly disputed regions (11:26). He leaves aside the intervening, seemingly extraneous, allusion to the case of the Moabite King Balak who never ventured to attack Israel (11:25), just he did the early references to Moab in Jephthah's speech; see note to "this too" at 5.262.

[712] Compare Judg 11:27b, where Jephthah concludes his 2nd message to the Ammonite king with an appeal to the Deity ("the Lord, the Judge, decide this day between the people of Israel and the people of Ammon").

[713] This concluding notice to the "negotiations report" of 5.261-262 (= Judg 11:12-28) takes the place of the statement of Judg 11:28 that the Ammonite king paid no heed to Jephthah's message. Josephus likewise leaves aside Judg 11:29, which tells of the coming of the divine spirit upon Jephthah and the latter's resultant movements. Here again (see previous note), Josephus diminishes the explicit presence of God in the Jephthah story.

[714] In Judg 11:30 Jephthah "vows to the Lord." On Josephus' handling of Jephthah's vow and its sequels, see Feldman 1998a: 182-91.

[715] Via his neuter formulation (ὅ τι), Josephus indicates that Jephthah anticipates meeting "something" (i.e. an animal) rather than "someone." By contrast the participial form of MT Judg 11:30 (היוצא) leaves the matter open, while LXX (ὃς ἂν ἐξέλθῃ) and Pseudo-Philo (*Bib. Ant.* 39.10: "*omnis qui mihi primus obviaverit*") specify that Jephthah was indeed thinking of a human being as his promised victim. Definitely presupposing as he does that the object of his promise will be an animal, the Josephan Jephthah appears a more pre-

cise speaker than in MT and less ready to shed human blood than he does in LXX and Pseudo-Philo.

[716] Characteristically, Josephus leaves aside the notice of Judg 11:32b (which Pseudo-Philo [*Bib. Ant.* 40.1] retains): "and the Lord gave them into his hand."

[717] MT (Judg 11:33) מנית (Eng.: "Minnith"); LXX A Σεμωιθ; LXX B Ἀρνών; Josephus Μανιάθης.

[718] Compare the more expansive indications concerning Jephthah's movements given in Judg 11:33 (MT): "from Aroer to the neighborhood of Minnith... and as far as Abel-keramim."

[719] Judg 11:33 specifies 20 cities; *Bib. Ant.* 40.1 reads 60.

[720] This item lacks a counterpart in Judg 11:33.

[721] Compare Judg 11:33b: "So the Ammonites were subdued before the people of Israel." Josephus' substitute conclusion to the battle account features his characteristic use of "liberation language" throughout his account of the Judges period (and his history generally); see note to "desert" in 5.34. He derives his datum concerning the duration of the Ammonite oppression from Judg 10:8b.

[722] The mention of Jephthah's return "to his home at Mizpah" in Judg 11:34aα lacks the ominous foreshadowing Josephus interjects here.

[723] Pseudo-Philo (*Bib. Ant.* 40.1) gives a name, i.e. "Seila," to the nameless daughter of the Bible and Josephus. On this figure in Josephus and Pseudo-Philo, see Brown 1992: 93-139.

[724] As Feldman (1998a: 185) points out, the Greek term used by Josephus here (μονογενής) is the same one employed by him of Isaac (see *Ant.* 1.222), another child facing immolation at the hands of his father. Thereby, he makes an implicit link between the 2 biblical stories of (near) human sacrifice.

[725] Josephus anticipates this datum from Judg 11:39b. He leaves aside the source detail (11:34aβ) about the girl coming to meet her father "with timbrels and dances" (cf. *Bib. Ant.* 40.1, where "Seila" leads a

her solicitude in meeting him, seeing that he had consecrated her to God.[727]

265. That which was to happen did not, however, come upon her against her will, namely that she was to die for the victory of her father and the freedom of her fellow-citizens.[728] She did, however, appeal to him to award her two months to bewail her youth with her fellow-citizens and then to do according to his vow.[729] **266.** He granted her the time just mentioned;[730] once this was past,[731] he sacrificed the child as a holocaust.[732] The sacrifice he offered was neither lawful not pleasing to God; for he did not carefully weigh through reason what would happen nor how his deed would appear to those who heard of it.[733]

Jephthah punishes Ephraimites

(7.11) 267. The tribe of Ephraim then made war against him, because he had not given them a part in the expedition against the Ammanites, but rather alone retained the plunder and the glory for what had been done.[734] He, for his part, first said that

---

whole group of dancing women to meet Jephthah).

[726] In Judg 11:35 Jephthah first "rends his clothes," while in *Bib. Ant.* 40.1 he "grows faint" upon seeing "Seila" emerge from the house.

[727] Josephus' (re-) formulation of Jephthah's words in Judg 11:35 tones down the father's expression of deep distress and leaves aside his closing statement ("I cannot take back my vow"), both points where Pseudo-Philo (*Bib. Ant.* 40.1) adheres more closely to the Bible's wording.

[728] This editorial statement replaces the daughter's own (initial) word as cited in Judg 11:36, in which she urges Jephthah to do as he had vowed, given that the Lord has in fact avenged him on his enemies. Pseudo-Philo (*Bib. Ant.* 40.2) expatiates on the daughter's discourse of 11:36. Feldman (1998a: 190, n. 24) points out that, in contrast to the Bible, both Josephus and Pseudo-Philo make mention of the daughter's willingness to die now that the people have recovered their "freedom." The daughter's willing acceptance of her fate here constitutes another implicit parallel between her story and that of Isaac, whom Josephus, going beyond the Bible itself, represents (*Ant.* 1.232) as urging his father to proceed with the sacrifice.

[729] In Judg 11:37 the daughter asks her father for 2 months to "go down on the mountains" and bewail "her virginity" with her companions. Josephus' concluding "appendix" to this request underscores her submissiveness to her fate. Pseudo-Philo (*Bib. Ant.* 40.3) greatly expands on the daughter's appeal.

[730] See Judg 11:38a: "And he said, 'Go'." Josephus leaves aside the subsequent notice (11:38b) on the daughter's doing as she had proposed. By contrast, Pseudo-Philo expands the content of 11:38b into a 4-paragraph (*Bib. Ant.* 40.4-5) "citation" of her words of lamentation.

[731] Compare 11:39a: "and at the end of two months, she returned to her father...."

[732] Josephus here renders more explicit the wording

of Judg 11:39bα ("he did to her according to his vow which he had made") in light of the language of Jephthah's actual vow in 11:31 (and his own rendering of this in 5.263). Thereby, he leaves readers in no doubt that the daughter actually was sacrificed, rather than, e.g., living on in a state of perpetual virginity as some commentators have understood the biblical text to indicate; see Feldman 1998a: 183-35. Compare *Bib. Ant.* 40.8 ("he [Jephthah] did everything that he had vowed and offered burnt offerings"), which continues with an "unbiblical" mention of "Seila" being buried and wept over by the assembled virgins of Israel.

[733] This editorial comment concerning the wrongfulness of Jephthah's vow and its execution has no counterpart in the "neutral" presentation of the affair in Judges 11 (MT and LXX). On the other hand, Josephus' censure is paralleled in the Targumic addition at the end of Judg 11:39, where Jephthah is faulted for not consulting Phineas the priest about his vow, in Rabbinic tradition (for references, see Ginzberg 1928: 6:203, n. 109), and in Pseudo-Philo (*Bib. Ant.* 39.11), where immediately upon Jephthah's making his vow (39.10) there is mention of God's "anger" at this. The above comment takes the place of the etiological notice of Judg 11:39bβ-40 concerning the annual 4-day commemoration of the daughter's fate by the Israelite women, which, Feldman (1998a: 184-85) suggests, Josephus may have found overly reminiscent of pagan mourning ceremonies for "deceased" divinities. In reproducing the notice, Pseudo-Philo (*Bib. Ant.* 40.8) specifies that the occasion was observed in the month of Seila's death, beginning on the 14th day of the month.

[734] Josephus here modifies Judg 12:1 in several ways: he omits the name of the site (MT Zaphon, LXX AL Sephim) where the confrontation occurs, recasts the Ephraimites' speech in indirect discourse, and replaces their concluding threat ("we will burn your house over you with fire") with their charge about Jephthah's hav-

it was not concealed from them that their relatives were being warred upon; when called to [join] the alliance, they had not come, though, even prior to his plea, they ought to have known of this and attacked.[735] **268.** Furthermore, what they were doing was wrong. Not having ventured to attack the enemy themselves, they had rushed upon their relatives.[736] With [the help] of God he threatened to impose judgment on them, unless they became prudent.[737]

269. When he did not persuade them,[738] he encountered their coming with an army that had come, summoned from Galadene. He inflicted a great slaughter upon them;[739] pursuing them as they turned to flight, he killed about 42,000 of them, having previously occupied the fords of the Jordan by sending ahead a certain contingent.[740] **(7.12) 270.** After ruling six years,[741] he died and was buried in his ancestral *Jephthah dies* city of Sebee that is in Galadene.[742]

(7.13) 271. Once Iaphthas died, Apsan[743] of the tribe of Iouda and the city of *Judge Ibzan* Bethlemon[744] assumed the rulership. He had sixty children, thirty sons and the re- *(Apsan)* mainder daughters, all of whom he left behind alive, after having giving them in marriage to husbands and taking wives for them.[745] Having done nothing worthy of

---

ing kept to himself the benefits of the campaign (for the "plunder," see the inserted reference to Jephthah's taking this in 5.263). Pseudo-Philo leaves aside the entire episode of Jephthah's dispute with the Ephraimites, Judg 12:1-6.

[735] Cf. Judg 12:2.

[736] In this version of Jephthah's words, drawn from Judg 12:3, Josephus supplies a reason why Jephthah felt bound to attack the Ammonites even without the Ephraimites' support, omits the reference to the Lord's giving the former into his hand (cf. his non-use of the similar notice in 11:32b), and turns his accusatory final question into a statement of rebuke.

[737] This concluding threat/warning has no parallel in Jephthah's reply as cited in Judg 12:2-3. It underscores the hero's effort to dissuade the Ephraimites from their projected initiation of civil war. Josephus' depiction of Jephthah functioning in this capacity recalls his similar presentation of Gideon's (successful) efforts at dissuading the same Ephraimites from fighting against him in 5.230-231.

[738] This mention of the failure of Jephthah's efforts at mollifying the Ephraimites is, like his immediately preceding warning at the end of 5.268, a Josephan insertion. It serves to place the blame for the Ephraimites' subsequent disaster squarely on them and their refusal to pay heed to Jephthah's warning.

[739] Like LXX Judg 12:4, Josephus lacks an equivalent to the obscure MT "motivation" for the Gileadites' slaughter of the Ephraimites, i.e. "because they said, 'You are fugitives of Ephraim, you Gileadites, in the midst of Ephraim and Manasseh'."

[740] Josephus here combines elements of Judg 12:6b (the Ephraimite casualties) and 12:5a (the Gileadites'

seizure of the Jordan fords). He omits the "Shibboleth-test" of the Ephraimites' identity (12:5b-6a), which could not readily be reproduced in Greek, as the (varying) LXX renderings of the MT sequence attest. Josephus introduced an explicit foreshadowing of the Ephraimites' calamity here with the notice he appends to Gideon's earlier mollifying of the tribe (Judg 8:1-3) in 5.230-231.

[741] Josephus' figure for Jephthah's length of rule agrees with that given in MT and LXX AL Judg 12:7. LXX B reads 60 years, while *Bib. Ant.* 40.9 assigns him 10.

[742] MT Judg 12:7 has Jephthah buried "in the cities of Gilead." LXX AB read "in his town in Galaad," while LXX L offers "in his town in Seph in Galaad." Schalit (*s.v.*) opines that the name of Jephthah's place of burial as found in the MSS of Josephus, i.e. Σεβέη, is a corruption of the form, namely Μασφαθή, which appears in the near context; see 5.261. Barthélemy (1982: 106), on the other hand, suggests that Josephus' Hebrew text of Judg 12:7 read בצפה.

[743] MT (Judg 12:8) אבצן (Eng.: "Ibzan") LXX A Εσεβων; LXX B Ἀβαισάν; Josephus Ἀψάνης. Pseudo-Philo does not mention this judge.

[744] Having introduced the specification that "Ibzan" was a "Judean," Josephus naturally identifies his biblical home-town with "Bethlehem" of Judah (see 5.136), whereas some commentators hold that the place intended in Judg 12:8 is rather the Bethlehem of Zebulon cited in Josh 19:15; see Harlé 1999: 196.

[745] See Judg 12:9a, from which Josephus omits the additional notice about Ibzan's "bringing in" 30 wives for his 30 sons from outside his clan.

mention or memory for a period of seven years, he died, an old man, and was buried in his ancestral [city].[746]

Judge Elon

(7.14) **272.** Upon the death of Aspan, Elon,[747] of the tribe of Zeboule, who assumed leadership after him and exercised it for ten years,[748] likewise did nothing worthy of enthusiasm.[749]

Judge Abdon

(7.15) **273.** Abdon,[750] the son of Elon[751] of the Ephramite tribe[752] and of the city of the Pharathonites,[753] who was appointed sole ruler[754] after Elon, is remembered solely for having had good children; he too accomplished no splendid deed, given the peace and tranquility of affairs.[755] **274.** He had, however, forty sons who left behind thirty progeny. He rode with the seventy of them, all of them being outstanding horsemen.[756] Leaving them all still on earth, he died as an old man and received a splendid burial in Pharath.[757]

Philistine oppression

(8.1) **275.** After his death the Palestinoi subjugated the Israelites and exacted tribute from them for forty years.[758] They were freed from this necessity in the following way:[759]

Manoah and his wife

(8.2) **276.** A certain Manoch[760] of the Danites, a man outstanding even among their elite and acknowledged to be preeminent in his ancestral place,[761] had a wife[762]

---

[746] Josephus embellishes the data of Judg 12:9b-10 on Ibzan's term of office, death and burial with a negative evaluation of his tenure and an indication about his age at death. He infers that Ibzan—as also the 2 following minor judges, see below—did nothing "memorable" from the fact that his biblical source reports no victory won by him of the sort it attributes to the "major judges."

[747] MT (Judg 12:11) אילון (Eng.: "Elon"); LXX AB Αἰλών; Josephus Ἤλων. Reversing the biblical order, Pseudo-Philo (*Bib. Ant.* 41.2) mentions this judge after his successor "Abdon" of Judg 12:13-15.

[748] See Judg 12:11b. Pseudo-Philo (*Ant. Bib.* 41.2) assigns him a judgeship of 20 years.

[749] This negative evaluation, echoing that supplied by Josephus for "Ibzan" in 5.271, takes the place of the death and burial notice for "Elon" of Judg 12:12. By contrast, Pseudo-Philo (*Bib. Ant.* 41.2) credits the latter figure with taking 12 Philistine cities.

[750] MT (Judg 12:13) עבדון (Eng.: "Abdon"); LXX A Λαβδων; LXX B and Josephus Ἀβδών.

[751] MT (Judg 12:13) הלל (Eng.: "Hillel"); LXX A Σελλημ; LXX B Ἑλλήλ; Josephus Ἤλων. In contrast to the Bible, where "Abdon's" father is called "Hillel," etc. Josephus gives this figure the same name as the preceding judge, i.e. "Elon," likewise, however, assigning the first "Elon" to the tribe of Zebulon (5.272), the second to that of Ephraim (5.273).

[752] Josephus anticipates this notice on Abdon's tribal affiliation from Judg 12:14, where his hometown, Pirathon, is said to be "in the land of Ephraim."

[753] MT (Judg 12:13) הפרעתוני (Eng.: "the Pirathonite"); LXX AB ὁ Φαραθωνίτης; Josephus τῆς Φαραθωνιτῶν.

[754] Greek: αὐτοκράτωρ ἡγεμών. On the word αὐτοκράτωρ as the Greek equivalent of the Latin *imperator*, see Mason BJP 9: 140-41, n. 1403.

[755] This negative evaluation of Abdon's judgeship lacks a biblical basis. By contrast, Pseudo-Philo (*Bib. Ant.* 41.1) ascribes to him a resounding victory over the Moabites in the manner of Jephthah's defeat of the Ammonites.

[756] See Judg 12:14; the equestrian excellence of Abdon's descendants is Josephus' embellishment. Pseudo-Philo omits the biblical details concerning Abdon's family.

[757] Compare the more expansive geographical indications of Judg 12:15: "at Pirathon in the land of Ephraim, in the hill country of the Amalekites (LXX A: Lanak)." Pseudo-Philo (*Bib. Ant.* 41.1) has Abdon buried "in his city Effrata." The reference to Abdon's "splendid" burial is a typical Josephan embellishment of the biblical burial notice.

[758] From Judg 13:1 Josephus leaves aside the double mention of the Lord as the one against whom the Israelites offended and who, in turn, handed them over to Philistine domination.

[759] Josephus inserts this transitional phrase between the source notice on the Philistine domination (Judg 13:1) and the following Samson story (13:2ff.).

[760] MT (Judg 13:2) מנוח (Eng.: "Manoah") LXX AB Μανῶε; Josephus Μανώχης. On Josephus' version of the Samson story of Judges 13-16 in 5.276-317, see Feldman 1998: 461-89.

[761] Judg 13:2 says nothing concerning Manoah's social standing; Josephus' indications on the matter have a counterpart in Pseudo-Philo (*Bib. Ant.* 42.1), who traces his ancestry back 10 generations to Dan, the

who was notable for her beauty and who stood out among the women of her time.[763] He had no children, however, and distraught at his childlessness, kept begging God, during his constant visits with his wife to the outskirts of the city where there was a great plain,[764] to give them legitimate offspring.[765]

277. He was madly in love with his wife and therefore immoderately jealous of her.[766] There appeared to the woman, who had been left alone, an apparition, an angel[767] of God, similar to a handsome, tall youth.[768] He told her the good news that, in accordance with God's providential care, a child was to be born who would be handsome and of extraordinary vigor. It would be through him, once he had reached manhood, that he [God] would defeat the Palestinoi.[769] **278.** He likewise urged her not to cut his hair.[770] He was to abstain from all other drink, since God had ordered this, and be familiar only with water.[771] Once he said these things, he departed, having come in accordance with God's will.[772]

Angelic apparition

---

ancestor of his tribe, the Danites. The indications recall Josephus' (likewise inserted) reference to Gideon's high standing within the tribe of Manasseh in 5.213.

[762] In Josephus, as in the Bible, she remains nameless. Pseudo-Philo (*Bib. Ant.* 42.1) calls her "Eluma the daughter of Remac."

[763] These indications concerning Manoah's wife are Josephan embellishments of Judg 13:2; in Pseudo-Philo (*Bib. Ant.* 42.1b-2a) the couple quarrels about which of them is responsible for their childlessness. His inserted mention of the woman's beauty recalls Josephus' presentation of the Levite and his wife in 5.136. In both instances, Josephus amplifies the romantic/erotic elements of the source account; see Feldman (1998: 475-82) on this feature of Josephus' retelling of the Samson story overall.

[764] Judg 13:2a simply mentions "Zorah" as Manoah's home-town. Josephus may have drawn his reference to the "great plain" visited by the couple from Judg 13:9, where the woman is sitting "in the field" when the angel appears to her a 2nd time.

[765] Josephus here elaborates the summary statement of Judg 13:2b ("and his wife was barren and had no children"), keeping the focus on Manoah—his childlessness, his feelings, his prayer. In Pseudo-Philo (*Bib. Ant.* 42.2) the wife is the one who prays regarding the couple's situation.

[766] Josephus' accentuation of the story's erotic features and his echoing of the language of 5.136-137 concerning the Levite and his wife continue.

[767] Greek: ἄγγελλος. This word is textually unsure. It is found in MSPLauE and is printed as part of the text by Marcus (who, however, relegates the translation of it to a note ["a spectre, an angel of God"], omitting it in the body of his translation, where he reads "a spectre... from God"). Niese's text omits the word; RO reads "a vision of a star from God."

[768] Judg 13:3 (like *Bib. Ant.* 42.2) designates the figure as "the angel of the Lord." Josephus here embellishes his corresponding designation of the figure (but see previous note) with terminology reminiscent of that used by him in 5.213 for Gideon's (angelic, see Judg 6:12) visitor, i.e. φάντασμα ("vision") and "young man" (νεανίας); see note to "Gedeon" at 5.213. His appended allusions to the apparition's appearance pick up on his previous highlighting (see 5.276) of the woman's own beauty.

[769] Josephus combines elements of the biblical angel's opening (Judg 13:3b, the birth of a son to the woman) and closing (13:5b, the son's role in effecting deliverance from the Philistines) words to Manoah's wife. Between these, he inserts indications of his own concerning the child's physical attributes, of which the reference to its "vigor" (Greek: ῥώμη) looks ahead to the explanation of the name "Sampson" in terms of the child's "strength" he will give in 5.285. In *Bib. Ant.* 42.3 the angel, in accord with the woman's prayer (42.2b), begins by addressing the couple's dispute (see 42.1b-2a) about which of them is responsible for their childlessness, ascribing this to her.

[770] Compare Judg 13:5aβ ("no razor shall come upon his head"); Josephus leaves aside the appended source statement, "the boy shall be a Nazirite to God [MT נזיר אלהים, LXX A ναζιραῖος θεοῦ, LXX B ἅγιος θεοῦ] from birth" (which Pseudo-Philo does reproduce in *Bib. Ant.* 42.2).

[771] In Judg 13:4 it is the mother-to-be who is told not to drink wine or strong drink (and to eat nothing impure). Pseudo-Philo's angel instructs the woman (*Bib. Ant.* 42.3) to see to it to that her son does not drink grape drinks or eat anything unclean.

[772] Both Josephus and Pseudo-Philo (*Bib. Ant.* 42.3 *in fine*) go beyond the Bible in making explicit mention of the heavenly visitor's departure.

Wife's report   **(8.3) 279.** The woman went to her husband and related the things [told her] by the angel. She enthused over the young man's handsomeness and height[773] so that her husband, in his jealousy, was driven to distraction by these accolades and conceived the suspicion provoked by this sort of passion.[774]

Angel's reappearance   **280.** She, desirous that her husband's irrational grief might subside, kept begging God to send the angel again, so that he might be seen also by her husband.[775] By the favor of God, the angel did come again while they were in the suburbs, and appeared to the woman whom the husband had left by herself.[776] She asked him to remain until she fetched her husband. Upon his granting this, she went after Manoah.[777] **281.** When he beheld him, he did not then cease from his suspicion,[778] but requested that he disclose to him whatever he had informed his wife.[779] When he stated that it sufficed that he had made it known to her alone,[780] Manoch directed him to say who he was, so that, once the child was born, they might award him thanks and a gift.[781]

282. He, however, stated to him that he had no need of anything, for it was not

---

[773] Josephus' wording of the woman's report reutilizes the language of his own description of the angel in 5.277. The appended reference to the woman's admiration for the angel's appearance takes the place of her largely verbatim report of his words to her (Judg 13:4-5) in 13:6-7. In *Bib. Ant.* 42.4 the wife acknowledges to Manoah, on the basis of the angel's announcement, that she had been in the wrong in their earlier dispute (see 42.1b-2) about the responsibility for their childlessness.

[774] Judges 13 says nothing about the emotional effect of his wife's report upon Manoah; Josephus' insertion echoes his mention of Manoah's "immoderate jealousy" towards his wife in 5.277. *Bib. Ant.* 42.5 relates the Manoah "did not believe" his wife's report, which left him "confused and sad."

[775] In Judg 13:8 it is Manoah who asks for the angel's return in order that he might instruct them about a matter that has seemingly already been sufficiently elucidated, i.e. what they are to do with the promised son. Josephus transfers the prayer request to the woman, likewise providing it with a new, more compelling motivation/content; elsewhere as well, he accentuates the woman's role in the proceedings, see note to "containers" at 5.283. Pseudo-Philo (*Bib. Ant.* 42.5) retains Manoah as the one praying, but has him ask whether he too is not worthy of hearing and seeing the angel.

[776] In Judg 13:9 the woman is alone "in the field" when the angel reappears. Josephus' mention of the "suburbs" echoes his localization of Manoah's initial prayer in 5.276.

[777] The woman's request to the angel here makes her appear more respectful than in Judg 13:10a, where she simply runs off to find her husband once the angel manifests himself to her; in *Bib. Ant.* 42.6b the angel takes the initiative himself in commanding the woman

to fetch her husband. Josephus leaves aside the woman's actual report to her husband as cited in 13:10b.

[778] This inserted reference to Manoah's feelings as he approaches the angel echoes the mention of his "suspicion" prompted by his wife's report concerning her visitor in 5.279.

[779] This formulation of Manoah's initial query to the angel takes the place of his rather obvious question ("are you the man who spoke to this woman?") and the angel's affirmative answer in Judg 13:11. In *Bib. Ant.* 42.7 the angel initiates the exchange, directing Manoah "to go in to his wife and do all these things," whereupon Manoah assents, asking that the angel ensure the realization of his promise, and the later promises to do so.

[780] Compare Judg 13:11bβ, where the angel responds affirmatively to Manoah's question about his identity; see previous note. Josephus (negatively) aligns the angelic response with his version of Manoah's opening question.

[781] Compare Manoah's final word to the angel in Judg 13:17 ("what is your name, so that, when your words come true, we may honor you?"). Josephus leaves aside the former's preceding question about his son's future (and the angel's reply to this which largely duplicates the wording of vv. 4 and 7) of 13:12-14. He likewise repositions Manoah's attempt to detain the angel and prepare a kid for him (= 13:15) to after his inquiry about his name with a view to honoring him (13:17); see 5.282. Pseudo-Philo (*Bib. Ant.* 42.8) combines and elaborates Manoah's 2 proposals about showing his appreciation for the angel (Judg 13:15, 17); he likewise supplies the angel's name, i.e. "Fahdael," in a concluding note to the reader, 42.10.

due to any lack that he had announced the good news of these things concerning the birth of the child.[782] When he then appealed to him to remain and share their hospitality, he did not assent.[783] He was, however, persuaded by his persistent entreaty to stay until some [mark of] hospitality might be brought to him.[784]

283. Manoch slaughtered a kid and directed his wife to roast this. Then, when everything was ready, he ordered her to set down loaves of bread and the pieces of meat on the rock, apart from their containers.[785]

Angel's ascent

284. When they had done this, [the angel] touched the pieces of meat with the staff that he held;[786] a fire blazed up and consumed them, together with the loaves.[787] The angel ascended to heaven in their presence through the smoke, as if in a vehicle.[788] Manoch feared that something threatening would happen to them as a result of their vision of God.[789] His wife, however, appealed to him to be of good cheer; for it was to their benefit that God had been seen by them.[790]

(8.4) 285. She became pregnant and observed the [angel's] commands.[791] When the child was born, they called[792] him Sampson,[793] a name that signifies "strong."[794]

Samson's birth and growth

---

[782] Josephus' rendering of the angel's answer replaces his (rhetorical) question of Judg 13:18 as to why Manoah has asked to be told his "wonderful" name with an explanation of his refusal of the proffered "gift" (cf. 13:16).

[783] This is Josephus' (repositioned, see note to "gift" at 5.281) version of Judg 13:15-16a, where Manoah tries to "detain" the angel with the offer of a "kid," only to be rebuffed by him.

[784] In Judg 13:16a the angel, on his own, suggests that, instead of trying to feed him, Manoah offer a sacrifice to the Lord. Josephus depicts an angel who, ultimately, is more responsive to the man's desire to show him honor. He omits the appended parenthetical notice of 13:16b, "for Manoah did not know that he was the angel of the Lord." On the "hospitality" theme in Josephus, see note to this word at 5.141.

[785] Josephus avoids representing the "offerings" of the non-priest Manoah as a sacrifice to the Lord; contrast Judg 13:19 (and *Bib. Ant.* 42.9). He likewise gives the wife a role in the proceedings; compare his making her, rather than Manoah himself (so Judg 13:8), the one to pray for the angel's return in 5.280, cf. note to "husband" at 5.280.

[786] In Judg 13:20, which does not mention this initiative by the angel, the sacrifice seems to ignite of itself. Josephus' addition has a parallel in Pseudo-Philo's *Bib. Ant.* 42.9; both authors have, it seems independently, introduced a reminiscence of Judg 6:21, where the angel "ignites" Gideon's sacrifices by touching them with his staff.

[787] Like *Bib. Ant.* 42.9, Josephus goes beyond Judg 13:20 in making explicit mention of the fire's consuming the offerings.

[788] Judg 13:20aβ speaks of the angel's ascending "in the flame," as does *Bib. Ant.* 42.9. Josephus leaves

aside the reference to the couple's falling on their faces of 13:20b (and *Bib. Ant.* 42.10). He likewise passes over the parenthetical notice of 13:21 about the angel appearing no more and Manoah's recognizing his identity (compare the remark of 13:16b about Manoah's not knowing his visitor to be "the angel of the Lord," also omitted by Josephus).

[789] This is Josephus' indirect discourse version of Manoah's words to his wife as cited in Judg 13:22: "We shall surely die for we have seen God," with their identification of the angel previously seen by them with the Deity himself; *Bib. Ant.* 42.10 takes over and elaborates the biblical Manoah's statement. See next note.

[790] Josephus here generalizes the catalogue of benefits received cited by the woman in Judg 13:23 to show her husband that the Lord did not in fact intend to kill them (Pseudo-Philo omits the wife's response). In having the woman refer to God's being seen by them (compare 13:23, where she alludes to the Lord's showing them "these things"), Josephus has her identify their visitor as God himself, just as Manoah did previously; see previous note.

[791] Josephus inserts these preliminaries to Samson's actual birth (= Judg 13:24); they accentuate the woman's role in his version of the story.

[792] In Judg 13:24 (and *Bib. Ant.* 43.1) the mother alone names the child.

[793] MT (Judg 13:24) שמשון (Eng.: "Samson"); LXX and Josephus Σαμψών.

[794] Neither Judg 13:24 nor Pseudo-Philo offers an explicit interpretation of Samson's name. Josephus' explanation picks up on his version of the angelic announcement (5.277) that the child to be born would be "of extraordinary vigor (ῥώμη)." On the meaning of the Hebrew name "Samson" and Josephus' interpretation of it, see Rappaport 1930: xxxii and Feldman 1998: 465-

Samson en-gaged

The child grew quickly, and it was clear that he would be a prophet from the prudence of his manner of life[795] and his letting his hair grow freely.[796]

(8.5) 286. Going with his parents[797] to Thamna,[798] a city of the Palestinoi, where a festival was being held,[799] he fell in love with a virgin among the inhabitants, and appealed to his parents to take the young woman as a wife for him.[800] Though they refused because she was not a compatriot,[801] he succeeded in betrothing the virgin,[802] God viewing the marriage as advantageous to the Hebrews.[803]

Honey from a lion

287. As he[804] was constantly going to her parents, he met a lion,[805] which he, though unarmed, assaulted and strangled with his bare hands;[806] then he tossed the beast into a wooded site on the side of the road.[807] **(8.6) 288.** As he was going off again to the young woman, it happened that a swarm of bees was nesting in the breast of that lion.[808] He removed three honeycombs[809] and brought these, along with his other gifts, and gave them to the girl.[810]

466, nn. 8-12. The noun "strength" (ἰσχύς) and the cognate adjective "strong" (ἰσχυρός) are key words in Josephus' presentation of Samson (5.276-317), in which the former term occurs 5 times (5.289, 307, 311, 312, 317) and the latter 6 times (5.277, 285, 302, 308, 309, 311).

[795] Or "regimen" (Greek: δίαιτα). On this word, which appears in a testimony of Clearchus of Soli concerning Aristotle's being impressed by the "manner of life" of a Jew whom he met as cited by Josephus in *Apion* 1.182; see Feldman 1998: 112, 486; Mason in BJP 1, note to "regimen" at *War* 2.137. The term recurs in 5.305, where Josephus introduces a new, negative stage of Samson's life.

[796] These indications about the young Samson represent Josephus' adaption of the triple notice of Judg 13:24b-25: "and the boy grew, and the Lord was with him, and the Spirit of the Lord began to stir him...." to which Pseudo-Philo has no equivalent. Throughout his retelling of the Samson story, Josephus systematically eliminates the recurrent references to the operation of the Spirit upon him. The reference to the boy's long hair echoes the angel's command to his mother in 5.278. Feldman (1998: 483) notes that Josephus is unique among the ancient sources in according prophetic status to Samson.

[797] In Judg 14:1 Samson travels to "Timnah" alone. Josephus' mention of his parents' accompanying him there is anticipated from 14:5. It would seem in fact to make more sense to have the parents go with Samson on his first trip to the foreign city rather than only on his subsequent one(s)—as one finds in the Bible.

[798] MT (Judg 14:1) תמנה (Eng.: "Timnah"); LXX Θαμνάθα; Josephus Θάμνα.

[799] Judg 14:1 does not mention this occasion; compare Josephus' inserted reference to a "festival" in his version of Judg 9:7 in 5.235.

[800] See Judg 14:1b-2.

[801] From the parents' rhetorical question of Judg

14:3, pointing up the inappropriateness of Samson's request given the availability of women of his kin and people for him to marry, Josephus leaves aside, as he does consistently elsewhere, their derogatory reference to the "uncircumcised Philistines" that would likely cause offense to his (also uncircumcised) Gentile readers; see Höffken 2001: 400-401.

[802] This notice takes the place of Samson's renewed appeal to his father (Judg 14:3b) that he get the woman for him.

[803] Compare the parenthetical notice of Judg 14:4a according to which the parents did not know that Samson's desire for the Philistine woman was "from the Lord" who was "seeking an occasion against the Philistines."

[804] In Judg 14:5 his parents accompany Samson on his 2nd trip to Timnah; see note to "parents" at 5.286.

[805] Judg 14:5 sets the encounter in "the vineyards of Timnah."

[806] Judg 14:6a attributes Samson's successful assault upon the lion to the Lord's Spirit coming upon him; Josephus omits this indication, just as did the earlier mention of the Lord's Spirit "stirring" Samson in Judg 13:25; see note to "freely" at 5.285.

[807] This notice on Samson's disposal of the lion's cadaver takes the place of the double statement of Judg 14:6b-7 (Samson does not inform his parents of his exploit with the lion; he speaks with the woman who pleases him).

[808] According to MT Judg 14:8 the bees were in the lion's "body/carcass," while LXX places them in its "mouth/gullet."

[809] Josephus' specification of 3 honeycombs lacks an equivalent in Judg 14:8-9a, which simply speaks of Samson's removing "the honey" present in the lion's corpse.

[810] Josephus here modifies the presentation of Judg 14:9, where, after eating some of the honey on the way,

289. At the wedding banquet, the Thamnites—for he was entertaining all of them—[811] in their anxiety over[812] the youth's strength,[813] gave him thirty robust men, purportedly as companions, but in fact to be his guards, should he wish to cause any trouble.[814] The drinking bout was prolonged and there were amusements (as usually happens on such occasions).[815] **290.** Sampson said: "I will propose a riddle; if you can solve it after investigating for seven days, you will individually receive from me fine linens and garments as a reward for your sagacity."[816] They were all ambitious both to appear sagacious and to acquire the reward,[817] and so they requested him to tell [the riddle]. He stated that what had eaten everything had, of itself, generated sweet food, though [having been] quite unpleasant.[818]

291. When after three days[819] they were unable to find out the solution to the riddle,[820] they appealed to the young woman to learn it from her husband and inform them, threatening to burn her if she did not provide this.[821] When the young woman asked him to tell her, Sampson initially resisted.[822] **292.** When, however, she importuned him and fell to weeping, alleging that his not telling her was a sign of his dislike for her,[823] he informed her of his dispatch of the lion and how he had taken away the three honeycombs generated from it and brought them to her.

293. Suspecting no deceit, he explained everything,[824] and she brought word to those who had asked her. Accordingly, on the seventh day, on which they had to

---

Samson gives a part of it to his parents, though without telling them where he obtained it (cf. Judg 14:6b, also omitted by him). Josephus' version accentuates Samson's attachment to the Philistine woman to whom he brings not only (all) the honey, but also "other gifts."

[811] From Judg 14:10 Josephus omits the role of Samson's father who "goes down" to the woman as well as the statement that Samson's providing a feast was in accord with the practice of young people of the time.

[812] Josephus' mention of the townsfolk's "anxiety" is in accord with the LXX AL reading in Judg 14:11, whereas the vocalized form of MT (and LXX B) refers rather to their "seeing."

[813] On this key word of Josephus' Samson story, see 5.277, 285, and the note to "strong" at 5.285.

[814] Josephus embellishes Judg 14:11, which does not mention the physical condition of the 30 attendants or the motivation behind their being assigned to Samson. Thereby, he underscores how great a threat Samson poses to the Philistines: 30 robust men are needed to keep him under restraint.

[815] This remark, leading into Samson's posing of his riddle in Judg 14:12, has no biblical equivalent.

[816] From Samson's "proposition" in Judg 14:12-13a Josephus omits the negative alternative with which it closes, i.e. the Philistines will have to pay him what he is offering them for elucidating the riddle, should they be unable to do this.

[817] This mention of the Philistines' state of mind as they urge Samson to tell them his riddle is Josephus'

embellishment of Judg 14:13b.

[818] Compare Judg 14:14a: "out of the eater came something to eat; out of the strong came something sweet." Josephus' substitution of "unpleasant" for "strong" makes for a better contrast with "sweet."

[819] Josephus' chronological indication here is equivalent to the "on the fourth day" of LXX Judg 14:15, whereas MT reads "on the seventh day."

[820] Cf. Judg 14:14b, which states that the Philistines "could not in 3 days tell what the riddle was."

[821] In Judg 14:15 the Philistines threaten to burn the house(hold) of the woman's father as well. Josephus likewise omits their (obscure) concluding question to the woman: "Have you invited us here to impoverish us?"

[822] Josephus summarizes the initial exchange between Samson and his wife (Judg 14:16), omitting, for example, the former's reference to his not having told the riddle to his parents, just as earlier he left aside the notices on Samson's not telling his parents about his killing of the lion (14:6b) and the source of the honey (14:9b).

[823] In the biblical presentation (Judg 14:16a) the wife's reference to Samson's "hating" her comes in her initial words to him. Josephus, more effectively, has her reserve this emotionally charged claim to a later point in her attempt.

[824] In Judg 14:17aβ Samson simply "tells" his wife. Josephus spells out what he tells her and supplies a reason for his readiness to do this, i.e. his "suspecting no deceit" on her part.

make known the solution of the riddle to him, assembling before sunset, they said:[825] "nothing is more unpleasant than meeting a lion, nor sweeter than honey to those who taste it."[826]

Samson's reaction

294 Sampson then said: "neither is anything more deceitful than the woman who brought this word of ours to you."[827] And he gave them what he had promised, after plundering the Askalonites who met him on the road (they too were Palestinoi).[828]

Marriage dissolved

He voided that marriage, while the girl herself, despising him for his wrath, was married to his friend who had been the best man.[829]

Vengeance by Samson and Philistines

(8.7) 295. Sampson was enraged by this outrage and decided to take it out on all the Palestinoi, as well as on her.[830] Now it was summer and the crops were already ripe for harvest.[831] He caught 300 foxes and, tying lighted torches to their tails, turned them loose in the fields of the Palestinoi.[832]

296. With their crops thus devastated, the Palestinoi, realizing that the deed was Sampson's and his reason for having done it,[833] sent their rulers to Thamna and burnt alive his former wife and her relatives as the ones responsible for their calamities.[834]

Judeans hand Samson over to Philistines

(8.8) 297. Sampson, after killing many Palestinoi in the plain,[835] settled down at Aita;[836] this is a solid rock belonging to the tribe of Iouda.[837] The Palestinoi, for their part, campaigned against that tribe. The latter said that it was not just for them, who

---

[825] See Judg 14:17b-18aα. In speaking of "sunset" rather than "sunrise," Josephus agrees with MT LXX AL Judg 14:18 against LXX B and Tg.

[826] Josephus reverses the sequence of the Philistines' answer in Judg 14:18aβ: "What is sweeter than honey? What is stronger than a lion?," likewise retaining his substitution of "unpleasant" for "strong" from 5.290; see note to "unpleasant" at 5.290.

[827] This retort replaces the (obscure) reply by Samson in Judg 14:18b: "If you had not plowed with my heifer [Tg. examined my wife], you would not have found out my riddle."

[828] In Judg 14:19 Samson's initiative is provoked by the Spirit's "coming mightily upon him"; for the 3rd time (see notes to "freely" at 5.282, "hands" at 5.287) Josephus passes over a source mention of the Spirit acting on Samson. He further modifies the presentation of 14:19, where Samson "kills" the men of Ashkelon (apparently in the city itself) and appends the identification of this group as "Philistines."

[829] Compare Judg 14:19b-20, where Samson's "anger" prompts him to return to his father's house, leaving his wife to be married to the best man. Josephus inserts the reference to the contempt for Samson's anger by his former wife.

[830] This introduction to the following episode of Samson's burning the Philistines' crops (Judg 15:4-5), with its reference to Samson's anger (see 14:19b), replaces the exchange between Samson and his (former) father-in-law concerning the latter's daughter(s) that eventuates in Samson's announcement of his intention to harm the Philistines without incurring blame himself (15:1-3).

[831] This inserted notice about the time of year serves to prepare the following episode.

[832] See Judg 15:4-5, from which Josephus omits the catalogue of agricultural products destroyed by the fire.

[833] In Judg 15:6a the Philistines have to be told, by an unidentified "they," that Samson, reacting to the loss of his wife, is the culprit. Josephus makes them, more plausibly, figure things out for themselves.

[834] In specifying that the Philistines burnt the ex-wife's "relatives," Josephus goes together with LXX Judg 15:6b against MT which has them (only) burn her "father." Josephus further spells out the reason for the Philistines doing as they do to the wife's family. Having mentioned Samson's acquiring his Philistine wife (cf. Judg 14:10) in *Bib. Ant.* 43.1, Pseudo-Philo (*ibid.*) proceeds immediately to the Philistines' burning of her (Judg 15:6b) in retaliation for their having been "humiliated" by Samson.

[835] Josephus passes over Samson's preceding address (Judg 15:7) to the Philistines, in which he states that he will avenge himself upon them and then "quit" From Judg 15:8a he omits the idiom ("hip and thigh" [Tg.: horsemen along with footmen]) used to describe Samson's slaughter of the Philistines.

[836] MT (Judg 15:8) עיטם (Eng.: "Etam"); LXX Ἠτάμ; Josephus Αἰτά.

[837] In speaking of "Aita" as a "rock" Josephus agrees with MT LXX B Judg 15:8 ("in the cleft of the rock of Etam") against LXX AL that refer to Samson's living "near the stream in the cave of Etam." He bases his assignment of the site to Judah on 15:9, where the Philistines respond to Samson's previous initiatives against them (15:8) by invading "Judah."

paid them tribute, to suffer punishment for Sampson's offenses.[838] [The Palestinoi] then stated that, if they did not wish to bear responsibility, they were to give Sampson into their hands.[839]

298. They, wishing to be held blameless, came with 3,000 troops to the rock.[840] They reproached him for what he had dared to do to the Palestinoi, men who were capable of bringing misfortune upon the whole Hebrew race.[841] They further said they had come to take him and to give him into their hands, and requested that he voluntarily endure this.[842] **299.** He, for his part, took oaths from them that they would do nothing else, but simply hand him over to the enemy.[843] He then came down from the rock and placed himself under the authority of the men of the tribe.[844] Binding him with two cords, they led him to turn him over to the Palestinoi.[845]

300. When they were at a certain site that is now called "Siagon"[846]—though of old it was nameless—on account of the brave deed done there by Sampson,[847] the Palestinoi encamped not far away.[848] They met them with joyful shouts, as though at the realization of what they wished.[849] Sampson, however, tore off his bonds[850] and, snatching the jaw-bone of an ass that was at his feet, rushed into the enemy.[851]

Samson massacres Philistines

---

[838] Compare Judg 15:10a, where the Judeans simply ask the Philistines: "why have you come up against us?" Josephus' interjected reference to their status as Philistine "tributaries," underscores the wrongfulness of the Philistine invasion of their territory.

[839] In Judg 15:10b the Philistines inform the Judeans that they have come to bind Samson in order that they might do to him as he had done to them. Josephus' version of their answer provides a more compelling motivation for the Judeans' following initiative regarding Samson, i.e. the Philistines spelling out what they must do to avoid being blamed by them.

[840] See Judg 15:11a, into which Josephus inserts a motive for the Judeans' acting as they do that itself harks back to the Philistines' warning to them in 5.297.

[841] From the Judeans' words in Judg 15:11bα Josephus omits their opening question ("do you not know that the Philistines are rulers over us?"), replacing this with an accusatory statement about what Samson has done to the Philistines and its potentially negative consequences, not simply for the Judeans themselves (so 15:11bα), but for all the Hebrews. He further passes over Samson's initial reply ("As they did to me, I have done to them," 15:11bβ), which interrupts the 2 parts of the Judeans' address to him (15:11bα, 12a).

[842] The Judeans' request for Samson's cooperation is Josephus' addition to their statement of their intentions regarding him as cited in Judg 15:12a. The addition suggests the Judeans' awareness that, given Samson's strength, they would be unable to take him without such cooperation on his part.

[843] Compare Samson's word to the Judeans in Judg 15:12b: "Swear to me that you will not fall upon me yourselves." Josephus leaves aside the Judeans' affirmative response to Samson's request as cited in 15:13a.

[844] This Josephan insertion underscores the fact that Samson did indeed voluntarily submit himself—as the Judeans ask him to do in his presentation (see 5.298 and note to "endure this" there).

[845] Josephus leaves aside the specification of Judg 15:13b that the ropes were "new," and substitutes an indication of the purpose of the Judeans' "leading" him for the source reference to their "bringing him up from the rock."

[846] This is the term used in LXX Judg 15:14 to translate the Hebrew place name "Lehi," meaning "Jawbone."

[847] These indications concerning the strange place name "Jawbone" are Josephan additions to the mention of the site in Judg 15:14.

[848] This item has no biblical equivalent.

[849] Josephus provides both a characterization ("joyful") and a motivation for the "shouting" of the Philistines mentioned in Judg 15:14a.

[850] Judg 15:14b attributes the "dissolving" of Samson's bonds to the action of the Lord's "spirit" upon him. Characteristically, Josephus attributes Samson's liberation rather to his own strength; see notes to "freely" at 5.285, "hands" at 5.287, "Palestinoi" at 5.293.

[851] Josephus' mention of Samson's finding the jaw-bone "at his feet" has a certain counterpart in LXX AL Judg 15:15: "([a jawbone] which have been discarded on the road"; cf. Tg.: "in the mud"); compare the qualification of it as "fresh" in MT. Mention of Samson's "rushing" into the massed Philistines is his dramatic embellishment.

Striking them with the jaw-bone, he killed about 1,000, while the rest took to flight in their consternation.[852]

God relieves Samson's thirst

(8.9) 301. Sampson, however, became more prideful than he should have over this. He did not say that this had happened due to God's cooperation,[853] but rather attributed the outcome to his own valor, boasting that he had felled some of the enemy with the jawbone, and put the others to flight due in their anxiety about him.[854]

302. When, however, he was overcome by a strong[855] thirst, he acknowledged that it was not a matter of human valor, and ascribed everything to God whom he implored not to hand him over to his enemies in his wrath at what he had said, but rather to provide him help in his terrible [torment] and rescue him from this calamity.[856] **303.** God, moved by his supplications, caused a sweet and abundant spring of water[857] to gush forth from a certain rock;[858] for this reason Sampson named the place "Siagon," and it is called this down till today.[859]

Samson escapes from Gaza

(8.10) 304. After this battle, Sampson, in his contempt for the Palestinoi,[860] went to Gaza and stayed in one of the inns.[861] When the rulers of the Gazaites learned of his presence at that very spot, they set ambushes in front of the gates so that his leaving would not be concealed from them.[862]

305. Because, however, these schemes of theirs were not concealed from him,[863]

---

[852] The flight of the surviving Philistines is a Josephan embellishment of Judg 15:15.

[853] With these editorial comments on Samson's pride, Josephus attempts to account for the source sequence of events, in which, following Samson's poetic claims about his exploit (Judg 15:16), a severe thirst afflicts him (15:18), in terms of the hubris of his words. He has used the word "cooperation" (Greek: συνεργία) for God's assisting Joshua in battle in 5.60; see note to "cooperation" at 5.60.

[854] This is Josephus' prose rendition of the miniature poem ascribed to Samson in Judg 15:16: "With the jawbone of an ass, heaps upon heaps, with the jawbone of an ass have I slain a thousand men." The reference to the Philistines' "flight" picks up on Josephus' earlier inserted mention of this in 5.300.

[855] Greek: ἰσχυρός. With his use of this term to characterize Samson's thirst, Josephus introduces a wordplay on the meaning of the hero's name, i.e. "strong" as given by him in 5.285; see note to "strong" at 5.285.

[856] From Samson's prayer of Judg 15:18 Josephus omits, as he did in his rendering of 14:3 in 5.286, the pejorative reference to the "uncircumcised Philistines"; see note to "compatriot" at 5.286.

[857] The references to God's motivation for providing the water and the character of the water provided by him are Josephus' elaboration of Judg 15:19a.

[858] In MT and LXX B Judg 15:19 the water emerges from the "cavity" at Lehi, whereas in LXX AL Tg. its source is a protrusion in the jawbone of the ass itself.

[859] MT Judg 15:19b cites a double place name, i.e. "the spring of him who called [Hebrew: אֵין הַקּוֹרֵא]; it is at Lehi to this day." Josephus' single Greek name for

the site echoes that used by him in 5.299. His reproduction of the source's etiological notice about the place name perduring down until "this day" is exceptional; generally, he leaves such indications aside. In contrast to Josephus, Pseudo-Philo (*Bib. Ant.* 43.4) limits his utilization of the material of Judges 15 to a brief allusion to a few selected items: Samson's killing the Philistines with the jawbone of an ass (15:15) the dissolving of his bonds (15:14), and his capture of the foxes (15:4), which items, he states, are written "in the Book of Judges."

[860] This motivation for Samson's going to Gaza at this point (Judg 16:1) is Josephus' own.

[861] With this formulation, Josephus "improves on" the presentation of Samson, who in Judg 16:1 sees a "harlot" in Gaza and goes in to her. Compare 5.7, where he has the spies go, not to the house of the harlot Rahab (so MT LXX Josh 2:1), but to "a certain inn"; see note to this phrase at 5.7. In *Bib. Ant.* 43.2 Samson's Gaza exploit (Judg 16:1-3) is introduced with the simple notice "afterwards Samson got angry at Gaza."

[862] In Judg 16:2 it is the Gazaites as a whole who lie in ambush against Samson. Josephus replaces the source's mention of their remaining quiet all night and its statement about their intending to kill him in the morning with a specification concerning the purpose of the rulers' ambushes.

[863] This insertion provides an explanation of what prompted Samson to arise in the middle of the night (so Judg 16:3). *Bib. Ant.* 43.2 ascribes to Samson a prayer or statement of intention prior to his uprooting the city gates.

Sampson got up when it was already about the middle of the night and flung himself against the gates. He lifted these up, along with the posts, the bars, and the other wood-work that was around them, onto his shoulders, and carried them to the mountain above Hebron where he set them down.[864]

(8.11) 306. He had, however, already violated the ancestral [customs] and altered his own manner of life[865] by his imitation of foreign ways, and this was the beginning of his calamity.[866] For he fell in love with a female prostitute[867] among the Palestinoi whose name was Dalal[868] and had a liaison with her.

Samson's liaison with Delilah

307. The heads of the Palestine commonwealth came to her and convinced her by promises to learn from Sampson the cause of his strength in virtue of which he was invincible against his enemies.[869] At drinking bouts and such occasions she marveled over his deeds, and kept cleverly plotting to learn how it was that he so excelled in valor.[870]

Delilah's unsuccessful efforts to learn Samson's secret

308. Sampson, however, since his mind was still strong, deceived[871] Dalal in his turn, stating that if he were bound with seven vine-tendrils[872] that could still be woven around, he would become totally weak. **309.** At that point she kept quiet, but then, having given a signal to the rulers of the Palestinoi, she positioned some of the soldiers inside. Once Sampson was drunk, she bound him with the vines as strongly as possible.[873] Then rousing him, she disclosed that some men were coming against him.[874]

310. But he tore off the vines, and prepared to help [himself] as though some

---

[864] In Judg 16:3 Samson transports the gates to "the top of the hill that is before Hebron." Josephus' explicit mention of his setting them down at the spot corresponds to the LXX plus at the end of 16:3 (and to *Bib. Ant.* 43.3, which further has Samson using one of the gate doors to kill 25,000 Philistines *en route*).

[865] Or "regimen." Greek: δίαιτα, the term used by Josephus in his introduction of Samson in 5.285, where it is the prudence of his "manner of life" that intimates the boy's prophetic status; see note to this phrase there. He re-introduces the term at this juncture where a new, negative period of Samson's career is beginning.

[866] With this editorial comment Josephus orients readers to the negative outcome of the following Delilah story (Judg 16:4-22) and the reason for this. Pseudo-Philo (*Bib. Ant.* 43.5) offers a comparable introduction to the story in which God pronounces advance sentence upon Samson for his "mingling" with Philistine women.

[867] Greek: ἑταιριζομένης. Josephus' only other use of the verb ἑταιρίζω is in *Ant.* 8.417 (the "prostitutes" bathe in the pool stained by the blood of Ahab).

[868] MT (Judg 16:4) דלילה (Eng.: Delilah"); LXX A Δαλιλά; LXX B Δαλιδά; Josephus Δαλάλης. Josephus, like Pseudo-Philo, omits the biblical indication that she was living "in the valley of Sorek."

[869] Josephus' reference to the Philistine leaders' "promises" to Delilah are a generalization of the statement made to her by "the lords of the Philistines," i.e. "we will each give you eleven hundred pieces of sil-

ver" in Judg 16:5. In Pseudo-Philo—who has no equivalent to 16:5—Delilah acts on her own initiative in trying to discover Samson's secret.

[870] Josephus elaborates on Delilah's opening request (Judg 16:6) that Samson disclose the secret of his strength with mention of the occasions on which she made her initial attempts.

[871] Elaborating on Judg 16:7, Josephus points up both the falsity of the answer Samson gives Delilah and the reason for this.

[872] Josephus here agrees with the wording of LXX L Judg 16:7, whereas MT speaks of "(fresh) bowstrings" and LXX AB of "cords." See Harlé 1999 *ad loc*.

[873] Josephus rearranges the sequence of Delilah's preliminary measures as cited in Judg 16:8-9a, adding mention of her getting Samson drunk (a detail which serves to confirm Josephus' previous statement about Samson's "altering his own manner of life" in 5.306, in that his drinking violates the divine prohibition issued even before his birth; see 5.278), and her binding him "as strongly as possible" (the use of the superlative form of the adjective ἰσχυρός here echoes the meaning of the name "Samson," i.e. "strong" given by Josephus in 5.285; see note to "strong" there). Conversely, he leaves aside the source statement (16:8a) that the Philistine rulers brought Delilah the bowstrings/cords she will use.

[874] Judg 16:9aβ: "and she said to him, 'The Philistines are upon you, Samson'."

assailants were upon him.[875] The woman, however, with whom Sampson was constantly associating, kept saying she took it amiss, that he, from disbelief in her loyalty to him, did not tell her those things that she asked, as though she would not keep to herself what she knew would not be to his advantage to have divulged.[876]

311. He again deceived[877] her, however, stating that if were bound with seven[878] ropes he would lose his strength. Doing this as well, she had no success.[879] The third time he informed her that she was to plait his hair.[880] **312.** When the truth was not found by this either,[881] Sampson, in response to her asking—for it was necessary that he fall into misfortune—and wishing to gratify Dalal,[882] finally said: "God protects [me] and since birth I have been under his providential care.[883] I let my hair grow, not cutting it according to his injunction. For my strength lies in its growth and preservation."[884]

Samson shaved and subdued

313. Having learned these things and shaved off his hair, she turned him over to his enemies whose assault he was no longer strong enough to resist.[885] They gouged out his eyes and turned him over to be led away bound.[886]

Samson's heroic death

(8.12) 314. In the course of time, however, Sampson's hair grew;[887] this was dur-

---

[875] From Judg 16:9b Josephus omits the comparison used of Samson's freeing himself from his bonds ("as a string of tow snaps when it touches the fire"), as well as its closing statement that the "secret of his strength was not known."

[876] Josephus elaborates on the woman's words as cited in Judg 16:10 by, e.g., having her evoke her "loyalty" (Greek: εὔνοια) to him and her ability to keep his secret.

[877] This extrabiblical qualification of Samson's 2nd response echoes Josephus' introductory remark concerning his first reply to Delilah in 5.308.

[878] Josephus shares this figure for the number of ropes to be used with LXX AL Judg 16:11, whereas MT LXX B do not specify a number. Unlike the biblical witnesses, Josephus does not qualify the ropes to be used as "new."

[879] This notice summarizes the more detailed description of the failure of Delilah's 2nd attempt in Judg 16:12 with its repetitions of the account of her first try in 16:8-9.

[880] Josephus passes over Delilah's 3rd appeal to Samson to disclose his secret to her (Judg 16:13a); his summary formulation of Samson's instructions to her regarding his hair reflects the short MT reading in 16:13b as opposed to the more expansive LXX one.

[881] As he did with Judg 16:12 in 5.311, Josephus here reduces to a mere allusion the source account of the failure of Delilah's 3rd attempt (Judg 16:14, where MT lacks LXX's opening reference to her weaving the 7 locks of Samson's hair into a web; see previous note). In the same line Pseudo-Philo (*Bib. Ant.* 43.6) confines his rendition of Judg 16:6-14 to a single inquiry by Deliah and the notice that Samson "tricked her three times."

[882] These editorial remarks, where the reference to Samson's necessary "falling into misfortune" echoes Josephus' statement of 5.306 about his involvement with Delilah being "the beginning of his calamity," take the place of the quotation of Delilah's words (Judg 16:15) and the notices on her pressuring Samson and the effect of this upon him (16:16).

[883] Greek: πρόνοια; the word here echoes the announcement to Sampson's mother by the angel that she will have a son "in accordance with God's providential care" in 5.277.

[884] From Samson's reply in Judg 16:17 Josephus omits his statement about being a "Nazirite to God from my mother's womb" (which itself picks up on the angel's announcement concerning Samson's future status in 13:5, also omitted by him). The closing declaration about his "strength" lying in his hair replaces the biblical Samson's informing Delilah (16:17b) that if he is shaved, he will be left as weak as other men.

[885] Josephus drastically abridges the source narrative (Judg 16:18-20) of the subduing of Samson, leaving aside, e.g., the Philistines' bringing Delilah her reward money (16:18bβ; cf. 16:5b, also omitted by him), Delilah's causing Samson to sleep on her knees (16:19aα), her cry that the Philistines are upon him (16:20aα), and Samson's "not knowing that the Lord had left him" (16:20bβ). In having Delilah herself shave Samson, he diverges from 16:19aβ, where she summons "a man" (so MT LXX B; "a barber," LXX AL [and *Bib. Ant.* 43.6]) to do this.

[886] From Judg 16:21 Josephus omits the mention of Samson's being taken to Gaza and the degrading detail about his "grinding at the mill in the prison"; Pseudo-Philo lacks these items as well.

[887] See Judg 16:22.

ing a national festival of the Palestinoi at which their rulers and leading men were feasting together at one place[888]—a house whose two pillars supported the roof.[889] At their summons, Sampson was brought to the banquet so that they might make fun of him during the drinking.[890]

315. But he, supposing it the most terrible of calamities to be unable to avenge oneself when one has been outraged, persuaded the boy who was leading him by the hand to bring him near the pillars, saying that he needed to rest from his fatigue.[891] **316.** When he got there, he threw himself upon them and caused the house to collapse, its pillars being overturned upon 3,000 men. All died, including Sampson himself.[892] Thus he ended, after having ruled the Israelites for twenty years.[893] **317.** He is deserving of admiration for his valor and strength as well as the sublimity of his death and for his wrath against his enemies until the end. His being captivated by women should be ascribed to human nature that easily gives in to offenses; in all other respects, the abundance of his valor is a testimony to him.[894] His relatives took up his body and buried it in his ancestral city of Sarasa alongside his relatives.[895]

(9.1) 318. After the death of Sampson Helei[896] the high priest[897] presided over the Israelites. Under him their country suffered the misfortune of a famine.[898] Abime-

Elimelech's (Abimeleh's) family goes to Moab

---

[888] In Judg 16:23a the occasion of Samson's final exploit is a "sacrifice to the Philistine god Dagon." Josephus likewise leaves aside the assembled Philistines' declarations ascribing Samson's capture to this deity in 16:23b-24.

[889] Josephus anticipates this parenthetical remark from Judg 16:26, where Samson asks to be allowed to feel "the pillars on which the house rests."

[890] See Judg 16:25. Josephus' introduction of the term "banquet" (Greek: συμπόσιον) gives a distinctly Hellenistic flavor to the proceedings.

[891] Josephus expands Samson's request to his attendant (Judg 16:26) with mention of the thoughts that prompt his initiatives at this point. He omits the figures for the assembled Philistines given in 16:27 (which, however, he will incorporate subsequently). Continuing the overall "detheologizing" trend of his Samson narrative, he likewise leaves aside the hero's final prayer in 16:28 (upon which Pseudo-Philo elaborates in *Bib. Ant.* 43.7).

[892] Into his version of Judg 16:29-30 Josephus incorporates the figure, i.e. 3000 (so MT AL LXX; LXX B 700), drawn from 16:27, for the Philistines on the roof, turning this into the number—left unspecified in 16:29-30 itself—of the Philistine dead (*Bib. Ant.* 43.8 gives the figure as 40,000). He omits the (exaggerated) claim of Judg 16:30b that in dying Samson killed more Philistines than he had while alive.

[893] See Judg 16:31b. Pseudo-Philo (*Bib. Ant.* 43.8) reproduces this chronological item as well.

[894] As often, Josephus here appends a final "eulogy" for a biblical character which underscores certain features of his preceding presentation of that character.

Thus, e.g., his allusion to Samson's "strength" is a final echo of the key word of his entire Samson story; see the note to "strong" at 5.285. On Josephus' penchant for balancing good and bad in his evaluation of the figures of his history, as evidenced here in his eulogy for Samson, see Mason in BJP 3: xxxii.

[895] Judg 16:31a localizes Samson's burial in the paternal grave at a point "between Zorah and Estaol." Josephus' name (Σαρασᾶ, which Schalit *s. v.* views as a corruption of an original Σαρά) for Samson's hometown in which he is buried seems to reflect the LXX form of the MT's initial place name, i.e. Σαραά. Pseudo-Philo (*Bib. Ant.* 43.9) does not localize the paternal tomb in which he has Samson buried.

Having anticipated the 2 concluding segments of the Book of Judges (chaps. 17-18 and 19-21) at the opening of his own version of the book (see 5.136-178), Josephus concludes his rendering of Judges with the figure of Samson, the protagonist of chaps. 13-16 (= 5.276-317). Immediately thereafter, in line with the arrangement of the LXX Bible (where Ruth stands as an appendix to the Book of Judges), he begins his parallel to the Book of Ruth (= 5.318-337). On Josephus' (greatly abridged) version of Ruth, see Levison 1991: 31-44; Feldman 1991: 45-52; 1998a: 193-202; Sterling 1998.

[896] MT (1 Sam 4:18b) עֵלִי (Eng.: "Eli"); LXX 'Ηλί; Josephus 'Ηλείς.

[897] Eli's title in 1 Sam 1:9 is simply "the priest." Josephus, who (see 5.361) traces his ancestry back to Ithamar, son of Aaron, the first high priest, assigns him a higher dignity.

[898] Ruth 1:1 dates, in general terms, the famine of

lech[899] of Bethlemon (this city belongs to the tribe of Iouda),[900] unable to withstand this terrible [occurrence],[901] led forth his wife Naamis,[902] along with Chellion[903] and Malaon,[904] the two sons whom he had by her, and resettled in the land of Moab.

Widow Naomi's (Naamis') planned return

319. Things went according to plan for him, and he married[905] his sons to Moabite women, Orpha[906] to Chellion and Routhe[907] to Malaon. When ten years had passed, Abimelech died and, shortly after him, his sons did as well.[908] **320.** Naamis was depressed at these events and, unable to endure the deprivation of those she loved most—and for the sake of whom she had come out of her ancestral place—was ready to depart for this again, for she had found out that things were now going well for it.[909]

Ruth (Routhe) accompanies Naomi

321. Her daughters-in-law would not, however, let themselves be separated from her, nor by her pleas could she persuade them who wished to go away with her.[910] As they importuned her, she prayed that they might make more fortunate marriages for themselves than those of which her sons had deprived them when they married them and acquire other good things. **322.** Given her own situation, however, she appealed to them to remain there and not to wish to share in her uncertain affairs by leaving their ancestral land.[911] Accordingly, Orpha did remain;[912] she took along Routhe, however, who was not persuaded, to be part of whatever was to happen to her.[913]

---

which it speaks "in the days when the judges ruled." Josephus draws the name of the specific judge under whose rule he situates this happening from 1 Sam 4:18b, which ascribes to "Eli" a judgeship of 40 years, this, in the biblical sequence, taking place between those of Samson who preceded (see Judg 16:31) and Samuel who followed him (see 1 Sam 7:15). Tg. Ruth 1:1 dates the famine rather to the days of the judge Ibzan, while other Rabbinic writings place it under either King Eglon of Moab or Deborah; see Rappaport 1930: 44, #185; 129, nn. 203-205.

[899] MT (Ruth 1:2) אלימלך (Eng.: "Elimelech"); LXX Ἀβιμέλεχ; Josephus Ἀβιμέλεχος.

[900] See Ruth 1:2; Josephus makes this same linkage of Bethlehem and Judah in *Ant.* 5.271. He omits the further specification of 1:2 that Elimelech's family were "Ephrathites."

[901] Josephus inserts this "motivation" for the move by Elimelech's household as cited in Ruth 1:2b; the insertion accentuates the severity of the famine.

[902] MT (Ruth 1:2) נעמי (Eng.: "Naomi"); LXX Νωεμείν; Josephus Ναάμις.

[903] MT (Ruth 1:2) כליון (Eng.: "Chillion"); LXX Κελαιών; Josephus Χελλίων.

[904] MT (Ruth 1:2) מחלון (Eng.: "Mahlon"); LXX Μααλών; Josephus Μααλών. Josephus reverses the biblical order of the sons' names.

[905] According to Ruth 1:4 the sons marry, seemingly on their own initiative, *after* the death of their father.

[906] MT (Ruth 1:4) ערפה (Eng.: "Orpah"); LXX and Josephus Ὀρφά.

[907] MT (Ruth 1:4) רות (Eng.: "Ruth"); LXX Ῥούθ; Josephus Ῥούθη. According to Tg. Ruth 1:4 Ruth was

the daughter of Eglon, king of Moab (see Judg 3:12); some rabbinic sources make the same identification, while others call her Eglon's granddaughter; for references, see Beattie 1994: *ad loc.*

[908] In Ruth 1:3-4 Elimelech dies before his sons, who then survive him for 10 years.

[909] Cf. Ruth 1:6, where Naomi hears in Moab "that the Lord had visited his people and given them food." Feldman (1998a: 196) points out that, whereas the Book of Ruth features 22 explicit mentions of the Deity, Josephus' version contains only a single such mention, this coming at the very end of his rendition in 5.337.

[910] Josephus here summarizes the initial exchange between Naomi and her daughters-in-law (Ruth 1:7-10), turning its direct into indirect discourse, and eliminating the poignant reference to Naomi's kissing them and their weeping (1:9b).

[911] This is Josephus' abbreviated rendition of Naomi's 2nd address to her daughters-in-law (Ruth 1:11-13), in which he characteristically (see note to "for it" at 5.320) passes over Naomi's accusatory reference to "the hand of the Lord having gone forth against me" (1:13b).

[912] In Ruth 1:14b Orpah simply "kisses" Naomi; Josephus replaces this notice on Orpah's initiative with one based on Naomi's word to Ruth in 1:15, "see, your sister-in-law has gone back to her people...." As in the case of Ruth 1:9b (see note to "with her" at 5.321), Josephus omits the pathetic detail of 1:14a about the daughters-in-law "lifting up their voices and weeping."

[913] Josephus limits himself to this generalized allusion to Ruth's reply to Naomi in Ruth 1:16-17. In par-

(9.2) 323. When Routhe came to Bethleemon with her mother-in-law, Booz,[914] a relative of Abimelech, received her hospitably.[915] But Naamis, when they greeted her by her name, said, "it would be more just for you to call me Mara."[916] ("Naamis" means "good luck" in Hebrew, while "Mara" signifies "pain").[917]

Women's arrival in Bethlehem

324. Now that it was harvest-time,[918] Routhe went out to glean the ears of grain with her mother-in-law's permission in order to supply them with food,[919] and, luckily,[920] came to Booz' parcel. Booz arrived shortly afterwards; beholding the young woman he asked the field overseer about the girl.[921] The overseer, who just previously had found out everything from her, disclosed this to his master.[922] **325.** Out of loyalty to her mother-in-law and mindful of her son to whom Routhe had been married,[923] Booz greeted her and prayed that she might experience good things.[924] He not only allowed her to glean the ears of grain, but even permitted her to reap and to take whatever she could. He also ordered the field overseer not to prevent her and to provide her the midday meal and drink such as he supplied to the reapers.[925]

Ruth works in field of Boaz

326. Receiving barley-meal from him, Routhe kept some of it for her mother-in-law; at evening she went to her, bringing this, along with the ears of grain.[926] Naamis

---

ticular, he makes no reference to Ruth's affirmation, at the end of v. 16, "your God shall be my God." His suppression of this element likely reflects Josephus' awareness of Roman sensitivities on the subject of Jewish proselytism; see Feldman 1998a: 198-199. By contrast the Targum on Ruth greatly accentuates the implicit biblical picture of Ruth as a proselyte. As he does regularly, Josephus also passes over the words of Ruth's "oath" in 1:17.

[914] MT (Ruth 2:1) בעז (Eng.: "Boaz"); LXX Βόος; Josephus Βοώζης (subsequently the name will appear under the form Βόαζος; see 5.327ff.). Josephus omits the characterization of Boaz found in 2:1, as "a mighty man/man of wealth" (which the Tg. interprets as "strong in the Law"). Tg. Ruth 1:6 further identifies Boaz with the judge Ibzan (see Judg 12:8-10) and accords him the epithet "the Pious."

[915] Rappaport (1930: 44, #186) points out that Ruth 2:1 does not mention an initial reception of the women by Boaz and that Josephus' own notice on the matter here seems to not cohere with his subsequent presentation (see 5.324// Ruth 2:5), where Boaz has to ask about Ruth's identity. In any case, the notice replaces the reference to Bethlehem's being "stirred" by the pair's appearance and the women's question "Is this Naomi?" in Ruth 1:19b.

[916] MT (Ruth 1:20) מרא (Eng.: "Mara"). LXX translates the word with Πικρά, while Josephus first transliterates with Μαρά and then translates with ὀδύνη ("pain").

[917] Josephus' explanation of the meaning of the 2 Hebrew names replaces Naomi's reproachful assertions concerning the Lord (Ruth 1:20b-21), which themselves echo her assertion about the hand of the Lord being

against her in 1:13b (also omitted by him).

[918] Ruth 1:22b specifies that Ruth and Naomi came to Bethlehem "at the beginning of the barley harvest."

[919] See Ruth 2:2-3a.

[920] In Ruth 2:3b Ruth "happens to come" to the field of Boaz. Josephus' adverb τυχαίως ("luckily") here introduces a word play with the noun εὐτυχία used by him in 5.323 in explaining the name "Naomi" as meaning "good luck."

[921] See Ruth 2:4a, 5. Josephus omits Boaz' initial exchange of greetings with the reapers (2:4b). On the seeming discrepancy between Boaz' "inquiry" here and Josephus' previous mention of his hospitable reception of Ruth and her mother-in-law in 5.323, see note to "hospitably" there.

[922] Ruth 2:6-7 cites in direct discourse the overseer's words concerning Ruth. Josephus inserts the indication as to how he knew about her.

[923] Josephus supplies this motivation for Boaz' subsequent gracious words to Ruth (Ruth 2:8-9).

[924] Boaz' prayer for "good things" (Greek: ἀγαθά) for Ruth echoes Naomi's earlier prayer that her daughters-in-law acquire "other good things" in 5.321.

[925] This is Josephus' version of Boaz' words to Ruth as cited in Ruth 2:8-9 (from which he omits, e.g., the former's rhetorical question of 2:9aβ: "have I not charged the young men not to molest you?"). Thereafter, he passes over the entire subsequent exchange between them (Ruth 2:10-13); in so doing he downplays the roles of both Ruth (who in his presentation has nothing to say in response to Boaz' opening words to her) and of God (compare the invocation of him in Boaz' blessing of 2:12) in the story.

[926] Josephus here combines (elements of) Ruth 2:14

too had kept for her some portions of the food with which the neighbors had abundantly provided her.[927] **327.** Routhe also related to her the things Boaz[928] had said to her.[929] When Naamis disclosed that he was a relative and might perhaps take care of them out of piety,[930] Routhe again went out on the following days to glean the ears of grain alongside Boaz' female attendants.[931]

Ruth sleeps beside Boaz

(9.3) 328. Not many days later Boaz came and, once the barley had been winnowed, slept on the threshing floor.[932] When she found out about this,[933] Naamis devised a plan to have Routhe lay down beside him—for he would be kind[934] towards them once he had intercourse with the girl—and sent the young woman to sleep at his feet.[935]

329. But she, since she thought it a holy [obligation] not to oppose anything her mother-in-law had directed,[936] went and, for the time being, was concealed from Boaz who had fallen into a deep sleep.[937] Waking up, however, in the middle of the night and noticing a human figure lying beside him, he inquired who she was.[938] **330.** When she told her name and asked that he, as her master, pardon her,[939] he kept silent for the moment.[940] At daybreak, however, before the servants began to

---

(Boaz offers Ruth "parched grain" to eat) and 2:17-18 (in the evening Ruth repairs to Naomi with the grain she had gleaned and her left-over food), passing over the intervening instructions (2:15-16) Boaz gives his young men about not impeding Ruth's activities.

[927] This notice on Naomi's solicitude for Ruth and the generosity of the townsfolk towards the former has no biblical counterpart. It accentuates the reciprocal concern of the women for each other; see Rappaport 1930: 44, #187, likewise taking the place of Naomi's opening words to the returned Ruth in Ruth 2:19.

[928] In what precedes Josephus' form of the name has been "Booz"; see note to this name at 5.323.

[929] In Ruth 2:19b Ruth first tells Naomi with whom she has worked, giving his name as "Boaz." Josephus leaves aside Naomi's initial response (2:20a) to her report with its "blessing" of the provident Lord.

[930] Josephus appends this statement of hope by Naomi regarding Boaz' "piety" (Greek: εὐσέβεια; compare the Targumic epithet "the Pious" for Boaz/Ibzan cited in note to "Booz" at 5.323) to her identification of him as a near relative in Ruth 2:20b. Thereafter, he omits the further exchange (2:21-22) between the women concerning where Ruth is to work henceforth.

[931] In Ruth 2:23a Ruth gleans with Boaz' women through both the barley and wheat harvests. Josephus omits the notice of 2:23b about Ruth's continuing to live with Naomi.

[932] Josephus turns into a narrative notice Naomi's words to Ruth concerning Boaz' activities as cited in Ruth 3:2b (Boaz is winnowing barley on the threshing floor that night) and 3:4a (once Boaz lies down...).

[933] This Josephan insertion addresses the source difficulty as to how Naomi, sitting at home, could have known what Boaz was/would be doing, as is presupposed by her words to Ruth in Ruth 3:1-4; cf.

previous note.

[934] Greek: χρήστος. On Josephus' use of this term as an epithet for many of the good characters in his writings, see Feldman 1998a: 251-53.

[935] Josephus abbreviates Naomi's series of instructions to Ruth regarding her dealings with Boaz at the threshing floor (Ruth 3:3-4). At the same time, he spells out more explicitly what Naomi has in mind with her instructions (sexual intercourse between the pair) and her hopes as to what this will lead to (Boaz' being "kind" to them).

[936] Josephus turns Ruth's response to Naomi ("All that you say I will do") of Ruth 3:5 into a notice on her motivation in acting as she now does. Thereby, he suggests that Ruth's subsequent (planned) fornication with Boaz was in no way her own idea/desire, but simply an ultimate display of her whole-hearted obedience to her mother-in-law—even in this. See Levison 1991: 37.

[937] Josephus abridges the notices of Ruth 3:6-7 concerning Ruth's carrying out Naomi's instructions regarding the sleeping Boaz. His statement about Ruth's initially being "concealed" from him draws on Naomi's relevant directive as cited in 3:3b. From both Naomi's instructions (3:4) and Ruth's execution of these (3:7) Josephus eliminates the sexually "loaded" phrase about her "uncovering" Boaz' "feet" (penis?).

[938] See Ruth 3:8-9a.

[939] Compare Ruth 3:9b, where, after identifying herself, Ruth more assertively tells Boaz "spread your skirt over your maidservant; for you are next of kin."

[940] By contrast, Boaz in Ruth 3:10-13 immediately responds to Ruth's reply (3:9) with an extended discourse concerning his intentions in her regard that itself picks up her designation of him as "next of kin" in her reply. Josephus has Boaz wait until the morning to make his announcement to Ruth about what he envis-

stir for their work, he woke her up and directed her to take what she could of the barley and go to her mother-in-law before anyone should see that she had slept there.[941] For in these matters it was prudent to guard against slander—all the more so since nothing had happened.[942] **331.** "But now," he stated, "as to the whole matter, this is how things are to be. The one who is a closer relative than I has to be asked whether he is willing for you to be his lawful wife; should he assent, you are to follow him. But if he refuses, I shall make you my wife according to law."[943]

(9.4) 332. Routhe disclosed these things to her mother-in-law,[944] and they found confidence in the hope of Boaz' taking care of them.[945] Since it now already midday,[946] he went down to the city and assembled the senate.[947] Having summoned Routhe,[948] he also called the relative. When he arrived,[949] he said: **333.** "Are you in possession of the inheritances of Abimelech and his sons?"[950] When the relative declared that this is what the laws granted him in virtue of his near kinship,[951] Boaz

Boaz enabled to marry Ruth

---

ages doing; see 5.331 and note to "law" there.

[941] Josephus utilizes elements of the biblical description of Boaz' initiatives once morning comes: his directive that Ruth's visit to the threshing floor not be known (Ruth 3:14b) and his giving her 6 measures of barley to take back with her (3:15a).

[942] Josephus appends a motivation for Boaz' injunction as related in Ruth 3:14b, i.e. concern about "slander"; elsewhere too, he often interjects references to (good) biblical characters as victims of slander, thereby establishing a parallelism between them and himself whom he represents as having been lied about by his fellow Jews to his Roman imperial patrons (see *Life* 424-425, 429). He likewise goes beyond the Bible in making explicit that, contrary to Naomi's instructions (see 5.328) and Ruth's own readiness to act on these (5.329), Boaz and Ruth did not in fact have premarital relations.

[943] In the Bible's presentation the corresponding words of Boaz (Ruth 3:12-13) are delivered by him already the night before (see note to "moment" at 5.330). In transferring his words to the following morning, Josephus likewise modifies their formulation. In MT Ruth 3:12-13 Boaz speaks of both the nearer relative and himself as "doing the part of the next of kin" (Hebrew: גאל) with Ruth. Josephus, who avoids this terminology throughout his version of Ruth, substitutes references to the relative's legally "marrying" her; see Levison 1991: 38-39.

[944] See Ruth 3:16b. Josephus omits both Naomi's opening question to Ruth about how she has fared (3:16a) and the latter's specific mention of the barley given her by Boaz (3:17; cf. 3:15).

[945] This editorial remark seems inspired by Naomi's confident affirmation in Ruth 3:18 that Boaz "will settle the matter today." It likewise echoes Naomi's reference to Boaz as someone who might "take care" of them in virtue of his "piety" in 5.327.

[946] The account of Boaz' preliminary initiatives given in Ruth 4:1-2 does not specify the time at which he undertakes these.

[947] Josephus here combines Ruth 4:1aα (Boaz goes up "to the gate") and 4:2a (he directs "ten men of the elders of the city" to sit down). Josephus' introduction of the term "senate" (Greek: γερουσία) here reflects his version of the law of levirate marriage (Deut 25:5-10) in *Ant.* 4.254-256, where (4.255) it is this body before which disputes—such as will occur in his rendition of Ruth 4 (see 5.335)—concerning this law are to be conducted.

[948] The biblical account does not mention Ruth's presence at the proceedings explicitly. Josephus brings her on the scene here since he will give her an active part in the legal formalities to follow (see 5.335).

[949] In Ruth 4:1aβbα the relative chances on the scene, whereupon Boaz directs him to take a seat.

[950] Josephus abbreviates and simplifies Boaz' words to the nearer relative in Ruth 4:3-4a, which raise legal (and other) difficulties. First, Boaz' statement in 4:3 about Naomi's "selling" Elimelech's property presupposes, contrary to Pentateuchal inheritance law (see Num 27:5-11), that Naomi would have received her late husband's property. Secondly, Naomi's possession of that property seems at variance with the previous depiction of her as one living in desperate poverty, dependent for her subsistence on whatever Ruth can glean in the fields of other people; see Levison 1991: 38. In view of these difficulties, Josephus has Boaz simply ask the next of kin whether he is currently "in possession of" the inheritances of Elimelech and his sons (the latter are not mentioned in Ruth 4:3).

[951] In Ruth 4:4b, the nearer relative, in response to Boaz' urging (4:3), states "I will redeem it [Naomi's property]." The "law(s)" to which the relative refers there is that of Lev 25:25 concerning the next of kin's obligation to "redeem" the property that his impover-

stated, "you ought then not only recall half of those laws, but do everything in accordance with them. For Maalon's wife has come here, so that if you wish to possess their fields, you must, according to the laws, marry [her]."[952]

334. He, however, ceded to Boaz both the inheritance and the woman as one who was himself also a relative of those who had died, saying that he already had a wife and children.[953]

335. After then taking the senate as a witness,[954] Boaz directed the woman to approach the other man, and, having removed his shoe in accordance with the law, to spit in his face.[955] When this was done,[956] Boaz married Routhe and a year later a male child was born to him.[957]

336. Naamis nursed him[958] and, in accordance with the counsel of the women, called him[959] Obed[960] as one who would provide support for her in her old age[961] (in

Boaz' descendants

---

ished relative has been forced to sell (Josephus does not reproduce this law in his version of Leviticus 25 in *Ant.* 3.281-285).

[952] Boaz' words to the nearer relative in Ruth 4:5 pose a further legal difficulty in that, whereas he there states that, as the prospective buyer of Elimelech's property, the nearer relative is also bound to "buy" Ruth "in order to restore the name of the dead to his inheritance," the law of Lev 25:25 itself (see note to "kinship" at 5.333) does not mention any such obligation for the property buyer. Accordingly, Josephus has Boaz now invoke a distinct law, i.e. that of levirate marriage (Deut 25:5-10= *Ant.* 4.254-256) that is also incumbent on the next of kin. See Levison 1991: 38-39.

[953] Compare Ruth 4:6a, where the relative's stated rationale for declining to redeem Elimelech's property is "lest I impair my own inheritance."

[954] In Ruth 4:9 Boaz calls "the elders and all the people" to witness only after the procedure with the sandal (4:7-8) has been completed. Josephus reverses this sequence, thus making the procedure one that is performed before the official witnesses as prescribed in Deut 25:9.

[955] Josephus here markedly modifies the presentation of Ruth 4:7-8, where there is reference to the nearer's relative's acting in accordance with a purportedly general "custom"—though one unknown to Pentateuchal law—whereby one entering into a agreement with another attests to that agreement by removing his sandal and handing this to the other party. Given the lack of legal basis for this custom, Josephus—who throughout his version of Ruth 4 has introduced repeated references to the "laws" that are (or should be) operative—substitutes another procedure involving a "sandal" (and one having to do with the precise case at issue, i.e. the relative's obligation to marry the widow Ruth), namely, the levirate marriage requirement of Deut 25:9 (= *Ant.* 4.256, whose wording Josephus fol-

lows closely here in 5.335), which prescribes that the spurned widow, in the presence of the elders, is to remove her recalcitrant brother-in-law's sandal and spit in his face. See Levison 1991: 39-40; and the notes on *Ant.* 4.254-256 in Feldman 2000 *ad loc.*

[956] This brief transitional phrase takes the place of the extended exchange (Ruth 4:9-12) between Boaz and the assembly concerning his intended marriage to Ruth.

[957] See Ruth 4:13. Josephus eliminates the source verse's mention of the Lord's "giving Ruth conception," while inserting an indication concerning the time of the child's birth that seems designed to underscore the fact that (so 5.330) "nothing happened" between Boaz and Ruth prior to their marriage; see Levison 1991: 37. One notes a similar concern on the part of Tg. Ruth in its handling of the nocturnal threshing floor scene (Ruth 3:6-14).

[958] See Ruth 4:16. Josephus omits the women's lengthy benediction of Naomi cited in 4:14-15 at this point, although he will incorporate an element of it into his explanation, later in the paragraph, of why the child is given the name he is.

[959] In Ruth 4:17 it is the neighborhood women who themselves name the son and who go on to make the curious statement, omitted by Josephus, that "a son has been born to Naomi," whereas, of course, the son is in fact Ruth's.

[960] MT (Ruth 4:17b) עובד (Eng.: "Obed"); LXX Ὠβήδ; Josephus Ὠβήδης.

[961] This phrase reflects the women's benediction of Naomi (Ruth 4:14-15) earlier passed over by Josephus; see 4:15a: "he shall be to you a restorer of life and a nourisher of your old age." It likewise echoes Josephus' previous references to Naomi's preoccupation with being "taken care" of by Boaz; see 5.327, 332. Josephus' one other use of the word γηροκομία ("old age") is in *Ant.* 7.183.

Hebrew "Obed" means "one who serves").[962] Of Obed Jesse[963] was born, and of him David[964] who reigned as king and all those to whom he left the leadership for twenty-one generations of men.[965] **337.** It was therefore necessary for me to relate these matters concerning Routhe.[966] In so doing, I wished to show the power of God, that it is easy for him to advance [anyone] to the splendid dignity and successes to which he elevated David, whose origins were from these kind [of people].[967]

Moral of Ruth story

(10.1) 338. The Hebrews' affairs declined again when, for the following reason, they made war on the Palestinoi.[968] Helei the high priest[969] had two sons, Hophni[970] and Phinees.[971] **339.** They were arrogant to people and impious towards the Deity,[972] refraining from no transgression.[973] They carried off some shares of the sacrifices as an honor [due them], while others they took for themselves by way of spoil.[974] They likewise outraged the women who came for worship, raping some, inflicting violence on others, and seducing still others with gifts.[975] Thus their lives differed in no way from that of a tyrant.[976]

Eli's degenerate sons

---

[962] Josephus supplies this etymology for the Hebrew name.

[963] MT (Ruth 4:17) יִשַׁי (Eng.: "Jesse"); LXX Ἰεσσαί; Josephus Ἰεσσαῖος.

[964] MT (Ruth 4:17) דּוִד (Eng.: "David"); LXX Δαυείδ; Josephus Δαβίδης.

[965] By means of this appendix to the mention of David with which Ruth 4:17 concludes, Josephus encompasses the whole series of kings Solomon through Zedekiah descended from David; he will repeat the same figure for the series in connection with the deposition of Zedekiah in *Ant.* 10.143. Conversely, Josephus omits the Book of Ruth's own appendix (4:18-22) enumerating the generations from Perez to David.

[966] With this notice Josephus responds to the question of why he chose to include the digressive story of Ruth, devoid as it is of noteworthy political/military events, at all: he did so given its account of the birth of a figure ("Obed") from whom a series of key personages of his history, namely David and his 21 royal descendants, with whom his subsequent history will be so largely concerned, originated. See Feldman 1998a: 193-94.

[967] On this concluding sentence of Josephus' version of Ruth as an echo of his opening statement concerning the purpose of *Antiquities* as a whole (*Ant.* 1.20), see Levison 1991: 31-33. As Feldman (1998a: 196) remarks, with its stress on God's "power" as exemplified in the story of Ruth, the sentence reads rather oddly given the fact that, up till this point, Josephus has systematically eliminated all the Book of Ruth's mentions of the Deity.

[968] This transitional phrase looks ahead to the story of the Israelites' defeat at the hands of the Philistines in 1 Samuel 4 (// 5.352-362), the background to which Josephus will now relate in dependence on 1 Samuel 1-3 (// 5.338b-351).

[969] Josephus introduced this figure as the ruler of the Israelites at the opening of 5.318, prior to his "digressive" reproduction of the Ruth story in 5.318b-337.

[970] MT (1 Sam 1:3) חׇפְנִי (Eng.: "Hophni"); LXX B Ὀφνεί; LXX L Ὀφνί; Josephus Ὀφνῆς.

[971] MT (1 Sam 1:3) פִּנְחׇס (Eng.: "Phineas"); LXX BL Φινεές; Josephus Φινεέσης. Josephus leaves aside the designation of the sons as "priests of the Lord" from 1:3b. He will reproduce the preceding material of 1 Samuel 1, i.e. vv. 1-3a, dealing with Elkanah and his family in 5.341ff., following his portrayal of Eli's renegade sons in 5.338-340(341), which he anticipates from 1 Sam 2:12-25.

[972] Josephus uses this same combination of epithets for the Sodomites in *Ant.* 1.194. In thus assimilating Eli's sons to those notorious evildoers, Josephus highlights their depravity.

[973] Josephus embellishes 1 Sam 2:12, which characterizes Eli's sons as "worthless men who had no regard for the Lord."

[974] Josephus here (like Pseudo-Philo in *Bib. Ant.* 52.1) summarizes the detailed description (1 Sam 2:13-17) of the way in which Hophni and Phineas used their "servants" to seize portions of the Israelites' sacrifices in spite of the protests made. He likewise highlights the enormity of the pair's misdeed by having them personally perform the sacrilegious theft.

[975] Josephus derives this additional offense—which Pseudo-Philo leaves unmentioned in *Bib. Ant.* 52— committed by the pair from 1 Sam 2:22b (which speaks of "the women who served [Tg.: came to pray] at the entrance to the tent of meeting"), passing over the intervening digressive material focussed on the boy Samuel of 2:18-21. To the source notice he adds the remark about the pair's giving "gifts" to those women whom they "seduced."

[976] On Josephus' use of "tyranny language," earlier applied by him to Abimelech's rule in 5.234, see note to "tyranny" at 5.234.

Fate of Eli's sons foretold

340. Therefore their father himself was disturbed by these things,[977] continually expecting that God's punishment would come upon them for their deeds,[978] while the crowd too was displeased.[979] When God revealed to Helei and to the prophet Samouel,[980] who was then a boy, the bad luck that would come upon his children,[981] Helei openly mourned for his sons.[982]

(10.2) 341. I wish, however, to speak first about this prophet and then tell of Helei's children and the disaster that happened to the whole Hebrew people.[983]

Elkanah (Alkan) and his wives

342. Alkan,[984] a Levite,[985] a man of moderate status in the inheritance of the citizens of Ephraim, and living in the city of Ramatha,[986] married two wives, Anna[987] and Phenanna.[988] He had children by the latter, although he continued to love the former,[989] who was childless.

343. Now this Alkan came with his wives to the city of Silo[990] to sacrifice[991] (for the tent of God had been set up there, as we said before).[992] At the feast that followed,[993] he divided up portions of meat among his wives and children.[994] Anna,

---

[977] This notice on Eli's sentiments regarding his sons' deeds takes the place of the account of his (unsuccessful) attempt to remonstrate with them in 1 Sam 2:23-25. Pseudo-Philo, after mentioning, at the start of *Bib. Ant.* 52.2, that the sons' behavior "displeased" Eli, goes on to elaborate upon his remonstrance with them (52.2-3= 1 Sam 2:23-25a) and their rejection of this (52.4= 2:25b).

[978] Eli's "expectation" regarding his sons' fate at this juncture is Josephus' addition.

[979] The Bible does not mention the people's reaction to the sons' doings. Josephus' notice on the point has a counterpart in *Bib. Ant.* 52.2.

[980] MT (1 Sam 1:20) שמואל (Eng.: "Samuel"); LXX BL Σαμουήλ; Josephus Σαμούηλος. On the Josephan Samuel see Feldman 1998: 490-508, who points out (ibid: 491) that whereas the Bible itself uses the term "prophet" of Samuel only once (1 Sam 3:20), Josephus employs the noun and the corresponding verb of him no less than 45 times. Pseudo-Philo likewise makes multiple applications of "prophet terminology" to Samuel in *Bib. Ant.* 50-65.

[981] Josephus here foreshadows the divine announcement (1 Sam 3:11-14) of the doom of Eli's house that Samuel transmits to Eli. Like Pseudo-Philo, he leaves aside the previous such announcement delivered by a nameless "man of God" to Eli personally in 1 Sam 2:27-36, given its similarity of content with 1 Sam 3:11-14, the climatic effect of which it accordingly greatly diminishes. Subsequently, however, he does evidence familiarity with the content also of 2:27-36; see notes to "single day" and "Eleazar" at 5.350.

[982] In 1 Sam 3:18b (as also in *Bib. Ant.* 53.13) Eli responds rather with words of submissive resignation to Samuel's informing him of the Lord's intended overthrow of his house.

[983] This parenthetical remark serves to introduce the remainder of *Antiquities* 5, in which Josephus will re-

late, in turn, the origins of Samuel (5.342-351) and Israel's defeat by the Philistines (5.352-362).

[984] MT (1 Sam 1:1) אלקנה (Eng.: "Elkanah"); LXX BL Ἐλκανά; Josephus Ἀλκάνης.

[985] Neither 1 Sam 1:1 nor Pseudo-Philo mentions Elkanah's Levitical status. Josephus derives the datum from 1 Chr 6:18-19 (Eng. 6:33-34). Contrary to his usual practice with significant biblical figures, Josephus (like Pseudo-Philo) does not reproduce the 4-member genealogy of Samuel's future father from 1:1.

[986] MT (1 Sam 1:1) הרמתים צופים (Eng.: "Ramathaim-zophim"); LXX Ἀρμαθάιμ; Josephus Ῥαμαθά (Niese; Marcus *ad loc.* and Schalit *s.v.* read Ἀρμαθά with SPLauE).

[987] MT (1 Sam 1:2) חנה (Eng.: "Hannah"); LXX BL Ἄννα; Josephus Ἄννα. On the figure of Hannah in Josephus and Pseudo-Philo, see Brown 1992: 140-73.

[988] MT (1 Sam 1:2) פננה (Eng.: "Peninnah"); LXX Φεννάνα; Josephus Φέναννα.

[989] Josephus' inserted reference to Elkanah's love for the childless Hannah anticipates the mention of this in 1 Sam 1:5.

[990] MT (1 Sam 1:3) שלה (Eng.: "Shiloh"); LXX Σηλώ; Josephus Σιλώ.

[991] Josephus omits the indication of 1 Sam 1:3a that Elkanah's sacrificial pilgrimage to Shiloh was an annual affair.

[992] Josephus' parenthetical explanation of Elkanah's going on pilgrimage specifically to Shiloh harks back to 5.68 (= Josh 18:1). In 1 Samuel 1-3 the reference is to the "temple" (1:9; 3:3) or "house" (1:24) of the Lord at Shiloh, i.e. a permanent, stationary structure, rather than the portable tent spoken of by Josephus (who, however, will subsequently make reference to the "temple" at Shiloh; see 5.347).

[993] 1 Sam 1:4 speaks simply "of the day when Elkanah sacrificed." *Bib. Ant.* 50.2 identifies the occasion as Passover. The "feast" mentioned by Josephus

however, beholding the other woman's children sitting around their mother, was reduced to tears and lamented her own childlessness and loneliness.[995]

344. Her grief outweighing her husband's consolation,[996] she rushed off to the tent of God[997] whom she begged to give her progeny and make her a mother.[998] She promised that she would consecrate her firstborn to the service of God and that he would make his manner of life[999] dissimilar to that of the common people.[1000]

Prayer of Hannah (Anna) and Eli's assurance

345. She spent much time in her prayers,[1001] and Helei the high priest—for he was sitting in front of the tent[1002]—directed her to go away, as though she were drunk.[1003] When, however, she stated that she was drinking water and that, in her grief over her lack of children, she was begging God,[1004] he appealed to her to be of good cheer, promising that God would award her children.[1005]

(10.3) 346. Full now of hope,[1006] she went to her husband[1007] and joyfully par-

Samuel's birth and dedication

---

here is the one in which portions of the "communion sacrifice" were eaten by the offerers (see Lev 7:15), following the burning up of the Lord's portion on the altar.

[994] Josephus omits 1 Sam 1:5b, which states that Elkanah gave the childless Hannah only one portion "because the Lord had closed her womb," since this might seem to conflict with his prior mention (see 5.343 // 1:5a) of Elkanah's "love" for Hannah. Pseudo-Philo completely omits the division of the sacrificial portions.

[995] In 1 Sam 1:6-7 Hannah's "weeping" (v. 7b) is provoked rather by the taunts of Peninnah (the content of which Pseudo-Philo, *Bib. Ant.* 50.1-2, develops at considerable length).

[996] Josephus here turns into a narrative allusion to Elkanah's attempted "consolation" of his wife the series of solicitous, direct-discourse questions that Elkanah addresses to Hannah in 1 Sam 1:8 (and which Pseudo-Philo reproduces, with various modifications, in *Bib. Ant.* 50.3). The biblical account does not explicitly mention the (non-) effect of Elkanah's words upon Hannah.

[997] 1 Sam 1:9b states merely that Hannah "rose"; Josephus' supplying of a destination for her movement (this echoing his mention of the "tent of God" at Shiloh in 5.343) has a parallel in *Bib. Ant.* 50.3, where Hannah rises and goes "to Shiloh to the house of the Lord."

[998] Josephus reduces Hannah's lengthy conditional appeal in 1 Sam 1:11a to its core element, i.e. the plea that God give her a son. He likewise leaves aside the mention of her "deep distress" and her "weeping bitterly" from 1:10. In Pseudo-Philo's version of her prayer (*Bib. Ant.* 50.4) Hannah invokes her past life of devotion as a reason why God should heed her appeal.

[999] This term (Greek: δίαιτα) serves to connect the future Samuel with Samson, of whom Josephus uses the term twice; see 5.285, 306; cf. note to "life" at 5.285.

[1000] Josephus here generalizes Hannah's 2nd, more

particular promise in 1 Sam 1:11b ("no razor shall touch his head" [+ and wine and strong drink he shall not drink," LXX BL]); he will, however, make allusion to its wording in 5.347; see note to "drink" at 5.347. From her initial promise he omits the explicit indication that the child's dedication will last his entire life.

[1001] 1 Sam 1:13a speaks rather of Hannah's praying "to herself," with only her lips moving. Pseudo-Philo (*Bib. Ant.* 50.5) explains this unusual mode of praying in terms of Hannah's concern that if she prayed aloud and her prayer went unanswered, this would lead to further mockery of her by Peninnah and blasphemy of God himself by any who might learn of the matter.

[1002] In 1 Sam 1:9b Eli is seated "on the seat before the doorpost of the temple of the Lord." Pseudo-Philo lacks an equivalent.

[1003] Compare 1 Sam 1:13b-14 (cf. *Bib. Ant.* 50.6), where Eli, witnessing Hannah's lips moving as she prays silently, and supposing her to be drunk, enjoins her to "put away your wine from you."

[1004] Josephus' version of Hannah's response to Eli (1 Sam 1:15-16) inserts an explicit mention of her childlessness as the reason for her prayer. In *Bib. Ant.* 50.6 Hannah picks up on Eli's calling her a "drunken woman" (see 1 Sam 1:14), affirming that she is "drunk with sorrow."

[1005] In 1 Sam 1:17 Eli tells Hannah to "go in peace" and expresses the prayerful wish that God will answer her appeal. Like Josephus, Pseudo-Philo (*Bib. Ant.* 50.6) has him more definitely promise Hannah the fulfillment of her prayer, having himself (so 50.7) been informed by God that a "prophet" was to be born to her. Neither writer reproduces Hannah's response ("let your maidservant find favor in your eyes") from 1 Sam 1:18a.

[1006] Hannah's "hope" is not mentioned by either the Bible or Pseudo-Philo (who, however, adds [*Bib. Ant.* 50.7] that "she told no one what she had prayed").

[1007] In 1 Sam 1:18bα Hannah simply "goes her way"; *Bib. Ant.* 50.7 has her coming "to her house."

took of food.[1008] When they returned to their ancestral town[1009] she became pregnant, and a child was born to them whom they called Samouel, as if to say "asked of God."[1010] They therefore went to sacrifice in return for the birth of the child,[1011] likewise bringing their tithes.[1012]

347. Recalling the prayer she had made about the child,[1013] the woman turned him over to Helei, dedicating him to God as one who would be a prophet.[1014] He let his hair grow freely and water was his drink.[1015] Samouel remained in the temple,[1016] being raised there,[1017] while Alkan had other sons by Anna, as well as three daughters.[1018]

Samuel called   **(10.4) 348.** When Samouel had already completed his twelfth year, he began
by God

[1008] Compare 1 Sam 1:18bβ: "... she ate, and her countenance was no longer sad." Pseudo-Philo does not mention Hannah's "eating" at this point; in *Bib. Ant.* 50.3 she eats already before making her prayer at the Shiloh sanctuary.

[1009] From the notice on the family's return to Ramah in 1 Sam 1:19a, Josephus omits the reference to their first worshipping before the Lord; Pseudo-Philo leaves aside the entire sequence. Josephus likewise passes over the statements about Elkanah "knowing" his wife and the Lord's "remembering" her of 1:19b.

[1010] According to 1 Sam 1:20a (and *Bib. Ant.* 51.1) Hannah (alone) named the child. Whereas Josephus follows 1:20b in its (problematic) derivation of the name "Samuel" from the word "ask," Pseudo-Philo (ibid.) avers that the name means "mighty" (Latin: *fortis*). In fact, the name "Samuel" means "God has *heard*."

[1011] Josephus here seems to conflate the family's double pilgrimage subsequent to the birth of Samuel spoken of in 1 Sam 1:21-24, the first without Hannah, the 2nd, following Samuel's weaning, including her. Pseudo-Philo too mentions only one pilgrimage after Samuel's birth; see *Bib. Ant.* 53.1.

[1012] Josephus draws his mention of the "tithes" from the reference to these in the LXX plus at the end of 1 Sam 1:21, which relates the initial pilgrimage of Elkanah's household following Samuel's birth. Conversely, he does not reproduce the list of victims subsequently brought by Hannah herself as cited, with variations among the witnesses, in 1 Sam 1:24a (MT has a total of 5, LXX 3). Pseudo-Philo too (*Bib. Ant.* 51.1) merely states that Hannah "brought gifts in her hands." Josephus further passes over the (self-evident) remark of 1:24b about Samuel's being "young" at this point; Pseudo-Philo (ibid.) avers rather that he was "very handsome" and that the "Lord was with him."

[1013] This allusion to the motivation for Hannah's subsequent action replaces the notice on the slaying of the sacrificial bull (see 1 Sam 1:24a) in 1:25a.

[1014] Josephus combines 1 Sam 1:25b (Hannah's presenting the child to Eli) and 1:28a (her declaration

about "lending" the child to the Lord for life), passing over her intervening words to the priest in 1:26-27 and the family's subsequent worship of God (1:28b). Pseudo-Philo (*Bib. Ant.* 51.2) gives a short version of Hannah's statement to which he appends a more extended response by Eli, speaking of the future role of her son.

[1015] This notice has no equivalent at this juncture in the sequence of the biblical account. It appears to represent a delayed use by Josephus of the longer text of Hannah's vow in LXX BL 1 Sam 1:11b (see note to "common people" at 5.344), where she promises that her asked-for son will observe both these practices (cf. too the plus at the end of 4QSamᵃ 1 Sam 1:22, according to which Samuel was a lifelong "Nazirite").

[1016] Greek ἱερός. Earlier (see 5.343, 345), Josephus spoke of the "tent of God" at Shiloh; see note to "before" at 5.343. Here, under the influence of 1 Sam 1:9; 3:3, he mentions the "temple" at the site that became the boy Samuel's home.

[1017] See 1 Sam 2:11b. Josephus thus passes over the entire "Song of Hannah" (1 Sam 2:1-10) in accord with his tendency to either omit entirely or drastically reduce such biblical poetic pieces (cf. his non-reproduction of the Song of Deborah, Judges 5, in his version of the Deborah-Barak story in 5.200-209). By contrast, Pseudo-Philo expatiates on Hannah's Song in *Bib. Ant.* 51.3-5, to which he further appends an extra-biblical account of the people's acclamation of the youthful Samuel as their prophet in 51.6. Josephus likewise dispenses with the notice on Elkanah's return home of 1 Sam 2:11a.

[1018] See 1 Sam 2:21a, where, as a result of the Lord's "visiting" Hannah, she has 3 additional sons, plus *2* daughters; Pseudo-Philo does not mention these younger siblings of Samuel's. In directly juxtaposing the content of 1 Sam 2:11b and 21a, Josephus passes over the segments 2:12-17 (on Eli's depraved sons, already used by him in 5.339) and 2:18-20 (Samuel's clothing and Eli's benediction of Elkanah and Hannah that he simply drops).

prophesying.[1019] It was then, while he slept,[1020] that God called him by name.[1021] He, however, thinking that he had been summoned by the high priest, went to him.[1022] When the high priest stated that he had not called him, God did this three times.[1023]

349. Then Helei, having been enlightened,[1024] said to him: "Now Samouel, I have kept silent as I did before; God is the one calling you; indicate to him: 'I am available'."[1025] So when he heard God talking again, he requested him to speak in oracles, for he would not delay regarding the service that he desired.[1026]

350. And God said: "since you are available,[1027] learn of the misfortune—beyond the words and belief of those involved—that will happen to the Israelites:[1028] Helei's sons will die on a single day[1029] and the high priesthood will be transferred to the house of Eleazar.[1030] For Helei has—in a way that was not to their advantage—given preference to his sons over my cult."[1031]

God's an-nouncements to Samuel

[1019] This is Josephus' heading, employing the "prophetic language" characteristic of his account of Samuel (see note to "people" at 5.341), to the story of 1 Samuel 3 concerning the Lord's initial communication with Samuel. It takes the place of the complex of preliminary notices in 3:1-3a (Samuel's ministering before the Lord, the rarity of divine communications at this time, Eli's blindness, and "the lamp of God" having not yet been extinguished). The Bible does not specify Samuel's age at the time of the revelation related in 1 Samuel 3; *Bib. Ant.* 53.1 states that he was 8 years old.

[1020] 1 Sam 3:3b specifies that Samuel was sleeping "in the temple of the Lord, where the ark of God was" (MT; LXX lacks the words "of the Lord," while 4QSam^a has only "in the temple"; cf. "in the temple of the Lord," *Bib. Ant.* 53.2).

[1021] In 1 Sam 3:4a the Lord calls Samuel's name twice, to which he immediately responds "here I am." Pseudo-Philo (*Bib. Ant.* 53.2) prefaces God's initial call with a lengthy divine reflection wherein God decides not to identify himself immediately to the boy Samuel, lest he be overwhelmed by this.

[1022] Josephus provides a motivation for Samuel's going to Eli (1 Sam 3:4b), as does also Pseudo-Philo (see *Bib. Ant.* 53.3: when God speaks, Samuel "recognizes this as the voice of Eli").

[1023] This is Josephus' compressed version of 1 Sam 3:6-8a, where a 2nd and 3rd call by God and Samuel's resultant going to Eli are related. Pseudo-Philo (*Bib. Ant.* 53.5-6) expatiates on the 2nd call sequence (3:6-7), while in response to the Lord's 3rd call, he has Samuel respond to him, rather than going to Eli yet again (as in 3:8a).

[1024] Greek: διαυγασθείς. This participial form is Josephus' only use of the verb διαυγάζω ("to be enlightened"). The codices SPE read the participle διυπνισθείς, a form of the verb διυπνίζω ("to awaken"), another *hapax* in Josephus.

[1025] See 1 Sam 3:8b-9a. Josephus, in contrast to the

Bible, has Eli aver, this time too (see 5.348) that he has not called Samuel. In Pseudo-Philo, where Samuel addresses God directly after his 3rd call to him (see note to "times" at 5.348), there is no mention of this 3rd intervention by Eli.

[1026] Josephus expatiates on Samuel's response to God's 4th and final call in 1 Sam 3:10b, where he simply declares "speak, for thy servant hears."

[1027] This inserted opening phrase of God's response picks up on Eli's instructing Samuel to make known his "availability" to God in 5.349.

[1028] Compare the opening, figuratively-worded divine announcement in 1 Sam 3:11: "Behold, I am about to do a thing in Israel, at which the two ears of every one that hears it will tingle."

[1029] In 1 Sam 3:12-13 God speaks in general terms of his intention of punishing the house of Eli. Josephus draws his more specific announcement of the joint death of Eli's sons from the word of the anonymous "man of God" (earlier passed over by him; see note to "children" at 5.340) in 2:34 (foreshadowed by him already in 5.340). Pseudo-Philo's expanded version of God's word to Samuel in *Bib. Ant.* 53.8-10 likewise contains reminiscences of the man of God's announcement of 1 Sam 2:27-36, which he too does not reproduce as such.

[1030] This announcement has no counterpart in the divine discourse of 1 Sam 3:11-14 itself. Here again, Josephus appears to be drawing on the word of the man of God in 1 Sam 2:27-36; see, in particular, v. 35 where, after the prediction of the death of Eli's sons (v. 34), one reads: "I will raise up for myself a faithful priest...." The reference to Eleazar's line succeeding that of Eli here likewise serves to prepare Josephus' appendix on the high priestly succession (5.361-362) to his account of the Elides' demise (= 1 Samuel 4) in 5.352-360.

[1031] Josephus accentuates Eli's personal, active responsibility for the fate of his house vis-à-vis 1 Sam 3:13, where God charges him merely with failure to "restrain" his sons' blasphemy against him, doing so per-

Samuel as- sumes prophet- ic role

351. Helei strongly adjured the prophet to tell him, for the latter did not wish to grieve him by speaking;[1032] he then expected the loss of his sons with still greater assurance.[1033] Samouel's reputation grew greater, all that he prophesied being seen to be true.[1034]

Israel's initial defeat

(11.1) 352. At this same time the Palestinoi were campaigning against the Israelites;[1035] they pitched camp at the city of Ampheka.[1036] Within a short time the Israelites were confronting them,[1037] and on the following day battle was joined. The Palestinoi were victorious and killed about 4,000 of the Hebrews; the rest they pursued to their camp.[1038]

Ark brought to Israelite camp

(11.2) 353. Anxious about a total [disaster],[1039] the Hebrews[1040] sent to direct the senate and the high priest to bring the ark of God in order that, with it present, their battle-lines might overcome the enemy.[1041] [They did this], not knowing that he who had pronounced the sentence of misfortune upon them was still greater than the ark, seeing that it was through him that it too existed.[1042]

---

haps under the influence of the question of the man of God to Eli in 1 Sam 2:29: "... why honor your sons above me....?" From the divine word to Samuel of 3:11-14, Josephus leaves aside God's concluding sworn declaration (v. 14) that "the iniquity of Eli's house shall not be expiated by sacrifice or offering for ever." He likewise passes over the appended notices (3:15a) on Samuel's... "laying until morning" and then "opening the doors of the house of the Lord." In contrast to both the Bible and Josephus, Pseudo-Philo (*Bib. Ant.* 53.11) does mention a verbal response by Samuel to God's word to him in which the former bewails his having to be the bearer of so harsh a message.

[1032] Josephus makes Samuel's reluctance (see 1 Sam 3:15b) the reason for Eli's adjuring him (3:17) to tell him what he has heard from God, while leaving aside both Eli's summoning of Samuel (3:16) and the wording of Eli's oath with which he calls on Samuel to disclose the revelation (v. 17b). By contrast, Pseudo-Philo (*Bib. Ant.* 53.12-13) expatiates on the Samuel-Eli exchange of 3:16-18.

[1033] This notice, picking up on the reference to Eli's earlier "expectation" of God's punishment coming upon his sons' deeds (5.340), replaces the content of 1 Sam 3:18, where Samuel tells Eli everything and the latter responds with words of resignation concerning the Lord's intentions.

[1034] This summary conclusion to the story of the Lord's first revelation to Samuel takes the place of the complex of notices on Samuel's subsequent career and reputation in 1 Sam 3:19-4:1a (to which Pseudo-Philo also has no equivalent). With its use of the verb προφητεύω ("to prophesy") it forms an inclusion, framing the intervening story of Samuel's call (5.348b-350) with the occurrence of the same verb in 5.348a.

[1035] In 1 Sam 4:1b it is the Israelites who initiate the war (as they are said to do in 5.338, to which 5.352

alludes back). Pseudo-Philo (*Bib. Ant.* 54.1) agrees with Josephus on the matter. On Josephus' version of 1 Samuel 4 in 5.352-362, see Begg 1996a.

[1036] MT (1 Sam 4:1) אֲפֵק (Eng.: "Aphek"); LXX BL Ἀφέκ; Josephus Ἀμφεκᾶ (this is the reading adopted by Niese and Marcus; Schalit *s.v.* prefers that of P, i.e. Ἀμφέκα).

[1037] Like Pseudo-Philo (see *Bib. Ant.* 54.1), Josephus leaves aside the source mention (1 Sam 4:1b) of the Israelites' camping place, i.e. "Ebenezer" (which LXX BL transliterate).

[1038] Josephus inserts mention of the Philistine "pursuit" of the surviving Israelites into the summary battle account of 1 Sam 4:2 (at the opening of 4:3 the defeated Israelites simply "come to the camp"). Pseudo-Philo (*Bib. Ant.* 54.1) leaves aside the casualty figures given by both the Bible and Josephus.

[1039] Josephus inserts this motivation for the Israelites' sending for the ark as related in 1 Sam 4:3.

[1040] 1 Sam 4:3 specifies that it is "the elders of Israel" who take the following initiative; like Josephus, *Bib. Ant.* 54.1 ascribes it to the entire people. Josephus' designation of the Philistines' opponents as "Hebrews" here (and in 5.353) may be inspired by the Philistines' own use of that designation for their adversaries in 1 Sam 4:6, 9.

[1041] In 1 Sam 4:3 (and *Bib. Ant.* 54.1) the Israelite elders propose to simply "bring" the ark from Shiloh on their own; Josephus' rendering has them recognize the need to act through the proper political and religious authorities. In *Bib. Ant.* 54.1 the Israelites express confidence in the efficacy of the ark's presence due to its containing the "testimonies" given by the Lord at Horeb.

[1042] This ominous note of foreshadowing, with its allusion back to the divine words of doom cited in 5.340, 350, is appended by Josephus to the notice of

354. So the ark arrived along with the sons of the high priest whose father had instructed them that, if the ark were taken, they should not come into his presence if they wished to remain alive.[1043] (Phinees was already exercising the high priesthood, which his father had ceded to him on account of his advanced age.)[1044]

355. The Hebrews grew very confident that, due to the arrival of the ark, they would prove superior to their enemies[1045] who were themselves dismayed, anxious over the presence of the ark among the Israelites.[1046] **356.** The outcome, however, did not correspond to the expectations of either side.[1047] Rather, when battle was joined, the Palestinoi won the victory that the Hebrews hoped for, while the latter suffered the defeat the former feared, realizing now that they had put their confidence in the ark in vain.[1048] For, immediately upon their engaging the enemy, they were defeated and lost about 30,000 men; among them there also fell the sons of the high priest, while the ark was carried off by the enemy.[1049]

Israel defeated again

(11.3) 357. When word of the defeat and the capture of the ark was brought to Silo—for a certain Benjamite youth who had been present for what had happened came to them as a messenger—the whole city was filled with mourning.[1050]

Word brought to Shiloh

358. Helei the high priest—for he was sitting at one of the two gates on a lofty throne[1051]—hearing the wailing and supposing that some disaster had occurred involving his sons,[1052] summoned the young man. When he knew of the result of the battle,[1053] he was not unduly distressed about his sons and disaster inflicted on the army, since what was to occur had been made know in advance and predicted by

Death of Eli

---

1 Sam 4:4a on the bringing of the ark to the Israelite camp. Compare *Bib. Ant.* 54.2, where, upon the arrival of the ark in the camp, the Lord responds by himself pronouncing doom on the sinful Israelites.

[1043] Josephus appends his remark on Eli's warning his sons to the mention of their accompanying the ark in 1 Sam 4:4b. The remark serves to underscore Eli's own attachment to the ark and so helps to account for his subsequent collapse upon hearing of its loss; see 5.359.

[1044] This parenthetical remark has no biblical counterpart; it serves to the answer the question of why Eli himself did not accompany the ark. Rabbinic tradition also speaks of Phineas replacing his father already during the latter's lifetime; see Ginzberg 1928: 221, n. 27.

[1045] This reference to the Israelites' state of mind upon the ark's arrival replaces the mention of the "mighty shout" raised by them in 1 Sam 4:5.

[1046] Josephus reduces to this brief allusion the extended reflections concerning the ark attributed to the Philistines in 1 Sam 4:6-9. Pseudo-Philo has no equivalent to the entire sequence of 1 Sam 4:5-9 on the 2 sides' reactions to the arrival of the ark. Josephus' shift from the designation "Hebrews" (see 5.352) to "Israelites" for the people within this paragraph might reflect the allusion to "all Israel" crying out in 1 Sam 4:5.

[1047] This inserted foreshadowing echoes that appended by Josephus to his rendering of 1 Sam 4:4-5 at the end of 5.353; see note to "existed" at 5.353.

[1048] Josephus prefaces the summary notice of 1 Sam 4:10a ("so the Philistines fought and Israel was defeated") with this foreshadowing remark concerning the reversal of the 2 sides' expectations as mentioned by him at the opening of 5.356.

[1049] See 1 Sam 4:10b-11. As he did with those of the first one, Pseudo-Philo omits the Israelite casualty figures for the 2nd battle. On the other hand, he identifies (*Bib. Ant.* 54.3) the giant Goliath as the Philistine who both seizes the ark and kills Eli's 2 sons.

[1050] Josephus combines into a continuous sequence the data of 1 Sam 4:12 (the Benjamite's race to Shiloh, omitting the source mention of his rent clothes and earth-covered head) and 13b (his report in Shiloh and the effect of this). Pseudo-Philo identifies (*Bib. Ant.* 54.4) the Benjamite messenger as the future King Saul (whom he earlier, 54.3, mentions as having held the ark along with Eli's sons).

[1051] Josephus here makes delayed use of the reference to Eli (1 Sam 4:13a) which, in the source "interrupts" the account of the messenger's activities (4:12, 13b). His specification that Eli was sitting "at one of the two gates" reflects the LXX plus ("beside the gate") in 4:13a (to which Pseudo-Philo has no equivalent).

[1052] Josephus adds a reference to Eli's "inference" to the mention of his hearing the uproar in Shiloh of 1 Sam 4:14a.

[1053] In 1 Sam 4:14b (and *Bib. Ant.* 54.4) the messenger approaches Eli on his own, once he hears the latter asking about the reason for the outcry in the city.

God (for one is most affected by terrible things that occur unexpectedly).[1054]

359. When he heard, however, that the ark too had been captured by the enemy, he was appalled at this unexpected news reaching his ears;[1055] tumbling down from his throne, he died.[1056] He had lived ninety-eight years in all,[1057] for forty of which he exercised the rulership.[1058]

Birth of Icha-bod

(11.4) 360. On that day there also died the wife of his son Phinees who could not bear to live in the face of her husband's bad luck.[1059] Being pregnant when it was announced to her what her husband had suffered, she gave birth to a seven-month old child[1060] who survived[1061] and whom they named[1062] Iachob,[1063] a name meaning "lack of glory," on account of the disgrace that had happened to the army.[1064]

The high priestly succession

(11.5) 361. Helei was the first the house of Ithamar, the family of Aaron's other son, to hold office.[1065] For at first the house of Eleazar exercised the high priesthood, a son receiving the honor from his father. Eleazar himself turned it over to his son Phinees.[1066] **362.** After him his son Abiezer[1067] assumed the honor that he left

---

[1054] Josephus turns the messenger's summary report of the Israelites' defeat and the death of Eli's sons (1 Sam 4:17) into an elaborate psychological description of Eli's response to this that itself harks back to the divine announcements made to Eli regarding their fate as cited in 5.340 and 350.

[1055] The Bible does not report Eli's emotional reaction to his hearing that the ark too had been lost (see 1 Sam 4:17). Josephus' insertion on the matter has a counterpart in *Bib. Ant.* 54.5 that speaks of him as "greatly despairing" when told of the ark's loss.

[1056] Josephus (like Pseudo-Philo, *Bib. Ant.* 54.5) leaves aside the additional details concerning Eli's fall and death given in 1 Sam 4:18a, i.e. the breaking of his neck by the fall, and his being an old man and "heavy."

[1057] Josephus here makes use of the parenthetical reference, already alluded to by him in 5.354, to Eli's age found in 1 Sam 4:15 (while omitting its further mention of Eli's blindness). His figure for the priest's age corresponds to that cited in MT and LXX L, whereas LXX B reads "90."

[1058] Josephus' figure for the duration of Eli's rulership (a topic introduced by him in 5.318) agrees with MT 4:18b, whereas LXX BL give him a 20-year judgeship. Pseudo-Philo mentions neither Eli's age at death nor his length of tenure.

[1059] Josephus supplies this "reason" for the fact of the woman's death as alluded to in 1 Sam 4:20 ("and about the time of her death..."). The reference to Phineas' "bad luck" (Greek δυστυχία) here echoes the mention of the "bad luck" that is to come upon Eli's sons according to the divine announcement cited in 5.340, this underscoring the fulfillment of that announcement.

[1060] See 1 Sam 4:19b, to which Josephus adds the specification concerning the child's age at birth. He leaves aside the attending women's word to the mother

about the birth of her son and her own lack of response to this of 1 Sam 4:20; Pseudo-Philo does reproduce the first part of this sequence in *Bib. Ant.* 54.6.

[1061] 1 Samuel 4 does not explicitly mention the newborn child's surviving his mother.

[1062] In 1 Sam 4:21-22 it is the dying mother who names the child. Josephus' modification reflects the fact that he has already mentioned her having died.

[1063] MT (1 Sam 4:21) אי־כבוד (Eng.: "Ichabod"); LXX B Οὐαὶ Βαρχαβώθ; LXX L Οὐαὶ Βαρ᾿Ιωχαβὴλ; Josephus ᾿Ιαχώβης (this is the reading adopted by Niese; Marcus and Schalit read rather ᾿Ιωχάβης).

[1064] The duplicate explanation of the name "Ichabod" given in 1 Sam 4:21-22 (see also *Bib. Ant.* 54.6) connects the departed "glory" (Hebrew: כבוד) to which the name alludes rather with the capture of the ark (and the death of Eli and Phineas, 4:21). On the name and the explanations of it given in the various biblical witnesses and in Josephus, see Grillet and Lestienne 1997: 169-70. Josephus will now round off his version of 1 Samuel 4 with an appendix, prepared by his earlier insertion within the divine announcement cited in 5.350 (see note to "Eleazar" at 5.350), concerning the high priestly succession.

[1065] The Bible itself nowhere represents Eli as a descendant of Aaron's son Ithamar (the younger of the 2 who survived their father, Nadab and Ahihu having predeceased him; see Lev 10:2// *Ant.* 3.209). Josephus' linkage of the 2 figures is, however, paralleled in Rabbinic (e.g., *S. Eli. Rab.* (11) 12, p. 57) and Samaritan tradition; see Begg 1996a: 181, n. 94.

[1066] This notice echoes 5.119, where Josephus, in line with the plus of LXX Josh 24:33, mentions Eleazar's bequeathing the high priesthood to Phineas.

[1067] Josephus derives the name of Phineas' successor from 1 Chr 5:30 (Eng. 6:4): MT אבישוע (Eng.: "Abishua"); LXX B ᾿Αβεισού; LXX L ᾿Αβιούδ; Josephus

behind to his son named Bokki[1068] from whom his son Ozi[1069] received it. After him Helei, of whom we have been speaking just now, held the high priesthood,[1070] as did his line until the times of Solomon's kingship. Then, Eleazar's descendants recovered it once again.[1071]

Ἀβιεζέρης. According to Pseudo-Philo (*Bib. Ant.* 48.2; 50.3), Phineas was succeeded as high priest directly by Eli; see further Begg 1996a: 182, n. 101.

[1068] MT (1 Chr 5:31) בֻּקִּי (Eng.: "Bukki"); LXX B Βωέ; LXX L Βοκχεί; Josephus Βόκκι.

[1069] MT (1 Chr 5:32) אֻזִּי (Eng.: "Uzzi"); LXX B Ὀζεί; L'Οζί; Josephus Ὄζις. In *Ant.* 8.12 Josephus gives a list of the first 3 successors of Phineas (i.e. Iesous-Bokias-Jotham) that differs notably, not only from that cited in 1 Chr 5:30-31 (Eng. 6:4-5), but also from his own list (Abiezer-Bokki-Ozi) here in 5.362.

[1070] According to 1 Chr 5:32 (Eng. 6:6) "Uzzi" was succeeded by his son "Zerahiah," while "Eli" does not appear in the continuation of the high priestly list. As mentioned in the note to "Abiezer" at 5.362, Pseudo-Philo makes Eli the direct successor of Phineas himself.

[1071] Josephus here looks ahead to *Ant.* 8.10-12, where, in connection with Solomon's dismissal of David's chief priest Abiathar and his replacement by Zadok (see 1 Kgs 2:26-27, 35b) he will pause, picking up on the language of 5.361-362, to trace the high priestly succession from the time of the Ithamaride Eli down to its recovery for Eleazar's descendants by Zadok. The priest Josephus' interest in the topic of priestly genealogy is further reflected in *Ant.* 10.151-153; 20.224-251; and *Apion* 1.30-36, 53.

BOOK SIX

(1.1) 1. Having taken captive the ark of their enemies, as we mentioned just previously,[1] the Palestinoi brought it to the city of Azotus.[2] There they placed it beside their god—who was called Dagon—as a kind of trophy.[3]

Ark humiliates Dagon

2. But when on the next day at daybreak all entered the sanctuary[4] to pay homage to their god,[5] they found him doing this very thing to the ark.[6] For he was lying in front of it, having fallen down from the pedestal on which he used to stand.[7] They picked him up and placed him again on his pedestal, troubled by what had happened.[8] But when they had often visited Dagon's house and found him in a similar pose, lying prostrate in homage to the ark,[9] they fell into terrible embarrassment and sorrow.[10]

3. Finally, the Deity struck both the city of the Azotians and their region with destruction and disease.[11] For they died of dysentery, a severe suffering and one bringing quick disintegration even before the soul was separated from the body by a welcome death.[12] For they vomited up their insides that had been consumed and completely destroyed by the disease.[13] A swarm of mice likewise came up over the

Ashdod (Azotus) afflicted

---

[1] Here at the beginning of a new book of the *Antiquities*, Josephus introduces an explicit cross-reference to the concluding event of Book 5 (see 5.356), i.e. the Philistine capture of the ark. On Josephus' version of 1 Samuel 5, the story of the ark's devastating stay in Philistia in 6.1-6, see Begg 1996b.

[2] Josephus uses the same name ("Azotus") for the ark's first stop in Philistia as does LXX 1 Sam 5:1; MT reads "Ashdod" (*Bib. Ant.* 55.3 leaves the site of Dagon's temple unidentified). He omits the source mention of the starting point of the ark's transport (i.e. "Ebenezer,") just as earlier—see *Ant.* 5.352—he left aside the reference of 1 Sam 4:1b to this site as Israel's pre-battle camping place.

[3] Josephus elaborates 1 Sam 5:2 with an identification of "Dagon" and mention of the ark's "trophy" status. The former item has an equivalent in *Bib. Ant.* 55.3.

[4] Josephus' explicit mention of the Philistines' "entry" into the sanctuary of Dagon here corresponds to the plus of LXX 1 Sam 5:2.

[5] Josephus inserts this indication concerning the purpose of the Philistines' coming to Dagon's sanctuary; in *Bib. Ant.* 55.3 they come to "inquire of their fate from" Dagon.

[6] This inserted phrase spells out the import of the following description of Dagon's "posture" vis-à-vis the ark; it also introduces an ironic contrast with the immediately preceding reference to the Philistines' intentions regarding Dagon: they come to pay homage to a deity who is himself paying homage to the ark.

[7] See 1 Sam 5:3a; Josephus derives his appended

reference to Dagon's "pedestal" from 5:3b, which speaks of Dagon being restored to his "place."

[8] See 1 Sam 5:3b; Josephus appends the reference to the Philistines' emotional response to their god's discomfiture.

[9] Josephus here modifies 1 Sam 5:4, where, on their 2nd visit to Dagon's temple, the Philistines discover his head and hands lying on the threshold, separate from his "trunk." He likewise leaves aside the appended etiological notice of 5:5 on the custom of visitors' stepping over the temple's "threshold." *Bib. Ant.* 55.3 conflates Dagon's 2 "falls" as described in 1 Sam 5:3, 4 into one, and has the Philistines respond to their seeing him both fallen and dismembered on their first visit by "crucifying" Dagon's priests. Thereafter, in a way analogous to Josephus' presentation, it refers to the Philistines' finding things "as on the day before" when they visit the temple the following day.

[10] Josephus' statement on the effect of the Philistines' seeing Dagon paying homage to the ark on their follow-up visits echoes (and intensifies) the language used by him at the opening of 6.2 to describe their initial visit.

[11] Josephus avoids the anthropomorphic language of 1 Sam 5:6a according to which "the hand (Tg.: stroke) of the Lord was heavy upon the people of Ashdod."

[12] Greek: εὐθανάτως; this adverb occurs only here in Josephus. On the Hellenistic anthropology (man as a composite of "body" and "soul") presupposed here, see Schlatter 1932: 17-18.

[13] Josephus here dramatizes the brief (and unclear)

country from beneath;[14] they ravaged it, leaving neither plants nor crops un-
touched.[15]

Ark sent to
Askalon

4. Overwhelmed by these calamities and unable to withstand their misfortunes, the
Azotians realized that these were emanating from the ark against them and that their
victory and the ark's capture had not been for their good.[16] They therefore sent to
the Askalonites and requested them to receive the ark from themselves.[17]

5. The latter were not displeased at the Azotians' plea and agreed to do them this
favor.[18] Having taken the ark, however, they fell into the same horrors. For the ark
carried the sufferings of the Azotians along with itself to those who received it from

Ark makes the
rounds of Phi-
listine cities

them.[19] So likewise the Askalonites sent it away from themselves to others.[20] 6. It
did not, however, remain among those people; for, compelled by their sufferings,
they dismissed it to the neighboring cities. In this way the ark made the rounds of
the five cities of the Palestinoi, demanding tribute, as it were, from each of those to
which it came, namely the things that they suffered because of it.[21] (1.2) 7. Unable

Philistines de-
liberate about
ark

to bear their calamities any longer, those who had been sorely tried became a lesson

---

notice of 1 Sam 5:6b concerning the nature of the inhabitants' affliction. MT (*ketiv*) speaks of the Lord's
smiting them with עפלים ("tumors"?, "hemorrhoids"?),
while LXX employs the term ἕδραί whose meaning is
also disputed (in addition to "tumors/hemorrhoids," the
renderings "buttocks" and "residences" have been proposed; see Begg 1996b: 389, and nn. 34-35). In his earlier reference to the Philistines' affliction in his speech
to the defenders of Jerusalem, as cited by him in *War*
5.385, Josephus uses different language in describing
this.

[14] Josephus' reference to "mice" (or "rats") here reflects the plus of LXX (cf. also OL) 1 Sam 5:6 about
the vermin's "going up into the land," after having
"swarmed in ships."

[15] In the plus of LXX 1 Sam 5:6 the mice infesta-
tion leads rather to a "mortal panic in the city."

[16] See 1 Sam 5:7, where the afflicted inhabitants
declare that the ark can no longer remain with them,
given the weight of the Lord's "hand" (see 5:6) upon
them.

[17] As with his "Azotus" for MT's "Ashdod" (see
note to "Azotus" at 6.1), Josephus here reflects the LXX
("Askalon") as opposed to the MT ("Ekron") name for
the ark's new destination as cited in 1 Sam 5:10. At the
same time he conflates the biblical account in which
the ark is dispatched—without any prior request to
the inhabitants as in Josephus—to "Ekron/Askalon"
(5:10a), only after having been first sent to Gath as the
result of a consultation between the Azotians and the
Philistine "lords" (5:8-9; like Josephus, Pseudo-Philo
makes no mention of the ark's intermediate stop in
Gath). This consultation, in turn, is the first of 3 such
deliberations concerning the disposition of the ark featured in the Bible (see 5:8, 11; 6:2-8). Josephus (as
does Pseudo-Philo) limits himself to a single, climactic

consultation, corresponding to one related in 1 Sam
6:2-8 (see 6.8-12).

[18] In 1 Sam 5:10a the ark is simply sent to "Ekron/
Askalon" without the inhabitants either being asked to
receive it (compare 6.4) or giving their assent to this.
(In fact, in 5:10b, the inhabitants respond to the ark's
arrival with the cry that the ark has been sent to them
in order that the Lord might "slay" them.) In *Bib. Ant.*
55.4 the Philistines gather in Ekron without there being any prior mention of the ark's coming there, as happens in the Bible and Josephus.

[19] Cf. the notices of 1 Sam 5:11b-12 on the baleful
effects of the ark's presence in Ekron/Askalon and the
inhabitants' response to this.

[20] As in the case of the Azotians (see 6.4), Josephus
has the Askalonites act on their own initiative in ridding themselves of the ark. By contrast, in 1 Sam 5:11a
the latter appeal to the lords of the Philistines to send
the ark away and let it "return to its place." The Bible
does not relate an explicit response to this appeal on
the part of the "lords" such that it remains unclear
whether, in fact, the ark did depart Ekron/Askalon prior
to its ultimate return to Israel. Josephus' formulation
here in 6.5 (and its sequel in 6.6) clarifies the matter.

[21] This paragraph has no precise equivalent in the
biblical account itself, although it might be viewed as
Josephus' "filling in" of the summary notice of 1 Sam
6:1 about the ark's spending 7 months in the Philistine
country. In specifying that the ark made its way to each
of the 5 (major) Philistine cities, Josephus may have
been inspired by the subsequent account in 1 Samuel
6, where the ark is accompanied by 2 sets of 5 golden
objects, these representing (vv. 17-18) the 5 Philistine
cities, instead of merely the 3 cities that the ark is explicitly said to have visited in 1 Samuel 5. Josephus
will mention the 5 cities by name in 6.8.

to those who heard of these [calamities] not to admit the ark to themselves at such a cost and consequence. From this point on, they were searching for a device and a means of deliverance from it.[22]

8. The rulers of the five cities, Gitta, Akkaron, Askalon, as well as Gaza and Azotos, came together and considered what they ought to do.[23] Their first thought[24] was to send the ark away to its own people, since God was exacting extreme vengeance for it and therefore horrors were accompanying it, entering their cities along with it.[25]

9. There were some, however, who said not to do this nor be deceived as to the cause of their calamities by attributing these to the ark, for it had no such force and strength. For if God were protecting it, it would not have fallen into human hands. They urged them to endure patiently and with resignation what had happened, reasoning that the cause was simply nature that, at times, generates regular changes of these sorts in bodies, the earth, plants, and everything that is present on earth.[26]

10. However, the counsel of men who in the past had been credited with outstanding sagacity and intelligence and who now especially seemed to be saying what accorded with the present situation was victorious over the just-mentioned plans.[27] These said to neither send the ark away nor retain it.[28] Rather, let five golden images[29] for each city[30] be dedicated to God as a thank-offering,[31] because he had

---

[22] This description of the "pan-Philistine" reaction to the ark's continued presence has no biblical equivalent. It functions as a "lead-in" to the following account of the climactic conference concerning the disposition of the ark in 6.8-12 (= 1 Sam 6:2-8). On Josephus' version of 1 Samuel 6, see Begg 1998a.

[23] In 1 Sam 6:2 those who assume the leading position in the final consultation concerning the ark are the Philistine "priests and diviners" (MT; LXX and 4QSam^a add one or more additional similar category). Josephus, with an eye to the 2 earlier biblical consultations (see 5:8, 11), previously passed over by him, assigns the dominant role rather to the Philistine "lords" themselves. Neither 5:8 nor 5:11 mentions the cities which these lords head; Josephus derives his enumeration of their cities from the listing in (LXX) 6:17 (where the 5 golden tumors represent the 5 cities), while also varying its sequence.

[24] In 1 Sam 6:2-8 there is a double question-and-answer exchange between the Philistines and their priests and diviners about whether the ark should be sent back to Israel. In *Bib. Ant.* 55.4-6 2 sets of Philistine "wise men" offer complementary proposals for determining whether or not the ark has been the cause of their troubles. Josephus turns the proceedings into a 3-way discussion among the Philistine "rulers" as to what should be done with the ark and the reasons for/ intended outcome of their respective proposals. On this device of "trichotomy" and Josephus' recurrent introduction of it for purposes of dramatic effect, see Begg 1998a: 18 and nn. 16-17, and cf. the previous instance in *Ant.* 5.169-171 (the question of how wives for the

remaining 200 Benjamites are to be obtained).

[25] The motivation cited by the first group of speakers for their proposal here has a counterpart in *Bib. Ant.* 55.4, where the Philistines, assembled at Ekron, ask rhetorically concerning their present plight: "Is it not because of the Lord?"

[26] Josephus' 2nd group of speakers seem to advocate an Epicurean-like outlook according to which the gods do not concern themselves with human affairs. On Josephus' references to/critique of Epicureanism, mostly notably in *Ant.* 10.278-290, see Van Unnik 1973; Feldman 1998: 192, 273-274, 640.

[27] This introductory characterization of the 3rd group of speakers serves to highlight their proposal as the one that deserves the acceptance it will obtain.

[28] With this opening affirmation the 3rd group appears to set itself in opposition to the proposals of both previous groups. As will emerge, however, their suggestion is, in fact, a further refinement of the first group's suggestion that the ark be returned.

[29] At this point Josephus finally rejoins the biblical presentation, i.e. 1 Sam 6:4, after going his own way in what precedes. In the biblical verse the first set of golden objects whose production is advocated by the Philistine priests and diviners (6:2) is designated by the same terms used for that with which the Lord is said to afflict the Philistines in 1 Sam 5:6, i.e. עפלים (MT)/ ἕδραι (LXX B); see note to "disease" at 6.3. Josephus derives his designation ("images") for these items from the more expansive phrase used of them in LXX L 6:4 and MT 6:5, i.e. "images of your tumors" (?).

[30] Josephus' wording here seems to reflect that of 1

cared for their safety and retained them in life when they were being forced out of this by their sufferings that they could no longer sustain.[32] Let them also make the same number of golden mice,[33] similar to those that had devastated them and destroyed their country.[34] **11.** Then placing these things in a box and putting [this] on top of the ark, let them prepare a new cart for it.[35] Let cows who had just calved[36] be harnessed before the cart and their calves be shut up and retained so that they [the calves] would not become impediments to their mothers by following them; out of longing for them they [the mothers] would make the journey more quickly.[37] Once they had driven them out, carrying the ark to a three-road junction, they should leave them, allowing them to go off on whichever of the roads they wished.[38] **12.** If they [the cows] proceeded by that of the Hebrews and went up to their country, they should conclude that the ark was the cause of their calamities.[39] "If, however, they take another turn, we should pursue after it," they stated, "having learned that it does not have this strength."[40]

Ark sent back to Israel

(1.3) **13.** [The hearers] judged these things well said and immediately endorsed the plan by their actions.[41] Having made the items mentioned above, they went ahead of the cart to the three-road junction, where they left it and drew back.[42] But when the cows, as though someone were leading them, proceeded by the direct road,[43]

Sam 6:17-18 (the objects are offered for the Philistine cities) rather than 6:4 (where they are rather to be presented "according to the number of the Philistine lords").

[31] In MT 1 Sam 6:3-4a (as also in 6:8) the objects to be made are designated as a "guilt offering" (אשׁם; compare LXX: "offering for the plague") that will cause the people "to be healed" (MT 6:3; + "and atonement shall be made for you," LXX).

[32] This motivation for the proposed "thank offering" has no biblical equivalent.

[33] In specifying the number (i.e. 5) of the mice in this way, Josephus goes together with MT 1 Sam 6:4 (and LXX L 1 Sam 6:5), whereas LXX B 6:5 leaves the figure indeterminate.

[34] Compare 1 Sam 6:5a "... your mice that ravage the land." Josephus omits the speakers' appended theological exhortations of 1 Sam 6:5b-6 with their call to the Philistines to give glory to God in hopes that he might "lighten his hand" upon them (v. 5b), rather than hardening their hearts like the Egyptians of old who were nonetheless compelled to release the Israelites (v. 6).

[35] Josephus here rearranges the sequence of 1 Sam 6:7-8a, where the cart (v. 7aα) is mentioned prior to the ark, the "box" (which is itself to be placed "beside" the ark in the cart), and the latter's contents, i.e. the golden objects (v. 8a).

[36] In MT 1 Sam 6:7 (and *Bib. Ant.* 55.6) the cows are called "milch/milking," whereas LXX, followed by Josephus, refers to them as ones which have "calved for the first time." Like LXX too, Josephus has no equivalent to the further MT requirement concerning the

cows, i.e. they are never to have borne a yoke.

[37] Josephus supplies a rationale for the proposed procedure with the cows and calves as laid down in 1 Sam 6:7b.

[38] See 1 Sam 6:8b, into which Josephus inserts the specification about the ark's being brought to the intersection of 3 roads; this insertion has an equivalent in the proposal of the 2nd group of Philistine wise men in *Bib. Ant.* 55.7.

[39] See 1 Sam 6:9a, from which Josephus eliminates the more specific destination mentioned ("to Bethshemesh"); in *Bib. Ant.* 55.7 the speakers refer to the ark's proceeding "straight to Judaea."

[40] In 1 Sam 6:9b the speakers aver that the ark's taking the alternative route would show that "chance" was responsible for the Philistines' afflictions. In *Bib. Ant.* 55.7 the lesson is rather that they have been smitten for neglecting their own gods. The proposal about "pursuing" the ark, should the 2nd hypothetical possibility materialize, is unique to Josephus.

[41] This transitional phrase, underscoring the persuasiveness of the 3rd group of speakers' words, has no biblical counterpart.

[42] These 2 items relating to the execution of the proposed plan take the place of the various preliminary measures carried out in accordance with the priests' and diviners' injunctions given in 1 Sam 6:7-8a, as cited in 6:10-11. Also Pseudo-Philo (*Bib. Ant.* 55.8) introduces explicit mention of the ark's being conducted to "the head of the three roads."

[43] In 1 Sam 6:12 the cows proceed directly to Bethshemesh (see 6:9), lowing as they go and not deviating "either to the right or left." Pseudo-Philo (*Bib. Ant.*

the rulers of the Palestinoi kept following, wishing to learn where they would stop and to whom they would go.[44]

14. Now there is a certain village of the tribe of Iouda called Bethes.[45] The cows arrived there and, a great and beautiful plain[46] receiving them on their journey, they ceased going further, stopping the cart there.[47] This was a sight for those in the village and they were overjoyed. Because it was summertime, they were all engaged in bringing in the harvest of the crops in the fields.[48] When they saw the ark, they were overcome with delight;[49] putting aside their manual labor, they immediately ran to the cart.[50] **15.** They took down the ark[51] and the vessel that contained the images and the mice and placed these on a certain rock that was in the plain.[52] They sacrificed splendidly to God, holding a sacrificial feast and offering up the cart and the cows as a holocaust.[53] When the rulers of the Palestinoi saw these things, they turned back.[54]

(1.4) 16. However, God's wrath and anger[55] castigated[56] seventy persons[57] of the village of Bethes. These were not worthy to touch the ark for they were not priests; as they approached it, he struck and killed them.[58] The villagers wept over those

Ark's arrival at Beth-shemesh (Bethes)

God punishes Bethshemeshites

55.8) specifies that the cows proceeded by the "right-hand" road.

[44] In 1 Sam 6:12b the Philistine "lords" follow the ark as far as "the border of Beth-shemesh." Josephus supplies a rationale for their action. In *Bib. Ant.* 55.9, the Philistines, once they have seen the ark proceeding towards Judaea, "return the ark to Shiloh with timbrels, pipes and dances."

[45] MT (1 Sam 6:12, etc.) בית השמש (Eng.: "Beth-shemesh"); LXX Βαιθσάμυς; Josephus Βήθης (Schlatter *s.v.* reads Βήθσιμις, while Schalit *s.v.*, with reference to Lat's "Bethsamis," proposes Βηθσάμη). Josephus perhaps derives his localization of the site from Josh 15:10, where "Beth-shemesh" figures among the boundary points for Judah's territory.

[46] Josephus embellishes 1 Sam 6:13's simple mention of the "valley" in which Beth-shemesh is situated.

[47] See 1 Sam 6:14, whose reference to "the field of Joshua" as the cows' precise stopping point Josephus omits.

[48] 1 Sam 6:13a specifies that the occasion was the wheat harvest.

[49] See 1 Sam 6:13bβ: "they rejoiced to see it."

[50] This notice, effecting a transition between the villagers' joyful seeing of the ark (6:13b) and their subsequent initiatives regarding it (6:14-15), has no biblical counterpart.

[51] Josephus rearranges the sequence of 1 Sam 6:14-15, in which the taking down of the ark and the box (6:15a) is preceded and followed by references to the villagers' sacrificing (6:14b, 15b). In his presentation, the sacrifices come after the removal of the ark from the cart as a climax to its reception in Beth-shemesh.

[52] In 1 Sam 6:15a "Levites" appear, seemingly "out of nowhere," to remove the ark and the box with its

"golden figures" and place these on the stone. Josephus has the villagers themselves, in their enthusiasm, perform these operations. He adds mention of the "mice" as a content of the box in light of the reference to these in 6.10, while deriving his localization of the rock from 6:14bα.

[53] Josephus here combines the Bible's duplicate mention of the villagers' "sacrifice" (1 Sam 6:14b, 15b). His inserted reference to their "holding a sacrificial feast" is perhaps inspired by the biblical mention of the "feasts" held in connection with subsequent movements of the ark; see Begg 1998a: 27, n. 80.

[54] 1 Sam 6:16b specifies that they returned "that day to Ekron." Josephus omits the parenthesis-like complex of appended notices of 6:17-18 (the representative function of the golden tumors [vv. 17-18a] and the continued presence of the stone in the field of Joshua at Beth-shemesh [v. 18b; cf. 6:14a, also omitted by him]).

[55] Greek ὀργὴ καὶ χόλος. Josephus uses this combination once elsewhere, i.e. in *Ant.* 9.288, where the worship of their native deities by those resettled in Samaria evokes God's "wrath and anger" towards them.

[56] Josephus here follows the MT reading at the opening of 1 Sam 6:19 ("he [God] slew some of the men of Beth-shemesh..."), while prefacing this with a reference to the divine emotions ("wrath and anger") that led to the villagers' punishment. LXX ("The sons of Jechonias were displeased with the men of Baith-samus...") reads quite differently at the start of 6:19.

[57] All textual witnesses to 1 Sam 6:19 read an additional, very high casualty figure, i.e. "50,000 men" to which Josephus has no equivalent.

[58] According to 1 Sam 6:19a the Bethshemites' offense was their "seeing" the ark (Tg. elaborates with a

Ark moved to Kiriath-jearim

who suffered these things. They made mourning for them as was appropriate for a God-sent calamity, and each one sorrowed for his own [relatives].[59] **17.** Declaring themselves unworthy to have the ark remain among them,[60] they sent to the Hebrews' general assembly[61] and disclosed that the ark had been given back by the Palestinoi.[62] Once they knew this, they carried it off to Kariathiareim,[63] a city near the village of Bethes.[64] **18.** Since a certain Aminadab,[65] a Levite by ancestry,[66] who had a reputation for justice and devotion,[67] lived there, they brought the ark into his house[68] as to a place suitable for God, in which a just[69] man resided. His sons looked after the ark and were in charge of its maintenance[70] for twenty years.[71] For throughout this time it remained in Kariathiareim, after spending four months among the Palestinoi.[72]

Israelites' turn to God; Samuel's address

(2.1) 19. The entire people, during that time in which the city of the Kariathiarimites held the ark, turned to God with prayers and sacrifices and manifested much devotion and readiness towards him.[73] The prophet Samouel saw their eager-

---

reference to the villagers' "rejoicing" to see the exposed ark). Josephus' alternative "rationale" for their punishment assimilates the incident to another episode involving the ark as he will present this, i.e. God's slaying the non-priest Uzzah for reaching out to steady the ark; see *Ant.* 7.81 (cf. 2 Sam 6:7// 1 Chr 13:10), cf. Rappaport 1930: 45, #190a.

[59] See 1 Sam 6:19b. This is Josephus' only use of the adjective θεόπεμπτος ("God-sent").

[60] This transitional phrase echoes Josephus' (likewise inserted) characterization of the villagers as "not worthy to touch the ark..." in 6.16.

[61] Greek: τὸ κοινόν. Josephus frequently uses this term to designate the Jerusalem governing body during the revolt in the *Life* and *War*; see Mason 2001: 48-49, n. 346.

[62] This sending by the villagers takes the place of the emotionally-charged questions they ask themselves in 1 Sam 6:20 ("Who is able to stand before Lord....? And to whom shall he go up away from us?"). Josephus' substitution underscores the pan-Israelite significance of the ark and its placement.

[63] MT (1 Sam 6:21) קרית־יערים (Eng.: "Kiriath-jearim"); LXX BL and Josephus Καριαθιαρείμ.

[64] In 1 Sam 6:21-7:1aα the inhabitants of Kiriath-jearim remove the ark to their town when called upon to do so by the people of Beth-shemesh. Josephus makes the move a pan-Israelite initiative, just as he appends a localization for Kiriath-jearim itself (compare his localization of "Bethes" in 6.15).

[65] MT (1 Sam 7:1a) אבינדב (Eng.: "Abinadab"); LXX BL Ἀμιναδάβ; Josephus Ἀμινάδαβος. Josephus' form of the name thus corresponds to that of LXX against MT.

[66] 1 Sam 7:1a itself does not speak of "Abinadab" (MT; LXX "Aminadab") as a Levite. Josephus likely derives his Levitical status from 1 Chr 15:10-11, where

a Levite named "Amminadab" figures among those whom David commissions to carry the ark to Jerusalem. Compare his similar awarding of Levitical status to "Elkanah" in *Ant.* 5.342.

[67] Greek: δικαιοσύνη καὶ θρησκεία. This combination recurs in *Ant.* 8.120, where Solomon prays that his people may continue to exhibit these qualities.

[68] Josephus omits the specification of 1 Sam 7:1a that the "house" to which the ark was brought was "on the hill."

[69] Greek: δίκαιος. On Josephus' overall use of the terms δικαιοσύνη ("justice") and δίκαιος ("just") of 6.18 and their word-field, see Feldman 1998: 113-26; Mason 1991: 142-49, 213-21. Josephus' inserted indications concerning Abinadab's character provide an explanation as to why the ark was brought precisely to his house.

[70] 1 Sam 7:1b speaks of the consecration of Abinadab's one son Eleazar as custodian of the ark. Josephus' generalized reference to the former's "sons" functioning in that capacity may have in view the fact that subsequently (see 2 Sam 6:3// 1 Chr 13:7) there is reference, not to the "Eleazar" of 1 Sam 7:1b, but to 2 other sons of Abinadab, i.e. Uzzah and Ahio, who attend the ark as its transport to Jerusalem begins.

[71] Josephus derives this indication concerning the duration of the ark's stay at Abinadab's house from 1 Sam 7:2a.

[72] This chronological indication represents Josephus' delayed use of 1 Sam 6:1, where, however, the ark's stay in Philistia lasts 7 months.

[73] Josephus here seems to base himself on, while also greatly elaborating, the LXX reading(s) in 1 Sam 7:2b (B: the people "looked after the Lord"; L: they "turned to the Lord in peace"). Compare MT ("they lamented after the Lord"). The word "devotion" (Greek: θρησκεία) was used of Abinadab in 6.18; his devotion

ness as an opportune occasion to speak of freedom and the good things it entails while they were in this state. He used words that he supposed would especially win over and persuade their minds.[74]

20. "Men," he thus said, "for whom even now the Palestinoi are a burdensome enemy, seeing that God is beginning to be benevolent and friendly,[75] you ought not merely long for freedom, but should also do that by which it may come to you.[76] Nor should you wish to be delivered from your masters even while you go on doing those things by which they remain such.[77] **21.** Rather, be just;[78] expel vileness from your souls, and having purged them,[79] direct your minds entirely towards the Deity and persevere in honoring him.[80] For to do these things will bring you good things: deliverance from slavery and victory over the enemy. These things are possible to attain neither by weapons, nor by bodily prowess, nor by a crowd of fellow-fighters—for God does not promise to award those [benefits] to these things—but for those who are good and just.[81] I myself am the guarantor of these promises of his."[82]

22. When he said these things, the crowd applauded, gratified by his exhortation, and pledged to make themselves pleasing to God.[83] Samouel then assembled them at a certain city called Masphate[84] (this means "that which is visible" in the Hebrew

Israelite response

---

has now become that of the people as a whole. On Josephus' version of 1 Samuel 7, see Begg 1997d.

[74] Josephus expatiates on the simple reintroduction of Samuel in 1 Sam 7:3aα ("Then Samuel said to all the house of Israel..."), appending a motivation for his speaking at this particular moment and underscoring the care with which he chooses his words.

[75] Greek: εὐμενὴς... καὶ φίλος. Josephus employs the first of these adjectives some 40 times for God; on it see Schlatter 1910: 62; 1932: 30, and cf. the cognate noun εὐμενεία ("benevolence") used of God in *Ant.* 5.213. On φίλος as an epithet for God in Josephus, see note to "friend" at 5.116.

[76] Samuel's summons to the Israelites to act for the sake of "freedom" here recalls the similar exhortation of the angel, urging Gideon to "exert himself for freedom" in *Ant.* 5.214.

[77] This extended opening word of Samuel, with its focus on Israel's recovering its lost "freedom," has no counterpart in the address attributed to him in 1 Sam 7:3.

[78] Greek: δίκαιοι. This term echoes the use of the words "justice" and "just" of Abinadab in 6.18.

[79] Josephus here generalizes the more specific call made by Samuel in 1 Sam 7:3 that Israel "put away its foreign gods and the Astaroth" (MT; LXX BL "the groves" [τὰ ἄλση]), likely out of deference to the sensibilities of his Gentile readers; see Feldman 1998: 304.

[80] Compare 1 Sam 7:3bα: "direct your heart to the Lord, and serve him only."

[81] Josephus elaborates on the conditional promise

with which Samuel concludes his address in 1 Sam 7:3: "... and he [God] will deliver you out of the hand of the Philistines." The expansion echoes Josephus' own discourse to the defenders of Jerusalem as cited in *War* 5.376-401, where he avers that, throughout Jewish history, the people's own military efforts have proved unavailing, while their preservation and deliverance has been effected directly by God in those times when the people showed themselves worthy of such divine aid. Here, as often, Josephus thus intimates a parallel between himself and a great biblical figure, in this case Samuel. In addition, this shared message of himself and Samuel serves to highlight the implied warning to Josephus' contemporaries about the futility of further military initiatives against Roman domination on their part, even as it holds out the hope that, should Jews of his own time endeavor to "be good and just," God could and would free them from the Romans, as he had freed their ancestors; see Begg 1997d: 203, n. 30; 216.

[82] This concluding affirmation has no equivalent in 1 Sam 7:3. It focusses attention on the person of Samuel himself, a recurrent feature in Josephus' rewriting of 1 Samuel 7 overall.

[83] Josephus modifies the biblical notice (1 Sam 7:4) on the execution of Samuel's directives by the people, accentuating his effectiveness as an orator in line with his remarks introducing the prophet's speech in 6.19; see Feldman 1998: 496-97.

[84] MT (1 Sam 7:5) המצפתה (Eng.: "Mizpah"); LXX B Μασσηφάθ; LXX L Μασσηφά; Josephus Μασφατή.

language).[85] Drawing water there, they offered a libation to God;[86] they fasted the whole day and turned to prayer.[87]

23. It was not, however, concealed from the Palestinoi that they were assembled there. Once they learned of their mustering, they set out with a great armed force in the hope of falling upon the unexpectant and unprepared Hebrews.[88] **24.** This dismayed the latter, reducing them to confusion and anxiety. Running to Samouel,[89] they stated that their souls were downcast due to fear and their earlier defeat. It was because of these things that they had remained inactive, "so as not to arouse the enemy's force. When you, however, brought us up for prayers and sacrifices and oaths, the enemy campaigned against us, who are defenseless and unarmed.[90] We therefore have no other hope of safety; it is only through you and the God whom you beg that it will be granted us to escape the Palestinoi."[91]

25. He, for his part, exhorted them to take courage and announced that God would help them.[92] He took a suckling lamb and sacrificed it on behalf of the mob,[93] appealing to God to extend his right hand over them in their battle with the Palestinoi and not be indifferent to their being defeated a second time.[94] God was receptive to his prayers;[95] accepting his sacrifice with the mind of a benevolent ally,[96] he indicated victory and conquest for them.[97]

26. While the sacrifice was still on God's altar and not yet completely consumed by the sacred flame, the enemy force went forward from its camp and drew up for

---

[85] Josephus' explanation of the site's name takes the place of Samuel's promise to pray for the people in 1 Sam 7:5b. The explanation itself involves a rather loose rendering of the Hebrew place name (see previous note) that would more literally translate as "the watchtower."

[86] Like MT 1 Sam 7:6, Josephus lacks an equivalent to the LXX BL plus specifying that the water of the libation was poured "on the ground."

[87] This reference to the people's all-day prayer replaces the confession attributed to them in 1 Sam 7:6aβ ("We have sinned against the Lord"); cf. the mention of their "turning to God with prayers and sacrifices" in 6.19. Josephus leaves aside the seemingly extraneous notice about Samuel's "judging" Israel at Mizpah of 7:6b.

[88] Josephus expatiates on the summary reference to the Philistines' hearing of the Mizpah assembly and advancing against Israel of 1 Sam 7:7a. In so doing, he accentuates the magnitude of the Philistine threat (and so, ultimately, the greatness of God's thwarting this).

[89] Josephus highlights the Israelites' consternation in face of the Philistine threat in comparison with the simple mention of their being "afraid of" the Philistines in 1 Sam 7:7b.

[90] These opening words of the people, highlighting their feelings of helplessness before the Philistines, are unparalleled in 1 Sam 7:8, which begins directly with their appeal that Samuel not desist from interceding with God for them. The "former defeat" to which the Israelites allude here is the battle(s) of Aphek (see 1 Samuel 4 = *Ant.* 5.352-362).

[91] In this rendition of the people's appeal for Samuel's continued intercession of 1 Sam 7:8, Josephus, remarkably, has them mention Samuel prior to God himself as the source of their hoped-for deliverance.

[92] Josephus supplies this verbal response by Samuel to the people's appeal to him of 1 Sam 7:8.

[93] See LXX BL 1 Sam 7:9a, which, apparently misunderstanding MT's reference to Samuel's sacrificing the lamb as "a whole [Hebrew: כליל] offering," speak of his sacrificing it "with the whole people." Josephus' reformulation of the LXX reading underscores Samuel's preeminence as one who acts for, rather than with, the people.

[94] Josephus elaborates on the mention of Samuel's "crying to the Lord for Israel" of 1 Sam 7:9bα, spelling out what the prophet is asking God to do for the people. Once again (see 6.24), he inserts an allusion to the earlier Aphek debacle. His introduction of the biblical anthropomorphic expression "(God's) right hand" (see, e.g., Exod 15:6) here is noteworthy, given his tendency to avoid such anthropomorphisms.

[95] Josephus' wording here corresponds to that of LXX BL 1 Sam 7:9bβ ("and the Lord heeded him"), whereas MT speaks of the Lord's "answering him."

[96] Greek: εὐμενὴς καὶ σύμμαχος. Josephus uses this adjectival combination also in *Ant.* 4.296; 9.259 (both times of God, as here in 6.25). The initial term of the combination appears as a qualification of God in 6.20.

[97] Josephus supplies this content to the summary allusion to the Lord's "answering" (MT)/ "heeding" (LXX) Samuel's plea in 1 Sam 7:9bβ.

battle.[98] It did so in hope of victory, [supposing that] the Judeans[99] to be caught in a difficult situation, not having weapons nor having lined up for battle there. They, however, encountered things of which, had someone predicted them, they would not easily have been convinced.[100] **27.** For God first disconcerted them by an earthquake, agitating the ground, making it sway and become unsteady for them, such that as it tottered their steps staggered and as it gaped open they sank down into its various chasms. Then making a loud noise with thunder, flashing round with fiery lightning as if to burn their faces, and striking the weapons from their hands, he turned them, defenseless, to flight.[101]

28. Samouel[102] now set out with the crowd and, after butchering many, pursued them to a certain place called "Korraea."[103] There he raised up a stone[104] as a landmark of the victory and the enemy's flight,[105] and named it "the Strong One"[106] as a symbol of the strength given them by God against the enemy.[107]

(2.3) 29. After that blow, they [the Palestinoi] no longer campaigned against the Israelites;[108] in their anxiety and memory of what had happened, they kept quiet. The Palestinoi's old self-confidence towards the Hebrews became the latter's after this victory.[109] **30.** Samouel campaigned against them; he did away with many, and their pride was completely humbled.[110] He also took away the territory they had

---

[98] Josephus dramatizes the notice of 1 Sam 7:10a about the Philistines advancing while Samuel offers the holocaust: they come on the scene at the climactic moment of the sacrificial process.

[99] Greek: οἱ Ἰουδαῖοι (alternative translation: the Jews). This designation takes the place of the term "Hebrews" used for the people in 6.17, 23. On Josephus' use of the designation in his writings overall, see Harvey 1996: 47-61; Spilsbury 1998: 37-42.

[100] Josephus supplies these remarks on the Philistines' state of mind and the reversal of their expectations; they are reminiscent of his comments in *Ant.* 5.355 on the expectations of the Hebrews and Philistines prior to the (2nd) battle of Aphek, both of which get reversed.

[101] Josephus notably elaborates and dramatizes the 3-part notice on God's dealings with the Philistines of 1 Sam 7:10b (he thunders against them and throws them into confusion; they are routed before Israel). His presentation underscores the ironic reversal in which the Israelites earlier complain of being "defenseless" (Greek: γυμνός) before the Philistines (6.24), who, however, are themselves left "defenseless" by God (6.27).

[102] 1 Sam 7:11 does not mention Samuel's involvement in the pursuit of the Philistines. Once again, Josephus accentuates his leadership role, this time as a general.

[103] According to 1 Sam 7:11 the pursuit extended "as far as below Bethcar" (MT בֵּית כַּר; LXX Βαιθχόρ). Josephus' site-name (Κορραίων) reflects the 2nd component of the biblical one.

[104] Josephus thus has Samuel erect the stone at the point where the pursuit of the Philistines terminates. According to 1 Sam 7:12 he erected it rather between Mizpah and a 2nd site that is variously denominated in MT (הַשֵּׁן, "the tooth") and LXX (τῆς παλαιᾶς, "the old").

[105] This indication concerning the purpose of the erected stone is peculiar to Josephus.

[106] In MT 1 Sam 7:12b Samuel names the stone "Ebenezer," i.e. "stone of help" (LXX both transliterates and translates this Hebrew form). The Bible mentions "Ebenezer" twice previously as the site of Israel's camp in its battle with the Philistines (1 Sam 4:1; 5:1), neither of which mentions are reproduced by Josephus. Marcus (*ad loc.*) suggests that Josephus might have read the *'ezer* ("help") component of the Hebrew name "Eben*ezer*" as *'oz* ("strength").

[107] Josephus' explanation of the stone's name picks up on his rendering of that name itself; see "the Strong One" at 6.28 and compare 1 Sam 7:12bβ ("for he said, 'hitherto the Lord has helped us'.")

[108] This is Josephus' 3rd distinct designation for his people in the course of his version of 1 Samuel 7; see "Hebrews" (6.23) and "Judeans" (6.26).

[109] Josephus elaborates on the summary statements of 1 Sam 7:13a ("the Philistines were subdued [MT; LXX the Lord humbled the Philistines] and did not again enter the territory of Israel"). His expansion underscores the overwhelming effect of the Philistines' defeat upon them and the role-reversal—foreshadowed in 6.26—that took place between them and Israel as a result.

[110] This notice, featuring the military initiative of Samuel (compare 6.28), replaces the anthropomorphic

previously cut off from the Judeans whom they had defeated in battle,[111] this extending from the boundaries of Gitta to the city of Akkaron.[112] At that time there was also friendship between the Israelites and the remnant of the Chananaians.[113]

Samuel the judge

(3.1) 31. The prophet Samouel reordered the people and assigned to them[114] a city to which he directed them to come together for judgment concerning their differences with one another.[115] He himself, setting out annually to these cities,[116] gave judgment for them, and over a long period of time, established much in the way of a sound legal system.[117]

Samuel's reprobate sons

(3.2) 32. Then, being weighed down by old age and impeded from performing his normal activities,[118] he turned over the rule and oversight of the nation to his sons.[119] Of these, the older was named Iulus,[120] while the younger's name was Ebia.[121] He ordered the one to sit as judge in the city of Bethel, the other in Bersoube,[122] dividing up the people who would be under the jurisdiction of each.[123]

33. They themselves, however, were an example and a proof that some children

---

reference to God's "hand being against the Philistines" throughout Samuel's lifetime of 1 Sam 7:13b.

[111] 1 Sam 7:14a makes no mention of Samuel's role in the recovery of the Israelite cities, attributing this rather to God (see the "divine passive," "[the cities] were restored [to Israel]" of v. 14aα) and Israel (v. 14aβ). Josephus continues to accentuate the military initiative of Samuel.

[112] Josephus' indication concerning the boundary points of the recovered territory reflects the reading of MT and LXX L 1 Sam 7:14aα ("from Ekron to Gath") as opposed to LXX B ("from Askalon to Azob").

[113] In 1 Sam 7:14b the reference is to the "peace" between Israel and "the Amorites." Josephus' phrase concerning "the remnant of the Chananaians" echoes similar formulations in *Ant.* 5.68, 90.

[114] This form (αὐτοῖς) is the reading of the codices, which Niese follows. Marcus (*ad loc.*) suggests the emendation ἑκάστοις ("to each [group]").

[115] The Bible does not mention such a reordering of the people by Samuel for judicial purposes. By means of this insertion, Josephus highlights the authoritative figure of Samuel in yet another of his capacities, i.e. as supreme legal authority.

[116] Josephus leaves aside the names of the 3 cities (Bethel, Gilgal, Mizpah) making up Samuel's "circuit" as cited in 1 Sam 7:16a. The reading "annually," corresponding to the Bible's phrase "year by year," is that of RO, followed by Niese and Marcus. The remaining witnesses have Samuel making his visitation "twice a year."

[117] Greek: πολλὴν ἐβράβευεν εὐνομίαν; this same phrase recurs in *Ant.* 7.185, where Absalom claims that as king he would do for the people what Samuel is credited with doing here. Josephus elaborates on the notices of 1 Sam 7:16b ("and he [Samuel] judged Israel in all these places") and 7:17aβ ("there also [i.e. in Ramah]

he administered justice to Israel"), making Samuel the overall artificer of Israel's legal system. Conversely, he leaves aside the references to Samuel's coming to his home in Ramah and his building an altar there of 7:17aαb.

[118] 1 Sam 8:1a speaks simply of Samuel's "becoming old."

[119] Compare 1 Sam 8:1b: "he made his sons judges over Israel."

[120] MT (1 Sam 8:2) יוֹאֵל (Eng.: "Joel"); LXX Ἰωάλ; Josephus Ἰοῦλος. Josephus' form of the name would appear to be a Latinization of the biblical one, being reminiscent of the alternate name of Aeneas' son Ascanius, i.e. "Iulus" (see Virgil, *Aen.* 6.32). Feldman (1998: 498) finds here an indication that Josephus viewed Samuel as a "Jewish Aeneas."

[121] MT (1 Sam 8:2) אֲבִיָּה (Eng.: "Abijah"); LXX B Ἀβιά; LXX L Ἀβιρά; Josephus Ἐβία (this is the reading of RO followed by Niese; Marcus *ad loc.* reads Ἀβίρα with M).

[122] MT (1 Sam 8:2) בְּאֵר שֶׁבַע (Eng.: "Beersheba"); LXX Βηρσάβεε; Josephus Βερσουβεί. On Josephus' version of 1 Samuel 8, see Begg 1997e; Spilsbury 1998: 161-70.

[123] 1 Sam 8:2 represents both sons functioning at a single site, i.e. Beersheba. Josephus' modification might be based on the consideration that it would have been highly inconvenient for the people as a whole to bring their cases to only one place, itself located in the extreme south of the land. Accordingly, in a way reminiscent of what Samuel did in the case of his own judicial activity (6.31), he has him partition the people between the 2 sites, one in the center of the country (Bethel; Josephus may have drawn this name from 1 Sam 7:16), the other in the south (Beersheba), each presided over by one of his sons.

are not similar in character to their parents; rather, kind and moderate ones stem from vile parents, just as those born from good [parents] show themselves depraved.[124] **34.** For they, deviating from their father's ways of acting and going off on the opposite path of gifts and shameful bribes, deserted what is just. They passed judgment, not according to truth, but for gain.[125] Inclining to luxury and an opulent manner of life, they acted first of all, in opposition to God and secondly to their own father the prophet who, with much solicitude and care, was educating even the crowd[126] to be just.[127]

(3.3) 35. The people,[128] however, resented the outrages that the prophet's sons were committing against their earlier form of government and constitution[129] and ran together to him—he was residing in the city of Armatha.[130] They spoke of the sons' transgressions and [added] that he, being already old and weakened by time, was no longer capable of administering their affairs as previously.[131] **36.** They asked and begged him[132] to appoint someone as their king who would rule over the nation and punish the Palestinoi with the judgments they still had coming to them for their previous misdeeds.[133]

Israelites ask for a king

Their words greatly grieved Samouel on account of[134] his innate justice and ha-

Samuel's reaction

---

[124] Josephus supplies this "moral" to the story of Samuel's reprobate sons. It serves to preclude readers' blaming Samuel himself for the way his sons turned out (as they might well be inclined to do in light of Josephus' previous story of Eli and his reprobate sons in *Ant.* 5.338-362). The pattern to which Josephus calls attention here has already been exemplified in the case of the liberator Gideon who engendered the tyrant Abimelech (see *Ant.* 5.239) and will further be illustrated in the succession of Israelite monarchs where good kings have bad sons and vice versa. One finds comparable remarks about the degeneracy of the Roman youth of the day in Cicero, *Cael.* 11.25; 12.28-29.

[125] Josephus' indictment of the sons here corresponds rather closely to that set out in 1 Sam 8:3.

[126] Feldman (1998: 503) sees Josephus' language here ("*even* the crowd") as another expression of his pervasive contempt for the masses.

[127] The above sentence, highlighting the sons' depravity, represents Josephus' elaboration of the charges made against them in 1 Sam 8:3 (and reproduced by him in what precedes); it recalls his remarks concerning the Israelites' descent into degeneracy under the influence of luxury, pleasure, and obsession with money in *Ant.* 5.132-135. By contrast, Rabbinic tradition tends to downplay the sons' offenses; see Begg 1997e: 333, n. 34.

[128] In having the people as a whole approach Samuel at this juncture Josephus follows the reading of LXX 1 Sam 8:4 as against MT (where "all the elders of Israel" take the initiative). Likewise Pseudo-Philo (who has no parallel to the whole sequence 1 Sam 7:3-17) reflects the LXX reading of 1 Sam 8:4 in *Bib. Ant.* 56.1.

[129] Josephus interjects this reference to the people's state of mind that prompts them to approach Samuel.

[130] MT (1 Sam 8:4) הרמתה (Eng.: "Ramah"); LXX Ἀρμαθάιμ; Josephus Ἀρμαθᾶ. Pseudo-Philo (cf. *Bib. Ant.* 56.1) does not specify where the people approach Samuel.

[131] In 1 Sam 8:5 Samuel's age is mentioned before the deviance of his sons. Josephus' reversed order highlights the latter point, even while it spells out the implications of Samuel's age in a way reminiscent of his previous portrayal of the aged Samuel in 6.32.

[132] In 1 Sam 8:5 (as also in *Bib. Ant.* 56.1) the elders (MT)/ people (LXX) simply command Samuel, "appoint for us a king." Josephus depicts the people acting in a more deferential manner.

[133] In 1 Sam 8:5 the asked-for king is characterized as one who will govern Israel "like all the nations." Josephus replaces this characterization with a reference to the king's military function (this perhaps inspired by the divine word to Samuel concerning the king in 1 Sam 9:16b). The substitution is likely prompted by the consideration that Gentile readers might well take offense at the Bible's presentation where the "assimilationist ideal" implicit in the request that Israel be given a king "like all the nations," evokes unqualified condemnation by both Samuel and God; see Feldman 1998: 508. Pseudo-Philo (*Bib. Ant.* 56.1) has the people invoke Moses' "word" of Deut 17:15 ("one from among your brethren you shall set as king over you...") as the basis for their demand that Samuel now appoint them a king.

[134] 1 Sam 8:6 leaves Samuel's "displeasure" at the people's request unexplained. Josephus supplies a (political) rationale for his negative response.

tred of kings.[135] For he delighted intensely in aristocracy as something divine that renders blessed those who use it as their constitution.[136] **37.** In his agitation and distress over what had been said, he thought of neither food nor sleep; throughout the entire night he continued turning over thoughts about public affairs.[137]

God's response   **(3.4) 38.** With things standing thus, the Deity appeared[138] and admonished him not to be disturbed at what the crowd had requested in that they had rejected not him, but rather himself so that he might not rule as sole king.[139] They had devised such deeds since the day when he brought them out of Egypt;[140] it would not be long, however, before a painful change of mind would take hold of them by which, nonetheless, nothing would be undone of what was to be. "They would rather be convicted of having been contemptuous and taking ungrateful decisions regarding me and your prophesying.[141] **39.** I direct you, however, to appoint for them whomever I shall nominate as king, once you have forewarned them of what calamities they will experience when ruled by kings and solemnly testified concerning the sort of change into which they are rushing."[142]

---

[135] Feldman (1998: 502) points out that the "hatred of kings" that Josephus attributes to Samuel here would have resonated with Roman readers whose own tradition featured an early expulsion of kings from Rome and an ongoing concern over attempts to revive the institution as expressed, e.g., in the comment Cicero (*Resp.* 1.40.62; cf. also 2.30.52) places on the lips of Scipio: Tarquin, the last of Rome's kings, "made the title of king odious (*in odium venisse*) to our people."

[136] Josephus' editorial comment concerning Samuel's attachment to "aristocracy" harks back to the affirmation with which he has Moses introduce the "law of the king" (Deut 17:14-20) in *Ant.* 4.223: "Now aristocracy and the life therein is best." See note to "already destroyed," at *Ant.* 5.135.

[137] This elaboration of the summary source reference to Samuel's "displeasure" over the elders/ people's request (1 Sam 8:6a) takes the place of the mention of Samuel's "praying to the Lord" in 8:6b. Also Pseudo-Philo elaborates on Samuel's reaction to the people's word, having him (*Bib. Ant.* 56.2) reflect that their proposal that he now activate Moses' word about appointing a king (56.1; cf. note to "misdeeds" at 6.36) is premature.

[138] Greek: ἐμφανίζω. 1 Sam 8:7 makes no mention of a such an "epiphany" by the Deity who now addresses Samuel. Also elsewhere Josephus introduces divine "appearances" where the Bible itself refers only to God's speaking to a person; see Begg 1993: 54-54, n. 300. Pseudo-Philo (*Bib. Ant.* 56.3) specifies that God spoke to Samuel "by night." On the epiphany theme in ancient literature generally, see Pax 1955; Lührmann 1971.

[139] From the opening divine word of 1 Sam 8:7 Josephus omits God's initial injunction that Samuel hearken to the people's voice in everything. The ideal of rule by God alone to which Josephus alludes here—

and in *Apion* 2.165, where he states that in his theocracy Moses placed "all sovereignty and authority in the hands of God"—might seem reminiscent of the views, rejected, of course, by Josephus himself, of Judas, the leader of the Sicarii, whom he portrays in *War* 2.118 as denouncing the Jews for acquiescing in Roman rule and human dominion when they had God as their true "master." However, according to Josephus in a later reference to the Sicarii (see *War* 7.253-256), their purported concern for rule by God alone was in fact simply a cloak for their own avarice and cruelty; unlike Samuel (and Moses) then the Sicarii abused the ideal of God's sole kingship for their own purposes.

In contrast to both the Bible and Josephus, Pseudo-Philo (*Bib. Ant.* 56.3) "motivates" God's urging Samuel not to be distressed over the people's request in terms of the divine intention of sending a king, who after "destroying" the people, will himself be destroyed.

[140] From the Lord's allusion to the people's past history of sin going back to the time of the Exodus (1 Sam 8:8) Josephus leaves aside the specific charges about their having forsaken him and served "other gods."

[141] This negative foreshadowing of what the request for a king will lead to for Israel has no equivalent in God's word to Samuel in 1 Sam 8:7-9 (compare, however, the divine announcement of the coming king who will both destroy the people and be himself destroyed in *Bib. Ant.* 56.3; cf. note to "king" at 6.38). It might, on the other hand, be seen as an anticipation/adaptation of Samuel's own word to the people in 8:18, where he warns them that their complaints to God about their king will meet with no response from him.

[142] Josephus elaborates—in negative fashion—on the conclusion of God's address (1 Sam 8:7-9) to Samuel, which ends (8:9; cf. 8:7) with his enjoining Samuel to hearken to the people's voice after first set-

(3.5) 40. When he heard these things, Samouel called the Judeans together at dawn[143] and declared that he would appoint a king for them.[144] He said, however, he must first precisely inform them of what would be with their kings and how many calamities they would get themselves into.[145] "For know, first of all, that they will seize your sons by force and direct some of them to be their charioteers, others their horsemen and bodyguards.[146] Others will be runners[147] and commanders of thousands and hundreds.[148] They will also make them fashioners of weapons and chariot-makers, and artificers of instruments, as well as farmers and caretakers of their own fields and diggers of vineyards.[149] **41.** There is nothing they [the sons] will not do, being directed in the manner of slaves purchased for money.[150] Your daughters too they will designate as ointment-makers and cooks and bakers, and will impose on them every work at which maids serve under compulsion, fearing blows and torture.[151] They will take away your possessions and give these as gifts to their eunuchs and bodyguards,[152] and will hand over your herds of cattle to their own entourage.[153]

Samuel's warning about the king

---

ting before them "the ways" of their coming king. Pseudo-Philo (*Bib. Ant.* 56.3) concludes his version of the divine address (and of 1 Samuel 8 as a whole) with God's announcement, inspired by 1 Sam 9:16, that Israel's future king will appear before Samuel on the following day.

[143] In 1 Sam 8:10 Samuel begins addressing the people immediately, nothing being said of his first (re-) convening them. Josephus' insertion regarding the latter point is appropriate in that, in his presentation, an entire night has intervened (6.37) between the people's initial request and the reply Samuel will now make to them in God's name, during which time the people would not likely have remained around the prophet.

[144] This initial announcement by Samuel, echoing God's injunction to him in 6.39, has no equivalent in his address to the people as cited in 1 Sam 8:10-18. It serves to make clear, right at the outset, that the people will in fact get the king they had requested.

[145] The biblical Samuel introduces his announcements concerning the king in more neutral fashion in 1 Sam 8:11 ("these will be the ways of the king who will rule over you..."); Josephus' alternative wording picks up on the command given him by God in 6.39 (// 8:9). Whereas 1 Sam 8:11 speaks only of "the (one) king" the people have asked for and his way, Josephus accentuates the warning element of Samuel's speech by having him refer to "kings" in the plural, all of whom will abuse their subjects in the same way. In line with this modification Josephus has Samuel (mainly) speak in what follows of what "they" (the kings) will require of their subjects, whereas in 1 Sam 8:11b-17 the reference is to "he" (the one king). Towards the end of his speech (see 6.42), however, there will be a shift to mention of the king in the singular.

[146] Josephus' rendering of 1 Sam 8:11b accentuates the "highhandedness" with which the king(s) will impose various military roles on the Israelites' sons. To

its listing of these roles he adds that of "bodyguard(s)," a group who will figure prominently in his account of the various kings.

[147] 1 Sam 8:11b specifies that the Israelites' sons will be required to "run before his [the king's] chariot(s)."

[148] In mentioning "commanders of hundreds" here, Josephus follows LXX BL 1 Sam 8:12a as against MT, which speaks rather of "(commanders) of fifties."

[149] Josephus reverses the order of the 2 types of activities spoken of in 1 Sam 8:12b, i.e. agricultural labor and the manufacture of armaments. In so doing, he more logically links the latter directly with the preceding mention of the military roles the Israelites' sons will be forced to assume. His reference to "diggers of vineyards" replaces the Bible's mention of the enslaved Israelites "reaping the king's harvest."

[150] This announcement concerning the enslavement of the (male) Israelites is an initial anticipation of Samuel's climactic warning of 1 Sam 8:17b "and you shall be his slaves," that Josephus will reproduce in 6.42. Josephus makes his anticipation of the warning serve as a transition between Samuel's warnings about what awaits the Israelites' sons and their daughters.

[151] Josephus expatiates on the announcement of 1 Sam 8:13 about the 3-fold service that will be imposed on the Israelites' daughters, underscoring, as he did in the case of the sons (see note to "bodyguards" at 6.40), the highhanded brutality involved.

[152] Josephus here generalizes the notices of 1 Sam 8:14-15, which enumerate the various agricultural items the king will award to his retainers. Josephus' use of the term "bodyguards" as one of the categories among these retainers replaces the double source mention of the king's "servants"; the term echoes (his likewise "unbiblical") reference to the Israelites' sons being appointed royal bodyguards in 6.40.

[153] With his mention of the kings' appropriating

42. To sum up, you will be slaves to the king, together with all that is yours, along with your own servants.[154] When he comes, he will remind you of my words and by your suffering these things [he will cause you], regretting your decision,[155] to beg God to have mercy on you and grant you quick deliverance from your kings.[156] He, however, will not accept your pleas; rather, turning a deaf ear, he will allow you to undergo judgment for your own folly."[157]

People rebuff warning

(3.6) 43. Yet even to these predictions of what would happen the crowd remained impervious and stubbornly refused to rid their minds of a decision that was already established in their thinking. For they did not allow themselves to be convinced by, nor to concern themselves with, the words of Samouel. Instead, they incessantly pressed him, requesting that he appoint the king right away, and give no thought to what would be.[158] **44.** For it was a matter of necessity that they should have someone who would wage war along with themselves for the punishment of their enemies[159]; nor was there anything improper about their having the same constitution as their neighbors who were ruled by kings.[160]

People dismissed

Samouel, seeing that they had not been dissuaded by his previous words, but were persisting, said:[161] "Let each one now go off to his home; I will summon you as

---

their subjects' "cattle" here Josephus aligns himself with the LXX BL reading in 1 Sam 8:16aβ, whereas MT refers to "your young men." He has no equivalent to 8:16aα, where the king's taking of the Israelites' "menservants and maidservants" is announced (nor to the mention of their donkeys in 8:16bα).

[154] Josephus elaborates on the brief, climactic statement of 1 Sam 8:17b ("and you shall be his slaves"), already anticipated by him in 6.41.

[155] This Josephan insertion serves to make the transition between Samuel's announcements concerning what the king will do to the Israelites (1 Sam 8:11-17) and his prediction of their response to this (8:18). Its language echoes that of Josephus' expansion of the divine word to Samuel (1 Sam 8:7-9) in 6.38, where God announces the Israelites' eventual (vain) change of mind.

[156] Josephus supplies a content to the Israelites' future "crying out" because of their king as announced in 1 Sam 8:18a, likewise generalizing this into a reference to (all their) "kings."

[157] Josephus elaborates on the divine response to the people's "cry" as announced in 1 Sam 8:18b: "but the Lord will not answer [MT; LXX give heed to] you in that day" (MT; LXX and 4QSamᵃ in those days; + for it is you who will have chosen a king, LXX). His expansion, e.g., underscores the people's stupidity in wanting a king, once again suggesting Josephus' disdain for the masses; see Feldman 1998: 503.

[158] Josephus notably expands on the people's dismissal of Samuel's warnings and their renewed demand for a king as cited in 1 Sam 8:19, their obstinacy on this occasion contrasting with their ready acceptance of Samuel's call to reform their lives in 6.22. Josephus'

embellishments further underscore that the people's renewed demand for a king was not the one-time affair it appears to be in 8:19, but rather something that they kept pressing upon Samuel.

[159] This opening motivation for the people's renewed demand for a king is Josephus' rendering of the people's closing characterization of the king as one who "will go out before us and fight our battles" in 1 Sam 8:20. Its wording echoes that used by the people in formulating their initial request to Samuel in 6.36, where they ask for the appointment of a king who "would punish the Palestinoi with the judgments they still had coming to them...."

[160] This is Josephus' delayed (see previous note) rendition of the people's opening rationale for their demand for a king, echoing that voiced by them already in 1 Sam 8:4, of 8:20: "... that we also may be like all the other nations." Josephus has the people spell out what such being "like the other nations" consists in, i.e. "being ruled by kings." Thereby, he underscores the opposition between them and Samuel with his "hatred of kings" (see 6.36).

[161] In having Samuel respond immediately to the people on the basis of his perception of their obduracy, Josephus leaves aside the intervening exchange between him and God of 1 Sam 8:21-22a, in which Samuel "repeats" the people's reaction "in the ears of the Lord," who, in turn, tells him to go ahead and appoint them a king. The effect of this omission is to accentuate the status of Samuel as one who knows what needs to be done at this point without additional divine instructions; see Feldman 1998: 494. The omission also eliminates the anthropomorphic reference of v. 21 to God's "ears," with its suggestion that God would not have

needed, when I learn from God whom he is giving you as king."[162]

(4.1) 45. Now there was a certain man of the Benjamite tribe, well-born[163] and of good character,[164] named Keis.[165] He had a son, a youth of outstanding appearance and tall in body; his intelligence and mind were superior to these visible [qualities.][166] He was called Saoul.[167]

Saul intro-duced

46. Now this Keis, when some of his beautiful donkeys, in which he took greater pleasure than in any of his other possessions, wandered off from their pasture, sent out his son with a single attendant to look for the animals.[168] Having gone round his father's tribe,[169] he went to the others.[170] Not meeting them in these, he decided to return, so as not to cause his father concern about himself for the future.[171]

Saul's search for donkeys

47. When, however, they were opposite the city of Armatha,[172] the attendant who followed him stated that there was a truthful prophet[173] in it, and advised going to him; for through him they would find out what had become of the donkeys. [Saoul then] said that if they went to him, they had nothing to award him in exchange for his prophecy, for their provisions were already used up.[174] 48. But the servant stated that he had available the fourth of a shekel and would give him this (for they were in error, due to their ignorance that the prophet did not take recompense).[175]

Prophetic con-sultation sug-gested

---

known of the people's response without Samuel's in-forming him of this.

[162] Josephus elaborates on 1 Sam 8:22b, where Samuel simply enjoins the people to go home. The elements appended by him serve to confirm that Samuel does indeed intend to appoint a king for them eventually (see 6.40) and to prepare God's revelation of the king's identity that will follow in 6.49 (= 1 Sam 9:15-16).

[163] Josephus omits the 4 ancestors of "Kish" cited in 1 Sam 9:1, just as in *Ant.* 5.342 he passed over the extended genealogy of Elkanah given in 1 Sam 1:1.

[164] 1 Sam 9:1 characterizes Kish rather as an impor-tant/wealthy man.

[165] MT (1 Sam 9:1) קִישׁ (Eng.: "Kish"); LXX B and Josephus Κείς; LXX L Κίς.

[166] Josephus' reference to Saul's preeminent mental qualities takes the place of the detail about his being "a head taller" than all the other Israelites (MT; than all the earth, LXX) in 1 Sam 9:2b.

[167] MT (1 Sam 9:2) שָׁאוּל (Eng.: "Saul"); LXX Σαούλ; Josephus Σαοῦλος. On Josephus' treatment of Saul, see Feldman 1998: 509-36.

[168] Josephus' insertions about the "beauty" of Kish's donkeys and his delight in them serves to moti-vate his sending his son Saul himself to look for them as related in 1 Sam 9:3.

[169] With RO Niese omits the words "seeking the donkeys" that follow at this point in the other wit-nesses and that Marcus incorporates into his text.

[170] According to 1 Sam 9:4, Saul's journey began in the hill country of Ephraim and ended up in the "land of Benjamin" with 2 additional named regions intervening. Josephus' generalization of this itinerary

begins, more logically, with Saul traversing the territory of his own tribe of Benjamin (see 6.45).

[171] In 1 Sam 9:5 Saul's decision to return is taken "in the land of Zuph" (MT; Siph, LXX) and is an-nounced by him to his servant.

[172] In 1 Sam 9:6 the servant speaks only of "this city," where the "man of God" is present and where the subsequent encounter between him and Saul will occur. Josephus names "the city" in question on the basis of 7:17, which designates "Ramah" (Josephus' "Ar-matha") as Samuel's "home." *Bib. Ant.* 56.4 offers a cor-responding localization for the encounter, i.e. "Ramathaim."

[173] The Josephan servant's characterization of Samuel as a "truthful prophet" takes the place of the phrase used of him by his biblical counterpart, i.e. "a man of God... a man held in honor; all that he says comes true" of 1 Sam 9:6. The modification reflects Josephus' recurrent stress on Samuel's status as a "pro-phet"; see note to "Samouel" at *Ant.* 5.340. Josephus' other uses of the phrase "truthful prophet" (Greek: προφήτης ἀληθής) are *Ant.* 8.296 (the potential lack of such a figure in the future); 8.408 (Micaiah); 9.23 (Elisha); 9.34 (ironically, of the "prophets" of Ahab and Jezebel).

[174] Like his servant (see 9:6) Saul in 1 Sam 9:7 speaks of the "man of God"; here too, Josephus uses alternative language (see note on "prophet" at 6.47) that underscores Samuel's prophetic status.

[175] Josephus' appended comment concerning the servant's reply in 1 Sam 9:8 elevates the status of Samuel by making clear that, in fact, he did not accept recompense for his prophetic services. Josephus has no equivalent either to the parenthetical remark about the terminological change from "seer" to "prophet" of 9:9

Saul at Samuel's house

They went off and meeting up at the gates with some virgins[176] who had come for water, questioned them about the prophet's house.[177] They indicated this,[178] and appealed to them to hurry before he reclined at the supper, for he was feasting many people and would recline prior to those who had been invited.[179] **49.** The reason for Samouel's having brought many together for the feast at that time was this: on the previous day God[180] had informed him—who had been praying every day to God to foretell to him whom he was going to make king[181]—that he would send a certain youth of the Benjamite tribe at this same hour.[182] Samouel, sitting on the roof, was waiting for this time to come; once it arrived, he came down and went to the supper.[183] **50.** Upon his meeting Saoul, God indicated to him that this was the one who was to rule.[184] Saoul approached Samouel and, having greeted him, asked him to inform him about the house of the prophet.[185] For he stated that as a stranger he was ignorant [of this].[186] **51.** Samouel then stated that he was [the prophet],[187] and conducted him to the supper.[188] As for the donkeys that he had been sent out to look

---

or to Saul's assent to the servant's proposal in 9:10a.

[176] In 1 Sam 9:11a Saul and his servant meet the maidens as they are "going up the hill to the city."

[177] This question replaces the one—to which Saul and his servant would already appear to have the answer—of 1 Sam 9:11b, i.e. "Is the seer here?" The substitution seems inspired by the query about the whereabouts of the "seer's house" that Saul will pose to Samuel himself in 1 Sam 9:18 (and that Josephus will reproduce in 6.50). As he did with the "man of God" language of 9:6-10, Josephus substitutes the term "prophet" for the alternative designation of Samuel, i.e. "seer" of 9:11. In *Bib. Ant.* 56.4 Saul encounters Samuel while walking "near the shrine" and asks, not the maidens, but Samuel himself, about the seer's whereabouts. When Samuel identifies himself as that seer, Saul inquires whether he can tell him about the lost donkeys.

[178] This initial response by the maidens, relating back to the question Josephus has the visitors pose to them in what precedes, has no equivalent in the Bible, where the maidens begin their answer (1 Sam 9:12a) by stating that the seer is "here" and indeed is "just ahead" of the pair of visitors.

[179] According to the maidens' answer in 1 Sam 9:12b-13, the people are waiting for the seer to bless their sacrifice on the high place (so MT; LXX renders as a proper place name, i.e. "in Bama"), after which the guests will eat. Josephus eliminates any reference to a sacrifice or a "high place" from their answer, turning the occasion into a secular "supper," held in Samuel's own house, at which, in Hellenistic fashion, one "reclines" to eat.

[180] Josephus now indicates the reason for Samuel's inviting people to his home for the supper, i.e. that they might be witnesses of the first appearance of the king whose imminent coming God has just announced to him; see 1 Sam 9:15.

[181] 1 Sam 9:15 does not mention such daily prayer

by Samuel prior to God's announcement; the insertion underscores the prophet's piety. Compare *Bib. Ant.* 56.5, where following his encounter with Saul (56.4), Samuel asks the Lord to instruct him about his plans concerning the people.

[182] Josephus considerably abridges God's announcement as cited in 1 Sam 9:15b-16, passing over the directive that Samuel anoint the one who will come to him and the divine statement concerning the military leadership the latter will provide against the Philistines (this role of Saul's has already been anticipated in the people's words about the king they are requesting of 6.35, 44).

[183] 1 Samuel 9 does not specify where Samuel was during and immediately after God's communication to him in vv. 15-16. Josephus derives his reference to "the roof" (i.e. apparently that of Samuel's own house; see 6.48) from 9:25, where Saul sleeps "on the roof" after eating. The reference to Samuel's "coming down and going into the supper" picks up on the virgins' mention (see 6.48) of his imminent "reclining at the supper."

[184] See 1 Sam 9:17.

[185] In 1 Sam 9:18 Saul, speaking to Samuel, poses—for the first time—his question concerning the whereabouts of the seer's house. Josephus has already had him put the same question to the maidens in 6.48. He leaves aside the indication of 9:18 concerning the site of the pair's meeting, i.e. the gate (MT)/ the town (LXX 4QSam^a).

[186] Josephus supplies this rationale for Saul's asking his question of Samuel about the seer's "house," as he does in 1 Sam 9:18.

[187] In MT 1 Sam 9:19aα Samuel responds "I am the seer," while in LXX 4QSam^a he answers "it is I myself."

[188] This notice, anticipating that of 1 Sam 9:22a, takes the place of the series of directives and promises given Saul by Samuel in 1 Sam 9:19aβb (to which

for, these were safe,[189] just as all things had been arranged to go well for himself.[190] [Saoul] replied: "But I, O master, am inferior to this hope; my tribe is too small to produce kings, and my ancestral clan is humbler than the other ancestral clans.[191] You, however, are joking and making a fool of me by speaking of things greater than what accords with my position."[192]

52. The prophet, however, conducted him to the meal and made him and his companion recline above those invited (who were seventy in number).[193] He ordered the servers to set a kingly portion before Saoul.[194] Then, when the bed-time hour approached, they arose and each went off to his own home,[195] while Saoul and his attendant slept at the prophet's house.[196]

(4.2) 53. When it was day, Samouel roused him from his bed and accompanied him.[197] Once they were outside the city, he directed him [Saoul] to make the attendant go on ahead, but himself to stay behind, for he had something to tell him in the other's absence.[198]

Saul's anointing

54. When Saoul had sent his companion off,[199] the prophet took the holy oil[200]

Pseudo-Philo has a partial equivalent in *Bib. Ant.* 56.4).

[189] See 1 Sam 9:20a.

[190] This announcement replaces Samuel's double question to Saul in 1 Sam 9:20b: "And for whom is all that is desirable in Israel? Is it not for you and for all your father's house?"

[191] Josephus spells out more directly and emphatically Saul's modest objection to Samuel's promises to him that in 1 Sam 9:21a is voiced by the former in the form of 2 rhetorical questions about his being from the least tribe of Israel (Benjamin) and the least family of that tribe. Compare Gideon's objection to his commissioning by the angel in *Ant.* 5.214.

[192] The translation "position" here follows the reading χῶραν adopted by Niese and Marcus; MSP have χρείαν ("need"). Once again, Josephus makes more emphatic Saul's modest demurral regarding Samuel's promises; compare his concluding question in 9:21b: "Why then have you spoken to me in this way?" On Josephus' treatment of Saul's quality of modesty, see Feldman 1998: 524-25. In *Bib. Ant.* 56.6, Saul, having alluded to the insignificance of himself and his house, goes on to affirm that, given his youth, he does not understand what Samuel has just told him (i.e. the Lord's choice of him as ruler, 56.5= 1 Sam 10:1). Samuel then predicts that Saul's word will prove to be like that of Jeremiah, who in Jer 1:6 objects to God's call with the words "I am only a youth."

[193] Josephus has already mentioned Saul's being brought to the supper by Samuel at the beginning of 6.51 (= 1 Sam 9:22a); he now resumes the point after the intervening exchange between the pair in the remainder of 6.51. His figure for the guests agrees with that of LXX BL 1 Sam 9:22b against MT ("about 30"). Conversely, Josephus follows MT in having Saul and his servant placed "at the head of the guests," rather than merely "among them" (so LXX).

[194] Josephus compresses the sequence of 1 Sam 9:23-24, where, at Samuel's direction (v. 23), the "cook" places the "leg (MT; LXX shoulder) and the upper portion" (? MT LXX L, > LXX B) before Saul, who is then urged to eat by Samuel, and does so (v. 24). Josephus' use of the expression "royal portion" to designate that which is given Saul accentuates the new status he is imminently to receive.

[195] This reference to the departure of the other guests at bedtime replaces the transitional notice of 1 Sam 9:25a: "and when they came down from the high place (LXX from Bama) into the city...," which would not correspond to Josephus' portrayal of the supper taking place in Samuel's own house within the city; see note to "invited" at 6.48.

[196] Josephus' wording here seems to reflect that of LXX BL 1 Sam 9:25b-26a ("... and they spread out for Saul on the roof something in which to wrap himself, and he went to sleep...") vs. MT's "and he [Saul] spoke with Samuel on the roof. And they arose early...." Josephus supplies the indication concerning the servant's sleeping arrangements.

[197] In 1 Sam 9:26 Samuel calls to Saul "on the roof" (see 9:25 LXX) so as to "rouse" him.

[198] Compare 1 Sam 9:27, where Samuel speaks, more portentously, of "a word of God" that he has for Saul.

[199] This statement corresponds to the LXX L plus at the end of 1 Sam 9:27: "and Saul spoke to his servant and he passed on before them."

[200] Greek: τὸ ἅγιον ἔλαιον; this is the majority reading of the witnesses that Niese follows. Marcus (*ad loc.*) adopts the alternative reading of ROE Lat, i.e. τὸ αγγεῖον, ἔλαιον ("[taking] his vial, [poured] oil"), this corresponding to the wording of 1 Sam 10:1: "he took a vial of oil and poured it...."

Signs for Saul

and poured it on the youth's head and kissed him.[201] "Know," he said, "that you have been appointed king[202] by God against the Palestinoi and for vengeance on the Hebrews' behalf. There will also be a sign of these things for you that I wish you to know in advance.[203] **55.** When you go away from here, you will encounter three persons on the road who are going to pay homage to God at Bethel.[204] You will see the first of them carrying three loaves,[205] the second a kid,[206] while the third will follow bearing a wineskin. They will greet you and address you in a friendly way and give you two loaves—that you are to take.[207] **56.** From there you will come to the so-called "tomb of Rachel,"[208] where you will meet [someone][209] who will tell you the good news that the donkeys have been saved.[210] Then coming from there to Gabatha,[211] you will run into assembled prophets[212] and, becoming inspired,[213] will

---

[201] See 1 Sam 10:1a.

[202] In having Samuel speak of Saul as "king," Josephus diverges from MT and LXX 1 Sam 10:1b, both of which use "lesser" titles for him, i.e. "prince" (נגיד) or "ruler" (ἄρχων; cf. the Latin *princeps* of *Bib. Ant.* 56.5), respectively. Conversely, his Samuel refers to Saul's having been "appointed" by God rather than "anointed" by him (so both MT and LXX 10:1b). This modification is in line with the frequent practice of Josephus who rewords biblical mentions of the "anointing" of Israelite kings with their messianic connotations that might well grate on Roman sensibilities, given the Jews' recent efforts at regaining their independence. On Josephus' "anti-messianism," see Feldman 1998: 151-54.

[203] Josephus' wording of Samuel's statement to Saul at the moment of the latter's designation clearly reflects the longer LXX form of 1 Sam 10:1b. In particular, his reference to Saul's having been appointed "against the Palestinoi and for vengeance on the Hebrews' behalf" seems to echo the LXX plus "you shall save them [the Israelites] from the hand of their enemies round about," just as the announcement of a "sign" for Saul corresponds to the continuation of this plus.

[204] In the sequence of 1 Samuel 10, Saul's encounter with the 3 pilgrims is the 2nd of the 3 "signs" that Samuel foretells to him. Josephus makes this, as the least dramatic of Saul's 3 upcoming experiences, the first in the series, thereby giving the whole complex a more clearly climactic movement. In addition, he leaves aside the specification concerning the site of Saul's announced encounter with the 3 men from 1 Sam 10:3, i.e. "the oak of Tabor" (MT LXX B; "the choice oak," LXX L).

[205] So MT 1 Sam 10:3; LXX speaks of 3 "*containers of* bread." In both MT and LXX the loaves are mentioned by Samuel in 2nd place. Josephus' shifting the item to the head of the list may have in view the fact that of the 3 items mentioned in 10:3, this is the only one that will actually be offered to Saul (see 10:4).

[206] Both MT and LXX 1 Sam 10:3 have the 2nd man carrying *3* kids. Josephus' modification might be inspired by the practical consideration that it would be difficult for one person to actually carry *3* kids.

[207] This remainder of Josephus' version of Samuel's announcement to Saul in 1 Sam 10:3-4 corresponds quite closely to the biblical wording.

[208] In 1 Samuel 10 what is to transpire at Rachel's tomb is the first of the 3 signs; Josephus makes it rather the 2nd; see note to "Bethel" at 6.55. The Bible makes earlier mention of that tomb in Gen 35:19-20 (cf. *Ant.* 1.343); 48:7. As he did with the localization "at the oak of Tabor" of 1 Sam 10:3, Josephus leaves aside the source placement of Rachel's tomb, i.e. "in the territory (MT; LXX mountains) of Benjamin (at Zelah [?] MT, > LXX)."

[209] According to 1 Sam 10:2, Saul is to meet *2* men; Josephus lacks an equivalent to the LXX plus describing the pair as "walking with great strides."

[210] Josephus omits the man's further announcement as predicted by Samuel in 1 Sam 10:2b, i.e. his father's anxiety about Saul has subsided, now that the donkeys have been found. In so doing he aligns the upcoming announcement with Samuel's own previous assurance concerning the donkeys in 6.51 (= 1 Sam 9:20) that mentions only the donkeys' safety, not the effect of this on Kish.

[211] MT (1 Sam 10:5) גבעת האלהים (Eng.: "Gibeah-elohim"); LXX BL (translating) (εἰς) τὸν βουνὸν τοῦ θεοῦ; Josephus Γαβαθά. Josephus omits the appended source mention of the presence of Philistine "garrisons" (or "prefects," Hebrew: נצבים; LXX both "translates" and transliterates this word: "[where there is] the construction of the Philistines and Nasib the Philistine") at the site as irrelevant to Samuel's prediction of what will happen to Saul there.

[212] Josephus leaves aside the catalogue of musical instruments carried by the prophets in 1 Sam 10:5. He likewise passes over the notation that the prophets will be "coming down from the high place" (MT; "from Bama," LXX); compare his reworking of the reference

prophesy along with them.[214] Hence, whoever sees all these things will be astonished and wonder, saying: 'How is that the son of Keis has attained such well-being?'[215] **57.** When these signs happen to you, know that God is with you; greet your father and your relatives.[216] You are to come to Galgala[217] when summoned by me[218] that we may offer thanksgiving sacrifices to God for these things."[219] Having said these things and made these announcements, he sent the youth away;[220] everything turned out for Saoul in accordance with Samouel's prophecy.[221]

(4.3) 58. When he came to the house of his relative[222] Abenar[223] (for he cherished

Saul's report to Abner

---

of 1 Sam 9:12b-13 to the people's sacrifice "on the high place," which Samuel is to bless, see note to "invited" at 6.48.

[213] Greek: γενόμενος ἔνθεος. This phrase substitutes for Samuel's announcement in 1 Sam 10:6 ("then the spirit of Lord will come mightily upon you"). The word ἔνθ(ε)ος, is absent in the LXX, but appears, e.g., in Plato, *Ion* 534B and Dionysius of Halicarnassus, *Ant. rom.* 2.48.1. Josephus uses the term ἔνθεος 6 times elsewhere: *War* 3.353 (of Josephus himself); 4.33 (Vespasian), 4.388 ("inspired men"); *Ant.* 6.76 (Saul); 8.346 (Elijah); 9.35 (Elisha), in all these instances (except for *War* 4.388) as part of the expression "to become inspired" of 6.56. See Begg 1993: 186, n. 1231.

[214] Josephus leaves aside the added indication of 1 Sam 10:6 according to which Saul will not only prophesy with the group, but will himself "be turned into another man."

[215] This statement by Samuel concerning the effect of Saul's prophesying upon those who witness it has no equivalent at this point in the biblical sequence. It might, however, be viewed as Josephus' anticipation/ positive reformulation of the (derogatory) question placed on the lips of those who see Saul prophesy in 1 Sam 10:11: "what has come over the son of Kish?"

[216] Josephus renders more definite the vague instruction given Saul by Samuel in 1 Sam 10:7, i.e. "do whatever your hand finds to do."

[217] MT (1 Sam 10:8) הגלגל (Eng.: "Gilgal"); LXX B Γαλαάδ; LXX L and Josephus Γάλγαλα (this is also A. Rahlfs' emendation of B). In 10:8a Samuel tells Saul "come down before me to Gilgal" (MT LXX L; LXX B: come down before Galaad).

[218] This interjected remark seems intended to obviate the difficulty that whereas 1 Sam 10:8 appears to envisage Saul's proceeding immediately to "Gilgal," in what follows he will be found at a variety of other sites before finally arriving there (see 1 Sam 11:14-15). Accordingly, at this point Josephus simply has Samuel tell Saul that he is to come to Gilgal whenever Samuel will summon him there.

[219] In 1 Sam 10:8a Samuel announces his intention of offering "burnt offerings and peace offerings" at Gilgal. Josephus has him speak rather of "thanksgiving sacrifices" to be offered "for these things" (i.e. Saul's

designation and its sequels). He likewise accentuates the status of Saul by making him a co-sacrificer along with Samuel (as also by omitting Samuel's imperious concluding words to him—which will themselves only be picked up much later in 13:8—of 1 Sam 10:8b: "seven days shall you wait, until I come and show you what you shall do"; compare *Bib. Ant.* 56.7, where Samuel prescribes a 7-day wait, nor for Saul, but rather for the people who have come forward to demand that he give them the promised king).

[220] In 1 Sam 10:9aα Saul takes the initiative in leaving Samuel; Josephus portrays a more deferential Saul, who waits to be "dismissed" by Samuel. He passes over the mention of 10:9aβ about God's "giving Saul another heart" as he leaves Samuel, just as he earlier omitted the similar phrase of 10:6: "you [Saul] shall be turned into another man."

[221] Compare 1 Sam 10:9b: "and all these signs came to pass that day"; Pseudo-Philo (who has no equivalent to the sequence of 1 Sam 10:2-7) reproduces this summary notice in *Bib. Ant.* 56.7 and adds "are these [the signs] not written in the Book of Samuel?" Following his version of the summarizing statement of 1 Sam 10:9b, Josephus leaves aside the sequence of 1 Sam 10:10-13a, which relates the fulfillment of the 3rd of the "signs," i.e. Saul's prophesying (10:5-6), predicted by Samuel and the effects of this on those who witness it. The omission (Pseudo-Philo has no parallel to it either) might have been motivated by the fact that it represents something of a duplicate of the episode related in 1 Sam 19:18-24 (which Josephus will reproduce in 6.220-223). Recall too that in 6.56 Josephus seems to anticipate the onlookers' words ("what has come over the son of Kish?") of 10:11, making his version of these part of Samuel's own prediction to Saul of what awaits him.

[222] MT 1 Sam 10:14 designates Saul's interlocutor as his "uncle." Like LXX, Josephus here employs a more general word, i.e. συγγενής, with the meaning "relative"; in 6.129 he will qualify Abner more specifically as the son of Saul's uncle, i.e. his cousin.

[223] Saul's "uncle" remains nameless throughout their exchange in 1 Sam 10:14-16. Josephus derives the name of this figure from 1 Sam 14:50 (// 6.130) which mentions "Abner" as the uncle (or cousin) of Saul.

him more than any of his other relations),[224] the latter inquired repeatedly about his travels and the things that had happened during them.[225] He, however, did not answer concerning the other matters, but only stated that he had been with the prophet Samouel who told him that the donkeys had been saved.[226] **59** About the kingship, however, and what this involved, he, supposing that the hearing of these things would be a source of envy and disbelief, kept silent.[227] For it did not seem riskless or prudent to inform him, even though he seemed very loyal and was more cherished by him than all his blood [relatives]. He reasoned, I suppose, that human nature is what it is in truth: neither is loyalty reliable, nor does anyone, whether friend or relative, retain his affection in the face of splendid [honors] from God; rather, they at once become malicious and begrudging towards those obtaining such distinctions.[228]

Samuel ad-dresses people about kingship

    (4.4) 60. Samouel called the people together to the city of Masphata[229] and addressed them in words that, he said, he spoke at God's command.[230] They had been unmindful of his benefits in awarding them freedom and enslaving their enemies,[231] and had deposed God from his kingship, not knowing that it is most advantageous to be ruled over by the best one of all, namely God who is best of all.[232] **61.** They preferred to have a human king, who would treat his subjects as possessions accord-

---

[224] With this inserted phrase—compare 1 Sam 10:13 where, after prophesying, Saul goes to "the (which?) high place")—Josephus provides a transition to the exchange between Saul and his relative, which in the Bible begins quite abruptly with the latter suddenly addressing Saul in 10:14. The insertion likewise offers a rationale for Saul's going in first place to this figure's house (rather than—as might be expected—to that of his own father, Kish).

[225] In 1 Sam 10:14a Saul's uncle/relative asks both Saul and his servant, "Where did you go?"

[226] Josephus at this point compresses the sequence of 1 Sam 10:14b-16a, in which Saul (so MT; LXX they: Saul and the servant) responds to his uncle's question ("where did you [pl.] go?," v. 14a) that, after unsuccessfully searching for the donkeys, he and his servant had repaired to Samuel (v. 14b), whereupon the uncle asks what Samuel had told him (v. 15), Saul responding that the former had assured them that the donkeys had been found (v. 16a).

[227] Josephus expatiates on the closing notice of 1 Sam 10:16b ("but about the matter of the kingdom about which Samuel had spoken, he did not tell him anything," MT LXX L [LXX B lacks the phrase "about which Samuel had spoken"]) with an indication concerning Saul's motivation in keeping silent about Samuel's other communications to him that he will develop in what follows.

[228] This typical Josephan moralizing reflection with its highly negative view concerning humans generally serves to further motivate Saul's silence about the kingship he has been awarded by Samuel. It recalls the warning that "human nature is self-loving and hostile

to those of outstanding virtue" that Josephus has God deliver to Gideon in *Ant.* 5.215. "Envy" (φθόνος) its sources, objects, and consequences, is a major theme throughout Josephus' story of Saul, his histories generally, and his own autobiography. On the topic see: Mason 1991: 225-27; 2001: 78-79, n. 591; Feldman 1998: 198-203. As these authors point out, the theme is also prominent in Greco-Roman historiography and biography. Cornelius Nepos (*Chabrias* 3), e.g., notes the "envy" (*invidia*) that the achievements of various Athenian generals evoked among their compatriots.

[229] In mentioning "Mizpah" here (see 6.22 = 1 Sam 7:5), Josephus omits the further specification of 1 Sam 10:17 that Samuel summoned the people "before the Lord" at that site. On Josephus' version of 1 Sam 10:17-27, see Begg 1996c.

[230] This formulation takes the place of the "messenger formula" ("thus says the Lord...") with which Samuel opens his discourse in 1 Sam 10:18a and which Josephus consistently avoids.

[231] Josephus generalizes Samuel's words in 1 Sam 10:18, where he recalls God's bringing Israel out of Egypt and delivering it from the hand of the Egyptians. The reference to "freedom" here echoes Samuel's summoning the people to act on behalf of their freedom in 6.19-20.

[232] To Samuel's reminiscence of Israel's "rejection" of its God as expressed in its demand for a king in 1 Sam 10:19a, Josephus has him append a remark underscoring the people's "ignorance" concerning their own best interests in making that demand. The remark recalls God's declaration that the people had rejected him "so that he might not rule as sole king" in 6.38.

ing to his will and desire and the urging of the other passions, and ruthlessly exploit his boundless authority.[233] Since the human race was not his own work[234] and production, he [the king] would not be concerned to preserve it, whereas God, for that same reason, would watch out for it. "But since these things have seemed good to you and since arrogance towards God has prevailed,[235] all of you take your positions according to your tribes and families[236] and cast lots."[237]

(4.5) 62. When the Hebrews did this, the lot fell out for the Benjamite tribe; from this the ancestral [clan] called Matris[238] was taken by lot.[239] The lot being cast man by man,[240] it was determined by lot that Saoul, the son of Keis, should rule as king.[241]

Saul's selection and disappearance

63. Once he knew that he had been taken, the youth hid himself,[242] not wishing, I suppose, to appear eager to take the rulership. He evidenced, rather, such self-control and prudence, in contrast to most people who cannot restrain their joy at even minor successes, but are in a hurry to manifest these to everyone. Not only did he not display such [pride] in the kingship and his being appointed master of such great and large nations, but even removed himself from the sight of those over whom he was to rule as king and made them seek him and exert themselves in this.[243]

64. When they were at a loss and distressed because Saoul had become invisible,[244] the prophet[245] begged God to show where the youth might be and to cause him to appear.[246] **65.** When he learned from God the place where Saoul had hid-

Saul's return and acclamation

---

[233] In developing the contrast between the human king and the "best of all" divine king (6.60), Josephus has Samuel hark back to his warning concerning the ways of the former in 6.40-42.

[234] Greek: οὐχ . . . ἴδιον ἔργον. Compare *Ant.* 8.280, where King Abijah designates God as "his own work" (ὃς ἔργον . . . αὐτοῦ).

[235] Josephus here has Samuel sum up on his charges concerning the wrongfulness of the people's opting for a human king and rejecting their divine one (6.60-61) as a transition to the command he will now give them.

[236] The word translated "families" is σκῆπτρα, literally "staffs," but often used in the LXX in the meaning of either "tribes" or "families." In LXX B 1 Sam 10:19b Samuel calls on the people to group themselves κατὰ τὰ σκῆπρα καὶ τὰς φυλὰς ὑμῶν ("according to your families and tribes"; compare MT and LXX L: "by your tribes and your thousands"). Josephus uses the same 2 designations as LXX B, while reversing their order.

[237] Josephus has Samuel command the people not only to take their positions by groups (so 1 Sam 10:19b), but to also cast lots (as they do in the continuation of the biblical account).

[238] MT (1 Sam 10:21) המטרי (Eng.: "the Matrites"); LXX B Ματταρεί; LXX L Ἀματταρί; Josephus Ματρίς.

[239] In specifying that first the tribe and then the family was taken "by lot," Josephus follows LXX 1 Sam 10:20-21 with its use of the verb κατακληρόω, whereas MT speaks simply of their being "taken."

[240] This formulation reflects the plus of LXX 1 Sam 10:21aβ: "and he [Samuel] brought the family of

Mattarei (B)/ Amattari (L) near man by man."

[241] 1 Sam 10:21bα reads simply "and Saul the son of Kish was taken (by lot)." Josephus spells out the import of his being thus "taken."

[242] Josephus anticipates his mention of Saul's "hiding himself" in response to his being "taken" from 1 Sam 10:22b, where God informs the Israelites that Saul "has hidden himself among the baggage."

[243] This extended insertion, highlighting Saul's modesty, provides a motivation for his self-concealment that 1 Sam 10:21-22 itself leaves unexplained. It recalls Josephus' accentuation of Saul's modesty in response to Samuel in 6.51 (see note to "position" there) in comparison with his words in 1 Sam 9:21. The depiction of Saul here in 6.63 further serves to establish an association between him and such Roman heroes as King Numa, Cincinatus and Cato the Elder who showed reluctance to assume the offices that were pressed upon them.

[244] Josephus elaborates on Saul's "unfindability" (so 1 Sam 10:21bβ) with mention of the emotional effect of this upon the people.

[245] In making Samuel the subject of the "inquiry" of 1 Sam 10:22aα, Josephus agrees with LXX against MT, where "they," i.e. the people as a whole, undertake the inquiry of God.

[246] Josephus gives a more definite content to Samuel's "inquiry" than one finds in the rather allusive question he poses to God in 1 Sam 10:22aβ ("is there yet a man to come hither?" [MT]/ "did the man come hither?" [LXX]).

den,[247] he sent to fetch him;[248] upon his arriving, he set him in the middle of the crowd.[249] He stood taller than everyone and was very kingly in his height.[250]

(4.6) 66. The prophet said: "This is the one whom God has given you as your king.[251] See how superior he is to all, and how worthy of rule!"[252] When the people acclaimed the king's safety,[253] the prophet wrote down[254] for them the things that were to happen[255] and read [these] as the king listened.[256] He placed the book in the tent of God as a witness to what he had predicted for later generations.[257]

Differing stances towards Saul

67. When he had finished these things, Samouel dismissed the crowd.[258] He himself went to the city of Armatha (for this was his ancestral town),[259] while Saoul departed for Gabatha,[260] from which he originated. Many good people went with him, rendering the king the honor due him.[261] There were, however, even more vile persons who despised him and kept jeering at the others. These neither brought him gifts nor did anything, either by their solicitude or word, to please Saoul.[262]

---

[247] From the divine answer of 1 Sam 10:22b Josephus omits the detail that Saul was hiding "among the baggage," given that this might appear degrading for a future king (and has, in any case, not been mentioned in what precedes).

[248] MT and LXX 1 Sam 10:23a differ as to who it is who "runs" and brings Saul back: in the former it the people as a whole, in the latter rather Samuel acting alone. Josephus seems to conflate the 2 divergent presentations with his reference to Samuel's taking the initiative in dispatching men to fetch Saul.

[249] According to MT 1 Sam 10:23bα Saul "takes his stand among the people," whereas in LXX Samuel "sets him in place." Josephus follows the LXX in his ongoing highlighting of Samuel's active role in the proceedings.

[250] 1 Sam 10:23bβ specifies that Saul was "taller than any of the people from his shoulders upward."

[251] This affirmation takes the place of Samuel's question to the people of 1 Sam 10:24aβ: "do you see him whom the Lord has chosen?," which might appear otiose given Saul's actual presence among them (10:23).

[252] This is Josephus' equivalent to Samuel's affirmation in 1 Sam 10:24bα: "there is none like him among the people."

[253] In 1 Sam 10:24bβ the people shout "Long live the king."

[254] Josephus reverses the sequence of 1 Sam 10:25a, where Samuel first speaks to the people and then writes his words down.

[255] In 1 Sam 10:25a Samuel first presents orally and then writes down the "ordinance of the kingship" (MT מִשְׁפַּט הַמְּלֻכָה; LXX B "ordinance of the king"). Seeing that Samuel has already discoursed at length on the "ordinance of the king" (מִשְׁפַּט הַמֶּלֶךְ, MT 1 Sam 8:9) in 1 Sam 8:10-18 (= 6.40-42), Josephus provides a new, more general content to his words here, i.e. future events.

[256] Josephus' reference to Samuel's "reading" his words to the people reflects the fact that in his presentation Samuel writes his words down before delivering them. 1 Sam 10:25a does not explicitly mention Saul as being among Samuel's hearers.

[257] In 1 Sam 10:25aβ Samuel simply lays the book up "before the Lord." Josephus replaces this vague indication with mention of a specific locale, i.e. "the tent of God" (see the references to this having been erected at Shiloh in *Ant.* 5.68, 343). He likewise supplies a rationale for such a storing of the book, i.e. its projected "witness" for later generations concerning the "predictions" Samuel has just made (on these as the content of his book/address, see note to "were to happen" at 6.66). Josephus' presentation of Samuel's initiatives here further serves to associate him with both Moses (see *Ant.* 3.38; 4.303) and Joshua (see *Ant.* 5.61), whose respective documents concerning the future are both laid up "in the temple."

[258] See 1 Sam 10:25b.

[259] With this inserted notice Josephus responds to the question of what Samuel himself did following the breakup of the Mizpah proceedings as related in 1 Sam 10:17-25 (= 6.60-66). For "Armatha" as Samuel's "hometown," see 6.35, cf. 1 Sam 7:17.

[260] MT (1 Sam 10:26a) גִּבְעָתָה (Eng.: "Gibeah"); LXX B Γαβαά; LXX L (translating) τὸν βουνόν; Josephus Γαβαθή. Josephus had Samuel announce Saul's coming to this site in 6.57 (// 1 Sam 10:5).

[261] From 1 Sam 10:26b Josephus eliminates the reference to God's "touching the hearts" of the "mighty men" who then simply accompany Saul to his home, while also accentuating the respect "good persons" accorded him.

[262] Josephus highlights both the extent of the opposition to Saul (this comprises the majority of the people; compare 1 Sam 10:27aα, where Saul is opposed only by "some worthless fellows") and its all-encompassing manifestations (they not only "despise" him

(5.1) **68.** A month later,[263] however, [Saoul's] war against Naas,[264] king of the Ammanites, was the beginning of universal honor for him.[265] For this king had inflicted many calamities on those Judeans[266] living across the Jordan river, invading them with a large and bellicose army.[267] **69.** He reduced their cities to slavery, subduing them for the present by strength and violence. Moreover, by his astuteness and cunning, he weakened them so that they would be unable thereafter to escape from their slavery to him by revolting. For he cut out the right eyes of those who surrendered to him under oath and those whom he took by the law of war.[268] **70.** He did this, so that, when their left eye was covered by their shields, they would be completely helpless.[269] **71.** When he had done these things to those beyond the Jordan,[270] the king of the Ammanites campaigned against those called the Galadenes and pitched camp at the mother-city of the enemy, that is Jabis.[271] He sent messengers to direct them to give themselves up[272] on the condition that their right eyes would be gouged out.[273] Otherwise, he threatened to lay siege to and wreck their

Invasion of Nahash (Naas)

Exchange between Nahash and Jabeshites

---

and bring him no presents [so 10:27aβbα], but also ridicule his supporters and show complete indifference to securing his favor). Like LXX B and 4QSam[a], Josephus has no equivalent to the plus of MT LXX L 10:27bβ, according to which Saul, in response to his opponents' treatment of him, "held his peace."

[263] This chronological indication (absent in MT) stands at the same point in Josephus' presentation as in LXX 1 Sam 11:1, i.e. at the very beginning of the account of Saul's Ammonite war. By contrast, the corresponding notice of 4QSam[a] appears only at a later point.

[264] MT (1 Sam 11:1) נחש (Eng.: "Nahash"); LXX Ναάς; Josephus Ναάσης.

[265] This notice marks the transition from and contrast between the time of Saul's being despised by many (6.67) and the "universal honor" that he subsequently acquired through his victory over the Ammonites. In what follows Josephus will give his amplified version of the 4QSam[a] plus concerning Nahash's Transjordanian campaign as found at the beginning of its 1 Samuel 11. This text reads in the translation of McCarter (1980: 199): "Now Nahash... had been oppressing the Gadites and the Reubenites grievously, gouging out the right eye of each of them and allowing Israel no deliverer. No men of the Israelites who were across the Jordan remained whose right eye Nahash... had not gouged out. But seven thousand men had escaped from the Ammonites and entered into Jabesh-gilead." On Josephus' version of 1 Samuel 11, see Begg 1997f.

[266] This general term for Nahash's victims replaces mention of "the Gadites and the Reubenites" in the plus of 4QSam[a]; see note to "for him" at 6.68.

[267] Josephus goes beyond 4QSam[a] itself in magnifying the Ammonite threat with this reference to the size and character of Nahash's army.

[268] In the above sequence only Josephus' reference to Nahash's gouging out the Transjordanians' right eyes has an actual parallel in 4QSam[a]. What precedes in 6.69 is a further elaboration of the severity of the Ammonite threat, featuring the astuteness of Nahash and his readiness to mutilate all without distinction, the result being that the Transjordanians are thoroughly subjugated by him, not only for the present, but also for the future. The phrase "law of war" (Greek πολέμου νόμος; cf. Latin *ius belli*) used by Josephus here refers to the rights which success in war gave to the victor over the lives and property of the vanquished.

[269] Josephus' (military) rationale for Nahash's practice of gouging out precisely the right eye of his victims has no parallel in the plus of 4QSam[a] (compare MT 1 Sam 11:2bβ, where Nahash spells out the intended purpose of his threatened removal of the Jabeshites' right eyes, i.e, "and thus put disgrace upon all Israel"). The notice takes the place of 4QSam[a]'s own reference to the 7,000 Transjordanians who previously escaped to Jabesh-gilead (and who have no role in the continuation of the story).

[270] With this transitional phrase, Josephus, after his preceding use of the 4QSam[a] plus, reconnects with the joint story line of MT LXX 1 Samuel 11.

[271] MT (1 Sam 11:1) יבש גלעד (Eng.: "Jabesh-gilead"); LXX B 'Ιαβεὶς Γαλαάδ; LXX L 'Ιαβὶς Γαλαάδ; Josephus 'Ιαβίς (called by him the "metropolis" of Nahash's enemies, the Galadenes [Γαλαδηνούς]).

[272] In 1 Sam 11:1b the Jabeshites take the initiative in asking Nahash for a treaty and promising to serve him. Josephus transfers the initiative in the negotiations to Nahash himself, once again underscoring his (current) control of events, likewise having him begin his message to the Galadenes with a call for their surrender.

[273] See 1 Sam 11:2a, where Nahash mentions his doing this as "the condition" for the "treaty" previously

cities.[274] The choice was theirs: did they prefer to have only a small part of their bodies cut off, or be slain completely?[275] **72.** The Galadenes were thrown into consternation; they did not dare to say anything, either that they would give themselves up or that they would fight.[276] Instead, they requested to receive a reprieve of seven days so that, sending messengers to their compatriots, they might appeal to them to ally themselves with them.[277] If help came, they would fight;[278] if, however, no help was [forthcoming] from them, they stated that they would give themselves up to him to suffer whatever might seem good to him.[279]

(5.2) 73. Naas, despising the Galadene crowd and their answer, gave them the reprieve and allowed them to send to whatever allies they wished.[280] They therefore immediately sent to the Israelites, city by city, to report Naas' [threats] and the helpless situation in which they had been placed.[281]

Israelite reaction to Jabeshites' plea

74. They [the Israelites] were reduced to tears and grief by the report concerning the Jabisenes. Anxiety, however, kept them from doing anything beyond this.[282] When the messengers came also to the city of King Saoul[283] and told of the dangers in which the Jabisenes found themselves, the people, like their fellows, suffered on account of these things, for they bewailed the misfortune of their relatives.[284]

Saul takes charge

75. Now Saoul, upon coming into the city from his agricultural labors,[285] met his fellow-citizens weeping. When he inquired about the reason for their sorrow and dejection, he learned the things [told] by the messengers.[286]

---

asked for by the Jabeshites (11:1b). Josephus leaves aside Nahash's appended indication that the eye-gouging is intended to "put disgrace upon Israel" (11:2bβ), having already cited an alternative military rationale for the measure in 6.70.

[274] This warning as to what awaits the Jabeshites should they fail to surrender has no equivalent in Nahash's words to them as cited in 1 Sam 11:2. The addition highlights the threat facing the Jabeshites, whatever response they make to Nahash.

[275] This conclusion to Nahash's message, underscoring the hopeless dilemma the Jabeshites face, is Josephus' own. With Nahash's alternative here between the "minor" loss of a body part (the right eye) and total destruction, compare the word of Jesus in Matt 5:29 (and parallels): "If you right eye causes you to sin, pluck it out and throw it away; it is better that you lose one of your members than that your whole body be thrown into hell."

[276] This inserted notice concerning the disorienting first effect of Nahash's message upon the recipients underscores the terrifying gravity of the threat posed by him.

[277] Josephus' Jabeshites spell out what the messengers mentioned by them in their request of Nahash in 1 Sam 11:3a are to ask of their compatriots. Like LXX, Josephus has the entire population (rather than simply the city "elders," so MT) make the request of Nahash.

[278] This possible positive outcome to the Jebeshites' embassy is not mentioned in 1 Sam 11:3b, which they refer only to its negative outcome and the

consequences for themselves.

[279] To the Jabeshites' statement in 1 Sam 11:3b about what they will do should their embassy generate no help for them, Josephus appends this concluding reference to Nahash's, getting to do whatever he wishes with them, should they end up surrendering.

[280] Josephus inserts this response by Nahash to the Jebeshites' appeal, whereas in 1 Sam 11:4 the messengers simply proceed to Gibeah without his permission being obtained. As in 6.71 (compare 11:2) Josephus accentuates the king's domination of the proceedings.

[281] This reference to the messengers' visitation of all Israel lacks a counterpart in 1 Samuel 11, where (see v. 4) only their going to Saul's hometown is mentioned.

[282] This description of the pan-Israelite response to the messengers' report has no source basis. It serves to highlight Saul's own subsequent efficacious initiative in the face of such universal paralysis.

[283] Compare the various designations used for the messengers' destination in 1 Sam 11:4: "Gibeah of Saul" (MT); "Gabaa (to Saul)" (LXX B); "to the hill of Saul" (LXX L).

[284] Josephus embellishes the reference of 1 Sam 11:4b to the inhabitants of Saul's town "weeping aloud."

[285] The witnesses for 1 Sam 11:5a differ as to how Saul "comes from the field": "behind the oxen" (MT), "after the morning" (LXX B), "early after the oxen" (LXX L).

[286] See 1 Sam 11:5b.

76. Becoming inspired,[287] he sent the Jabisenes away, promising that he would come to them as their helper on the third day and would conquer the enemy before sunrise so that the rising sun might see them already victorious and delivered from their fears.[288] He then directed some of them to stay behind who would serve as guides on the way.[289]

(5.3) 77. Wishing by fear of retribution to incite the people to war against the Ammanites and to assemble them more quickly,[290] Saoul cut through the tendons[291] of his oxen[292] and threatened to do the same to those of everyone,[293] if they did not go out to meet him armed at the Jordan on the next day[294] and follow him and the prophet Samouel wherever they might lead them.[295]

78. In their dread of the threatened retribution,[296] they assembled at the designated time[297] and the crowd was mustered at the city of Bala.[298] The number of those gathered, apart from the tribe of Iouda, was found to be 700,000,[299] while from that tribe there were 70,000.[300]

79. Crossing the Jordan and covering a distance of ten *schoenoi*[301] throughout the entire night, he arrived before sun-up.[302] Dividing his army into three parts, he fell

Saul's victory over Nahash

---

[287] In 1 Sam 11:6 the reference is to God's spirit "coming mightily upon Saul" with the result that his "anger is greatly kindled." Josephus' substitute phrase (Greek: ἔθεος γενόμενος) is the same used by him in place of the mention of God's spirit "coming mightily upon" Saul of 1 Sam 10:6; see note to "becoming inspired" at 6.56.

[288] In the biblical sequence Saul (so LXX; MT: they, i.e. the Israelites as a whole) dispatches the messengers back to Jabesh (1 Sam 11:9) only after the king has initiated a variety of other measures (11:7-8). Josephus' reversal of this sequence reflects the consideration that the besieged Jabeshites would have been in desperate need of immediate reassurance. Whereas in 1 Sam 11:9 Saul promises deliverance "tomorrow," Josephus, reflecting that it would have taken more time to assemble the Israelite forces (cf. 11:7-8), makes this "on the third day."

[289] In 1 Sam 11:9 Saul seems to send back all the Jabeshite messengers. Josephus' having him retain some of them as guides accentuates his status as a general who "thinks of everything."

[290] Josephus supplies this motivation for Saul's initiative with the oxen as reported in 1 Sam 11:7a.

[291] In 1 Sam 11:7 Saul cuts the oxen "in pieces" rather than simply "hamstringing" them.

[292] 1 Sam 11:7aα (where MT speaks of "a yoke of oxen," LXX of "two cows") does not specify that it was Saul's own beasts that were used by him. Josephus' clarification of the point highlights Saul's readiness to sacrifice personally for the cause of his compatriots.

[293] According to 1 Sam 11:7aβ Saul dispatched the pieces of the cut-up beasts throughout Israel with the threat to do the same to the oxen/cows of whoever did not join him. In Josephus the oxen are only hamstrung, not dismembered, and so cannot be practicably carried

from place to place. Accordingly, Josephus turns Saul's threat into a purely verbal one, minus the Bible's accompanying visual reinforcement of this.

[294] Josephus supplies a specification, lacking in 1 Sam 11:7bα, as to where, when and how (i.e. "armed") the Israelites are to meet Saul and Samuel.

[295] This indication concerning the intended sequel to the Israelites' joining Saul and Samuel is Josephus' addition to the wording of 1 Sam 11:7bα.

[296] In 1 Sam 11:7bβ the people's fear is a divinely-sent one; Josephus grounds it rather in Saul's preceding threat; cf. the opening words of 6.77.

[297] Josephus' reading here reflects the final verb of MT 1 Sam 11:7 ("they came out") as against LXX's "they shouted." His inserted reference to "the designated time" picks up on Saul's directing the Israelites to assemble "on the next day" in 6.77.

[298] The witnesses for 1 Sam 11:8a differ as to where, and by whom, Israel is mustered, compare: "he [Saul] mustered them in Bezek" (MT); "Abiezek mustered them in Bama" (LXX B); "Saul mustered them in Rama" (LXX L). According to Schalit (*s.v.*) the place name "Bala" read by Niese and Marcus in 6.78 is a corruption of the LXX B reading, i.e. Βαμά.

[299] Josephus gives a higher figure for the non-Judean Israelites than do either MT (300,000) or LXX and 4QSamᵃ (600,000) 1 Sam 11:8.

[300] Josephus' figure for the Judean forces agrees with that of LXX 1 Sam 11:8 (and that reconstructed for 4QSamᵃ) as opposed to the 30,000 of MT.

[301] 10 *schoenoi* are equivalent to *ca.* 40-50 miles; see Marcus *ad loc.*

[302] These indications on Saul's march are peculiar to Josephus; they portray Saul as an energetic general, determined to reach his goal by the stated time, i.e. before sunrise (see 6.76).

suddenly upon the unprepared enemy from all sides.[303] Joining battle, he killed
many others of the Ammanites, in addition to King Naas.[304] **80.** This splendid deed
accomplished by Saoul disseminated his praise to all the Hebrews and [caused him
to] enjoy a marvelous reputation for courage.[305] For even if there were some who
previously despised him, they now switched over to honoring him and thinking him
the best of all.[306] For he was not merely content to have saved the Jabisenes; he also
campaigned against the country of the Ammanites that he subjugated in its entirety.
Taking much plunder, he returned home in splendor.[307]

People's re-
sponse to
Saul's victory

81. Now the people, in their pleasure at Saoul's achievements, rejoiced that they
had designated such a king.[308] They cried out,[309] however, against those who said
he would be of no advantage to the state: "Where are they now?"[310] and "Let them
pay the penalty," and all the things that a mob, elated by successes, loves to say
against those who were recently disparaging the ones responsible for these [suc-
cesses].[311] **82.** Saoul,[312] however, although he welcomed their loyalty and eagerness
regarding himself, swore that he would not tolerate any of his compatriots' being
done away with on that day.[313] For it would be improper to defile by bloodshed the
victory God had given and to celebrate the festival by the mutual murder of their
relatives.[314]

Saul spares op-
ponents

---

[303] See 1 Sam 11:11, which Josephus characteristically embellishes with mention of the suddenness of
the attack and the unpreparedness of the enemy; compare, e.g., his description of Ahab's victory over the
Syrians in *Ant.* 8.377.

[304] 1 Sam 11:11bα does not mention Nahash himself being killed in the battle; Josephus' insertion on
the point satisfies readers' curiosity concerning the
king's fate (and their sense of poetic justice regarding
one who had himself caused such harm to the Israelites).

[305] This notice on the reaction to Saul's victory is
biblically unparalleled; it accentuates Saul's status as a
successful general, just as it recalls the reference (6.68)
to the "universal honor" Saul's conduct in the upcoming Ammonite war was to bring him.

[306] Greek: πάντων ἄριστος; this is the same expression used of God as Israel's king by Samuel in 6.60.
Josephus' insertion here in 6.80 underscores the univer-
sality of the popularity (see 6.68) that Saul's victory
won him: even his erstwhile confirmed detractors (see
6.67) now join in recognizing his abilities.

[307] These statements on Saul's following up his victory portray him as a general who knows how to make
full use of the opportunity afforded him by his success
to definitively eliminate the Ammonite threat and gain
riches thereby. Compare 1 Sam 11:11bβ, where there is
no mention of Saul's personal role in the post-battle
situation: "... those who survived [i.e. of the Ammo-
nites] were scattered so that no two of them were left
together."

[308] This inserted statement concerning the general
satisfaction with Saul's kingship serves as a lead-in to
the people's subsequent demand regarding his detractors (see 1 Sam 11:12).

[309] In 1 Sam 11:12 the crowd addresses itself to
Samuel.

[310] This rhetorical question takes the place of the
one ascribed to the people in 1 Sam 11:12: "Who is it
that said, 'Shall Saul (+ not, LXX) reign over us'?"
Josephus has already reintroduced Saul's former detractors (see 6.67= 1 Sam 10:27) in 6.80.

[311] This appendix to the crowd's words as cited in 1
Sam 11:12 is another expression of Josephus' contempt
for the masses; see note on "even the crowds" at 6.34.

[312] Josephus follows MT and LXX L 1 Sam 11:13
in making Saul the one to respond to the crowd's demand (which in 1 Sam 11:12 is addressed rather to
Samuel); in LXX B+ Samuel is the respondent.

[313] Josephus embellishes Saul's refusal to permit the
death of his detractors (1 Sam 11:13) with mention of
his initial expression of appreciation for the crowd's
attachment and by having him confirm his rejection of
their demand with an oath.

[314] The translation follows the reading of RO as
printed by Niese. Marcus adopts the rather different
reading of SP, which he renders as follows: "... it were
monstrous to defile that God-given victory with bloodshed and murder of men of their own race, and it better
beseemed them to keep feast in a spirit of mutual good-
will." Whichever reading is preferred, one has here a
Josephan expansion of the biblical Saul's words of 1
Sam 11:13, in which he makes the king the mouthpiece
for his oft-voiced condemnation of intramural Jewish
violence; see Feldman 1998: 556. As one who attempts
to mollify tensions within the people, Saul stands in the
line of both Gideon (*Ant.* 5.230-231) and Jephthah
(5.267-268).

(5.4) 83. When Samouel now stated that it was necessary to confirm Saoul's king-ship by a second designation, all assembled at the city of Galgala, for it was there that he directed them to come.[315] In the presence of the crowd the prophet again anointed Saoul with the holy oil and proclaimed him king a second time.[316] And thus the Hebrews' constitution was changed into a kingship.[317] **84.** For in the time of Moyses and his disciple,[318] the general [Iesous],[319] they continued living under an aristocratic form of government.[320] After the latter's death, anarchy prevailed over their people for a whole eighteen years.[321] **85.** After this, they reverted to their earlier constitution,[322] entrusting the administration of the whole to the one who seemed the best[323] in warfare and courage. And therefore, they called this constitutional period that of the Judges.[324]

86. Summoning an assembly of the Hebrews,[325] the prophet Samouel said: "I adjure you,[326] by the greatest God,[327] who imparted life to those [good][328] brothers—

Saul reanointed

Constitutional changes

Samuel's apologia and its acceptance by people

---

[315] See 1 Sam 11:14-15aα.

[316] Josephus agrees with LXX 1 Sam 11:15aβ in making Samuel (rather than the people as a whole, so MT) the subject of the action regarding Saul. He likewise follows LXX in speaking of Samuel's "anointing" Saul, whereas in MT "they make Saul king." In introducing mention of the "holy oil" with which Samuel anoints Saul here, Josephus harks back to his own presentation in 6.54 (cf. 1 Sam 10:1), where this same phrase appears (at least in the Niese reading); see note to "oil" there. On that earlier occasion, however, Samuel "pours" the oil on Saul's head rather than "anointing" him as here in 6.83.

[317] Josephus rounds off his whole segment 6.32-83 (= 1 Samuel 8-11) dealing with the emergence of the monarchy with this phrase, which likewise serves as a lead-in for his following remarks on the evolution of the Israelites' constitution in 6.84-85.

[318] Greek: μαθητής. This is Josephus' only use of the term as a designation of Joshua in relation to Moses. On his 14 total uses of the word (which occurs only 3 times in the LXX), see Begg 1993: 197, n. 1307.

[319] The name is absent in RO and bracketed by Niese; Marcus reads it without brackets, following the other witnesses.

[320] This is Josephus' only use of the verb ἀριστοκρατέομαι ("live under an aristocratic form of government"). The term here echoes the cognate noun found in 6.36, where Josephus speaks of kingship as being much inferior to "aristocracy"; see note to "constitution" at 6.36.

[321] Josephus' one remaining use of term ἀναρχία ("anarchy") is in *Ant.* 5.185, where, following the death of the judge Kenaz, Israel falls into this condition. The only 18-year period cited in Josephus' account of the Judges epoch is the time of Israel's subjugation to Eglon king of Moab; see 5.187 and cf. Marcus *ad loc.* Whereas, however, the anarchy spoken of in 5.187 begins only after the death of Keniaz when Israel fell un-

der the power of Moab, 6.84 suggests that such anarchy set in directly after the death of Joshua.

[322] According to Josephus' account of the Judges period, this constitutional shift occurred with the overthrow of King Eglon of Moab by "Ioud" (Ehud) (see *Ant.* 5.197)—which itself ended the 18 years of "anarchy" that set in after the death of Keniaz (see previous note)—and prevailed down to the new change of constitution that occurred with Saul's accession to kingship (see 6.83).

[323] Greek: ἄριστος. The use of this term sets up a word-play with the verbal form ἀριστοκοκρατούμενοι ("living under an aristocratic form of government") of 6.84, thereby reinforcing Josephus' statement that the period of the Judges as spoken of in 6.85 did represent a "return" to the "aristocracy" of the time of Moses and Joshua. The term further echoes the references to God and Saul as "the best of all" in 6.60 and 6.80, respectively; see note to "the best of all" at 6.80.

[324] In the above reflective interlude Josephus thus distinguishes 4 distinct governmental stages in the period between Moses-Joshua and Saul's accession: aristocracy, anarchy, return to aristocracy with the Judges, and kingship. According to *Ant.* 11.111 the Jews reverted to "aristocracy" (now combined with "oligarchy") a 2nd time following the exile when the high priests assumed power, they, in turn, giving way to a revived kingship under the Hasmoneans.

[325] 1 Sam 12:1 makes no mention of Samuel's "calling an assembly" prior to his speaking to the people (i.e. apparently in connection with their gathering at Gilgal, 1 Sam 11:14-15). Josephus' inserted reference to the prophet's convening of a (new) assembly confers extra solemnity on his following words; it has a parallel in *Bib. Ant.* 57.1. On Josephus' version of 1 Samuel 12, see Begg 1997g.

[326] In moving immediately to Samuel's summoning the people to give their testimony against him (// 1 Sam 12:3aα), Josephus passes over the leader's opening

I speak of Moyses and Aaron—and who liberated our ancestors from the Egyptians and slavery under them,[329] that, showing neither partiality out of deference nor keeping things secret from fear nor yielding to any other emotion, to say[330] whether I have done anything bad or unjust or for the sake of gain or covetousness or [to win] favor with others.[331] **87.** Make an accusation if I have accepted any of those things— a calf or sheep[332]—that are considered permissible to take as food, or if I have caused grief to anyone by seizing his beast of burden for my own needs.[333] Charge me with any of these things in the presence of your king."[334] But they shouted that he had done none of these things; rather, he had presided over the nation in a holy and just[335] way.[336]

---

words as cited in 1 Sam 12:1-2, i.e. the reminder that he has given them their asked-for king (v. 1), reference to the current presence among them of that king, himself, and his sons (v. 2a), and allusion to his own life-long leadership of the people (v. 2b). By contrast, Pseudo-Philo (*Bib. Ant.* 57.2) precedes Samuel's call to testify in 57.3 with a reminiscence of God's earlier punishment of the company of Korah (see Numbers 16), who had falsely claimed, in response to Moses' question, that he had "taken" things from them.

[327] Greek: ὁ μέγιστος θεός. This is Josephus' first use of this designation for God in *Antiquities*. On it, see Begg 1993: 156, n. 1010.

[328] The words "the good" [Greek: τοὺς ἀγαθούς] as a qualification of "the brothers" are missing in RO and not printed in Niese's text. Marcus includes them with the other witnesses.

[329] In 1 Sam 12:3aα Samuel summons the people to testify "before the Lord and his anointed." Leaving the mention of Saul's presence for a later point (see 6.87), Josephus expatiates on the source's reference to the Deity, anticipating the allusion in 12:6, 8b to God's delivery of the ancestors from Egypt through the agency of Moses and Aaron.

[330] Josephus' elaborations of Samuel's simple summoning of the people to "testify" against him in 1 Sam 12:3aα underscore the confidence of his vindication with which Josephus' Samuel issues that summons—he has no doubt that the people will have nothing to charge him with.

[331] This sequence corresponds to the last 3 questions in the 5-question series Samuel addresses to the people in 1 Sam 12:3: "Or whom have I defrauded? Whom have I oppressed? Or from whose hand have I taken a bribe [+ or a pair of shoes, LXX] to blind my eyes with it [MT LXX L; LXX B lacks these closing words]?" Like MT then Josephus has no equivalent to the LXX mention of the "shoes" that Samuel did not take.

[332] Niese includes these words—compare the "ox" and "ass" about which Samuel asks in 1 Sam 12:3— within brackets in his text, affirming that they "appear

to be spurious." Marcus (*ad loc.*) reads them without the brackets; they are present in all witnesses.

[333] Josephus here expatiates on Samuel's opening 2 questions according to 1 Sam 12:3 ("Whose ox have I taken? Or whose ass have I taken?"), likewise placing these at the end of the series of his possible misdeeds about which the people are being invited to testify. Pseudo-Philo's development of Samuel's call to "testify" in *Bib. Ant.* 57.3 is quite different from the biblical and Josephan ones: his prophet challenges the people to say whether their asking him for a king was prompted by his mistreatment of them.

[334] Josephus' reserves until the end of Samuel's discourse his parallel to the words which the leader opens his summoning the people to testify in 1 Sam 12:3: "testify against me before the Lord and his anointed." In making this exhortation the conclusion of Samuel's speech, Josephus omits his final words in 1 Sam 12:3, i.e. his promising to "restore" whatever the people might charge him with having "taken." Thereby, he once again (see 6.86) underscores Samuel's total confidence in his vindication by them, this excluding even the idea that might be anything that he will need to restore to them.

[335] Greek: ὁσίωσς... καὶ δικαίως. This adverbial collocation has an adjectival counterpart in *Ant.* 8.245, 295 (reverse order); 9.35 (here predicated of King Jehoshaphat).

[336] Josephus amplifies the people's negative statement about Samuel's having done no wrong (1 Sam 12:4) with this positive affirmation on their part. Josephus lacks an equivalent to the summary recapitulation of the Samuel-people exchange of 1 Sam 12:3-4 in 12:5. In *Bib. Ant.* 57.4 the people respond to Samuel's call for them to testify (57.3) by declaring themselves and their king to be his "servants" and confessing that it was their unworthiness to be ruled by a prophet that prompted them to demand a king. Pseudo-Philo's version of 1 Samuel 12 then concludes with the people weeping, acclaiming Samuel as prophet as Saul stands by, and sacrificing.

(5.6) 88. When Samouel had received this testimony from everyone, he stated: "Since you have acknowledged to me that you are unable to tell of anything improper done by me against you, allow yourselves now to hear me speaking with frank speech[337] because you have been very impious towards God in requesting a king.[338] **89.** It is, however, appropriate for you to remember that, with only seventy persons of our race, Jacob our ancestor went, due to a famine, to Egypt.[339] There, many ten thousands were later born[340] whom the Egyptians brought under slavery and harsh outrages.[341] When our ancestors prayed,[342] God, in the absence of a king,[343] granted the crowd rescue from their necessity, sending them the brothers Moyses and Aaron, who brought them into this same land that you now have.[344] **90.** But, even as you enjoyed these [benefits] from God, you have neglected devotion and piety.[345] Nevertheless, when you were subject to your enemies, he first freed you[346] from the Assyrians, making you victorious over their strength.[347] Then he granted you to overcome the Ammanites,[348] the Moabites,[349] and finally the

Samuel reviews Israel's history

---

[337] In place of the Bible's summary introduction ("and Samuel said to the people," 12:6a) to Samuel's following admonition, Josephus introduces this elaborate transition that picks up on his previous exchange with the people and highlights the significance of what he will now say. Samuel's "speaking with frank speech (Greek: παρρησία)" to the people in God's name here is reminiscent of Joshua's "using frank speech (Greek: παρρησία)" with God on behalf of the people in *Ant.* 5.38.

[338] Within his discourse of 1 Sam 12:6-25 Samuel comes to castigate the people's demand for a king only in 12:17b. By having him mention the matter already at the outset of his speech, Josephus signals that the wrongfulness of that demand will be the speech's main theme. By contrast, the biblical Samuel opens his discourse in 12:6-7 by recalling God's appointment of Moses and Aaron in Egypt and his delivery of the people from there (v.6, already anticipated by Josephus in 6.86) and stating his intention of reminding the people of the Lord's great deeds on behalf of their ancestors (v. 7).

[339] In mentioning that not only Jacob himself but also his household went down to Egypt, Josephus reflects the plus ("and his sons") of LXX 1 Sam 12:8aα. At the same time, drawing on Gen 46:27 (// *Ant.* 2.176); Exod 1:5, he supplies a figure for those who accompanied Jacob to Egypt, just as he inserts a reference to the motivation ("famine"; see Gen 42:1-3 [// *Ant.* 2.95]; 43:1-2 [// *Ant.* 2.114]) for his going there.

[340] Josephus inserts this reminiscence of the people's multiplication in Egypt on the basis of Exod 1:7.

[341] Once again (see note to "to Egypt" at 6.89) Josephus' reading reflects a LXX plus in 1 Sam 12:8, i.e. "and the Egyptians humbled them."

[342] In 1 Sam 12:8aβ the ancestors "cry to the Lord."

[343] This Josephan insertion picks up on the thesis statement of Samuel's discourse as formulated by

Josephus in 6.88, i.e. the wrongfulness of the people's demand for a king—in whose absence God had delivered their ancestors.

[344] See 1 Sam 12:8b. In making Moses and Aaron—already cited in 6.86—the ones who bring the people into their land, Josephus follows the wording of MT as against LXX, where God himself is the subject of this action.

[345] Greek: θρησκεία καὶ εὐσέβια; Josephus' one other use of this combination is in *Ant.* 16.115, where the terms occurs in reverse order. He expands on the summary charge of 1 Sam 12:9a ("but they forgot the Lord their God") in a way paralleled in the Tg.'s rendering ("they forgot the service of their God"). He likewise makes Samuel's own hearers—rather than their ancestors (so 12:9)—the object of Samuel's accusation.

[346] 1 Sam 12:9b speaks of God's "selling the Israelites into the hand of" 3 enemy leaders/peoples, i.e. Sisera, the Philistines, and the king of Moab. Avoiding this formulation just as he did its occurrences in the Book of Judges, Josephus turns the allusion into a positive statement about God's "freeing" Israel from the domination of 4 foreign nations.

[347] This initial entry in Josephus' catalogue of the 4 nations from whose dominion God freed Israel (see note to "freed you" at 6.90) has no equivalent in 1 Sam 12:9b, whose opening allusion to Israel's subjection to the Canaanite Sisera it replaces. The mention of "the Assyrians" here is a reference to Othniel's (Josephus: Keniaz') victory over King Cushan-rishathaim of Mesopotamia (Judg 3:7-11), whom Josephus calls "king of Assyria" in *Ant.* 5.180.

[348] Like the previously mentioned Assyrians, this people is absent from the catalogue of 1 Sam 12:9b. The allusion is to Jephthah's victory over the Ammonites as described in Judg 11:32-33 (// *Ant.* 5.263).

[349] In 1 Sam 12:9b Israel's subjugation to "the king of Moab" is mentioned after its domination by the

Palestinoi.[350] You accomplished these things, not with a king as your leader,[351] but with Iaphthas and Gedeon as your generals.[352]

91. What madness then caused you to flee from God, wishing to be under a king?[353] Nonetheless, I have appointed this man whom he chose.[354] In order, however, to make clear that God is wrathful and displeased at your request for kingship,[355] I shall induce God to clearly disclose this to you through signs. For, what none of you has previously known to happen until now, namely, a rainstorm in midsummer,[356] God, at my request, will cause you to perceive."[357]

92. Once Samouel had said these things to the crowd, the Deity indicated by thunder, lightning and the descent of hail[358] the truth[359] of the prophet regarding everything. Astounded and terrified at this, they declared they had offended, having fallen into this through ignorance, and begged the prophet, as a kind and gentle[360] father, to make God benevolent to them and forgive this offense[361] of theirs that they had committed in addition to their acting outrageously and transgressing in other respects.[362]

Philistines. Josephus reverses this order, given that the Book of Judges treats Israel's oppression by the Moabites (see Judg 3:14) prior to that by the Philistines (Judg 13:1). In addition, he turns the source's negative reference to Israel's submission to the Moabite king into a positive one concerning its triumph over the Moabites, as effected by Ehud ("Ioud") in Judg 3:30 (// *Ant.* 5.197).

[350] The Philistines are the 2nd of the peoples/kings to be cited in 1 Sam 12:9b. The reference is to Samson's exploits against the Philistines as related in Judges 13-16 (// *Ant.* 5.276-317).

[351] This phrase, echoing the wording of 6.88, 89, takes the place of the mention of the people's confession/appeal in 1 Sam 12:10, which, in turn, prompted the Lord's sending of the Judges cited in 12:11. In omitting the former item, Josephus underscores the gratuity of God's saving intervention, which occurs without any preceding repentance by Israel.

[352] Josephus 2-member list of Israel's generals contrasts with the 4 names cited, with variations, in the witnesses to 1 Sam 12:11a, i.e. Jerubbaal, Bedan, Jephthah, Samuel (MT); Jeroboam, Barak, Jephthah, Samuel (LXX B); Jerubbbaal, Barak, Jephthah, Samuel (LXX L); and Gideon [see Josephus], Samson, Jephthah, Samuel (Tg.). For more on Josephus' list in comparison with the biblical ones, see Begg 1997g, 66, n. 66.

[353] This question, reiterating Samuel's reference (6.89) to God, "in the absence of a king," freeing the people from their Egyptian slavery, takes the place of the immediate continuation of the Judge list of 1 Sam 12:11a, i.e. v. 11b (Israel's dwelling in safety following the initiatives of the various Judges) and 12 (the threat of the Ammonite king Nahash [1 Samuel 11] prompts Israel's demand for a king). Josephus' omission of the latter item is readily understandable given the fact that in both the Bible (1 Samuel 8) and his own presenta-

tion (6.32-44) that demand is inspired rather by Samuel's age, the unworthiness of his sons, and concern for future military leadership against the Philistines.

[354] Cf. 1 Sam 12:13, where Samuel makes parenthetical reference to King Saul's presence at the assembly.

[355] Josephus anticipates this phrase concerning the purpose of the "sign" Samuel is about to announce (see 1 Sam 12:16-17a) from 12:17b. In thus proceeding directly from 12:13 (the presence of the king) to 12:16-17 (the announced sign and its purpose), Josephus reserves for a later point Samuel's conditional promise/warning of 12:14-15.

[356] Compare Samuel's question in 1 Sam 12:17a: "Is not wheat harvest today?" (which in Palestine takes place in early summer, when the rains have ceased to fall).

[357] See 1 Sam 12:16-17a.

[358] Compare 1 Sam 12:18, which, less dramatically, mentions only "thunder and rain."

[359] Greek: ἀλήθεια. This reference to God's confirming the "truth" of Samuel's words echoes the designation of Samuel as a "truthful prophet" (προφήτης ἀληθής) in 6.47.

[360] Greek: χρηστός καὶ ἐπιεικής. This combination occurs only here in Josephus; the word χρηστός ("kind") recurs in Josephus' own eulogy for Samuel in 6.294. On the noun ἐπιείκεια and its cognates, see Spicq 1978 (I): 263-68.

[361] Greek ταύτην ἀφεῖναι τὴν ἁμαρτίαν (alternative translation: "to forgive this sin"). This phrase occurs only here in Josephus. Compare Luke 11:4, where the petition of the "Our Father" reads ἄφες ἡμῖν τὰς ἁμαρτίας ἡμῶν ("forgive us our sins"). On the parallels between Josephus and Luke-Acts overall, see Krenkel 1894; Mason 2003: 251-95.

[362] This sequence represents an amplification, ac-

93. He, for his part, promised that he would appeal to—and persuade—God to pardon[363] them for these things.[364] He advised them, however, to be just and good and always to remember both the calamities that had happened to them on account of their deviation from virtue as well as God's signs[365] and the legislation of Moyses,[366] if their desire was for safety and well-being with their king.[367] **94.** If, however, they disregarded these things, this would, he said, bring a great blow from God upon them and their king.[368]

When Samouel had prophesied these things to the Hebrews, he dismissed them to their homes, having ratified the kingship of Saoul a second time.[369]

(6.1) 95. Now [Saoul][370] selected from the crowd about 3,000 men, of whom he took 2,000 as his bodyguards,[371] and resided in the city of Betheb.[372] He gave the remainder to his son Ionathes[373] to be his bodyguard and sent him to Gebal.[374] Ionathes took by siege a certain garrison[375] of the Palestinoi not far from Gebal.[376]

Samuel's closing words

Saul's initiatives and Jonathan's success

---

centuating the status of Samuel, of the sequence concerning the people's response to the God-sent storm in 1 Sam 12:18b-19, i.e. their "fear" of the Lord and Samuel, appeal for Samuel's intercession, and confession of their additional sin in asking for a king.

[363] Greek: συγγιγνώσκω. Josephus' one other use of this verb with God as subject is in *Ant.* 11.129 (object: the Judeans). On the use of the term, its cognates, and word-field in Greek literature overall, see Metzler 1991.

[364] Josephus anticipates this promise by Samuel from 1 Sam 12:23a, making it the very first component of his response (12:20-25) to the people's appeal for his intercession (12:19).

[365] This phrase echoes Samuel's statement that he is going to induce God to make the wrongfulness of the people's request for a king clear to them "through signs," i.e. the "rainstorm in midsummer" in 6.91.

[366] Greek: ἡ Μωυσέως νομοθεσία. This is Josephus' only use of this phrase. On his recurring (16 times in *Antiquities* 1-4) use of the cognate term νομοθέτης ("legislator") for Moses, see Feldman 1998: 399.

[367] With this exhortation Josephus sums up and combines the conditional promises that Samuel makes his hearers in 2 different contexts of his biblical speech, i.e. 12:14 and 12:20-22, 23b-24.

[368] This conditional warning synthesizes those voiced separately by Samuel in 1 Sam 12:15, 25. Compare in particular 12:15, where Samuel warns that if the people prove rebellious, then "the hand of the Lord will be against you and your king." Josephus' substitution of "blow" for the anthropomorphic "hand" of MT has a counterpart in Tg.

[369] With this narrative notice Josephus provides suitable closure to Samuel's farewell discourse (which, biblically, ends abruptly in 1 Sam 12:25, with Samuel still speaking). Its formulation harks back to Josephus' (likewise inserted) mention of Samuel's convening an assembly in 6.86 and to the prophet's statement about the need to reconfirm Saul's kingship in 6.83

(cf. 1 Sam 11:14).

[370] Like LXX B, Josephus has no equivalent to the (problematic) chronological indications of MT LXX L 1 Sam 13:1, which read literally: "Saul was a year old [Tg. glosses: there was no sin in him; cf. *Bib. Ant.* 57.5: "afterwards Saul fought with the Philistines *for one year*..."] when he became king, and he reigned... two years over Israel." Josephus nowhere specifies Saul's age at accession; subsequently, however, he will provide (divergent) figures for his length of reign, i.e. 40 years (6.378= Acts 13:21) vs. 20 years (10.143).

[371] 1 Sam 13:2aα speaks more generally of the 2,000 "being with" Saul at Michmash. The specific mention of Saul's taking "bodyguards" echoes the Josephan Samuel's announcement about the kings' compelling certain of the Israelites' sons to be their bodyguards in 6.40.

[372] In 1 Sam 13:2aβ Saul and the 2,000 establish themselves "in Michmash and the hill country of Bethel." Schalit (*s.v.*) qualifies the place name read by Niese and Marcus in 6.95 (βέθηβος) as certainly erroneous and proposes substituting the form Βήθηλος in line with the biblical reference to "Bethel."

[373] MT (1 Sam 13:2) יונתן (Eng.: "Jonathan"); LXX Ἰωναθάν; Josephus' Ἰωνάθης.

[374] MT (1 Sam 13:2bα) גבעת בנימים(ב) (Eng.: "Gibeah of Benjamin"); LXX B Γαβεὲ τοῦ Βενιαμείν; LXX L Γαβαὰ τοῦ Βενιαμίν; Josephus Γεβάλ. Schalit (*s.v.*), in accordance with the variant of MSP Lat, reads τῆς Γαβὰς Παλαιστῖνοι. Josephus omits the concluding notice of 1 Sam 13:2 concerning Saul's dismissal of the remainder of the people.

[375] MT 1 Sam 13:3aα mentions Jonathan's defeating a Philistine נציב ("prefect"? "garrison"? [so LXX L and Josephus]) which, as in 1 Sam 10:5, LXX B understands as a proper name, "Nasib."

[376] 1 Sam 13:3aα locates the site of the Philistine garrison at "Geba" (MT; LXX "translates" as "on the hill") itself.

Philistine measures against Israelites

96. For the Palestinoi, when they vanquished the Judeans, took away their weapons and occupied the most solid places of the country with garrisons;[377] they likewise forbade them to carry iron weapons or to make any use of iron whatever.[378] For this reason the farmers, whenever they needed to repair any of their tools—whether a plowshare, or a mattock, or anything else that was agriculturally useful—went to the Palestinoi to have this done.[379]

Philistine invasion

97. Now when the Palestinoi heard of the annihilation of their garrison, they were indignant.[380] Thinking such contempt a terrible outrage,[381] they campaigned against the Judeans with 300,000 foot soldiers[382] and 30,000 chariots;[383] they also led out 6,000 cavalry.[384]

Saul's and Israelites' reaction

98. They encamped at the city of Machma.[385] When Saoul, the king of the Hebrews, learned of this, he went down to the city of Galgala.[386] He made a proclamation throughout the whole country,[387] calling the people to war against the Palestinoi for the sake of their freedom.[388] He disparaged their force and ridiculed it as not worth mentioning, such that they should have no fear of risking a fight against them.[389]

---

[377] To his notice on Jonathan's capture of the Philistine garrison (6.95= 1 Sam 13:3aα) Josephus attaches an explanation ("for") concerning the Philistines' current occupation of Israel that this notice presupposes. The first part of the explanation is peculiar to Josephus; it speaks of the Philistines' occupation of Israelite sites with their garrisons—like the one just recaptured by Jonathan. The past "vanquishing of the Judeans" mentioned here is presumably that inflicted on them at the battle(s) of Aphek, 1 Samuel 4= *Ant.* 5.352-362.

[378] This continuation of Josephus' "explanation" concerning the current Philistine presence in Israel is an anticipated adaptation of the Philistines' words as cited in 1 Sam 13:19b: "... lest the Hebrews make themselves swords or spears." Josephus' specification of the weapons as ones "made of iron" reflects the LXX's reference to there being no "ironsmith" in Israel in 13:19a, where MT simply refers to a "smith."

[379] See 1 Sam 13:20. Josephus omits the attached detail of 13:21 concerning the charges levied by the Philistines for work on the various kinds of implements brought them.

[380] See 1 Sam 13:3aβ, to which Josephus adds mention of the Philistines' emotional reaction to what they hear.

[381] This additional (see note to "indignant" at 6.97) reference to the Philistines' state of mind that prompts their move against Israel (1 Sam 13:5) might reflect the reference to Israel's "having become odious to the Philistines" in 13:4a; see 6.98. Josephus anticipates his mention of the Philistine advance here from 13:5, reserving the intervening notices concerning Israel's own follow-up to Jonathan's exploit (13:3b-4) for a later point; thereby, he keeps together in a continuous sequence (the biblically interrupted) references to the Philistine response to Jonathan's initiative in 13:3aβ + 5.

[382] 1 Sam 13:5 speaks in vague, poetic terms of the Philistine troops being "like the sand on the seashore in multitude." As he does elsewhere, Josephus turns this indication into a "precise" (and very large) figure.

[383] This figure for the Philistine chariots corresponds to that read by MT LXX B 1 Sam 13:5; LXX L has 6,000.

[384] This figure for the Philistine cavalry accords with that read by both MT and LXX 1 Sam 13:5.

[385] MT (1 Sam 13:5b) מכמש (Eng.: "Michmash"); LXX B Μαχεμάς; LXX L Μαχμάς; Josephus Μαχμά. Josephus leaves aside the source specification that the city was located "to the east of Bethaven" (MT; "opposite Baithoron, to the south," LXX).

[386] 1 Samuel 13 does not explicitly record such a move by Saul to "Gilgal" in response to his hearing of the Philistine advance (13:5). That city is, however, mentioned in 13:4 as the site where the Israelites are called—seemingly prior to the Philistines' own move—to join Saul, while 13:7b mentions Saul's still being "at Gilgal."

[387] Cf. 1 Sam 13:3bα ("and Saul blew the trumpet throughout all the land..."), which precedes the mention of the Philistines' own advance in 13:5.

[388] Josephus conflates the source's separate references to Saul's summons—issued by him prior to the mention of the Philistine advance in 1 Sam 13:5—of 13:3bβ ("let the Hebrews hear" [MT; "the slaves have revolted," LXX]) and 13:4b (the people are called to join Saul at Gilgal). The reference to the recovery of "freedom" as the intended goal of the upcoming conflict echoes that of Israel's earlier wars in the time of the Judges in Josephus' presentation; see *Ant.* 5.182 (Keniaz), 194 (Ehud); and 6.20 (Samuel).

[389] Josephus' mention of this psychological warfare tactic whereby Saul seeks to stimulate the Israelites'

99. When, however, they observed the crowd of Palestinoi, Saoul's men were dismayed.[390] Some hid themselves in caves and underground passages,[391] while most fled to the land beyond the Jordan that belonged to Gad and Roubel.[392]

(6.2) 100. Saoul, for his part, sent to the prophet and called him to himself to confer about the war and public affairs.[393] Samouel directed him to remain there and to prepare sacrificial victims,[394] for he would come to him after seven[395] days in order that, after sacrificing on the seventh day, they might then engage the enemy.[396] **101.** Saoul initially stayed put, as the prophet had commanded;[397] then, however, he no longer abided by his command.[398] Rather, when he saw that the prophet was delaying, and that he himself was being deserted by his soldiers,[399] he took the victims and offered the sacrifice.[400]

Saul's premature sacrifice

Then, when he heard that Samouel was approaching, he went out to meet him.[401] **102.** [Samouel], however, stated that he had not done rightly in disobeying what he had commanded him and by anticipating his coming,[402] which, in accordance with the Deity's will, was so that he might conduct prayers and sacrifices on behalf of the people; he [Saoul] had rather sacrificed wrongfully and acted rashly.[403]

Samuel–Saul exchange

---

courage has no explicit counterpart in 1 Samuel 13. Conceivably, however, it was inspired by the (LXX L) reading in 1 Sam 13:4aβ: "Israel held the Philistines in contempt" (MT: had become odious to the Philistines; LXX B: had been put to shame by the Philistines). For another possible allusion to this formulation by Josephus, see note to "outrage" at 6.97.

[390] In 1 Sam 13:6a the Israelites see themselves "in straits" (MT; LXX: saw the difficulty of advancing into battle). Josephus adds mention of the emotional effect of what the Israelites see upon them.

[391] See 1 Sam 13:6b, where 5 different Israelite hiding places are mentioned.

[392] According to 1 Sam 13:7a, the Israelites crossed the Jordan "to the land of Gad and Gilead." For the latter territory, Josephus substitutes mention of the tribe possessing it. He likewise omits 13:7b ("Saul was still at Gilgal, and all the people followed him trembling") whose 2nd element, in particular, seems not to accord with the mention of the people's hiding themselves and fleeing across the Jordan in 13:6-7a.

[393] This notice on Saul's summoning the prophet to him takes the place, at this juncture in Josephus' presentation (see, however, 6.101), of 1 Sam 13:8a, where Saul is said to "wait seven days" in accordance with the command previously given him by Samuel, i.e. in 1 Sam 10:8bα (Josephus does not reproduce this command in his own rendition of Samuel's words to Saul of 10:8 in 6.57 that has Saul simply being told that he is come to Gilgal when summoned by Samuel that they might offer sacrifices there). Accordingly, it is now necessary for him to have Saul take the initiative in bringing himself and Samuel together at this point. On Josephus' version of the episode of Saul's "first sin" (1 Sam 13:8-15a) in 6.100-105a, see Begg 1999.

[394] This initial directive by Samuel in response to

Saul's "summons" has no equivalent in 1 Sam 13:8 itself. It converts into a command for the present Samuel's announcement concerning the sacrifice that will be offered at Gilgal as cited in 6.57 (// 1 Sam 10:8aβ; whereas in this source text Samuel speaks of himself as the sole future sacrificer, Josephus' version of his saying in both 6.57 and 6.100 magnifies Saul's status by having Samuel mention him as co-sacrificer.)

[395] This is the reading adopted by Niese in accordance with the *septem* of Lat (and the period specified by Samuel in 1 Sam 10:8). RO lack a corresponding figure. Marcus reads "6" with SPE.

[396] These concluding words of Samuel in answer to Saul's summons represent Josephus' "delayed" use of the prophet's final directive to Saul in 1 Sam 10:8b ("Seven days shall you wait, until I come to you and show you what you shall do"). Josephus likewise renders the vague source formulation concerning what Samuel will do once the 7 days are up more definite, introducing an allusion to the current war context.

[397] See 1 Sam 13:8a (Saul's 7-day wait in accordance with the time previously fixed by Samuel in 10:8).

[398] This inserted phrase foreshadows both the course and the wording of the subsequent episode.

[399] See 1 Sam 13:8b. Josephus adds the reference to Saul's "seeing" the 2 developments mentioned, this serving to motivate his following initiative.

[400] In 1 Sam 13:9 Saul first commands that victims be brought to him and then offers the sacrifice. Josephus' formulation depicts Saul performing both operations himself.

[401] See 1 Sam 13:10.

[402] Greek: παρουσία. On this word, see Spicq 1978 (II): 673-76.

[403] This extended opening discourse by Samuel, anticipating his subsequent charges about the king's

103. Saoul excused himself, saying that he had stayed put for the days he had fixed. Then, however, out of necessity and given the withdrawal of his own soldiers due to their fear, as also to the encampment of the enemy at Machma and the report of their coming down against him to Galgala,[404] he had been compelled [to offer] the sacrifice. **104.** Samouel, however, replied: "On the contrary, if you were just and had not disobeyed me nor been contemptuous of that which God advised me concerning the present situation by acting more hastily than was suitable in these matters,[405] then it would have been granted by him to you and your descendants to rule as kings for a very long time."[406]

Israel's precarious state
105. Irritated at what had happened,[407] Samouel departed for his home,[408] while Saoul went to the city of Gabaon with his son Ionathes, having only 600 men with him.[409] Most of these had no weapons[410] since the country was destitute of iron and those capable of forging weapons, for the Palestinoi did not allow this, as we mentioned a short while ago.[411]

Saul's and Jonathan's reactions to Philistine advance
106. The Palestinoi divided up their army into three parts and, advancing by as

---

transgression of God's commandment (see 1 Sam 13:13a, 14b), takes the place of his short initial question ("what have you done?") of 13:11a. Josephus' substitution of an accusatory statement for this question might be inspired by the consideration that, as a prophet, Samuel would/should have known what Saul had done, without having to ask him about this.

[404] 1 Sam 13:11b-12a features 5 extenuating circumstances cited by Saul in attempting to excuse his deed: the dispersal of his army, Samuel's own failure to arrive, the Philistines' mustering at Michmash, his supposition that they would come against him at Gilgal, and his own not yet having entreated the favor (literally: face) of the Lord. Of these 5 alleged motivations, Josephus' version diplomatically passes over the 2nd (Samuel's non-appearance) and 5th (with its anthropomorphic language). As for the remaining 3, Josephus "reinforces" the king's invocation of the Philistines' advance by having Saul state that he had actually received a report to this effect. In addition, he makes Saul begin his *apologia* by reminding Samuel that he had, at any rate, remained the 7 days prescribed by him, and then had acted as he did under the pressure of "necessity."

[405] Josephus derives the content of Samuel's charges from 1 Sam 13:13a, 14b, where the prophet twice accuses Saul of having failed to "keep" God's commandment.

[406] Compare 1 Sam 13:13b, where the reference is to the kingship (potentially) remaining in Saul's line "forever." With Roman sensibilities concerning Jewish messianic aspirations in mind, Josephus reduces the kingship's (possible) duration to a "very long time." He likewise leaves aside Samuel's further announcement of 13:14a ("But now your kingdom shall not continue; the Lord has sought out a man after his own heart; and the

Lord has appointed him to be prince over his people"). The omission might have in view the fact that this announcement reads like a (premature) duplication of what Samuel will tell Saul in 1 Sam 15:28 (// 6.150).

[407] Josephus inserts this reference to Samuel's emotional response to Saul's misdeed.

[408] In having Samuel go to his "home" (i.e. Ramah/Armatha; see 1 Sam 7:17 and 6.35, 67) at this juncture, Josephus offers a more plausible scenario than does MT 1 Sam 13:15a, where the prophet proceeds from Gilgal to "Gibea of Benjamin," i.e. the likely residence of Saul (see 1 Sam 10:26; 11:4) with whom he has just had a dramatic altercation. Josephus' presentation here likewise differs from that of LXX 13:15a, where, once Samuel "goes his way," the remaining Israelite troops follow Saul, proceeding from Gilgal to "Gabaa of Benjamin."

[409] Josephus draws his mention of the persons involved here (Saul, Jonathan, the 600) from 1 Sam 13:15b-16a. In referring, however, to Saul's "going" with Jonathan to "Gabaon" (in 6.95 Jonathan was stationed at "Gebal"), he differs from 13:16a, which has king, prince, and people "staying in Geba (LXX Gabaa) of Benjamin."

[410] Josephus anticipates the notice on the Israelites' lack of weapons from 1 Sam 13:22. At the same time, he tones down the source's implausible statement that Saul and Jonathan, alone among all the Israelites, had a sword or spear.

[411] Here Josephus explains the Israelites' current lack of weapons via an explicit reminiscence of his earlier remarks (6.96), themselves drawn from 1 Sam 13:19-21, concerning the Philistine prohibition of the Israelites' carrying iron weapons or making any use of iron.

many routes, were devastating the country of the Hebrews.[412] Though they saw this, their King Saoul and his son Ionathes were unable to repel [them] from the land since they only had 600 men.[413]

107. He, his son, and the high priest Echias,[414] a descendant of the high priest Helei,[415] as they sat on a lofty hill[416] and saw the land being ravaged, fell into a terrible agony. Saoul's son then suggested to his weapon-carrier that they secretly go and assault the enemy's camp in order to bring confusion and turmoil [upon them].[417] **108.** The weapon-bearer said that he would eagerly follow him, wherever he might lead, even if he had to die.[418]

Having thus secured the youth's cooperation, Ionathes, descending from the hill, proceeded towards the enemy.[419] The enemy's camp was on a steep slope, with three summits that tapered to a long narrow [ridge]. It was encircled by rocks, bulwarks, as it were, to ward off attacks.[420] **109.** Now it happened that the camp guards were careless because the site was endowed with security by nature, and it was considered impossible for anyone even to approach those [summits]—much less ascend them.[421]

Jonathan and companion approach Philistine camp

110. When then they had come to the camp, Ionathes encouraged his weapon-bearer and said, "Let us fall upon the enemy;[422] if, seeing us, they direct us to come up to them, let us take this as a sign of victory. But if they utter no sound, as if not calling us, let us return."[423]

---

[412] Josephus summarizes the indications concerning the Philistines' movements found in 1 Sam 13:16b-18 (+ 23), eliminating the source place names, while also inserting mention of the devastation they perpetrated during their advance.

[413] This notice on Saul's (non-)response to the Philistine movements lacks a parallel in 1 Samuel 13. In acknowledging the king's inactivity, Josephus also highlights the extenuating circumstance, i.e. his having a mere 600 men available to him (see 1 Sam 13:15b// 6.105).

[414] MT (1 Sam 14:3) אחיה (Eng.: "Ahijah"); LXX Ἀχιά; Josephus Ἐχίας (this is the reading of RO followed by Niese; Marcus [ad loc.] reads Ἀχίας with the other codices and Lat).

[415] Josephus omits the names of the priests between Eli and "Ahijah" cited in 1 Sam 14:3 (which makes him Eli's great-grandson). He likewise passes over the mention of Ahijah's "wearing an ephod."

[416] 1 Sam 14:2 places Saul "in the outskirts of Gibeah [MT; LXX: the hill; cf. Josephus] under the pomegranate tree which is at Migron" (MT; LXX B: of the magi; LXX L: in Mageddo). Feldman (1998: 518) calls attention to the similarity between Josephus' description of the scene (including the threesome's emotional response to what they see) and Aeschylus' portrayal (*Pers.* 465-70) of King Xerxes mourning his men lost at Salamis, while seated on a lofty spot.

[417] See 1 Sam 14:1. Josephus' supplies a motivation for Jonathan's projected move against the Philistines mentioned in this verse, while leaving aside Jonathan's

reiteration of his proposal—this time in highly theological language and with use of the objectionable phrase "these uncircumcised [Philistines]"—of 14:6. The above bracketed words "upon them" are absent in RO.

[418] See 1 Sam 14:7; Josephus accentuates the readiness of the armor-bearer to join Jonathan by having him aver that he will follow him even to the point of death.

[419] The biblical presentation does not narrate this initial movement by Jonathan. The "hill" in question is that cited in 6.107.

[420] 1 Sam 14:4-5 gives a somewhat different description of the site of the Philistine garrison, i.e. as positioned between 2 named crags (v. 4), one to the north facing Michmash, the other to the south, facing Geba (v. 5, MT LXX L; LXX B speaks, not of the crags of v. 4, but rather of 2 "routes").

[421] Josephus' remark on the guards' negligence and the reasons for this has no parallel in 1 Samuel 14. The insertion serves to magnify Jonathan's subsequent feat in seizing the site.

[422] Compare 1 Sam 14:8: "Behold we will cross over to the men, and we will show ourselves (MT; LXX fall upon) to them."

[423] Josephus both modifies and rearranges the 2 alternatives as set out by Jonathan in 1 Sam 14:9-10: (a) they will not advance if the Philistines summon them to wait until they (the Philistines) come to them or (b) they will advance, should they urged by them to "come up." He eliminates the theological allusion at-

Jonathan routs
Philistines

111. They approached the enemy camp as dawn was breaking.[424] When the Palestinoi saw [them], they said to one another that the Hebrews were coming out of their underground passages and caves.[425] To Ionathes and his weapon-bearer they said: "Come on, ascend to us, so that we may duly punish you for your daring deeds."[426] **112.** Saoul's son welcomed their cry as indicating victory for him,[427] and they immediately withdrew from the place where they had been seen by the enemy. Leaving this behind, they came to the rock that, due to its solidity, was bereft of guards. **113.** From there they crept up; with great difficulty they forcibly overcame the nature of the site in order to ascend to the enemy.[428] Falling upon them as they slept,[429] they killed about twenty,[430] and filled them with confusion and distress.[431] As a result, some fled, casting off their armor. **114.** Most, however, not recognizing one another because of their being from many nations, supposed each another to be enemies—for they did not imagine that only two of the Hebrews had come up to them—they took to fighting [among themselves]. So, killing one another, they died; some of the fugitives, having been pushed against the rocks, were thrown down.[432]

Victory predict-
ed

(6.3) 115. When Saoul's scouts notified the king that the camp of the Palestinoi was in a state of confusion, Saoul questioned whether any of his own men had gone out.[433] When he heard that his son had left along with his weapon-bearer,[434] he directed the high priest[435] to take the high priestly garment[436] and prophesy to him about what was to come.[437] Upon his saying that there would be victory and con-

---

tached to the 2nd alternative in v. 10b ("for the Lord has given them into our hand"), while adapting Jonathan's appended statement, i.e. "and this shall be the sign to us."

[424] Josephus appends this time indication to the mention of the pair's "showing themselves to" (MT; entering, LXX) the Philistine garrison in 1 Sam 14:11a.

[425] See 1 Sam 14:11b. The Philistines' words here echo those used to describe the Israelites' self-conceal-ment in 6.99 (// 1 Sam 13:6).

[426] Josephus provides a more definite conclusion to the Philistines' "invitation" as cited in 1 Sam 14:12a ("[come up to us], and we will show you a thing").

[427] This notice, echoing Jonathan's words to his weapon-bearer in 6.110 ("let us take this as a sign of victory"), substitutes for his theological affirmation in 1 Sam 14:12b ("the Lord has given them into the hand of Israel").

[428] The above sequence represents Josephus' elabo-ration, magnifying the difficulty of the enterprise, of the brief notice of 1 Sam 14:13a: "Then Jonathan climbed up on his hands and feet and his armor-bearer after him."

[429] Compare 1 Sam 14:13bα: "they [the Philistines] fell before Jonathan" (MT; LXX: they beheld Jona-than's face).

[430] Josephus compresses the indications of 14:13bβ-14a concerning Jonathan and his weapon-bearer's as-sault. He leaves aside the indication of 14:14b about the dimensions of the massacre site (MT)/ the weapons used (LXX).

[431] This phrase echoes that used by Josephus con-cerning the purpose of Jonathan's enterprise in 6.107 (i.e. to bring "confusion and turmoil" on the Philis-tines), thus underscoring its success.

[432] Josephus embellishes with a variety of vivid touches (e.g., the presence of different peoples in the Philistine camp, the tossing of some off the rocks) the general notice on the Philistines' panic of 1 Sam 14:15 (from which he does, however, omit the reference to the "earthquake").

[433] See 1 Sam 14:16-17a, which does not explicitly mention the lookouts' reporting what they see of the state of the Philistine camp to the king.

[434] In 1 Sam 14:17b a "census" of the army, con-ducted at Saul's command (v. 17a), reveals the absence of the pair.

[435] 1 Sam 14:18a repeats the priest's name ("Ahijah") from 14:3 (= 6.107, where, in Niese's read-ing, he is called "Echias"; see note to "Echias" at 6.107).

[436] Josephus here clearly reflects the reading of LXX 1 Sam 14:18, where Ahijah is told to bring "the ephod" as opposed to MT, where he is to fetch "the ark of God." He leaves aside the attached parenthetical notice about Ahijah being the one who "bore the ephod in his hand in those days" (LXX; MT speaks of the ark being among the Israelites at that time).

[437] With this appended phrase Josephus spells out what it is Saul intends "Ahijah" to do by means of the priestly garment (cf. LXX 1 Sam 14:18a) he tells him to take. On "prophesying" as a characteristic (high)

quest of the enemy,[438] Saoul went out against the Palestinoi and fell upon them who were in a state of confusion and slaughtering one another.[439]

116. Once they heard that Saoul had been victorious, those who had earlier fled together to the underground passages and caves also approached him.[440] Now having about 10,000 Hebrews with him, he pursued the enemy who were scattered over the entire country.[441] Then, however, either due to his joy at so unexpected a victory (for it happens that those who have good luck in this way do not stay in control of their reason), or through ignorance, he was plunged into a terrible and very reprehensible action.[442] **117.** For, wishing to personally punish and impose judgment on the Palestinoi, he put the Hebrews under a curse:[443] if anyone should desist from slaughtering the foe and eat before the onset of night halted their annihilation and pursuit of their enemies, he would be accursed.[444]

Saul's prohibition/curse

118. Once Saoul said this, they arrived at a certain dense, bee-filled forest belonging to the allotment of Ephraim.[445] Now Saoul's son, who had not heard his father's curse nor the crowd's approbation of this, broke off a portion of a honeycomb and ate it.[446]

Jonathan violates prohibition

119. Afterwards, when he found out that his father had, by way of a terrible curse, forbidden anyone to taste anything before sundown, he stopped eating.[447] He said, however, that his father had not been right to prevent [their eating], for they would

---

priestly activity in Josephus, see note to "prophesied" at *Ant.* 5.120.

[438] In supplying this answer by the priest to Saul's inquiry, Josephus notably modifies 1 Sam 14:19, where, in the face of the increasing turbulence in the Philistine camp, Saul instructs Ahijah to "withdraw his hand," even though no response has yet been obtained.

[439] See 1 Sam 14:20; the allusion to the Philistines' mutual slaughter recalls the description of enemy forces' fighting among themselves in 6.114.

[440] See 1 Sam 14:22 (where the reference is to "those who had hid themselves in the hill country of Ephraim"). Josephus' wording echoes his earlier mentions of the Israelite fugitives in 6.99 (// 1 Sam 13:6) and 6.111. He omits the source's preceding notice (1 Sam 14:21) concerning those "Hebrews" who had previously joined the Philistines—a development nowhere mentioned in what precedes—now attaching themselves to Saul's forces.

[441] Josephus' figure for the Israelites involved in the pursuit corresponds to that of the LXX plus at the end of 1 Sam 14:23 (from which he omits the opening theological affirmation "so the Lord delivered Israel that day," as well as the various place names cited).

[442] This foreshadowing remark represents an elaboration, alluding to the familiar Greek linking of prosperity and hubris (on which see Feldman 1998: 180-81), of the LXX reading at the opening of 1 Sam 14:24 ("and Saul committed a great mistake in ignorance [Greek: ἄγνοια, the same word used by Josephus] on that day"; compare MT: "and the men of Israel were distressed that day"). Josephus' elaborated version

makes clear, from the start, e.g., the reprehensibility of Saul's subsequent initiative; compare his (also inserted) censure of Jephthah's vow in *Ant.* 5.266.

[443] Josephus supplies this prefatory motivation for Saul's "curse" of 1 Sam 14:24aβ.

[444] See the quotation of Saul's imprecatory words in 1 Sam 14:24bα. Josephus omits the statement with which 14:24 ends up, i.e. the entire people did in fact refrain from food in accord with Saul's curse.

[445] See 1 Sam 14:25-26, which does not cite either the presence of bees or the forest's being part of Ephraim (conceivably Josephus derived this localization from the mention of Ephraim in 14:22 and/or the LXX plus at the end of 14:23). Conversely, Josephus does not reproduce the source reference to the "honey" the people encountered in the forest, nor their refraining from eating this.

[446] See 1 Sam 14:27, from which Josephus omits mention of Jonathan's using his "staff" to extract the honey from the honeycomb and the result of his eating it, i.e. "his eyes became bright." Josephus has not previously mentioned the people's approving Saul's curse; compare 14:24bβ, which states that, following Saul's uttering of the curse, the people did, in fact, refrain from food.

[447] Josephus' statement about Jonathan's ceasing to eat upon hearing of Saul's prohibition is his addition to the notice of 1 Sam 14:28a, where he is simply informed of that prohibition; the expansion underscores Jonathan's filial piety. Josephus has no equivalent to the (seemingly displaced) mention that "the people were faint" of 14:28b.

have pursued with greater strength and eagerness if they had ingested food, and would have taken and slaughtered many more of their foes.[448]

Israelite sacri-
lege

(6.4) 120. Having, nonetheless, cut down many ten thousands of the Palestinoi,[449] they turned at dusk to plundering the Palestinoi's camp. Taking much plunder and livestock, they butchered the latter and consumed them with the blood in them.[450] It was then reported to the king by the scribes that the crowd was offending against God in that, having sacrificed, they were eating before they had duly washed away the blood and made the flesh clean.[451] **121.** Saoul directed that a large stone be rolled into their midst[452] and issued a proclamation that the mob should sacrifice the victims upon this and not consume the sacrificial pieces along with their blood, for this was not pleasing to God.[453] When everyone had done thus in accordance with the king's order, Saoul erected an altar there and offered holocausts to God on it. This was the first altar he built.[454]

God's silence
and Saul's vow

(6.5) 122. Wishing now to immediately lead his army to the enemy camp in order to plunder the things in it before daybreak, and with his soldiers not hesitating to follow, but rather displaying much eagerness for what he ordered,[455] the king called Achitob[456] the high priest and directed him[457] to find out whether God would grant and permit them to go to the camp of their foes and destroy those in it.[458]

123. When the priest said that God did not answer,[459] Saoul said "It was not without cause that God—who earlier announced all things beforehand and spoke without our questioning—gives us no response when we do inquire. Rather, it is some

---

[448] From Jonathan's words of disapproval for his father's order in 1 Sam 14:29-30 Josephus leaves aside his statement in v. 29b: "see how my eyes became bright, because I tasted a little honey," which itself harks back to the notice, likewise omitted by Josephus, at the end of 14:27 about Jonathan's eyes "becoming bright" after eating the honey.

[449] See 1 Sam 14:31a, whose place indications (MT: from Michmash to Aijalon; LXX at Michmash) Josephus leaves aside, just as he does the renewed (see 14:28b) mention of the people's being "faint" in 14:31b.

[450] Compare 1 Sam 14:32, which specifies that the Israelites slaughtered the captured sheep, oxen and calves "on the ground."

[451] Josephus (anachronistically) identifies the indeterminate "they" who inform Saul of the people's offense in 1 Sam 14:33a (whose wording he likewise elaborates) as "the scribes" in light of this group's status as *the* legal authorities of his own time. Josephus reproduces the biblical prohibition of eating blood (see Lev 17:11, etc.) in *Ant.* 3.260.

[452] From Saul's response in 1 Sam 14:33b to the report made him about the people's eating of the blood (14:33a), Josephus omits his opening words, i.e. "you have dealt treacherously" (MT; LXX (mis)reads this as "in Geththaim").

[453] Josephus supplies the concluding motivation for Saul's directive about the sacrificial procedure laid

down by him in 1 Sam 14:34a, this grounded in the biblical prohibition of eating blood; see note to "clean" at 6.120.

[454] See 1 Sam 14:34b-35 (into which Josephus inserts the reference to Saul personally sacrificing upon the altar that he erected).

[455] Josephus turns into an extended narrative notice the words of Saul's proposal and the people's response as reported in 1 Sam 14:36abα, accentuating the latter's readiness to follow the king's lead.

[456] *Ant.* 6.107 called Saul's priest "Echias" (cf. Ahijah, MT 14:3; Achia, LXX). Schlatter (*s.v.*; compare Schalit *s.v.* ['Εχίαν τοῦ] 'Αχιτώβου) reads this same form also here in 6.122 (where the name "Achitob," read by Niese and Marcus, corresponds to that of Ahijah's father, i.e. "Ahitub" in 14:3). The priest is nameless in 1 Sam 14:36bβ.

[457] In 1 Sam 14:36bβ it is the (nameless) priest himself who takes the initiative at this juncture with his admonition "let us draw near hither to God." Josephus accentuates the status of Saul who, just as he had earlier (see 1 Sam 14:18= 6.115), issues orders to the attending priest.

[458] Compare Saul's double "inquiry" in 1 Sam 14:37a: "Shall I go down after the Philistines? Wilt thou give them into the hand of Israel?"

[459] Josephus inserts explicit mention of the priest's mediatorial role into his rendering of 1 Sam 14:37b: "But he [God] did not answer him [i.e. Saul, the questioner in 14:37a] this day."

concealed offense of ours against him that is the cause of his silence.[460] **124.** And I swear by him that if anyone, even it is my son Ionathes, has committed this offense, I shall kill him and thus placate[461] God, as if I were imposing judgment on his behalf upon a stranger unrelated to myself."[462]

125. When the crowd cried out that he should do this,[463] he immediately made everyone stand in one place. He himself stood with his son in a separate spot,[464] seeking by means of the lot to learn the one who had offended.[465] By lot, this appeared to be Ionathes.[466]

Jonathan the culprit

126. When he was questioned by his father in what he had erred and what he acknowledged having done in his life that was not right or holy,[467] he said: "Father, there is nothing but this: yesterday, in ignorance of your curse and oath, I tasted honey while pursuing the enemy."[468] Saoul, for his part, swore that he would kill him and so honor his oath above birth and the nature of kinship.[469]

Saul–Jonathan exchange

127. [Ionathes], however, was not dismayed at the threat of death, but showed himself noble and magnanimous.[470] "Nor would I," he stated, "beg you to spare me, father; death on behalf of your piety and following a splendid victory is most pleasing to me. For it is the greatest consolation to leave behind Hebrews who have conquered the Palestinoi."[471]

---

[460] This statement elaborates on Saul's summary allusion to "this sin which has arisen today" that he summons the leaders of the people to recognize according to 1 Sam 14:38. The expansion accentuates Saul's stature as one conversant with God's way of acting.

[461] Greek: ἱλάσκομαι. Josephus' other uses of this verb are in *War* 5.385; *Ant.* 8.112; 10.59; *Apion* 1.308.

[462] As he did with Saul's "sin allusion" of 1 Sam 14:38 (see 6.123), Josephus considerably elaborates upon the king's oath as cited in 14:39a.

[463] Josephus turns the statement of 1 Sam 14:39b that no one responded to Saul's oath (14:39a) into a general approbation of this oath, basing himself on the mention of the people's assent to the king's plans in the immediately following 14:40b: "And the people said to Saul, 'Do what seems good to you'."

[464] Compare the corresponding directives given by Saul in 1 Sam 14:40a.

[465] This appended indication concerning the purpose of the "division" prescribed by Saul in 1 Sam 14:40a takes the place of the notice on the people's urging Saul to do whatever seems good to him of 14:40b (which Josephus has anticipated earlier in 6.125). The indication is inspired by the following account of the use of the lot procedure in 14:41-42 (where the LXX is considerably more expansive than the MT).

[466] With this equivalent to 1 Sam 14:42b ("and Jonathan was taken") Josephus confines himself to the end process of the lot-procedure whose application is described in detail in 14:41-42. Perhaps the differences between the shorter MT and the longer LXX texts of these verses prompted Josephus to limit himself to an item that both witnesses have in common.

[467] The Josephan Saul's high-flown questions replace the king's blunt command in 1 Sam 14:43a: "Tell me what you have done."

[468] Josephus embellishes the opening words of Jonathan's response in 1 Sam 14:43b with mention of his being unaware of the king's earlier pronouncement and having violated this during the course of his pursuing the enemy. As in his version of 14:27 in 6.118, he omits reference to Jonathan's use of his staff in obtaining the honey. Finally, he reserves Jonathan's closing declaration of his readiness to die to a later point; see 6.127.

[469] Josephus' expansion of Saul's words sentencing Jonathan to death (1 Sam 14:44) highlights the king's determination to respect his earlier oath at all costs. As usual, he leaves aside the actual "oath formula" ("God do so to me and more also...") the source attributes to the king.

[470] Greek: εὐγενῶς καὶ μεγαλοφρόνως. This combination occurs only here in Josephus; on the word εὐγενής, see Spicq 1978 (I): 301-4. This characterization of Jonathan as he faces death is Josephus' own.

[471] Josephus develops Jonathan's brief closing statement of 1 Sam 14:43bβ ("here I am, I will die") into a discourse expressive of his magnanimity. Feldman (1998: 526-27) points out the similarities between Jonathan's words and those that Josephus attributes to Isaac when facing death at the hands of his father in *Ant.* 1.232 as well as both texts' reminiscences of a variety of Greco-Roman passages involving the killing of a child by a father, e.g., Livy 2.5 and Aeschylus, *Ag.* 228-30.

*People save
Jonathan*

128. At this, the entire people became indignant and sympathetic; they swore that they would not allow Ionathes, the cause of their victory, to die.[472] Thus they liberated him from his father's curse and made prayers to God on the youth's behalf that he would absolve him from his offense.[473]

*Saul's military
success and
family*

(6.6) 129. Saoul then returned to his own city, having destroyed about 60,000 of the enemy.[474] He reigned as king with good luck and subjugated the neighboring nations by making war on them: the Ammanites, the Moabites, the Palestinoi, the Idumeans [and the Amalekites] and the king of Soba.[475] He had three male children, Ionathes, Iesous,[476] and Melchis,[477] while Merobe[478] and Michaal[479] were his daughters.[480]

130. As his general he had Abenar,[481] the son of his uncle.[482] The latter was called Ner,[483] and both Ner and Keis, the father of Saoul, were brothers, sons of Abeli.[484] Saoul also had a supply of chariots and horsemen; with whomever he fought, he came back victorious. He brought the Hebrews to the height of success and well-being and caused them to be more powerful than the other nations.[485] He made those youths who were outstanding in size and beauty his bodyguards.[486]

---

[472] See 1 Sam 14:45a. Josephus prefaces the people's "vetoing" of Saul's intention to execute Jonathan with an allusion to their state of mind at this juncture. He omits the (superfluous) re-affirmation of their resolution in 14:45bα ("as the Lord lives, there shall not one hair of his head fall to the ground") with its use of an oath formula and the figurative language that Josephus regularly avoids.

[473] Josephus' formulation here seems to conflate the readings of MT (the people "ransom" Jonathan) and LXX (they "pray for" him) 1 Sam 14:45bβ.

[474] Josephus introduces a double specification of the notice of 1 Sam 14:46a ("then Saul went up from pursuing the Philistines"), mentioning both his present destination and the impressive number of those slain by him (the figure is without biblical parallel). He leaves aside the reference of 14:46b to the Philistines also "going to their own place."

[475] In MT 1 Sam 14:47 the 5 peoples/kings subjugated by Saul appear in the following order: Moab, Ammonites, Edom [+ Beth-rehob, LXX L, + Baitheor, LXX B], the kings [LXX: king] of Zobah [LXX: Souba], and the Philistines. Josephus adds the "Amalekites" from 14:48 (the name is missing in Lat and bracketed by Niese, though not by Marcus).

[476] MT (1 Sam 14:49) ישׁוי (Eng.: "Ishvi"); LXX B Ἰεσσιούλ; LXX L Ἰεσσιού; Josephus Ἰησοῦς (in 6.369 the name of Saul's 2nd son appears as "Aminadab").

[477] MT (1 Sam 14:49) מלכי־שׁוע (Eng.: "Malchi-shua"); LXX B Μελχεισά; LXX L Μελχισέδδε (L adds an additional son, i.e. Εἰσβαάλ); Josephus Μέλχισος.

[478] MT (1 Sam 14:49) מרב (Eng.: "Merab"); LXX Μερόβ; Josephus Μερόβη.

[479] MT (1 Sam 14:49) מיכל (Eng.: "Michal"); LXX Μελχόλ; Josephus Μιχαάλ.

[480] Josephus omits both the specification of the birth order of Saul's 2 daughters from 1 Sam 14:49b and the name of his wife, i.e. "Ahinoam, daughter of Ahimaaz" from 14:50a.

[481] MT (1 Sam 14:50) אבינר (Eng.: "Abner"); LXX Ἀβεννήρ; Josephus Ἀβήναρος.

[482] In 6.58 (// 1 Sam 10:14) when he first introduces "Abner," Josephus designates him more generally as a "relative" of Saul. 1 Sam 14:50b is ambiguous as to which figure is Saul's "uncle": is it Abner or rather Ner, his (Abner's) father? Josephus clearly opts for the later alternative, thus making Abner himself Saul's cousin.

[483] MT (1 Sam 14:50) נר (Eng.: "Ner"); LXX Νήρ; Josephus Νῆρος.

[484] MT (1 Sam 14:51) אביאל (Eng.: "Abiel"); LXX Ἀβιήλ; Josephus Ἀβέλιος. 1 Sam 14:51 does not explicitly state, as does Josephus, that not only Ner, but also Kish was a son of Abiel (MT; LXX makes Ner the grandson of Abiel, inserting an additional name between them, i.e. Ἰαμείν [B]/ Ἰαβίν [L]). In 1 Sam 9:1, on the other hand, Kish is called son of Abiel (Josephus does not reproduce this genealogical indication in his introduction of "Keis" in 6.45, but seems to have it in mind here in 6.130).

[485] This concluding notice to Josephus' account of Saul's conflict with the Philistines (1 Samuel 13-14// 6.95-130) represents an amplification and synthesis of the references to his combat successes in 1 Sam 14:47-48, 52a, to which he adds, e.g., mention of Saul's extensive military resources.

[486] The "beauty" of those selected by Saul is Josephus' addition to 1 Sam 14:52b (where the chosen are designated as "strong and valiant"), as is the specification that they were intended to serve as royal "bodyguards." Josephus introduces this same specifica-

(7.1) 131. Samouel now came to Saoul[487] and stated that he had been sent by God *Samuel tells* to remind him that God had appointed him king[488] in preference to all [others], and *Saul to exter-* therefore he should be obedient and attentive to him since, whereas he had leader- *kites* ship over the nations, God had this over him and all affairs.[489] **132.** God had then, he said, spoken thus: "Since the Amalekites inflicted many calamities upon the Hebrews in the desert when they, having come out of Egypt, were journeying to the country they now possess,[490] I direct you to punish the Amalekites by means of war and, having conquered them, to leave no [trace] of them. **133.** Rather, put to death those of every age; kill them, beginning with the women and infants, and in this way avenge what they did to your ancestors. Spare neither the beasts of burden nor other livestock for personal profit and possession. Dedicate everything to God and obliterate the name of Amalek in accordance with the commands of Moyses."[491]

(7.2) 134. Saoul declared that he would do what he had been ordered, thinking to *Saul's cam-* manifest his obedience to God, not only in undertaking the campaign against the *paign* Amalekites, but still more by his alacrity and speed, allowing no delay.[492] He mustered his whole force and when he numbered this in Galgala he found that there were about 400,000 of the Israelites, apart from the tribe of Iouda, while this tribe by itself comprised 30,000 soldiers.[493] **135.** Invading the Amalekite country, Saoul set many ambushes and traps around the brook. In so doing, his aim was not only to do them harm by fighting openly, but also, by falling upon them on the roads when they were not expecting it, to encircle and annihilate them.[494] Joining battle with them, he put the enemy to flight and destroyed all of them, following after those who fled.[495]

---

tion concerning the 2,000 men earlier chosen by Saul in his version of 1 Sam 13:2 in 6.95, which thus constitutes an inclusion with his notice on Saul's choice of bodyguards here in 6.130.

[487] With this inserted transitional notice Josephus "reconnects" Samuel and Saul, the former having separated himself from the king in 6.105 (// 1 Sam 13:15a) in view of their interaction throughout 1 Samuel 15. On Josephus' version of this chapter, see Begg 1996d.

[488] In 1 Sam 15:1 Samuel reminds Saul of his having been sent by the Lord to "anoint" him; here, as frequently elsewhere, Josephus avoids that "Messianically-loaded" term. Samuel here alludes back to his words to Saul in 6.54 (// 1 Sam 10:1).

[489] Josephus supplies a motivation for Samuel's summons of 1 Sam 15:1a that Saul heed the Lord's words. On the theme of divine "leadership" (Greek: ἡγεμονία) in Josephus, see Schlatter 1932: 48.

[490] See 1 Sam 15:2. To Samuel's reminiscence of Amalek's past offenses against Israel as cited in Exod 17:8-16 (// *Ant.* 3.39-61); Deut 25:17-19 (// *Ant.* 4.304) Josephus appends mention of the goal of the Israelites' journey that Amalek had tried to impede. On Josephus' treatment of the Amalekites overall, see Maier 1994; Begg 1997n.

[491] Josephus rounds off his reproduction of Samuel's directives from 1 Sam 15:3 with an explicit reference to that Mosaic "law" whose execution God is now enjoining, i.e. Deut 25:19 (// *Ant.* 4.304; cf. 3.60). The version of God's instructions to Samuel about what he is to tell Saul in *Bib. Ant.* 58.1 quotes the actual words of Deut 25:19 rather than simply alluding to them, as Josephus does.

[492] Josephus inserts this reference to Saul's initial verbal response to the directives given him and the state of mind underlying his response. The insertion highlights the king's piety. By contrast, such rabbinic texts as *Midr. Samuel* 18.2; *b. Yoma* 22.5 represent Saul as challenging the divine command of 1 Sam 15:3 that he kill also the cattle and children. Thereupon, a heavenly voice replies in the words of Qoh 7:16: "be not righteous overmuch."

[493] Josephus' rendering of 1 Sam 15:4 agrees with LXX against MT in a whole series of particulars: the muster-site (Galgala vs. "Telaim") and the number of the 2 bodies of troops available to Saul, i.e. the 400,000 (MT: 200,000; both MT and LXX simply designate the first contingent as "infantry" without specifying that they were "Israelites" as Josephus does) and an additional 30,000 (MT: 10,000) men of Judah.

[494] Josephus expatiates on the summary reference to Saul's "laying in wait in the valley" of 1 Sam 15:5b, thereby accentuating his status as a general. Neither he nor the Bible identifies the "brook/valley" in question.

[495] Josephus combines (and embellishes) the notices on Saul's defeat and slaughter of the Amalekites of

136. Once he had accomplished that task of his in accordance with the prophecy of God,[496] he assaulted the Amalekite cities. He besieged and took them by storm, some by machines, some by underground tunnels and outer walls constructed over against them, some by hunger and thirst, and still others in other ways;[497] then, he proceeded to the massacre of the women and infants.[498] Nor did he think that he was acting cruelly or in a way harsher than accords with human nature, because, first of all, he was doing these things to enemies and also because it was by the order of God—whom it would be dangerous not to obey.[499]

Sparing of King Agag and livestock

137. He likewise took prisoner the enemy king Agag.[500] Marveling at his beauty and size of his body, he judged him worthy of safety.[501] He did this, no longer now in accordance with the will of God, being overcome by his own emotion and giving in to an untimely pity with regard to matters over which he did not have an authority that was without danger.[502] **138.** For God so hated[503] the nation of the Amalekites that he had directed him not to spare even the infants—to whom it was more natural to show mercy. Saoul, nevertheless, saved their king—and the leader in the Hebrews' calamities—preferring the beauty of the enemy to the memory of what God had commanded.[504]

The crowd too offended along with him.[505] **139.** For they spared and plundered the beasts of burden and the livestock,[506] whereas God had directed them not to keep

---

1 Sam 15:7, 8b, leaving the material of 15:6 (Saul's warning to the Kenites) and 15:8a (his capture of Agag) for a later point.

[496] Josephus inserts this transitional clause. Its phrase "prophecy of God" (Greek τοῦ θεοῦ προφητεία) occurs twice elsewhere in his writings, i.e. *Ant.* 8.289; 9.129. The phrase likewise recalls Josephus' version of Exod 17:14 in *Ant.* 3.60: "Moses predicted (Greek προφητεύω) that the Amalekites would perish with utter annihilation"; see Feldman: 2000 *ad loc.*

[497] Josephus embellishes 1 Sam 15:5a ("he came to the city [MT; LXX, like Josephus, reads cities] of Amalek") so as to build up Saul's military stature. His inserted references to the siege devices employed by Saul against the Amalekite cities are reminiscent of those with which he elaborates the notice of 2 Kgs 25:1 concerning the Babylonian siege of Jerusalem in *Ant.* 10.132-134. In both instances Josephus is doubtless drawing on his personal experience as a general of contemporary siege practices.

[498] The "massacre notice" of 1 Sam 15:8b (already anticipated by Josephus in 6.135) speaks in general terms of Saul's killing "all the people." Josephus' specific mention of "women and infants" here in 6.136 echoes his notice of these persons in the divine command of 6.133 (// 15:3) and thus underscores Saul's fulfillment—up till this point—of that command in all its details.

[499] With this attached comment Josephus seeks to explain and extenuate Saul's readiness to kill even the Amalekite "women and infants" as enjoined by God in 6.133 (// 1 Sam 15:3). See previous note.

[500] MT (1 Sam 15:8a) אגג (Eng.: "Agag"); LXX Ἀγάγ; Josephus Ἄγαγος.

[501] Josephus supplies an "aesthetic" motive for Saul's sparing of Agag as cited in 1 Sam 15:9a, this echoing his mention (6.130) that Saul chose youths of outstanding "size and beauty" for his bodyguards. Pseudo-Philo, in contrast, attributes (*Bib. Ant.* 58.2) Saul's sparing of the Amalekite king to the latter's promising to show him "hidden treasures." In *Bib. Ant.* 58.3 God informs Samuel that Saul, having been "corrupted by silver," also spared Agag's wife.

[502] This editorial comment serves to prepare readers for God's following condemnation of Saul.

[503] Josephus uses the verb "hate" (Greek: μισέω) with the Deity as subject 4 times elsewhere: *War* 3.376 (object: suicide); *Ant.* 8.129 (passive, the unfaithful Hebrews), 318 (the vile); and 20.166 (the impiety of the Jewish rebels).

[504] These additional editorial comments on Saul's sparing of Agag develop the contrast between God's perspective and that of the king, further preparing readers for the former's upcoming condemnation of the latter.

[505] With this mention of the people's role in the proceedings Josephus returns to the source story-line (see 1 Sam 15:9), adding an explicit, negative evaluation of their initiative, comparable to the one previously supplied by him concerning Saul's misguided actions in 6.137.

[506] Like MT 1 Sam 15:9, Josephus mentions only the animals taken by the people; LXX speaks also of food and vineyards.

these things. They also carried off other valuable goods and riches. They did, how-ever, destroy whatever was not worthy of attention as a possession.[507]

(7.3) 140. Saoul, having been victorious over everything extending from Pelousion in Egypt to the Red Sea,[508] destroyed the enemy. He did, however, pass over the nation of the Sikimites[509] for these were settled in the middle of the country of Madiene.[510] Prior to the battle he sent to exhort them to withdraw, so that they would not share the misfortune of the Amalekites.[511] For, seeing that they were rela-tives of Ragouel, the father-in-law of Moyses, he had cause to save them.[512]

Saul's advance warning to Sikimites

(7.4) 141. Now Saoul, just as though he had not disobeyed anything of what the prophet had commanded him when he was about to launch war on the Amalekites, and as if he had guarded all those things exactly once he had been victorious over the enemy, returned to his own home, rejoicing over his achievements.[513]

Saul's return

142. But God was displeased at the safety of the king of the Amalekites and the crowd's plundering of the livestock, because these things were done without his giving permission. For he thought it terrible that, whereas it was he who gave them the strength to be victorious and prevail over the enemy, he should be despised and disobeyed, as no human king would be.[514]

God's anger against Saul

143. He therefore said to the prophet Samouel that he had changed his mind[515] about having designated Saoul who had not at all done as he had directed, but had acted in accordance with his own will, as king.[516] Samouel was very distressed when

God–Samuel exchange

---

[507] This paragraph represents Josephus' amplified version of 1 Sam 15:9 concerning the people's differ-entiated way of dealing with the Amalekites' property, depending on its quality.

[508] Here Josephus picks up on the indication con-cerning the extent of Saul's conquest in 1 Sam 15:7, where MT reads "from Havilah (LXX B Εὐειλάτ; LXX L Εὐιλάτ) as far as Shur (LXX B Ἀσσούρ, LXX L Σούρ), which is east of Egypt." Marcus (*ad loc.*) comments: "Josephus reverses the direction [i.e. of 15:7, this pro-ceeding east-to-west], assuming that Shur corresponds to Pelusium and that Havilah is somewhere near the Red Sea."

[509] In 1 Sam 15:6 Saul issues an advance warning to the "Kenites." Schlatter (1913 *s.v.*) reads this same name here in 6.140, while Rappaport (1930: 129, n. 12) proposes that, having the targumic reading in 15:6 (where Saul speaks to "the Shalmaite") before him, Josephus made a connection between that form and the "Sikimites" (i.e. Shechemites) of whom he speaks here in 6.140, on the basis of Gen 33:18, where "Salem" is called "a city of Shechem."

[510] 1 Sam 15:6 makes no mention of "Madiene," i.e. "Midian," referring only to the Kenites' departure "from among the Amalekites." Josephus' introduction of the place name has in view his subsequent reference to Moses' father-in-law Raguel/Jethro, whom both the Bible (see Exod 2:16; 3:1; Judg 1:16) and he (see *Ant.* 5.127) designate as a "Midianite."

[511] See Saul's warning the "Kenites" to separate from the Amalekites lest they suffer the same fate in 1 Sam 15:6a.

[512] Josephus supplies a different motivation for Saul's special treatment of the Kenites/Sikimites than does 1 Sam 15:6b, where it is their (ancestors') "kind-ness" to Israel on its journey from Egypt that prompts Saul's timely warning to them. Conceivably, Josephus' modification reflects the fact that the Bible does not explicitly mention the Kenites' previous showing favor to the Israelites, a point noted in rabbinic tradition; see Begg 1996d: 397, n. 79.

[513] 1 Samuel 15 does not directly relate Saul's homecoming (in MT 15:12 Samuel is informed of the king's movements that have taken him towards Gilgal). Josephus not only fills this lacuna, but also provides a detailed description of Saul's (deluded) state of mind as he returns to be confronted with the divine perspec-tive on his acts. Pseudo-Philo (*Bib. Ant.* 58.2) has Saul bring Agag to "Ramaathaim," i.e. "Ramah," the home-town of Samuel according to 1 Sam 7:17, where their run-in occurs.

[514] As in 6.138, Josephus pauses to take readers into the mind of God himself in order to highlight the con-trast between the king's self-evaluation (see 6.141) and the Deity's view of his conduct.

[515] This is Josephus' only use of the verb μετανοέω ("change one's mind, repent") with God as subject; he likely derives the term from LXX 1 Sam 15:29, where it twice appears in that usage.

[516] See 1 Sam 15:10-11. Characteristically, Josephus avoids the Bible's introductory phrase "the word of the Lord came to...," making God speak to Samuel directly.

he heard this,[517] and all night long kept appealing to God to be reconciled to Saoul and not be angry.[518]

144. He, however, did not agree to a pardon[519] for Saoul despite the prophet's request, thinking it not just to indulge offenses [in response] to intercession. For there is nothing by which these are more increased than by the showing of leniency on the part of those wronged, for they, in their striving after a reputation for gentleness and kindness,[520] engender them, concealed though this is from themselves.[521]

Samuel–Saul exchange

145. When therefore God rebuffed the prophet's prayer and made clear that he had thought better [of things],[522] Samouel, as soon as it was day, went to Galgala to Saoul.[523] When he beheld him, the king rushed up and embraced him. "I thank God," he said, "who has given me the victory. For my part, I have done everything directed by him."[524]

146. To this Samouel responded: "Tell me then, from where am I hearing cattle and the noise of beasts of burden in the camp?"[525] He answered that the people had kept these for sacrifice. The entire race of the Amalekites had, however, been exterminated in accordance with the command and none remained alive.[526] But he had, he said, brought their king to him, whom alone he had kept, so that they might confer with each other about what should be done with him.[527]

Pseudo-Philo's version of God's word to Samuel in *Bib. Ant.* 58.3 is quite different, with the Deity first informing the prophet of Saul's sparing both Agag and his wife. The royal pair are—Samuel is next informed—to be allowed a final coupling that night that will produce a son who will prove a "stumbling block" to Saul. Agag is then to be killed on the following day by Samuel, while his wife is to be preserved until her son is born.

[517] Josephus follows LXX 1 Sam 15:11bα in describing Samuel's reaction as one of "grief," whereas MT speaks of him rather as "angry."

[518] In 1 Sam 15:11bβ Samuel simply "cries to the Lord" throughout the night. Josephus supplies a definite content to his "cry."

[519] Greek: συγγνώμη. This is the noun cognate of the verb συγγιγνώσκω used in 6.93 (see note to "pardon" at 6.93), where Samuel confidently informs the people that he will persuade God to "pardon" them. Here in 6.144 Samuel fails in his effort to win God's "pardon" for Saul.

[520] Greek: ἐπιείκεια καὶ χρηστότης. This noun combination echoes that of the cognate adjectives used of Samuel himself in 6.92; see note on "kind and gentle" at 6.92.

[521] 1 Samuel 15 does not record a divine response to Samuel's all-night cry (15:11bβ). Josephus not only does so, but also offers a motivation for the Deity's negative response and an editorial comment that draws a moral about the perils of leniency from the divine response.

[522] This transitional phrase prolongs Josephus' extended insertion concerning God's rejection of Samuel's plea in 6.144. It likewise echoes the Deity's

statement to Samuel of 6.143 about "changing his mind" concerning his appointment of Saul. In 6.143 the verb used is μετανοέω, here in 6.145 rather μεταμέλεω (neither verb is elsewhere used by Josephus with God as subject; see note to "changed his mind" at 6.143).

[523] Josephus' notice on Samuel's movement draws on 1 Sam 15:12-13a (MT LXX L) where, having heard of Saul's descent to Galgala, Samuel goes to him. He lives aside the preceding (irrelevant) details concerning Saul's coming to Carmel and erecting a "monument" (literally: hand) there.

[524] See 1 Sam 15:13b.

[525] Samuel's question in 1 Sam 15:14 asks specifically about the noise of sheep and oxen and does not mention the camp.

[526] See 1 Sam 15:15.

[527] Josephus anticipates Saul's further admission concerning his sparing of Agag from 1 Sam 15:20b, likewise having the king offer a rationale for this, which, however, does not agree with Josephus' own editorial explanation of Saul's initiative in 6.137 (i.e. his delight in Agag's "beauty"). The effect of this discrepancy is thus to call Saul's veracity into question. In passing from 1 Sam 15:15 (sparing of the beasts) to 15:20b (sparing of Agag), Josephus leaves aside the intervening sequence 15:16-20a, which for the most part seems simply to recapitulate the previous exchange between king and prophet in 15:13-15. Also Pseudo-Philo abridges the repetitious biblical exchange between Samuel and Saul. In *Bib. Ant.* 58.4, in response to Saul's affirmation concerning the fulfillment of the prophet's prediction about the Lord's handing over of

147. But the prophet said that the Deity was not pleased by sacrifices, but by those who are good and just.[528] Such were those who followed his will and commands, and who thought nothing to have been done well by themselves other than what they did at God's direction. For it is not by not sacrificing to him that one despises [God], but by seeming to disobey him. **148.** "From those who do not obey or offer the true worship that alone is pleasing to God[529]—even if they sacrifice many fat victims, or present magnificent dedicatory offerings made from silver and gold—he does not receive these things benevolently, but rejects them and regards them as proofs of vileness rather than of piety.

149. Rather, it is those who keep in mind only what God has uttered and directed and who choose to die rather than transgress any of these things in whom he takes pleasure.[530] From them he seeks no sacrifice, and, if they do sacrifice anything, however humble, he will more readily accept the honor [given him] by poverty than by the wealthiest.[531]

150. Know therefore that you yourself are subject to God's wrath, for you have despised and ignored what he commanded.[532] How then can you imagine that he will look upon a sacrifice made from what he condemned to be annihilated—unless you think that sacrificing these things to God is equivalent to their extermination?[533] Expect then that you will be deprived of your kingship and authority you have taken for granted in neglecting God who awarded it to you."[534]

151. Saoul declared that he had done wrong and did not deny his offense; for he had transgressed the prophet's commands.[535] It was, however, out of anxiety and fear of the soldiers that he had not prevented or hindered them from despoiling the plunder.[536] "But pardon and be indulgent," for he would keep himself from offend-

---

the enemy, Samuel first reiterates his lament over Israel's premature demand for a king from 56.2 and then proceeds to denounce Saul for his transgression as a result of which Agag, who is about to be executed, will not show him his hidden treasures (as he had previously promised; see 58.2), just as the posthumous son to be born to Agag will be a stumbling block for Saul.

[528] Greek: ἀγαθοὶ καὶ δίκαιοι. This same adjectival combination occurs (in reverse order) in Samuel's speech to the people in 6.93, where he urges them to be "just and good."

[529] Compare *Apion* 2.192, where Josephus avers that God is to be worshiped by the practice of virtue, this being "the most holy way of worshiping" him.

[530] This affirmation echoes many other statements by Josephus (see, e.g., *Apion* 2.150, 183) concerning the supreme importance of keeping the Law for Jews—an emphasis calculated to win the sympathy of Roman readers, given their own tradition's stress on respect for law; see Feldman 1998a: 552; Spilsbury 1998: 57-58.

[531] The above 3-paragraph sequence (6.147-149) represents Josephus' elaboration of Samuel's remarks concerning the superiority of "obedience" over sacrifice in 1 Sam 15:22. Conversely, Josephus does not reproduce Samuel's equating "rebellion" with "divination" and "stubbornness" with "iniquity and idolatry"

from 15:23a. One might see Josephus' emphasis on the point that God can be "pleased" apart from any sacrifice as reflecting the situation of Jews in his time who had lost the possibility of offering sacrifice (and been, in many cases, reduced to poverty), but who, he wishes to make clear, can still attain God's favor by consistent obedience of the kind Saul himself failed to evidence.

[532] Josephus amplifies Samuel's charge of 1 Sam 15:23bα about Saul's having "rejected the word of the Lord" with mention of the divine "wrath" against him that this provoked.

[533] This question, with its ironic reference to Saul's "thinking" his proposed "sacrifice" of the beasts to be equivalent to their "extermination" as ordered by God, has no source equivalent.

[534] As he did with the summarizing accusation of 1 Sam 15:23bα, Josephus also elaborates upon the prophet's "sentence" against Saul of 15:23bβ: "he [God] also has rejected you from being king (+ over Israel, LXX)."

[535] In 1 Sam 15:24a Saul confesses transgressing not only Samuel's words, but also those of the Lord himself.

[536] The conclusion of Saul's assertion about the people in 1 Sam 15:24b is, not that he allowed them to plunder (so Josephus), but rather that he had "obeyed their voice"—a point not mentioned in what precedes.

Samuel's sacri-
ficing

ing in the future.[537] He then appealed to the prophet to return and offer thanksgiving sacrifices to God.[538] But he, having seen that God remained unappeased,[539] departed for his home.[540]

(7.5) 152. Saoul, however, wishing to restrain Samouel, took hold of his cloak, and pulled so forcibly—since Samouel was in a great hurry to depart—that he tore[541] the garment in two.[542] 153. But the prophet stated that in the same way his kingdom had been torn from him and that a good and just[543] man would receive it.[544] For God was abiding by what he had decided concerning him, since to change one's mind and reverse one's intention are characteristics of human emotion, rather than of divine strength.[545] 154. Saoul, for his part, said that, while he had acted impiously, it was impossible to undo what had been done.[546] He nevertheless appealed to him to show him honor in the sight of the crowd and to come with him to pay homage to God.[547] Samouel granted him this; having accompanied him, he payed homage to God.[548]

King Agag
killed

155. Agag, the king of the Amalekites, was also brought to him.[549] Upon his inquiring how bitter his death would be,[550] he said: "Just as you made many Hebrew mothers lament and mourn for their children, so you will cause your own mother to

---

[537] Josephus amplifies and intensifies Saul's plea for "forgiveness" (1 Sam 15:25a) with a promise of amendment for the future.

[538] Saul in 1 Sam 15:25b requests that Samuel return with him so that he (Saul) might worship God. The Josephan Saul expresses greater deference towards Samuel as the one who would offer the sacrifice.

[539] The word rendered "unappeased" is the participle of the verb διαλλάττω. *Ant.* 7.153 will introduce a verbal contrast between Saul here and David in stating that God "was appeased" (διαλλάττεται) after the latter's sin with Bathsheba.

[540] This transitional phrase, with its echo of Samuel's earlier realization of God's unwillingness to forgive Saul (see 6.145), takes the place of 1 Sam 15:26, where Samuel rebuffs Saul's plea that he accompany him (15:25b), reiterating his condemnation of 15:23b.

[541] Like LXX and 4QSam^a 1 Sam 15:27, Josephus specifies that Saul was the one to tear Samuel's cloak, whereas MT leaves it ambiguous whether the subject of this action is Saul or Samuel himself.

[542] Josephus embellishes 1 Sam 15:27 with mention both of the motivation for Saul's initiative and Samuel's "haste" to be gone.

[543] This qualification of David as Saul's successor recalls the same combination of terms used for those who please God in 6.147; see note to "good and just" at 6.147.

[544] Samuel's announcement in 1 Sam 15:28 is that the Lord has awarded Saul's kingdom to "a neighbor of yours, who is better than you."

[545] See 1 Sam 15:29 (which in MT contains a reference to the Deity's "not lying" unparalleled in the LXX and Josephus). Both the Bible and Josephus leave un-

clear how their affirmations about divine immutability in 15:29 // 6.153 cohere with the statement they earlier (15:11// 6.143) attribute to God himself about his "thinking better of/ repenting of" having made Saul king.

[546] To Saul's renewed confession of sin in 1 Sam 15:30aα Josephus appends an expression of resignation by the king in the face of the divine refusal to forgive him, in which he submits to the immutability of God's decisions as just affirmed by Samuel.

[547] In 1 Sam 15:30aβb Saul asks that Samuel also honor him "before the elders of my people," a group nowhere mentioned earlier in the chapter. As in 15:25, he likewise speaks of himself as the (only) one who will worship God. In line with his modification of that earlier formulation (see 6.151), Josephus has Saul allude to Samuel's being the one to worship.

[548] Josephus follows LXX 4QSam^a 1 Sam 15:31 (and his own formulations of Saul's plea in 6.151, 154) in having Samuel be the one to worship. In MT it is Saul himself who worships.

[549] In 1 Sam 15:32aα Samuel commands that Agag be brought to him, while in *Bib. Ant.* 58.4 he himself goes to him with sword in hand.

[550] In having Agag pose a question expressive of his realization of what awaits him at Samuel's hands here, Josephus reflects the reading of LXX 1 Sam 15:32b as opposed to MT, where he makes rather the confident assertion "surely the bitterness of death is past." Josephus has no equivalent to the (divergent) indications concerning the manner of Agag's approach to Samuel in the various witnesses to 15:29aβ: "cheerfully" (?, MT), "trembling" (LXX), "imperiously" (Tg.).

weep over you, once you are destroyed."[551] Then he immediately directed that he *Samuel and* be killed[552] in Galgala,[553] while he himself went away to the city of Armatha.[554] *Saul separate*

(8.1) 156. King Saoul, aware of the calamities he was experiencing since he had made God hostile to him,[555] went up to his palace in Gaba (a name that means "hill"),[556] and from that day on no longer entered the prophet's presence.[557]

157. God directed Samouel, who was still grieving over him, to cease mourning.[558] *God sends* He was to take the holy oil[559] and go off to the city of Bethleme, to Jesse, the son of *Samuel to* Obed,[560] and anoint[561] one of his sons whom he would point out as the one who *Bethlehem* was to be king. Samouel, however, said that he was afraid that when Saoul learned of this he would do away with him, whether in secret or openly.[562] But when God counseled him and gave him a secure journey,[563] he went to the above-mentioned city.[564]

---

[551] Josephus substitutes another formulation of the "measure for measure" (*talion*) principle for the one enunciated by Samuel in 1 Sam 15:33a according to which just as Agag's sword had rendered women [Josephus specifies these as "Hebrews"] childless, so also his mother is about to be made childless.

[552] Both 1 Sam 15:33b and *Bib. Ant.* 58.4 have Samuel kill Agag personally. Josephus' modification, which makes the prophet's involvement in the gory deed a more indirect one, has a parallel in his handling of Elijah's killing of the 450 prophets of Baal (see 1 Kgs 18:40 and compare *Ant.* 8.343). In both instances, Josephus may have felt qualms about the source depictions of prophetic figures personally perpetrating "Zealot-like" deeds of violence. By contrast, rabbinic tradition elaborates on the variety of techniques employed by Samuel in killing Agag; see Begg 1996d: 409, n. 161.

[553] Josephus omits the further specification of 1 Sam 15:33b concerning the place of Agag's execution, i.e. "before the Lord."

[554] MT (1 Sam 15:34a) הרמתה (Eng.: "Ramah"); LXX Ἀρμαθάιμ; Josephus Ἀρμαθά. Josephus has previously mentioned this city in connection with Samuel in *Ant.* 5.342; 6.35, 47, 67.

[555] Josephus inserts this ominous indication concerning Saul's state of mind following his confrontation with Samuel.

[556] In MT 1 Sam 15:34b Saul goes to his home "in Gibeah of Saul." Josephus' rendering reads like a conflation of LXX B ("Gabaa") and LXX L's "translation" of this ("the hill").

[557] 1 Sam 15:35a states in global terms that Samuel "did not see Saul again until the day of his death." In both the Bible and Josephus the pair actually do encounter each other once again during Samuel's lifetime; see 1 Sam 19:24 (// 6.223).

[558] Josephus here combines Samuel's grieving for Saul (1 Sam 15:35bα) and God's calling on him to desist from this (16:1a). In the Bible itself these 2 items

are separated from each other by the "repetition" of the notice of 15:11 in 15:35bβ concerning God's "repenting" of having made Saul king that Josephus leaves aside. Josephus likewise omits—as something obvious from what precedes—the "motivation" God gives for his ordering Samuel to desist from his mourning, i.e. the fact of his (God's) having "rejected" Saul as king. Pseudo-Philo's version of the exchange between God and Samuel at the opening of 1 Samuel 16 in *Bib. Ant.* 59.1 is distinctive: God begins forthwith by telling Samuel to go anoint the one whom he will tell him, since the time for that one's kingship has now come.

[559] 1 Sam 16:1b speaks simply of the "oil" with which Samuel is to fill his "horn." Josephus' specification of the oil as "holy" recalls his similar qualification of the oil used to anoint Saul in 6.54; see note to "holy oil" at 6.54. On Josephus' version of the story of David's anointing in 1 Sam 16:1-13, see Begg 1996e.

[560] Josephus inserts the name of Jesse's father from Ruth 4:17, 21-22 (// *Ant.* 5.336). In having God send Samuel to "Bethlehem," Josephus agrees with LXX 1 Sam 16:1b, whereas in MT he is to go to "Jesse the Bethlehemite."

[561] Josephus anticipates God's use of this term from 1 Sam 16:3bβ. In 16:1b Samuel is simply told to "go to" Jesse.

[562] Josephus' elaboration of Samuel's response in 1 Sam 16:2a ("How can I go? If Saul hears of it, he will kill me") underscores the magnitude of the (perceived) danger facing the prophet.

[563] This statement concerning the divine response to Samuel's objection to his mission takes the place of God's directive to the prophet in 1 Sam 16:2b: "Take a heifer with you, and say, 'I have come to sacrifice to the Lord'." Josephus' version does seem to address Samuel's security concerns more satisfactorily than does his biblical source—how in fact would Samuel's acting in accord with God's directive about the heifer in 16:2b serve to protect him against Saul's intended violence? Pseudo-Philo (*Bib. Ant.* 59.1) replaces the ex-

Samuel mis-
takes God's in-
tended king

158. When all greeted him and asked the reason for his coming,[565] he said that he had come to sacrifice to God. Having therefore made the sacrifice,[566] he called Jesse, together with his children, to the sacred [feast].[567] Beholding his eldest son,[568] who was tall and handsome,[569] he concluded from his good looks that this was the one who was to rule as king.[570]

159. He, however, misread God's providential design,[571] for, when he questioned him whether he should anoint with the oil the youth whom he had admired and judged worthy of the kingship,[572] God said that humans and God do not see the same things.[573]

160. "You, for your part, are looking to the youth's beauty and thinking him worthy to rule as king.[574] I, however, do not make kingship the prize of bodily good looks, but rather of virtue of soul. I seek one who is altogether outstanding in this

---

change of 1 Sam 16:2-3 with one of his own, wherein Samuel asks whether God is now going to "destroy the kingdom of Saul" and God responds affirmatively.

[564] See 1 Sam 16:4a. Josephus leaves aside the continuation of the divine instructions to Samuel cited in 16:3 (which he has partially anticipated in 6.157).

[565] Josephus eliminates the note of—unexplained—menace that marks Samuel's encounter with the Bethlehemites in 1 Sam 16:4b-5, where they come "trembling" to meet him, asking whether he has come "in peace," whereupon he assures them that he has. The Tg. does something analogous with its "neutral" rendering, "the elders of the city *gathered* to meet him," while Pseudo-Philo leaves aside the "meeting scene" of 16:4b-5a completely. In having Samuel met, not simply by "the elders of the city" as in 16:4b, but by "all" (i.e. the Bethlehemites) Josephus accentuates the prophet's status.

[566] This statement that Samuel did in fact offer the sacrifice announced by him in 1 Sam 16:5a has no explicit biblical parallel.

[567] In contrast to 1 Sam 16:5, where Samuel invites first the elders, and then Jesse and his sons, "to the sacrifice" Josephus introduces a distinction between the sacrifice (which Samuel alone offers) and the following sacred feast in which Jesse's family is to participate (his reference to the latter occasion may have been suggested to him by Samuel's reference to the company's not "sitting down/coming to the table" until David arrives in 1 Sam 16:11). Given this modification, Josephus likewise leaves aside the cultic detail about Samuel's "consecration" of both the elders and Jesse and his sons prior to their participation in the sacrifice of 16:5 (which Pseudo-Philo does reproduce in *Bib. Ant.* 59.2).

[568] Unlike 1 Sam 16:6 and *Bib. Ant.* 59.2, Josephus does not mention the son's name, i.e. "Eliab" at this point. He supplies the specification about his being Jesse's "eldest" on the basis of 1 Sam 17:13 and

1 Chr 2:13.

[569] Josephus anticipates his allusion to the first son's appearance from God's comment concerning him in 1 Sam 16:7.

[570] Josephus supplies a motivation, i.e., the youth's appearance, for Samuel's surmise (1 Sam 16:6) about his suitability for kingship, drawing this from the divine allusion to Eliab's physique in 16:7 (see note to "handsome" at 6.158). In addition, Josephus reformulates Samuel's surmise itself ("surely the Lord's anointed [MT מָשִׁיחַ; LXX (ὁ) χριστὸς αὐτοῦ] is before him") so as to eliminate its use of the term "messiah," which as Schlatter (1932: 257) notes, occurs only once in Josephus' writings, i.e. in *Ant.* 20.200, where it is applied to Jesus in the so-called *Testimonium Flavianum*. By contrast, Pseudo-Philo (*Bib. Ant.* 59.2) does reproduce the Messiah designation of 16:6.

[571] Greek: πρόνοια. This inserted editorial comment intimates the upshot of the following exchange between God and Samuel.

[572] In 1 Sam 16:7 God responds directly to Samuel's "thoughts" concerning Eliab (16:6), without a preceding question by the prophet.

[573] Josephus reverses the sequence of God's words in 1 Sam 16:7, where an analogous general statement about the divine as opposed to the human perspective ("for the Lord sees not as man sees," LXX) follows the divine admonition to Samuel personally about not focussing on Eliab's appearance.

[574] This statement about what Samuel is (wrongly) doing is Josephus' equivalent to the prohibition issued Samuel at the opening of God's word to him in 1 Sam 16:7. Pseudo-Philo (*Bib. Ant.* 59.2) turns God's word to Samuel into a divine censure for the latter's lack of vision regarding Eliab's (non-) suitability, notwithstanding Samuel's earlier claim to be a "seer" (*Bib. Ant.* 56.4// 1 Sam 9:18), whereupon God immediately commands Samuel to anoint Jesse's youngest son.

respect, endowed with piety, justice, courage, and obedience, in which beauty of soul consists."[575]

161. When God said these things, Samouel directed Jesse to show him all his sons.[576] He made five[577] others come, of whom the eldest was Taliab,[578] the second Aminadab,[579] the third Samal,[580] the fourth Nathanael;[581] the fifth was called Rael,[582] and the sixth Asam.[583]

Process of elimination leads to David

162. Seeing that none of these were inferior to the eldest in appearance, the prophet questioned God which of them he chose as king. When he said that it was none of them,[584] he inquired of Jesse whether he did not have other children in addition to these.[585] **163.** He stated that there was one, named David, who was shepherding and taking care of guarding the flocks;[586] [Samouel] directed him to call him quickly. For they could not recline for the feast in his absence.[587]

164. When David came at his father's summons—a ruddy[588] boy with a vivacious

Samuel anoints David

---

[575] With the above conclusion to the divine discourse Josephus spells out what God is seeking when, as 1 Sam 16:7bβ puts it, he "looks on the heart." The list enumerates 3 of the 5, i.e. the standard 4 plus piety, cardinal virtues enumerated by Plato (see *Prot.* 349B), with "obedience" taking the place of "wisdom" and "prudence/temperance." Of the 3 qualities, 2, i.e. "justice" and "courage" that the Lord states he seeks in a king here in 6.160 are attributed to David in the Josephan eulogy for him of 7.390-391.

[576] Josephus streamlines the Bible's narration, where it is only after (1 Sam 16:8-9) Jesse—on his own—has presented his next 2 sons (Abinadab, Shammah) to Samuel and seen them too rejected by him, that Jesse exhibits (16:10) all 7 of his (older) sons to Samuel, only to hear that God had chosen none of them. Pseudo-Philo, who has God instruct Samuel to anoint Jesse's youngest son (*Bib. Ant.* 59.2) in direct connection with the former's "misapprehension" of Eliab and Samuel then immediately summoning (59.3) that youngest son, lacks a parallel to the entire sequence 16:8-10.

[577] 1 Sam 16:10 speaks of Jesse's 7 sons other than David himself, 3 of whom (Eliab, Abinadab, Shammah) are mentioned by name in 16:6-9. Josephus, on the contrary, has a total of 6 sons brought before Samuel prior to David, i.e. the eldest (6.158) plus the next 5 in age (6.161), all of whom he will now proceed to name on the basis of the list in 1 Chr 2:13-15.

[578] This is the reading of the codices RO, which Niese adopts. Both Marcus (*ad loc.*) and Schalit (*s.v.*) read rather "Eliab" following the codices MSP and in accordance with the name of Jesse's eldest son as given in 1 Chr 2:13 (cf. 1 Sam 16:6).

[579] MT (1 Chr 2:13; cf. 1 Sam 16:8) אבינדב (Eng.: "Abinadab"); LXX Ἀμιναοδάβ; Josephus Ἀμινάδαβος. Josephus' form thus corresponds to that of LXX against MT.

[580] MT 1 Chr 2:13 (cf. 1 Sam 16:9) שמעא (Eng.: "Shimea"); LXX Σαμμά; Josephus Σάμαλος.

[581] MT (1 Chr 2:14) נתנאל (Eng.: "Nethanel"); LXX Ναθαναήλ; Josephus Ναθαναῆλος.

[582] MT (1 Chr 2:14) רדי (Eng.: "Raddai"); LXX Ῥαδδαί; Josephus Ῥάηλος.

[583] MT (1 Chr 2:15) אצם (Eng.: "Ozem"); LXX B Ἄσομ; LXX L Ἄσαμ; Josephus Ἄσαμος. Josephus' insertion of this list of all David's brothers here is contrary to his usual practice of leaving aside the names of minor biblical personages. The exception points up the importance of David's family for his entire history.

[584] In 1 Sam 16:10b there is no such "inquiry" of God by Samuel; rather, the prophet simply announces on his own that God has not "chosen" any of Jesse's 7 (16:10a) sons, who have just been presented to him. Compare 6.159, where Josephus also introduces an explicit consultation of God by Samuel concerning Jesse's firstborn, whereas 16:6 has him thinking to himself.

[585] See 1 Sam 16:11aα, in which Samuel asks Jesse: "Are all your sons here?" Compare *Bib. Ant.* 59.3, where Samuel, who already knows of the youngest son's existence from God (59.2), simply commands Jesse to fetch him.

[586] Josephus inserts this name (Δαυίδης; MT דוד; LXX B Δαυείδ; LXX L Δαυίδ) of the youngest son into Jesse's reply (1 Sam 16:11aβ) to Samuel's question (16:11aα), anticipating the name from 16:13. On Josephus' portrayal of David, see Feldman 1998: 537-69.

[587] See 1 Sam 16:11b. Josephus' inserted reference to "the feast" harks back to his mention of the "sacred (feast)" in 6.158.

[588] Feldman (1998: 542-43) notes that Josephus' adjective here, i.e. ξανθός ("tawny"; cf. LXX 1 Sam 16:12 πυρράκης, "fiery red") is the same one used by him to designate the "reddish" pottage that gave Esau his nickname in *Ant.* 2.2-3. Thereby, Josephus insinuates a connection between David and Rome whose origins Jewish tradition traces back to Esau and his

complexion and eyes, and otherwise handsome[589]—Samouel said quietly to himself: "this is the one whom it has pleased God to have rule as king."[590] He reclined and made the youth and Jesse recline beside him, along with his [other] children.[591]

165. Then, taking the oil, with David looking on, he smeared it on him[592] and spoke softly in his ear, indicating that God had chosen him to rule as king. He further urged him to be just and receptive[593] to his orders, for thus the kingship would remain his for a long time and he would have a splendid and famous house.[594] He would also overthrow the Palestinoi and would be victorious over and prove superior in battle to whatever nations he might war against. He would acquire a fame that would be celebrated in song[595] during his lifetime and leave this behind to those after him.[596]

Saul's afflic-tion

(8.2) 166. Samouel urged these things and departed.[597] The Deity then abandoned Saoul[598] and went over to David.[599] Once the divine spirit transferred to him,[600] he began to prophesy.[601] A certain suffering beset Saoul and demons[602] caused him to

---

descendants, the Edomites. Feldman (ibid: 543) further notes that the same term is used to describe the great heroes Achilles (*Il.* 1.197; 23.141) and Odysseus (*Od.* 13.399, 431) in Homer.

[589] See 1 Sam 16:12a; like MT, Josephus has no equivalent to the LXX specification that David was handsome "in the Lord's sight." Pseudo-Philo omits any mention of David's appearance.

[590] According to 1 Sam 16:12b it is God who informs Samuel that the lad is the one he is to anoint (MT LXX L; in LXX B he is told to anoint David "for he is good"). Josephus has Samuel make this determination on his own (contrast his 2 inserted mentions of a consultation of God by Samuel concerning Jesse's older sons in 6.159, 162), thereby intimating the prophet's growth in spiritual insight over the course of the episode. Pseudo-Philo anticipates God's directive of 16:12b to an earlier point, i.e. in connection with his word to Samuel concerning Eliab in *Bib. Ant.* 59.2.

[591] The fact of the whole party's "reclining" at this point is not mentioned explicitly in 1 Samuel 16 (cf., however, 16:11b, where Samuel states that they cannot do this until David appears and 16:13aα, where Samuel anoints David "in the midst of his brothers"). In specifying that Samuel placed David beside himself Josephus accentuates the latter's status.

[592] See 1 Sam 16:13aα (cf. 16:1b), which mentions the "horn of oil" Samuel uses to anoint David. In recounting Samuel's application of the oil to David, Josephus does not use the verb "anoint" (LXX χρίω) of 16:13 (and of God's order to Samuel in 6.157), but rather an alternative term, i.e. ἀλείφω (whose other 2 occurrences in his writings are in *War* 2.123; 5.565). Compare his avoidance of the reference to "his [God's] messiah" of 16:7 in 6.158.

[593] This adjectival combination picks up on God's statement that he is looking, *inter alia*, for "justice" and "obedience" from the new king in 6.160.

[594] Greek: ὁ οἶκος λαμπὸς καὶ περιβόητος. The same phrase recurs in *Ant.* 7.94, where, responding to Nathan's dynastic promise, David rejoices to know that he will have such a "house."

[595] Greek: ἀοίδιμος. Josephus' only other use of this term is in *Ant.* 19.53. As used here in 6.165, the term foreshadows the women's chant, exalting David's killing of ten thousands of the Philistines in 1 Sam 18:7 (// 6.193).

[596] Neither the Bible nor Pseudo-Philo records such an address spoken by Samuel to David at the moment of his anointing. Josephus' insertion spells out the import of that anointing and prepares readers for the subsequent unfolding of David's career.

[597] 1 Sam 16:13bβ specifies that he went to Ramah.

[598] 1 Sam 16:14a states that the "Spirit of the Lord departed from Saul."

[599] Compare 1 Sam 16:13bα: "the Spirit of the Lord came mightily upon David from that day forward." Once again, Josephus, in accord with his general tendency (see note to "freedom" at *Ant.* 5.182)—cf., however, the continuation of the paragraph and next note—reformulates a biblical reference to the operation of God's spirit.

[600] Josephus here makes delayed (and exceptional; see previous note) use of the reference in 1 Sam 16:13bα to "the Spirit of the Lord coming mightily upon David from that day forward"; compare *Bib. Ant.* 59.3: "The Lord was with him from that day." His other uses of the phrase "divine spirit" (τὸ θεῖον/πνεῦμα) are in *Ant.* 4.108, 118 (recipient: Balaam); 6.222 (// 1 Sam 19:21: the 3 groups of messengers sent by Saul to apprehend David); 8.354 (the prophet Micaiah); and 10.239 (Daniel).

[601] 1 Sam 16:13bα does not mention such activity by David as a result of his reception of the Spirit. Josephus' addition of the item has a counterpart in *Bib.*

suffocate and choke,[603] so that the physicians[604] could conceive of no other way of curing him than to direct that there be a search for someone capable of breaking the spell by singing[605] and playing on the harp.[606] Whenever the demons assaulted him and threw him into confusion, this person should be made to stand over his head to play his instrument and sing songs to its accompaniment.[607]

167. Saoul did not neglect [their advice], but ordered that such a person be sought.[608] One of those on hand said to him that he had beheld in the city of Bethleeme a son of Jesse who though still a boy in age, was of pleasing appearance and handsome, and otherwise deserving of attention. He also knew how to play an instrument and sing songs and was an exceptional warrior.[609] Sending then to Jesse, Saoul directed him to dispatch David to him, releasing him from his flocks. For he wished to see him, having heard of the youth's good looks and courage.[610]

168. Jesse sent his son, giving him gifts to bring to Saoul.[611] When he came, Saoul was pleased with him. Making him his armor-bearer, he held him in the greatest honor,[612] for he broke his spell by his singing. Against the confusion caused by the demons whenever these assaulted him, he was his sole physician who, by reciting his songs and playing on the harp, made Saoul himself again.[613]

David becomes Saul's musical therapist

Ant. 59.4, where, following his anointing, David sings a lengthy song praising the Lord for his dealings with him (to this song, Pseudo-Philo appends a further extra-biblical addition in 59.5, this concerning David's killing, by means of stones, a lion and a bear which have attacked his "oxen," whereupon God announces that this exploit portends David's future killing of Israel's enemy [Goliath] with stones). As Feldman (1998: 450-61) notes, Josephus twice elsewhere interjects references to David's prophetic status; see *Ant.* 7.334; 8.109. The title "prophet" is likewise applied to him in Acts 2:30. For another instance of Josephus' linking the divine "spirit" and "prophesying," see 6.222.

[602] Greek: δαιμονία. In line with his tendency to avoid biblical references to the (supernatural) "spirit," Josephus substitutes this designation for the phrase "evil spirit" (LXX: πνεῦμα πονηρόν) of 1 Sam 16:14-16 here and in 6.168. Subsequently, when having Jonathan recall his father's affliction, Josephus will combine his alternative designation with that of the source; see note to "demons" at 6.211. In all cases, however, he leaves aside the further specification of 16:14-16 that the force tormenting Saul was "from God/the Lord." Thereby, he avoids attributing Saul's malady to God personally. On "demonology" in Josephus, see Deines 2003.

[603] In describing the "demons" as "suffocating" Saul, Josephus aligns himself with the reading of LXX 1 Sam 16:14 against MT's more general reference to the evil spirit's "tormenting" him. Pseudo-Philo (*Bib. Ant.* 60.1) speaks of an "evil spirit" that "terrified" (Latin: *prefoco*) Saul.

[604] In 1 Sam 16:15-16 it is Saul's "servants" who approach him with their advice. Pseudo-Philo (*Bib. Ant.*

60.2) has Saul himself take the initiative in securing the healing services of David.

[605] Greek: ἐξᾴδω; Josephus' 2 remaining uses of this verb are in 6.168, 214 (both times in connection with Saul's treatment). The servants' proposal to Saul in 1 Sam 16:15-16 does not mention such a "spell-breaking" by means of song.

[606] Like LXX 1 Sam 16:16, Josephus transliterates the Hebrew term for the musical instrument in question, i.e. כנור (RSV: "lyre").

[607] Josephus modifies the concluding words of the proposal made to Saul in 1 Sam 16:16: "when the evil spirit from God (> LXX) is upon you, he will play it [the lyre] and you will be well (+ and he will relieve you, LXX)," introducing mention of where David's musical therapist is to position himself and of the "songs" that he is to sing as he plays.

[608] See 1 Sam 16:17, where Saul assents to the servants' proposal of 16:15-16.

[609] Josephus' reproduction of the report given Saul about David in 1 Sam 16:18 omits the latter's speaking ability and the concluding reference to the Lord's being "with" him, while inserting mention of his age and deserving of attention.

[610] Josephus appends this motivation for Saul's directing Jesse to send David to him as reported in 1 Sam 16:19. The addition echoes his earlier references to the king's eye for (masculine) beauty; see 6.130, 137-138.

[611] 1 Sam 16:20 enumerates the gifts in question: bread, wine, and a kid.

[612] See 1 Sam 16:21, which states that Saul "loved" David greatly.

[613] See 1 Sam 16:23. Josephus' insertion about David's being Saul's "sole physician" both highlights

169. He sent therefore to Jesse, the boy's father, directing that he leave David with him; for it pleased him to see him and have him on hand.[614] Jesse did not refuse Saoul, but agreed to let him retain him.[615]

New Philistine invasion

(9.1) 170. Not long afterwards,[616] the Palestinoi again[617] assembled and mustered a great force; they moved against the Israelites and camped, occupying [a site] between Socho[618] and Azeko.[619] Saoul likewise led out his army against them; camping on a certain mountain,[620] he compelled the Palestinoi to abandon their first camp and to likewise camp on a certain mountain over against the one that had been occupied by Saoul.[621]

Goliath challenges Israel

171. The camps were separated from each other by a valley in between the mountains on which they were situated.[622] There came down then a certain man from the camp[623] of the Palestinoi, named Goliath[624] from the city of Gitta,[625] a very tall man.[626] For he was four cubits plus a span [in height],[627] and equipped with weapons whose size corresponded to the nature of his body.[628] He wore a breastplate

---

the latter's stature and recalls the mention of the royal "physicians" (6.166)—whom David completely overshadows at this point. Unlike the Bible and Josephus, Pseudo-Philo (*Bib. Ant.* 60.4-5) "quotes" the words of the song that David played for Saul, this comprising a "rebuke" of the king's evil spirit.

[614] As with his initial summons to Jesse (6.167), Josephus also provides a motivation for the king's new directive (1 Sam 16:22) that David be permitted to stay with him. Josephus' rearrangement of the sequence of 16:22 (Saul's retention of David) and 16:23 (mention of David's services to himself) in 6.168-169 appears more logical in that before deciding to keep David on, the king would naturally first test the youth's ability to help him.

[615] 1 Samuel 16 does not mention Jesse's response to Saul's 2nd directive concerning David (v. 22).

[616] Josephus inserts this indication, thereby establishing a chronological link between the preceding events and those to follow.

[617] This insertion reminds readers of the previous Philistine advance mentioned in 6.97 (// 1 Sam 13:5).

[618] MT (1 Sam 17:1) שׂוכה (Eng.: "Socoh"); LXX Σοκχώθ; Josephus Σωκώ.

[619] MT (1 Sam 17:1) עזקה (Eng.: "Azekah"); LXX Ἀζηκά; Josephus Ἀζηκώ. Josephus simplifies the indications of 1 Sam 17:1, where the Philistines first gather at "Socoh which belongs to Judah" (MT LXX L; LXX B: Idoumaia) and then encamp "between Socoh and Azekah, in Ephesdammim" (MT). On Josephus' version of 1 Samuel 17, which stands intermediate between the longer text of MT (and such Greek witnesses as A and L) and the shorter text of LXX B (which entirely lacks the MT verses 12-31, 41, 50, 55-58), see Begg 1999a.

[620] In the Bible's presentation Israel first (1 Sam 17:2) camps "in the valley of Elah" (MT; LXX B lacks the name of the valley, while LXX L translates this as

"of the oak"), and then (17:3) "on the mountain" opposite the Philistine camp. Josephus passes over the initial camp site.

[621] 1 Sam 17:3 represents both armies as eventually camping on facing mountains after having previously encamped at other sites (see 17:1-2). Josephus magnifies Saul's stature by ascribing the Philistines' camp change to pressure exerted on them by him.

[622] Josephus derives his mention of the "valley" between the 2 mountain camps from the closing words of 1 Sam 17:3 (MT LXX L; LXX B speaks rather of both sides taking up their positions at the foot of their respective mountains, with Israel in a "circular formation" beneath its mountain). Pseudo-Philo (*Bib. Ant.* 61.4) has a very different opening to his David and Goliath story from the biblical and Josephan ones. In it, David returns to his flocks (see 1 Sam 17:15), which he then successfully defends against Midianite raiders.

[623] Josephus follows MT 1 Sam 17:4 in having Goliath proceed from the Philistine "camp"; in LXX he comes "from the ranks."

[624] MT (1 Sam 17:4) גלית (Eng.: "Goliath"); LXX Γολιάθ; Josephus Γολιάθης.

[625] MT (1 Sam 17:4) גת (Eng.: "Gath"); LXX Γέθ; Josephus Γίττα.

[626] The various witnesses to 1 Sam 17:4a offer divergent opening characterizations of Goliath: "a man of the betweens" (so literally MT; RSV: "champion"); "a capable man" (LXX); "a bastard" (*vir spurius*, Vulg.). Josephus' qualification has in view the notice on Goliath's height that will follow immediately in 17:4b.

[627] Josephus' figure for Goliath's height agrees with that of LXX 1 Sam 17:4b against MT's "*six* cubits and a span." Marcus (*ad loc.*) notes that the figure given by Josephus is equivalent to 6 ft. 8 in.

[628] This indication concerning the dimensions of Goliath's weapons has no biblical equivalent.

weighing 5,000 bronze shekels.[629] He had a helmet[630] and bronze greaves of a sort suitable to protect the limbs of a man of such extraordinary size.[631] His spear was not light [enough] to be carried in his right hand; instead, he bore it suspended on his shoulders.[632] He also had a lance [weighing] 600 shekels.[633] Many followed him, carrying his weapons.[634]

172. This Goliath now took his stand between the ranks. Loudly raising his voice, he said to Saoul[635] and the Hebrews: "I am relieving you of battle and dangers. For what necessity is there for our entire army to engage and suffer harm?[636] **173.** Give someone of yours to fight with me and the outcome of the war will be decided by the one who alone has been victorious; those whom he has vanquished will be slaves to the others.[637] It is, I believe, much better and most prudent that you get what you wish by the danger of one man rather than of all."[638]

174. Having said these things, he returned to his own camp. On the following day he came again and spoke the same words.[639] For forty days he did not stop challenging the enemy with the above-mentioned [words],[640] so that he dismayed both

---

[629] Josephus anticipates this item of Goliath's equipment from 1 Sam 17:5b, where it follows mention of his helmet in 17:5a. Like MT LXX L, he lacks a parallel to the plus of LXX B in 17:5b according to which Goliath's armor was made, not only of bronze, but also "of iron."

[630] Like LXX B 1 Sam 17:5a, Josephus lacks an equivalent to the specification of MT LXX L that Goliath's helmet was made "of bronze."

[631] Josephus elaborates on the mention of Goliath's "greaves" in 1 Sam 17:6a with his indication concerning their size and purpose.

[632] The precise identity of the item carried on Goliath's shoulders according to 1 Sam 17:6b is uncertain; MT calls it a כידון ("javelin"?, "shield"?), LXX an ἀσπίς ("shield"). Josephus leaves aside the specification, common to all the biblical witnesses, that the item was made of bronze.

[633] 1 Sam 17:7aβ specifies that it was Goliath's "spear*head*" that weighted "600 shekels of iron." Josephus leaves aside the comparison of the spear(head) with a "weaver's beam" from 17:7aα.

[634] Josephus magnifies the threat posed by Goliath in speaking not of a single attendant for the giant, as does 1 Sam 17:7b, but of "many." His generalizing indication that the person(s) in question bore Goliath's "weapons" corresponds to LXX, whereas MT calls him a "shield-bearer." Pseudo-Philo leaves aside the entire description of Goliath's size and weaponry given in 1 Sam 17:4b-7.

[635] 1 Sam 17:8a speaks only of Goliath's addressing the "ranks of Israel." As he does throughout his version of 1 Samuel 17, Josephus accentuates Saul's role in the proceedings; compare *Bib. Ant.* 61.2, where, having come forth from the Philistine camp, Goliath "looks upon Saul and Israel" and then proceeds to address each separately.

[636] This initial "invitation" to the Israelites to consult their own interests takes the place of Goliath's—seemingly superfluous—opening double question to them in 1 Sam 17:8bα: "Why have you come out to draw up for battle? Am I not a Philistine, and are you not servants of Saul?" (MT; LXX: "and you Hebrews of Saul"). In *Bib. Ant.* 61.2 Goliath asks the Israelites, with reference to his own role in the Battle of Aphek (1 Samuel 4), as described by Pseudo-Philo in *Bib. Ant.* 54.3, "are you not the Israel who fled before me when I took the ark from you and killed your priests?"

[637] See 1 Sam 17:8bβ-9. In *Bib. Ant.* 61.2 Goliath specifically challenges King Saul to be the one to come and fight with him, threatening that otherwise he himself will come and capture him and subjugate Saul's people to the Philistine gods.

[638] This renewed appeal to the Israelites' self-interest, unparalleled in 1 Samuel 17, echoes the opening of the Josephan Goliath's speech in 6.172. It takes the place of Goliath's bombastic concluding words in 1 Sam 17:10 with their partial repetition of what has already been said by him in 17:9: "I defy the ranks of Israel this day; give me a man that we may fight together."

[639] Neither Goliath's retiring to the camp nor his reappearance before the Israelites on the following day is mentioned explicitly in 1 Samuel 17.

[640] Josephus anticipates this notice on the duration of Goliath's challenge from 1 Sam 17:16 (MT LXX AL, > B). Pseudo-Philo too brings forward the "40 days" of Goliath's challenging from 17:16, having (*Bib. Ant.* 61.2) Goliath announce, in his initial address to Israel and Saul, that he intends to "mock" for this period of time, equaling the number of days Israel rejoiced over its reception of the Law in the desert.

Saoul and his army.[641] Though they were drawn up as if for battle, it did not come to actual combat.[642]

David volun-
teers to fight
Goliath

(9.2) 175. Now when war broke out between the Hebrews and the Palestinoi,[643] Saoul dismissed David to his father Jesse,[644] being satisfied with the three sons whom he [Jesse] had sent to share in the fighting and its dangers.[645]

176. At first David went again to the flocks and livestock pastures.[646] Not long afterwards, however, he came to the Hebrews' camp, having been sent by his father to bring provisions to his brothers and find out what they were doing.[647]

177. Goliath came again and was challenging and insulting them because there was no one among them courageous enough to dare to come down for battle with him. When David, who was conversing with his brothers about the things his father had commanded him, heard the Palestinos defaming and abusing the army,[648] he became indignant[649] and said to his brothers that he was ready to fight the enemy in single combat.[650]

178. At this, the eldest of the brothers, Ianab[651] reprimanded him, saying that he

---

[641] The source equivalent to this notice on the reaction of Saul and his people is appended directly to Goliath's initial challenge to them (17:8-10) in 1 Sam 17:11 (as also in *Bib. Ant.* 61.2). Josephus makes mention of their reaction only after they have been subjected to multiple challenges by Goliath.

[642] Josephus may have found inspiration for this picture of the 2 armies drawn up, but not venturing to fight, from 1 Sam 17:21: "And Israel and the Philistines drew up for battle, army against army" (MT LXX AL, > B).

[643] Josephus inserts this transition to, and occasion for, Saul's following initiative regarding David.

[644] Highlighting Saul's role, Josephus has him take the initiative concerning David's "placement" at this juncture. By contrast, in 1 Sam 17:15 David, on his own initiative, either "commutes" between Saul's camp and his father's sheep in Bethlehem (so MT) or returns permanently to Bethlehem (so LXX AL, > B; see also *Bib. Ant.* 61.1, where David's return occurs prior to Goliath's challenge). In line with LXX B, Josephus has no equivalent to the notices, reintroducing David, his father, and older brothers, and duplicating the presentation of 1 Samuel 16, of MT 17:12, 13b-14a.

[645] Josephus suggests a reason for Saul's readiness to dismiss David (see previous note), i.e. the presence with himself of the 3 older brothers, as mentioned in 1 Sam 17:13a, 14b (whose indication that they had "followed Saul to the battle" and names and birth order he omits).

[646] In speaking of such an initially full-time return by David to his sheep-tending duties, Josephus follows the formulation of LXX AL 1 Sam 17:15 (> LXX B) as opposed to MT, which portrays David commuting between his flocks and the Israelite camp; see note to "Jesse" at 6.175.

[647] Josephus abridges the detailed instructions given David by Jesse in MT LXX AL 1 Sam 17:17-18, omitting, e.g., the specific items he is to bring his brothers (and their commander).

[648] See 1 Sam 17:23 (MT LXX AL, > LXX B). In thus combining his version of 17:23 (Goliath's renewed challenge) directly with his rendering of 17:17-18 (Jesse's dispatch of David), Josephus passes over the intervening (MT LXX AL) sequence 17:19-22, which relates, in circumstantial detail, David's journeying to the site of the Philistine-Israelite standoff where, having deposited what he had brought with the baggage-keeper, he runs to greet his brothers.

[649] Josephus inserts this reference to David's emotional response to his hearing Goliath's words (whose offensiveness ["defaming and abusing the army"] he accentuates in comparison with the bland formulation of 1 Sam 17:23a, which has the giant simply "speaking the same words he had said before").

[650] In having David address himself to his brothers upon hearing Goliath's challenge and forthrightly declare his own readiness to meet that challenge at this juncture, Josephus notably modifies the account given in 1 Sam 17:24-27 (MT LXX AL), where the exchange is rather between David and the Israelite troops, the brothers not being mentioned as such, and where David, in a rather self-centered way, asks them (v. 26) what the one who kills Goliath would gain from this, without, however, affirming his own readiness to take on the task. Josephus thus depicts David in a considerably more disinterested, heroic light. Somewhat similarly, Pseudo-Philo has (*Bib. Ant.* 61.3) David respond to his hearing of Goliath's provocations with the words: "Is this the time about which God said to me [see *Bib. Ant.* 59.5] 'I will deliver into your hands by stones the enemy of my people'?"

[651] This is the reading (Greek Ἰάναβος) of RO that

was too bold for his age and ignorant of what was appropriate.[652] He then directed him to go to his flocks and father.[653] Deferring to his brother, David withdrew,[654] but let it be known to some of the soldiers that he wanted to fight the challenger.[655]

179. They immediately disclosed the youth's intention to Saoul.[656] The king summoned him and, when he inquired what he wished to say,[657] David said "Do not let your mind be dejected or fearful, O king,[658] for I will eliminate the enemy's boastfulness. Advancing against him for battle, I will strike him down—tall and great as he is—beneath me.[659] **180.** He would thus become an object of derision and your army would be more famous should he be killed, not by a man already competent in war and entrusted with battle-command, but by one who seems—and in fact is—still a boy in age."[660]

Saul–David exchange

(9.3) 181. Saoul admired his boldness and high spirits,[661] but did not put full confidence in him because of his age. He said, rather, that on that account he was too weak to fight with one who was an expert in warfare. But David said, "I promise these things, confident that God is with me, **182.** for I have had experience of his help.[662] For once, when a lion[663] came against my flocks and carried off a lamb,

---

Niese adopts. Marcus (*ad loc.*) and Schalit (*s.v.*) follow MSP, which, in line with the "Eliab" of 1 Sam 17:28, read Ἐλίαβος, just as they do in 6.161 (where Niese reads Ταλίαβος with RO; see note to "Taliab" at 6.161).

[652] Josephus leaves aside the mention of Eliab's "indignation" over David's words from 1 Sam 17:28a and replaces his opening question to him ("Why have you come down?")—which he will end up answering himself at the end of 17:28b—with a statement spelling out the nature of David's offense.

[653] This "order" replaces Eliab's question in 1 Sam 17:28aβ (MT LXX AL): "where have you left those few sheep of yours in the wilderness?"

[654] In 1 Sam 17:29 (MT LXX AL) David responds rather petulantly to Eliab's remonstrance: "What have I done now? Was it not but a word?" Josephus portrays a David who shows due deference to his eldest brother.

[655] This conclusion to the brothers' exchange as reported in 1 Sam 17:28-30 MT LXX AL (to which Pseudo-Philo has no counterpart) represents Josephus' modification of 17:30, where there is a reprise of the earlier discussion between David and the "people" (see 17:24-27) concerning the reward awaiting the one who kills Goliath. Josephus has David now reiterate his previous (see 6.177) readiness to take on the giant without any mention of such reward.

[656] See 1 Sam 17:31 (MT LXX AL). In Pseudo-Philo (*Bib. Ant.* 61.4) Saul overhears David's words himself and so does not need to be informed of these.

[657] 1 Sam 17:32 (where LXX B picks up after its long "minus" corresponding to MT LXX AL 17:11-31) represents David as initiating the conversation with Saul. Josephus portrays proper protocol being followed with Saul being the first to speak (as he does also in *Bib. Ant.* 61.4).

[658] In having David urge Saul personally not to be

dispirited, Josephus follows the LXX reading in 1 Sam 17:32 ("let not the heart of my lord fail...") as against MT's more general "let no man's heart fail...."

[659] In 1 Sam 17:32b David simply offers to go fight the Philistine. Amplifying his words, Josephus portrays a more self-confident (and "prophetic") David. Pseudo-Philo gives a similar expansion to David's opening statement (*Bib. Ant.* 61.4): "(.... I will go and fight the Philistine), and God will take away the hatred and disgrace from Israel."

[660] This added embellishment of David's opening words of 1 Sam 17:32 highlights, once again, David's disinterestedness: the fame to be anticipated from his elimination of Goliath will be, not his personally, but rather that of Saul's army as a whole. In Pseudo-Philo the (initial) exchange between David and Saul ends with a reproduction of the former's word of 1 Sam 17:32 in *Bib. Ant.* 61.4. Thereafter, David immediately sets out against Goliath, 61.5// 17:40, the whole intervening continuation of their exchange, 17:33-39, being passed over.

[661] This notice concerning the positive impact of David's words upon Saul is biblically unparalleled. It serves to heighten the stature of David, whose outstanding qualities are recognized by the king, even as he (initially) resists giving David permission to fight.

[662] By placing David's recognition of God's help in his life at the very beginning of his reply to Saul, rather than only at the end of this (as in 1 Sam 17:34-37a), Josephus accentuates his piety.

[663] In 1 Sam 17:34 David makes back-to-back reference to "a lion or a bear" so that in what follows one is uncertain which animal in fact he is speaking of. Josephus clarifies by having David refer to the 2 beasts separately.

I pursued and overtook him and liberated the lamb from the mouth of the beast. When he rushed upon me, I lifted him up by the tail[664] and destroyed him by dashing him against the ground.[665] **183.** I dealt in the same way with a bear on which I took vengeance.[666] Let the enemy, who for so long has been insulting our army and defaming our God—who will make him subject to me—, be thought of as one of those beasts."[667]

David's weapons

(9.4) **184.** Saoul, praying that there might indeed be a commensurate recompense from God for the boy's eagerness and daring, said: "Go off to battle."[668] He put his own breastplate upon him and girded his sword around him; placing his helmet on his head, he sent him off.[669] **185.** But David was weighed down by the weapons, for he was not familiar with them, nor had he learned how to bear weapons.[670] "Let these things, O king," he said, "be for your own adornment, for you are able to carry them. Please, however, permit your slave to fight as I wish."[671] At that, he put off the weapons[672] and took up his staff and put five stones from the brook in his shepherd's bag;[673] bearing a sling in his right hand, he went towards Goliath.[674]

Goliath–David exchange

186. The enemy despised him when he saw him coming in this way, and ridiculed him for not having the weapons with which it is customary to fight against humans, but rather those with which we drive away and guard against dogs.[675] Did he indeed think him a dog, rather than a human?[676] [David] answered that he thought of him, not as this, but as worse than a dog.[677] He thus roused Goliath to wrath;[678]

---

[664] David speaks of taking the lion by the "beard" in MT 1 Sam 17:35, and by the "throat" in LXX.

[665] Josephus dramatizes David's dispatch of the beast as compared with his final words in 1 Sam 17:35: "I smote him and killed him."

[666] Compare 1 Sam 17:36a: "your servant has killed both lions and bears."

[667] See 1 Sam 17:36b. Josephus' rendition, in which not only the God's "army" (as in 6.177), but also God himself is the object of Goliath's abusive words, heightens the Philistine's offense.

[668] Josephus expatiates on Saul's wish ("... the Lord be with you," MT)/ affirmation ("the Lord will be with you," LXX) of 1 Sam 17:37b, likewise reversing the biblical order of the king's prayer and command that David "go."

[669] Josephus agrees with LXX B 1 Sam 17:39aα in having Saul place the sword upon David, while in MT LXX L David does this himself. In contrast to both these witnesses to 17:38-39aα, he mentions David's receiving the sword in 2nd place, before the helmet. Finally, like LXX, Josephus has no equivalent to MT's 4th item of apparel (this appearing 3rd in its listing), i.e. "a coat of mail" (RSV).

[670] Cf. 1 Sam 17:39aβ.

[671] David's word to Saul about the latter's weapons in 1 Sam 17:39bα is rather brusque: "I cannot go with these; for I am not used to them." Josephus here, as throughout the passage, depicts a more deferential David.

[672] Josephus agrees with MT LXX L 1 Sam 17:39bβ

in making David himself doff the weapons; in LXX B the subject is an indeterminate "they, one."

[673] Josephus inserts the indication concerning the origin of the 5 stones that David takes according to 1 Sam 17:40a; conversely, he leaves aside the source description of these as "smooth" (MT LXX L)/ "perfect" (LXX B). Pseudo-Philo (*Bib. Ant.* 61.5) speaks of 7 stones on which David writes the names of his various "ancestors," himself, and God. He adds that, at this point, God sent the angel "Zeruel" to David.

[674] See 1 Sam 17:40b. Josephus specifies that David carried the sling in his "right" hand. Like LXX B, he has no equivalent to the MT LXX AL plus of 1 Sam 17:41: "And the Philistine came on and drew near to David, with his shield-bearer in front of him."

[675] In 1 Sam 17:42 it is Goliath's catching sight of David's youthfully handsome appearance that causes him to despise him. Josephus' alternative motivation, with its reference to the giant's beholding David's unusual "weapons," is inspired by Goliath's question in 17:43: "Am I a dog, that you come to me with sticks (MT; LXX: with a stick and stones)?"

[676] Josephus amplifies Goliath's opening question to David of 1 Sam 17:43a ("Am I a dog...?") with an alternative, "rather than a human."

[677] For this interjected reply by David Josephus is clearly dependent on the plus of LXX B 1 Sam 17:43: "And David said: 'But worse than a dog'." MT and LXX L have no equivalent.

[678] Josephus supplies this notice of the emotional impact of David's answer on Goliath.

he cursed him in the name of his god[679] and threatened to give his flesh to the beasts of the earth[680] and the birds of the air[681] to devour.[682] **187.** David, for his part, replied to him: "You come against me with a sword, spear, and breastplate,[683] but I proceed against you with God as my weapon,[684] he who will utterly destroy you and your entire army by our hands.[685] For I will behead you today and will cast off the rest of your body to the dogs, your compatriots[686] so that all may learn that the Deity defends the Hebrews and that his concern for us is our weapon and strength,[687] and that where God is not present, other equipment and force is useless."[688]

188. Now the Palestinos was hindered from running quickly by the weight of his weapons. He came slowly towards David, contemptuous and confident that he would easily do away with him, who was both defenseless and still a boy in age.[689]

David kills Goliath

(9.5) 189. The youth met him, however, with an ally whom the enemy did not see, namely God.[690] He lifted out of his bag one of the stones from the brook that

---

[679] Compare 1 Sam 17:43b, where both MT and LXX speak of Goliath's "cursing David by his god*s*" (Tg. has "idol").

[680] Greek: ἐπιγείοι (literally: "on the earth"). Josephus' one other use of this term for land animals is in *Ant.* 8.44.

[681] Greek: μετάρσια. Josephus' uses this paraphrastic expression ("the raised-aloft ones") for "birds" also in *Ant.* 1.32, 102.

[682] Josephus reverses the order of 1 Sam 17:44 (first birds, then beasts) and adds the specification concerning the purpose of Goliath's leaving David's body to these predators.

[683] Josephus' list of the 3 weapons with which, David states, Goliath is coming against him agrees for the first 2 (sword, spear) with 1 Sam 17:45a, whereas its 3rd item ("breastplate") differs from that cited in both MT (javelin? shield?) and LXX (shield). Josephus' previous enumeration of Goliath's weaponry (6.171) did not refer to a sword. He introduces mention of it here because of its function in David's subsequent beheading of Goliath.

[684] In 1 Sam 17:45b David states that he is coming against Goliath "in the name of the Lord..." whom Goliath has defied. Josephus' formulation ("with God as weapon") prolongs the "weapons-language" with which his David's reply opens, contrasting his one divine weapon with the 3 man-made ones available to Goliath.

[685] To David's announcement in 1 Sam 17:46a about God's handing Goliath into his hand and his striking him down, Josephus appends a further, wider prediction by David, i.e. God's overthrow also of the Philistine army. In so doing, he accentuates both David's confidence about what is to happen and his prophetic foresight.

[686] David's announcement in 1 Sam 17:46bα is that he is going to behead Goliath and then give the corpses

of the (other) Philistines to the birds and the beasts (cf. Goliath's threat to do this to David himself in 17:44). Josephus keeps attention focussed on the fate of Goliath himself, at the same time picking up on the "dog language" used earlier in the exchange between him and David. Feldman (1998: 563) notes that the term ὁμόφυλοι ("compatriots"), which Josephus almost invariably uses as a designation for Jews, is here exceptionally (and pejoratively) applied to the Philistines.

[687] Josephus combines and rewords David's double statement concerning the purpose of Goliath's upcoming overthrow by God in 1 Sam 17:46bβ-47a: "that all the earth may know that there is a God in Israel and that all this assembly may know that the Lord saves not with sword and spear..."

[688] This concluding statement by David takes the place of that of 1 Sam 17:47b: "for the battle is the Lord's and he will give you into our hand." In Pseudo-Philo (*Bib. Ant.* 61.6) the extended biblical exchange between David and Goliath (1 Sam 17:43-47) is replaced by David's monologue in which he informs the giant that they are descendants, respectively, of the 2 sisters, Ruth and Orpah. Once David kills, not only Goliath but also his 3 brothers, Orpah will be told (by the dead Goliath!) that his sister's son has not spared his cousins.

[689] 1 Sam 17:48a speaks only of Goliath's advancing to meet David. Josephus offers a more vivid picture, with mention of the giant's physical and mental state.

[690] MT LXX AL 1 Sam 17:48b (> LXX B) only mention David's "running to meet Goliath." Josephus highlights God's presence with David at this moment, as he has in previous moments of the story; see 6.187, where the image of God as David's "weapon" is used. On Josephus' recurrent designation of God as an "ally" (Greek: σύμμαχος) of individuals or the people as a whole, see note to "ally" at *Ant.* 5.98.

he had put in it and placed this in the sling. Then he hurled it against Goliath's fore-head. The shot passed through to his brain so that Goliath, stunned, immediately fell on his face.[691] **190.** David ran and stood over the prostrate enemy; with the latter's sword—for he did not have one of his own—he cut off his head.[692]

Rout of Philis-tines

191. Goliath's fall led to the defeat and flight of the Palestinoi, for they, seeing their most outstanding [champion] overthrown and anxious about total [disaster], decided not to remain any longer. Rather, abandoning themselves to a shameful and disorderly flight, they tried to liberate themselves from the dangers.[693] Raising the battle cry, Saoul and the whole army of the Hebrews rushed out against them.[694] Cutting down many, they pursued them to the boundaries of Gitta and the gates of Askalon.[695]

192. About 30,000 of the Palestinoi were killed and twice as many wounded.[696] Returning to their camp, Saoul[697] tore down and burnt its stockade.[698] David brought the head of Goliath to his own tent and dedicated his sword to God.[699]

Women pro-voke Saoul's envy of David

(10.1) 193. The women,[700] however, stirred up Saoul's envy and hatred[701] against

---

[691] See 1 Sam 17:49. Like MT, Josephus has no equivalent to the LXX plus, specifying that the stone passed through Goliath's helmet.

[692] Josephus combines (selected) sequels to David's felling of Goliath (1 Sam 17:49) as related in 17:50 (MT LXX AL, > LXX B: David's not having a sword of his own) and 51a (David's running forward, standing over Goliath, using the giant's own sword to behead him). Pseudo-Philo's version of the scene (*Bib. Ant.* 61.7-8) adds a final exchange between Goliath and David: the fallen giant urges David to quickly dispatch him and then rejoice. In response, David enjoins Goliath to behold his true slayer (i.e. the angel Zeruel; see 61.5). When Goliath does this, he confesses that it was not David alone who killed him, but also the su-perhuman figure accompanying him.

[693] Josephus embellishes the summary notice of 1 Sam 17:51b on the Philistines' flight with, e.g., indica-tions concerning their state of mind and the ignominy of their behavior.

[694] 1 Sam 17:52a speaks only of the response to the Philistines' flight on the part of the Israelites and Judeans, without mention of Saul himself. Josephus, as he does throughout his version of 1 Samuel 17, high-lights the active role of the king.

[695] Josephus' indications concerning the end points of the pursuit agree with those of LXX 1 Sam 17:52 (where the sites "Geth" and "Askalon" are actually mentioned twice). Compare MT ("as far as Gai and the gates of Ekron... on the way from Shaaraim as far as Gath and Ekron").

[696] Here, as often, Josephus introduces "precise" casualty figures where the Bible lacks these.

[697] As with the pursuit of the Philistines (see 6.191; compare 1 Sam 17:52), so also with the "return" from this, Josephus highlights the initiative of Saul, whereas

the source (17:53a) speaks only of the Israelites' return-ing.

[698] In 1 Sam 17:53 the Israelites "plunder" the Phil-istine camp. Josephus' reference to Saul's "burning" it is perhaps inspired by the MT plus in 17:53, which cites the Israelites' "ardently pursuing after" (מדלק אחרי) the Philistines; cf. the mention of the Israelites' "burning" (Latin: *comburo*) in their pursuit of the Philistines in various OL MSS. See Skehan 1976.

[699] According to 1 Sam 17:54 David deposited Goliath's head in Jerusalem and installed the giant's sword in his own tent. Josephus' modifications have in view the difficulties posed by the biblical account: Je-rusalem is not in Israelite hands at this point, and 1 Sam 21:10 will speak of Goliath's sword being rather at Nob. Josephus, further reflecting that the giant's sword would be a more appropriate (and much less "messy") offering to God, has him dedicate this to him at an un-specified site, while keeping the head for himself.

Like LXX B, Josephus has no equivalent to the MT LXX AL paragraph 1 Sam 17:55-58, where, in striking contrast with the account of Saul's personally taking David into his service given in 1 Sam 16:14-23 (// 6.169), the king appears to know nothing of David's identity and has to send his general Abner to inquire about him. Pseudo-Philo, conscious of the problem, as-serts (*Bib. Ant.* 61.9) that Saul's ignorance of David's identity as recorded in 17:55-58 was due to the Lord's angel (i.e. Zeruel)'s having "changed his [David's] ap-pearance."

[700] For his version of 1 Samuel 18, dealing with the beginnings of the rift between Saul and David, in 6.193-204, Josephus essentially follows the shorter text of LXX B, which lacks vv. 1-5, 10-11, 17-19, 29b-30 of MT (and LXX AL), segments that (mostly) duplicate what is found in other contexts of 1 Samuel. Thus, at

him. For they went out to meet the victorious army[702] with cymbals and timbrels, and the utmost joy.[703] The women sang of how Saoul had slain many thousands of the Palestinoi, the virgins of how David had annihilated ten thousands.[704]

194. When the king heard these things, namely that he was receiving the lesser testimony, while the [greater] figure of the ten thousands was being ascribed to the youth, reasoning that, after such a splendid acclamation, nothing remained for him except the kingship,[705] he began to fear and suspect David.[706]

195. Since in his anxiety he thought that David was too near to himself (for he had made him his armor-bearer),[707] he removed him from his previous position,[708] and appointed him commander of a thousand giving him a better post, but also, as he thought, one more secure for himself. For he wished to send him out against the enemy and into battles so that in those dangers he would be killed.[709]

David reassigned

(10.2) 196. Having God with him everywhere he went, David, however, achieved [things] and proved fortunate,[710] so that, by his surpassing courage he won the love both of his people and of the daughter of Saoul[711] who was still a virgin. Her ex-

Princess Michal loves David

---

the outset he has no equivalent to the MT segment 1 Sam 18:1-5 featuring Jonathan's covenant with David (and paralleling 1 Samuel 20). Like B, he also lacks a parallel to the transitional phrase of (MT) 1 Sam 18:6a: "as they were coming home, when David returned from slaying the Philistine...." In place of this material, he begins immediately with a version of 18:6b, the women's response to Israel's victory.

[701] Greek: φθόνος καὶ μῖσος. This combination (in this or reverse order) occurs also in *War* 2.82 (subject: the friends of Archelaus' relatives; object: Archelaus); 4.566 (subject: the Idumeans; object: John of Gischala); *Ant.* 2.10 (subject: Joseph's brothers; object: Joseph); 20.29 (subject: the nobles of Adiabene; object: Izates); cf. also *Ant.* 13.288, 296, 401, 402.

[702] In MT 1 Sam 18:6b the women go to meet Saul, in LXX rather David. Josephus' rendering avoids choosing between these 2 divergent readings.

[703] 1 Sam 18:6 (MT LXX B) cites 3 (LXX L has 5) "accompaniments" to the women's reception: timbrels/tambourines, songs of joy, and a 2nd musical instrument, of uncertain meaning in MT (Hebrew: שָׁלִשִׁים, RSV: "instruments of music"), which LXX renders by "cymbals." Josephus rearranges the source sequence of the 3 items, while following LXX in its mention of "cymbals" as one of these.

[704] 1 Sam 18:7 refers in general terms to the "women" who sing to one another. Josephus introduces the distinction between the 2 groups of women.

[705] See 1 Sam 18:8. Like LXX B, Josephus has no equivalent, at this juncture, to the verse's opening words in MT LXX AL: "And Saul was very angry..." Cf., however, his possible anticipation of these—as also of the verse's continuation, i.e. "and this saying displeased him"—at the opening of 6.193, with its notice on Saul's being roused to "envy and hatred" against David.

[706] 1 Sam 18:9 speaks, more cryptically, of Saul's "eyeing" David from then on. Like LXX B, Josephus lacks an equivalent to the segment 18:10-11 of MT LXX AL, which, in its description of Saul trying to pin David with his spear, represents a duplicate of 19:9-10.

[707] 1 Sam 18:12 offers a theological explanation of Saul's fear of David, i.e. the fact of the Lord's being "with" the latter, after abandoning the former (cf. 1 Sam 16:13-14). Josephus' alternative explanation (Saul's feeling David to be in too close proximity to himself) has in view Saul's subsequent distancing David from himself. To this explanation he appends a further one, this recalling how David came to be in such proximity to the king, i.e. through Saul's appointing him his armor-bearer (see 1 Sam 16:21b// 6.168).

[708] 1 Sam 18:13 has Saul remove David "from his presence"; Josephus rewords in line with his preceding reminiscence of Saul's appointing David his armor-bearer.

[709] Josephus' comment concerning Saul's intentions in appointing David commander of a thousand (1 Sam 18:13a) takes the place of the notice on the latter's "going out and coming in before the people" in 18:13b.

[710] Greek: διευπραγέω; the word is a Josephan *hapax*. See 1 Sam 18:14, the order of whose elements (David's success, God's being with him) Josephus reverses. Having spoken at length of Saul's intentions in 6.195, he leaves aside the attached notice (1 Sam 18:15) on the "awe/fear" David's success caused Saul.

[711] Josephus here combines the notices concerning the "love" that David aroused on the part of both people (1 Sam 18:16a) and Saul's daughter, i.e. Michal (18:20a). Like LXX B, he has no parallel to the intervening MT LXX AL sequence 18:17-19 concerning the first, abortive effort at marrying David to a daughter of Saul, i.e. the elder Merab, which "duplicates" the at-

ceedingly strong passion for him became manifest and reached the ears of her father.[712]

*Marriage nego-
tiations*

197. The king, for his part, heard of this gladly, [thinking to] use it as an opportunity for plotting against David.[713] He said to those who informed him of her love that he would eagerly give the virgin to him, since this would be a cause of annihilation and dangers for him, should he take it.[714] "For I pledge him," he said, "my daughter in marriage, if he brings me 600 heads of the enemy.[715] **198.** Having been offered so splendid a distinction and wishing to gain renown by an audacious and unbelievable deed, he will rush to do it and be destroyed by the Palestinoi and my [plots] against him will proceed under a good pretext. For I will be delivered from him through others, rather than through his being killed by me."[716]

199. He therefore directed his servants to sound out David's mind as to where he stood on marriage to the young woman.[717] They began to say to him that King Saoul and all the people cherished him and that he wished to give him his daughter in marriage.[718] **200.** But he said: "Does it seem a little thing to you to become a king's son-in-law? To me, in any case, it does not appear such, especially since I am lowly[719] and lacking in glory and honor."[720]

---

tempt involving the king's younger daughter, Michal (whose name Josephus himself will not cite until 6.204) in 18:20-27. On Josephus' overall portrayal of the David-Michal relationship, whose romantic dimensions he highlights, see Feldman 1998: 564-5.

[712] Josephus here elaborates on the summary notice concerning the figure of "Michal" and her "love" for David of 1 Sam 18:20a with mention of his virginal status and the strength of her feelings for David. The latter item, in turn, helps explain how it was, as 18:20bα ("and they told Saul") reports, those feelings became public.

[713] See 1 Sam 18:20bβ. Josephus appends the "explanation" of Saul's "delight" in hearing of his daughter's love for David.

[714] In contrast to 1 Sam 18:21a, which reports an inner monologue by Saul, in which he voices his anticipation that the marriage would prove a "snare" for David and turn the "hand of the Philistines" against him, Josephus makes the king's perfidious intentions part of his address to his retainers. Thereby, he highlights Saul's open cynicism. Like LXX B, Josephus has no equivalent to the attached notice—itself harking back to the account of the abortive previous match between David and Merab in 18:17-19 (MT LXX AL, no parallel in LXX L and Josephus; see note to "Saoul" at 6.196)—of MT LXX AL 18:21b: "therefore Saul said to David a second time, 'you shall now be my son-in-law'."

[715] In proceeding immediately to this condition (// 1 Sam 18:25a) attaching to Saul's promise to give his daughter to David (18:21), Josephus reserves for a later point (see 6.199-200) the Bible's initial, 3-way exchange (18:22-24) between Saul's servants, David, and the king featuring David's reminder to the servants of

his lowly status. Josephus' version of the condition of 18:25 has Saul ask for both a much larger number (600 vs. 100) and a different, less vulgar portion of the Philistines' anatomy (heads rather than foreskins). In addition, it omits Saul's (purported) reason for his request as cited at the end of v. 25a, i.e. desire for vengeance on his enemies.

[716] Josephus incorporates into Saul's words to his servants an expanded version of the editorial comment of 1 Sam 18:25b: "Now Saul thought to make David fall by the hand of the Philistines" (cf. 18:21). Thereby, he highlights, yet again (see note to "take it" at 6.197) the brazen cynicism of the king.

[717] This directive is an expansion of the message— which Josephus will reproduce in what follows—Saul enjoins his servants to convey to David in 1 Sam 18:22, where they are told to inform him of the favor he enjoys with Saul and his retainers, and to urge him to become the king's son-in-law. In addition, Josephus, rearranging the biblical sequence, has Saul entrust this (purportedly friendly) message to his servants (// 18:22) only after he has already informed them of his plans for ridding himself of David with the proposed marriage as a pretext (// 18:25). Thereby, he highlights the king's deceitfulness; see 6.197,198.

[718] Josephus combines the wording of Saul's directive to his servants in 1 Sam 18:22 (they are to tell David of the favor he enjoys with the king and his servants and urge him to become Saul's son-in-law) with the notice on the servants' delivery of the message to David of 18:23a. His rendering expands the circle of those said to "cherish" David from "all the king's servants" to "all the people," this echoing the language of 6.196 (// 18:16).

[719] Greek: ταπεινός. On this adjective and its cognates, see Spicq 1978 (II): 878-85.

When the servants reported David's answers to him,[721] Saoul said: "Tell him that I am not asking for possessions or wedding gifts—for that would be to barter my daughter rather than give her in marriage—but rather for a son-in-law who has courage and every other virtue that I see him to possess.[722] **201.** I wish then to receive from him, in exchange for the marriage of my daughter, neither gold nor silver, nor things of that sort such as he might bring from the house of his father, but rather the punishment of the Palestinoi and 600 of their heads. **202.** For myself there could be no more welcome or splendid gift than these. And, as for my child, marriage to such a man, accredited by the defeat of the enemy, would be far more desirable than the customary wedding gifts."[723]

(10.3) 203. When they brought these words to David, he was pleased, thinking that Saoul was solicitous about being related to him.[724] Not pausing to reflect or pondering rationally whether the assigned deed was possible or difficult, he immediately[725] marched with his comrades against the enemy [to perform] the action promised in exchange for the marriage. Since God made everything easy and possible for David, he, having killed many and cut off the heads of 600,[726] went to the king and by displaying these claimed the marriage in exchange for them.[727]

David's exploit and marriage

204. Saoul, having no way of backing out of his promises, since he regarded it as something shameful that he should seem to have lied or to have promised the marriage as a plot so that David would undertake the impossible and die,[728] gave him his daughter, whose name was Melcha.[729]

(11.1) 205. Saoul, however, was not ready to resign himself to what had happened for any length of time.[730] For, seeing that David was held in esteem by God and by

Saul decides to kill David

---

[720] See David's reply to the servants in 1 Sam 18:23b, which Josephus' rendering follows rather closely.

[721] See 1 Sam 18:24.

[722] Saul's statement here about David's possession of "courage and every other virtue" echoes the catalogue of virtues, including "courage," that God prescribes for the king desired by him in 6.160. Saul, in spite of himself, recognizes that David possesses this range of virtues.

[723] Saul's above response, extending over 2.5 paragraphs, to the servants' report of David's initial, non-committal reply (1 Sam 18:23b) to his offer of his daughter, represents Josephus' vastly expanded version of the king's words in 18:25a ("The king desires no marriage present, except a hundred foreskins of the Philistines, that he may be avenged of the king's enemies"), which Josephus has already anticipated in 6.197 (in both instances he makes Saul prescribe 600 Philistine heads as opposed to the 100 foreskins of 18:25). The expansion here in 6.200b-202 (fraudulently) insists on Saul's personal "disinterestedness"; his one concern is, he claims, not his own enrichment, but obtaining a worthy son-in-law and husband for his daughter. Once again, Josephus underscores the king's deceitfulness; see 6.197, 198, 199.

[724] See 1 Sam 18:26a, which Josephus elaborates with mention of David's being taken in by Saul's

deceptive words.

[725] Josephus' emphasis on David's eagerness to undertake the mission proposed by Saul seems to reflect—while also expatiating on—the (MT LXX AL) phrase (> LXX B) "before the time had expired" at the end of 1 Sam 18:26, which serves to introduce the mention of David's setting out in 18:27.

[726] Josephus elaborates on David's successful exploit against the Philistines as reported in 1 Sam 18:27a. In particular, he interjects a "theological explanation" of David's success and mention of his "beheading" those he kills. He likewise brings the number of those actually slain by David (600) into line with the figure specified by the king in 6.197, 201 (compare the 200 foreskins David is said to bring back in 18:27 [MT; LXX: has 100] as opposed to the 100 prescribed by Saul himself in 18:25).

[727] See 1 Sam 18:27bα. Josephus interjects the reference to David's "display" of what he has brought back.

[728] Josephus supplies this motivation as to why Saul, however unwillingly, does proceed with the marriage, as he is said to do in 1 Sam 18:27bβ.

[729] See 1 Sam 18:27bβ. In 6.129 Josephus called the woman "Michaal" in line with the biblical form of her name (which he does not mention when reintroducing her in 6.196// 1 Sam 18:20).

[730] Josephus inserts this transitional phrase, fore-

the crowds, he was highly alarmed.[731] Unable to hide his fear about two weighty matters, namely his kingdom and his life—it being a terrible misfortune to be deprived of either[732]—he decided to kill David and ordered his elimination by Ionathes his son and his most trusted servants.[733]

Jonathan warns David

206. [Ionathes], however, was astonished at his father's change regarding David, which was not from extreme loyalty towards moderate [feelings], but towards his death itself.[734] Himself moreover loving the youth and deferring to his virtue,[735] he told him of his father's secret design and intention.[736] **207.** He further advised him to keep on guard and hide himself on the next day.[737] For he himself would greet his father and, when the opportunity presented itself, would speak to him about him. He would learn the cause [of his hostility] and downplay this by saying that **208.** on that account he ought not to kill one who had done so many good things for the crowd and had been a benefactor to himself [Saoul] as well. For the sake of these things, it was proper that he find pardon for even the gravest of offenses. "And I will disclose to you my father's plans."[738] David, persuaded by his kind advice, avoided the king's presence.[739]

Jonathan reconciles Saul and David

(11.2) 209. On the next day Ionathes came to Saoul; when he found him seemingly cheerful and in good humor, he began to speak to him about David:[740] "What wrongdoing, father, whether small or great, did you note in him that you have ordered the doing away with of a man[741] who has been of great advantage to your own safety, and greater still in punishing the Palestinoi?[742] **210.** He has delivered

---

shadowing Saul's subsequent initiatives against David.

[731] See 1 Sam 18:28-29a. In citing Saul's perception of the people's positive stance towards David, Josephus aligns himself with LXX B 18:28 ("all Israel loves" David) against MT ("Michal, the daughter of Saul, loves" him; LXX L conflates the 2 readings).

[732] This statement spells out the nature of Saul's "fear" as cited in 1 Sam 18:29a, while likewise foreshadowing the king's next attempt to rid himself of David. Like LXX B, Josephus has no equivalent to the complex of notices making up MT LXX AL 1 Sam 18:29b-30 (Saul's ongoing hostility towards David; David's proving more successful than Saul's servants in his battles with the Philistines and so gaining high repute).

[733] In 1 Sam 19:1a Saul's command to kill David is issued to Jonathan and "all his servants." Josephus, more plausibly, has the directive addressed to a smaller, more reliable group.

[734] Josephus inserts this reference to Jonathan's surprise over his father's changed disposition towards David, thereby underscoring the magnitude of the change.

[735] Josephus expands the mention of Jonathan's "love" for David in 1 Sam 19:1b with a reference also to his respect for David's moral qualities. On Josephus' portrayal of the David-Jonathan relationship overall, in which he heightens the pathos of the biblical depiction, while also downplaying the homosexual suggestions of that depiction, see Feldman 1998: 565-7.

[736] See 1 Sam 19:2a, where Jonathan informs David "Saul... seeks to kill you."

[737] See 1 Sam 19:2b. Josephus' use of the phrase "on the next day" corresponds to LXX's "tomorrow morning" against MT's "in the morning."

[738] In 1 Sam 19:3 Jonathan simply states that he will speak to his father about David and will report whatever he might learn; Josephus has him spell out what he intends to say to the king. Conversely, he leaves aside Jonathan's reference to his intending to speak to his father "in the field" where David himself is hiding, since this would seem to make a report to David about their conversation unnecessary.

[739] Josephus adds this notice on the effect of Jonathan's advice upon David.

[740] Josephus expands the introductory notice on Jonathan's speaking to Saul (1 Sam 19:4) with indications concerning the time and Saul's state of mind. The latter item serves to motivate Jonathan's venturing to speak to him at this particular moment and picks up on Jonathan's reference to the "opportunity presenting itself" in 6.207.

[741] Josephus makes Jonathan begin his discourse with a question reminiscent of the one with which he concludes his plea in 1 Sam 19:5bβ: "why then will you sin against innocent blood by killing David without cause?"

[742] Jonathan's invocation of David's benefits both to the king personally and to all Israel by his overthrow of the Philistines draws on 1 Sam 19:4bβ-5a. His refer-

the Hebrew people from their arrogance and mockery that they endured for forty days when no one dared to take up the enemy's challenge.[743] After this he had brought to him as many heads of the enemy as he was instructed, obtaining my sister in marriage as his recompense for this.[744] Thus his death would be painful for us, not only on account of his virtue,[745] but also because of our kinship. For by his death your daughter would be wronged as well, experiencing widowhood before they had even lived together, when she was about to attain delight.[746] **211.** Considering these things, change to a greater moderation. Do not harm a man who,[747] first of all, has done us the great benefit of restoring your safety; when the evil spirit and the demons[748] settled upon you, he drove them out, granting your soul peace from them.[749] Secondly, [he has inflicted] vengeance upon the enemy.[750] For it would be shameful to forget these things."[751]

212. By these words Saoul was won over and swore to his son that he would do no wrong to David (for a just word is indeed superior to wrath and fear).[752] Ionathes summoned David and informed him of the kindness and safety [granted him] by his father, to whom he then brought him. David then remained with the king as before.[753]

(11.3) 213. Around this time the Palestinoi again encamped against the Hebrews. [Saoul] sent David with an army to make war on the Palestinoi.[754] Joining battle, he killed many of them and returned victoriously to the king.[755] Saoul, however, did

Saul assaults victorious David

---

ence to David's role in "punishing the Palestinoi" adroitly reminds Saul that this is just what he had claimed to want from David in 6.201. Josephus leaves aside mention of God's role in David's victory as well as the appended notice about Saul's (MT; LXX: Israel's) seeing and rejoicing over this in 19:5bα.

[743] Josephus has Jonathan expatiate on his allusion to David's slaying "the Philistine" in 1 Sam 19:5a. The mention of the "40 days" of Goliath's challenge harks back to 6.174 (// 1 Sam 17:16).

[744] Continuing to amplify Jonathan's words, Josephus now has him recall David's most recent exploit, i.e. winning Michal's hand at the price of the Philistine heads; see 6.203.

[745] See Josephus' (likewise inserted) reference to Jonathan's "deferring to David's virtue" in 6.206 and to Saul's feigned desire for a son-in-law who has "courage and every other virtue" in 6.200.

[746] With this, the 3rd and last of the (initial) series of "extrabiblical" arguments Josephus attributes to Jonathan, he represents him appealing to the king's sense of family, particularly as regards his daughter.

[747] With this appeal, Jonathan reaches the core component of his discourse, towards which the preceding and following "arguments" are all directed. See Jonathan's opening exhortation in 1 Sam 19:4bα: "let not the king sin against his servant David."

[748] When referring to Saul's tormentor(s) earlier, Josephus designated these simply as "demons" (see 6.166, 168). He now combines that designation with the one used of them in 1 Sam 16:14-16, i.e. "evil spirit";

see note to "demons" at 6.166.

[749] Elaborating on his previous reminiscence of David's benefaction to Saul personally (see 6.209), Josephus' Jonathan now specifies the nature of that benefaction, i.e. his relieving Saul when he was possessed; see 6.168.

[750] With this statement Jonathan recapitulates his earlier references to David's exploits in 6.209-210 (cf. 1 Sam 19:5a). The remark likewise points back to Jonathan's mention of David's role in "punishing the Palestinoi" at the opening of his discourse in 6.209, this, in turn, echoing Saul's own claim about desiring this from David in 6.201.

[751] Josephus supplies this concluding affirmation with its allusion to the whole range of David's merits for his greatly expanded version of Jonathan's brief speech in 1 Sam 19:4-5.

[752] See 1 Sam 19:6; Josephus appends the proverb-like moral that serves to motivate Saul's positive response to Jonathan's appeal.

[753] In his version of 1 Sam 19:7 Josephus underscores the positive outcome of Jonathan's initiative; whereas in 19:7aβ Jonathan simply "shows David all these things," Josephus has him informing him of the "kindness and safety" Saul has now awarded him.

[754] 1 Sam 19:8a depicts David going on his own initiative to fight the Philistines. Josephus has him act on the king's orders; thereby he accentuates the wrongfulness of Saul's subsequent attempt to kill David, who has just demonstrated his obedience to him.

[755] Josephus' mention of David's "return" as the

not receive him as he hoped, given his achievement. Rather, he was grieved by his success, as though he himself were still more imperilled by his actions.[756]

214. Because the demon[757] again came upon him, his spirit was sorrowful and confused.[758] He called him [David] to the room in which he was lying sick and, holding his spear, ordered him to break the spell by his harp and songs. As David was doing what he was directed,[759] Saoul hurled the spear with all his might.[760] David, seeing it coming, eluded it.[761] He fled to his own house and remained there the whole day.[762]

Michal saves David

(11.4) 215. Sending by night,[763] the king directed that he be kept under guard until dawn so that he would not conceal himself and disappear completely.[764] [He did this] in order that he might be brought into the law court, handed over for judgment, and be killed.[765] When Melcha, David's wife and daughter of the king, learned of her father's state of mind, she stood by her husband. She had anxious expectations concerning him and agonized about her own life as well. For she could not endure to live if she were deprived of him.[766] **216.** "Let not," she said [to David], "the sun encounter you here. For it will not see you again. Flee while the present night that is still with us grants you to do so and may God make it longer for you. For know that if you are found by my father, you are lost."[767] Letting him down through a window, she secured his safety.[768]

217. Then she made up the bed as though for a sick person[769] and placed the liver

---

necessary preparation for what follows replaces the reference to the Philistines' flight in 1 Sam 19:8b.

[756] Josephus interjects this foreshadowing remark (and the attached allusion to Saul's state of mind), thereby preparing readers for what now awaits the victorious David at Saul's hands. On envy in the face of others' success as a recurrent theme of Josephus' account of Saul, see note to "distinctions" at 6.59.

[757] In contrast to his earlier usage (see 6.166, 168,211), Josephus here speaks of "the demon" in the singular.

[758] Josephus amplifies the biblical notice on the evil spirit's assault (1 Sam 19:9aα) with reference to its effect upon Saul and an allusion ("again") to the demons' previous attacks (see 6.166,168). As in his version of 1 Sam 16:14-23 in 6.166-169, he avoids the source qualification of the evil spirit as "from the Lord."

[759] In comparison with 1 Sam 19:9aβb ("... as he [Saul] sat [MT LXX L; LXX B: slept] in his house with his spear in his hand, and David was playing the lyre"), Josephus, here too, highlights David's acting in conformity with Saul's orders; see note to "Palestinoi" at 6.213. As in 6.166, he portrays David, not simply playing his instrument, but singing as he does so.

[760] Josephus' emphasis on the force of Saul's throw replaces the statement concerning his intention in 1 Sam 19:10a ("Saul sought to pin David to the wall" [MT; LXX lacks to the wall]).

[761] Josephus leaves aside the detail of 1 Sam 19:10bα about the spear that David eludes "sticking in the wall."

[762] Josephus' inserted specification as to where David flees (1 Sam 19:10bβ) has in view 19:11, which speaks of Saul's sending messengers "to David's house." His appended indication concerning the period David remains in his house likewise looks to the (LXX) timing of Saul's initiative, i.e. "that night." See next note.

[763] Josephus agrees with LXX in connecting this temporal indication with the opening of 1 Sam 19:11 (Saul sends messengers to David "that night") against MT, which links the phrase rather with the end of 19:10 (David escapes "that night").

[764] Josephus inserts this additional, negative indication concerning Saul's intentions in sending his men to David's house (see 1 Sam 19:11a).

[765] According to 1 Sam 19:11a, Saul's intention is simply to "kill" David the next morning. Josephus represents the king as concerned to give his intended murder the appearance of a legally sanctioned act.

[766] Josephus prefaces Michal's warning David as recounted in 1 Sam 19:11b with these inserted background notices on her learning of Saul's plan and the state of mind this provokes in her. The insertion underscores Michal's attachment to David that prompts her subsequent exertions on his behalf.

[767] Josephus elaborates on Michal's brief warning in 1 Sam 19:11b ("If you do not save your life tonight, tomorrow you will be killed") with, e.g., a reference to the divine aid she hopes will be given her husband.

[768] See 1 Sam 19:12.

[769] This mention of Michal's making up the bed "as

of a goat beneath the covers.[770] When it was day, her father sent to her regarding David.[771] She told those who came that he had passed a restless night, and showed them the bed that had been covered up. By agitating the covering with a jerking motion of the liver, she convinced them that the one lying sick was the ill David.[772]

218. When the messengers reported that he had been very sick throughout the night,[773] Saoul directed that he be brought just as he was, for he wished to do away with him.[774] They came therefore and uncovered the bed; finding the woman's trick, they reported it to the king.[775]

219. When her father reproached her for having saved his enemy while tricking[776] him, she contrived a convincing defense.[777] For she said that he had threatened to kill her so as, through anxiety, to secure her cooperation in regard to his safety.[778] Because of this, she deserved to be pardoned since she had acted under necessity rather than intentionally. "For," she said, "I cannot think that you were seeking to kill your enemy more than you were to save me." With that, Saoul pardoned the young woman.[779]

*Michal par-
doned by Saul*

220. Now David, fleeing the danger, came to the prophet Samouel at Armatha[780] and disclosed the king's plot to him and how he had came close to being killed when he threw his spear,[781] even though he had not been bad to him nor cowardly in the struggles against the enemy, but rather both spirited[782] and lucky[783] in all things. This

*David reports
to Samuel*

---

though for a sick person" (compare 1 Sam 19:14b, where she informs Saul's men that "he [David] is sick") replaces the reference of 19:13a to her placing a first object, of uncertain meaning and variously denominated in the textual witnesses, in the bed, i.e. התרפים (MT; RSV: "an image"); "empty sarcophagoi" (LXX); "statues" (Tg.).

[770] Josephus' specification that the item was a goat "liver" corresponds to LXX 1 Sam 19:13b. MT's phrase כביר העזים (RSV: "a pillow of goats' hair") is of uncertain meaning (Tg. reads "a goatskin").

[771] Josephus prefaces his notice on Saul's sending to David's house (see 1 Sam 19:14a) with a chronological indication that picks up on the reference to its still being night in 6.216.

[772] Josephus considerably embellishes Michal's summary declaration ("he is sick") of 1 Sam 19:14b: she confirms her verbal assertion with a "demonstration" of David's condition, making use of the goat liver (19:13), and succeeds in persuading her hearers. Here, as in 6.215, Josephus goes beyond the Bible in highlighting the person, mental state, words, and effective initiatives of Michal.

[773] This report by the messengers to Saul is simply presupposed in the presentations of MT and LXX L. It does have a certain equivalent in LXX B 1 Sam 19:14, where the word "he (David) is sick" is attributed, not as in MT and LXX L (as also in Josephus; see 6.217) to Michal, but rather to the messengers themselves ("and they said that he was sick").

[774] See 1 Sam 19:15; cf. Josephus' previous notice on Saul's intentions regarding David in 6.215.

[775] 1 Sam 19:16 does not mention a report by the messengers of their "discovery" to the king. Josephus' inserted reference to their doing so serves to prepare the following confrontation between Saul and Michal (19:17).

[776] Greek: κατασοφίζομαι; there is a play on words here with the term σόφισμα ("trick") used of Michal's ruse in 6.218.

[777] To his reproduction of Saul's accusatory words from 1 Sam 19:17a, Josephus prefaces this notice, intimating that by her subsequent response Michal will succeed in hoodwinking her father, just as she had earlier duped the royal messengers (see 6.217).

[778] Josephus expands on Michal's report of David's death threat (1 Sam 19:17b) with mention of his (purported) purpose in making that threat.

[779] 1 Sam 19:17 says nothing concerning the effect of Michal's reply upon Saul. Josephus' appendix on the point underscores the effectiveness of Michal's self-defense.

[780] Josephus mentioned Samuel's departure for this, his home-town (MT: Ramah), in 6.155 (// 1 Sam 15:34) following his confrontation with Saul concerning the king's Amalekite campaign.

[781] See 1 Sam 19:18a. Josephus concretizes the source's general reference to David's informing Samuel of "all that Saul had done to him" with specific mention of the spear-throwing incident of 6.214 (// 19:10).

[782] This rendering follows the reading of RO (μετὰ [τοῦ] θυμοῦ) adopted by Niese; Marcus (*ad loc.*) reads μετὰ τοῦ θεοῦ (literally: "with God") on the basis of MSP.

was the cause of Saoul's hostility towards David.[784]

Saul's efforts to arrest David frustrated

(11.5) 221. When the prophet learned of the king's wrongdoing, he left the city of Armatha; he led David to a certain place called Galbouath[785] and resided there with him.[786] When it was reported to Saoul that David was with the prophet, he sent troops against him whom he ordered to arrest and fetch him.[787]

222. When they came to Samouel, they encountered an assembly of prophets.[788] Becoming possessed by the divine spirit, they [Saul's troops] too began to prophesy.[789] On hearing this Saoul sent others against David. These suffered the same thing as the first ones; once again, [Saoul] dispatched others. When these third ones prophesied as well,[790] Saoul, in his wrath, finally marched out himself.[791]

223. When he was already nearby, Samouel, even before he saw him, made him prophesy.[792] As he came to him, Saoul, overcome by much spirit, lost his mind.[793] Removing his clothes[794] and throwing himself down, he lay prostrate for an entire day and night with Samouel and David seeing [this].[795]

---

[783] Greek: ἐπιτυχής. This adjective is *hapax* in Josephus.

[784] To his elaboration of David's "report" to Samuel (1 Sam 19:18a), Josephus appends this summarizing remark concerning the basis of the king's animosity towards David. The remark recalls Josephus' earlier statement (6.213) that Saul "was grieved by his [David's] success, as though he himself were still more imperilled by his actions."

[785] MT (1 Sam 19:18) נוית(ב) (= *ketiv*; *qere* has ניות(ב)); commentators disagree as to whether this is a proper place name [RSV: "Naioth"] or a common noun, i.e. "[the] camps"); LXX Αυαθ ἐν Ραμά; Tg. "in the house of study"; Josephus Γαλβουάθ (Schalit *s.v.* sees this form as a corruption of the Greek transcription of the name, itself reflecting a Hebrew בגיות, actually read by Josephus).

[786] See 1 Sam 19:18b, which Josephus elaborates with mention of Samuel's departing his home-town in response to David's report.

[787] See 1 Sam 19:19-20a.

[788] Compare 6.56, where Samuel informs Saul that he will meet "assembled prophets." Josephus omits the detail of 1 Sam 19:20bα about Samuel "standing as head" over this group, just as he does the specification that the group itself was "prophesying." In Tg. the reference is to "a band of teachers singing," with Samuel "standing teaching them."

[789] Here exceptionally, Josephus does reproduce a source reference (see 1 Sam 19:20bβ) to God's "spirit." His wording echoes that used by him in 6.166, where, once "the divine spirit" transfers from Saul to David, the latter begins to prophesy. In Tg. the Spirit prompts Saul's messengers to "sing praise."

[790] See 1 Sam 19:21.

[791] Josephus' mention of Saul's "wrath" reflects the LXX plus at the opening of 1 Sam 19:22. He leaves

aside the following sequence (19:22aβb-23a) concerning Saul's movements as well as the intervening exchange between Saul and an unidentified person concerning Samuel and David's whereabouts (v. 22b); this exchange might appear otiose, given that in 19:19 Saul has already been informed about the pair's current residence.

[792] In 1 Sam 19:23b it is God's Spirit which prompts Saul's prophesying (Tg. has him "singing praise"). Josephus' formulation underscores the stature of Samuel who, even at a distance, can elicit prophesying from others. *Bib. Ant.* 62.2 provides a content for Saul's prophesying on this occasion according to which the spirit, speaking through him, informs him that he and his son are to die and that David will succeed as king. Thereupon, Saul, as directed by the prophetic spirit, departs, unaware that he has prophesied.

[793] Greek: ἔκφρων γίνεται. Josephus' other uses of the term ἔκφρων are *War* 1.443, 544; *Ant.* 6.246. 1 Sam 19:23 lacks an equivalent indication.

[794] While he does reproduce the unseemly detail of 1 Sam 19:24 about King Saul stripping naked, Josephus stresses that his doing this was due to the extraordinary circumstances that had befallen him (the pressure of "much spirit" and his resultant loss of mind); see Feldman 1998: 527.

[795] In specifying that Saul lay stripped before both Samuel and David Josephus reflects the reading of LXX B 1 Sam 19:24bα, where Saul prophesies "before them," as opposed to MT LXX L, where he does so only before Samuel. Josephus omits the cryptic question, "is Saul also among the prophets?," with which the biblical account of the king's prophesying concludes in 1 Sam 19:24bβ (Tg. replaces "prophets" with "scribes" in its version of the saying), likely given the fact that this same question has already been cited previously (see 1 Sam 10:12// 6.56) in connection with Saul's initial

(11.6) 224. From there David went to Ionathes, the son of Saoul, and bewailed his father's plot, saying that, though he had done no wrong or committed any offense, he was being chased after by his father in order that he might be murdered.[796] Ionathes, however, appealed to him not to believe either this suspicion of his or slanderers—if in fact there were some who were acting as such[797]—but rather to look to himself and take courage.[798] For his father was not scheming any such thing against him. For otherwise, he would have told him about this and taken him as his counsellor, seeing that in everything else he acted according to their joint plan.[799]

David–Jonathan exchange

225. David, however, swore[800] that matters indeed stood thus, and requested him to believe him and care for him instead of despising the truth of his words and only admit them to be true when he should behold [him murdered][801] or find out [about this].[802] He further stated that his father had said nothing to him [Ionathes] about these matters, because he knew of his friendship and affection for himself.[803]

(11.7) 226. Grieved because his reassuring David concerning Saoul's intentions did not convince him,[804] Ionathes questioned what he wished to obtain from him.[805] [David] then said: "I know that you will grant and confer on me everything that I wish.[806] Tomorrow is the new moon, and it is my custom to have supper seated with the king.[807] **227.** If it seems good to you, I shall go outside the city and keep myself concealed in the plain.[808] If you are interrogated by him, say that I have gone to my ancestral city of Bethleeme where my tribe is celebrating a feast, and add that you had given me permission.[809] If he says that it is appropriate and customary to say

---

"prophesying" after his anointing by Samuel.

[796] See 1 Sam 20:1, whose 3 short, direct questions by David to Jonathan Josephus transposes into a series of affirmations by him in indirect discourse. Pseudo-Philo (*Bib. Ant.* 62.3-8) greatly elaborates on David's opening word to Jonathan of 20:1.

[797] This "appeal" is Josephus' expansion of Jonathan's opening assurances (1 Sam 20:2) to David; Josephus' subsequent portrayal of the David-Saul relationship will feature recurrent references to those who "slander" David to the king; the emphasis likely reflects Josephus' own experience of the "slanders" of his fellow Jews to his Roman patrons as alluded to by him in *Life* 424-429.

[798] These exhortations have no counterpart in Jonathan's reply to David as cited in 1 Sam 20:2.

[799] Cf. Jonathan's statement in 1 Sam 20:2: "Behold, my father does nothing either great or small without disclosing it to me, and why should my father hide this from me?"

[800] Josephus' mention of David's "swearing" at this juncture reflects the opening words ("David swore again") of MT 1 Sam 20:3 as opposed to LXX's "David replied."

[801] The words "him murdered," bracketed by Niese, are absent in RO Lat. Marcus retains them without brackets.

[802] This portion of David's reply, with its sharp rejoinder to Jonathan's efforts at soothing him, has no counterpart in the response of David cited in

1 Sam 20:3.

[803] This is Josephus' rendering of David's response (1 Sam 20:3) to Jonathan's claim (20:2) that Saul would not withhold anything from him, including his intentions regarding David: "Your father knows well that I have found favor in your eyes; and he thinks, 'Let Jonathan not know this, lest he be grieved (MT; LXX B: not wish it; LXX L: not report it to David)'." Josephus leaves aside David's concluding sworn statement "there is but a step between me and death."

[804] Josephus inserts this reference to the emotional effect of David's response upon Jonathan.

[805] Compare 1 Sam 20:4, where Jonathan tells David: "whatever you say (MT; LXX desire), I will do for you."

[806] Josephus prefaces David's proposed plan of action that he presents to Jonathan in 1 Sam 20:5-7 with this affirmation by David of his awareness of the extent of Jonathan's willingness to assist him.

[807] See 1 Sam 20:5a. Josephus' having David make explicit mention of his dining "with the king" corresponds to the plus of MT.

[808] Josephus leaves aside the chronological indication, "till the third day at evening" (MT; LXX till evening) that David appends to his proposal about staying hidden in the field in 1 Sam 20:5b.

[809] Josephus' specification of the feast in question as a "tribal" one corresponds to LXX 1 Sam 20:6 ("a sacrifice... for the entire tribe") as against MT's "a sacrifice for all the family." He leaves aside the further

about traveling friends 'May he have gone for his good,' know that there is nothing perfidious or hostile in him.[810] But if he answers otherwise, this will be a portent of what has been planned against me.[811] **228.** Inform me of your father's state of mind, doing this out of pity and the friendship[812] on account of which you have seen fit to take pledges from me and even to give these to me yourself, though you are the master to your servant.[813] If, however, you find anything vile in me, do away with me yourself and thus anticipate your father."[814]

229. Although he was distressed by the last of [David's] words,[815] Ionathes promised that he would do these things and would inform him, even if his father should answer something rough and indicative of his hostility.[816] So that he might have greater confidence in him, he brought him out into the open, clear air and swore that he would neglect nothing affecting David's safety.[817]

230. "For I make this God," he said, "whom you see to be great and universally extended and who, before I have expressed my mind in words, already knows this,[818] the witness[819] of my agreements with you,[820] namely that I shall not cease

---

qualification of the occasion as "yearly" (MT)/ "of the days" (LXX). Finally, in Josephus' version of David's proposal Jonathan is not only to say that he was asked permission by David (so 20:6), but that he actually gave that permission.

[810] Compare 1 Sam 20:7a, where Saul's single-word (hypothetical) response ("good") is to be taken, according to David, as a sign that things will go well with him.

[811] In 1 Sam 20:7b it is rather Saul's "anger" (MT; LXX his answering harshly) that will portend a threat for David.

[812] David's plea in 1 Sam 20:8aα is simply that Jonathan "deal kindly with your servant." The Josephan David's alternative appeal for a report concerning Saul's state of mind might reflect David's subsequent question to Jonathan in 20:10: "who will tell me if your father answers you roughly?"

[813] Compare 1 Sam 20:8aβ, where David invokes the "covenant of the God/the Lord" existing between himself and Jonathan. In accord with his consistent practice, Josephus replaces the biblical mention of a "covenant" (LXX: διαθήκη), in the sense of a solemn agreement regulating the relationship between 2 parties, with alternative terminology, here "pledges" (πίστεις). Like LXX B, Josephus has no equivalent to the account given in MT LXX L 1 Sam 18:1-4 of a previous covenant-making between David and Jonathan to which the former's words here in 20:8 are alluding; see note to "women" at 6.193.

[814] Compare 1 Sam 20:8b, where David's word to Jonathan concludes with the question "for why should you bring me to your father?"

[815] Josephus prefaces Jonathan's response to David (1 Sam 20:9) with this notice concerning the (negative) effect of the latter's final word with its reference (6.228) to his killing David himself upon Jonathan. See the

comparable indication inserted by him at the opening of 6.226.

[816] Josephus conflates Jonathan's answer promising to disclose to David whatever might be his father's evil intentions regarding him (1 Sam 20:9) and David's follow-up question—which would appear to have just been answered by Jonathan—of 20:10: "who will tell me if your father answers you roughly?" Thereby, he eliminates the source's seeming "mismatch" between Jonathan's assurance and David's response.

[817] See 1 Sam 20:11-12aα, whose wording Josephus modifies, amplifies and compresses. Thus, he has the pair go out into "the open air" rather than the "field" of 20:11, conflates Jonathan's directive and its realization (compare 20:11), and introduces an explicit mention of Jonathan's "swearing." He likewise supplies a purpose for Jonathan's new initiative regarding David and an opening, general content for his discourse.

[818] Josephus has Jonathan expatiate on the "universal" characteristics of God in contrast to 1 Sam 20:12, which simply calls him "the God of Israel." Elsewhere too he calls attention to the ubiquity and omniscience of God (see, e.g., *Ant.* 1.20; 6.263; 8.108, 227) in terms reminiscent of the Stoic belief in the all-pervading cosmic world-soul; see Feldman 1998: 194.

[819] This use of the term "witness" for God aligns Josephus' version of Jonathan's reply with that of LXX 1 Sam 20:12 ("The Lord... be witness") against MT, which lacks the term.

[820] This reference to the pair's "agreements" (Greek: συνθῆκαι) picks up on David's invocation of the "pledges" (πίστεις) exchanged between them in 6.228. Josephus' use of the term "agreements" here in 6.230 reflects, while also modifying, the MT reading at the opening of 1 Sam 20:16: "and Jonathan cut [a covenant] with the house of David."

sounding out my father regarding his intentions until I have fully ascertained what these are and gotten near the secret designs of his soul. Having ascertained this, I shall not hide it, but shall fully inform you, whether his disposition be mild or malevolent.[821] **231.** This God knows how I pray that he will be with you in everything. For he is now [with you] and will not abandon you, but rather will make you superior to your enemies, whether they be my father or myself.[822] **232.** Only remember these things and, should I die, save my children, and in return for my present [aid] recompense them."[823]

After he had sworn to these things, he dismissed David,[824] telling him to go off to a certain place in the plain where he [Ionathes] used to exercise;[825] for, once he knew how matters stood with his father, he would, he said, come to him there, bringing along only a servant boy.[826] **233.** And if, after hurling three javelins at the target, I order the boy to bring the javelins (for they will be lying in front of it),[827] you will know that there is nothing amiss with my father. If, however, you hear me saying the opposite of these things, then expect the opposite from the king as well.[828] **234.** You, however, will obtain security from me and will suffer no harm. See to it, though, that you remember these things in the time of your success and be kind to my sons."[829] David, having received these pledges from Ionathes, departed for the agreed-upon spot.[830]

Jonathan's proposed plan

---

[821] Josephus compresses Jonathan's statement concerning Saul's 2 possible stances towards David—both of which he is ready to report to him—of 1 Sam 20:12b-13a.

[822] Josephus here combines 2 distinct components of Jonathan's discourse: "May the Lord be with you, as he has been with my father" (1 Sam 20:13b) and "... when the Lord cuts off every one of the enemies of David from the face of the earth..." (20:15b).

[823] Josephus transposes into positive terms Jonathan's plea in 1 Sam 20:15a: "do not cut off your loyalty from my house for ever (cf. 20:16a: "let not the name of Jonathan be cut off from the house of David"). Conversely, he leaves aside Jonathan's appeal for himself personally: "if I am still alive, show me the loyal love of the Lord, that I may not die" (1 Sam 20:14, RSV following LXX).

[824] This reference to Jonathan's "dismissal" of David replaces the notice of 1 Sam 20:17 about Jonathan's making David swear again by his love for him whom he "loved as his own soul." Feldman (1998: 366-67) sees Josephus' omission of this biblical statement as indicative of his concern that the friendship of Jonathan and David not be viewed as a homosexual love affair.

[825] In reproducing Jonathan's parting words to David (1 Sam 20:18-23), Josephus passes over the recapitulation of David's own earlier remarks to Jonathan (20:5) about the upcoming feast and his absence from this being "missed" by Saul of 20:18-19aα. From Jonathan's directive about what David is now to do (20:19aβb) he omits the closing mention of David's

remaining beside "the stone (heap)" (to which MT gives the name "Ezel," LXX L transcribing with *ergab*).

[826] This component of Jonathan's discourse have no biblical equivalent. Josephus introduces it in order to provide more of a preparation for the continuation of Jonathan's speech.

[827] In 1 Sam 20:20 (MT) Jonathan speaks of the "3 arrows" which he will shoot. Josephus adds the specification about what the boy is to do with the javelins/arrows once, at Jonathan's command, he has "found" them (20:21a). Marcus (*ad loc.*) points out that Josephus' form αὐτοῦ leaves it unclear what or who the arrows will lie before: is it the target ("it") or rather the lad ("him")?

[828] Josephus modifies the 2 alternatives set out by Jonathan in 1 Sam 20:21-22a (Jonathan's telling the lad that the arrows are on this side of him signifies safety for David, whereas his telling him that they are beyond him indicates that David is to depart). In Josephus' rendition the directive that the lad fetch the arrows and deposit them in front of Jonathan has positive significance for David, whereas "the opposite" of this (presumably, Jonathan's telling the lad not to bring him the javelins) points to danger for David.

[829] This conclusion to Jonathan's discourse, with its renewed appeal for his descendants (see 6.232), takes the place of 1 Sam 20:23, where, as in 20:12, Jonathan invokes the Lord (+ as witness, LXX).

[830] Josephus expands 1 Sam 20:24a with mention of the departing David's taking Jonathan's (verbal) "pledges" (πίστεις; see 6.228), i.e. those given him in 6.229-234, with him.

235. The next day was the new moon. The king, having purified himself according to his custom, came to the supper;[831] his son Ionathes sat down next to him on his right, with Abener, the commanding general, on his left.[832] Seeing David's seat vacant, he kept silent, supposing that he would come later, not yet having cleansed himself from sexual intercourse.[833] **236.** When, however, on the second day of the new moon he was still not present, he inquired of his son Ionathes why the son of Jesse was absent from the festival supper on the previous day and this one as well.[834] Then he, according to their agreements, stated that he had gone to his own ancestral city where his tribe was celebrating a festival and that he had given him permission for this.[835] "[David] had, moreover, appealed to him to come to the sacrifice and, if he were allowed, he would go. "For you are aware of my loyalty towards him."[836]

237. It was then that Ionathes perceived his father's malevolence towards David and clearly saw his entire purpose, for Saoul did not restrain his wrath.[837] Rather, he defamed him [Ionathes], calling him a descendant of deserters and an enemy, and said that he was a accomplice and collaborator of David.[838] In thinking that way, and not wishing to be convinced that, so long as David survived, the kingship would be insecure for them,[839] he showed no respect either for himself or his mother.[840] "Therefore summon him," he said, "so that he may pay the penalty."[841]

---

[831] See 1 Sam 20:24b; Josephus interjects the reference to Saul's customary self-purification.

[832] Josephus' indications concerning the seating arrangements follow (with modifications) those of LXX 1 Sam 20:25abα, where Jonathan sits facing Saul (whose own seat is "by the wall"), while Abner sits at Saul's side. In MT Jonathan is not "seated," but rather "stands up."

[833] In his rendition of 1 Sam 20:25bβ-26 concerning David's absence from the table and Saul's initial response to this, Josephus spells out the king's vague reference ("something has befallen him," v. 26aβ) to the source of David's (supposed) current impurity, i.e. sexual intercourse, as does also Rabbinic tradition; see *b. Pesaḥ* 3a. He likewise interjects mention of the king's expectation that David would eventually appear.

[834] See 1 Sam 20:27, which Josephus follows in having Saul call David, not by his name, but rather "the son of Jesse."

[835] See 1 Sam 20:28-29a. In accordance with his version of David's request in 6.227 (compare 20:6), Josephus has Jonathan state explicitly that he did grant David's plea. Conversely, he passes over David's (alleged) statement (20:29aβ) about being "commanded by his brother" to attend the affair in Bethlehem—a point not mentioned in David's own proposal (20:6) about what Jonathan is to tell his father concerning his absence.

[836] This conclusion to Jonathan's response to Saul

takes the place of 1 Sam 20:29b, where, after citing David's plea to him that he be allowed to go visit his brothers, Jonathan rounds off his reply with the words "for this reason he [David] has not come to the king's table." Josephus' rendition underscores the bond between Jonathan (who has himself been invited to attend the feast in Bethlehem and wishes to do so) and David. In so doing, he likewise prepares for the vehemence of Saul's outburst in what follows.

[837] Josephus amplifies the introductory narrative notice of 1 Sam 20:30a: "Then Saul's anger was kindled against Jonathan...." with mention of Jonathan's resultant perception.

[838] Josephus replaces Saul's invective against Jonathan's mother in 1 Sam 20:30aβ, in which he calls Jonathan "the son of a perverse, rebellious woman" (RSV) with a denunciation of the "culprit" Jonathan himself.

[839] See 1 Sam 20:31a: "For as long as the son of Jesse lives upon the earth, neither you nor your kingdom shall be established." Josephus' Saul interjects a reference ("for them") also to his own kingship that is endangered by David.

[840] See 1 Sam 20:30b: "do I [Saul] not know that you have chosen the son of Jesse to your own shame, and to the shame of your mother's nakedness?" Josephus tones down the vulgarity of the king's language.

[841] See 1 Sam 20:31b, where Saul more emphatically avers "he shall surely die."

238. When Ionathes replied: "For what misdeed do you wish to punish him?,"[842] Saoul did not vent his wrath merely in words and defamations but, seizing his spear, lunged at him, wishing to kill him.[843] He did not succeed in this endeavor, being restrained by his friends.[844] It was, however, clear to his son that he hated David and desired to get rid of him, seeing that because of him he had come very close to doing this even to his son with his own hand.[845]

(11.10) 239. Then the king's son rushed out of the supper, unable to eat anything because of his grief.[846] He spent the night lamenting that he himself had narrowly escaped being slain and that David had been condemned to death.[847] At daybreak, he went out into the plain in front of the city, ostensibly to exercise, but in fact to disclose to his friend his father's state of mind, as he had agreed.[848]

Jonathan–David encounter

240. After doing what had been arranged,[849] Ionathes dismissed the boy who followed him back to the city; thus it was now safe for David to come forth to be seen by him and hear [his words].[850] When he appeared, he fell at Ionathes' feet and paid him homage, calling him the savior[851] of his life.[852]

241. [Ionathes] raised him up from the ground.[853] Embracing one another, they kissed long and tearfully.[854] They lamented their youth and the comradeship that was envied them and their imminent separation that seemed to them no different from death.[855] Then, with difficulty recovering from their laments,[856] and appealing to

---

[842] Josephus conflates Jonathan's double question of 1 Sam 20:32: "Why should he [David] be put to death? What has he done?"

[843] See 1 Sam 20:33a, where Saul is said to "hurl" (MT; LXX: brandish) his spear.

[844] This reference to the "friends'" intervention is Josephus' insertion; it serves to explain how it was that Saul did not succeed in killing Jonathan. Here, as frequently elsewhere, Josephus introduces mention of the Greco-Roman institution of the royal "friends" where the Bible has no counterpart to this; see Begg 1993: 16, n. 54.

[845] See 1 Sam 20:33b. Josephus spells out the grounds for Jonathan's realization concerning his father's intentions, likewise interjecting the reference to Saul's "hatred" for David.

[846] Josephus' reference to Jonathan's "rushing out" reflects the vivid verbs used by LXX and 4QSam[a] 1 Sam 20:34a as opposed to MT's bland "he arose." In the Bible, Jonathan leaves the table "in anger," in Josephus rather in grief.

[847] Josephus' mention of Jonathan's "lamenting" over his own and David's situation seems to reflect the double motivation for Jonathan's not eating found in MT LXX L 1 Sam 20:34b, i.e. "for he was grieved for David (> LXX B), because his father had disgraced him."

[848] In 1 Sam 20:35 Jonathan proceeds to "the field" and takes "a little lad" with him. Josephus spells out

the purpose of his move, with reference back to Jonathan's proposal in 6.232 (which mentions the plain as the place where he used to exercise).

[849] With this transitional phrase, Josephus sums up the biblical narration (1 Sam 20:36-39) concerning Jonathan's shooting the arrows and the boy's collecting these in accordance with what he had earlier proposed to David (20:20-22// 6.233).

[850] See 1 Sam 20:40-41aα. MT 20:41aα mentions David's rising "from beside the south," while LXX has him rise "from beside the stone heap."

[851] Greek σωτήρ. On this term and its word-field, see Spicq 1982 (III): 629-43.

[852] Josephus adds a word of recognition by David to his (silent) gesture of homage to Jonathan as mentioned in 1 Sam 20:41aβ (where David falls "to the ground" [MT LXX L, > LXX B], doing this "three times").

[853] Josephus inserts this action by Jonathan as a necessary transition between David's prostration and the 2 friends' subsequent embrace.

[854] See 1 Sam 20:41bα.

[855] Josephus provides a verbal content for the friends' lament, thereby augmenting the pathos of the scene. Pseudo-Philo (*Bib. Ant.* 62.9-11) does something analogous via the extended, tearful discourse that he has Jonathan deliver on this occasion.

[856] This notice seems to reflect the obscure final words of 1 Sam 20:41, where David (so MT) finally

David asks Abimelech's assistance

each other to remember their oaths, they went their separate ways.[857]

(12.1) 242. David, fleeing the king and death at his hands, went to Naba,[858] the city of the high priest Abimelech.[859] When he saw him coming alone, with no friend beside him or servant present,[860] Abimelech wondered[861] and wished to learn the reason why no one was with him.[862] **243.** David then stated that he was undertaking a secret operation for the king for which he did not need an entourage, since he wished to be concealed.[863] "I have, however, ordered my attendants to meet me at a certain place."[864] He requested to receive provisions,[865] for in doing this he [Abimelech] would show himself a friend and would be assisting with his assigned task.[866]

244. Once he had obtained these things, [David] further asked that he might have whatever weapon—whether sword or short spear—he had available.[867] (Now there was on hand a slave of Saoul, by race a Syrian,[868] named Doeg,[869] the keeper of the

---

"recovers" or "exceeds" himself. In speaking of the 2 men's joint "recovery," Josephus aligns himself with LXX.

[857] In 1 Sam 20:42 it is Jonathan alone who reminds David of their joint "oath" (and quotes its wording). Josephus accentuates the mutuality involved in the friends' interaction, while by contrast, in Pseudo-Philo's version of the scene (*Bib. Ant.* 61.9-11) Jonathan does all the talking. Josephus' generalized reference to the pair's "separating" takes the place of the more expansive notice of 1 Sam 21:1 (MT; Eng. 20:42bβ): "And he [David] rose, and departed; and Jonathan went into the city."

[858] MT (1 Sam 21:2 [Eng. 21:1]) נבה (Eng.: "Nob"); LXX Νόμβα; Josephus Ναβά. On the Josephan and Pseudo-Philonic versions of the story of the "Nob massacre" and its sequels (1 Samuel 21-22), see Begg 1997h.

[859] MT (1 Sam 21:2= Eng. 21:1) אחימלך; LXX B Ἀβιμέλεχ; LXX L Ἀχιμέλεχ; Josephus Ἀβιμέλεχος. Josephus' form of the name thus corresponds to that of LXX B ("A*b*imelech") as opposed to MT and LXX L's "A*h*imelech" (Pseudo-Philo also calls him "Abimelech" in *Bib Ant.* 63.2). The Bible designates him simply as "priest."

[860] For this description of what the priest "sees," Josephus draws on 1 Sam 21:2bβ, where Ahimelech asks David: "why are you alone, and no one with you?"

[861] Ahimelech's "wondering" here corresponds to the LXX reading in 1 Sam 21:2bα, where he is "astounded" to meet David (in MT he comes "trembling" to meet him).

[862] Josephus transposes into narrative Ahimelech's direct discourse questions to David as quoted in 1 Sam 21:2bβ (see note to "present" at 6.242).

[863] Cf. 1 Sam 21:3a.

[864] In 1 Sam 21:3b David speaks of the "young men" with whom he has "made an appointment" (MT?

4QSam[b]; LXX: has adjured). Josephus' vague allusion to the site corresponds to the Hebrew idiom used by David, which the LXX first "translates" and then transcribes.

[865] In 1 Sam 21:4 David asks more specifically for "five loaves of bread."

[866] Josephus supplies this motivation, designed to persuade Ahimelech to accede to David's request. It replaces the extended discussion in 1 Sam 21:5-7 (MT= Eng. 21:4-6) between David and Ahimelech regarding the conditions for the priest's giving—as he ends up doing—David and his men the holy bread/ bread of the Presence, since this is all he has in hand at the moment. Josephus' passing over this sequence may reflect his concern not to bore gentile readers with such esoteric cultic particulars. It could likewise be prompted by a more intra-Jewish concern that the high-priest not appear a party to a violation of the stipulation of Lev 24:9 reserving the Bread of the Presence to the descendants of Aaron. Compare the controversy story featuring this prescription in Mark 2:23-28 and parallels.

[867] Josephus anticipates this further request by David from 1 Sam 21:9a; thereby, he keeps together in a continuous sequence David's 2 requests, for food and weapons, which in 1 Samuel 21 are separated by the parenthetical notice on the presence of Doeg in v. 8 (that Josephus himself appends to his version of David's double request). He leaves aside the source's motivation (21:9b) for the request, i.e. due to the urgency of his mission, David had not taken along any weapons.

[868] Josephus' specification of Doeg's ethnicity corresponds to that of LXX B 1 Sam 21:7 (= MT 21:8) and *Bib. Ant.* 63.2, as against MT and LXX L, which call him an Edomite/Idumean.

[869] MT (1 Sam 21:8= Eng. 21:7) דאג (Eng.: "Doeg"); LXX Δωήκ; Josephus Δώηγος.

royal mules.[870]) The high priest said that he did not have anything of this sort, but the sword of Goliath that he himself had dedicated to God after killing him was there.[871]

(12.2) 245. David took this[872] and escaped outside the country of the Hebrews to Gitta of the Palestinoi,[873] where Anchous[874] ruled as king. He was recognized by the king's servants who made his presence known to the king, informing him that David was the one who had killed many ten thousands of the Palestinoi.[875] David then became anxious that the king would kill him and that, having escaped danger from Saul, he would be exposed to this from his side.[876] Therefore he feigned madness and frenzy, in order that, by foaming at the mouth and manifesting other symptoms of madness, he might make the king of Gitta believe that he was ill.[877]

David's stay in Gath (Gitta)

246. The king got angry at his servants for having brought him a man who was out of his mind[878] and directed them to expel David as quickly as possible.[879]

(12.3) 247. Having thus escaped from Gitta, David went to the tribe of Iouda and took up residence in a cave near the city of Adollame.[880] Sending to his brothers, he disclosed to them that he was there;[881] they came to him with all their relatives.[882] Likewise whoever else was in need or in fear of King Saoul gathered to him,[883] and

David's further movements

---

[870] LXX 1 Sam 21:7 and Pseudo-Philo (*Bib. Ant.* 63.2) give Doeg this same title; MT (21:8) calls him "the chief of Saul's herdsmen." Like Pseudo-Philo, Josephus has no equivalent to the obscure mention of Doeg's being "detained before the Lord" of MT 21:8.

[871] Josephus rearranges the sequence of Ahimelech's reply (1 Sam 21:10a) to David's request for weapons (21:9). He likewise omits various particulars of the reply (the site of David's killing Goliath; the sword being wrapped in a cloth and located "behind the ephod" [this last item is absent in LXX B as well]). Conversely, he introduces an allusion to his own earlier notice on David's dedicating—at an unspecified site—Goliath's sword to God in 6.192 (compare 1 Sam 17:54, where what David takes to Jerusalem is Goliath's head).

[872] This transitional notice takes the place of 1 Sam 21:10b, where David first affirms that Goliath's sword has no counterpart, and then asks Ahimelech to give it to him (LXX adds that he actually did so).

[873] Josephus expands the mention of "Gath" (MT)/ "Geth" (LXX) in 1 Sam 21:11 (Eng. 21:10) with indications concerning its being outside Hebrew territory and belonging to the Philistines.

[874] MT (1 Sam 21:11= Eng. 21:10) אכיש (Eng.: "Achish"); LXX B Ἀγχούς; LXX L Ἀκχούς; Josephus Ἄγχους.

[875] Josephus reduces the servants' report to the king of 1 Sam 21:12 to its core component, i.e. the fact of David's having killed numerous Philistines. He leaves aside all that precedes this in the source report, i.e. the reference to David as "king of the land," the allusion to the women's song, and the first part of their couplet (itself drawn from 1 Sam 18:7 // 6.193) mentioning Saul's exploits.

[876] Josephus supplies a content for David's "fear" of Achish as mentioned in 1 Sam 21:13.

[877] Josephus appends this indication concerning the purpose of David's behavior to his reproduction of 1 Sam 21:14 (from which he omits the reference to David's "marking" [MT]/ "drumming on and falling upon" [LXX] "the doors of the gate" and whose mention of David's "spittle running down his beard" he turns into a notice on his "foaming at the mouth").

[878] Greek ἔκφρων. This is the same word used of Saul in the presence of David and Samuel in 6.223. Whereas, however, Saul actually was "out of his mind" on that occasion, David only pretends to be so here.

[879] Josephus inserts the reference to the king's "anger"; the expulsion command he ascribes to Achish stands closer to the affirmation of LXX B 1 Sam 21:15 ("this fellow shall not come into my house") than to the rhetorical question of MT (21:16) LXX L ("shall this fellow come into my house?").

[880] MT (1 Sam 22:1) עדלם (Eng.: "Adullam"); LXX Ὀδολλάμ; Josephus Ἀδολλάμη. Josephus' inserted reference to the site's being located in Judah corresponds to Josh 15:35.

[881] With this addition Josephus explains how David's relatives "hear" of his whereabouts—as they are said to do in 1 Sam 22:1bα.

[882] See 1 Sam 22:1bβ.

[883] Josephus introduces mention of Saul as the source of the distress that prompts people to join David. He likewise tones down, by generalizing these, the unflattering qualifications used of these persons in 1 Sam 22:2 (debtors, malcontents), perhaps as Feldman (1998: 562) suggests, so as not to have the hero David surrounded by Zealot-like figures.

said that they were ready to do whatever seemed good to him.[884] There were in all about 400.[885]

248. Encouraged that a group of collaborators had already joined him,[886] David marched off from there and came to the king of the Moabites.[887] He appealed to him to receive his parents into his own country until he should finally recognize what awaited him.[888] The king awarded this favor, and showed David's parents every honor during the time they were with him.[889]

Saul denounces his retine

(12.4) 249. [David], however, was directed by the prophet[890] to leave the desert and go live in the inheritance of the tribe of Iouda.[891] He obeyed, and coming to the city of Saris[892] remained there.

250. When Saoul, however, heard that David had been seen with a crowd, he fell into an extraordinary sorrow and confusion.[893] Knowing the mind of the man and his determination, he conjectured that he would cause him not a little work and that, due to him, he would greatly lament and be afflicted.[894]

251. He gathered his friends and leaders and the tribe to which he himself belonged[895] to the hill on which he had his palace.[896] Seated at a certain place called "Aroura"[897] with his office-holders and the ranks of his bodyguards around him,[898] he said to them: "My compatriots,[899] you surely remember my benefactions, how I made some of you masters of fields, and awarded others honors and offices among

---

[884] Compare 1 Sam 22:2aβ: "and he became captain over them."

[885] Josephus' figure for David's retinue corresponds to that given in 1 Sam 22:2b.

[886] Josephus interjects this reference to David's new-found confidence (contrast the "anxiety" ascribed to him in 6.245).

[887] From 1 Sam 22:3 Josephus omits the name (MT Mizpeh; LXX Massepha) of the Moabite site to which David comes.

[888] David's request in 1 Sam 22:3 is that his parents might be with (LXX; MT go out to) the king "till I know what God will do for me."

[889] The biblical account does not record a response by the king to David's request, simply noting (1 Sam 22:4) that David left them with the king (MT; in LXX 22:4a David "beseeches the face of the king of Moab") with whom they stayed the whole time "David was in the stronghold."

[890] 1 Sam 22:5 supplies this figure with a name, i.e. "Gad."

[891] The prophet Gad in 1 Sam 22:5a directs David not to remain in the "stronghold" (see 22:4), but to go to "the land of Judah."

[892] Josephus' designation for David's destination ("the city of Saris") clearly stands closer to that of LXX 1 Sam 22:5b ("the city of Sar(e)ik") than to MT's "the forest of Hereth." According to Schalit (*s.v.*), the original reading of both LXX and Josephus was Χάρις.

[893] Josephus supplies this notice on Saul's response to the reports brought him about the sighting of David's and his men (1 Sam 22:6a).

[894] This mention of Saul's state of mind is peculiar to Josephus; it prepares readers for the king's upcoming large-scale crime, i.e. the massacre of the priests of Nob.

[895] In 1 Sam 22:6b Saul's entourage consists simply of his "servants." For the royal "friends" see 6.238 and see note to "friends" at 6.238. Josephus' allusion to Saul's tribal affiliation recalls 6.45 (// 1 Sam 9:1), where Saul's father Kish is identified as belonging to the tribe of Benjamin.

[896] Josephus' reference to Saul's "palace on the hill" recalls 6.156 (where this is further localized as "in Gaba"). His mention of "the hill" corresponds to the LXX 1 Sam 22:6b translation of MT's "Gibeah."

[897] This is the same Greek term (meaning "field") used by LXX 1 Sam 22:6b to designate the place under which (rather than on which, as in Josephus) Saul sits (MT has him sitting "under the tamarisk tree"). Josephus omits the further specification that Saul's sitting place was "on the height" (MT; + in Bama, LXX).

[898] 1 Sam 22:6 speaks more generally of the "servants" who stand around Saul. Josephus cited the king's "bodyguards" previously in 6.95, 130. He leaves aside the source mention of Saul's holding his spear, given that the spear will have no function in what follows.

[899] In 1 Sam 22:7 Saul addresses his entourage as "Benjamites" (MT)/ "sons of Benjamin" (LXX). The Josephan Saul's designation of his addressees as "compatriots" echoes Josephus' earlier reference to Saul's summoning "the tribe to which he himself belonged."

the crowd.[900] **252.** I therefore inquire whether you have received greater and more such gifts from the son of Jesse.[901] For I know that all of you have joined that one.[902] My own son Ionathes is so disposed and has convinced you of these things.[903] **253.** For I am not ignorant[904] of the oaths and agreements he has made with David,[905] or that Ionathes is the advisor and collaborator of those conspiring against me.[906] None of you is concerned about these matters; rather, you are silently looking to what will happen."[907]

254. When the king fell silent, none of those present answered,[908] except for Doeg the Syrian, who looked after his mules.[909] He said that he had seen David coming to the city of Naba to Abimelech, the high priest,[910] in order to learn from his prophesying about the future;[911] he received provisions and the sword of Goliath, and was then sent off in security to those to whom he wished to go.[912]

Doeg reports Ahimelech to Saul

(12.5) 255. Saoul therefore summoned the high priest and his entire family.[913] "What terrible and unfriendly [thing]" he said, "did you suffer at my hands[914] that

Saul–Ahimelech confrontation

---

[900] The biblical Saul's discourse contains no such mention of the king's previous favors to his hearers. Josephus' insertion of the item serves to magnify their (purported) treachery in defecting from their benefactor.

[901] In 1 Sam 22:7 Saul asks his hearers whether the "son of Jesse" is planning to award them various properties ("fields and vineyards") and positions ("commanders of thousands and hundreds"). In Josephus' rendition Saul has just recalled that he himself conferred such benefactions upon them. Accordingly, he now has the king ask if his rival has actually outdone him in this regard. As in the source, Josephus' Saul avoids calling David by his name.

[902] Compare Saul's charge in 1 Sam 22:8aα: "all of you have conspired against me."

[903] This initial assertion about Jonathan and his influence upon Saul's retainers has no counterpart in the king's biblical speech.

[904] In 1 Sam 22:8 Saul twice asserts that "no one has disclosed to him" Jonathan's intrigues with David, this leaving the question of how then Saul could know of these. Josephus replaces this problematic assertion with a claim by Saul that he is "not ignorant" of Jonathan and David's dealings with each other, even though he too leaves it unexplained how the king came by this knowledge.

[905] In LXX 1 Sam 22:8 Saul charges Jonathan with having "cut a covenant" (Greek: διαθήκη; MT lacks an equivalent noun). In accord with his invariable practice, Josephus replaces the Greek word in its meaning "covenant" with an alternative rendering.

[906] In 1 Sam 22:8bβ Saul's 2nd charge against his son is that he has "stirred up my servant to lie in wait (MT; LXX to become a enemy)...." Josephus' formulation applies to Jonathan the same conspiracy charge Saul has already made against his retainers.

[907] Compare 1 Sam 22:8bα: "None of you is sorry

(MT; LXX exerts himself) for me or discloses to me..."

[908] Josephus inserts this transitional phrase which serves to highlight Doeg's own tale-bearing in what follows.

[909] See 6.244, whose qualifications of Doeg Josephus recapitulates here. Josephus' designation of him as "keeper of Saul's mules" at this juncture corresponds to LXX 1 Sam 22:9 (cf. 21:8), whereas MT refers to him as "standing by the servants of Saul."

[910] As he does throughout his version of 1 Samuel 22, Josephus leaves aside the name of Ahimelech's father, i.e. Ahitub that Doeg cites in 22:9.

[911] This is Josephus' equivalent to the Doeg's assertion "he [Ahimelech] consulted the Lord for him [David]" of 1 Sam 22:10a. For "prophesying" as a characteristic (high) priestly activity in Josephus, see *Ant.* 5.120 (Phineas); 6.115 (Ahitub). Neither Josephus nor the Bible, in their respective versions of the David-Ahimelech exchange, mentions David's seeking such a "consultation" from Ahimelech.

[912] Josephus expands Doeg's report of Ahimelech's giving David food and the sword (1 Sam 22:10b) with mention of his dismissal of him. In Pseudo-Philo's presentation Doeg takes the initiative in reporting Ahimelech to Saul, *Bib. Ant.* 63.2 (this notice is itself preceded [*Bib. Ant.* 63.1] by a biblically unparalleled announcement by God of his intention to destroy Nob, given its priests' practice of taking the first fruits for themselves).

[913] See 1 Sam 22:11a. Compressing, Josephus omits the notice on the family's arrival before Saul (22:11b), as well as the king's call to the priest to "hear" and the latter' statement that he is at the former's disposition (22:12).

[914] In prefacing Saul's accusations (see 1 Sam 22:13) with this reminder that Ahimelech has not been wronged by himself, Josephus' Saul highlights the

you should have received the son of Jesse and supplied with food and weapons a plotter against my kingdom? Why did you give him an oracle concerning the future?[915] For indeed it was not concealed from you that he was a fugitive from me and hates my house."[916]

256. The high priest did not have recourse to denial about what had happened, but with frank speech declared that he had awarded these things, granting them, not to David, but to [Saoul] himself:[917] "For," he stated, "I did not know him as your enemy, but as your especially faithful slave, and commander of thousands, and now in addition your son-in-law and relative.[918] **257.** Humans do not award such things to enemies, but to those who are outstanding in their loyalty and honor towards themselves.[919] Moreover, this was not the first time I prophesied for him; I have repeatedly done so also on other occasions.[920] He, for his part, said that he had been sent by you with much urgency on a task, such that if I did not award him what he was asking for, I would think that I was refusing, not him, but you in these matters.[921] **258.** Do not then suppose anything vile of me nor, because of what you now hear David is undertaking, suspect me of what at the time seemed to me [an act of] humanity.[922] For I made my award, not to an enemy, but to your friend, son-in-law, and commander of thousands."[923]

Ahimelech punished

(12.6) 259. In saying these things the high priest did not convince Saoul (for fear is so terrible that it does not believe even a truthful self-defense.)[924] He directed the troops[925] to surround him [with his family] and kill [them].[926] When they, however, did not have the courage to lay hands on the high priest, being more afraid of the

---

latter's (alleged) crimes. Compare Saul's (also inserted) recalling of his benefactions to his retinue prior to his making his charges against them in 6.251.

[915] Saul's 3 charges against Ahimelech correspond to those leveled by Saul in 1 Sam 22:13.

[916] This conclusion to Saul's accusation takes the place of the king's final words in 1 Sam 22:13: "... so that he [David] has risen against me to lie in wait as at this day." Josephus' keeps the focus on Ahimelech himself and his allegedly conscious offenses.

[917] Josephus elaborates on the summary opening formula of 1 Sam 22:14 ("then Ahimelech answered the king"), accentuating the priest's confidence in his own innocence.

[918] Ahimelech's 3-fold characterization of David in relation to Saul here corresponds to the priest's opening words in 1 Sam 22:14 (where as its 2nd item LXX has "charged with carrying out all your orders" for MT's "chief [emended text for the extant verbal form "and turned aside to"] of your bodyguard").

[919] This reflective aside by Ahimelech lacks a biblical equivalent.

[920] Josephus turns Ahimelech's rhetorical question —which he then proceeds to answer in the negative— of 1 Sam 22:15a ("Is this the first time I have consulted God for him?") into a definite affirmation by him.

[921] This further exculpatory affirmation by Ahimelech, harking back to David's declaration to him in

6.243, has no biblical parallel. Its wording reflects Ahimelech's opening statement that in doing what he did for David he supposed himself to be acting in favor of Saul himself (6.256).

[922] Greek: φιλανθρωπία. On this noun and its wordfield, see Spicq 1958; 1978 (II): 922-27. Josephus' version of Ahimelech's appeal in 1 Sam 22:15bα ("let not the king impute anything to his servant or to all the house of my father") underscores the total good faith with which he claims to have acted earlier.

[923] These concluding words of Ahimelech's self-defense echo his opening characterization of David in 6.256. They take the place of the priest's closing declaration in 1 Sam 22:15bβ: "for your servant has known nothing of all this, much or little."

[924] This editorial notice on the non-effect of Ahimelech's words and the reason for this takes the place of Saul's condemnation of Ahimelech and his house in 1 Sam 22:16 (which Pseudo-Philo does [*Bib. Ant.* 63.2] reproduce, immediately following his notice on the king's summoning of the priest [// 22:11]).

[925] In 1 Sam 22:17a Saul commands his "runners" to kill the priests.

[926] The codices other than RO read the bracketed words "with his family" in line with Saul's order as cited in 1 Sam 22:17a, prescribing the execution, not of Ahimelech personally, but of "the priests." Niese omits the words, while Marcus makes them part of his text.

Deity than of disobedience to the king,[927] he ordered the Syrian Doeg [to under-take] the murder.[928]

260. The latter, taking men as vile as himself, killed Abimelech and his family[929] (they were in all about 305[930]). Saoul[931] likewise sent to Naba, the city of the priests, and killed them all, sparing neither women, nor infants, nor those of any other age, and burned it.[932]

261. One son of Abimelech, named Abiathar,[933] did escape, however.[934] Now these things happened as God had prophesied to the high priest Helei, saying that his descendants would be destroyed because of the transgressions of his two sons.[935]

Abiathar escapes

(12.7) 262. King Saoul perpetrated this so cruel deed,[936] butchering an entire family of high priestly rank and not even taking pity on infants, nor showing respect for age.[937] He likewise overthrew a city that was the ancestral [home] and nurse of priests and prophets,[938] the very spot the Deity had chosen and exclusively appointed to produce such men.[939]

Reflections on Saul's deed

---

[927] Josephus supplies the motivation for the soldiers' refusal to obey Saul's command as mentioned in 1 Sam 22:17b. Conversely, he leaves aside, as something already sufficiently known, the rationale for the command Saul gives in 22:17aβ (i.e. the priests' support for David and failure to report his flight to Saul).

[928] See 1 Sam 22:18a. In Pseudo-Philo Saul's commands to both the soldiers and to Doeg (1 Sam 22:17-18a) are passed over, and he proceeds to kill the priests himself (*Bib. Ant.* 63.2).

[929] 1 Sam 22:18b says nothing about Doeg's having assistants in killing the priests. Josephus' introduction of these may be based on the consideration that it would have been difficult for one man to perform the task alone, given the large number of victims involved.

[930] This is the figure for the murdered priests read by Niese and Marcus on the basis of Lat and corresponding to LXX 1 Sam 22:18. RO read 85 (with MT 1 Sam 22:18); MSP have 385 (as does *Bib. Ant.* 63.4), while E gives 530. Josephus leaves aside the biblical specification that the slain priests "wore the linen (> LXX) ephod."

[931] 1 Sam 22:19 does not specify the subject when mentioning that Nob was "put to the sword"; the immediately preceding context would seem to suggest that it was Doeg who did this (cf., however, 1 Sam 22:21, where, in reporting the Nob massacre to David, Abiathar attributes this directly to Saul; cf. also *Bib. Ant.* 63.2, where Saul personally kills the priests). Josephus' formulation insists on Saul's (ultimate) responsibility in view of the extended subsequent denunciation of the king he will append in 6.262-268.

[932] From the catalogue of the Nob slain in 1 Sam 22:19, Josephus omits the oxen, donkeys, and sheep. Conversely, he adds mention of the burning of the city.

[933] MT (1 Sam 22:20) אביתר (Eng.: "Abiathar"); LXX Ἀβιαθάρ; Josephus Ἀβιάθαρος.

[934] See 1 Sam 22:20. Also Pseudo-Philo reproduces the biblical notice on Abiathar's escape (*Bib. Ant.* 63.3).

[935] Josephus appends this cross reference to God's announcement to Samuel—which the latter in turn conveys to Eli—concerning the fate of Eli's house (*Ant.* 5.350// 1 Sam 3:11-14) to his account of Saul's massacre of all but one of Eli's line. In Pseudo-Philo the massacre is the realization of a different divine announcement, i.e. that cited by him in *Bib. Ant.* 63.1, pronouncing doom on the priests of Nob for their arrogation of the first fruits.

[936] Josephus here begins his lengthy, 7-paragraph (6.262-268) appendix to the biblical account of the Nob massacre (1 Samuel 21-22). In this segment he both provides an evaluation of Saul's deed (which the Bible itself leaves without explicit comment) and portrays the king as exemplifying the familiar tragic pattern in which good fortune evokes hubris that in turn leads to doom; see Feldman 1998: 531. Likewise Pseudo-Philo rounds off the story of the Nob massacre with an appendix of his own in which God pronounces judgment first on the people for their failure to show due outrage over the priests' deaths (*Bib. Ant.* 63.3) and then on the informant Doeg (whose tongue will be attacked by a fiery worm, 63.4), the whole being rounded off with a summary source notice for Saul's deeds (63.5).

[937] Josephus here echoes his mention of Saul's "sparing neither infants, nor those of any other age" in 6.260.

[938] Neither the Bible nor Josephus himself makes previous mention of the presence also of "prophets" at Nob. Josephus' introduction of these figures here might reflect his ascription of "prophetic" activity to the priest Ahimelech (and to the priesthood in general); see note to "prophets" at 6.268.

[939] This (non-biblical) description of Nob's God-given status as the sole legitimate sanctuary accentuates the wrongfulness of Saul's deed.

This gives everyone [the opportunity] of learning about and discerning the ways of humans: **263.** as long as they are private, humble citizens, incapable of exercising their [true] nature or daring to do as they wish, such persons are gentle and moderate; pursuing only what is just, they devote all their loyalty and solicitude to this. As for the Deity, they are convinced that he is present to everything that happens in life, and not only sees the deeds that are done, but already knows the thoughts themselves from which those deeds will [flow].[940] **264.** When, however, they attain to authority and dynastic power,[941] they set all these things aside. Taking off, like masks on a stage,[942] these habits and manners, they put on audacity, insanity, contempt of things human and divine.[943] **265.** And now, when piety and justice are especially needed by them who are most exposed to envy with their thoughts and actions manifest to all, then it is that they—as though God no longer saw them[944] or as if he were anxious before their authority—act without restraint.[945] **266.** What they hear, they fear; or they either willingly hate or cherish irrationally.[946] To them these things seem certain and confirmed, and likewise true and pleasing to both humans and to God, while to the future they give no thought.[947] **267.** [Initially], they honor those who have put themselves out in many ways for them, but having honored them, they then envy them.[948] Having incited them to [gain] renown, they deprive those who had attained it, not only of this, but even, because of it, of life itself,[949] doing so for vile reasons that are unbelievable in their exaggerations.[950] They do not punish deeds worthy of judgment, but rather on the basis of slanders and unexamined accusations.[951] They kill, not those who ought to suffer thus, but whomever they can.

268. Now Saoul,[952] the son of Keis, who was the first to rule as king over the

---

[940] This description of the ways of the mere "private citizen" recalls Josephus' portrayal of Saul's own exemplary modesty and reticence prior to his accession; see 6.59, 63.

[941] Greek: δυναστεία. This is Josephus' only use of this term in *Antiquities* 1-11; he employs it with some frequency of rulership—both Jewish and Gentile—in the post-biblical period.

[942] Josephus inserts a Hellenistic touch into his reflections with this use of the term προσωπεῖον ("actor's mask") drawn from the language of the Greek theater. This is his only employment of the term in *Antiquities*; elsewhere, he uses it twice (*War* 1.471; 4.156).

[943] With this reference to the double "contempt" exhibited by those who have gained power, Josephus underscores the contrast with the earlier ways of such people, who in 6.263 are described as acting appropriately in their relations both with fellow humans and with God.

[944] This illusion on the part of the powerful contrasts with their earlier faithfulness to God, motivated by their awareness that he knows not only deeds but thoughts; see 6.263.

[945] Such lack of "restraint" by the powerful is the reverse of their earlier "moderation" (6.263).

[946] As Marcus (*ad loc.*) points out, the text appears defective at this point.

[947] The allusion here is, of course, to Saul's taking

Doeg's insinuations about Ahimelech's support of the renegade David at face value. The mention of the "fear" of the powerful at what they hear echoes Josephus' attribution of Saul's refusal to entertain Ahimelech's protestations of innocence to his "terrible fear" in 6.259.

[948] This "envy language" echoes that introduced by Josephus in 6.265, intimating that "envy" is the powerful's decisive motivation in their dealings with their intimates—as was the case between Saul and David.

[949] This is precisely what Saul tried to do with David, whom he removed from his position as his armor-bearer and sent out to face death at the hands of the Philistines; see 6.195.

[950] This allusion to the mendacious reports that prompt people like Saul to deal with those closest to them as they do picks up on the mention of the powerful's giving unwarranted credence to what they "hear" in 6.266.

[951] The 2 components of this general statement about the ways of the powerful have in view Saul's dealings with Doeg and Ahimelech, respectively.

[952] After the intervening, generalizing reflections on the ways of the powerful in 6.263-267, Josephus now returns to his opening focus on Saul himself (6.262), portraying him as an egregious example of everything he has been saying in the interval.

Hebrews after the aristocracy and the constitution of the Judges,[953] made this clear by his killing 300 priests and prophets[954] because of his mistrust of Abimelech.[955] He likewise overthrew their city and took pains to make what was, as it were, their sanctuary[956] bereft of priests and prophets. He did this by doing away with so many of them and by not permitting even their ancestral [home] to remain for others who would come after them.[957]

(12.8) 269. But Abiathar, the son of Abimelech—who alone of the priestly family that was murdered by Saoul was able to escape—fled to David[958] and disclosed the misfortune of his household and his father's elimination.[959] **270.** [David], for his part, said that he was not unaware that these things would happen to them when he saw Doeg. For he suspected that the high priest would be slandered to the king by him.[960] He blamed himself for this disaster of theirs.[961] He asked him nonetheless to remain there and dwell with him, since in no other place would he be so concealed.[962]

David welcomes Abiathar

(13.1) 271. At this time David heard that the Palestinoi were advancing against the country of the Killanians[963] and plundering it.[964] He undertook to campaign against them, having inquired of God, through the prophet,[965] whether he would award him victory.[966] When he [the prophet] stated that God so indicated,[967] he

David defends Keilah (Killa) against Philistines

---

[953] This allusion to the constitutional change that occurred with Saul following the preceding period of the aristocracy/the Judges harks back to 6.84-85, where Josephus pauses to call attention to a series of such changes that took place over the course of Israel's earlier history.

[954] This combination echoes the reference to Nob as the "ancestral home and nurse of priests and prophets" in 6.262. Josephus rounds off the figure of 305 for those slain given in 6.260.

[955] Cf. Josephus' interjected remark (6.259) on Ahimelech's failure to convince Saul who, due to his fear, did not believe the former's self-defense.

[956] Neither the Bible nor Josephus himself speaks of an actual, physical "sanctuary/temple" at Nob. Given the city's status as the residence of priests and prophets one might, however, call the site a virtual sanctuary, as Josephus does here.

[957] The qualification of Nob as the priests and prophets' "ancestral [home]" here echoes the same phrase at the start of Josephus' reflection in 6.262. The remark about Saul's precluding the city from serving as such a site in the future recalls Josephus' inserted notice about his "burning" Nob in 6.260.

[958] After the long reflective interlude inserted by him in 6.262-268, Josephus now resumes the biblical story line with a recapitulation of his notice on Abiathar's escape of 6.261 (// 1 Sam 22:20).

[959] In 1 Sam 22:21 Abiathar attributes the killing of the priests directly and explicitly to Saul.

[960] See 1 Sam 22:22a. The verb "to slander" (Greek: διαβάλλω), used by David of Doeg's report to Saul here (the Bible speaks more blandly of his "telling" the king), echoes Josephus reflection in 6.267, where he

speaks of the powerful punishing on the basis of "slanders" (Greek: διαβολαί) that they hear. See also Jonathan's urging David not to heed "slanderers" (Greek: οἱ διαβάλλοντες) in 6.224.

[961] See David's confession as cited in 1 Sam 22:22b: "I have occasioned the death of all the persons of your father's house."

[962] From David's concluding word to Abiathar in 1 Sam 22:23 Josephus omits his MT statement: "he that seeks my life seeks your life."

[963] 1 Sam 23:1 mentions the name of the threatened city, rather than its people, i.e. "Keilah." On Josephus' version of 1 Samuel 23, see Begg 1998b.

[964] Josephus omits—for the moment—the further precision of 1 Sam 23:1 that the Philistine attack was directed against the site's "threshing floors." He will, however, use this item subsequently; see 6.272.

[965] Josephus introduces this figure as the medium of David's "inquiring of the Lord" (1 Sam 23:2) in line with his overall tendency to insert references to "prophets" and "prophesying" where the Bible itself lacks such; compare his replacement of biblical mentions of Ahimelech's "inquiring of the Lord" for David (1 Sam 22:10, 15) with statements about the priest's "prophesying" in 6.254, 257. As in 6.249, David's prophet remains anonymous.

[966] In 1 Sam 23:2 David's question reads: "Shall I go and attack these Philistines?"

[967] 1 Sam 23:2-4 features a double inquiry by David and (positive) response by God (vv.2, 4) with an admission of fear by David's men intervening (v.3). Josephus limits inquiry and response to a single one, likewise eliminating the confession by David's troops that does not reflect well on the courage of his compatriots—es-

marched out against the Palestinoi with his companions; he perpetrated a great slaughter and carried off plunder.[968]

Saul's move against David fails

272. He stayed on with the Killanians until, once they had fearlessly secured their threshing floors and crops,[969] King Saoul was informed that he was among them.[970] For his deed and achievement did not remain [confined to] those among whom it occurred. Instead, a general rumor was disseminated to the hearing of others and reached the king's ears, this praising the deed and the one who had done it.[971]

273. Saoul rejoiced to hear that David was in Killa.[972] He said: "God has now delivered him into my hands since he has compelled him to enter a city having walls, gates and bars."[973] He ordered all the people to march out against Killa and, once they had besieged and taken it by storm, to kill David.[974]

274. David, however, got wind of these things;[975] once he learned from God that if he remained among them the Killanians would hand him over to Saoul,[976] he took along the 400[977] and went away from the city to the desert situated above [the site] called Engedon.[978] The king, hearing that he had fled from the Killanians, ceased his campaign against him.[979]

Final Jonathan–David encounter

(13.2) 275. David set out from there and came to a certain place called "Kaine" [New] of Ziphene.[980] There Ionathes, the son of Saoul, met him; embracing him, he appealed to him[981] to have good hopes for the future and not be discouraged by his

---

pecially since David has already received the divine commission to proceed against the Philistines.

[968] Josephus reverses the order of the slaughter and plunder notices in 1 Sam 23:5a, likewise generalizing the source's "cattle" into "plunder." Like MT, he has no equivalent to the LXX plus mentioning the Philistines' "flight before" David.

[969] These indications concerning the duration of David's stay bring together the notice on his delivery of Keilah (1 Sam 23:5b) and the mention of the "threshing floors" from 23:1 (see note to "plundering it" at 6.271). Josephus leaves aside the reference to Abiathar's coming to David at Keilah with ephod in hand of 23:6, since in his version of the sequels Abiathar and his device have no part to play.

[970] See 1 Sam 23:7a.

[971] Josephus appends this explanation of how it was that also Saul heard of David's exploit (1 Sam 23:7a), while likewise underscoring its noteworthy character.

[972] Josephus interjects this reference to Saul's emotional response to what he hears (1 Sam 23:7b).

[973] Josephus' rendering of Saul's statement in 1 Sam 23:7b adds mention of Keilah's "walls."

[974] To Saul's command to his forces in 1 Sam 23:8 Josephus appends the directive that they are to kill David. Thereby, he accentuates the tension surrounding David's fate at this juncture.

[975] See 1 Sam 23:9a.

[976] Josephus here reduces the biblical account of 1 Sam 23:9-12 with its double consultation of the Lord by David, using Abiathar and his ephod (see 23:6), and the corresponding divine responses (so MT LXX L;

LXX B has only a single inquiry and reply by God) to its core content, i.e. God's informing David that the Keillians will surrender him to Saul (// MT LXX L 23:12; compare LXX B 23:11, where David's single question is whether the town will be "closed," God answering that it will be). In Josephus' rendering of 1 Samuel 23 the figure of Abiathar thus disappears completely, with God taking the initiative himself in warning David about the inhabitants' intentions here in 6.274.

[977] This figure for David's men corresponds to that given in LXX 1 Sam 23:13 (as well as in 6.247// 1 Sam 22:2); MT has 600.

[978] This designation for the site to which David repairs after leaving Keilah replaces the plethora of topographical indications (themselves varying from one textual witness to another) of 1 Sam 23:(13aβ)14a (RSV= MT: "in the strongholds in the wilderness, in the hill country of the Wilderness of Ziph"). Josephus apparently derives his own site name from 1 Sam 24:1 (MT; Eng. 23:29 // 6.282), where David takes up residence in the "strongholds (MT; LXX passes) of Engedi."

[979] See 1 Sam 23:13b. Josephus leaves aside the subsequent, seemingly discordant notice of 23:14b: "And Saul sought him every day, but God did not give him into his hand."

[980] Josephus' designation for David's next stopping place reflects that of LXX 1 Sam 23:15, where MT's form בחרשה (RSV: "at Horesh") seems to have been misread as בחדשה and so rendered "the New."

[981] Compare the obscure phrase of 1 Sam 23:16b:

present situation,[982] for he was to rule as king and would have the entire force of the Hebrews under him.[983] Such things, however, usually required great exertions.[984] **276.** He once again[985] swore to lifelong loyalty and mutual fidelity and called on God to witness [the curses] that he invoked upon himself should he transgress the agreements and turn them into their opposite.[986] He left him there, a little relieved of his worry and anxiety, while he himself returned to his own home.[987]

277. But the Ziphenes curried favor with Saoul by informing him that David was residing among them and by saying they would hand him over to him, should he come against him.[988] For if the Ziphene passes were occupied, he would not be [able] to flee to others.[989] **278.** The king, for his part, commended them, declaring his gratitude for their having informed him about his enemy. Promising them that the reward of their loyalty would not be long in coming,[990] he then sent men to seek for David and to comb the desert. He himself, he said, would follow them.[991]

Ziphites report David's presence to Saul

279. Thus they incited the king to the pursuit and arrest of David,[992] being solicitous not only to inform him of the enemy, but also to provide him with an even more evident proof [of their loyalty to him],[993] by delivering him into his authority.[994] But they failed in their unjust and vile desire.[995] **280.** For, whereas they would have run no risk by not revealing these things to Saoul, in their obsequiousness and expectation of gain from the king they slandered[996] and promised to turn over a man

---

Jonathan "strengthened his [David's] hand in God."

[982] Josephus expatiates on Jonathan's opening exhortation of 1 Sam 23:17: "Fear not."

[983] This announcement corresponds to the 2nd ("you shall be king over Israel") of the 4 predictions/assurances Jonathan offers David in 1 Sam 23:17.

[984] This concluding reminder by Jonathan replaces the remaining assurances delivered by him in 1 Sam 23:17: "the hand of Saul... shall not find you... I shall be next to you; Saul my father also knows this." Josephus' omission of Jonathan's statement about his having 2nd place to David once the latter becomes king (see previous note) perhaps reflects the consideration that this, in fact, constitutes a "false prophecy" in that Jonathan was to die simultaneously with his father and so never attained the position alongside David of which he speaks here.

[985] Josephus' insertion of this phrase represents a cross reference to the earlier sworn agreements between the friends as recorded by him in 6.241 (// 1 Sam 20:42).

[986] These concluding words of Jonathan to David replace the mention of the pair's "making a covenant before the Lord" in 1 Sam 23:18a.

[987] See 1 Sam 23:18b into which Josephus inserts an allusion to the emotional impact of Jonathan's words upon David. Thereby, he underscores the former's status as an effective speaker.

[988] 1 Sam 23:19 narrates the Ziphites' report in neutral terms. Via his reference to their "currying favor" with Saul, Josephus interjects a criticism of the Ziphites' motivations that he will amplify in what follows.

[989] Josephus appends this claim to the Ziphites' report of 1 Sam 23:19-20, thereby providing a ground for their confidence that they will indeed be able to apprehend David—as they assert they will in 23:20b. In reproducing the Ziphites' report Josephus leaves aside most of the various geographical indications concerning the current whereabouts of both Saul and David given in 23:19.

[990] Compare the opening words of Saul's response in 1 Sam 23:21: "May you be blessed by the Lord; for you have had compassion on me." Josephus' wording eliminates the notion of God as the rewarder of evil-minded informants—such as he represents the Ziphites to be.

[991] In the line of the shorter LXX B text of 1 Sam 23:22-23, Josephus drastically compresses the string of directives issued the Ziphites by Saul regarding David and announcements by him of what he himself intends to do found in MT LXX L.

[992] Compare 1 Sam 23:24a, which speaks of the Ziphites going to Ziph "ahead of Saul."

[993] This phrase is missing in the codices RO. Unlike Niese, Marcus reads the words without brackets.

[994] These remarks pick up on the reference to the Ziphites' "currying favor" with Saul of 6.277.

[995] This parenthetical remark within Josephus' extended appended critique of the Ziphites' actions (6.279-280) foreshadows David's frustrating of their schemes.

[996] This term picks up on the "slander language" introduced by Josephus in 6.244, 267, 270.

David's narrow
escape

who was beloved by God[997] and whose death was being unjustly sought, when they could have concealed him. For David, having found out about the malice of the Ziphenes and the king's approach,[998] left the passes of their country and fled to a great rock situated in the desert of Simon.[999]

(13.3) 281. Saoul marched out to pursue him there; for as he was underway, he learned that David had withdrawn from the passes; therefore he went off to another part of the rock.[1000] But just as David was on the point of being caught, those who had heard that the Palestinoi were again campaigning against the Hebrews' country caused Saoul to desist from his pursuit.[1001] For he turned back against them as his natural enemies, judging it more urgent to resist them than, in his solicitude to take his personal enemy, to disregard the devastation of his country.[1002]

Saul enters Da-
vid's hiding
place

(13.4) 282. Thus unexpectedly escaping danger, David came to the passes[1003] of Engedene.[1004] Certain people came to Saoul after he had driven out the Palestinoi, reporting that David was residing inside the boundaries of Engedene.[1005]

283. Taking 3,000[1006] picked troops, Saoul pressed after him. When he was not far from the place,[1007] he saw from the road a deep, hallow cave, of great size in both length and breadth.[1008] It happened that David had hidden inside with his 400 men.[1009] Saoul, being compelled by what is in accordance with nature,[1010] entered it

---

[997] Josephus' other uses of this accolade (Greek: θεοφιλής) are in *War* 1.331 (= *Ant.* 14.455, of Herod in the popular estimation); *Ant.* 1.106 (the antedeluvians); 1.346 (Isaac); 8.49, 190 (Solomon); 9.182 (Elisha); 10.215 (Daniel's companions), 264 (Daniel himself); and 14.22 (the high priest Onias).

[998] Josephus expatiates on the mention of David's "being told" in 1 Sam 23:25aβ with a final jab at the Ziphites and their reprehensible motives. Conversely, he leaves aside the complicated (and textually variable) indications concerning David's initial place of refuge in the preceding 23:24b.

[999] According to 1 Sam 23:25bα the "rock" to which David escapes was situated in the "desert of Maon" (MT; LXX B Maan; LXX L τῇ Ἐπηκόῳ, i.e. "[the desert of] Hearing"). Josephus' site name (Greek: Σίμωνος ἔρημος) likely reflects a form that figures among the topographical indications concerning David's flight in 23:24b (earlier passed over by him), i.e. הישׁימון (MT; Eng.: "Jeshimon");Ἰεσσαιμού (LXX B; LXX L renders with the same form it employs in 23:25b; see above). For further discussion, see Begg 1998b: 39, n. 72.

[1000] See 1 Sam 23:25bβ-26a, where Saul pursues David around "the mountain." Josephus brings this indication into line with his previous mention (6.280// 23:25bα) of a "rock" as David's place of refuge. His inserted reference to the "passes" from which David "withdraws" echoes the mention of these in 6.277, 280.

[1001] See 1 Sam 23:26b-27, which quotes (v. 27) the words of the messenger who reports the Philistine incursion to Saul.

[1002] Josephus expands the mention of Saul's return (1 Sam 23:28a) with a reference to his motivation in re-

turning. As Feldman (1998: 518) points out, the addition accentuates Saul's magnanimity and patriotism. Conversely, he leaves aside the etiological notice of 23:28b: "therefore that place was called the Rock of Escape."

[1003] Like LXX 1 Sam 24:1 (Eng. 23:29), Josephus speaks of "passes" rather than the "strongholds" of MT.

[1004] MT (1 Sam 24:2= Eng. 1 Sam 24:1) עין־גדי (Eng.: "Engedi"); LXX B Ἐνγάδδει; LXX L Γαδδί. Josephus uses the adjective form Ἐνγεδηνή (whose nominal counterpart, i.e. Ἐνγεδών, he anticipated in 6.274; see note to "Engedon" at 6.274). On Josephus' version of 1 Samuel 24, see Begg 1998c.

[1005] In 1 Sam 24:2 (MT; Eng. 24:1) Saul is informed as "he returned from following the Philistines."

[1006] This is the figure for Saul's forces given by both MT and LXX 1 Sam 24:3a.

[1007] Josephus leaves aside the topographical particulars of 1 Sam 24:3b-4aα: "in front of the Wildgoats Rocks... to the sheepfold (MT; LXX: sheepflocks) by the way...."

[1008] Josephus expatiates on the size of the cave (compare 1 Sam 24:4aα) that needs to be so large in order to hold David and his 400 men, as will be mentioned in what follows.

[1009] Josephus anticipates this notice from 1 Sam 24:4b, where it follows, as a kind of afterthought, the mention of Saul's entry into the cave (24:4aβ). He likewise specifies the number of those with David in the cave, drawing the figure from 6.274 (= 1 Sam 23:13 LXX).

[1010] This is Josephus' version of the euphemism of 1 Sam 24:4aβ, where MT speaks of the king's "cover-

alone,[1011] where he was observed by one of those with David.[1012]

284. David was told by the one who observed him[1013] that he had a God-given chance[1014] to avenge himself on his enemy; he further counseled him to cut off his head and thus deliver himself from his many wanderings and afflictions.[1015] Rising up, David only removed the fringe of the garment Saoul was wearing,[1016] but immediately had a change of mind:[1017] "It is not just," he said, "to murder one's own master, nor the one found worthy of kingship by God.[1018] For even if he is vile towards us, I should not be the same to him."[1019]

David refuses to kill Saul

285. When Saoul left the cave, David advanced and cried out, requesting Saoul to hear [him].[1020] Once the king turned round, he paid him homage, falling on his face, as the custom was,[1021] and said: "One ought not, O king, lend an ear to vile people and liars who fabricate slanders, nor show them favor by believing those [slanders], while holding one's best friends in suspicion.[1022] Rather, one should seek to discern the dispositions of everyone from their actions.[1023] **286.** For while slander deceives, things done are a manifestation of genuine loyalty. A word has a double character; it can be either true or false, but deeds make a person's mind open to be seen.[1024] **287.** Know therefore from these things that I am well-disposed towards you

David–Saul exchange

---

ing his feet" and LXX of his "preparing himself."

[1011] With this inserted indication Josephus makes explicit what is presupposed in the biblical account, i.e. Saul's (3,000, 1 Sam 24:3) troops did not go into the cave with him, thereby leaving the king defenseless before David and his men.

[1012] This notice has no biblical counterpart. It constitutes the presupposition for the suggestion made to David by his men regarding Saul in 1 Sam 24:5a.

[1013] In 1 Sam 24:5a it is David's men as a group who make the suggestion to him. Josephus attributes the proposal to the one man who, in his presentation (see 6.283) actually witnesses Saul's entry.

[1014] In the proposal made by David's men in 1 Sam 24:5a reference is made to a previous divine word to David, promising to give his enemy into his hand so that he might do as he wished with him. Given that such a word has not been cited beforehand, Josephus turns the quotation of what God had (purportedly) said to David earlier into an allusion to the "God-given chance" Saul's appearance in the cave represents for him.

[1015] Josephus' conclusion to the man's proposal as to what David ought to do with Saul is quite different from the divine word quoted by David's men in 1 Sam 24:5a (see previous note). The phrase "cut off his head" used by the Josephan speaker is the same one employed of David's dispatch of Goliath in 6.190 (// 1 Sam 17:51): David is being urged to do with Saul exactly what he had done with his (and Israel's) arch-enemy.

[1016] See 1 Sam 24:5b.

[1017] This is Josephus' equivalent for the phrase of 1 Sam 24:6a: "David's heart smote him."

[1018] These designations for King Saul replace the phrase "the Lord's anointed" of 1 Sam 24:7b that

Josephus tends to avoid.

[1019] This reflection, motivating David's previous statement about the wrongfulness of assaulting the king, substitutes for David's closing words in 1 Sam 24:7b with their use of "messiah terminology": "... seeing he is the Lord's anointed." The substitution introduces the contrast between Saul's and David's ways of dealing with each other, which is a marked feature of both 1 Samuel 24 and Josephus' version. Josephus leaves aside the attached notice of 24:8a concerning David's restraining his men from attacking Saul by his words.

[1020] See 1 Sam 24:8b-9a. In his explicit mention of Saul's leaving the cave, Josephus agrees with MT LXX L 1 Sam 24:8b against LXX B, which lacks the item.

[1021] See 1 Sam 24:9b, to which Josephus adds the reference to David's gesture before Saul being in accordance "with custom."

[1022] Josephus here begins his greatly expanded version of David's opening word to Saul in 1 Sam 24:10 ("why do you listen to the words of men who say, 'Behold, David seeks your hurt'?"), likewise turning the Bible's question into an admonition about what Saul should not do. The term "slander" harks back to Josephus' reflection on Saul's career in 6.262-268.

[1023] This positive alternative to the wrongful course of action against which David warns Saul in what precedes is part of Josephus' elaboration of David's opening word in 1 Sam 24:10.

[1024] These appended reflections serve to explain the wrongfulness of the first course of action spoken of by David in 6.285 (i.e. listening to purveyors of slander) and the appropriateness of the 2nd (i.e. focusing on persons' actions).

and your house, and that you ought to believe me and not those who maliciously accuse me of things I never thought to do nor ever could have done. Those ones seek my life; day and night they have no other thought than of my elimination that you are unjustly pursuing.[1025] **288.** For how could that opinion you entertain about me, namely that I wish to kill you, not be false? Or how are you not impious towards God when you are so desirous of making an end of and supposing to be your enemy a man who, though capable of punishing today and executing judgment on you, did not wish to do so or make use of an opportunity, which, if it had presented itself to you against me, you yourself would not have passed up?[1026] **289.** For when I cut off the fringe of you garment, I was then also able [to cut off] your head." Then displaying the piece for him to see, David conferred credibility [on his words]. "I, however," he said, "refrained from just vengeance, whereas you did not hesitate to nourish unjust hatred against me.[1027] May God judge these things and examine the ways of each of us."[1028]

290. Saoul marveled at his unexpected safety; astonished at the youth's moderation and nature,[1029] he groaned.[1030] Once David had done the same,[1031] Saoul replied that it was just of him to sigh. "For you indeed," he said, "have been a source of good things for me, but I of misfortunes for you.[1032] You have shown yourself today to possess the justice[1033] of the ancients[1034] who instructed those who took enemies in the desert to save them.[1035] **291.** I am now convinced that God is guarding the

---

[1025] In this final part of his elaboration of David's word in 1 Sam 24:10, Josephus has David draw practical conclusions for the case at hand from the general reflections developed by him in 6.285-286.

[1026] The above series of reproachful questions represents Josephus' expansion of David's opening, single query to Saul in 1 Sam 24:10: "Why do you listen to the words of men who say 'Behold, David seeks your hurt'?"

[1027] After his preceding elaboration of David's opening reproachful question of 1 Sam 24:10, Josephus now presents a condensed version of David's words informing Saul of how he has just refrained from killing him in 1 Sam 24:11-12, leaving aside, e.g., the quotation of his earlier words to his men (24:11b= 24:7). Conversely, with the phrase "I was able [to cut off] your head," he introduces a reminiscence of the proposal made to David by his companion in 6.284.

[1028] This conclusion to David's speech conflates his double appeal for divine vindication found in 1 Sam 24:13a and 16. Josephus leaves aside the intervening source segment 24:13b-15, where David twice avers that his own hand will not be against Saul (v. 13b, 14b), quotes a ancient proverb about wickedness emanating from the wicked (v. 14a), and points up, using the imagery of a "dead dog" and a flea, just how little of a threat he poses to Saul (v. 15). On the possible reasons for Josephus' omission of this segment, see Begg 1998c: 464, n. 77.

[1029] This indication concerning the emotional impact of David's words upon Saul take the place of

Saul's—seemingly otiose—question to David once the latter has finished speaking in 1 Sam 24:17a: "Is this your voice, my son David?" The replacement accentuates the positive image of David developed throughout Josephus' version of 1 Samuel 24.

[1030] Compare 1 Sam 24:17b: "And Saul lifted up his voice and wept."

[1031] 1 Samuel 24 says nothing about David joining in Saul's lamentation. This is one among a number of such items that Josephus interjects into his version of 1 Samuel 24 so as to accentuate the positive—here his capacity for sympathy, even with a dangerous adversary—image of David; see note to "nature" at 6.290.

[1032] See 1 Sam 24:18b: "... you have repaid me with good, whereas I have repaid you with evil." The moral contrast between the 2 men, previously developed by David (6.284, 288, 289), is now picked up by Saul himself.

[1033] Compare the opening of Saul's address to David in 1 Sam 24:18a: "you are more righteous than I."

[1034] The term "ancients" does not figure in Saul's own address in 1 Sam 24:18-22. Josephus may have found inspiration for its use here in 24:14, where David cites "a proverb of the ancients."

[1035] Leaving aside Saul's reminiscence of David's words to him of 1 Sam 24:11-12 in 24:19, Josephus directly connects the "justice of the ancients" (cf. 24:18a and see note to "justice of the ancients" at 6.290), which the king ascribes to David, with his rendition of 24:20a. In that rendition he turns into a pre-kingship for you and that domination over all the Hebrews awaits you.[1036] Give me, though, sworn pledges that you will not wipe out my family, nor, from resentment against me, annihilate my descendants, but will preserve and save my house."[1037] Having sworn as requested, David dismissed Saoul to his own kingdom,[1038] while he himself went up to the pass of Masthera along with those with him.[1039]

(13.5) 292. At this time Samouel the prophet died, a man who enjoyed extraordinary honor among the Hebrews.[1040] For the mourning over him which the people carried on for a long time manifested both his virtue and the crowd's loyalty to him, as did also the pomp and attention surrounding his burial and the fulfillment of the customary rites.[1041] 293. For they buried him in his ancestral city, Armetha[1042] and wept over him for many days, not suffering through this together as if at the death of an alien, but each mourning as though it were a member of his own family.[1043] 294. By nature he was a just and kind[1044] man, and therefore especially a friend of God.[1045] He ruled and presided over the people alone for twelve years after the death of Helei the high priest, and then for an additional eighteen years together with King Saoul.[1046] Thus did Samouel's life end.[1047]

(13.6) 295. Now there was a certain man of the Ziphenes[1048] from the city of

Samuel's death

Nabal and Abigail introduced

scription laid down by the ancients concerning the treatment to be accorded one encountered in the desert (which David has followed in Saul's own case, thereby manifesting his righteousness) the statement (so LXX) or rhetorical question expecting a negative answer (so MT) of 1 Sam 24:20a about what one would do with the "enemy" one encounters. He leaves aside 24:20b, where Saul invokes the Lord's recompense for David's treatment of him (MT; in LXX the Lord's rewarding the one who treats his enemy in the way portrayed in 24:20a is announced for the future).

[1036] See 1 Sam 24:21. Saul's acknowledgement here recalls that attributed to Jonathan in his words to David in 6.275 (// 1 Sam 23:17): "He [David] was to reign as king and have the entire force of the Hebrews under him." David's coming rule has now been affirmed by both son and father.

[1037] See 1 Sam 24:22. Josephus inserts the reference to David's (presumed) "resentment," the effects of which Saul is trying to preclude by getting David to swear not to harm his family.

[1038] In 1 Sam 24:23a Saul, once David has sworn, returns home on his own initiative. Josephus' reformulation depicts David as already now exercising that kingly role with regard to Saul that the latter had just recognized (6.291) will one day be given him by God.

[1039] Josephus' indication concerning the destination of David and his men clearly reflects that of LXX 1 Sam 24:23b: "to the pass of Messera" (MT: "to the stronghold").

[1040] Josephus appends this mention of the people's regard for Samuel to the notice of his death that he derives from 1 Sam 25:1a. He likewise inserts, as he does repeatedly throughout his presentation, the title "prophet" for Samuel. On Josephus' version of 1 Samuel

25, see Begg 1996f.

[1041] Josephus markedly embellishes the summary notices on Samuel's being "mourned" (so MT; LXX B: they beat their breasts for him; LXX L: they beat their breasts for him and mourned for him) and "buried" in 1 Sam 25:1b.

[1042] MT (1 Sam 25:1bα) הרמה(ב) (Eng.: "in Rama"); LXX Ἀρμαθάιμ; Josephus Ἀρμεθᾶ (Marcus [ad loc.] reads Ἀρμαθᾶ with MSP). Josephus mentions "Armatha" as the hometown of Samuel's father in Ant. 5.342.

[1043] Josephus appends the reference to the "weeping" for Samuel and its character to the notice on his burial of 1 Sam 25:1bα. The addition establishes an implicit connection between Samuel and Moses, who likewise is wept over at his death (see Ant. 4.323// Deut 34:8).

[1044] This qualification of Samuel as "kind" (Greek: χρηστός) in Josephus' (inserted) epithet recalls his earlier characterization of him as a "kind (Greek: χρηστός) and gentle father" in 6.92.

[1045] Josephus uses this same designation (Greek: φίλος τοῦ θεοῦ) for Gideon in Ant. 5.213.

[1046] Neither of these chronological indications on Samuel's tenure has a biblical basis. Josephus reiterates the 2nd of them in connection with his closing notices for Saul in 6.378.

[1047] Josephus' extended epithet for Samuel in 6.294 takes the place of the closing words of 1 Sam 25:1, which mention David's going "to the wilderness of Paran" (MT; LXX B: of Maan; LXX L: τὴν Ἐπήκοον)."

[1048] 1 Samuel 25 does not use this qualification for Nabal, David's antagonist. Josephus may have been inspired to apply the term to him given that the context (see 1 Sam 23:19 and 26:1) features the Ziphites as David's opponents.

Emman[1049] who was rich and possessed much livestock, having a flock of 3,000 sheep, and 1,000 goats.[1050] David instructed those who were with him to keep these [animals] unharmed and unimpaired and not to inflict injury on them either out of desire or hunger, or given their ability to conceal themselves in the desert. Rather, they should regard the avoidance of wrongdoing to anyone as more important than any of these things; they were to consider it as something terrible and repugnant to God to steal what belonged to others.

296. David taught them these things,[1051] supposing that he was dealing with a good man and one worthy of this care of his.[1052] Nabal,[1053] however—for that was his name—was a harsh and vile man who conformed his manner of life to Cynic practice.[1054] He had, nonetheless, a good and prudent wife of desirable appearance.[1055]

David rebuffed by Nabal

297. David therefore sent ten of the men who were with him to this Nabal at the time when he was shearing his sheep. Through them, he greeted him and joined in his prayer that he might continue doing this for many years.[1056] He likewise appealed to him to award him what he could from what he had, once he had learned from his shepherds that they had done them no wrong, but were guarding them and their flocks over the long time they had already spent in the desert.[1057] He would not have a change of mind about awarding something to David.[1058]

298. Those who had been sent to Nabal carried out their instructions, but he received them very inhumanely and harshly.[1059] He questioned them about who David

---

[1049] This place name is likely a corruption of the form "Maan" cited by LXX B 1 Sam 25:2 (MT reads "Maon") as Nabal's place of residence; see Begg 1996f: 8, n. 11. Josephus makes no mention of the other site associated with Nabal in 25:2, i.e. "Carmel," perhaps taking this to be, not the Judean town of that name (see Josh 15:55; 1 Sam 30:29)—which would fit the southern geographical context of the materials surrounding 1 Samuel 25—, but rather the (better-known) northern Carmel—a supposition that would entail a whole other setting for the Nabal story.

[1050] These figures correspond to those given for Nabal's 2 types of livestock in 1 Sam 25:2bα.

[1051] The Josephan David's lengthy "instruction" to his men in 6.295 has no counterpart in 1 Samuel 25. It accentuates both David's personal sense of justice and his concern to transmit this to his associates.

[1052] This motivation for David's preceding instructions to his men lacks a biblical basis. It serves to highlight the true character of Nabal as Josephus will go on to describe this as just the opposite of what David supposes it to be.

[1053] Josephus uses the declined form (Greek: Νάβαλος) of the name as read by MT and LXX, i.e. "Nabal."

[1054] Josephus' characterization of Nabal as a (proto) Cynic (Greek: ἐκ κυνικῆς ἀσκήσεως) picks up on the LXX's (mis-) translation (i.e. κυνικός) of the Hebrew gentilic found in the *qere* of MT 1 Sam 25:3b (כלבי, "Calebite," deriving from the proper name "Caleb,"

meaning "dog"; compare the *ketiv*, כלבו, "as his heart"). This is Josephus' only use of the word "Cynic." In 25:3 the characterization of Nabal follows that of his wife; Josephus reverses this sequence, thereby keeping together the data concerning Nabal that in 1 Samuel 25 are "interrupted" by the notice on Abigail of v. 3aββα.

[1055] Unlike 1 Sam 25:3, Josephus reserves mention of the woman's name, i.e. "Abigail," until a later point; see 6.301. To the listing of her intellectual and physical attributes in 25:3bα, Josephus appends a moral one, i.e. her being "good."

[1056] Josephus here combines the notices of 1 Sam 25:4 (David learns of Nabal's sheep-shearing) and 5-6 (his dispatch of 10 men with their words of greeting to the shearers), embellishing the latter item.

[1057] Josephus here reverses the sequence of 1 Sam 25:7-8, where it is only at the very end of his message that David formulates his request for a contribution from Nabal (v. 8b), this after he has expatiated on his services to Nabal's shepherds (v. 7), to which they will themselves attest.

[1058] This concluding assurance, providing an additional motive for Nabal to respond favorably to David's request, has no parallel in the message entrusted by him to his 10 messengers in 1 Sam 25:6-8.

[1059] Compare LXX 1 Sam 25:9b, where Nabal, in response to the messengers' words, "leaps up" (MT: and then they [the messengers] waited). Josephus' remark on the nature of his "reception" serves to prepare the ungracious words of Nabal that follow.

was and when he heard that he was the son of Jesse,[1060] he said: "Nowadays run-away slaves think highly of themselves and pride themselves on leaving their masters."[1061]

299. When they related this, David was wrathful[1062] and directed 400 armed men to follow him, while[1063] leaving behind 200 to guard the baggage[1064]—for by this point he had 600 men.[1065] He marched against Nabal, having sworn to wipe out his household and all his possessions that very night.[1066] For he was irate,[1067] not only because he had been ungracious to them, offering nothing in return for the much humanity shown him, but also because he had reviled and spoken abusively to them, even though he had in no way been grieved by them.[1068]

David sets out against Nabal

(13.7) 300. However, a certain slave, one of those guarding the sheep of Nabal, recounted to his own mistress, Nabal' wife, that when David sent to her husband, he did not obtain any sort of moderation, but had even been reviled with terrible defamations,[1069] although he had shown them every care and guarded their flocks.[1070] He further said that this would be a [source of] calamity for both his master and herself.[1071]

Abigail (Abigaia) goes to David

301. When he had stated these things, Abigaia[1072]—for that was her name[1073]—saddled her donkeys on which she loaded provisions of all sorts,[1074] and saying nothing to her husband—for he was unconscious from drink[1075]—went to David. As she

---

[1060] Compare Nabal's double opening question in 1 Sam 25:10a: "Who is David? Who is the son of Jesse?"

[1061] Josephus interjects a contemptuous allusion to the state of mind of the runaway servants into his version of Nabal's reply in 1 Sam 25:10b. He omits Nabal's attached rhetorical question about bestowing his provisions on such people, 25:11.

[1062] Josephus appends mention of David's emotional response to the report brought him as recounted in 1 Sam 25:12.

[1063] See 1 Sam 25:13abα. Josephus' rendition aligns itself with the shorter text of LXX B as against MT and LXX L.

[1064] See 1 Sam 25:13bβ.

[1065] Josephus' appendix to the indications concerning the 2 groups of David's men, these totaling 600, calls attention to the increase in David's forces, beyond the figure last mentioned by him in 6.283, i.e. 400 (// LXX 1 Sam 23:13; MT has 600 already here).

[1066] Josephus here anticipates the statement of intention parenthetically attributed to David in 1 Sam 25:22, long after he has begun his advance against Nabal in 25:13. From David's words in 25:22, Josephus eliminates (as he regularly does) its opening oath formula, just as he passes over the vulgar expression (literally: "all who piss against the wall") used there.

[1067] This allusion to David's emotional state picks up on the mention of his being "wrathful" at the opening of 6.299.

[1068] Also here (see note to "night" at 6.299), Josephus anticipates David's displaced statement of intention, in particular his expression of outrage at Nabal's

failure to requite his own benefits in kind, 1 Sam 25:21. He further amplifies David's affirmation with a reference to Nabal's having insulted his inoffensive messengers (see 6.298).

[1069] Josephus expatiates on the servant's report of Nabal's offense as cited in 1 Sam 25:14: "he railed at [MT; LXX: turned away from] them."

[1070] Josephus gives a shortened version of the informant's lengthy report to Abigail of all that David's men had done for Nabal's shepherds, 1 Sam 25:15-16. Its language echoes that used in David's own message to Nabal in 6.297.

[1071] See 1 Sam 25:17, from which Josephus omits the servant's exhortation that Abigail "consider what she should do" and his concluding statement that Nabal is "so ill-natured that one cannot speak with him."

[1072] MT (1 Sam 25:3) אֲבִיגַיִל (Eng.: "Abigail"); LXX B Ἀβειγαία; LXX L and Josephus Ἀβιγαία.

[1073] Josephus here for the first time, at the moment when she begins assuming an active role in the story, gives the name of Nabal's wife (which 1 Samuel 25 had cited already in v. 3).

[1074] Josephus generalizes the extended catalogue of assorted foodstuffs taken with her by Abigail in 1 Sam 25:18.

[1075] Anticipating the reference to Abigail's finding Nabal "drunk" on her return in 1 Sam 25:36, Josephus cites his condition as the reason for Abigail's not telling him of her departure (25:19b). He leaves aside her words to the young men of 25:19a: "go on before me; behold I come after you." In Josephus' presentation then, it appears that Abigail goes forth unaccompanied

descended the passes of the mountain, she met David with his 400 men coming against Nabal.[1076]

Abigail–David exchange

302. Observing him, the woman leapt down,[1077] fell on her face, and payed him homage.[1078] She asked him not to remember the words of Nabal [for she was not ignorant][1079] that he was like his name (since in the Hebrew language "Nabal" means "folly").[1080] As for herself, she apologized for not having observed those sent by him.[1081] **303.** "But now," she said, "pardon me and thank God,[1082] who has prevented your defiling yourself with human blood;[1083] for, as long as you remain clean of that, he will secure justice against those who are vile.[1084] May these calamities that are to happen to Nabal fall upon the heads of your enemies as well.[1085]

304. Be benevolent to me, judging me worthy of your accepting these things from me,[1086] and forego your fury and wrath against my husband and his household in my honor.[1087] For it is fitting that you, especially since you are to reign as king, be mild and humane."[1088]

305. He accepted her gifts[1089] and said: "The benevolent God has brought you,

---

to meet David, this highlighting the woman's fearlessness.

[1076] See 1 Sam 25:20, to which Josephus, recalling 6.299 (// 1 Sam 25:13), adds the figure (400) for those accompanying David. Thereby he accentuates the contrast between the solitary woman Abigail—he passed over the reference to the young men who precede her of 25:19a (see previous note))—and the large group of hostile men she encounters. Having already incorporated the statement of David's intentions cited parenthetically in 25:21-22 in 6.299 (see notes there), he will move directly from Abigail's encountering David (// 25:20) to her submissive gestures towards him (// 25:23).

[1077] Josephus' verb (Greek: καταπηδάω) is the same one used by LXX B 1 Sam 25:23; MT and LXX L employ a blander term, i.e. "she alighted."

[1078] See 1 Sam 25:23-24aα.

[1079] These words are absent from ROELat; they are bracketed by Niese, but not by Marcus.

[1080] In Josephus' rendition Abigail, leaving aside her opening confession of guilt and appeal for a hearing by David (1 Sam 25:24), begins immediately with the mention of her offending husband from 25:25a. Josephus supplies the meaning of his Hebrew name (of which the more precise rendering would be "fool"). Throughout, he notably rearranges the sequence of Abigail's words.

[1081] See 1 Sam 25:25b, where Abigail simply mentions the fact of her not having seen David's men; Josephus has her "apologize" for this failure on her part.

[1082] Josephus derives Abigail's plea for forgiveness from 1 Sam 25:28a, adding to this her exhortation that David "thank God."

[1083] Josephus draws this reference to God's restraining David from bloodshed from 1 Sam 25:26a (whose opening oath formula he omits).

[1084] This assurance might be seen as Josephus' compressed version of Abigail's (highly figurative) promises of what the Lord will do for David, should he refrain from evil in 1 Sam 25:28b-29.

[1085] See 1 Sam 25:26b.

[1086] See 1 Sam 25:27; Josephus' rendering shifts the focus from David's acceptance of her "gifts" to his favorable response to the giver of those gifts, Abigail herself.

[1087] This appeal lacks a biblical equivalent. It continues to focus attention on David's acting for Abigail's sake; see previous note.

[1088] Greek: φιλάνθρωπος. This adjective echoes the negative adverb ἀπανθρώπως ("inhumanely") used of Nabal's reception of David's delegation in 6.298, as well as the allusion to Nabal's having been shown "much humanity" (Greek: φιλανθρωπία) by David's men in 6.299. Abigail's concluding statement here has no direct equivalent in the words of her biblical counterpart (although it might be seen as a transposition into a positive key of her negative reference to David's not having to regret his shedding of blood and taking of vengeance in 1 Sam 25:31a). It does, however, incorporate her allusion to God's appointing David "prince over Israel" in 25:30b. Josephus leaves aside Abigail's closing plea (25:31b) that David "remember" her in the future.

The Josephan Abigail's final statement about what it is "fitting" (Greek: πρέπω) for David to do as designated king has a certain counterpart in the word addressed by John of Gischala to Titus in *War* 4.102, where he avers that it would be "fitting" (Greek: πρέπω) for the Roman commander to preserve not only the lives, but also the laws of those for whom is appealing.

[1089] See 1 Sam 25:35a. Josephus rearranges the biblical sequence in which David first addresses Abigail at

woman, to us today;[1090] for otherwise you would not have seen the coming day because I swore to exterminate the house of Nabal this very night and to leave alive none of you [associated with] that man who was vile and ungrateful to me and my companions.[1091] But now you have forestalled me and placated my rage, due to God's concern for you.[1092] But even though Nabal now avoids punishment because of you, he will not escape judgment; his own behavior will exterminate him, taking another pretext."[1093]

(13.8) 306. When he said these things, David dismissed the woman.[1094] When she came to her house and encountered her husband feasting along with many[1095] and already senseless,[1096] she did not, at the time, reveal anything of what had happened.[1097] But the next day when he was sober she disclosed everything to him.[1098] At this, he grew weak, his whole body rendered lifeless by her words and his grief over these.[1099] Not surviving more than ten days, Nabal ended his life.[1100]

Death of Nabal

307. When he heard of his death, David said that he had been well avenged by God who had killed Nabal due to his own vileness and given judgment for him whose right hand remained clean.[1101] He then also realized that those who are vile are afflicted by God who overlooks nothing of human affairs, repaying the good in kind, but bringing quick requital upon the vile.[1102]

308. Sending to Nabal's wife, [David] called her to himself to live with him in marriage.[1103] She said to those who came to her that she was unworthy to touch his feet;[1104] nevertheless, she went, together with all her attendants.[1105] Thus she lived with him as his wife, receiving this honor both because of her prudent and just

---

length (25:32-34), then takes what she has brought (25:35a), and finally resumes his speaking to her (25:35b).

[1090] See 1 Sam 25:32, where David begins his response by "blessing the Lord." David's characterization of God as "benevolent" (Greek εὐμενής) here echoes Abigail's plea that David be "benevolent" (εὐμενής) to her in 6.304.

[1091] See 1 Sam 25:34. Just as he did in the case of David's initial statement of his intentions in 6.299 (// 25:21), so here in 6.305 Josephus rewords the vulgar expression "those who piss against the wall." In addition, he appends a characterization of Nabal, reminiscent of that used in 6.299, which serves to justify David's intended severity towards him and his household.

[1092] This statement synthesizes David's acknowledgement (1 Sam 25:32-34) of the role of both the Lord and Abigail in preventing him from acting on his murderous intentions.

[1093] This announcement, in which David appears in the role of a (true) prophet of Nabal's imminent demise, takes the place of his concluding assurance that he has "heard" Abigail's appeal (1 Sam 25:35b).

[1094] 1 Sam 25:35aβ quotes David's words to her: "go up in peace to your house."

[1095] 1 Sam 25:36a represents Nabal feasting "like a king."

[1096] 1 Sam 25:36bα speaks of Nabal's heart being

"merry within him" and of his being "very drunk." Josephus has already anticipated this notice in 6.301, prior to Abigail's setting out; see note to "drink" at 6.302.

[1097] See 1 Sam 25:36bβ.

[1098] See 1 Sam 25:37a.

[1099] Compare 1 Sam 25:37b: "his heart died within him and he became as a stone."

[1100] From the notice of 1 Sam 25:38 on Nabal's dying 10 days after Abigail's report to him, Josephus eliminates the theological indication about the Lord's "smiting him."

[1101] See 1 Sam 25:39a.

[1102] This "lesson" learned by David from Nabal's fate has no counterpart in 1 Samuel 25. As often, Josephus appends an explicit moral to the biblical story, this reminding readers of the overarching purpose of his work as set out in *Ant.* 1.20.

[1103] See 1 Sam 25:39b-40.

[1104] Josephus eliminates the reference to Abigail's "prostration" before David's messengers in 1 Sam 25:41a, while also modifying her verbal response in 25:41b, where she speaks of herself as one whose task it would be to wash the feet of David's servants. In his version it is a question of her (not) "touching" David's own feet.

[1105] In 1 Sam 25:42abα (the circumstantiality of which Josephus reduces), Abigail is accompanied by "five maidens."

manner, but also obtaining it due to her beauty.[1106] **309.** Now David had an earlier wife, whom he had married, from the city of Abisar.[1107] Her father gave Melca,[1108] the daughter of King Saoul, who had been David's wife,[1109] in marriage to Pelti,[1110] the son of Lis,[1111] from the city of Gethla.[1112]

David approaches Saul's camp

(13.9) 310. After these things some of the Ziphenes came to Saoul[1113] and reported that David was back in their country and that they could arrest him if he were willing to cooperate with them.[1114] He set out with 3,000 troops against him[1115] and, once night came on,[1116] pitched camp at a certain place called Sikella.[1117] **311.** When David heard that Saoul was coming against him, he sent spies, directing them to disclose to him where in the country Saoul had now advanced.[1118] When they told him that Saoul was spending the night at Sikella,[1119] David, keeping this concealed from his own men,[1120] went to Saoul's camp, with Abisai,[1121] the son of his sister Sarouia,[1122] and Abimelech[1123] the Chettai[1124] accompanying him.[1125]

[1106] To the summary notice on Abigail's marrying David of 1 Sam 25:42bβ Josephus appends a motivation for this event, which picks up his triple characterization of her in 6.296 (// 25:3bα).

[1107] MT 1 Sam 25:43 calls David's earlier wife "Ahinoam (LXX B Ἀχεινάν; LXX L Ἀχιναάμ) of Jezreel (LXX B: Israel)." Josephus' name for the woman's hometown (Greek: Ἀβίσαρος) seems to represent a corrupted conflation of her personal name and that of her city; see Schalit *s.v.* Josephus cites her name as "Achima" in 6.320 (// 1 Sam 27:3).

[1108] MT (1 Sam 25:44) מיכל (Eng.: "Michal"); LXX Μελχόλ; Josephus Μελχά.

[1109] Josephus recounts Saul's marrying of "Michal" to David in 6.204 (// 1 Sam 18:27).

[1110] MT (1 Sam 25:44) פלטי (Eng.: "Palti"); LXX Φαλτί; Josephus Φέλτιος.

[1111] MT (1 Sam 25:44) ליש (Eng.: "Laish"); LXX B Ἀμείς; LXX L Ἰωάς; Josephus Λίσος.

[1112] MT (1 Sam 25:44) גלים (Eng.: "Gallim"); LXX B´ Ρομμά; LXX L Γολιάθ; Josephus Γεθλά (Schalit *s.v.* calls this a form corrupted to the point of irrecognizability). Josephus will relate David's "recovery" of "Michal" in *Ant.* 7.26 (// 2 Sam 3:15-16).

[1113] Josephus leaves aside the specification of 1 Sam 26:1 concerning Saul's current whereabouts, i.e. at "Gibeah" (MT; LXX: "at the hill"). Cf. his like omission in 6.282 (// 1 Sam 23:19), where the Ziphites make their initial report to Saul. On Josephus' version of 1 Samuel 26, see Begg 1997i.

[1114] Josephus gives a more straightforward content to the Ziphites' message, which in 1 Sam 26:1b consists of a rhetorical question concerning David's current hiding place, this featuring several (textually variable) place names: "on the hill of Hachilah, which is on the east of Jeshimon" (RSV).

[1115] See 1 Sam 26:2, from which Josephus eliminates the double reference to "the wilderness of Ziph" as the theater of operations.

[1116] Josephus anticipates this temporal indication from 1 Sam 26:7a, where David and Abishai approach Saul's encampment "by night."

[1117] According to 1 Sam 26:3, Saul encamped at the same spot where the Ziphites had reported David to be, i.e. "on the hill of Hachilah (LXX Ἐχελά)... on the east of Jeshimon." Josephus apparently derives his name for the king's campsite, i.e. "Sikella" from the LXX L reading in 1 Sam 26:4, where David learns that Saul had come "after him to Segelag"; see Marcus *ad loc.* (Alternatively, Schalit *s.v.* suggests that the original form here was Χίκελλα, this corresponding to the "Hachilah" of MT 26:3).

[1118] See 1 Sam 26:3b-4a, to which Josephus appends mention of the purpose of David's dispatching the spies.

[1119] Josephus' reading here reflects that of LXX L 1 Sam 26:4b (already anticipated by him in 6.310): "he learned that Saul had come after him to Sekelag." MT reads "he learned of a certainty that Saul had come," LXX B "he learned that Saul had come well-prepared from Keila."

[1120] This phrase appears to reflect LXX's specification in 1 Sam 26:5a that David rose "secretly" and went to Saul's camp.

[1121] MT (1 Sam 26:6) אבישי (Eng.: "Abishai"); LXX Ἀβεσσά; Josephus Ἀβισαῖος.

[1122] MT (1 Sam 26:6) צרויה (Eng.: "Zeruiah"); LXX and Josephus Σαρουία. Josephus leaves aside the further specification of Abishai as "brother of Joab" given in 26:6.

[1123] MT (1 Sam 26:6) אחימלך (Eng.: "Ahimelech"); LXX B´ Ἀβειμέλεχ; LXX L Ἀχιμέλεχ; Josephus Ἀβιμέλεχος. Josephus' name-form thus corresponds to that of LXX B against MT LXX L; compare the similar case of his name for the priest of Nob in 6.242.

[1124] MT (1 Sam 26:6) החתי (Eng.: "the Hittite"); LXX and Josephus ὁ Χετταῖος.

[1125] Josephus anticipates (and reverses the sequence

312. Saoul was sleeping, with his troops and his general Abenner lying around *David spares*
him in a circle.[1126] Upon entering the royal camp, David neither himself did away *Saul*
with Saoul—whose sleeping place he recognized from his spear (for this was stuck
in the ground beside him)[1127]—nor did he allow Abisai, who in his desire to murder
him rushed ahead for this purpose, to do so.[1128] Saying that it was a terrible thing to
kill the king who had been appointed by God even if he were vile,[1129] since in time
judgment would come upon him from the one who had given him rule,[1130] he
blocked his assault.[1131]

313. Nevertheless, as a proof that, though he could have killed him he had re- *David accuses*
frained from doing so, David took from Saoul the spear and the water jar that was *Abner*
lying beside him.[1132] He made his exit, unnoticed by any of all those lying asleep in
the camp, having safely perpetrated everything that he did to the king's men in virtue of the opportunity given him and his own daring.[1133] **314.** Once he crossed the
stream[1134] and ascended the top of the hill from which he would be audible,[1135]
David shouted to the soldiers of Saoul and his general Abenner; he woke them from
sleep and cried to the people as well.[1136] Once the general was listening and questioned who was calling him,[1137] David said: **315.** "It is I, the son of Jesse, who am
in flight from you.[1138] But why are you, sir, who are so great and have the first [place

---

of) the names of David's 2 companions from 1 Sam
26:6, where after David, seemingly alone, has approached Saul's camp (26:5), they suddenly appear and
are addressed by him. He thereby makes clear that the
2 were with him from the start; accordingly, he passes
over the actual dialogue of 26:6, in which David asks
who will accompany him to the camp and Abishai replies that he will do so. Moreover, in contrast to 26:7,
Josephus has not only Abishai, but also Ahimelech, go
with David to Saul's camp.

[1126] See 1 Sam 26:5. Josephus has no equivalent to
the (textually varying) specification as to where Saul
was sleeping of 26:5bα: "within the encampment" (MT)
vs. "in a chariot" (LXX).

[1127] See 1 Sam 26:7. Josephus' rendering highlights
the figure of David, who both "recognizes" the king
from his spear and refrains from harming him personally. Conversely, he leaves aside the repetitious (see
26:5// 6.312a) mention of the presence of Abner and
the army around Saul of 26:7bβ.

[1128] Josephus compresses the sequence of 1 Sam
26:8-9a, omitting the actual words of Abishai, declaring that God has handed Saul over to David and confidently volunteering to dispatch the king himself (v. 8).

[1129] David's affirmation here replaces the rhetorical
question attributed to him in 1 Sam 26:9b: "... who can
put forth his hand to the Lord's anointed and be guilt-
less?," likewise eliminating its "loaded" term "anointed." The allusion to Saul as "vile" (Greek: πονηρός) by
David here echoes his qualification of him with the
same term in 6.284.

[1130] In 1 Sam 26:10 David presents 3 different sce-
narios as to what might happen to Saul: "... the Lord
will smite (LXX B: correct) him; or his day shall come

to die; or he shall go down into battle and perish (LXX
B: be added)." Josephus' David limits his remarks to
the first of these eventualities, thereby intimating that
whatever befalls Saul will be God's doing.

[1131] This notice, echoing the earlier mention of
David's "not allowing" Abishai to assault Saul, replaces David's closing statement, emphatically refusing
to do violence to the "Lord's anointed" of 1 Sam
26:11a.

[1132] See 1 Sam 26:12a, to which Josephus adds a
motivation for David's taking of the items. He leaves
aside David's command (26:11b) to Abishai to "take"
the 2 objects, given that in 26:12a it is David himself
who ends up carrying them off.

[1133] Josephus' highlighting of David's daring replaces the statement of 1 Sam 26:12b about the divine
origin of the "deep sleep" that befell Saul's men and
kept them unaware of what was going on around them.

[1134] The description of David's movements in 1 Sam
26:13 does not mention such a stream; it speaks rather
of the "great space" between him and Saul's camp that
resulted from those movements.

[1135] Josephus appends this indication concerning
the purpose behind David's ascending the hill (see 1
Sam 26:13).

[1136] From 1 Sam 26:14 Josephus omits David's
opening query: "Will you not answer, Abner?," while
inserting reference to his waking Saul's whole force.

[1137] Josephus' rendition of Abner's question stands
closest to its form in LXX L 1 Sam 26:14b: "who are
you, the one calling me, who are you?" Compare MT
("who are you that calls the king?") and LXX B ("who
are you, the one who is calling?").

[1138] David's self-identification in response to Ab-of] honor beside the king, so careless in guarding the person of your master?[1139] Is sleep more agreeable to you than his safety and care?[1140] For this is a matter worthy of the death penalty that a little while ago some men entered into your camp, [going to] the king and all the others without your being aware of it.[1141] Search now for the king's spear and water jug and you will learn how great a calamity there was within [the camp], though concealed from you."[1142]

Final Saul–David exchange

316. But Saoul, when he recognized the voice of David[1143] and learned that though he had found him exposed due to sleep and the carelessness of the guards, he had not killed but spared him, when he might justly have done away with him,[1144] said that he was grateful to him for his safety[1145] and appealed to him to take courage and, without further fear of suffering something terrible from him, to return to his own house.[1146] **317.** For he was convinced that he did not love himself as much as he was cherished by him,[1147] given that he [Saoul] had expelled one who could have watched over him and who had provided many proofs of his loyalty, just as he had for so long a time compelled him to be a fugitive and, out of terror for his life, to live deprived of friends and relatives.[1148] He, nevertheless, had not ceased to be saved by him, repeatedly receiving his life back when this was clearly [marked for] annihilation.[1149]

318. At this, David directed him to send someone to take back the spear and water jar,[1150] further saying "God will be the arbitrator of the personal nature of each of us and of the [deeds] done in accordance with this.[1151] He knows that I, though able to kill you on the present day, refrained."[1152]

---

ner's question about who is calling him (6.314) takes the place of his odd opening counter-question in 1 Sam 26:15aα: "Are you not a man?"

[1139] See 1 Sam 26:15aββα. Josephus' rendering underscores both Abner's exalted status and his egregious failure to fulfill the responsibilities this entails.

[1140] This sarcastic question is Josephus' addition to David's words to Abner in 1 Sam 26:15-16.

[1141] Josephus compresses (and rearranges) the sequence of David's words in 1 Sam 26:15bβ-16abα, where he first informs Abner of the penetration of Saul's camp (v. 15bβ), then affirms that Abner's behavior was not "good" (v. 16aα), and finally avers that, given his failure to "to watch over... the Lord's anointed," Abner is deserving of death (v. 16aβbα). For the 3rd time in his version of 1 Samuel 26, Josephus eliminates a source use of the term "anointed."

[1142] To David's call to Abner to look for the 2 objects in question (1 Sam 26:16bβ), Josephus appends a indication of what this (vain) search is designed to disclose to him.

[1143] See 1 Sam 26:17aα.

[1144] This extended notice on what Saul now "realizes" concerning David takes the place of Saul's—seemingly superfluous—question whether the voice he has heard is that of David (1 Sam 26:17aβ) and David's lengthy response (26:17b-20) with its mixture of affirmations of innocence, reproaches, and appeals to the Lord.

[1145] This initial expression of gratitude by Saul, flowing out of the "realization" attributed to him in what precedes, has no biblical counterpart. The inserted mention of it by Josephus serves to accentuate the king's capacity for magnanimity.

[1146] Josephus reverses the order of Saul's command and attached motivation of 1 Sam 26:21aβ ("return... for I will no more do you harm").

[1147] Cf. Saul's acknowledgement in 1 Sam 26:21bα: "... my life was precious in your eyes this day."

[1148] Josephus has Saul spell out in detail the nature of the "wrong" and his "erring exceedingly" that he confesses with regard to David in 1 Sam 26:21.

[1149] This concluding statement, picking up on Saul's acknowledgement of David's solicitude for him of 6.317, represents a further elaboration of the king's words in 1 Sam 26:21bα: "... my life was precious in your eyes this day." It serves to accentuate the contrast between the 2 men's dealings with each other that Josephus develops throughout his version of Saul's discourse to David (6.316-317).

[1150] In 1 Sam 26:22 David mentions only the retrieval of Saul's spear. In Josephus he does not forget the other object taken by him in 6.313 (// 26:12).

[1151] Compare David's earlier statement to Saul in 6.289 (// 1 Sam 24:13a, 16): "May God judge these things and examine the ways of each of us."

[1152] See 1 Sam 26:23, from which Josephus yet again (see note to "of it" at 6.315) eliminates a men-

(13.10) 319. Saoul, now that he had escaped David's hands a second time, retired to his palace and his own [land].[1153] David, however, fearing that if he remained
there he would be arrested by Saoul, judged it expedient to go down[1154] to Palestine[1155] and live in it.[1156] Together with the 600[1157] who were around him, he went to
Anchous,[1158] king of Gitta[1159] (this is one of the five [Philistine] cities).[1160] **320.** The
king received him with his men and gave them a place to live.[1161] He also had with
him his two wives, Achima[1162] and Abigaia,[1163] and dwelt in Gitta. Saoul heard of
these things, but no longer thought of sending or going against him himself. For
already twice, as he was intent on arresting him, he had been in imminent danger
from him.[1164]

321. To David, however, it did not seem good to remain in the city of the
Gittoi.[1165] Instead, he asked their king, seeing that he had received him humanely,
to do him also this favor of giving him a certain place in his country for a residence.[1166] For he was ashamed of being burdensome and troublesome to him by living in the city.[1167]

322. Anchous gave him a certain village called Sekella[1168] that David so liked that

*David settles in
Gath (Gitta)*

*King Achish
(Anchus) gives
Ziklag (Sekella)
to David*

---

tion of the "Lord's anointed." He likewise leaves aside
David's appended prayer for God's protection (26:24),
as well as Saul's response with its "benediction" of
David and prediction of the great future that awaits him
(26:25a); compare his omission of David's earlier words
to Saul in 26:17b-20. In both instances, Josephus' compression of the 2 parties' words might be influenced by
the consideration that much the same ground has already been covered in the earlier scene between them
as related in 6.283-291 (// 1 Samuel 24).

[1153] 1 Sam 26:25b mentions David's "return" (this
duplicating the notice on his movements of 27:1) before that of Saul, and has the latter going "to his place"
(so MT LXX L; LXX B: on his way). Josephus eliminates the duplication of the biblical notices on David's
moves subsequent to his encounter with Saul.

[1154] This translation follows the conjecture of Niese
(καταβάς), inspired by Lat's *descendere* and adopted
by Marcus *ad loc.* The codices have ἀναβάς ("going
up").

[1155] MT 1 Sam 27:1a refers to "the land of the Philistines," LXX BL to "the land of the aliens (Greek:
ἀλλόφυλοι)."

[1156] See 1 Sam 27:1a. Josephus interjects the reference to David's "fear," while leaving aside his reflections of 27:1b concerning Saul's giving up his pursuit
of him and his own escape. On Josephus' version of 1
Samuel 27, see Begg 1997j.

[1157] This figure corresponds to that of MT LXX L 1
Sam 27:2; LXX B has 400. The figure harks back to
Josephus' statement (6.299) about David having as-
sembled 600 men by the time of his confrontation with
Nabal.

[1158] MT (1 Sam 27:2) אכיש (Eng.: "Achish"); LXX
B Ἀγχοῦς; LXX L Ἀκχοῦς; Josephus Ἀγχοῦς. He
omits the name of Achish's father (MT: Maoch).

[1159] Surprisingly, neither the Bible nor Josephus
makes reference at this juncture to David's earlier abortive approach to this same "Achish, king of Gath" as
related in 1 Sam 21:11-16 (// 6.245-246).

[1160] This inserted notation identifies "Gitta" (Gath)
as one of the 5 member cities of the Philistine
Pentapolis; see 1 Sam 6:17, cf. 6.20.

[1161] Mention of this "award" by the king is Josephus' replacement for the notice of 1 Sam 27:3a
that the "households" of David's men also settled in
Gath.

[1162] MT (1 Sam 27:3) אחינעם (Eng.: "Ahinoam");
LXX B Ἀχεινάαμ; LXX L Ἀχινάαμ; Josephus Ἀχιμά
(this is the reading of RO, which Niese and Marcus follow; Schalit *s.v.* reads Ἀχινά in line with Lat's
Achinam). Earlier (see 6.309; compare 1 Sam 25:44)
Josephus referred to this first wife of David as being
"from the city of Abisar," without naming her. Here, he
leaves aside her gentilic, i.e. "the Iezreelitess."

[1163] Josephus leaves aside the attached source indications concerning Abigail, i.e. her being a "Car-
melitess" and Nabal's widow. On David's marriage to
Abigail, see 6.308.

[1164] Josephus supplies a reason for Saul's failure, as
cited in 1 Sam 27:4, to pursue David further at this
point.

[1165] Josephus inserts a reference to David's state of
mind as he makes his request of Achish (1 Sam 27:5).

[1166] See 1 Sam 27:5a.

[1167] Josephus turns David's allusive, rhetorical question of 1 Sam 27:5b ("why should you servant dwell in
the royal city with you?") into a more straightforward
declaration on his part.

[1168] MT (1 Sam 27:6) צקלג (Eng.: "Ziklag"); LXX B
Σεκελάκ; LXX L Σεκελάγ; Josephus Σέκελλα (thus Niese
and Marcus; Schalit *s.v.* prefers the form Σίκελλα read

once he became king, he treated it as his personal property, as did his sons as well[1169] (we shall have something to say about these matters in another place).[1170] The time David lived in Sekella in Palestine was four months and twenty days.[1171]

David's raids

323. Secretly coming against the neighbors of the Palestinoi,[1172] the Serrites, and the Amalekites,[1173] he plundered their country; after taking much spoil in the form of livestock and camels, he returned.[1174] He refrained [from taking captive] the human inhabitants, out of anxiety that they would testify against him to King Anchous,[1175] to whom he sent a part of the plunder as a gift.[1176] **324.** When the king inquired whom he had attacked so as to lead away this plunder,[1177] he said that it was those situated south of the Judeans and living in the plain,[1178] and persuaded Anchous to think this. For he hoped that David hated his own nation and that he would have a slave in him as long as he lived settled among his [subjects].[1179]

Philistines muster against Israel

(14.1) 325. At this same time the Palestinoi, having decided to campaign against

---

by P and suggests that this form might reflect that of LXX A in 1 Sam 30:14). "Sekella/Sikella" was mentioned as Saul's earlier camping place in 6.310, 311.

[1169] Cf. 1 Sam 27:6b: "therefore Ziklag has belonged to the kings of Judah to this day." Josephus' reformulation reflects the fact that by his own time there had been no "kings of Judah" for centuries.

[1170] In fact, Josephus never does return to the subject, as Marcus (*ad loc.*) points out. For other instances of the historian's announcing that he will subsequently treat a given subject, but then failing to do so, see Begg 1997j: 6, n. 33.

[1171] Josephus' chronological indication does not fully agree with that of either MT ("a year [literally days] and four months") or LXX ("four months") 1 Sam 27:7. It might, however, be seen as an attempt to specify the indeterminate plus "days and" of MT, taken in its literal sense.

[1172] Josephus' opening, general reference to the "targets" of David's incursions corresponds to the LXX L plus at the start of 1 Sam 27:8: "(David and his men set forth) against everyone nearby."

[1173] Like LXX B 1 Sam 27:8, Josephus mentions only 2 particular peoples against whom David campaigns, having no equivalent to the "Girzites" which stands 2nd in the 3-member list of MT (LXX L reads "the Iezraite" at this point). Whereas his 2nd name, i.e. the Amalekites, corresponds to the 2nd designation in LXX B (and the 3rd of MT LXX L), his initial name, i.e. "the "Serrites" diverges from the first name of the various biblical witnesses, i.e. "the Geshurites" (Schalit *s.v.* does, however, see Josephus' form as reflecting the "Gesiri" of LXX B; alternatively, Schlatter *s.v.* traces it back to a Hebrew form השׁרי). Josephus omits the further precisions—which evidence much textual variation—regarding the extent of the territory raided by David given in 27:8b.

[1174] From the list of David's bellicose initiatives in

1 Sam 27:9 Josephus omits his killing of both men and women (which duplicates the notice on the matter of 27:11a), as well as the garments taken by him.

[1175] The translation reflects that of Marcus *ad loc.*, this agreeing with the statement of 1 Sam 27:11a (cf. 27:9) that David did not "leave alive" the inhabitants of the places he raided. As Marcus notes, however, the verb used by Josephus here (Greek: ἀπείχετο) could also mean "he spared." On this alternative understanding, Josephus would be contradicting the biblical notice, thereby depicting David as a more merciful figure. On the other hand, it remains difficult to see how David's sparing the inhabitants would further his goal of keeping them from reporting his raids to the king; see further Rappaport 1930: 50 #206. In any case, Josephus leaves aside the statement of 27:11b that David's killing the peoples he raided was his standard practice throughout his time in Philistia.

[1176] This item has no parallel in 1 Samuel 27. It underscores David's attempt to ingratiate himself with (and repay) his benefactor Achish. The addition is perhaps inspired by the notice of 1 Sam 30:26-31 (// 6.357) about David's dispatching spoil from his subsequent Amalekite campaign to the elders of various Judean cities.

[1177] Josephus provides a motivation (i.e. his seeing the plunder given him by David) for Achish's question about the targets of David's raids that in 1 Sam 27:10 itself lacks such motivation. The motivation, in turn, harks back to Josephus' previous insertion concerning David's sharing the plunder he had acquired with the king.

[1178] Josephus substitutes these general indications concerning the sites of David's incursions for the more specific localizations given in 1 Sam 27:10b (MT: the Negeb of Judah, the Negeb of the Jerahmeelites, the Negeb of the Kenites).

[1179] See 1 Sam 27:12.

the Israelites, sent round to all their allies[1180] [telling them] that they were to come to them for war at Rega,[1181] from which place, once they were mustered, they would march out against the Hebrews. Anchous, the king of Gitta, then directed David to join him as an ally, along with his own troops.[1182] **326.** He eagerly promised to do so, saying that this was his opportunity to repay his benefaction to him and his hospitality.[1183] Anchous, for his part, promised that he would make him his bodyguard following the victory—should the struggles against the enemy go favorably for them. By this promise of honor and trust, he increased David's eagerness still more.[1184]

(14.2) 327. Now it happened[1185] that Saoul, king of the Hebrews, had expelled from the country the mantics and the ventriloquists[1186] and every operative of that sort—except for the prophets.[1187] When he heard that[1188] the Palestinoi were already on hand and had encamped near the city of Soune[1189] in the plain, Saoul marched out against them with his force.

Saul's expulsion of mantics

Saul's response to Philistine invasion

328. Coming to a certain mountain called Gelboue,[1190] he pitched camp over

---

[1180] The cognate terms "ally" (Greek: σύμμαχος), "to be/ act as an ally" (Greek: συμμαχέω), and "alliance" (Greek: συμμαχία) occur a total of 7 times in Josephus' account of David's dismissal by the Philistines (// 1 Sam 28:1-2; 29:1-11) in 6.325-326, 351-355.

[1181] This name for the Philistine mustering site has no equivalent in either MT or LXX 1 Sam 28:1a. Possibly, it reflects the plus of 4QSam^a, i.e. [ה]יזרעל ("at Jezreel"). On this possibility (as well as alternative suggestions regarding the Josephan place name), see Begg 1997j: 10, n. 58.

[1182] See 1 Sam 28:1b.

[1183] Josephus expatiates on David's brief (and ambiguous) reply to Achish in 1 Sam 28:2a ("... you shall know what your servant can do"), stressing his concern to repay Achish's favors.

[1184] Josephus amplifies Achish's promise (1 Sam 28:2b) with mention of its effect on David who, much more so than in the Bible itself, appears enthusiastic about being part of the Philistine undertaking. On Josephus' retouching of the portrait of David in 1 Sam 27:1-28:2 as a way of legitimating his own comparable dealings with and stance towards the Romans, see Begg 1997j: 14-15.

[1185] Josephus omits the notice of 1 Sam 28:3a on the death, mourning for and burial of Samuel, given its duplication of the earlier mention of these same happenings in 25:1, expansively cited by him in 6.292-294. Pseudo-Philo, on the contrary, does reproduce the content of 28:3a within the context of his rendition of 1 Samuel 28 in *Bib. Ant.* 64.1. To this, in turn, he attaches a reflection by Saul who thinks to win himself lasting fame, like that of Samuel, by removing the diviners from the land (28:3b), only to have God pronounce judgment on him for his self-interested action. On Josephus' and Pseudo-Philo's versions of the

"Endor incident" (1 Sam 28:3-25), see Brown 1992: 181-211.

[1186] 1 Sam 28:3b speaks of 2 categories of mantics expelled by Saul: ואבות ואת־הידענים (MT; RSV: "the mediums and the wizards")/ οἱ ἐγγαστρίμυθοι καὶ γνῶσται (LXX: "the ventriloquists and the diviners"). Josephus designates the 2 groups as οἱ μάντεις καὶ οἱ ἐγγαστρίμυθοι ("the mantics and the ventriloquists"); Pseudo-Philo (*Bib. Ant.* 64.1) refers only to "wizards" (Latin: *malefici*). On Josephus' use of the term "mantic" (Greek: μαντίς) and its cognates, (primarily) in reference to pagan "prophets," see Feldman 1990: 416-18. Josephus' use of the term ἐγγαστρίμυθος ("ventriloquist"), drawn by him from LXX 28:3, is limited to his account of the Endor incident, where it occurs 3 times; see 6.327, 329, 330.

[1187] With these appended indications, Josephus generalizes the 2-member biblical list of 1 Sam 28:3b, while also, in view of what follows, making clear that Saul did exempt the prophets from his expulsion measure.

[1188] The reference to Saul's "hearing" of the Philistine move is Josephus' addition to 1 Sam 28:4a; it helps account for the king's counter-move as related in 28:4b.

[1189] MT (1 Sam 28:4) שׁונם (Eng.: "Shunem"); LXX Σωμάν; Josephus Σούνη. Pseudo-Philo does not mention the site of the Philistine camp. On the other hand, he appends a motivation (*Bib. Ant.* 64.2) for their advance, i.e. their thinking to profit from the fact that Israel at this point no longer enjoyed either the spiritual support of Samuel's prayer or the military leadership of David.

[1190] MT (1 Sam 28:4) גלבע (Eng.: "Gilboa"); LXX Γελβούε; Josephus Γελβουέ. Josephus' precision about the site being a "mountain" draws on 1 Sam 31:1.

against the enemy. He was, however, thrown into extraordinary confusion, seeing that the enemy's force was large and, he presumed, superior to his own.[1191] He therefore asked God through the prophets[1192] to tell in advance about the battle and what the outcome would be.[1193]

Saul goes to Endor medium

329. When God, however, did not answer,[1194] Saoul became still more anxious and lost heart, foreseeing an inescapable calamity since the Deity was not present to support him.[1195] He then directed that a woman from among the ventriloquists and those who conjure up the souls of the dead[1196] be sought out for him so that in this way he might know how matters would turn out for him.[1197] **330.** (For this class of ventriloquists bring up the souls of the dead, and through them they foretell what will occur to those who ask.)[1198] When he was informed by one of his servants that such a woman was in the city of Dor,[1199] Saoul, unbeknown to all in the camp,[1200] having laid aside his royal garments,[1201] and taking with him two of his servants whom he knew to be most trustworthy,[1202] went to Dor to the woman.[1203] He appealed to her to act as a mantic[1204] and to bring up for him the soul of whomever he should say.[1205]

Saul persuades medium

331. The woman was reluctant, however, saying that she would not despise the king[1206] who had expelled her class of mantics.[1207] Nor was it right for him, who

---

[1191] Josephus spells out what it is about Saul's seeing of the Philistine army that prompts his "fear" (1 Sam 28:5). In *Bib. Ant.* 64.3 Saul's distress is attributed rather to his consciousness of the death of Samuel and the absence of David.

[1192] 1 Sam 28:6 mentions 3 (legitimate) means used, without result, by Saul in his inquiring of the Lord: dreams, Urim, and prophets. Josephus, like Pseudo-Philo (*Bib. Ant.* 64.3), cites only the last of these (whose availability at this point he has prepared for by his inserted reference to their exemption from Saul's expulsion of the mantics in 6.327; see note to "prophets" at 6.327). He will, however, have Saul also mention "dreams" when recounting his attempted "consultation" to Samuel in 6.334 (// 28:15).

[1193] Josephus spells out the content of Saul's "inquiry of the Lord" as mentioned in 1 Sam 28:6a.

[1194] Cf. 1 Sam 28:6b. In *Bib. Ant.* 64.3 God is not explicitly mentioned; rather, when Saul "seeks" prophets, none "appear to him."

[1195] Josephus inserts this description of the emotional effect of God's silence (1 Sam 28:6b) on Saul.

[1196] Josephus expatiates on the designation used by Saul in 1 Sam 28:7a for the person he has in mind (MT אֵשֶׁת בַּעֲלַת־אוֹב, RSV: "a woman who is a medium"; LXX γυνὴ ἐγγαστρίμυθος), combining LXX's word "ventriloquist(s)," with the specifying phrase "those who conjure up the souls of the dead." In *Bib. Ant.* 64.3 Saul urges the people as a whole (compare 28:7a: his servants) to seek a "diviner" (Latin: *divinus*).

[1197] Josephus appends a specification as to what Saul intends to ask the "medium" whom he commands be sought out for him in 1 Sam 28:7a. Compare *Bib.*

Ant. 64.3, where Saul proposes to the people that they inquire of the "diviner" about "what I [Saul] should plan."

[1198] Josephus interjects this explanatory remark concerning the procedure used by the particular type of "ventriloquist" Saul is seeking.

[1199] MT (1 Sam 28:7) עֵין דּוֹר (Eng.: "En-dor"); LXX B Ἀελδώρ; LXX L Ἀενδώρ; Josephus Δῶρος. Pseudo-Philo (*Bib. Ant.* 64.3) places the diviner about whom Saul is informed by the people at "Endor." He likewise has Saul told that her name is "Sedecla," the daughter of a Midianite diviner who had earlier misled the Israelites (apparently the "Aod" of *Bib. Ant.* 34).

[1200] Josephus interjects this detail about Saul's journey (1 Sam 28:8a).

[1201] In 1 Sam 28:8aα Saul "disguises himself" (MT LXX L; LXX B: covers himself completely) and "puts on other garments." *Bib. Ant.* 64.4 has him "donning ordinary clothing." By contrast, Josephus focusses not on what Saul puts on, but what he takes off.

[1202] Josephus adds the qualification about the reliability of the 2 servants mentioned in 1 Sam 28:8aβ.

[1203] Josephus leaves aside the specification that the threesome's journey took place "by night" found in both 1 Sam 28:8bα and *Bib. Ant.* 64.4.

[1204] Greek: μαντεύομαι. Josephus' one other use of this verb is in *Apion* 1.306, where it has the sense "consult an oracle."

[1205] See 1 Sam 28:8bβ. In *Bib. Ant.* 64.4 Saul immediately commands the woman to bring up Samuel for him.

[1206] Josephus inserts mention both of the woman's hesitancy to do what Saul has just requested and an

had not been wronged by her, to be setting a trap for her to catch her in forbidden things in order that she might be punished.[1208] Saoul, however, swore[1209] that he would make nothing known nor tell anyone of her mantic prediction,[1210] and that she would not be endangered.[1211]

332. Having convinced her by his oaths not to be anxious,[1212] he directed her to bring up the soul of Samouel for him.[1213] Not knowing who Samouel was, she called him from Hades.[1214] When he appeared, the woman, beholding a venerable and god-like[1215] man, was thrown into confusion and alarmed by the vision.[1216] "Are you not," she said, "King Saoul?"—for Samouel had disclosed this to her.[1217]

Samuel brought up

333. When Saoul admitted this and questioned why she was in a state of confusion,[1218] she said that she saw one coming up with a form similar to God.[1219] Once Saoul directed her to describe the appearance and clothing of the one she

---

initial statement of her intention not to act against the king's earlier expulsion measure. In *Bib. Ant.* 64.4 the woman's reply is limited to the declaration: "I fear Saul."

[1207] With this allusion by the woman to Saul's earlier initiative, Josephus picks up on the biblical wording of her response (1 Sam 28:9a), following his inserted preface to this (see previous note).

[1208] Cf. the woman's comparable accusatory question in 1 Sam 28:9b, to which Josephus adds a statement of innocence by the woman that underscores the wrongfulness of Saul's current effort to entrap her.

[1209] Like LXX B 1 Sam 28:10a, Josephus lacks an equivalent to the specification of MT about Saul's swearing "by the Lord" (LXX L: by God). He likewise, in accord with his regular practice, leaves aside the source's oath formula ("as the Lord lives..."). In *Bib. Ant.* 64.4 Saul does not "swear," but simply assures (// 28:10b) the woman that she will not be harmed by Saul "in this matter." To the king's statement Pseudo-Philo further attaches an appendix (*ibid.*), which ends up with Saul weeping to discover that his appearance has so changed that the woman, who—as she informs him—had earlier seen him many times, no longer recognizes him, this being a sign that the "glory of Saul's kingship has passed from him."

[1210] Greek: μαντεία. Compare μάντεις in 6.327 and μαντεύεομαι in 6.330.

[1211] Josephus has Saul expatiate on his promise to the woman of 1 Sam 28:10b that "no punishment shall come upon you for this thing."

[1212] This mention of the effect of Saul's sworn assurance on the woman takes the place of her question to him about whom he wants her to "bring up" in 1 Sam 28:11a.

[1213] Whereas in 1 Sam 28:11b Saul simply asks that Samuel be brought up, Josephus has him specify that it is the latter's "soul" (Greek: ψυχή) he has in mind.

[1214] Neither 1 Samuel 28 nor Pseudo-Philo explicitly mentions the actual "calling up" of Samuel by the woman—as Josephus does here. This is Josephus' only use of the word ᾅδης ("Hades") in *Antiquities*; it occurs 4 times in the *War*: 1.596; 2.156, 165; 3.375. Josephus likewise interjects the indication concerning the woman's ignorance of Samuel.

[1215] Greek: θεοπρεπής. This term is *hapax* in Josephus.

[1216] Josephus inserts the reference to the appearance of Samuel (anticipated by him from 1 Sam 28:14) and its emotional effect upon the woman into the account of her reaction given in 28:12, where she simply "cries out," prior to addressing Saul. In *Bib. Ant.* 64.4, Pseudo-Philo, following his reproduction of the woman's words to Saul from 28:12, has her add that, in her 40 years of raising the dead for the Philistines, she had never beheld a sight like the one she has just brought up.

[1217] Josephus' supplies an "explanation" as to how the woman was able to recognize Saul's identity at this point; see her statement to this effect ("you are Saul") in 1 Sam 28:12b. The explanation, i.e. Samuel's informing her about the matter, takes the place of her preceding reproachful question to Saul ("why have you deceived me?") in the source verse. In *Bib. Ant.* 64.4 it is the woman's seeing Samuel and Saul together that prompts her recognizing the latter.

[1218] Compare 1 Sam 28:13a (// *Bib. Ant.* 64.5), where Saul replies: "Have no fear; what do you see?"

[1219] In both MT and LXX 1 Sam 28:13b the woman uses plural forms in referring to the apparition as "gods" (Tg.: the angel of the Lord). Like the Targum, Josephus eliminates the source's (potentially) polytheistic wording and plays down its attribution of divine status to Samuel's ghost. Compare *Bib. Ant.* 64.5, where the woman states that "his appearance is not that of a man" and then mentions that the figure is being led "by two angels."

beheld and his age,[1220] she indicated that he was an old and distinguished[1221] person, wearing a priestly cloak.[1222]

Saul–Samuel exchange

334. From these [indications] the king recognized that it was Samouel; falling on the ground he greeted him and paid him homage.[1223] But when the soul of Samouel inquired why he had disturbed his rest and forced him to come up,[1224] Saoul lamented his necessity, for the enemy was pressing him hard and he himself was at a loss in the present circumstances, having been abandoned by God and having obtained no prediction—whether through prophets or dreams.[1225] "And therefore I have turned to you as someone who will take care of me."[1226]

335. Samouel, seeing that his [Saoul's] change [of fortune] was now at an end,[1227] said: "it is pointless for you to wish to still learn from me, seeing that God has deserted you.[1228] But hear now that David must rule as king[1229] and be successful in war.[1230] You, however, will lose both your rulership and your life,[1231] **336.** you who disobeyed God in the war against the Amalekites and did not keep his commands, just as I predicted to you while I was still alive.[1232] Know then that the people too will be subjected to the enemy,[1233] and that tomorrow you, having fallen in battle along with your sons, will be with me."[1234]

[1220] Josephus expatiates on Saul's single, general question of 1 Sam 28:14aα (// *Bib. Ant.* 64.5): "what is his appearance?" (MT; LXX what do you recognize?).

[1221] In MT 1 Sam 28:14aβ the woman qualifies the figure as "old," in LXX rather as "erect."

[1222] Josephus' inserted specification of Samuel's "cloak" (1 Sam 28:14aβ) as "priestly" might reflect Samuel's childhood association with the priesthood of Shiloh (see *Ant.* 5.347), as well his own personal priestly interests.

[1223] See 1 Sam 28:14b. Pseudo-Philo (*Bib. Ant.* 64.6) emphasizes that it was Samuel's "mantle" in particular that caught the attention of Saul, who then recalled the incident of the rending of that mantle as described in 1 Sam 15:27.

[1224] See 1 Sam 28:15aα. As in 6.332, Josephus specifies that what is brought up is the "soul" (Greek: ψυχή) of Samuel. Pseudo-Philo (*Bib. Ant.* 64.7) has Samuel follow his initial question (// 1 Sam 28:15aα) with an extra-biblical statement, in which he informs Saul that his current manifestation is to be credited, neither to the king nor to the medium, but rather to an order given him by God prior to his death.

[1225] Josephus closely follows the wording of Saul's response to Samuel in 1 Sam 28:15aβbα. In particular, whereas in 6.328 (see note to "prophets" at 6.328), he, in contrast to 28:6, referred only to Saul's use of "prophets" in attempting to obtain an answer from God, he now, under the influence of 28:15, has the king mention his recourse to "dreams" as well.

[1226] Saul's words to Samuel in 1 Sam 28:15bβ end with him informing the latter that he has summoned him to "tell me what I should do." Pseudo-Philo has no equivalent to Saul's reply in 1 Sam 28:15aβb; in his presentation, Samuel speaks without interruption by

Saul throughout *Bib. Ant.* 64.7-8.

[1227] Josephus inserts the reference to Samuel's perceiving where things stand with Saul.

[1228] In 1 Sam 28:16 Samuel questions why Saul is querying him, seeing that God has "become his enemy" (MT; LXX: has placed himself on the side of your neighbor).

[1229] Josephus leaves aside Samuel's preceding statement in 1 Sam 28:17a, with its reminiscence of his earlier announcement in 1 Sam 15:28, about God's having "torn the kingdom out of your hand."

[1230] This announcement concerning David's coming military achievements is Josephus' addition to Samuel's statement in 1 Sam 28:17b. Pseudo-Philo has no equivalent to the biblical Samuel's declaration about Saul's loss of his kingship to David.

[1231] Josephus anticipates this announcement of Saul's death from Samuel's closing word to him in 1 Sam 28:19aβ.

[1232] To Samuel's reminiscence of Saul's transgression of the divine command concerning Amalek (1 Sam 28:18a), Josephus appends his version of the cross-reference of 28:17a to the former's earlier announcement of the latter's loss of kingship (6.150// 1 Sam 15:28). In Pseudo-Philo (*Bib. Ant.* 64.8) Saul's coming loss of kingship is attributed, not to his disobedience to the divine command about Amalek, but rather to his "envy," i.e. of David.

[1233] Josephus, like Pseudo-Philo (*Bib. Ant.* 64.8), reduces the double notice on the Lord's handing over the Israelite forces to the Philistines of 1 Sam 28:19 to a single one.

[1234] For this concluding announcement by Samuel Josephus seems to draw on the wording of both MT ("tomorrow you and your sons [will be] with me" = *Bib.*

(14.3) 337. When he heard these things, Saoul was rendered speechless by grief[1235] and sank down on the ground, either due to the pain that came upon him from what had been disclosed, or as a result of hunger—for he taken no nourishment the preceding day and night—and lay immobile, like a corpse.[1236]

Distraught Saul made to eat

338. Once he, with difficulty, regained consciousness, the woman joined in pressing him to taste [something], requesting this as a favor from him in exchange for her risky mantic activity, this being something she was not permitted to do because of her fear of him while she was ignorant of who he was, but which she had nevertheless undertaken and accomplished.[1237] In return for this she appealed to him [to permit her] to set a table with food for him, so that, having recovered his strength, he might return safely to his own camp.[1238] She compelled and helped persuade [Saoul], although he resisted and turned away completely in his dejection.[1239] **339.** She had a single tame calf that she had undertaken to look after and feed in her house—for the woman was a day-laborer and had to be satisfied with this as her only possession.[1240] Butchering the calf and preparing the meat, she set this before his servants and him.[1241] During the night Saoul then came to the camp.[1242]

(14.4) 340. It is just, however, to give credit to[1243] the woman for her friendly readiness because, even though she had been prevented by the king from exercising her craft that would had made things better and more abundant for her at home,[1244] and though she had never beheld him before, she did not hold it against him that her lore had been condemned by him. Nor did she turn away from him as

Encomium on medium

Ant. 64.8) and LXX B ("tomorrow you and your sons with you will fall") of 1 Sam 28:19aβ.

[1235] Josephus inserts this reference to Saul's "speechlessness" into the description of his reaction to Samuel's words in 1 Sam 28:20. By contrast, Pseudo-Philo (*Bib. Ant.* 64.9) has him repeat Samuel's announcement about himself and his sons, and affirm "my destruction will be atonement for my sins." Saul then immediately departs (// 1 Sam 28:25b), the whole intervening sequence of 28:20-25a, featuring the woman's ministrations to the king, being left aside.

[1236] Josephus offers a double, alternative explanation for Saul's collapse, the first, i.e. the impact of Samuel's words upon him, peculiar to himself, the 2nd, namely his preceding all-day fast, corresponding to that of 1 Sam 28:20bβ.

[1237] Josephus expatiates on the woman's summary statement in 1 Sam 28:21: "I have taken my life in my hand." On the ambiguity in the woman's word concerning the connection between her "fear" of Saul and her not "recognizing" him, see Marcus *ad loc.*

[1238] See 1 Sam 28:22, where the woman speaks only of Saul's eating the "morsel of bread" she will set before him. Josephus has her allude to a more elaborate repast in view of the hospitality the woman will subsequently offer to her visitors; see 28:24-25a.

[1239] Josephus here compresses the circumstantial account (1 Sam 28:23) of the eventual success of the woman's plea. In particular, he makes no explicit mention of the role of Saul's servants in the proceedings

(although his use of the verb "helped persuade" [Greek: συνπείθω; see also συναναγκάζω ("joined in pressing")] in reference to the woman's initiatives seems to allude to their involvement).

[1240] Josephus expatiates on the summary source reference to the woman's "fatted calf in the house" (1 Sam 28:24a), thereby accentuating her generosity in using this to feed Saul. Brown (1992: 199) suggests that his elaboration has been influenced by Nathan's account of the poor man's beloved "ewe lamb" in 2 Sam 12:3.

[1241] From the account of the woman's measures on behalf of her guests in 1 Sam 28:24aβ-25aα, Josephus leaves aside the notices on her preparing unleavened bread to accompany the calf's flesh.

[1242] This notice on Saul's successful return to the Israelite camp, echoing the woman's plea that he eat and thereby regain the strength to get back to camp (6.338), renders more definite the concluding words of 1 Sam 28:25: "they (Saul and his servants) rose and went away that night."

[1243] Josephus here pauses to interject a 3-paragraph (6.340-342) praise of the woman. On this eulogy and its portrayal of the woman as a (Jewish) exemplar of key Stoic virtues, e.g., *clementia*, *humanitas*, and hospitality, see Brown 1992: 200-203.

[1244] The reference here is to Saul's expulsion of the various classes of mantics, including the "ventriloquists" of whom the woman is one, as described in 6.327 (// 1 Sam 28:3b) that resulted in her loss of livelihood.

a stranger and someone not of her acquaintance.[1245] **341.** Rather, she sympathized with and consoled him, and encouraged him [to do] what he himself was very reluctant [to do];[1246] she likewise generously and humanely bestowed on him the only thing that she, in her poverty, had on hand. Nor did she do this in return for some past benefaction or striving after a future favor—for she was aware that he was about to die,[1247] even though it is but human nature either to do good to those who have previously shown friendly readiness or to exert oneself in advance for those from whom one might be able to benefit.[1248] **342.** It is noble therefore to imitate this woman and to do good to all who are in need and not expect a reward, nor suppose anything more fitting for the human race than this or that by anything else shall we have God benevolent and conferring good things.[1249] But concerning this woman, it suffices to have reported these things.[1250]

Encomium on Saul's heroism

343. But at this point I shall say something that is advantageous to cities, peoples and nations and of relevance for good persons, by which all will be moved to pursue virtue and be zealous[1251] for those things that are capable of conferring glory and an everlasting memory. In addition, I will cause kings of nations and rulers of cities to be inspired with a great desire and solicitude for noble deeds, incite them to confront dangers and death for their country's sake, and teach them to despise all that is terrible.[1252] **344.** I find an occasion for such a word in Saoul, king of the Hebrews, for he, though he knew what was to happen and the death awaiting him—the prophet having foretold [this][1253]—gave no thought to flight, nor was he so attached to life as to hand over his people to the enemy and thus dishonor the dignity of his kingship.[1254] **345.** Instead, he thought it noble to expose himself, his house, and his sons to these dangers, to fall with them, fighting on behalf of those ruled by him.[1255] He likewise thought it better that his sons die as good men rather

---

[1245] In this initial part of his eulogy, Josephus commends the woman for what she did not do, i.e. requite Saul in kind for the harm he had done her or refuse to assist him, despite his being a stranger to her.

[1246] The reference here is to Saul's unwillingness to eat; see 6.338.

[1247] Josephus' eulogy now turns to positive praise of the woman, i.e. for her compassion for one in distress, generosity despite her extreme poverty, and her unselfish motivation in acting on behalf of the doomed Saul.

[1248] This appended maxim about how humans generally operate highlights the extraordinary character of the woman's benefactions to Saul, who had previously done nothing for her and from whom she knew she had nothing to gain in the future.

[1249] Josephus now draws a general moral from his praise of the woman, urging readers to do as she did with the assurance that those who so act are sure to be rewarded by God. His admonition about doing good to others without any expectation of recompense by them is reminiscent of Jesus' exhortation in Luke 6:35: "... do good, and lend, expecting nothing in return; and your reward will be great...."

[1250] With this formula Josephus provides a clear conclusion to his interjected eulogy (6.340-342) of the woman.

[1251] Greek: ζηλόω. Here, in contrast to his usage in, e.g., *Ant.* 8.316, Josephus uses the verb in a positive sense. On Josephus' tendency to avoid "zeal terminology," given its appropriation by the "Zealots," see Begg 1993: 152, n. 983; Spilsbury 1998: 143-44.

[1252] Josephus now introduces a second appendix (6.343-350) to his account of the "Endor scene," this one focussed on the person of Saul as an hero in the Greco-Roman mold and as lesson in right living and dying, especially for his fellow kings. On the passage—whose grandiloquent introduction aims to underscores its significance—see Feldman 1998: 521-22.

[1253] After the preceding general introduction, Josephus redirects attention to the figure of Saul, the source of the lesson he now wishes to impart, recalling in particular Samuel's prediction of inescapable doom for him in 6.336.

[1254] Josephus here goes beyond his own earlier account in spelling out how Saul might have responded, but in fact did not, to Samuel's announcement. This is Josephus' only use of the verb φιλοψυχέω ("to be attached to life") in *Antiquities*; it occurs 3 times in the *War* (1.357, 650; 4.164). The cognate noun is used in *Ant.* 19.261, the cognate adjective in *War* 7.378.

[1255] Josephus here anticipates his account of the heroic deaths of Saul and his sons in 6.368-378.

than to leave them behind, in uncertainty as to how they would turn out.[1256] For, as his successor and family he would thus have praise and an ageless memory.[1257]

346. He therefore seems to me a uniquely just, courageous, and prudent man,[1258] and if anyone has been or will be worthy of reaping the testimonial of virtue from all, it is he. For others go forth to battle in the hope that they will prevail and return safely. When such persons perform some splendid deed, it does not seem appropriate to me to call them courageous, however much they may have been spoken of in histories and other writings.[1259] **347.** Though these are justly praised, only those are justly said to be "great-souled",[1260] "greatly daring"[1261] and "despisers of terrors" who have imitated Saoul. For in the case of those who, not knowing what will happen to them in war, do not weaken in the face of it, but expose themselves to an uncertain future and are tossed about by it, this is still not bravery, however many deeds they may happen to perform.[1262] **348.** Those, on the contrary, who anticipating nothing favorable in their minds, but instead foreseeing that they must die, and who suffer this [fate] while fighting, neither fearing nor being dismayed by the terror, but proceeding towards this as something foreknown—they, I judge, truly give evidence of courage.[1263] **349.** This then is what Saoul did, thus showing that it is fitting for all who yearn for fame after their deaths to do these same things, whereby they will leave it behind for themselves.[1264] This is the case above all with kings, who, given the greatness of their rulership, are not allowed, not simply not to be a source of calamities to their subjects, but even to be only moderately kind [to them].[1265] **350.** I could say still more than this about Saoul and his greatness of soul, as a topic supplying us with a great deal of material, but in order that I not seem to exaggerate in my praise of him, I revert to the point from which I digressed to these matters.[1266]

[1256] With this statement Josephus provides an answer to the question of why Saul did not at least try to protect his sons from the fate he knew awaited himself.

[1257] On concern for the posthumous fame to be won by exposing oneself to certain death as a hallmark of Greco-Roman heroes—of whom Saul is the worthy Jewish counterpart in Josephus' presentation—see Feldman 1998: 521.

[1258] As Feldman (1998: 521) points out, Josephus here attributes to Saul 3 of the 4 Greek cardinal virtues.

[1259] Josephus now begins developing a contrast between the supposed courage of other warriors and that of Saul himself, which alone deserves to be called such. The difference between them, as he will proceed to show, lies not in what they do, but rather in the state of mind with which they enter into the conflicts they face.

[1260] Greek: εὔψυχος. On the word-field of this term, see Spicq 1978 (I): 337-38. The cognate noun εὐψυχία occurs at the conclusion of Josephus' panegyric for Saul in 6.350.

[1261] Greek: μεγαλότολμος. Josephus uses this adjective of Joshua in *Ant.* 5.118. These are the only certain occurrences of the term in the Josephan corpus; it is conjectured by Niese in *Ant.* 12.433.

[1262] Josephus continues presenting the case of the only apparently courageous—those who engage in battle with some hope that they may emerge alive.

[1263] Having spoken of those whose courage is only apparent given that they confront danger with a hope of survival and victory (6.346-347), Josephus now focuses on the truly courageous, i.e. those who enter battle without any such hope.

[1264] Josephus here reaches the culminating point of his eulogy of Saul, representing him as one of those truly courageous fighters whose only hope as they go into battle is of posthumous fame (see 6.345). As the woman's disinterested generosity is commended for imitation in 6.342, so is Saul's "hopeless" courage here.

[1265] Josephus' concluding focus on kings as the primary addressees of his reflection regarding Saul's career echoes the mention of "kings of nations" as those whom he aims to inspire by means of that reflection in 6.343.

[1266] This closing formula, with its recognition that readers might well have had enough of Josephus' foregoing exaltation of Saul, makes the transition back to the Philistine threat introduced in 6.325, which will eventuate in Saul's heroic death. The foregoing posi-

*David's pres-
ence in Philis-
tine army chal-
lenged*

(14.5) 351. For the Palestinoi, as I said before,[1267] set up camp,[1268] and mustered their force by nations, kingdoms, and satrapies.[1269] Finally, King Anchous presented himself with his own army; David with his 600 troops followed.[1270]

352. When the Palestinoi generals[1271] beheld him, they questioned the king about where the Hebrews had come from and who had called them.[1272] Anchous said that it was David who was a fugitive from his own master Saoul and that he had received him when he came to him.[1273] David, now wishing to repay this favor and punish Saoul, was an ally to them.[1274]

353. Anchous was, however, censured by the generals[1275] for having admitted into alliance a man who was an enemy,[1276] and they advised him to sent him away, so that he would not, on his account, inadvertently cause his friends great calamity.[1277]

---

tive eulogy of Saul for the manner of his death serves to counterbalance Josephus' extended negative exposé of his fall into hubris, envy, and paranoia in 6.262-268. Not all readers have found the sequence as soul-stirring as Josephus evidently intended it to be. See the tart comment of Montgomery (1920-21: 305, n. 45): "I doubt if there in any better example in all literature of absurd homiletics... than his moral reflections on Saul and the witch of Endor in *Ant.* 6.14.4."

[1267] The cross-reference here is to the account of the Philistine movements in 6.325 (// 1 Sam 28:1). On Josephus' version of 1 Samuel 29, see Begg 1998d.

[1268] Josephus leaves aside the indications of 1 Sam 29:1 concerning the site of both the Philistine and Isra-elite camps, i.e. "Aphek" and "the fountain which is in Jezreel" (MT; LXX B: Aeddon [LXX L Ain] which is in Israel), respectively. He has previously assigned alter-native camping sites to both sides, i.e. "Soune" for the Philistines (6.327) and Mount "Gelboue" for the Israel-ites (6.328).

[1269] In MT 1 Sam 29:2 the Philistine "lords" (LXX: satraps) pass on "by hundreds and thousands." Jose-phus' (anachronistic) use of the Persian term "satrapies" in reference to their divisions appears to be inspired by the LXX designation for the Philistine leaders; see Marcus *ad loc.*

[1270] See 1 Sam 29:2. Josephus specifies the number of David's companions in accordance with the figure given by him for those who took refuge with David in Gath; see 6.319// 1 Sam 27:2.

[1271] Josephus' term for these figures (Greek: στρα-τηγοί) is one of the 2 designations used by LXX L 1 Sam 29:3 (the other being "satraps," the LXX B term; MT has "princes," שרים). The Bible does not explicitly mention their "seeing" David.

[1272] The first part of the generals' question accord-ing to Josephus corresponds to the reading of MT 1 Sam 29:3 ("what are these Hebrews [Tg.: Jews] doing here?") as opposed to LXX ("who are these who are crossing over?"). Its 2nd part lacks a biblical counter-part.

[1273] From Achish's initial reply in 1 Sam 29:3b Josephus omits the variable indications concerning the duration of David's stay with himself: "days or these two years" (so literally MT [RSV: for days and years]); "(this makes) days (that he has been with us); it is the second year" (LXX B); "it is already the second year of days" (LXX L). Earlier (6.322; cf. 1 Sam 27:7), Josephus stated that David spent 4 months and 20 days in the Philistine city of "Sekella."

[1274] This statement concerning David's current in-tentions takes the place of Achish's declaration in 1 Sam 29:3b: "... since he deserted to me I have found no fault in him till this day." Achish's report here concern-ing David echoes the latter's own words to the king as cited in 6.326: "... he said that the time had come for him to repay his benefactions and make recompense for his hospitality." On "ally language" as a *Leitwort* of Josephus' version of 1 Sam 28:1-2; 29:1-11 in 6.325-326, 351-355, see note to "allies" at 6.325. On the apologetic thrust of this emphasis on David's being a (loyal) "ally" of the Philistines, i.e. as intimating that (also contemporary) Jews can indeed be good allies of foreign powers and as legitimating Josephus' own (David-like) role as "ally" of the Romans, see Begg 1998d: 118-19.

[1275] Josephus leaves aside the notice of 1 Sam 29:4aα concerning the emotional state of the Philistine generals, i.e. their "anger" at Achish (MT; LXX: "they were distressed because of him").

[1276] In having the Philistine commanders speak of David as (already) their "enemy," Josephus diverges from 1 Sam 29:4bα, where they refer to the possibility of his becoming an "opponent" (MT שטן; LXX ἐπί-βουλος, "plotter") in the upcoming battle.

[1277] In 1 Sam 29:4aβ the commanders begin by call-ing on Achish to send David back "to the place which you have assigned him (i.e. Ziklag; see 1 Sam 27:6)." Leaving aside the source specification about where the dismissed David is to go for the moment (but see 6.354), Josephus appends his own motivation for the generals' directive.

For he would be providing [David] with the opportunity of being reconciled to his master by bringing calamity on our force.[1278]

354. They therefore directed him, given this prospect, to send David, along with his 600 troops, away to the place he had given him to reside in.[1279] For this was that David about whom the virgins had sung as one who annihilated many ten thousands of the Palestinoi.[1280] Hearing these things and thinking them well said,[1281] the king of the Gittoi called David. **355.** "I, for my part," he said, "attest to your great solicitude for and loyalty to me,[1282] and therefore I brought you here as an ally.[1283] This did not, however, seem good to the generals.[1284] Depart now, within a day, to the place that I gave you, suspecting no wrong.[1285] Guard the country for me, so that some enemy does not invade it. This too is part of an alliance."[1286]

David dismissed by king Achish (Anchous)

356. David, as the king of the Gittoi had directed,[1287] went to Sikella.[1288] At the

David finds Ziklag (Sikella) plundered

[1278] Josephus turns into a single statement the generals' double question of 1 Sam 29:4bβ: "For how could this fellow reconcile himself to his lord? Would it not be with the heads of the men here?"

[1279] Josephus has the generals reiterate their call for David's dismissal from 1 Sam 29:4aβ, now reproducing the specification, based on 1 Sam 27:6 (// 6.355) about where David is to go. He likewise has them prescribe the dismissal of the 600 in David's entourage (see 6.351).

[1280] Josephus aligns his rendition of the quotation of the women's acclamation as first reported in 1 Sam 18:7// 6.195 with his earlier evocation of this in 6.245 (// 1 Sam 21:12). In particular, in both 6.245 and 354, he eliminates the (irrelevant) mention of Saul's exploits and specifies that those acclaiming David were "virgins" (compare 29:5a: "... they [the women] sang to one another...").

[1281] Josephus provides a more flowing transition between Achish's exchange with the Philistine generals (1 Sam 29:3-5) and his following dialogue with David (29:6-10), noting in particular the king's "agreement" with what the generals told him. In his subsequent report to David (6.355) Achish will, however, make no mention of his interior assent to the generals' words; see note to "generals" at 6.355.

[1282] From Achish's initial words to David in 1 Sam 29:6, Josephus eliminates the opening oath formula ("as the Lord lives"), while accentuating the king's acknowledgement of David's fidelity.

[1283] Josephus inserts this statement by Achish, echoing his affirmation to the Philistine generals in 6.352, about his having taken David along as an "ally" (see note to "ally to them" at 6.352), given the latter's impeccable behavior towards himself.

[1284] In having Achish thus contrast his own view of David and what should be done with him with that of the Philistine commanders, Josephus aligns himself with the reading of MT LXX L 1 Sam 29:6b, where the king informs David "the lords do *not* approve of you";

compare LXX B, which lacks the negation. At the same time, Josephus' king appears as less than candid in his words, distancing himself from the generals' opinion of him, to David, given that just previously in 6.354, Josephus inserts a reference to Achish's finding the generals' negative remarks concerning David "well said."

[1285] Josephus here conflates the double "dismissal order" given David by Achish, first in 1 Sam 29:7 and then in 29:10 (whose longer LXX version with its reference to David's going "to the place which I gave you" [see 29:4// 6.354] Josephus follows). In so doing, he passes over the (repetitious) intervening exchange between the 2 men of 29:8-9, where David (v. 8) voices a protesting question about Achish's having no reason to doubt his loyalty to him that the latter has already answered in v. 7, Achish then responding (v. 9) with a reiteration of his earlier statements about the diverging perspectives of himself and the Philistine commanders regarding David.

[1286] Achish's concluding remark to David about what an "alliance" involves has no counterpart in 1 Samuel 29. On the other hand, the king's directive that David "guard (Greek: φυλάσσω) the country" seems inspired by the LXX plus in 1 Sam 29:11, where David goes to "guard" (Greek: φυλάσσω) the Philistine country.

[1287] This inserted phrase serves to underscore David's continued, ready obedience to his overlord—he had come along at the latter's command (6.325) and now he goes back when so directed by him, without a word of demurral. In the same line, Josephus passes over David's earlier protest (see 1 Sam 29:8) about Achish's questioning his loyalty to him and directing him to depart; see note to "no wrong" at 6.355.

[1288] Josephus anticipates this specification about where David goes from 1 Sam 30:1. It takes the place of the notice of 29:11b: "but the Philistines went up to Jezreel" (MT; LXX: the Philistines went up to fight against Israel).

same time that he had departed from there to join the Palestinoi as an ally,[1289] the nation of the Amalekites came against Sikella and took it by storm.[1290] They burned it, and taking much plunder both from it and the rest of the Palestinoi's country, withdrew.[1291]

David's distress and danger

(14.6) 357. When he discovered that Sikella had been looted and everything plundered, just as his own wives (there were two of them) and the wives and children of his companions had been taken captive,[1292] David immediately tore his clothes.[1293] **358.** He wept and lamented with his friends, being so overcome by these calamities, that finally he had no tears left.[1294] He was then in danger of being stoned to death by his companions[1295] who were pained by the capture of their wives and children; for they blamed him for what had happened.[1296]

David told to pursue Amalekite raiders

359. Recovering from his grief and raising his mind to God,[1297] David appealed to the high priest Abiathar to put on his priestly garment[1298] and to inquire of God and prophesy[1299] whether, if he pursued the Amalekites, he would grant him to overtake them, save the women and children, and punish the enemy.[1300]

Egyptian guide procured

360. Once the high priest directed him to pursue,[1301] David rushed out with his 600[1302] troops and followed after the enemy. When he arrived at a certain brook called Basel,[1303] he ran into a certain wanderer, an Egyptian by race,[1304] who was

---

[1289] This transitional phrase, harking back to 6.325, where Achish summons David "to join him as an ally" on the Philistine campaign, substitutes for the notice of 1 Sam 30:1aα that David's party reached Ziklag "on the third day." On Josephus' version of 1 Samuel 30, see Begg 1997k.

[1290] See 1 Sam 30:1aβbα, where the Amalekites' "raid" encompasses "the Negeb" as well.

[1291] See 1 Sam 30:1bβ-2. Josephus inserts the reference to the Amalekites' taking plunder also from the remainder of the Philistine country, perhaps under the influence of 30:16, where the Amalekites are pictured enjoying the spoil they had taken "from the land of the Philistines."

[1292] For this notice on the losses that David and his men discover upon their arrival at Ziklag, Josephus combines elements of 1 Sam 30:3 and 5 (from which he omits the names of David's 2 wives, who had previously joined him at Ziklag; see 6.321// 1 Sam 27:3).

[1293] This action by David is not mentioned in 1 Samuel 30. Its insertion serves to highlight the emotional intensity of the scene, and David's own role therein.

[1294] See 1 Sam 30:4.

[1295] See 1 Sam 30:6aβ.

[1296] Josephus' addendum to the mention of the people's distress over the loss of their family members in 1 Sam 30:6bα clarifies why this should have prompted them to threaten to kill David (30:6aβ), i.e. they blame David for what had happened. Whereas 30:6bα speaks only of the people's grief for their children, Josephus, under the influence of 30:3, also mentions their "wives."

[1297] This transitional phrase is Josephus' clarifying rendition of 1 Sam 30:6bβ: "But David strengthened himself in God."

[1298] In 1 Sam 30:7a David commands Abiathar to bring him the "ephod." Like LXX B, Josephus lacks an equivalent to MT and LXX L 30:7b, which state that Abiathar did as directed. Josephus' last previous mention of Abiathar was in 6.261 (// 1 Sam 22:21).

[1299] Josephus' addition of this word to the source phrase "inquire of the Lord" (see 1 Sam 30:8a, where the grammatical subject is David himself) reflects both his tendency to introduce such terminology in contexts where the Bible lacks it and his characteristic linkage of priesthood and prophecy.

[1300] Josephus expands David's 2-part question in 1 Sam 30:8a about his pursuing and overtaking the raiders with 2 additional queries, these concerning his ability to "rescue" and "take vengeance," should he catch up with the Amalekites. The 2nd of these additional questions is likely inspired by the divine assurance of 30:8b that he would indeed "rescue."

[1301] Josephus limits the divine answer to David of 1 Sam 30:8b to its opening directive, i.e. "pursue," leaving aside the appended assurances about his "overtaking" and "rescuing" (already incorporated by him into the wording of David's question; see previous note).

[1302] Josephus' figure for those who accompany David agrees with that cited in MT LXX L 1 Sam 30:9aα, as opposed to the 400 of LXX B.

[1303] MT (1 Sam 30:9) בְּשׂוֹר (Eng.: "Besor"); LXX Βοσόρ; Josephus Βάσελος. Josephus leaves aside the indications of 1 Sam 30:9b-10 about 200 of David's men staying behind at the brook due to exhaustion while

worn out by lack of necessities and hunger, for he had spent three days wandering in the desert without food.[1305] Having first refreshed and revived him with drink and food,[1306] David interrogated him about who he was and from where he came.[1307] **361.** He indicated that he was of the Egyptian race and had been left behind by his master because he was unable to follow, due to illness.[1308] He further disclosed that he himself was one of those who had burned down and plundered both other [parts] of Ioudaia and Sikella.[1309]

362. David therefore used him as a guide to the Amalekites.[1310] He came upon them sprawled on the ground, some eating breakfast, others already drunk and relaxed from wine and enjoying their spoils and plunder.[1311] Falling suddenly upon them, he perpetrated a great slaughter of them; for being defenseless and not expecting anything of the sort and having given themselves up to drinking and feasting, they were all easily overcome. **363.** Some were caught unawares while still at the tables that had been spread out and dispatched on the spot; their blood washed away the provisions and food. Others he destroyed as they drank each other's health; still others had been put to sleep by the unmixed [wine]. Those who managed to put on their armor and make a stand against him were also butchered—no less easily than those lying around defenseless.[1312]

David massacres Amalekites

---

the remainder press on (MT LXX L; LXX B differs considerably). He will, however, make use of the subsequent biblical allusion to this development (1 Sam 30:21); see 6.365.

[1304] In 1 Sam 30:11a "they" find the Egyptian "in the open country" and lead him to David. Josephus' compressed presentation has him found by David himself "at the brook."

[1305] Josephus anticipates these particulars concerning the man's state from 1 Sam 30:12bβ.

[1306] Continuing to keep attention focused on David himself, Josephus ascribes the man's revival to David personally, whereas "they" attend to the Egyptian in 1 Sam 30:11b. He passes over the fig-cake and 2 clusters of raisins (> B) that are given the man according to 30:12a.

[1307] Having anticipated the notice of 1 Sam 30:12bβ about the man's state (see note to "food" at 6.360), Josephus directly links his revival (30:12bα) and David's double question to him (30:13a). In 30:13 David's initial question is "to whom do you belong?" The MSP variant in 6.360 features this same question.

[1308] From the man's reply (1 Sam 30:13b) Josephus leaves aside his mention of being the "servant to an Amalekite"—this answering David's opening question ("to whom do you belong?") previously reworded by him (see note to "where he came" at 6.360)—as well as the chronological indication about his sickness having overtaken him "three days ago" (which he incorporated into his initial presentation of the man in 6.360).

[1309] Josephus conflates and simplifies the man's statement in 1 Sam 30:14, where he acknowledges his involvement in raids on portions of the Negeb belong-

ing to 3 different entities (MT: the Cherethites, Judah, and Caleb), as well as in the burning of Ziklag itself. Continuing to streamline the biblical account, he leaves aside the appended exchange between David and the Egyptian of 30:15, in which David asks the latter whether he will conduct him to the Amalekites, and the Egyptian agrees to do so, provided that David swears neither to kill him or turn him over to his master. He will, however, incorporate David's "guide request" of 30:15a into his subsequent narrative; see note to "guide to the Amalekites" at 6.362.

[1310] With this rendering of 1 Sam 30:16aα ("and when he [the Egyptian] had taken him down..."), Josephus once again highlights David's initiative in and control over the course of events. His reference to the use of the man as a "guide" draws on David's question to him about his willingness to "take him down" to the raiders in 30:15a, previously passed over by him.

[1311] Josephus both elaborates on the picture of the Amalekites' camp given in 1 Sam 30:16aβb (e.g., with his interjected reference to their breakfasting and being "already drunk"), and simplifies this (he does not reproduce the notice on the 2 sources of the Amalekites' plunder, i.e. the land of Judah and the land of the Philistines—see, however, note to "withdrew" at 6.356).

[1312] Josephus greatly elaborates on the summary mention of David's "smiting" the Amalekites of 1 Sam 30:17a. Feldman (1998: 563-64) points out that his embellishment of the massacre scene with a variety of gory details has a counterpart in his treatment of Abraham's victory over the kings (Gen 14:14-15) in *Ant.* 1.177. He further suggests that, in both instances,

364. Those therefore who were with David continued dispatching them from early morning until the evening,[1313] so that not more than 400 of the Amalekites were left; these mounted their dromedaries and fled.[1314] David recovered everything the enemy had plundered, as well as his own wives and those of his companions.[1315]

Disposition of plunder

365. On their return they came to the place where they had left behind with the baggage 200 men who had been unable to follow them.[1316] The 400 were, however, unwilling to divide up any of their gain or plunder with them.[1317] For they said that since these had not followed along with them, but had given out during the course of the pursuit, they should be content to get back their wives who had been recovered.[1318]

366. David, for his part, declared this scheme of theirs a vile and unjust one.[1319] For, since God had enabled them to take vengeance on their enemies[1320] and bring [back] everything that was theirs, [it was incumbent on them] to divide their gains up equally among all who had taken part in the campaign—all the more so because these had remained behind to guard the baggage.[1321] **367.** From that [time] on this law has been in force among them that those guarding the baggage receive the same as those doing the fighting.[1322] Arriving at Sikella, David dispatched portions of the spoils to all his relatives and friends in the tribe of Iouda.[1323] This then is the story

---

Josephus may have found inspiration in Herodotus' account (1.211) of Cyrus' rout of his enemies.

[1313] 1 Sam 30:17a mentions only David's role in the massacre; Josephus gives credit to his men as well. Whereas the LXX seems to extend the massacre over 2 days ("from the early morning light until the evening of the next day"), Josephus, like MT, limits it to a single day.

[1314] See 1 Sam 30:17b.

[1315] Josephus compresses the circumstantial enumeration of the recovered plunder given in 1 Sam 30:18-20, omitting, e.g., mention of the flocks and herds and the designation of these as "David's spoil" from v. 20.

[1316] See 1 Sam 30:21a. As pointed out earlier (see note to "a certain brook called Basel" at 6. 360), Josephus does not reproduce the notices in 30:9b-10, to which this passage alludes. Here, he passes over the appended account—with its variations among the textual witnesses—of 30:21b concerning the encounter of David and his forces with the 200.

[1317] 1 Sam 30:22 attributes the refusal to "all the wicked and base fellows among the men" who had accompanied David. Josephus extends the refusal to the entire 400.

[1318] From the objectors' words in 1 Sam 30:22 Josephus omits the "children" of the 200 whom they would allow the latter to take back along with their wives.

[1319] With this qualification of the proposed scheme by David, Josephus "reapplies" the source characterization of the objectors themselves ("all the base and

wicked fellows," 1 Sam 30:22) to their proposal, substituting this for David's opening declaration in 30:23: "you shall not do so, my brothers (> B)."

[1320] Josephus' explicit mention of the "enemies" upon whom God has allowed David and his men to take vengeance aligns his wording with the plus of LXX L in 1 Sam 30:23, whereas in MT and LXX B David speaks generally of "what the Lord has given us."

[1321] See 1 Sam 30:24b. Josephus has no equivalent to David's (extraneous) question of 30:24a ("who would listen to you [the objectors] in this matter?") or to the attached plus of LXX ("they [the 200] are not inferior to you").

[1322] Josephus' impersonal formulation reflects that of LXX 1 Sam 30:25 ("that became an ordinance and legal prescription for Israel...") as opposed to MT's "he (David) made it a statute..." The biblical provision for the distribution of plunder among the participants in a campaign that Josephus reproduces here has a counterpart in Roman military history as reported by Polybius (10.16.5). According to this author, following his capture of New Carthage, Scipio directed that the spoils of the city be divided equally among his entire force, including the reserves, those left to guard the camp, and even the sick.

[1323] Josephus' wording follows MT 1 Sam 30:26a, which seems to identify David's "friends/neighbors" with the "elders of Judah" as the recipients of the spoils, whereas LXX L distinguishes the 2 groups, and LXX B speaks of David sending "the plunder of Judah" to the "elders" and "his neighbors." He leaves aside David's appended word of 30:26b designating his

of the overthrow of Sikella and the extermination of the Amakelites.[1324]

(14.7) 368. Once the Palestinoi joined battle, a fierce fight ensued; the Palestinoi were victorious and did away with many of their opponents.[1325] Saoul, the king of the Israelites, and his sons struggled bravely and displayed the utmost eagerness, as if their entire glory depended solely on their dying nobly and boldly battling the enemy, since they could do no more than this.[1326]

Saul's sons die in battle

369. Thus they drew upon themselves all the ranks of the enemy. Being surrounded, they were killed, after they had brought down many of the Palestinoi.[1327] When Saoul's sons Ionathes and Aminadab[1328] and Melchis[1329] fell, the crowd of Hebrews took to flight;[1330] there was disorder, shock, and slaughter as the enemy pressed hard [after them].[1331]

370. Saoul too fled, having the elite [troops] around himself.[1332] When the Palestinoi sent against him javelin-throwers and archers, he lost all but a few of these.[1333] He himself struggled splendidly and received many wounds, so that he was no longer able to hold out or resist due to these blows.[1334] Too weak to kill himself, he directed his weapon-bearer to draw his sword and run him through with this, before the enemy should catch him alive.[1335]

Saul's attempted suicide

371. Since, however, the weapon-bearer did not dare to kill his master, Saoul drew his own sword, and standing over the tip, threw himself down upon it.[1336] Incapable

Saul finished off by Amalekite

---

award as a "present for you from the enemies of the Lord" (MT LXX L; LXX B: "behold plunder taken from the enemies of the Lord").

[1324] This closing formula for Josephus' version of 1 Samuel 30 (6.356-367) takes the place of the list of 13 localities to which David dispatches the plunder in 1 Sam 30:27-31.

[1325] See 1 Sam 31:1// 1 Chr 10:1. Josephus reserves for a later point the sources' reference to the Israelites' flight; see 6.369. On Josephus' version of 1 Samuel 31 // 1 Chronicles 10, see Begg 1999b.

[1326] 1 Sam 31:2// 1 Chr 10:2 speak simply of the Philistines pursuing Saul and his sons and killing the latter. Josephus, in line with his earlier eulogy of Saul (6.343-350), accentuates the heroic resistance offered by both the king and his sons.

[1327] Josephus' embellishment of 1 Sam 31:2// 1 Chr 10:2 continues with this appended statement that, prior to being killed themselves, Saul and his sons inflicted many casualties.

[1328] Greek: Ἀμινάδαβος, the declined form of the name of Saul's 2nd son as read by LXX L 1 Sam 31:2 and LXX BL 1 Chr 10:2. The MT of both verses reads "Abinadab," while LXX B 1 Sam 31:2 has "Ionadab." In 6.129 Josephus calls Saul's 2nd son "Iesous."

[1329] MT 1 Sam 31:2// 1 Chr 10:2 read "Melchi-shua"; LXX B 1 Sam 31:2 has Μελχεισά, LXX L 1 Sam 31:2 and LXX BL 1 Chr 10:2 Μελ(ε)ισσούε, and Josephus Μέλχισος (as in 6.129).

[1330] This is Josephus' delayed version of the "flight notice" of 1 Sam 31:1aβ// 1 Chr 10:1aβ; he "motivates" the Israelites' flight as their response to the deaths of the 3 princes.

[1331] With this appended notice on the circumstances attending the Israelites' flight, Josephus heightens the drama of the scene.

[1332] This notice on Saul's fleeing along with his retinue has no counterpart in the biblical sources.

[1333] This reference to the decimation of Saul's retinue might represent an anticipation of the MT LXX L reading in 1 Sam 31:6, which states that "all his (Saul's) men" were killed that day. To 1 Sam 31:3// 1 Chr 10:3's mention of the Philistine "archers," Josephus adds "javelin-throwers."

[1334] The reference to Saul's being "wounded" reflects the LXX reading in 1 Sam 31:3 and 1 Chr 10:3, whereas the vocalized MT in both verses speaks of the king's "writhing in fear because of the archers"—not, in any case, the image of Saul Josephus wishes to convey. Josephus' attached remarks on the effect of his wounds on Saul prepare his following description of the king's inability to complete his attempted suicide.

[1335] Josephus explains the king's command to his armor-bearer as cited in 1 Sam 31:4a// 1 Chr 10:4a in terms of the former's being so weakened by his wounds that he is unable to kill himself. From Saul's command in the source texts he eliminates the derogatory designation of the Philistines as "these uncircumcised," while also compressing the enumeration of the reasons why Saul wishes to die at this point. In Pseudo-Philo Saul, prior to commanding his armor-bearer to kill him (*Bib. Ant.* 65.2), asks himself (65.1) while he is still trying to live, given Samuel's announcement (see 64.8) that he and his sons are to die this day.

[1336] See 1 Sam 31:4b// 1 Chr 10:4b.

of either forcing it in or of pressing himself against the iron so as to run himself through, he turned around.[1337] A certain youth was standing there and Saoul inquired who he was.[1338] When he learned that he was an Amalekite, he appealed to him to press the sword in, because he was unable do this with his own hands, and so provide him with the death he desired.[1339]

372. The Amalekite did this; he then removed his golden bracelet and the royal crown and hid himself.[1340] When the weapon-bearer observed that Saoul had been done away with, he killed himself.[1341] None of the king's bodyguards survived; all fell on the mountain called Gelboue.[1342]

Philistines occupy Israelite territory

373. When the Hebrews living in the valley beyond the Jordan and those having cities in the plain[1343] heard that Saoul and his sons had fallen and that the crowd with him had been lost, they abandoned their own cities and fled to strongholds.[1344] The Palestinoi, finding the abandoned [sites] deserted, settled in them.[1345]

Philistines' handling of remains of Saulides

(14.8) 374. The next day, when the Palestinoi were stripping the corpses of the enemy, they came upon the bodies of Saoul and his sons;[1346] stripping these, they cut off their heads.[1347] They dispatched the news that the enemy had fallen to their

---

[1337] At this point, Josephus begins incorporating elements of the alternative account of Saul's death, i.e. the report made to David by the Amalekite as cited in 2 Sam 1:6-10, into his version of 1 Samuel 31// 1 Chronicles 10. He does this out of a concern to harmonize the 2 apparently discordant narratives (Pseudo-Philo proceeds similarly in *Bib. Ant.* 65.3-4). Specifically, he draws here on 2 Sam 1:6, where the Amalekite speaks of his encountering Saul "leaning on his spear"—Josephus turning this into a "sword" in line with the presentation of 1 Sam 31:4b// 1 Chr 10:4b— and 1:7 (which mentions Saul's "looking behind him").

[1338] See 2 Sam 1:7-8a, from which Josephus omits Saul's calling to the youth and the latter's responding "Here I am." In *Bib. Ant.* 65.3-4, in a reversal of the sequence of 2 Sam 1:8-9, Saul asks the youth to kill him before inquiring who he is.

[1339] See 2 Sam 1:8b-9. Josephus modifies the motivation given by Saul for his request to be dispatched by the Amalekite in 1:9, i.e. "for anguish has seized me, and yet my life still lingers," which seems to detract from Saul's heroic image. In *Bib. Ant.* 65.4 the youth identifies himself more specifically as Edabus, the son of Agag, who was conceived just prior to his father's execution (see 58.3-4). Saul then recalls Samuel's words concerning this figure, whom he now commissions (65.5) to report his having killed him to David and to ask David "not to remember my hatred and injustice." For other identifications of Saul's killer elsewhere in Jewish tradition (Doeg, the son of Doeg), see Begg 1999b: 492, n. 53. Feldman (1998: 532-33 and nn. 32-33) draws attention to Josephus' lack of comment on Saul's (assisted) suicide, notwithstanding his emphatic condemnation of that practice in the speech delivered by him in *War* 3.361-383 (compare Eleazar's

discourse to the defenders of Masada urging their joint suicide cited, with apparent approval by Josephus in *War* 7.323-336, 341-388). Feldman attributes the lack of such negative commentary on Saul's deed to Josephus' desire not to detract in any way from the heroism of the king's death.

[1340] Josephus reverses the order of the 2 items that the Amalekite mentions having removed from Saul's body in 2 Sam 1:10. The reference to the youth's self-concealment is his own addition.

[1341] See 1 Sam 31:5// 1 Chr 10:5.

[1342] Josephus seems to be drawing here on the MT LXX L plus in 1 Sam 31:6 with its reference—already anticipated by him in 6.370—to the demise of "all Saul's men" (1 Chr 10:6 speaks of the death of all Saul's "house"). The mention of "Mt. Gilboa (Gelboue)" as the site of their death stems from 1 Sam 31:1 // 1 Chr 10:1; Josephus previously mentioned the mountain as Saul's camping place in 6.328.

[1343] Like 1 Sam 31:7, Josephus distinguishes between 2 groups of Israelites who respond to Saul's defeat, i.e. those across the Jordan and those living "in the plain," i.e. of Jezreel (1 Chr 10:7 mentions only this latter group), even while reversing the sequence in which they appear there.

[1344] To the notice on the Israelites' flight (1 Sam 31:7a// 1 Chr 10:7a) Josephus appends an indication as to where they headed.

[1345] See 1 Sam 31:7b// 1 Chr 10:7b.

[1346] See 1 Sam 31:8// 1 Chr 10:8.

[1347] In his explicit mention of the Philistines' "beheading" the bodies, Josephus goes together with MT LXX L 1 Sam 31:9 against LXX B 31:9 and 1 Chr 10:9. In both 31:9-10 and 10:9-10, the reference is to the Philistines' dealings with the remains of Saul alone.

BOOK SIX

203

entire country.[1348] They dedicated their armor in the temple of Astarte,[1349] while they impaled their bodies on the walls of the city of Bethsan[1350] that is now called Scythopolis.[1351]

375. Now the inhabitants of the city of Jabis in the Galaadite country heard that the corpse of Saoul and those of his sons had been mutilated.[1352] Thinking it a terrible thing to leave them unburied,[1353] their most courageous men, those outstanding for their daring—the city itself produces men valiant in both body and soul—set out.[1354] **376.** Traveling all night, they came to Bethsan and, advancing to the enemy's wall, took down the body of Saoul and those of his sons and brought them to Jabis,[1355] none of the enemy being capable of or daring to prevent them on account of their courage.[1356]

Jabeshites recover and bury Saulides' remains

377. Then the Jabesenians buried the bodies with public weeping[1357] in the most beautiful place in their country, called "Aroura."[1358] They mourned over them with their wives and children for seven days. Beating their breasts, they lamented the king and his sons, tasting neither food nor drink.[1359]

(14.9) 378. Saoul ended up in this way in accordance with the prophecy of Samouel[1360] because he disobeyed God's commandments regarding the Amalekites and because he did away with both the family of Abimelech and Abimelech himself, as well as the city of the high priests.[1361] He reigned as king eighteen years

Closing notice for Saul

Josephus, in 6.374-375, has their measures extend also to the sons' remains, given that in 31:8// 10:8 the Philistines discover the bodies of both Saul and his sons.

[1348] Josephus provides a content for the "good news" that the Philistines send their messengers to convey in 1 Sam 31:9// 1 Chr 10:9. He generalizes the recipients of that news in comparison with both sources, i.e. "the house of their idols and the people" (MT 31:9)/ "their idols and their people" (LXX 31:9 and 1 Chr 10:9).

[1349] Josephus uses the same form (Ἀσταρτεῖον) as does LXX 1 Sam 31:10 to designate the site where the armor is deposited (compare MT 31:10: the temple of Astaroth; 1 Chr 10:10: the temple of their gods).

[1350] MT (1 Sam 31:10b) בית שן (Eng.: "Beth-shan"); LXX B Βαιθέμ; LXX L Βαιθσάν; Josephus Βηθσάν (so RO, which Niese and Marcus follow). In 1 Chr 10:10b it is Saul's "skull" that is "nailed up" in the temple of Dagon.

[1351] Josephus had previously noted this newer, Greek name for Hebrew "Beth-shan" in *Ant.* 5.83.

[1352] 1 Sam 31:11// 1 Chr 10:11 designate the site as "Jabesh-gilead." Although neither the Bible nor Josephus make the connection explicit, the initiative on Saul's behalf undertaken by the town's population undoubtedly was inspired by his delivery of them from the threat by King Nahash of Ammon (see 1 Sam 11:1-11 // 6.68-80).

[1353] Josephus supplies this indication concerning the inhabitants' motivation for acting as they now do.

[1354] Josephus embellishes the biblical references (1 Sam 31:12// 1 Chr 10:12) to the "valiant men" of Jabesh, here again underscoring the courage of his

people for Gentile readers.

[1355] Josephus' wording here reflects that of 1 Sam 31:12 as opposed to 1 Chr 10:12 (which does not mention either the all-night march or the wall of Beth-shan). In referring to the bodies of Saul's "son*s*," Josephus aligns himself with MT 31:12 against LXX, which mentions only the body of Jonathan.

[1356] This further accentuation of the valor of the Jabeshites takes the place of the concluding words of 1 Sam 31:12 (otherwise followed by Josephus), i.e. "and they (the Jabeshites) burned them (the bodies of Saul and his sons) there," which is also lacking in 1 Chr 10:12. See, however, next note.

[1357] Greek: κλαύσαντες. Niese (*ad loc.*) conjectures καύσαντες ("burning") in light of the reference in 1 Sam 31:12b to the Jabeshites "burning" the bodies. See previous note.

[1358] Josephus' designation for the burial site represents an elaboration of that given in LXX BL 1 Sam 31: 13, i.e. "beneath the field (Greek: ἄρουρα) of Jabeis." MT 31:13 has the corpses buried under a tamarisk, 1 Chr 10:12 under a terebinth. Compare the similar case in 6.251 // 1 Sam 22:6.

[1359] As often in his burial accounts, Josephus embellishes the notice of 1 Sam 31:13b// 1 Chr 10:12b, which mentions only a 7-day fast by the Jabeshites for Saul and his sons.

[1360] See 6.336, where the soul of Samuel informs Saul: "... tomorrow you, having fallen in battle along with your sons, will be with me."

[1361] Josephus here adapts the reflection on the death of Saul in 1 Chr 10:13-14, where Saul is first charged

during the lifetime of Samouel and twenty-two after his death.[1362] Thus Saoul ended his life.[1363]

---

generally with unfaithfulness to the Lord and not keeping his "word," and then more specifically with "consulting a medium" (see 1 Sam 28:3-25, a passage not reproduced by the Chronicler). For the latter charge, Josephus, who nowhere explicitly condemns Saul's consultation of the medium, substitutes 2 others, i.e. Saul's disobedience to the command that he exterminate the Amalekites (6.131-15 // 1 Samuel 15) and his massacre of the priests of Nob (6.250-268// 1 Sam 22:6-19). *Midr. Samuel* 24.7, commenting on 1 Chr 10:13, states that Saul died for 5 sins, the 2nd and 3rd of which are those cited by Josephus here.

[1362] This chronological appendix has no equivalent in either 1 Samuel 31 or 1 Chronicles 10. Josephus has already mentioned the 18 years of Saul and Samuel's co-rule in 6.294. His further datum of 22 years for Saul's subsequent sole rule here gives the king an overall reign of *40* years; this agrees with the figure cited by Paul in Acts 13:21, but diverges from Josephus' own dating in *Ant.* 10.143, where Saul is assigned a reign of *20* years. Lat harmonizes 6.378 and 10.143 by reading, not 22, but rather 2 years for the time Saul reigned alone in the former text; Rappaport 1930: 51, #210 holds that the reading in 6.378 (40 years for Saul's total reign) stems from a Christian scribe, influenced by Acts 13:21. The 2nd century BCE Jewish historian Eupolemos (in the extract from Alexander Polyhistor cited by Eusebius in his *Preap. ev.* 9.30.2) assigns still another duration to Saul's reign, i.e. 21 years.

[1363] In contrast to 1 Chr 10:14 ("therefore the Lord slew him") Josephus avoids attributing Saul's death directly to God.

(1.1) 1. It happened that this battle occurred on the same day that David returned to Sikella after defeating the Amalekites.[1] He had already spent two days in Sikella when, on the third day,[2] the one who had done away with Saoul,[3] having survived the battle against the Palestinoi, arrived, his clothes torn and his head sprinkled with ashes.[4]

Saul's killer reports to David

2. When David, to whom he paid homage,[5] inquired from where he came in this state, he said that he had come from the Israelites' battle.[6] He also disclosed to him[7] its unfortunate outcome, with many ten thousands of the Hebrews having been done away with and their King Saoul and his sons having fallen.[8]

3. He stated[9] that he was indicating these things as someone who had been present for the rout of the Hebrews and had stood by the king, who had fled.[10] He declared that he had killed him when he [Saoul], about to be captured by the enemy, appealed to him.[11] For, having thrown himself upon his sword, Saoul had been too weak to finish himself off, because of the excess of his wounds.[12]

4. As evidence of his having dispatched him, he displayed the gold from the king's arms as well as the crown, which he had brought to him after stripping Saoul's corpse.[13] David could no longer disbelieve, seeing these vivid proofs of Saoul's

David's response

---

[1] 2 Sam 1:1 dates David's return to Ziklag "after the death of Saul." In synchronizing the battle of Mt. Gilboa in which Saul lost his life (1 Samuel 31// 1 Chronicles 10// *Ant.* 6.368-378) with David's coming back to Ziklag after his successful pursuit of the Amalekites (1 Samuel 30// 6.356-367), Josephus excludes any idea that David might have been present for the battle as an ally of the Philistines. On Josephus' version of 2 Samuel 1, see Begg 1999c.

[2] Josephus derives this double chronological indication from 2 Sam 1:1b and the opening words of 1:2.

[3] 2 Sam 1:2aα speaks simply of "a man from Saul's camp." Josephus' more definite designation reflects the fact that in his version of 1 Samuel 31// 1 Chronicles 10 in *Ant.* 6.368-378 he has, for the purpose of harmonizing the 2 accounts, introduced elements from 2 Samuel 1, in particular the figure of the Amalekite who claims to have slain Saul in this text (see 2 Sam 1:6-10// 6.371-372).

[4] See 2 Sam 1:2aβ.

[5] See 2 Sam 1:2b.

[6] See 2 Sam 1:3, where (v. 3b) the man responds that he has "escaped from the camp of Israel."

[7] In having the man continue his report here, Josephus passes over David's interjected question of 2 Sam 1:4a about the outcome of the battle.

[8] In 2 Sam 1:4b the man mentions only Jonathan as having perished along with his father. The plural "sons"

of Josephus' version reflects the notice of 1 Sam 31:2 // 1 Chr 10:2// *Ant.* 6.369 according to which 3 of Saul's sons perished with him.

[9] Here too (see note to "to him" at 7.2), Josephus passes over an interruption of the man's report by David, who in 2 Sam 1:5 asks how he knows that Saul and Jonathan are indeed dead.

[10] In 2 Sam 1:6 the man reports additional details about his encounter with the wounded Saul that Josephus leaves aside, given that he has already related that encounter in detail in *Ant.* 6.371.

[11] In proceeding immediately to the man's confession of having killed Saul at the latter's request (// 2 Sam 1:10a), Josephus passes over his report of the initial exchange between himself and Saul (1:8-9), given his anticipation of this in *Ant.* 6.371.

[12] The man's explanation of why Saul asked him to dispatch him and why he had agreed to do this (which replaces the indications on the matter given in 2 Sam 1:10b) harks back to Josephus' own description of Saul's inability to finish himself off due to his weakened condition in *Ant.* 6.370-371.

[13] See 2 Sam 1:10b, to which Josephus adds the opening indication concerning the purpose of the man's bringing the 2 items to David. Josephus has already introduced an anticipated mention of his taking these in *Ant.* 6.372; both there and here in 7.4 he specifies that the objects were of "gold."

death.[14] Tearing his clothes, he spent the entire day weeping and lamenting with his companions.[15]

5. [The thought of] Ionathes, the son of Saoul, who had been his most faithful friend and cause of his safety, made his grief even worse.[16] He himself showed such virtue and loyalty towards Saoul that, although he had many times been in danger of being deprived of life by him, he not only took his death hard, but also punished the one who had done away with him.[17] **6.** For David said to him that he would be his own accuser for having done away with the king;[18] upon learning that his father was of the Amalekite race, he directed that he be executed.[19] He also wrote laments and funeral songs for Saoul and Ionathes that have lasted down to my [own time].[20]

David goes to Hebron

(1.2) 7. Once he had honored the king in these ways, David ceased to mourn[21] and asked God through the prophet[22] which city of the tribe called Iouda he was giving him to live in.[23] When God stated that he was giving him Hebron, David left Sikella and went to that city,[24] bringing his wives—of whom he had two[25]—and the soldiers who were with him.[26]

Made king of Judah, David commends Jabeshites

8. The entire people of the tribe we have just mentioned [that is Iouda] assembled to him and appointed him king.[27] When David heard that the inhabitants of Jabes of Galaditis had buried Saoul and his sons,[28] he sent to them, praising and commending

---

[14] Josephus interjects this notice of the effects of the man's display upon David.

[15] From 2 Sam 1:11-12 Josephus leaves aside both the "fasting" of David and his retinue and the "occasion" of their mourning rites, the death of the king, princes, and people.

[16] This remark on David's particular sorrow for Jonathan has no explicit parallel in 2 Samuel 1; cf., however, his emotionally charged words concerning the latter in 1:25-26.

[17] This notice, highlighting the magnanimity of David, lacks an explicit biblical parallel. Its reference to David's distress over the death of his persecutor Saul does reflect the exclusively positive tenor of his eulogy for the king in 2 Sam 1:17-27, while the mention of his punishing the regicide looks ahead to what follows immediately in 1:13-16.

[18] Josephus anticipates this word of judgment from 2 Sam 1:16b, where it stands, rather illogically, after the man has already been put to death at David's command (1:15). He leaves aside David's preceding word of 1:16a ("your blood be upon your head").

[19] Josephus conflates the sequence of 2 Sam 1:13 (David's asking where the man is from [a question already posed by him in 1:3// 7.2] and the latter's reply that he is "the son of an Amalekite") and 15 (at David's direction, one of his men kills the Amalekite). He leaves aside David's intervening question of 1:14 to the man about his daring to "destroy the Lord's anointed" with its problematic "Messiah-language."

[20] This general notice takes the place of the "source reference" for David's lament (2 Sam 1:17) and the ac-

tual text of that lament in 1:18-27. In not reproducing the wording of the source poem, Josephus follows his earlier procedure regarding the Songs of Deborah (Judges 5) and of Hannah (1 Sam 2:1-10).

[21] Josephus inserts this transitional phrase.

[22] 2 Sam 2:1 speaks simply of David's "inquiring of the Lord." Josephus inserts mention of a (nameless) prophetic intermediary, just as he did in his rewriting of 1 Sam 23:3 in *Ant.* 6.271.

[23] Josephus compresses the double exchange between David and the Lord in 2 Sam 2:1, where David first asks whether he should go up to any of the Judean cities and then, when he is told to do so, asks which city it should be.

[24] See 2 Sam 2:1b-2a. Josephus interjects the reference to David's leaving "Sikella" (i.e. Ziklag; see 7.1) to go to Hebron.

[25] 2 Sam 2:2 gives the names of the 2 women, i.e. Ahinoam and Abigail; as in *Ant.* 6.357 (// 1 Sam 30:5) Josephus omits these. Similarly, in *Life* 1-6 he passes over the names of the women of his own family line.

[26] See 2 Sam 2:3a, which mentions "his men who with him, every one with his household" accompanying David. Josephus omits the notice of 2:3b about the whole party settling "in the towns of Hebron."

[27] In 2 Sam 2:4a the Judeans "anoint" David their king; characteristically, Josephus replaces this verb with one lacking its "messianic" associations.

[28] 2 Sam 2:4b mentions only the burial of Saul himself; Josephus' addition of his sons brings what David "hears" into conformity with the Jabeshites' deed as described by him in *Ant.* 6.377 (// 1 Sam 31:12-13// 1 Chr 10:12).

their deed,[29] and promising that he would repay their solicitude on behalf of the dead.[30] At the same time, he also disclosed that the tribe of Iouda had designated him king.[31]

(1.3) 9. When Saoul's commanding general, Abenner, son of Ner,[32] a man of energy and good by nature, found out that the king had fallen along with Ionathes and his two other sons,[33] he proceeded in haste to the camp,[34] and carried off his [Saoul's] remaining son, who was called Iebosthos.[35] He led him over to the other side of the Jordan,[36] and appointed him king of the entire crowd, except for the tribe of Iouda.[37]

Abner makes Ish-bosheth (Iebosthos) king

10. He established a royal capital for him at [a place] called "Manalis"[38] in our native language, meaning "Camps"[39] in that of the Greeks. From there Abenner marched with a picked army, intending to engage the men of the tribe of Iouda in battle, for he was wrathful at them for having designated David king.[40]

11. He was met by Joab,[41] David's commanding general[42] and the son of Saruia, the king's sister,[43] to whom he had been born (his father was Souri);[44] he had been sent by David,[45] along with his brothers Abessai[46] and Asael[47] and all David's

Encounter at Gibeon

---

[29] Josephus rewords David's message of 2 Sam 2:5-6a so as to eliminate its double invocation of the Deity, first in the benediction of v. 5 and then in the petitionary prayer of v. 6a.

[30] In 2 Sam 2:6b David alludes to "this thing" which the Jabeshites have done; Josephus has him spell out its content.

[31] See 2 Sam 2:7b whose verb "anoint," echoing that of 2:4a, Josephus replaces here as well (see note to "king" at 7.8). He leaves aside David's exhorting the Jabeshites to resolution and the motivation of this in terms of Saul's death of v. 7a.

[32] Josephus here recalls the personal data concerning Abner given by him in *Ant.* 6.129-130 (// 1 Sam 14:50b-51).

[33] Expatiating on the notice of 2 Sam 2:8 concerning Abner's initiative, Josephus inserts both a characterization of him and a reference to the report about the death of the king and the 3 princes (cf. *Ant.* 6.369) that prompts his action on behalf of Saul's surviving son.

[34] Josephus' reference to the "camp" from which Abner takes Saul's son corresponds to the plus of LXX BL 2 Sam 2:8.

[35] MT (2 Sam 2:8) אִישׁ בֹּשֶׁת (Eng.: "Ish-bosheth"); LXX B Ἰεβόσθε; LXX L Εἰσβάαλ (MS 93; emended text Ἰσβάαλ), Μεμφιβόσθε (MSS 19 108 82 127); Josephus Ἰέβοσθος.

[36] 2 Sam 2:8b does not explicitly mention the "Jordan"; Josephus introduces the term in light of source's use of the verb "bring over."

[37] In 2 Sam 2:9 Abner makes Ish-bosheth king over various named regions on both sides of the Jordan, summed up in the phrase "all Israel," while 2:10b notes that "the house of Judah followed David." Josephus leaves aside the series of (displaced) chronological no-

tices of 2:10a (Ish-bosheth accedes at age 40 and rules 2 years) and 2:11 (David rules at Hebron for 7 1/2 years).

[38] MT (2 Sam 2:8) מחנים (Eng.: "Mahanaim"); LXX B Μαναέμ (LXX L "translates" the Hebrew name with the phrase "in the camps"); Josephus Μάναλις.

[39] Josephus' "translation" of the Hebrew place name corresponds to that given in LXX L 2 Sam 2:8b; see previous note.

[40] Josephus, alluding back to 7.8, supplies both a purpose and a motivation for Abner's move as related in 2 Sam 2:12, where he advances from "Mahanaim to Gibeon."

[41] MT (2 Sam 2:13) יואב (Eng.: "Joab"); LXX Ἰωάβ; Josephus Ἰώαβος. On Josephus' (highly ambivalent) portrayal of Joab—whom he mentions for the first time here—see Feldman 1998a: 203-14.

[42] Josephus adds the indication concerning Joab's rank to the mention of him in 2 Sam 2:13, anticipating this from 8:15.

[43] Josephus previously mentioned "Souria" ("Zeruiah" in the Bible) as sister of David in *Ant.* 6.311 (cf. 1 Sam 26:6).

[44] The Bible nowhere names the husband of Zeruiah and the father of her 3 sons; cf., however, the reference to this figure's tomb in 2 Sam 2:32. Marcus (*ad loc.*) suggests that Josephus might have in mind the father of another biblical Joab, i.e. "Seraiah" (LXX: Σαραί) mentioned in 1 Chr 4:14. Alternatively, Σουρί might be seen as an erroneous partial duplication of the name of Joab's mother (Σαρουίας) cited a few words back in 7.11.

[45] In 2 Sam 2:13a Joab sets out on his own initiative; Josephus underscores his subordination to King David.

troops.[48] Encountering him by chance at a certain pool in Gabaon,[49] Joab formed his ranks for battle.[50]

Contest and battle

12. But when Abenner told him that he wished to learn which of them had the more courageous soldiers, it was agreed that twelve combatants from both [sides] would fight.[51] Accordingly, those selected for battle by each of the generals[52] advanced into the middle of the ranks. After hurling their spears[53] at each other, they drew their swords and, catching hold of one another's heads, held fast to these; they kept striking their opponents' ribs and sides with their swords until all were slain, as if by agreement.[54] **13.** Once they had fallen, the remainder of the armies rushed upon each other; a fierce battle ensued in which Abenner's men were defeated.[55]

Abner pursued

When they fled, Joab did not stop pursuing. Rather, he himself pressed forward, appealing to his troops to follow him on foot and not grow tired of slaughtering.[56]

14. His brothers eagerly exerted themselves and especially the youngest Asael[57]— who had a reputation for swiftness of foot—distinguished himself beyond the others. For it is said that he not only outran humans, but also horses when he competed with them in contests.[58] He pursued Abenner speedily in a straight-ahead movement,

Abner kills Asahel

not diverging to either side.[59] **15.** Turning round, Abenner tried to dissuade him from his impetuosity, first telling him to desist from his pursuit and to strip the armor off one of his soldiers.[60] Next, when he did not convince him to do this, he urged him to restrain himself and stop pursuing, so that he would not [need] to kill him and so ruin his frank relations with his brother.[61] He, however, did not assent to his words, but continued the pursuit. Fleeing though he was, Abenner struck him mortally with

---

[46] Josephus has mentioned this figure ("Abishai" in the Bible) as a companion of David in *Ant.* 6.311-312 (// 1 Sam 26:6-9).

[47] MT (2 Sam 2:18) אשהאל (Eng.: "Asahel"); LXX Ἀσαήλ; Josephus Ἀσάηλος. Josephus anticipates his mention of the presence of Joab's 2 brothers on the expedition from 2 Sam 2:18.

[48] 2 Sam 2:13a speaks of David's "servants" accompanying Joab.

[49] MT 2 Sam 2:13a designates the site of the encounter as "Gibeon." Josephus' form of the place name corresponds to that of LXX.

[50] This indication takes the place of the mention of the 2 forces sitting on opposite sites of the pool in 2 Sam 2:13b.

[51] Josephus provides a motivation for Abner's proposal (which in 2 Sam 2:14a reads: "let the young men arise and play before us") to which Joab gives his assent in 2:14b ("let them arise"), likewise clarifying the meaning of the term "play" used by Abner. He makes part of the agreement itself the number of those who are to fight, anticipating the figure from 2:15.

[52] Josephus inserts the detail about the generals' choosing the fighters.

[53] This preliminary action of the fighters is not mentioned in the account of the contest given in 2 Sam 2:16.

[54] See 2 Sam 2:16, from which Josephus omits the

etiological notice of v. 16b about the site being called "Helkath-hazzurim" (RSV note: "field of the sword-edges"; LXX: "field of the plotters").

[55] See 2 Sam 2:17.

[56] 2 Sam 2:18 simply mentions the presence of Joab along with his 2 brothers at the moment of Abner's defeat and then moves immediately to a focus on Asahel. Josephus highlights the initiative of the general Joab as the pursuit gets under way.

[57] In 2 Sam 2:19 Asahel seems to pursue Abner on his own initiative. In Josephus' presentation he does so in response to Joab's exhortation; see previous note.

[58] This notice, underscoring Asahel's speed, takes the place of the image used in 2 Sam 2:18b, which calls him "as swift of foot as a wild gazelle."

[59] See 2 Sam 2:19. Josephus leaves aside the (superfluous) initial exchange between the 2 men of 2:20, in which Abner asks Asahel if it is he, and the latter responds affirmatively.

[60] See 2 Sam 2:21. Josephus uses the same word (πανοπλία, "armor") as does LXX for that which Asahel is urged to "strip." The corresponding MT term (חלצה; RSV "spoil") is of uncertain meaning.

[61] In 2 Sam 2:22 Abner asks, rhetorically, how, if he kills Asahel, he could face his brother Joab. Josephus' rendition accentuates the 2 men's amity and hence Abner's unwillingness to do the deed to which Asahel's continued pursuit is driving him.

the spear [that he threw] backwards, and immediately killed him.[62]

16. When those who were pursuing Abenner with him came to the spot where Asael was lying, standing round his dead body, they ceased to pursue the enemy.[63] But Joab himself and his brother Abessai ran past the corpse, having, in their wrath over him who had been killed, even more reason for exertion against Abenner.[64] Using unbelievable speed and eagerness, they pursued Abenner to a certain place called "Ommat,"[65] it being now already about sunset. **17.** Ascending a certain hill that was at that place, Joab sighted Abenner along with those of the tribe of Benjamin who were with him.[66] [Abenner] then cried out and said that one ought not stir up compatriots to strife and battle.[67] His brother Asael had also committed an offense by not being persuaded when he was urged not to pursue, with the result that he died after being struck by him.[68] Assenting, Joab took these words as a consolation;[69] he sounded the trumpet, signalling to his troops, and halted any further pursuit.[70]

Hostilities cease

18. Joab pitched camp that night in that place,[71] while Abenner marched the whole night and, having crossed the Jordan river, reached Saoul's son Iebosthos at "The Camps."[72] On the next day Joab, having counted all the dead bodies, buried them.[73] **19.** There fell of the troops of Abenner about 360, while David's army lost nineteen in addition to Asael.[74] Joab and Abessai carried his body from there to Bethleem and buried it in their ancestral tomb; then they went to David at Hebron.[75]

Asahel buried

20. From that time on then there began a civil war among the Hebrews that lasted a long time. David's supporters grew ever stronger, prevailing in the face of dangers, whereas Saoul's son and his subjects became weaker almost by the day.[76]

David's dominance

(1.4) 21. Around this time David had sons, six in number[77] [by as many wives],[78]

David's family

---

[62] Josephus omits the gory details of 2 Sam 2:23aβbα, where Abner strikes Asahel with the butt of his spear with such force that it comes out his back.

[63] See 2 Sam 2:23bβ.

[64] Josephus provides a motive for the brothers' continued pursuit (2 Sam 2:24a) when the rest of the army abandons this (2:23bβ).

[65] MT (2 Sam 2:24) אמה (Eng.: "Ammah"); LXX B Ἀμμάν; LXX L Ἐμμάθ, Ἀμμαθ; Josephus Ὄμματον (this is the reading of M, which Niese follows; Marcus adopts that of SP, i.e. Ἀμμάταν). Josephus omits the designation of the site as a "hill" (cf., however, 7.17), as well as the indication about its location ("which lies before Giah on the way to the wilderness of Gibeon") of 2:24b.

[66] In 2 Sam 2:25 it is the Benjamites who take their stand as "one band" behind Abner "on top of a hill."

[67] Josephus turns Abner's threefold question to Joab of 2 Sam 2:26 into a characteristic statement by him, highlighting the wrongfulness of civil strife. On the theme of "civil strife" in Josephus, see Feldman 1998: 140-43, 610-11; 1998a: 556.

[68] This statement by Abner, justifying his killing of Asahel, has no biblical counterpart.

[69] This notice takes the place of Joab's initial (obscure) response to Abner in 2 Sam 2:27, in which he swears that if Abner had not spoken, his men would

have abandoned their pursuit only in the morning.

[70] See 2 Sam 2:28 whose concluding remark about there being no further fighting Josephus omits.

[71] Josephus inserts the reference to Joab's pitching camp.

[72] Josephus' "translation" of the site name is in accord with the LXX B reading in 2 Sam 2:29; compare "Mahanaim" (MT); "in the camps of Madaim" (LXX L). See 7.10, where Josephus gives the Hebrew site name as "Manalis" and provides the translation "Camps" for this.

[73] 2 Sam 2:32 mentions the burial of Asahel alone by an indeterminate "they." Josephus accentuates Joab's piety by making him the one to bury, not only Asahel, but all the fallen troops; see Feldman 1998a: 205.

[74] These figures correspond to those given in 2 Sam 2:30-31 for the losses on the 2 sides.

[75] See 2 Sam 2:32, from which Josephus omits mention of the all-night march from Bethlehem to Hebron by Joab and his men.

[76] See 2 Sam 3:1.

[77] Josephus omits the specification that the sons in question were born to David "in Hebron" (2 Sam 3:2a; see 3:5b). He supplies the total figure for the sons listed in 3:2b-5a.

[78] This phrase, bracketed by Niese (but not by Marcus) is absent in RO.

of whom the oldest, whose mother was Achina,[79] was called Amnon,[80] the second by his wife Abigaia,[81] Daniel,[82] the third, who was born to Machame,[83] daughter of Tholomai,[84] king of the Gesseroi,[85] had the name of Apsalom,[86] the fourth, by his wife Aethe,[87] he called Adonias,[88] the fifth Saphatias[89] by Abitale,[90] while the sixth, by Galaad,[91] he named Gethersas.[92]

Israelites' loyalty to Ish-bosheth

22. Once civil war broke out,[93] it often came to actual combat between the adherents of each of the two kings. Abenner, the commanding general of Saoul's son, being very clever and having the full loyalty of the crowd,[94] managed to keep them all attached to Iebosthos. They continued for some time in their willingness to support his cause.[95]

Abner turns against Ish-bosheth

23. Later, however, a complaint was made against Abenner on the grounds that he had had relations with Saoul's concubine, Raispha[96] by name, the daughter of Sibat.[97] When he was reproached about this by Iebosthos,[98] he became very indignant and angry, thinking he was not being justly recompensed by him for all the care he had used with him.[99] He threatened to transfer the kingship to David in or-

---

[79] MT (2 Sam 3:2b) אחינעם (Eng.: "Ahinoam"); LXX B Ἀχεινόομ; LXX L Ἀχινάαμ; Josephus Ἀχινά (the same form read by him in *Ant.* 6.320). Josephus leaves aside the source qualification of her as "of Jezreel."

[80] MT (2 Sam 3:2) אמנון (Eng.: "Amnon"); LXX and Josephus Ἀμνών.

[81] On "Abigail," see *Ant.* 6.295-309 (// 1 Samuel 25); 6.320 (// 1 Sam 27:3). Josephus leaves aside the notation of 2 Sam 3:3a about her being "the widow of Nabal of Carmel."

[82] MT (2 Sam 3:3a) כלאב (Eng.: "Chileab"); LXX Δαλουιά; Josephus Δανίηλος. Josephus derives his alternative name for David's 2nd son, born to him by Abigail, from 1 Chr 3:1.

[83] MT (2 Sam 3:3b) מעכה (Eng.: "Maacah"); LXX Μααχά; Josephus Μαχάμη.

[84] MT (2 Sam 3:3) תלמי (Eng.: "Talmai"); LXX B Θομμεί; LXX L Θολμί; Josephus Θολομαῖος.

[85] MT 2 Sam 3:3b calls him "king of Geshur" (LXX B "Geseir"; LXX L "Gessir").

[86] MT (2 Sam 3:3) אבשלום (Eng.: "Absalom"); LXX Ἀβεσσαλώμ; Josephus Ἀψάλωμος (this is the reading of RO that Niese and Marcus follow; the remaining witnesses read Ἀβεσ(σ)άλμος).

[87] MT (2 Sam 3:4a) חגית (Eng.: "Haggith"); LXX B Φεγγείθ; LXX L Ἀγγίθ; Josephus Ἀήθη (this is the reading of RO adopted by Niese; Marcus *ad loc.* and Schalit *s.v.* read Ἀγίθη with MSP).

[88] MT (2 Sam 3:4) אדניה (Eng.: "Adonijah"); LXX B Ὀρνείλ; LXX L Ὀρνιά; Josephus Ἀδωνίας.

[89] MT (2 Sam 3:4b) שפטיה (Eng.: "Shephatiah"); LXX B Σαβατεία; LXX L and Josephus Σαφατίας.

[90] MT (2 Sam 3:4b) אביטל (Eng.: "Abital"); LXX B Ἀβειτάλ; LXX L Ἀβιτάαλ; Josephus Ἀβιτάλη.

[91] MT (2 Sam 3:5a) עגלה (Eng.: "Eglah"); LXX B Ἀιγάλ; LXX L Ἀγλά; Josephus Γαλαάδ (this is the reading adopted by Niese; Marcus reads Ἀιγλᾶς with SP).

[92] MT (2 Sam 3:5) יתראם (Eng: "Ithream"); LXX B Ἰεθεραάμ; LXX L Ἰεθραάμ; Josephus Γεθερσᾶς (this is the reading of ROM followed by Niese; Marcus *ad loc.* and Schlatter *s.v.* read Ἰεθρόας with SE).

[93] This transitional phrase (see 2 Sam 3:6a) picks up the topic of the civil war from 7.20, after the interlude concerning David's family in 7.21.

[94] This inserted characterization of Abner echoes that of 7.9, where he is called "a man of energy and good by nature."

[95] These notices on Abner's influence on the people and the support for Saul's son this generated render more specific (and positive) the statement of 2 Sam 3:6b: "Abner was making himself great in the house of Saul."

[96] MT (2 Sam 3:7) רצפה (Eng.: "Rizpah"); LXX Ῥεσφά; Josephus Ῥαισφᾶ (this is the form read by Niese; Marcus adopts the "Respha" [= LXX] of Lat).

[97] MT (2 Sam 3:7) איה (Eng.: "Aiah"); LXX B Ἰάλ; LXX L Σιβά; Josephus Σιβάτης; Schalit *s.v.* Σιβάθης attempts a reconstruction of the original reading of the name in Josephus on the basis of Lat "Ansebath." In 2 Sam 3:7b there is no reference to some 3rd party "complaining" to Ish-bosheth about Abner's deed, this causing him to confront Abner. Josephus' insertion of such a reference accounts for the king's knowledge of the happening.

[98] In LXX BL 2 Sam 3:7-8 the name of the one confronting Abner is Μεμφιβόσθε, the son of Jonathan (and grandson of Saul) featured in 2 Samuel 9. Josephus reads the MT form of the name, as cited by him in 7.9.

[99] Josephus provides a motivation for Abner's "anger" as cited in 2 Sam 3:8aα (this inspired by Abner's

der to make clear that it was not in virtue of his vigor and cleverness that Iebosthos was ruling beyond the Jordan, but thanks to his own generalship and fidelity.[100] **24.** He then sent to David at Hebron[101] and asked him to swear and pledge that he would regard him as his companion and friend, once he induced the people to turn away from the son of Saoul and appointed him king of the entire country.[102]

Abner's overture to David

25. David made these declarations, for he was pleased at what Abenner had conveyed to him by his messengers.[103] As a first token of his fulfilling their agreements, he asked[104] that he safely return to him [Melchale],[105] the wife whom he had acquired by great dangers and by the heads of the 600 Palestinoi[106] that, for her sake, he had brought to her father Saoul.[107]

David gets Michal back

26. Abenner therefore sent Melchale to him, having taken her by force from Ophelti,[108] who was then her husband, Iebosthos also assisting in the matter,[109] for David had written to him that he had a just [claim] to get his wife back.[110]

Convening those of advanced age of the crowd, the subordinate commanders,[111] and the commanders of a thousand,[112] Abenner said to them **27.** that, whereas they

Abner secures Israelites' support for David

---

enumeration of his benefactions to the Saulides in v. 8bα). He leaves aside Abner's self-derogatory opening words of v. 8aβ: "Am I a dog's head of Judah?" (MT; LXX BL lack the words "of Judah"). He further omits Abner's reference to the "fault" with which he is being charged (v. 8bβ) and his oath formula at the beginning of v. 9.

[100] See 2 Sam 3:10 whose array of place names, demarcating the extent of David's prospective kingdom, Josephus omits, substituting an extended motivation for Abner's intended initiative. He further omits the notice of 2 Sam 3:11 on Ish-bosheth's failure to respond to Abner due to his fear of him.

[101] Josephus' specification of David's whereabouts reflects the LXX L reading in 2 Sam 3:12 (LXX B reads "to Thailam," while MT has "[Abner sent messengers to David] where he was"). Like LXX, Josephus has no equivalent to the opening words of Abner's message to David as cited in MT 3:12, i.e. "to whom does the land belong?"

[102] Josephus characteristically rewords Abner's proposal in 2 Sam 3:12 so as to eliminate its phrase "make a covenant (LXX: διαθήκη)."

[103] Josephus motivates David's acceptance of Abner's proposal (2 Sam 3:13a), while once again (see previous note) eliminating the source's use of the term "covenant."

[104] Josephus tones down David's peremptory demand as cited in 2 Sam 3:13b ("you shall not see my face, unless..."), while also spelling out the motivation behind David's request.

[105] The name, absent in Lat, is bracketed by Niese, but not by Marcus.

[106] In 2 Sam 3:14 David refers to the 100 Philistine foreskins procured by himself, while in 1 Sam 18:27 the figure given is 200. Josephus takes care to harmonize David's words here with his own previous account in

Ant. 6.202-203; in both instances David's required wedding gift is 600 Philistine heads.

[107] Josephus conflates the content of the separate orders given by David to Abner (2 Sam 3:13) and to Ish-bosheth (3:14) concerning the return of his wife. He delays mention of David's address to Ish-bosheth until a later point; see 7.26.

[108] MT (2 Sam 3:14) פלטיאל (Eng.: "Paltiel"); LXX B Φαλτιήλ; LXX L Φαλτίου; Josephus 'Οφέλτιος (this is the majority reading adopted by Niese and Marcus; Schalit *s.v.* suggests rather Φέλτιος, this corresponding to the form of the name found in *Ant.* 6.309// 1 Sam 25:44). Josephus leaves aside the name of Paltiel's father (MT 2 Sam 3:14: Laish), having given this as "Lis" in 6.309.

[109] In 2 Sam 3:15 it is Ish-bosheth who actually effects the return of Michal to David, in line with David's injunction to him in 3:14. Josephus makes the return a joint initiative of Abner and the king, with the former taking the leading role.

[110] This is Josephus' delayed use of David's order to Ish-bosheth as cited in 2 Sam 3:14, the wording of which he generalizes, given that he has already drawn on its allusion to the bridal price paid by David for Michal in formulating the king's command to Abner in 7.25. Josephus omits the pathetic biblical scene—reflecting badly on David's compassionate image—of Paltiel following his wife, weeping as he goes, until he is directed by Abner to return (2 Sam 3:16).

[111] Greek: ταξίαρχοι. As Mason (2001: 114, n. 1053) points out, the precise meaning of this term depends on the size of the "unit" (Greek: τάξις) that these officers are commanding. Here, as elsewhere, Josephus leaves the matter indeterminate.

[112] Abner's (single) interlocutor in 2 Sam 3:17 is "the elders of Israel."

had been ready to turn away from Iebosthos and go over to David, he had held them back from their impetuousness;[113] now, however, he would allow them to go do as they wished. For he knew that God, through the prophet Samouel, had designated David king of all the Hebrews.[114] He had further announced that he himself would punish the Palestinoi and, having overcome them, would make them their subjects.[115] **28.** When the elders and the leaders heard these things, they realized that Abenner's plan was in accord with what they themselves had previously thought about the situation, and switched to supporting David's cause.[116]

Abner received by David

29. Once they had been persuaded, Abenner called together the tribe of the Benjamites—for all Iebosthos' bodyguards were from this tribe[117]—and told them the same thing. Seeing that they made no resistance, but were won over to what he wished,[118] he took about twenty of his companions and came to David[119] so that he might receive his oath from him personally—for it seems that we all find more credible what we ourselves do than what is done by others[120]—and also to indicate to him the words he had spoken to the leaders and the entire tribe.[121] **30.** He was received by David in a friendly way, being splendidly and lavishly entertained by him at table for many days.[122] Then Abenner requested to go off to bring the crowd to him in order that, while he was present and visible, they might hand over the rule to him.[123]

Joab fails to discredit Abner with David

(1.5) 31. Shortly after David had sent Abenner off, the king's commander-in-chief, Joab came to Hebron.[124] When he learned that Abenner had been with the king and had departed a short time before with agreements and commitments about the lead-

---

[113] Abner's speech to the elders in 2 Sam 3:17 mentions only their desire to have David as their king. Josephus' inserted remark about Abner's past efforts to restrain their impulse picks up on the reference to his keeping the Israelites loyal to Ish-bosheth in 7.22.

[114] Abner's invocation of the divine promise to David in 2 Sam 3:18a does not mention Samuel as the mediator of that promise, nor speak explicitly of God's having appointed David "king." Josephus' formulation recalls his account of the anointing of David by Samuel in *Ant.* 6.164-165.

[115] Compare 2 Sam 3:18b, where there is reference to David's delivering Israel also from all its (other) enemies. Concentrating on the Philistine threat, Josephus has Abner recall God's word through Samuel (see *Ant.* 6.165) that David would not only defeat, but also "subdue" them.

[116] With this inserted notice on the audience's reaction, Josephus highlights Abner's effectiveness as a speaker.

[117] In his rendering of 2 Sam 3:19a, Josephus interjects a notice on the special status of the Benjamites that prompts Abner to speak to them separately. He plausibly infers that Ish-bosheth would have drawn his bodyguards from the tribe to which he himself, as a son of the Benjamite Saul (see 1 Sam 9:1// *Ant.* 6.45), belonged.

[118] Once again (see note on "cause" at 7.28), Josephus inserts mention of the persuasive effect of Abner's

words on his audience. Josephus delays to the end of the paragraph his rendition of the statement of 2 Sam 3:19b about Abner's going to report the mind of his audiences to David; see note to "entire tribe" at 7.29.

[119] From 2 Sam 3:20a Josephus omits the specification that Abner came to David "at Hebron."

[120] Josephus adds this reference to Abner's concern that he get an oath from David and the explanation as to why he wished to be given this personally rather than through intermediaries.

[121] See 2 Sam 3:19b. The "entire tribe" here is the Benjamites mentioned earlier in the paragraph.

[122] Josephus expatiates on the king's hospitality as mentioned in 2 Sam 3:20b.

[123] See 2 Sam 3:21a. Once again, Josephus eliminates the source's use of the phrase "make a covenant," likewise having Abner suggest a reason why the people need to be "brought" to David, i.e. that they might see the one on whom they are conferring the kingship for themselves.

[124] Josephus' conflation of 2 Sam 3:21b (David's dismissal of Abner) and 22a (Joab's arrival) omits the latter verse's mention of Joab and David's servants having been on a raid from which Joab had bought back much plunder. He likewise passes over the notice of 3:22b that Abner was no longer in Hebron at the moment of Joab's return, which seems to duplicate the reference to David's dismissing Abner in 3:21b.

ership,[125] Joab, anxious that he [Abenner] would be held in honor and given first rank as one who would be a supporter of David's kingship, and who was also adept in understanding political matters[126] and in making use of opportunities, while he himself would be put at a disadvantage and deprived of his generalship, embarked on a malicious and vile path.[127]

32. First, he undertook to slander him to the king,[128] urging him to be on his guard and not give credence to what Abenner had agreed to,[129] for he [Abenner] was doing all these things in order to strengthen the leadership of Saoul's son.[130] Having come to him with deception and deceit,[131] he [Abenner] had now gone off in the hope of [obtaining] what he wished and the realization of what he had prepared.[132]

33. When, however, he did not convince David by these words and saw that he was not enraged, Joab turned from these to a path that was still more daring than this, and decided to kill Abenner.[133] He dispatched men to pursue him, whom he ordered, once they caught up with him, to call him in the name of David, who had something to say to him about matters that he had not remembered when he was present.[134]

Joab assassinates Abner

34. When Abenner heard the messengers' words—for they caught up with him at a certain spot known as Besera, twenty *stadia* distant from Hebron[135]—he returned, having no inkling of what was about to happen.[136] Joab met him at the gate, wel-

---

[125] 2 Sam 3:23 merely reports that David had dismissed Abner, who had gone away "in peace." The more specific information given Joab about David and Abner's dealings according to Josephus serves to better motivate his subsequent reactions.

[126] Greek: δεινὸν ὄντα συνιδεῖν πράγματα. This same phrase recurs in *Ant.* 12.63 in reference to King Ptolemy.

[127] This editorial sequence goes beyond the biblical account in exposing the psychology behind Joab's subsequent deed and providing an evaluation of it. The comment reflects Josephus' sustained interest in jealous rivalry among commanders, a matter highlighted by him in *Life* 46-61.

[128] Earlier, Josephus had highlighted the "slandering" of David to Saul by various parties (see *Ant.* 6.267, 280, 285). Now yet another good character, Abner, is about to be slandered by an envious compatriot—just as happened to Josephus himself from the side of his fellow Jews (see *Life* 425, 428b-429).

[129] These words of warning take the place of the pointed, reproachful questions about why David dealt with Abner as he did with which Joab begins his address to the king in 2 Sam 3:24. The Josephan Joab appears more tactful in his approach to David.

[130] Joab's concluding charge in 2 Sam 3:25b is that Abner came to David in order to spy on his doings. Josephus substitutes a reference to the (purported) ultimate aim of his visit, i.e. the shoring up of Ish-bosheth's rule.

[131] Joab's initial charge against Abner in 2 Sam

3:25 is that he came to David to "deceive" him. The Josephan Joab intensifies the charge—and the irony, given that it is he himself who is trying to deceive David.

[132] Josephus amplifies Joab's charge that Abner has come to "deceive" David in 2 Sam 3:25a, appending a claim about the state of mind in which his rival has departed.

[133] Josephus interjects this notice on the failure of Joab's first initiative and his recourse to a still more outrageous one. The insertion sets up a contrast between Joab, the ineffectual speaker, and Abner, whose words did have their desired effect (see 7.28-29). It also contrasts David (and the Roman emperors) who did not believe the "slanders" told them concerning Abner and Josephus, respectively, and Saul who credited those made against David (see *Ant.* 6.285); cf. note to "the king" at 7.32.

[134] In recounting Joab's dispatch of his messengers (see 2 Sam 3:26a), Josephus underscores the deceitfulness of Joab, who fraudulently recalls Abner in David's own name on the alleged ground that there were things that the latter had forgotten to tell him—this from a man who has just charged Abner himself with "deception and deceit" (7.32).

[135] MT (2 Sam 3:26b) בור הסרה (RSV: "the cistern of Sirah"); LXX B τοῦ φρέατος τοῦ Σεειράμ; LXX L τοῦ φρέατος Σεειρά; Josephus (conflating the 2 Hebrew words of MT) Βησηρᾶ. Josephus supplies the indication concerning the site's distance from Hebron.

[136] Josephus inserts this notice on Abner's state of

coming him like an especially loyal friend—for those who undertake dishonorable actions often play the part of the truly good, so as to deflect suspicion from their plot.[137] **35.** Having separated him from his servants—as if to speak to him in private—Joab, alone except for his brother Abessai, conducted him to a remoter section of the gate. Drawing his sword, he struck him in the side.[138]

Reflections on Abner's murder

36. Thus Abenner died, having been ambushed in this way by Joab, who indeed said that he was punishing [him] for his brother Asael,[139] whom Abenner had taken and killed as he was pursuing him in the battle near Hebron.[140] In reality, however, he was anxious about the generalship and honor from the king, that he not be deprived of these things and that Abenner obtain the first rank from David.[141] **37.** From these things each will recognize what and how much people dare to do for the sake of ambition and rule, not yielding to anyone regarding these matters. For desiring to gain these things, they attain them by countless evils, and being anxious about losing them, they endeavor to secure their continuation for themselves by even worse acts, **38.** as if it is not as terrible not to obtain the supreme greatness of authority as to lose it, once one has become accustomed to the good things that come from it. Regarding this as the height of misfortune, they therefore devise even more evil things and venture on deeds, in constant fear of losing [these things]. But about these matters it suffices to have spoken briefly.[142]

David sees to Abner's burial

(1.6) 39. When David heard that Abenner had been done away with, he was grieved in soul.[143] He testified to all, stretching out his right hand to God and crying out that he had no part in Abenner's murder; nor was it at his command or by his wish that he had been killed.[144] He invoked terrible curses upon him who had murdered him and made his entire house and his accomplices liable to penalties on behalf of the one who had put to death.[145] **40.** For David was concerned that it not appear that he had done this thing in violation of the sworn pledges he had given to

mind, thereby accentuating both his vulnerability and the criminality of Joab, who will take advantage of that vulnerability.

[137] In introducing the notice of 2 Sam 3:27a on the encounter of the 2 men at the gate, Josephus interjects mention of the deceitful hypocrisy of Joab's "welcome," likewise making this the occasion for a moral maxim (cf. the likewise interjected maxim about people putting more faith in what they do themselves rather than what others do for them in 7.29).

[138] Josephus adds several details to the summary account of Abner's murder in 2 Sam 3:27: the dismissal of Joab's servants and the presence of Abishai (this last anticipated from 3:30, where Abishai appears unexpectedly as a co-assassin of Abner). He likewise has Abner struck in the "side" rather than in the "belly," thereby assimilating his killing to that of the 24 champions in 7.12, who strike each others' "ribs and sides."

[139] Josephus modifies the concluding words of 2 Sam 3:27, where the narrator reports, seemingly as his own view of things, that Abner died "for the blood of Asahel his [Joab's] brother." In Josephus' presentation this becomes a mere (and fraudulent) claim on Joab's part, as is evident from what follows.

[140] As Marcus (*ad loc.*) points out, Josephus' men-

tion of "Hebron" as the site of the battle in which Asahel lost his life is a "slip" for the actual site as reported both by the Bible (Gibeon, 2 Sam 2:12-13) and Josephus himself ("Gabaon," 7.11). Here in 7.36 Lat does, in fact, read "Gablon."

[141] Having cited Joab's alleged motive for killing Abner as suggested by 2 Sam 3:27, Josephus now goes on—without any (explicit) biblical warrant, but echoing his previous statements in 7.31—to adduce the real reason.

[142] Josephus' 2-paragraph reflection on the corrupting effects of the struggle both to attain and retain positions of power has no biblical counterpart. As Feldman (1998a: 212) points out, however, it is reminiscent of the extended remarks Josephus appends to Saul's killing of the priests of Nob in *Ant.* 6.262-268.

[143] Josephus inserts this reference to David's emotional response to Abner's killing.

[144] Josephus amplifies and dramatizes David's statement (2 Sam 3:28) disassociating himself from Abner's murder, with, e.g., mention of the hand gesture accompanying this.

[145] Josephus' reference to David's "terrible curses" generalizes 2 Sam 3:29, where David pronounces 5 particular imprecations against Joab's house.

Abenner.[146] Moreover, he ordered the entire people to weep and mourn for the man and to honor his body by the customary rituals of tearing their clothes and putting on sackcloth, and having done these things, to precede the bier.[147]

41. David himself, together with those of advanced age and those in leadership roles, followed.[148] Beating his breast[149] and evidencing by his tears both his loyalty to Abenner while he was alive and his grief for him when dead, he likewise made it clear that it was not in accordance with his plan that Abenner had been done away with.[150]

42. He buried him magnificently in Hebron;[151] having composed funeral songs, he first sobbed these out himself, standing by his grave, and then handed the role over to others.[152] The death of Abenner so tormented him[153] that he would not eat when his companions called on him to do so, but swore that he would taste nothing until sundown.[154]

43. These things won him the loyalty of the crowd. For those who cherished affection for Abenner were very pleased by his honoring of him when dead and loved his keeping his pledge, because he thought him worthy of the customary rites as though he were a relative and friend, rather than outraging him as if he were an enemy by a plain and careless burial. All the others rejoiced at his kind and affable nature, each one supposing that he [would receive] from the king, in similar circumstances, the same care as he had seen Abenner's corpse obtain.[155]

Popular response to David's solicitude for Abner

44. It was, moreover, natural that David should wish to deserve a good reputation by caring for [the dead] so that no one would suspect that Abenner had been murdered by him.[156] He also told the crowd that his grief for him, a good man who had

David's declaration about Abner's murder

---

[146] Josephus inserts this reference to the motivation behind David's preceding statements, underscoring the king's concern for his reputation as a respecter of oaths.

[147] See 2 Sam 3:31a. From David's directives concerning Abner's funeral there, Josephus omits the surprising and off-putting detail that the murderer Joab is himself to participate in the funeral.

[148] In 2 Sam 3:31b David alone is said to follow the bier; Josephus' inserted mention of the participation also of the aged and the leadership groups adds solemnity to the occasion.

[149] This inserted element accentuates the intensity of David's distress. It recalls Josephus' likewise inserted mention of the Jabeshites "beating their breasts" as they bury Saul and his sons in *Ant.* 6.377.

[150] Josephus embellishes the simple statement about David's "weeping" of 2 Sam 3:32aβ with mention of the intended effect of that weeping, this echoing the king' own earlier affirmation on the matter as cited in 7.39.

[151] 2 Sam 3:32aα simply states that "they buried Abner at Hebron." Josephus accentuates both David's personal role in the burial and its lavishness.

[152] As he did in the case of David's lament for Saul and Jonathan (2 Sam 1:17-27), Josephus does not reproduce the actual wording of his lament for Abner as cited in 3:34. On the other hand, he heightens the pa-

thos of the scene with mention of David's own "sobbing" and the eventual involvement of others in the lament.

[153] This inserted reference to the emotional impact of Abner's death upon David echoes the (also inserted) mention of his being "grieved in soul" in 7.39. Here, David's distress serves to motivate his subsequent refusal to eat.

[154] In 2 Sam 3:35a "all the people" urge David to eat. Josephus, more plausibly, has the request emanate from the king's intimates. In accord with his usual practice, he omits the actual wording of David's "oath" as cited in 3:35b.

[155] Josephus greatly expands on the summary notice of 2 Sam 3:36 about the people's being "pleased" by David's treatment of Abner's remains, as well as by everything he did. The phrase "keeping his pledge (Greek: πίστις)" echoes the reference to David's concern that he not appear to have "violated his sworn pledges (Greek: πίστεις)" in 7.40. It is now clear that David has convinced everyone that he is indeed not a pledge-breaker.

[156] This (inserted) remark picks up on Josephus' rendition of David's statement in 7.39: "He testified to all... that he had no part in Abner's murder...," as well as to the allusion to the king's concern for his reputation in 7.40.

been put to death, was not a passing one, even as the affairs of the Hebrews [had suffered] no slight loss by their being deprived of one who was capable of keeping them together and saving them by his excellent counsels and by his vigor in military operations.[157] **45.** "But God," he said, "who is concerned with everything, will not allow this thing to go unavenged for us.[158] You know that I myself am incapable of doing anything to Joab and Abessai, the sons of Sarouia, who are stronger than I.[159] The Deity will, however, repay them for their brazen deeds."[160] It was in this way that Abenner ended his life.[161]

Plot to kill Ish-bosheth

(2.1) 46. When Saoul's son Iebosthos[162] heard of his death, he did not take lightly his being deprived of a man who was a relative[163] and who had conferred the kingship on him; rather, the death of Abenner caused him exceeding suffering and great pain.[164] He himself did not survive much longer, but died as the result of a plot[165] by the sons of Eremmon,[166] one of whom was named Bana,[167] the other Thaenos.[168] **47.** These men were Benjamites by race[169] and of high rank.[170] They thought that if they killed Iebosthos they would receive great gifts from David and that their deed would be the cause of [their getting] a generalship or some other token of favor from him.[171]

Ish-bosheth assassinated

48. They found Iebosthos alone, resting at noon and lying asleep; the guards were

---

[157] This comment underscores, one last time, Josephus' positive depiction of Abner, just as it points up the loss his murder entailed for the whole people. Compare David's word to his servants as cited in 2 Sam 3:38: "Do you not know that a prince and a great man has fallen this day in Israel?"

[158] This opening affirmation concerning God's omniscience and his ability to requite all wrongs has no equivalent in David's final word concerning Abner's murder in 2 Sam 3:39. It does, however, echo similar statements elsewhere in Josephus' writings; see, e.g., *Ant.* 1.20; 10.278-281.

[159] From David's "confession" about his "weakness" vis-à-vis Joab and his brother in 2 Sam 3:39a, Josephus eliminates his designation of himself as "anointed king."

[160] Compare David's prayer in 2 Sam 3:39b: "the Lord requite the evildoer according to his wickedness."

[161] This closing formula to Josephus' story of Abner (7.9-45) has no biblical parallel.

[162] MT 2 Sam 4:1 leaves "Saul's son" unnamed. As they do throughout the chapter, LXX BL (wrongfully) designate the Israelite king as Μεμφιβόσθε. Josephus supplies the correct name when re-introducing him here. On Josephus' version of 2 Samuel 4, see Begg 1998e.

[163] According to *Ant.* 6.129, Abner was the son of Saul's uncle Ner, i.e. Saul's first cousin. This would make Ish-bosheth, the son of Saul, Abner's second cousin.

[164] 2 Sam 4:1a speaks of Ish-bosheth's "hands drooping" when he hears of Abner's death. Josephus'

description of his emotional response recalls his references to David's own reaction (see 7.39, 42) to that event, just as he intimates a reason for Ish-bosheth's responding as he does. Josephus leaves aside the notice of 4:1b that "all Israel was dismayed" by Abner's murder, thereby keeping attention focussed on Ish-bosheth.

[165] This inserted phrase prepares readers for what awaits Ish-bosheth at the hands of the pair who are about to be mentioned (// 2 Sam 4:2).

[166] MT (2 Sam 4:2) רמון (Eng.: "Rimmon"); LXX Ῥεμμών; Josephus Ἐρέμμων.

[167] MT (2 Sam 4:2) בענה (Eng.: "Banah"); LXX B Βαανά; LXX L Βαναία; Josephus Βανά (this reading, reflecting the "bana" (bena) of Lat, is the one adopted by Niese and Marcus).

[168] MT (2 Sam 4:2) רכב (Eng.: "Rechab"); LXX Ῥηχάβ; Josephus Θαηνός. On the possible origin of Josephus' form of the name, see Begg 1998e: 243, n. 17.

[169] Josephus leaves aside the further specification about the brothers' father being "from Beeroth" and the attached parenthetical information concerning this site and its inhabitants given in 2 Sam 4:2b-3.

[170] 2 Sam 4:2a designates the brothers as "captains of raiding bands."

[171] Josephus inserts this notice on the motivation for the brothers' subsequent deed. He has no equivalent, at this point, to the parenthetical and seemingly extraneous mention of Jonathan's crippled son Mephibosheth in 2 Sam 4:4. He will, however, reproduce its content in his version of 2 Samuel 9 in 7.113, where this figure comes to the fore.

not on hand,[172] nor was the doorkeeper awake. She too had fallen asleep, due to fatigue and the labor she had performed as well as the noonday heat.[173] When they entered the room in which Saoul's son was lying, they killed him.[174]

49. Cutting off his head, they marched the whole day and night;[175] thinking they were fleeing from those wronged by them to one who would receive [their] deed as a favor and would provide them with security, they came to Hebron.[176] They showed the head of Iebosthos to David, and presented themselves as loyal men who had done away with his enemy and the opponent of his kingship.[177]

Assassins come to David

50. But David did not react to their deed as they had hoped.[178] Instead, he said, "O most wicked men, who are immediately to undergo judgement,[179] did you not know how I took vengeance on the murderer of Saoul who brought me his golden crown[180]—even though his dispatch was done as a favor to him, so that the enemy would not catch him?[181] **51.** Or do you suppose that I have changed and am no longer the same man, such that I would rejoice over evildoers and view your regicidal deeds as a favor,[182] you who did away with on his bed a just man who had done no wrong to anyone, but had rather obligated you by his manifold loyalty and honor?[183] **52.** Therefore you will pay the penalty, being punished on his account.[184] You will likewise make satisfaction to me for having eliminated Iebosthos, supposing that I would be pleased at his death—for you could not have done my reputa-

David executes assassins

---

[172] Josephus' inserted reference to Ish-bosheth's being "alone" and "without guards" in his version of 2 Sam 4:5 helps account for the assassins' ability to gain access to the king (whom one would normally expect to be properly guarded).

[173] Josephus' reference to the state of the doorkeeper clearly reflects the LXX reading ("the doorkeeper of the house had been cleaning wheat, but she grew drowsy and slept") of 2 Sam 4:6 as opposed to MT's "and hither they [the assassins] came into the midst of the house fetching wheat; and they smote him [Ish-bosheth] in the belly."

[174] See 2 Sam 4:7a.

[175] From 2 Sam 4:7b Josephus omits the detail about the pair's march taking them "by way of the Arabah."

[176] Josephus' inserted notice on the expectations with which the brothers make their journey, recalls his notice on their reason for killing Ish-bosheth in 7.47; see note to "from him" at 7.47.

[177] The brothers' statement to David in 2 Sam 4:8 is ambiguous: is David's "enemy" Saul or Ish-bosheth? By omitting the former name from his version, Josephus eliminates the basis of the ambiguity. He likewise leaves aside the brothers' affirmation that "the Lord has avenged" David; in his presentation the pair claim all "credit" for themselves.

[178] This foreshadowing remark has a counterpart in that with which Josephus introduces the brothers in 7.46; see note on "plot" at 7.46.

[179] These opening words of David's response—which make clear from the start his evaluation of the brothers' deed and his intentions regarding them—take

the place of the king's oath formula of 2 Sam 4:9 ("as the Lord lives who redeemed my life from every adversity...").

[180] In 2 Sam 4:10 David refers to the one who reported Saul's death to him, thinking he was "bringing good news." Josephus' alternative allusion to this figure echoes his mention of the regicide's showing David Saul's crown in 7.4 (cf. *Ant.* 6.372).

[181] This acknowledgement of the extenuating circumstances surrounding the Amalekite's killing of Saul has no counterpart in 2 Sam 4:10. It recalls the regicide's statement in 7.3 (cf. *Ant.* 6.371) that Saul had "appealed to" him to dispatch him, while also underscoring the still greater reprehensibility of the brothers' deed, for which there are no such extenuating circumstances.

[182] Josephus interjects this rhetorical question as a lead-in to David's accusation of and pronouncing sentence on the pair in 2 Sam 4:11. The question highlights the brothers' miscalculation in supposing that they would be rewarded by David for their deed; see 7.47.

[183] Compare David's charging the pair with the killing of a "righteous man" in 2 Sam 4:11a. Josephus accentuates the accusation by adding mention of Ish-bosheth's past favor to the assassins, his own former clients.

[184] Compare David's statement to the assassins in 2 Sam 4:11b: "I shall [so LXX] now require his [Ish-bosheth's] blood at your hand and destroy you from the earth."

tion a greater wrong by surmising that."[185] When he had said this, he put them to death, torturing them with every sort of torture,[186] while he buried[187] the head of Iebosothos in the grave of Abenner, honoring it in every way.[188]

Israelite leaders approach David

(2.2) 53. Once these things had ended, all the chiefs of the Hebrew people, their commanders of thousands and their leaders, came to David at Hebron;[189] they entrusted themselves to him, recalling their loyalty to him when Saoul was still alive[190] and the honor they had not ceased to show him since he had been commander of a thousand.[191] They further affirmed that he and his sons had been designated king by God through the prophet Samouel[192] and that God had enabled him to save the country of the Hebrews by defeating the Palestinoi.[193]

54. David welcomed this eagerness of theirs and appealed to them to persevere in this, for in so doing, they would not have reason to change their minds. Having entertained[194] them and treated them considerately, he sent them off to bring the whole people to him.[195]

---

[185] These concluding words of David's response to the brothers have no equivalent in 2 Samuel 4. They highlight both David's resolve to do right by Ishbosheth in every respect and his concern for his own good name (compare 7.40).

[186] In 2 Sam 4:12aα David entrusts the execution of the brothers to "his young men." Josephus' formulation attributes the deed to David personally, thereby accentuating his passionate determination to requite their crime. He leaves aside the reference to the hanging up of the pair's hands and feet "beside the pool at Hebron" from 4:12aβ.

[187] Josephus' attribution of the burial to David personally corresponds to the 4QSamᵃ reading in 2 Sam 4:12b, whereas in both MT and LXX BL an indeterminate "they" see to the head's burial.

[188] Josephus accentuates the respect shown Ishbosheth's remains by David with the inserted reference to his "honoring" the head "in every way." Like LXX B 1 Sam 4:12b, he lacks an equivalent to the specification that Abner's tomb was located "in Hebron" (so MT, 4QSamᵃ [restored], LXX L).

[189] In 2 Sam 5:1a // 1 Chr 11:1a David is first approached by "all (the tribes of) Israel" and thereafter (5:3// 11:3) by "all the elders of Israel." Josephus reverses this sequence: the leaders come first (7.53) to David who subsequently dispatches them to bring the entire people (7.54).

[190] This reference to the leaders' long-time devotion to David replaces the opening affirmation of the Israelite tribes in 2 Sam 5:1b // 1 Chr 11:1b: "Behold we are your bone and flesh."

[191] In 2 Sam 5:2a// 1 Chr 11:2a the tribes recall David as one who "led out and brought in" during Saul's reign, the reference being to his military leadership role. Josephus clarifies and concretizes this formulation with an allusion to David's being appointed "chiliarch" by Saul; see *Ant.* 6.195// 1 Sam 18:13.

[192] In 2 Sam 5:2b// 1 Chr 11:2b the tribes evoke a divine word—not previously cited in either complex—addressed to David and designating him as one who is be "shepherd" of Israel and "prince" over the people. With his mention of Samuel as the mediator (for which he may have been inspired by the language of 1 Chr 11:3b: "[they anointed David as king over Israel] according to the word of the Lord by Samuel") Josephus turns the "missing" referent of the allusion in his sources into a clear-cut reminiscence of Samuel's word to David on the occasion of his anointing as quoted in *Ant.* 6.165 (and echoed by Abner in his address to the people in 7.27). From the double divine announcement cited in 2 Sam 5:2b// 1 Chr 11:2b, Josephus leaves aside the reference to David's future shepherd role, while also having him designated "king" rather than (mere) "prince."

[193] This element has no counterpart in the divine word to David as recalled by the tribes in 2 Sam 5:2b // 1 Chr 11:2b. It does, however, echo the announcement made by Samuel (*Ant.* 6.165) to David at his anointing concerning his future military role (as also the allusion to this by Abner in 7.27).

[194] Greek: κατευωχέω. Whereas this verb is used only infrequently by authors prior to Josephus (e.g., only once each by Herodotus and Philo), it is a Josephan favorite, occurring 12 times in his corpus. I owe this observation to Prof. Steve Mason.

[195] This sequence, featuring the initiatives taken by David in response to the leaders' preceding statement, replaces the series of events narrated in 2 Sam 5:3// 1 Chr 11:3, i.e. the coming of the Israelite elders to David, his "making a covenant" with them, and their anointing him king; see note to "Hebron" at 7.53. Josephus' alternative presentation of what happens at this juncture characteristically avoids the sources' "covenant" and "anointing" terminology, while also preparing for his use of the segment 1 Chr 12:24-41 in what follows.

55. There now assembled[196] from the tribe of Iouda about 6,800 soldiers who carried shields and lances as their weapons.[197] These men had stuck with the son of Saoul, for the tribe of Iouda had appointed David their king without them.[198]

56. From the tribe of Simeon 7,100.[199] From the Levites 4,700,[200] having Iodam[201] as their leader.[202] With them was the high priest Sadok,[203] together with twenty-two leaders who were his relatives.[204] From the Benjamite tribe 4,000 soldiers[205]—for the tribe was in suspense, still expecting that someone of the family of Saoul would rule as king.[206]

57. From the Ephraimite tribe 28,000 very capable men of outstanding strength.[207] From the Manassehite half-tribe 18,000[208] [very capable men].[209] From the tribe of Isachar 200 with foreknowledge of the future, along with 20,000 soldiers.[210]

58. From the tribe of Zebulon 50,000 picked soldiers,[211] for it was only this tribe that assembled to David in its entirety;[212] all these had the same weapons as the tribe of Gad.[213] From the tribe of Nephthali 1,000 notables and leaders equipped with

---

The reference to David's feasting of the leaders at this point is inspired by the notice of 1 Chr 12:40 concerning the 3 days of eating and drinking enjoyed by the crowds that came to Hebron; it likewise echoes Josephus' account of David's reception of Abner in 7.30.

[196] Josephus at this point begins making use of 1 Chr 12:24-41 (MT; Eng. 12:23-40), the list of the tribal forces who repair to David at Hebron in order to turn the kingship over to him (see 12:24). In so doing, he leaves aside—for the moment—both the intervening segment of 1 Chronicles (11:4-12:23) and the chronological notices concerning David's kingship of 2 Sam 5:4-5.

[197] See 1 Chr 12:25.

[198] This remark about the previous loyalties of the 6,800 Judeans has no counterpart in 1 Chr 12:25. It serves to answer the question of why these Judeans come to David at this point, seeing that, according to Josephus' other biblical source, i.e. 2 Sam 2:4, the "men of Judah" have already acknowledged David as their king at Hebron. The addition reflects Josephus' attempt to integrate the data of both Chronicles and Samuel.

[199] See 1 Chr 12:26.

[200] The figure given in 1 Chr 12:27 (both MT and LXX) is 4,600. Conceivably, Josephus' number, i.e. 4,700 is influenced by 12:28, where there is reference to the 3,700 men who accompany Jehoaida; see next note.

[201] MT (1 Chr 12:28) יהוידע (Eng.: "Jehoaida"); LXX B τωαδάς; LXX L Ἰωαδά; Josephus Ἰώδαμος.

[202] 1 Chr 12:28 designates "Jehoiada" as "prince/leader of the house of Aaron."

[203] MT (1 Chr 12:29) צדוק (Eng.: "Zadok"); LXX B Σαδώκ; LXX L Σαδδούκ; Josephus Σάδωκος. The source calls him "a young man mighty in valor." Josephus' alternative designation anticipates Zadok's

priestly service under David and Solomon.

[204] See 1 Chr 12:29b.

[205] 1 Chr 12:30a (MT and LXX) cites *3,000* Benjamites.

[206] Cf. 1 Chr 12:30b, which states that the majority of the 3,000 Benjamites who now approach David had "hitherto kept their allegiance to the house of Saul."

[207] See 1 Chr 12:31.

[208] See 1 Chr 12:32.

[209] Greek: τῶν δυνατωτάτων. This phrase, absent in MLat, is bracketed by Niese and omitted by Marcus. 1 Chr 12:32 designates the 18,000 Manassehites as "those who were expressly named to come and make David king."

[210] 1 Chr 12:33 mentions 200 "chiefs" of Issachar "who had understanding of the times to know what Israel ought to do," plus "all their kinsmen under their command." Josephus supplies a "precise" number for the latter group.

[211] See 1 Chr 12:34a.

[212] This statement represents Josephus' interpretation of the notice in 1 Chr 12:34b that the Zebulunites "came to help [David] with singleness of purpose." It further explains why the numbers of this tribe should be greater than those of any other individual tribe that came to David.

[213] This notice on the weapons of the tribes Simeon-Zebulun as listed in 7.56-58a has no biblical equivalent. In making "Gad" the basis of the comparison Niese follows the majority reading of the witnesses, this looking ahead to the catalogue of weapons carried by the Transjordanian tribes—on which Gad was one—in 7.59. Marcus (*ad loc.*) opts for the conjecture of Reinach, i.e. "Judah," which would connect the notice here with the mention of the Judeans' "shields and lances" in 7.55.

shields and spears as their weapons, whom countless others of the tribe were following.[214]

59. From the tribe of Dan 28,600 picked men.[215] From the tribe of Aser 40,000.[216] From the two Transjordanian tribes and the rest of the Manassehite tribe 120,000 armed with shields, spears, helmets and swords.[217] The remaining tribes were equipped with swords as well.[218]

Feasting at Hebron

60. This whole crowd assembled to David at Hebron, along with large supplies of grain and wine and every kind of foodstuff, and unanimously proclaimed David king.[219] After the people had feasted and celebrated for three days in Hebron,[220] David, departing from there with all of them, came to Hierosolyma.[221]

David captures Jerusalem (Jebus)

(3.1) 61. The Jebusites who inhabited the city—they were of the race of the Chananaians[222]—closed the gates to him and, in mockery of the king, stationed on the wall those whose faces and feet were mutilated and all who were deformed. Those afflicted with some infirmity would, they said, prevent him from entering.[223] They did these things being highly confident in the solidity of the walls.[224] In his wrath David then began to besiege Hierosolyma.[225]

62. Applying great solicitude and eagerness in order that by capturing it he might immediately demonstrate his strength and dismay others who might act towards him as they [the Jebusites] had,[226] he took the lower city by storm.[227]

---

[214] Compare 1 Chr 12:35, where the number of (ordinary) soldiers from Naphtali is specified as 37,000, and it is they (rather than the 1,000 leaders) who carry shields and spears.

[215] See 1 Chr 12:36.

[216] See 1 Chr 12:37.

[217] See 1 Chr 12:38, which speaks in general terms of the Transjordanians' having "all the weapons of war."

[218] This appended notice has no equivalent in the sequence of 1 Chr 12:24-41.

[219] Josephus here combines the data of 1 Chr 12:39 (the assembly's coming to David to make him king) and 12:41 (the victuals brought by the tribes to Hebron). He positions the latter item at a more logical point than does the Bible, where it appears only after the mention of the "feasting" at Hebron in 12:40. He likewise abbreviates the extended catalogue of provisions cited in 12:41.

[220] See 1 Chr 12:40. This feasting by the crowds recalls David's previous "entertaining" of the leaders in 7.54.

[221] Josephus here modifies the sequence of 1 Chronicles, where the Hebron banqueting scene (12:24-41) is immediately followed, in 13:1-8, by David's leading all Israel in procession with the ark with Jerusalem as the ultimate goal. He does so in order to first accommodate a source segment (2 Sam 5:6-10// 1 Chr 11:4-9) dealing with the prerequisite for David's ark-initiative, i.e. his capture of Jerusalem, which he had previously passed over in connecting the data of 1 Chr 11:1-3 (// 2 Sam 5:1-3) directly with those of 12:24-41; see note to

"assembled" at 7.55. In particular, he combines into a continuous sequence elements drawn from 2 distinct contexts in 1 Chronicles, i.e. the people's feasting at Hebron (12:40) and their proceeding as a body with David to Jerusalem (11:4, MT LXX L [in LXX B as well as in 2 Sam 5:6 David is accompanied by a smaller group, i.e. "his men"]). On Josephus' version of David's capture of Jerusalem, see Begg 1998f.

[222] Neither 2 Sam 5:6 nor 1 Chr 11:4 identifies the Jebusites as "Canaanites" (as Josephus does here, as well as in *War* 6.439 and *Ant.* 5.140). Cf., however, Gen 10:16 (// *Ant.* 1.138) where the Jebusites are listed among the descendants of "Canaan."

[223] Josephus' inspiration for this notice is clearly 2 Sam 5:6bα, where the Jebusites declare to David "the blind and the lame [Tg. the sinners and the guilty] will ward you off." Josephus dramatizes and reinforces this declaration by having the defective persons not simply referred to, but actually displayed before David on the walls. His presentation has a certain parallel in *Pirqe R. El.* 36.5, where the Jebusites mount idols on the walls, while informing David that he will not be able to enter until he removes these.

[224] Cf. the appended editorial remark concerning the Jebusites' declaration to David (2 Sam 5:6bα) in 5:6bβ: "... thinking, 'David cannot come in here'."

[225] Josephus interjects the reference to David's "wrath" that prompts his undertaking the siege.

[226] These remarks on David's state of mind as he undertakes the siege are without biblical parallel.

[227] Josephus' sources (see 2 Sam 5:7// 1 Chr 11:5) do not clearly distinguish such an initial stage in Da-

63. With the citadel still remaining, the king decided, by promising honor and awards, to make his troops more eager for the task. He promised to give the generalship over the entire people to the one who, by way of the ravines situated beneath, would ascend to the citadel and capture it.[228]

Joab wins generalship

64. All were ambitious to ascend and, in their desire for the generalship, did not shrink from any exertion.[229] But Joab, son of Sarouia, outstripped the others and, when he had ascended, shouted to the king, claiming the generalship.[230]

(3.2) 65. After David expelled the Jebusites from the citadel[231] and himself rebuilt the city of Hierosolyma,[232] he named it the City of David, and resided in it the whole time that he ruled as king.[233] Now the time that he ruled over the tribe of Iouda alone in Hebron was seven years and six months.[234] Once he had established his palace in Hierosolyma, he experienced ever more splendid successes in his affairs because, in his providential care, God made these greater and caused them to progress.[235]

David establishes himself in Jerusalem

66. Likewise Hierom,[236] king of the Tyrians, sent to him and proposed [a treaty of] friendship and an alliance.[237] He also sent him gifts of cedar wood and artisans,

King Hiram assists David

---

vid's conquest of the city, seeming rather to envisage a single-step seizure of "the stronghold of Zion/city of David" by him. Josephus' having David get possession first of the "lower town," and only then of the (more difficult) "citadel" (see 7.63-64), recalls his presentation in *Ant.* 5.124 (compare Judg 1:8), where the Israelites do occupy the "lower town" of Jerusalem, but are unable to gain control of the "upper town," given the strength of its walls. Reading 7.62-64 in light of 5.124 underscores the military achievement of David who accomplishes what the Israelites before him were unable to do, i.e. secure mastery of both the lower and the upper (the citadel) sections of Jerusalem.

[228] In relating the 2nd stage of David's campaign (7.63), Josephus elaborates on the king's promise of military command to whoever "smites the Jebusites" in 1 Chr 11:6a. In so doing, he leaves aside the (obscure) alternative version of 2 Sam 5:8, in which David urges anyone intending to smite the Jebusites to ascend the "water shaft" (?) in order to attack the blind and the lame (see 5:6) whom he hates, a directive which, the verse concludes, gave rise to the saying "The blind and the lame shall not come into the house (+ of the Lord, LXX)." Josephus' elaboration of 11:6 elucidates the king's ultimate intention (i.e. not simply "smiting the Jebusites," but capture of the citadel) in making his offer and spells how this is to be accomplished (i.e. by climbing up through the surrounding ravines—this indication might represent an interpretation of the Hebrew phrase בצנור, RSV: "the water shaft" of 5:8).

[229] This inserted remark underscores the effectiveness of David's preceding words.

[230] Josephus embellishes the summary notice of 1 Chr 11:6b: "Joab the son of Zeruiah went up first, so he became the chief."

[231] Neither biblical source mentions such an "ex-

pulsion," which, however, is also cited by Josephus in *War* 6.439.

[232] Josephus omits the specification of 2 Sam 5:9b // 1 Chr 11:8a that David's "building" of the city was "from the Millo (inward/ in complete circuit)."

[233] Josephus reverses the sequence of 2 Sam 5:9// 1 Chr 11:7 (David's dwelling in the citadel, its being called "the city of David"). He adds the specification concerning the duration of David's residence there.

[234] Josephus makes delayed use of this chronological datum reported in 2 Sam 2:11 and 5:5a now at the moment when David's "Hebron period" actually ends.

[235] This theological conclusion to the story of David's capture of and taking up residence in Jerusalem is Josephus' version of 2 Sam 5:10// 1 Chr 11:9, where David "grows stronger" due to the Lord's being "with him."

[236] MT (2 Sam 5:11) חירם (Eng.: "Hiram"); LXX Χειράμ; Josephus Ἱέρωμος (this form of the king's name corresponds to that used by Josephus' extra-biblical authorities, Menander and Dios, whom he cites in *Ant.* 8.136-150 and *Apion* 1.112-125). In making the overture of the Tyrian king come immediately after David's capture of Jerusalem, Josephus follows the sequence of 2 Samuel (5:11-12), whereas the parallel text of 1 Chronicles (14:1-2) mentions this only at a later point, i.e. after David's initial, failed attempted to bring the ark to Jerusalem (13:5-14).

[237] Neither 2 Sam 5:11-12 or 1 Chr 14:1-2 mentions such a proposed alliance between Hiram and David. Josephus' notice on the matter is likely inspired by (and designed to prepare for) the statement of 1 Kgs 5:1b (MT // *Ant.* 8.50): "Hiram always loved David." In any case, the fact of King Hiram's readiness to conclude such an alliance with David accentuates the latter's status.

carpenters and builders, who were to construct the palace in Hierosolyma.[238] Enclosing the lower city, David joined the citadel to it, making them one entity. Having surrounded this with a wall,[239] he appointed Joab overseer of the walls.[240]

Historical remarks on Jerusalem

67. It was David then who first expelled the Jebusites from Hierosolyma and named the city after himself.[241] For in the time of our ancestor Abram it was called "Solyma"[242] [some, however, say that Homer afterwards called it "Hierosolyma"].[243] The temple however, they named "Solyma," which in the Hebrew language means "security."[244] **68.** But the whole time from the campaigns and war of the general Iesous against the Chananaians, through which he subjugated them and awarded it [the city] to the Hebrews[245]—even though the Israelites were not yet able to expel the Chananaians from Hierosolyma[246]—, until David captured it by siege, was 515 years.[247]

David spares Ornan (Orona)

(3.3) 69. I shall also make mention of Orona,[248] a wealthy man of the Jebusites,

---

[238] See 2 Sam 5:11// 1 Chr 14:1. Josephus omits the appended theological notice on David's recognition of God's establishing and exalting his kingship of 5:12// 14:2, which appears to duplicate that of 5:10// 11:9, previously utilized by him in 7.65.

[239] This notice on David's further building activities, subsequent to Hiram's overture, lacks an explicit equivalent in the sources (it might represent, however, Josephus' further elaboration of the summary indications in 2 Sam 5:9b// 1 Chr 11:8a about David's "building of the city," already cited by him in 7.65).

[240] According to 1 Chr 11:8b Joab "repaired the rest of the city."

[241] This notice "resumes" elements of Josephus' previous statements in 7.65 by way of transition to his following discussion of the city's different names throughout history.

[242] Josephus mentions that the city's name was earlier "Solyma" also in *Ant.* 1.180, where "Abram" meets Melchizedek, "king of Solyma" (in the source text, Gen 14:18, Melchizedek is called rather "king of Salem"). Compare *War* 6.438, where Melchizedek is credited with renaming "Solyma" as "Hierosolyma."

[243] This is the reading of the codices, which Niese follows. Marcus (*ad loc.*) regards the reading as a gloss and suggests reconstructing the original text to read "afterwards they named it Hierosolyma," in line with Josephus' statements in *Ant.* 1.180 and *War* 6.438 (see previous note). The reference to Homer in the text printed by Niese is apparently inspired by *Od.* 5.283, where there is mention of the "Solymian hills." That allusion is picked up by the poet Choerilius (a contemporary of Herodotus), whom Josephus quotes in *Apion* 1.173, and then proceeds to affirm that Choerilius' reference is to "us" since the "Solymian hills are in our country"; see Marcus *ad loc.*

[244] The text is problematic here. Niese follows the reading τὸ... ἱεροῦ of RO, which yields the above translation, in which it is the word "temple," rather than

"Solyma," that is said to mean "security" (= Hebrew שלום). Given the obvious incorrectness of this etymology, Marcus (*ad loc.*) favors the reading ἱερὸν... (τὰ) Σόλυμα of MSP and renders "calling the temple (*hieron*) Solyma, which, in the Hebrew tongue, means 'security'," this making "Solyma" the word meaning "security." According to Eupolemus (in the excerpt from Alexander Polyhistor cited by Eusebius, *Praep. ev.* 34.11), the name "Jerusalem" and its Greek rendition "Hierosolyma" for the city are a corruption of the name originally given the temple built by Solomon, i.e. *hieron Solomonos*.

[245] Jebus/Jerusalem was assigned to the Benjamites in particular in Joshua's day; see Josh 18:28 (// *Ant.* 5.82, 129).

[246] This parenthetical notice draws on statements of Josh 15:63 and Judg 1:21, according to which the Judeans/Benjamites were unable to drive out the Jebusites who continued to dwell in Jerusalem "to this day." These statements appear to stand in tension with Judg 1:8, where Judah and Simeon capture and burn Jerusalem. On Josephus' attempt to resolve this biblical contradiction via a distinction between the "lower town" of Jerusalem, which the Judeans and Simeonites did capture, and the "upper town," which they could not, see *Ant.* 5.124 (cf. 5.129, where the Benjamites allow the population of Jerusalem to pay them tribute).

[247] On the biblical chronological indications drawn on by Josephus in arriving at this figure, see Marcus *ad loc.* Modern chronology would posit an interlude of *ca.* 200 years between Joshua's occupation of the land and David's capture of Jerusalem.

[248] This is the form of the name read by Niese. Marcus (*ad loc.*) follows the conjecture of J. Hudson, i.e. Ὀρόννα. Josephus anticipates his mention of this figure from 2 Sam 24:16// 1 Chr 21:15, where he is called "Araunah"/"Ornan," respectively (MT; LXX reads Ὀρνά in both instances).

who was not killed in the siege of Hierosolyma by David on account of his loyalty to the Hebrews and a certain favor and solicitude on his part towards the king himself, which I shall treat a little later at a suitable moment.[249]

70. David also married[250] other wives in his addition to his earlier ones and had concubines as well.[251] He likewise fathered nine[252] sons[253] whom he named Amase,[254] Amnou,[255] Seba,[256] Nathan,[257] Solomon,[258] Iebare,[259] Elies,[260] Phalnagees,[261] Naphes,[262] Ienaë,[263] and Eliphale,[264] plus a daughter Thamara.[265] Of these, nine were by his wives of noble birth, while the two mentioned last were by his concubines.[266] Thamara, for her part, had the same mother as Apsalom.[267]

Additions to David's family

---

[249] See *Ant.* 7.318-334, Josephus' version of the story of David's census (2 Samuel 24// 1 Chronicles 21). Josephus makes mention of the figure already at this point lest, after his double reference to the general expulsion of the Jebusites by David (7.65, 67), readers be subsequently surprised to learn of the continued presence of this particular Jebusite in Jerusalem.

[250] After the interlude of 7.67-69 concerning Jerusalem, its names and history and the figure of Arauna, Josephus now picks up, once again, on the sequence of his 2 biblical sources, in which the catalogue of David's later womenfolk and offspring (2 Sam 5:13-16 // 1 Chr 14:3-7// 7.70) follows immediately on the account of Hiram's initiative (5:11-12// 14:1-2// 7.66) in David's favor.

[251] Josephus reverses the sequence of 2 Sam 5:13, where David's concubines are mentioned before his (later) wives (the parallel text, 1 Chr 14:3 speaks only of wives).

[252] This is the reading of the codices, which Niese retains. Given the fact that the following list actually cites *11* names of David's sons, Marcus (*ad loc.*) follows the emendation of the *Ed. prin.*, i.e. ἕνδεκα ("ll"). Conceivably, the figure "9" read by Niese derives from 1 Chr 3:8, where the 2nd group of David's latter-born sons is said to total "9."

[253] The Bible contains no less than 3 listings of David's latter-born sons: 2 Sam 5:13-16 (11 names); 1 Chr 3:5-8 (9 names); and 1 Chr 14:4-7 (13 names). Each of these lists contains numerous textual variants, just as they all differ among themselves to some extent. The names on Josephus' own list, in several instances, have no recognizable counterpart in any of the biblical lists.

[254] The first name in the lists of 2 Sam 5:14// 1 Chr 14:4 is "Shammua," while 1 Chr 3:5 reads "Shimea." Schlatter (*s.v.*) views Josephus' initial name as a corruption of the former form.

[255] 2 Sam 5:14; 1 Chr 3:5; and 1 Chr 14:14 all read "Shobab" as their 2nd name. According to Schalit (*s.v.*) the first 2 names on Josephus' list as read by Niese originally constituted a single name, i.e. Σεαμμούαμα, which would itself be a corruption of the first name in 2 Sam 5:14// 1 Chr 14:4, i.e. "Shammua."

[256] This name (Greek: Σεβάς) conceivably reflects the form Ἰεσσεβάν in LXX L 2 Sam 5:14 (compare MT: "Shobab").

[257] Josephus' 4th name corresponds to the 3rd name in all 3 biblical lists (2 Sam 5:14; 1 Chr 3:5; 1 Chr 14:4).

[258] This 5th name in Josephus' list corresponds to the 4th name in all 3 biblical lists (2 Sam 5:14; 1 Chr 3:5; 1 Chr 14:4). Josephus has no equivalent to the notice—unique to 1 Chr 3:5—that the mother of David's first 4 latter-born sons was "Bathshua, daughter of Ammiel."

[259] This 6th name on Josephus' list reflects the 5th name in all 3 biblical lists (2 Sam 5:15; 1 Chr 3:6; 1 Chr 14:5), i.e. "Ibhar."

[260] Compare "Elishua" (2 Sam 5:15; 1 Chr 14:5)/ "Elishama" (1 Chr 3:6).

[261] Schalit (*s.v.*) suggests that this form is a conflation of the last name in LXX 1 Chr 14:5 (Ἐλειφάλεθ; MT "Elepelet") and the first name in LXX 14:6 (Νάγεθ; MT "Nogah").

[262] Schalit (*s.v*) suggests that this form might reflect a mis-rendering of the final consonant of the name "Nepheg" of 2 Sam 5:15; 1 Chr 3:7; 1 Chr 14:6.

[263] Mez (1895: 40) and Schalit (*s.v.*) see this form as a corruption of the Hebrew name "Japhia" of 2 Sam 5:15; 1 Chr 3:7; 1 Chr 14:6 in which the latter's middle consonant, i.e. פ, has been mistaken for a נ. Schlatter (*s.v.*) on the contrary, derives the form from the "Eliada" of 2 Sam 5:16; 1 Chr 3:8.

[264] This final son in Josephus' list corresponds to the last figure in all 3 biblical lists, i.e. "Eliphelet" (2 Sam 5:16; 1 Chr 3:8; 1 Chr 14:7).

[265] MT (1 Chr 3:9) תמר (Eng.: "Tamar"); LXX Θαμάρ; Josephus Θαμάρα. The lists of 2 Sam 5:13-16 and 1 Chr 14:3-7 do not mention this figure.

[266] None of the biblical lists—of which that of 2 Sam 5:13-16 is the only one (see v. 13) to mention David's "concubines" in addition to his wives—makes this distinction among David's latter-born sons.

[267] Josephus anticipates this notice about Absalom and Tamar being full siblings from 2 Sam 13:1 (// *Ant.* 7.162). He mentions the mother of Absalom, i.e.

Philistine advance

(4.1) 71. When the Palestinoi found out that David had been appointed[268] king by the Hebrews, they campaigned against him towards Hierosolyma.[269] Occupying the valley called that of the Giants[270]—the site is not far from the city[271]—they encamped there.[272]

David consults God

72. But the king of the Judeans[273]—who did not permit himself to do anything except by prophecy and at God's direction and after taking him as his guarantor for the future[274]—directed the high priest[275] to predict to him what God had in mind and what would be the result of the battle.[276]

Initial Philistine defeat

73. When the high priest prophesied[277] victory and triumph, David led out his force against the Palestinoi.[278] Once they engaged, he suddenly fell upon the enemy from the rear. He killed some of them, while the others he put to flight.[279] **74.** Let no one, however, suppose that the army of the Palestinoi that came against the Hebrews was small [or surmise] from the quickness of their defeat and their not displaying any brave deed or one worthy of mention, that this was [a matter of] sluggishness

---

"Machame," in 7.21 (// 2 Sam 3:3= Maacah).

[268] Here again, Josephus avoids the word "anointed" used in 2 Sam 5:17a// 1 Chr 14:8a. On Josephus' version of David's double victory over the Philistines (7.71-77// 2 Sam 5:17-25// 1 Chr 14:8-17), see Begg 1999d. In reporting that victory prior to David's initiative of bringing the ark to Jerusalem, Josephus follows the sequence of 2 Samuel 5-6 as opposed to 1 Chronicles 13-16 (where the Philistine wars are related [14:8-17] in the interlude between the first abortive [1 Chronicles 13] and the second, successful [1 Chronicles 15-16]) attempt at moving the ark).

[269] The notice on the Philistines' move against David in 2 Sam 5:17a// 1 Chr 14:8a does not mention "Jerusalem." Josephus leaves aside the reference to David's initial response to this threat, i.e. his "going down to the (which?) stronghold" (2 Sam 5:17b)/ "going out before [LXX to meet] them" (1 Chr 14:8b).

[270] In MT 2 Sam 5:18// 1 Chr 14:9 the Philistines operate in "the valley of the "Rephaim." Josephus' designation of the valley, i.e. τῶν Γιγάντων ("of the giants") corresponds to the LXX's rendering (i.e. "valley of the Titans [τῶν Γιτάνων]") of the Hebrew name.

[271] Josephus adds this indication concerning the location of the valley.

[272] In MT 2 Sam 5:18 the Philistines "spread out" in the valley, whereas in LXX BL 5:18 and 1 Chr 14:9 they "make a raid" there.

[273] Josephus' other uses of this title (Greek: ὁ τῶν Ἰουδαίων βασιλεύς) are in *War* 6.103 (Jehoiachin), 439 (David); 7.71 (Alexander Janneus); *Ant.* 14.9 (Herod), 36 (Alexander Janneus); and 15.373, 409; 16:291 (all of Herod). It corresponds to the designation used for Jesus in, e.g., Matt 27:29; Mark 15:18, 26; Luke 23:37, 38; John 19:3, 19, 21.

[274] The above parenthetical phrase, accentuating David's piety, lacks a counterpart in the bib-

lical sources.

[275] In 2 Sam 5:19a// 1 Chr 14:10a David consults God directly, without any human intermediary. With Josephus' interposition of such an intermediary here, compare 7.7, where he introduces "the prophet" as the one through whom David makes the "inquiry of God" cited in 2 Sam 2:1. Here in 7.72 Josephus leaves indeterminate which of the 2 "high priests" previously mentioned in connection with David, i.e. Abiathar (see *Ant.* 6.359) and Zadok (see 7.56) the king employed on this occasion.

[276] This formulation in indirect address replaces David's 2-part, direct-address question in 2 Sam 5:19a // 1 Chr 14:10a ("Shall I go up against the Philistines? Wilt thou give them into my hand?").

[277] In 2 Sam 5:19b// 1 Chr 14:10b God answers David's (unmediated) inquiry of him (5:19a// 14:10a; see note to "priest" at 7.72) directly. Josephus' reference to the high priest's "prophesying" recalls *Ant.* 5.120, where the priest Phineas "prophesies" God's directive that Judah take the lead in exterminating the Canaanites.

[278] Josephus leaves aside the name of the battle site as given in 2 Sam 5:20aα// 1 Chr 14:11aα, i.e. "Baal-perazim."

[279] Josephus embellishes the summary notice of 2 Sam 5:20aβ// 1 Chr 14:11aβ about David's "striking down" the Philistines. Conversely, having left aside the place name "Baal-perazim" from 5:20aα// 14:11aα (see previous note), he likewise passes over the attached etymological/etiological indications concerning that name of 5:20b// 14:11b. In addition, he leaves for the conclusion of his 2nd battle account (see 7.77) the sources' notices (2 Sam 5:21// 1 Chr 14:12) on the Israelites' handling of the Philistine "gods/idols" that fell into their hands following the first battle.

and cowardice on their part. Let it rather be known that Syria and Phoinike and many other bellicose peoples in addition to these jointly campaigned against them as well and participated in the war.[280]

75. This was the only reason[281] why, having been so often defeated and lost many tens of thousands, that they now came against the Hebrews with a still larger force. Indeed after they had been routed in these battles,[282] an army three times as large advanced against David and encamped in the same region.[283]

76. Once again, the king of the Israelites asked God about the outcome of the battle.[284] The high priest prophesied[285] that he should hold back his army in the groves called the "Weepers,"[286] not far from the camp of the enemy.[287] He was not to break camp or start the battle until the grove should be agitated, even though no wind was blowing.[288]

David consults God again

77. When the grove was thus agitated and the time that God had announced to him had arrived,[289] David no longer held back, but went out to a victory that was already prepared and manifest.[290] For the enemy ranks did not stand up against him; at the first engagement, they fled, David pressing after and killing them.[291] He pursued them as far as the city of Gazara, which is the border of their country.[292] He

Philistines routed again

---

[280] This sequence has no equivalent in the sources. It serves to underscore the magnitude of David's success by vastly augmenting the forces arrayed against him. Thereby, Josephus aims, as often elsewhere in *Antiquities*, to rebut claims about the Jews' lack of military distinction. Compare the similar case of *War* 1.7-8, where he insists the Judeans had posed a serious challenge to the forces of Vespasian and Titus. On the whole subject, see further Feldman 1998: 106-109.

[281] I.e. the fact that, contrary to what one might suppose from reading the source accounts of David's initial victory over them, the Philistines were energetic and courageous, rather than "sluggish" and "cowardly," in their dealings with the Israelites; see 7.74.

[282] The sources know of only one battle between David and the Philistines prior to the 2nd, decisive one. In introducing mention of multiple intervening Israelite victories, Josephus highlights both the continuing resolution of the Philistines and David's efficacy as a military leader.

[283] As in 7.71 (compare 2 Sam 5:18// 1 Chr 14:9; see note to "there" at 7.71), Josephus' reference to the Philistines' "encamping" replaces sources mentions of other operations now undertaken by them, i.e. "coming up and spreading out" (MT 2 Sam 5:22)/ "making raids" (1 Chr 14:13 and LXX 2 Sam 5:22).

[284] In contrast to 2 Sam 5:23a// 1 Chr 14:14a, Josephus spells out the content of David's (2nd) "inquiry." He likewise varies David's title from 7.72, where he is called "king of the Judeans."

[285] Just as in 7.73 (compare 2 Sam 5:19b// 1 Chr 14:10b; see note to "prophesied" at 7.73), Josephus replaces a direct divine answer to David with mention of a high priestly "prophecy."

[286] Josephus' phrase here (ἐν τοῖς ἄλεσει τοῖς... Κλαυθμῶσι) rather closely corresponds to that of LXX 2 Sam 5:23b// 1 Chr 14:14b, where David is told by God to approach the Philistines ἀπὸ τοῦ ἄλσους τοῦ κλαυθμῶνος ("from the grove of the weeper"). In MT, where David is instructed to come upon them opposite בכאים(ה), it is uncertain whether the reference is to some kind of tree (RSV: "balsam trees") or to a place name, i.e. "Beka'im," meaning "weepers."

[287] Josephus supplies this indication concerning the site referred to in the divine directive of 2 Sam 5:23b // 1 Chr 14:14b. Compare his inserted localization of "the valley of the Giants" in relation to Jerusalem in 7.71 (// 2 Sam 5:18// 1 Chr 14:9); see note to "city" at 7.71.

[288] Here again (see note to "Weepers" at 7.76), Josephus' wording (τὰ ἄλση σαλεύεσθαι) stands closer to that of LXX L 2 Sam 5:24 and LXX 1 Chr 14:15 ([τὴν φωνὴν] τοῦ συνεισμοῦ αὐτῶν ἄκρων τῶν ἀουῶν, "the sound of the *agitation* of the tops of the pear trees") than to the MT's "sound of *marching* in the tops of the balsam trees" (RSV). Josephus' reference to "no wind blowing" elaborates on the LXX reading.

[289] Josephus inserts this transitional phrase, picking up on his version of the divine order to David in 7.76.

[290] Josephus embellishes the notice (2 Sam 5:25a// 1 Chr 14:16a) about David acting in accord with his divine instructions, underscoring the certainty of his success in so acting.

[291] Once again (see note to "to flight" at 7.73), Josephus elaborates on the summary notices on David's "slaying the Philistines" (2 Sam 5:25b)/ "[the Israelites'] striking down the camp of the Philistines" (1 Chr 14:16b).

[292] Josephus omits the starting point of David's pur-

Deliberations about ark

likewise plundered their camp, in which he found much wealth[293] and their gods that he destroyed.[294]

(4.2) 78. After these developments and this battle,[295] David, having taken counsel with the aged as well as the leaders and the commanders of thousands,[296] decided to summon to himself[297] from the whole country those of his compatriots who were in the prime of life,[298] and then have the priests and Levites[299] go to Kariathiarim, in order to bring the ark of God with them from there to Hierosolyma.[300] There they were to hold it, showing devotion to it with sacrifices and other honors that would please the Deity.[301] **79.** For if they had done these things when Saoul was still ruling as king, they would not have suffered anything terrible.[302]

Procession with ark begins

When therefore the whole people had come together,[303] as they had decided,[304] the king approached the ark.[305] The priests lifted it up[306] from the house of

---

suit, i.e. Geba (MT 2 Sam 5:25b)/ Gibeon (LXX 2 Sam 5:25b// 1 Chr 14:16b). He adds the specification concerning the status of its end point, i.e. Gezer (MT)/ Gazara, Gazera (LXX).

[293] This notice about the copious plunder David obtained from the Philistine camp has no source counterpart. For a similar case, see *Ant.* 6.80.

[294] Josephus has transferred this notice on the fate of the Philistine sacred objects from the first (see 2 Sam 5:21// 1 Chr 14:12) to the 2nd battle (see note to "flight" at 7.73), thereby giving it a more climactic character. His wording of the notice reflects that found in 1 Chr 14:12 (the Philistine "gods" are burned with fire) as opposed to 2 Sam 5:21 (where the Philistine "idols" [MT; LXX: gods] are "carried off" by David and his men [in LXX L, there is a conflation of the 2 presentations, i.e. after carrying off the Philistine "gods," David commands that they be "burned"]).

Josephus has no equivalent to the closing theological notice, unique to 1 Chr 14:17, concerning the universal dissemination of David's "fame" and the Lord's causing the fear of him to befall all nations.

[295] Josephus supplies this transitional phrase, placing David's next initiative, i.e. his transporting the ark to Jerusalem, in explicit relation to his previous Philistine triumph. On Josephus' account of the ark's move to Jerusalem (7.78-89), see Begg 1997l.

[296] See 1 Chr 13:1, where David consults with "the commanders of thousands and of hundreds, with every leader." The parallel text, 2 Samuel 6 lacks mention of this prior consultation by David, who there (see 6:1) simply assembles the picked force that will accompany him and the ark on its way (6:2).

[297] In 1 Chr 13:2 David proposes such a "summoning" to "all the assembly of Israel" for its approval (which it does grant, 13:4).

[298] 1 Chr 13:2 designates the first group of those to be summoned as "our brethren who remain in the land of Israel." Josephus' designation might reflect the refer-

ence to "the chosen men of Israel" of 2 Sam 6:1.

[299] Josephus omits the (irrelevant) qualification of the priests and Levites as "in the cities that have pasture lands" of 1 Chr 13:2.

[300] Josephus renders more explicit David's proposal as cited in 1 Chr 13:3a ("let us bring again the ark of our God to us"). In so doing he draws the name of the ark's current place of residence from 1 Chr 13:5 (cf. his earlier mention of its stay there in *Ant.* 6.18// 1 Sam 7:1) and that of its intended new home from, e.g., 2 Sam 6:10// 1 Chr 13:13.

[301] David's positive prescription about the treatment of the ark once it reaches its destination has no equivalent in his words concerning it as cited in 1 Chr 13:3.

[302] Josephus has David spell out the consequences of the neglect of the ark during Saul's reign as confessed by him in 1 Chr 13:3. Having passed over David's making his proposal to the pan-Israelite assembly (1 Chr 13:2; see note to "to himself" at 7.78), Josephus likewise leaves aside the notice on the assembly's giving its assent from 13:4; see, however, 7.79.

[303] Compare 1 Chr 13:5, where David "gathers all Israel from the Shihor of Egypt to the entrance of Hamath...."

[304] This phrase, with its reference to what "*they*" had decided" might reflect the mention of the assembly's giving its assent to David's proposal in 1 Chr 13:4; see note to "to himself" at 7.78.

[305] This reference to the David (alone) approaching the ark takes the place of the mention of king and people proceeding to the site ("Baal-judah" [MT 2 Sam 6:2]/ "Baalah, Kiriathjearim which belongs to Judah" [1 Chr 13:6]) where the ark is currently stationed.

[306] 2 Sam 6:3// 1 Chr 13:7 attribute the "carrying" of the ark to an indeterminate "they." Josephus' specification concerning the carriers reflects the prescription cited by him in *Ant.* 3.136 (compare Deut 10:8),

Aminadab[307] and placed it on a new cart;[308] they[309] permitted all his brothers and sons[310] to pull it, along with the oxen.[311]

80. The king and with him the whole crowd went on ahead, singing hymns to God and intoning every kind of native song.[312] To the music of various stringed instruments,[313] with dancing and psalms,[314] as well as trumpets[315] and cymbals,[316] they brought the ark down to Hierosolyma.[317]

81. But when they had advanced as far as a certain spot, the so-called threshing-floor of Cheidon,[318] Ozas[319] died by the wrath of God,[320] for when the oxen tilted the ark,[321] he stretched out his hand,[322] wishing to steady [it].[323] Because he touched

Uzzah (Ozas) dies

---

making the priests the designated bearers of the ark.

[307] This form of the name corresponds to that read by LXX L 2 Sam 6:3 (and to that given by Josephus himself in *Ant.* 6.18). MT 6:3// 1 Chr 13:7 call the figure "A*b*inadab" in accord with his name in MT 1 Sam 7:1. As in his rendering of 1 Sam 7:1 in 6.18, Josephus leaves aside the mention of Abinadab's house being "on the hill."

[308] So 2 Sam 6:3a// 1 Chr 13:7a.

[309] I.e. the priests who previously carried the ark out of Abinadab's house.

[310] In MT 2 Sam 6:3b// 1 Chr 13:7b the reference is to 2, not further identified, individuals, i.e. "Uzzah and Ahio." The LXX of both verses reproduces the first of these proper names (i.e. as "Oza"), but then takes the MT's 2nd name as a (plural) common noun, i.e. "his [Oza's] brothers." Josephus will mention "Uzzah/Oza" only subsequently (7.81). Whereas his use of the term "brothers" here in 7.80 does reflect the LXX reading in 6:3// 13:7, given his non-mention of "Oza" as this point, the figures in question become "brothers" not of him, but rather of the one individual named in 7.79, i.e. "Aminadab" (just as the "sons" whom Josephus mentions here without biblical basis are likewise those of Aminadab). Given that Josephus has previously identified Aminadab himself as a "Levite" (see *Ant.* 6.18), his "brothers and sons" here in 7.79 are implicitly Levites as well.

[311] Josephus anticipates his mention of the "oxen" involved in the ark's transport from 2 Sam 6:6// 1 Chr 13:9. His notice here in 7.79 about the priests' entrusting the further transport of the ark to the (Levitical; see previous note) relatives of Aminadab and the oxen creates an implicit conflict with the prescription of *Ant.* 3.136, according to which the ark was "not carried upon a wagon but was borne by the priests." On the "anti-Levitical/ pro-priestly polemic" operative in the background here, see S. Schwartz 1990: 88-90.

[312] Josephus' reference to the assembly's "songs" reflects (and embellishes) 1 Chr 13:8 (and LXX 2 Sam 6:5), whereas MT 6:5 refers to "instruments of cypress wood(?)."

[313] This phrase generalizes the mention of "lyres and harps" in 2 Sam 6:5// 1 Chr 13:8.

[314] 2 Sam 6:5// 1 Chr 13:8 mention the assembly's "dancing," but not the recitation of "psalms."

[315] These instruments appear in the list of 1 Chr 13:8, but not that of 2 Sam 6:5.

[316] These instruments are also cited last in both 2 Sam 6:5 and 1 Chr 13:8. Whereas each of the 2 source verses mentions a total of 5 specific kinds of musical instruments (though differing somewhat as to which these were), Josephus lists only 2 (trumpets and cymbals).

[317] This phrase, without parallel in the account of the ark's progress in 2 Sam 6:5// 1 Chr 13:8, echoes Josephus' (likewise inserted) mention of the ark's intended destination in 7.78.

[318] Josephus' form (Greek: Χειδῶν) of the name of the owner of the threshing floor corresponds to that given in MT LXX L 1 Chr 13:9 (LXX B does not cite a name). Compare "Nacon" (MT 2 Sam 6:6), "Nodan" (4QSam^a), "Nodab" (LXX B 2 Sam 6:6), "Orna the Jebusite" (LXX L, a reading inspired by the reference to this figure's "threshing floor" in 2 Sam 24:16// 1 Chr 21:15).

[319] MT (2 Sam 6:6// 1 Chr 13:10) עֻזָּה (Eng.: "Uzzah") LXX Ὀζά; Josephus Ὀζᾶς. This is Josephus' first mention of this figure; see note to "sons" at 7.79.

[320] Cf. 2 Sam 6:7aα// 1 Chr 13:10a: "the anger of the Lord was kindled against Uzzah." Josephus reverses the sequence of 2 Sam 6:6-7// 1 Chr 13:9-10 by mentioning Uzzah's death, due to the Lord's anger, prior to the offense that provokes this.

[321] In supplying an object (i.e. the ark) for the oxen's action, Josephus aligns himself with LXX 2 Sam 6:6bβ// 1 Chr 13:9bβ against MT, where an intransitive verb is used (RSV: "the oxen stumbled").

[322] In making explicit mention of Uzzah's "hand" Josephus agrees with 1 Chr 13:9 (as well as 4QSam^a LXX 2 Sam 6:6) against MT 2 Sam 6:6, which lacks the specification.

[323] In making the "steadying" of the ark the purpose of Uzzah's action, Josephus follows 1 Chr 13:9 (and

Ark's stay with Obed-edom (Obadar)

it (though not a priest), [God] caused him to die.[324] **82.** Both the king and the people were distressed at the death of Ozas[325] (now the place where he expired is called the "breach of Ozas").[326] David was anxious, thinking that he might suffer the same thing as Ozas had if he received the ark into his house in the city, for he had died in this way, even though he only stretched out his hand to it [the ark].[327]

83. Therefore, he did not admit it into the city to his house.[328] Instead, he diverted it to the property of a just man,[329] named Obadar,[330] a Levite by birth,[331] and placed the ark with him. It remained there three whole months;[332] it prospered Obadar's household and conferred many good things upon him personally.[333]

Procession with ark resumed

84. When David heard[334] that these things had happened to Obadar, and that from

---

LXX L 2 Sam 6:6) against MT 2 Sam 6:6, which states that he actually did "steady" it (LXX B conflates both readings).

[324] Josephus' explanation of God's slaying Uzzah seems to conflate those given in 1 Chr 13:10 (and 4QSam[a] 2 Sam 6:7): "because he put forth his hand to the ark" and 2 Sam 6:7 (MT LXX L > LXX B): "because of his error/ rashness," while elucidating the latter in terms of his foregoing (implicit) identification of Uzzah as a (non-priestly) Levite who, as such, was not allowed to touch the ark (see *Ant.* 3.136 and cf. note to "oxen" at 7.79).

[325] Josephus' indication concerning David's emotional reaction to Uzzah's death reflects the term "dispirited" used in LXX 2 Sam 6:8 as opposed to the "he was angry" of MT 4QSam[a] 6:8 and 1 Chr 13:11. None of the biblical witnesses mentions a response by the people, as does Josephus.

[326] Here, exceptionally, Josephus does reproduce the etiological notice on the name for the place of Uzzah's death (MT: Perez-Uzzah, "breaking out against Uzzah") from 2 Sam 6:8b// 1 Chr 13:11b, even though in what precedes his rewording ("the king and people were distressed at the death of Ozas"; see 7.82) eliminates the preparation for this notice provided in 6:8a// 13:11a: "(David was angry dispirited because) the Lord had *broken forth* upon Uzzah."

[327] Josephus elaborates on the statement about David's being "afraid" of God and his attached rhetorical question concerning the (im)possibility of the ark's coming to him in 2 Sam 6:9// 1 Chr 13:12, spelling out what/why David "fears" at this point.

[328] Josephus follows 1 Chr 13:13a in stating as a fact that David did not bring the ark into the city to his house. 2 Sam 6:10a merely avers that David was "unwilling" to do this.

[329] This characterization of the ark's (temporary) host has no equivalent in the notice concerning "Obed-edom" as that host in 2 Sam 6:10b// 1 Chr 13:13b. Josephus' inserted qualification of him does serve to account for the ark's being placed with this figure in particular, just as its echoes his (likewise inserted) des-

ignation of Aminadab, the ark's earlier custodian, as "just" in *Ant.* 6.18 (// 1 Sam 7:1).

[330] MT (2 Sam 6:10// 1 Chr 13:13) עבד־אדום (Eng.: "Obed-Edom"); LXX B 2 Sam 6:10 (and LXX 1 Chr 13:13) Ἀβεδδαρά; LXX L 2 Sam 6:10 Ἀβεδδαδάν; Josephus Ὠβαδάρος.

[331] This designation takes the place of the sources' indication (2 Sam 6:10// 1 Chr 13:13) that Obed-edom was a "Gittite." Josephus could have found biblical inspiration for his attribution of Levitical ancestry to the ark's new host in 1 Chr 15:18, where an "Obed-Edom" figures in a list of Levitical singers appointed by David (cf. also 1 Chr 26:4, 8, where the sons of an Obed-edom appear in a context dealing [see 26:1] with the Levitical Korahites). In similar fashion, Josephus, drawing on 1 Chr 15:10-11, makes the ark's earlier custodian, Aminadab, a Levite (*Ant.* 6.18// 1 Sam 7:1). Rabbinic tradition as well designates the Obed-edom to whom David confides the ark as a Levite; see, e.g., *Num. Rab.* 4.20.

[332] See 2 Sam 6:11a// 1 Chr 13:14a.

[333] Josephus makes the ark itself the source of benefits to Obed-edom, whereas 2 Sam 6:11b// 1 Chr 13:14b have the Lord "blessing" him and his household.

[334] In passing directly from the benefits brought Obed-edom by the presence of the ark (2 Sam 6:11// 1 Chr 13:14// 7.83) to David's "hearing" of these (// 2 Sam 6:12a), Josephus follows the sequence of 2 Samuel 6 as opposed to that of 1 Chronicles, where between David's first (13:1-14) and 2nd (15:25-16:43) attempts at moving the ark, a long segment (14:1-15:24) supervenes. Within that segment, one can distinguish the Chronicler's parallel to 2 Sam 5:11-25, i.e. 14:1-17 (Hiram's overture, David's latter-born sons, and the Philistine wars), already reproduced by Josephus in 7.66-77, and a passage (15:1-24) unparalleled in 2 Samuel, featuring directions given by David and addressed to the Levites in particular, in view of the upcoming, 2nd attempt at moving the ark. Josephus' omission of this latter sequence is understandable, given its general highlighting of the Levites and its assigning them—rather than the priests (see *Ant.* 3.136

lowliness and poverty he had, all of a sudden, become happy and enviable to all those who saw and were informed about his household, being reassured that he would experience no calamity, he transferred the ark to his house.[335]

85. The priests lifted it up,[336] while seven choirs that the king had provided went ahead.[337] David himself was playing a stringed instrument and dancing,[338] with the result that when she saw him doing this Michale,[339] the daughter of Saoul the first king, jeered.[340]

86. When they brought in the ark, they placed it under the tent that David had set up for it.[341] He offered holocausts and peace offerings[342] and feasted the entire crowd, women, men, and infants,[343] giving them a small loaf, baked bread, a cake baked in a pan,[344] and a portion of sacrificial flesh.[345] After he had thus entertained

Feasting in Jerusalem

---

and cf. note to "oxen" at 7.79)—the carrying of the ark (see 1 Chr 15:12). On the other hand, Josephus does draw selectively on the segment in assigning a Levitical ancestry to the ark's 2 hosts, i.e. Aminadab (*Ant.* 6.18; cf. 1 Chr 15:10-11) and Obed-edom (7.83; cf. 1 Chr 15:18); see note to "Levite by birth" at 7.83.

[335] Josephus expatiates on 2 Sam 6:12a (David's hearing of the Lord's blessing Obed-edom and his household because of the ark), highlighting both the far-reaching extent of those blessings and the "message" they convey to David. To this elaboration he appends a summary version of 2 Sam 6:12b// 1 Chr 15:25 about David's resuming his transport of the ark.

[336] In specifying that it was the "priests" who lifted up the ark during the 2nd attempt at moving it, Josephus diverges from both 2 Sam 6:13 (the identity of the "bearers of the ark" is left indeterminate) and 1 Chr 15:26 (the Levites bear the ark; cf. 15:12). On the other hand, the specification is in accord with his own statements in *Ant.* 3.136 (the priests are to carry the ark) and 7.79 (the priests convey the ark out of Aminadab's house).

[337] Josephus' reference to these 7 "choirs" clearly reflects the plus of LXX BL 2 Sam 6:13. In contrast to all textual witnesses of 2 Sam 6:13 and 1 Chr 15:26, Josephus does not mention the offering of sacrifices *en route,* perhaps so as not to detract from the sacrifices that will take place at the climatic moment of the ark's actual arrival in Jerusalem (see 2 Sam 6:17b// 1 Chr 16:1// 7.86).

[338] Josephus here seems to conflate the wording of LXX 2 Sam 6:14 ("David was sounding with well-tuned instruments") and MT 6:14 ("David was dancing with all his might"). In contrast to both 2 Sam 6:14 and 1 Chr 15:27, he does not mention the "linen ephod" worn by David on this occasion, lest, perhaps, the king appear to have arrogated to himself this component of the high-priest's vesture (see Exod 28:39 and cf. Begg 1997l: 24, n. e). Josephus likewise has no parallel to the additional notice of 1 Chr 15:27 about both the king and the Levitical ark-bearers and musicians wearing

"robes of fine linen" on this occasion. Given the fact that he denounces the permission given the Levitical singers by King Agrippa II to wear "linen robes" just like the priests, as a violation of ancestral custom that was certain to provoke punishment of the people (see *Ant.* 20.216-218), it is not surprising that Josephus here leaves aside a "biblical precedent" for the Levites' wearing such linen robes. The historian further omits the mention of the "shouting" and the playing of one or more instruments that accompanies the ark's entry into Jerusalem in 2 Sam 6:15// 1 Chr 15:28.

[339] "Michal" has last been mentioned in 7.26 (// 2 Sam 3:14-15), where David's "recovery" of her from her 2nd husband is related.

[340] According to 2 Sam 6:16// 1 Chr 15:29, Michal "despised David in her heart."

[341] See 2 Sam 6:17a// 1 Chr 16:1. Like 2 Samuel 6, Josephus has not previously mentioned the erection of a tent for the ark by David. By contrast, 1 Chr 15:1 does provide such a notice.

[342] In making David the sacrificing subject, Josephus agrees with 2 Sam 6:17b against 1 Chr 16:1b, where an indeterminate "they" offers sacrifice. He passes over the appended notice of 2 Sam 6:18// 1 Chr 16:2 about David's "blessing" the people in the Lord's name, doing so out of concern that David not appear to be usurping a priestly prerogative, i.e. the cultic, public blessing of the people, which, e.g., Num 6:22-27; Deut 10:8 present as a task of the priests; see note to "house" at 7.86.

[343] 2 Sam 6:19// 1 Chr 16:3 do not mention "infants" among the recipients of David's largess.

[344] Josephus' Greek terms for the 3 kinds of "baked goods" distributed by David to the people are notably similar to those used in LXX 2 Sam 6:19; see Ulrich 1978: 248.

[345] In the list of foodstuffs given to the people by David in 2 Sam 6:19// 1 Chr 16:3 only 3 such items are mentioned. This 4th and final item on Josephus' list lacks a clear-cut counterpart in the sources. It may, however, reflect the rabbinic understanding of the He-

*Michal–David
confrontation*

the people, he dismissed them,[346] while he himself went to his own house.[347]

(4.3) **87.** His wife Michale, the daughter of Saoul,[348] stood beside him and, having congratulated him for everything else, prayed God to bestow on him all those things that he, in his benevolence, could confer.[349] She reproached him, however, because he, being so great a king, had danced unbecomingly, and in his dancing had exposed himself to his [slaves and][350] female attendants.[351] **88.** But David stated that he was not ashamed to have done these things that were gratifying to God,[352] who had honored him above her father and everyone else.[353] He intended to play and dance many [more] times, not worrying whether his doing this appeared shameful to the female attendants or to her.[354]

89. Michale herself, while married to David bore him no children.[355] Following, however, her subsequent marriage to the man to whom her father Saoul had handed her over—although David had taken her back and had her—she bore five chil-

---

brew term אֶשְׁפָּר (which stands 2nd in the MT of both verses and which the Greek witnesses take as designating some kind of pastry) as denoting a choice portion of meat (on this, see McCarter 1984: *ad* 2 Sam 6:19). Alternatively (or additionally), Josephus may have been inspired to mention the item given his previous reference to David's "peace-offerings," i.e. that (animal) sacrifice of which the worshippers also received a share.

[346] In 2 Sam 6:19b// 1 Chr 16:43a the people depart on their own. Josephus accentuates David's control of the entire proceedings by having him dismiss them. Josephus omits the whole segment of 1 Chronicles 16, i.e. vv. 4-42, that comes between the Chronicler's notices on David's feasting the people (16:3) and their departure (16:43a). This segment comprises a recitation by the Levites, at David's command (16:8), of portions of various psalms (16:9-36) and further cultic prescriptions concerning the Levites (16:37-42). Given the character of this material (focus on the Levites, an extended poetic interlude), its omission by Josephus accords with his practice elsewhere; see, e.g., his handling of 1 Chr 15:1-24 as mentioned in note to "heard" at 7.84.

[347] 2 Sam 6:20aα// 1 Chr 16:43b have David going to "bless his household." Josephus omits mention of this household blessing, just as he did David's blessing of the entire people; see note to "offerings" at 7.86.

[348] Drawing on 2 Sam 6:20aβb, Josephus resumes his reference to Michal from 7.85 (// 2 Sam 6:16// 1 Chr 15:29). The Chronicler has no parallel to the unseemly exchange between Michal and David of 2 Sam 6:20aβb-23// 7.87-89.

[349] These opening positive words of Michal to her husband represent an elaboration of the summary plus that follows the notice on her going out to meet David in LXX 2 Sam 6:20, i.e. "she blessed him." Josephus' elaboration of the queen's "blessing" is part of his over-all strategy of toning down Michal's aggressively sarcastic intervention in 6:20, with its

denigration of David.

[350] This phrase, bracketed by Niese, but not by Marcus, is missing in RO (and in Michal's words in 2 Sam 6:20, which mention only David's female servants).

[351] Josephus' indirect discourse version of Michal's words softens the intense sarcasm of her counterpart in 2 Sam 6:20: "How the king of Israel honored himself today, uncovering himself today before the eyes of his servants' maids, as one of the vulgar fellows [LXX dancers] shamelessly uncovers himself." His inserted reference to David's "dancing" picks up on the mention of this in 2 Sam 6:16// 1 Chr 15:29// 7.85.

[352] Josephus expatiates on David's opening statement concerning the "object" of his display as cited in 2 Sam 6:21aβ: "it was before the Lord" (MT; LXX: before the Lord I shall dance).

[353] From David's allusion to the Lord's giving him greater honor than Saul and his household in 2 Sam 6:21bα Josephus omits the specification that the Lord did this by making him [David] "prince over Israel." He likewise leaves aside David's declaration in 6:21bβ: "and I will make merry before the Lord."

[354] As in 2 Sam 6:22a, Josephus has David affirm his determination to persist in the behavior Michal finds objectionable. Whereas, however, in that verse David envisages a different response to his activity from Michal (i.e. contempt) and the maids (i.e. honor), Josephus' David asserts his indifference to their common assessment of his performance. Thereby, he underscores David's resolve to continue expressing his thanks to the Lord in his previous manner.

[355] Josephus modifies the seemingly absolute statement of 2 Sam 6:23 that Michal had no children "to the day of her death," given the mention of her children elsewhere in the Bible. In his presentation it was only during her marriage to David that she remained childless. See next note.

dren.[356] We shall disclose these matters in their proper place.[357]

(4.4) 90. When the king saw that in every respect his affairs, in accordance with the will of God, were improving virtually by the day, he supposed that he would be committing an offense if, while he himself was living in a lofty house constructed of cedars and excellently built in every other way, he neglected the ark, which was lying in a tent.[358]

David's temple plan

91. He thus wished to construct a sanctuary for God, as Moyses had predicted.[359] He talked about these matters with the prophet Nathas.[360] When Nathas then ordered him to do what he intended, as one who, in all things, had God as his present cooperator,[361] he became even more eager to construct the sanctuary.[362]

Nathan's (Nathas') approval

92. But that night God appeared to Nathas and told him[363] to inform David that

God's message for David

---

[356] This addition to the (problematic; see note on "no children" at 7.89) notice of 2 Sam 6:23 on Michal's childlessness poses problems of its own in light of what one reads in other biblical contexts. Marcus (*ad loc.*) takes "the man" referred to by Josephus here as Adriel the son of Barzillai, given that 2 Sam 21:8 (MT and LXX B) mentions Adriel's 5 sons by Michal (LXX L reads "Merob" in line with the statement of 1 Sam 18:19 [MT, no parallel in LXX B and Josephus], where Adriel's Saulide wife is not Michal, but her sister Merab). On the other hand, the further reference to David's taking Michal back from the man by whom she had her 5 children would seem to have in view, not Adriel, but rather Palti[el] to whom Saul gives her (1 Sam 25:44// *Ant.* 6.309) and from whom David recovers her (2 Sam 3:15// 7.26), seeing that the Bible does not mention either Saul's conferring Michal on Adriel (in 1 Sam 18:19 it is Merab whom he gives to him) or David's recuperation of her from him. By omitting the name of Michal's other husband, Josephus contrives to have his notice cover the case of both Adriel and Paltiel, apparently presuming that the casual reader would not notice the problems involved.

[357] In fact, as Marcus (*ad loc.*) points out, Josephus makes no further mention of Michal. In his version of 2 Sam 21:8 (see previous note) in 7.296 he speaks in general terms of "the 7 descendants of Saoul's family" rather than specifically of the 5 sons Michal bore Adriel. For a similar case of Josephus' announcing that he will treat some matter at a later point in his work, but then failing to do so, see on *Ant.* 5.31.

[358] Josephus develops this notice on the state of mind that prompts David to raise the possibility of building a house for the ark with Nathan on the basis of the narrative reference to the king's "residing in his house" of 2 Sam 7:1a// 1 Chr 17:1a and David's own allusion to the ark's current tent-dwelling in 7:2// 17:1b. His opening mention of David's affairs improving daily as willed by God might be seen as his adaptation of the phrase of 2 Sam 7:1b: "... the Lord had given rest from all his enemies round about." The Chronicler's

omission of this phrase and Josephus' modification of it likely reflect the fact in what follows many further wars by David with his enemies will be recounted. On Josephus' (highly abridged) version of 2 Samuel 7// 1 Chronicles 17 in 7.90-95, see Begg 2000b.

[359] Continuing his description of David's state of mind as he approaches Nathan, Josephus spells out in advance the import of the king's allusive words to the prophet as quoted in 2 Sam 7:2// 1 Chr 17:1b about his own dwelling in a cedar house, while the ark resides in a tent. Josephus' reference to Moses' earlier speaking of the building of a sanctuary lacks a counterpart in either 2 Samuel 7// 1 Chronicles 17, or the Pentateuch itself. On the other hand, the reference does have a basis in *Ant.* 4.200, where Moses ordains that there should be "one Temple" in the city that God would designate "through prophecy." The cross reference serves to invest David's project with Mosaic authority.

[360] MT (2 Sam 7:2// 1 Chr 17:1b) נתן (Eng.: "Nathan"); LXX Ναθάν; Josephus Νάθας. Josephus does not reproduce the actual words of the king to Nathan, having made use of these in describing David's state of mind in 7.90. In his (garbled) version of the David-Nathan exchange of 2 Samuel 7// 1 Chronicles 17, Eupolemus (in the excerpt of Alexander Polyhistor cited by Eusebius, *Preap. ev.* 30.5) has David ask God at the outset where he is to build the altar. Thereupon "an angel" appears above the site of the future altar and orders him not to proceed with the temple-building. Subsequently, this angel is identified as "Dianathan," apparently a corruption of the biblical "Nathan." It would appear that Eupolemus is conflating the accounts of 2 Samuel 7// 1 Chronicles 17 and 2 Samuel 24// 1 Chronicles 21, turning the prophet Nathan of the first pair of texts into the angel featured in the 2nd.

[361] See 2 Sam 7:3// 1 Chr 17:2.

[362] This notice, spelling out the effect of Nathan's response on David, lacks a biblical counterpart. It serves to underscore the king's piety.

[363] Compare 2 Sam 7:4// 1 Chr 17:3, where "the word of God comes to Nathan." On Josephus' penchant

he commended his intention and desire, seeing that whereas no one previously had thought of constructing a sanctuary for him, he had devised this very idea.[364] Nevertheless, he would not permit one who had fought with many enemies and who was defiled by the slaughter of numerous foes to make him a sanctuary.[365] **93.** However, after his death as an old man who had completed a long life,[366] the sanctuary would be built by his son, who would receive the kingship after him and who would be called Solomon.[367] He promised that he would protect and take care of him as a father does his son,[368] and would preserve and hand on the kingship to the descendants of his sons.[369] He would, however, punish him, if he offended, with disease and infertility of the soil.[370]

---

for inserting references to appearances by God where the Bible lacks them, see note to "appeared" at *Ant.* 6.38. Here in 7.92, Josephus' mention of such a theophany may be inspired by the statement of 2 Sam 7:17// 1 Chr 17:15 about Nathan's speaking to David "in accordance with all this vision."

[364] Neither 2 Samuel 7 nor 1 Chronicles 17 records God's approbation, in principle, of David's plan of building him a temple. Josephus anticipates the item from 1 Kgs 8:18// 2 Chr 6:18, where Solomon quotes the Lord's telling his father that "he did well" in thinking to build a temple. With this opening insertion, Josephus blunts the thrust of God's words in 2 Sam 7:5-7// 1 Chr 17:4-6, which reject David's plan out of hand.

[365] Josephus prefaces the rhetorical question of 2 Sam 7:5 and prohibition of 1 Chr 17:4, both expressing God's disavowal of David's temple plan, with a motivation for the divine veto. This motivation indicates that, whereas the project is as such a commendable one, nevertheless David personally will not be allowed to carry it out. Josephus draws the content of this motivation from a series of subsequent biblical statements about why David himself was prevented from building the temple; see 1 Kgs 5:17; 1 Chr 22:8; 28:3. Having now presented his (expanded) parallel to 2 Sam 7:5 // 1 Chr 17:4, he passes over the whole segment 7:6-11// 17:5-10 in which God elaborates on his rejection of a temple in principle and then speaks of his own past/ future benefits for David personally and for Israel as a whole. Josephus will make use of the latter item subsequently; see 7.95. In a similar way, Eupolemus (in the excerpt from Alexander Polyhistor cited by Eusebius, *Praep. ev.* 30.5) has the angel "Dianathan" (see note to "Nathas" at 7.91) forbid David to erect the temple in view of the bloodshed and wars in which he had been involved.

[366] Cf. 2 Sam 7:12a// 1 Chr 17:11a: "... when your days are fulfilled and you lie down with your ancestors." Josephus elucidates the biblical euphemism, adding an explicit promise of a long life for David, a promise that finds an implicit realization in 7.389, where Josephus, going beyond his biblical sources,

states that David lived 70 years.

[367] Josephus reverses the sequence of 2 Sam 7:12b-13// 1 Chr 17:11b-12, in which the Lord's raising up David's son as his successor is mentioned prior to that son's building a "house" for "my name" (2 Sam 7:13)/ "for me" (1 Chr 17:12). Thereby, he highlights the importance of the temple building vis-à-vis the Davidic succession. Neither source text names Solomon as David's promised successor; Josephus draws the name from 1 Chr 22:9; 28:6 where, in citing the divine promise of 17:11b-12 (// 7:12-13), Solomon introduces a mention of his own name. According to Eupolemus (in the excerpt from Alexander Polyhistor cited by Eusebius, *Praep. ev.* 30.6) the angel "Dianathan" (see note to "Nathas" at 7.91) commands David to entrust the temple building task to his (unnamed) son and to collect the necessary materials himself. David responds (30.7), in an extrabiblical elaboration, to the order by dispatching miners to an island in the Red Sea to procure the gold that will be needed.

[368] See 2 Sam 7:14a// 1 Chr 17:13a. Josephus spells out the implication for Solomon personally of the father-son relationship between the Lord and David's successors generally spoken of in the sources.

[369] Josephus' formulation of the repeated promise concerning the duration of David's dynasty of 2 Sam 7:12bβ, 13b, 16 // 1 Chr 17:11bβ, 12b, 14 eliminates the sources' allusion to the Davidic line enduring "forever." Thereby, he disposes of the problem that David's dynasty had, in fact, ceased to rule already centuries before his own time, as well as the promise of its eventual revival implicit in the use of the term "forever" that might well make his Roman patrons uneasy.

[370] This is Josephus' elucidation of the cryptic warning regarding David's successor found in 2 Sam 7:14b (but not in 1 Chronicles 17): "when he commits iniquity, I will chasten him with the rods of men, with the stripes of the sons of men." The announcement prepares for Solomon's subsequent defection and the disasters this will bring with it. Josephus has no equivalent to the additional plus of 2 Sam 7:15, where God announces that, while he will punish David's successor if

94. When David learned these things from the prophet,[371] he was overjoyed to find out that his rulership would endure among his descendants and that his house was to be splendid and famous.[372] He went to the ark,[373] and falling on his face,[374] began to worship and thank God for all these things,[375] **95.** namely his having already promoted him from the lowly [state] of being a shepherd, and advanced him to so great a position of leadership and glory,[376] as well as what he had promised his descendants and his providential care[377] that he had shown both for the Hebrews and for their freedom.[378] Having said these things and sung a hymn to God, he departed.[379]

David thanks God

(5.1) 96. When a little time had elapsed, he decided that it was necessary to campaign against the Palestinoi. He saw to it that there should be no slackness or negligence in his administration, in order that, as the Deity had foretold to him, he might, having conquered his enemies,[380] leave behind descendants to rule as kings in peace for the future.[381] **97.** He again assembled his army and enjoined it to be prepared

David's Philistine campaign

---

he sins, he will not withdraw his "favor" from him, as he did from Saul.

[371] This transitional phrase takes the place of the notice on Nathan's delivering God's message to David in 2 Sam 7:17// 1 Chr 17:15.

[372] This mention of David's initial, emotional response to Nathan's message has no biblical parallel. Its wording picks up on the promise concerning David's dynasty and its duration in 7.93.

[373] With this mention of his approaching the ark Josephus specifies where it is that David "goes in," as he is said to do at the opening of 2 Sam 7:18// 1 Chr 17:16. Cf. 7.79, which cites David's "approaching the ark" that is now to be brought to Jerusalem.

[374] In 2 Sam 7:18a// 1 Chr 17:16a David "sits before the Lord." Rabbinic tradition was divided as to whether this biblical phrase was to be taken literally and whether it provided biblical warrant for a special privilege of the Davidic kings; see Begg 2000b: 12-13, n. 39. Josephus, in any case, depicts David in a more reverential posture; compare *S. Eli. Rab.* 18, p. 89, where David first "prostrates himself" on the ground and then "seats himself before the Presence."

[375] Josephus compresses and generalizes the extended opening segment (2 Sam 7:18b-21// 1 Chr 17:16b-19) of David's prayer, in which he humbly acknowledges what God has done for him.

[376] For this portion of David's prayer Josephus makes delayed use of God's recalling that he took David from shepherding his flock to be prince over his people Israel in 2 Sam 7:8// 1 Chr 17:7. The wording used, with its reference to David's past "lowly [state]" (Greek: ταπεινός) is also reminiscent of the reference to Obed-edom's earlier "lowliness" (Greek: ταπεινότης) in 7.84. God prospers both of those who show due solicitude for the ark.

[377] Here Josephus has David echo God's promise

concerning the continuation of his dynasty in 7.93 and his own joy over this in 7.94. This component of the king's prayer likewise vaguely reflects David's references to the divine word concerning his "house" in 2 Sam 7:18b-19// 1 Chr 17:16b-17.

[378] This phrase synthesizes David's invocation of the Lord's past benefits for his people, above all his delivering them from slavery in Egypt, in 2 Sam 7:23-24 // 1 Chr 17:21-22.

[379] This concluding notice on David's "exit" following his response to God takes the place of the extended final segment of the king's prayer in 2 Sam 7:25-29// 1 Chr 17:23-27, where David implores the Lord to maintain his dynasty forever. Overall, in line with his consistent tendency, Josephus drastically shortens David's 12-verse biblical prayer.

[380] The reference here is to Samuel's promise of all-sided military success to the newly anointed David in *Ant.* 6.165.

[381] Josephus here alludes to the previous divine promises concerning David's "descendants" of *Ant.* 6.165 and 7.93. The entire above paragraph is Josephus' elaboration of the summary transitional formula of 2 Sam 8:1// 1 Chr 18:1: "... it came to pass after these things [i.e. the dynastic promise featured in 2 Samuel 7// 1 Chronicles 17]...." On Josephus' version (7.96-110) of David's conquests as described in 2 Samuel 8// 1 Chronicles 18, see Begg 1999e. Eupolemus (in the excerpt from Alexander Polyhistor cited by Eusebius, *Praep. ev.* 30.3-4) gives a summary version of the biblical accounts, in which, e.g., he introduces mention of place names ("Commagene") and peoples (e.g., the Itureans and Nabateans) of his own time. He likewise represents David as imposing tribute on "Souron" king of Tyre and Phoenicia and making a friendship treaty with "Vaphres" king of Egypt.

and in readiness against the enemy. When the army seemed to him to be in good shape, he set out with it from Hierosolyma and marched against the Palestinoi.[382] **98.** After defeating them in battle,[383] he cut off much of their territory and added this to the Hebrews' domain.[384] Then he redirected the war against the Moabites. Victorious in battle,[385] he killed two thirds of their army and took the remainder captive.[386]

Moabites sub-jected

Hadadezer (Artazar) de-feated

99. Having imposed annual tribute on them,[387] he campaigned against Artazar,[388] son of Araos,[389] king of Sophene.[390] Engaging him at the Euphrates river, he destroyed about 20,000 of his infantry,[391] as well as about 5,000 horsemen.[392] He seized 1,000 chariots from him,[393] most of which he obliterated, though ordering that a mere 100 of them be preserved for himself.[394]

Syrian king Hadad (Adad) routed

(5.2) 100. When Adad, the king of Damascus and Syria,[395] heard that David was making war on Artazar, whose friend he was,[396] he, acting as an ally, came with a strong force. He departed, however, differently than he had expected;[397] engaging

---

[382] 2 Sam 8:1a// 1 Chr 18:1a begin immediately with David's "defeat" of the Philistines. Josephus' insertion of the above preliminaries to David's victory accentuate his stature as a provident commander.

[383] Josephus now, finally, comes to reproduce the datum of 2 Sam 8:1a// 1 Chr 18:1a on David's defeat of the Philistines.

[384] The sources diverge as to what David "took" from the Philistines following his defeat of them. Josephus' own indication on the matter seems to reflect the reading of LXX BL 2 Sam 8:1b, where the object is "the appropriated/common (land)." Compare MT 8:1b: "Metheg-ammah" (rendered as a place name by RSV, but possibly meaning "supremacy") and 1 Chr 18:1b: "Gath and its villages."

[385] See 2 Sam 8:2aα// 1 Chr 18:2aα whose reference to David's "defeating" the Moabites Josephus elaborates.

[386] This notice reflects the plus of 2 Sam 8:2aββα, in particular the reading of MT LXX L, where the ratio of those killed/left alive by David is 2 to 1 (in LXX B it is rather 2 to 2). Josephus leaves aside the gruesome source details concerning the process employed (measuring off the Moabites with a cord, having them lie on the ground).

[387] See 2 Sam 8:2bβ// 1 Chr 18:2b.

[388] Greek: Ἀρτάζαρος; this is the reading of the codices ROE followed by Niese. Marcus (*ad loc.*) reads Ἀδράζαρος with MSP (and 7.105). Compare MT (2 Sam 8:3// 1 Chr 18:3) הדדעזר (Eng.: "Hadadezer"); LXX Ἀδραάζαρ.

[389] MT (2 Sam 8:3) רחב (Eng.: "Rehob"); LXX B Ῥαάβ; LXX L Ῥαάφ (1 Chr 18:3 does not mention Hadadezer's father); Josephus Ἄραός (Schalit *s.v.* suggests that this form reflects a metathesis of the first 2 letters of the original form, i.e. Ῥααός).

[390] MT (2 Sam 8:3// 1 Chr 18:3) צובה (Eng.: "Zobah"); LXX Σουβά; Josephus Σωφήνη (which Scha-

lit *s.v.* views as a corruption of an original Σωβᾶ, both here and in *Ant.* 8.204, 259). Josephus leaves aside the obscure indication of 2 Sam 8:3b// 1 Chr 18:3b that David's defeat of Hadadezer occurred as he (David? Hadadezer?) was going to restore/set up his monument/ power at the River (i.e. the Euphrates).

[391] This figure corresponds to that given in 2 Sam 8:4// 1 Chr 18:4, where, however, it appears in last place in the listing of casualties inflicted by David.

[392] This figure stands between the low number (1,700) for the slain horsemen/charioteers given in MT 2 Sam 8:4a and the much higher figure, i.e. 7,000, cited by LXX BL 8:4a and 1 Chr 18:4a (as also by the codices MSP in 7.99).

[393] This figure corresponds to the plus of LXX BL 4QSam[a] BL 2 Sam 8:4a// 1 Chr 18:4a, where it stands first in the listing of Hadadezer's casualties. MT 2 Sam 8:4a lacks the item.

[394] See 2 Sam 8:4b// 1 Chr 18:4b. MT's use of the term רכב leaves it ambiguous whether David "hamstrung" the captured "chariot horses" (so RSV) or rather "dismantled" the chariots themselves. By employing the same Greek term ἅρματα ("chariots") as does the LXX, Josephus clarifies the matter.

[395] 2 Sam 8:5a// 1 Chr 18:5a designate David's next opponent as a nation, i.e. "Aram of Damascus." In his naming the leader of that nation, as also for his designation of his domain, Josephus anticipates the wording of the notice drawn from Nicolas of Damascus that he will quote in 7.101.

[396] Josephus interjects these background details— also perhaps derived from Nicolas of Damascus (see previous note)—concerning the Syrian intervention in favor of Hadadezer as related in 2 Sam 8:5a// 1 Chr 18:5a, thereby providing a motivation for that intervention.

[397] With this inserted remark Josephus prepares readers for the outcome of the upcoming battle.

David at the Euphrates river, he was defeated in battle and lost many of his soldiers.[398] For 20,000 of Adad's army fell, done away with by the Hebrews, while all the rest fled.[399]

101. Nicolas[400] too makes mention of this king in the fourth book of his *Histories*, speaking as follows:

Excerpts from Nicolas of Damascus

> "After these things, a long time later, a certain one of the natives, named Adad,[401] growing stronger, ruled as king over Damascus and the rest of Syria,[402] except for Phoinike. He made war against David, the king of Judea, and contended with him in many battles, in the last of which, at the Euphrates, he was defeated.[403] He was regarded as the best of kings in terms of vigor and courage."

102. Concerning his descendants, he further states that, after his death, they inherited from one another both the kingdom and the name.[404] His words are:

> "Upon his death, his descendants ruled as kings down to the tenth generation, each one inheriting from his father the name along with rulership, like the Ptolemies in Egypt.[405] **103.** The most capable of them all was the third, who, wishing to make up for his grandfather's defeat, campaigned against the Judeans; he ravaged the territory now called Samaritis."

Nor did Nicolas deviate from the truth. For this is that Adad who campaigned against Samareia when Achab ruled as king over the Israelites, concerning whom we shall speak in the proper place.[406]

(5.3) 104. In his campaign against Damascus and the rest of Syria,[407] David subjected it all.[408] Having established garrisons in the country and fixed the tribute they were to pay,[409] he returned.[410] He dedicated the golden quivers[411] and suits of

David's dedicatory offerings

---

[398] Josephus elaborates the summary account of 2 Sam 8:5a// 1 Chr 18:5a, which does not explicitly mention either a battle or the Syrian defeat. Josephus draws his (extra-biblical) localization of the conflict at the Euphrates from the report of Nicolas that he will cite in 7.101.

[399] 2 Sam 8:5b// 1 Chr 18:5b speak of 22,000 Syrians slain by David; neither mentions a flight by the survivors.

[400] On Nicolas, the court historian of Herod the Great, and Josephus' use of his no longer extant *Histories*, see Wacholder 1962 and 1989: 147-72. Josephus cites this non-biblical author—as he does such other Greco-Roman historians as Herodotus—with a view to enhancing the credibility of his Bible-based account in the eyes of Gentile readers, whose own writers he can show attesting to events narrated in the Jewish Scriptures.

[401] See Josephus' anticipated use of this name for David's opponent in 7.100.

[402] Cf. Josephus' designation of Adad as king of "Damascus and Syria" in 7.100.

[403] Cf. Josephus' utilization of this wording of Nicolas' account in his elaboration of 2 Sam 8:5a// 1 Chr 18:5a in 7.100: "joining battle at the Euphrates river, he was defeated..."

[404] This editorial remark introduces Josephus' following, additional quotation from Nicolas whose wording it echoes.

[405] In *Ant.* 8.156 Josephus, this time writing on his own, calls attention to the succession of Alexandrian kings, each named "Ptolemy" after the founder of the dynasty.

[406] In this instance (contrast that of Michal's progeny in 7.89), Josephus does follow through on his promise of relating the matter at a later point; see *Ant.* 8.363-392 (// 1 Kings 20). Cf. note to "for them" at 7.105.

[407] Josephus derives this phrase from Nicolas as quoted by him in 7.101.

[408] Compare 2 Sam 8:6bα// 1 Chr 18:6bα, where the Syrians "become servants to David." Josephus' formulation highlights David's own active role in the process.

[409] See Sam 8:6a// 1 Chr 18:6a, where the Syrians take the initiative in paying tribute rather than having David impose this on them; see previous note.

[410] This mention of David's "return" prepares the following notice on his activities in Jerusalem. It takes the place of the allusion to the divine source of David's victories in 2 Sam 8:6bβ// 1 Chr 18:6bβ (which Josephus will, however, utilize subsequently; see 7.105 and cf. note to "his wars" at 7.105).

[411] This is Josephus' (correct?) rendering of the Hebrew term שלטים of 2 Sam 18:7// 1 Chr 18:7, which has often been understood to mean "shields" (see RSV; cf. Begg 1999e: 157, n. 56); he shares the rendering with

armor[412] that Adad's bodyguards had worn[413] to God in Hierosolyma.[414] **105.** Later, Susak, king of Egypt, when he campaigned against David's grandson Roboam, took these, just as he carried off much other wealth from Hierosolyma.[415] We shall disclose these things when we reach the appropriate point for them.[416]

Cities of Hadadezar plundered

But the king of the Hebrews, with God supporting him and giving him success in his wars,[417] campaigned against Adrazar's most beautiful cities,[418] Battaia[419] and Machon.[420] Taking them by storm, he plundered them.[421] **106.** Much gold and silver was found in these cities,[422] as well as that bronze which is said to be better than gold[423] from which Solomon[424] made the large vessel that is called the "Sea"[425] and those beautiful wash-basins[426] when he constructed the sanctuary for God.[427]

Symmachus. LXX 8:7 speaks of golden "bracelets/anklets," LXX 18:7 of "collars."

[412] None of the biblical witnesses mentions these items (compare the plus of LXX L 2 Sam 8:7: "and the golden weapons and the spears").

[413] In 2 Sam 8:7// 1 Chr 18:7 the objects are removed by David from "the servants of Hadadezer" (see 8:3// 18:3). Josephus substitutes Nicolas' form of the king's name.

[414] 2 Sam 8:7// 1 Chr 18:7 refer simply to David's bringing the objects to Jerusalem. Josephus' formulation prepares for that of *Ant.* 8.259 (// LXX 1 Kgs 14:26), where he will speak of Pharoah Shishak's removing the golden quivers that "David had dedicated to God."

[415] This foreshadowing notice reflects the 4QSam^a LXX and OL plus at the end of 2 Sam 8:7, which NAB renders "these [i.e. the golden objects spoken of earlier in the verse] Shishak [LXX: Susakeim], king of Egypt, took away when he came to Jerusalem in the days of Rehoboam [LXX B: Jeroboam], son of Solomon." Josephus' added reference to Shishak's removal of "much other wealth" has in view his presentation in *Ant.* 8.258-259 (// 1 Kgs 14:26), where the king carries off a variety of items from Jerusalem.

[416] As with the "announcement" of 7.103, Josephus does make good on this editorial promise; see *Ant.* 8.258-259.

[417] This parenthetical phrase represents Josephus' delayed use of the theological notice on the source of David's victories of 2 Sam 8:6b// 1 Chr 18:6b; see note to "returned" at 7.104.

[418] This phrase reflects the LXX reading ("from the elect cities") in 2 Sam 8:8// 1 Chr 18:8, where it substitutes for MT 8:8's 2nd proper place name, i.e. "Berothai." On the name of David's opponent, see note to "Artazar" at 7.99.

[419] MT (2 Sam 8:8) בטח (Eng.: "Betah"); MT (1 Chr 18:8a) טבחת (Eng.: "Tibhah"); LXX B (2 Sam 8:8) Μασβάκ; LXX L (2 Sam 8:8) Ματεβάκ; LXX B (1 Chr 18:8a) Μεταβηχάς; LXX L (1 Chr 18:8a) Ταβαάθ; Josephus Βαττάια.

[420] MT (2 Sam 8:8) ברתי (Eng.: "Berothai"); MT (1 Chr 18:8a) כון (Eng.: "Cun"); Josephus Μάχων (Schalit *s.v.* traces this form back to the name found in Chronicles, where it is preceded by the preposition מ, thus מכון). LXX does not have a 2nd proper place in either 2 Sam 8:8 or 1 Chr 18:8a, but rather the phrase "from the elect cities"; see note to "beautiful cities" at 7.105. Josephus appears to conflate the readings of both MT and LXX 2 Sam 8:8// 1 Chr 18:8a with his 2 proper place names, plus an equivalent to the LXX phrase "elect cities."

[421] These actions of David, preparatory to his taking the cities' metals to Jerusalem, have no equivalent in 2 Sam 8:8// 1 Chr 18:8a. Josephus' insertion of them accounts for David's being able to remove the cities' riches and accentuates his success as a general.

[422] 2 Sam 8:8// 1 Chr 18:8a speak only of the cities' bronze. Josephus' mention also of their precious metals accentuates the wealth their capture by David brought the Israelites.

[423] This characterization of the cities' bronze lacks a counterpart in 2 Sam 8:8// 1 Chr 18:8a. The insertion intimates an explanation as to why David bothered to remove the captured bronze, especially since, according to his own presentation, David obtained precious metals from the cities as well (see previous note).

[424] Josephus' allusion to various cultic objects later made by Solomon here corresponds to the plus, lacking in MT 2 Sam 8:8, of LXX 8:8 and MT LXX 1 Chr 18:8b.

[425] Josephus relates Solomon's making of the "Sea" in *Ant.* 8.79-80. Here, he prefaces mention of the object's odd name with an indication of its nature, i.e. a "large vessel."

[426] Josephus describes Solomon's fabrication of these objects in *Ant.* 8.85. His mention of them here reflects the reading of LXX 2 Sam 8:8 and 1 Chr 18:8b against MT, which lacks them. Josephus' 2-member list of Solomon's constructions does not mention the various additional bronze objects made by him according to one or other of the biblical textual witnesses, i.e. pillars (BL OL 2 Sam 8:8; MT LXX 18:8b); "all (B OL

(5.4) 107. When the king of Amathe[428] found out what had happened to Adrazar and heard that his army had been destroyed, he became anxious for himself; before David should come against him, he decided to request a [treaty of] friendship and a pledge.[429] He sent his son Adoram[430] to him, declaring his thanks to him for having made war on Adrazar, who was his enemy, and proposing to make an alliance and [treaty of] friendship with him.[431] **108.** He also sent him golden, silver, and bronze vessels of antique workmanship as gifts.[432] David made the alliance with Thain[433]— for that was the name of the king of Amathe—and accepted his gifts.[434] He then dismissed his son with the honor befitting them both. He brought the things which Thain had sent, as well as the rest of the silver and gold he had taken from the cities and the nations he had subjugated and dedicated them to God.[435]

109. God did not confer on him [David] alone victory and success in his waging war and leading his army.[436] Rather, when David sent Abessai,[437] the brother of his commanding general Joab,[438] with a force against Idumea, God, through Abessai, gave him victory, over the Idumeans.[439] For Abessai destroyed 18,000 of them in

King of Hamath submits to David

Abishai subjugates Idumeans

8:8) the vessels (of bronze)" (LXX L OL 8:8; MT LXX 18:8b; LXX B 8:8 lacks of bronze); and the altar (OL 8:8).

[427] This chronological notice as to when Solomon fabricated the objects in question has no biblical counterpart.

[428] MT (2 Sam 8:9//1 Chr 18:9) חמת (Eng.: "Hamath"); LXX 2 Sam 8:9 and LXX B 1 Chr 18:9 Ἡμάθ; LXX L 1 Chr 18:9 Αἱμάθ; Josephus Ἀμάθη. Josephus reserves mention of the king's own name until 7.108.

[429] Josephus expatiates on the notice of 2 Sam 8:9 // 1 Chr 18:9, where the king simply learns of David's destruction of the entire army of Hadadezer (see 8:3// 18:3// 7.100). In particular, he introduces reference to the emotional effect of the news on the king and his objective in subsequently dispatching his son to David.

[430] MT (2 Sam 8:10) יורם (Eng.: "Joram"); MT (1 Chr 18:10) הדורם (Eng.: "Hadoram"); LXX BL (2 Sam 8:10) Ἰεδδουράν; LXX B (1 Chr 18:10) Ἰδουραάμ; LXX L (1 Chr 18:10) Ἀδωράμ; Josephus Ἀδώραμος.

[431] See 2 Sam 8:10a // 1 Chr 18:10a, to which Josephus adds the appeal for an alliance with David, this picking up his earlier insertion concerning the king's objective in sending to David; see 7.107a.

[432] To the catalogue of the various metal vessels sent to David in 2 Sam 8:10b// 1 Chr 18:10b, Josephus appends the detail concerning their antique character, thereby heightening the value of the gift.

[433] MT (2 Sam 8:10) תעי (Eng.: "Toi"); MT (1 Chr 18:10) תעו (Eng.: "Tou"); LXX B (2 Sam 8:10) Θόουου; LXX L (2 Sam 8:10) Ἐλιάβ; LXX BL (1 Chr 18:10) Θῶα; Josephus Θαῖνος. Josephus has held over the king's name until this point, where he introduces it as a kind of afterthought.

[434] These 2 preliminary actions by David in response to the emissary from Hamath are Josephus' additions. The first of them offers an appealing image of a Jewish leader responding favorably to a appeal for a friendship pact from the side of a weaker Gentile party, this serving to rebut contemporary charges about Jewish xenophobia. On such charges and their refutation as a recurrent concern throughout Josephus' writings, see Feldman 1998: 121; 1998a: 557-58.

[435] See 2 Sam 8:11-12// 1 Chr 18:11, from which Josephus omits the list of the nations that supplied David's spoils (8:12// 18:11b). His mention of David's drawing these from both "cities" and "nations" conflates the variant readings of LXX BL 8:11 and MT 8:11// MT LXX 18:11a, respectively.

[436] This affirmation draws on the closing notice of 2 Sam 8:14b// 1 Chr 18:13b: "The Lord gave victory to David wherever he went." As formulated by Josephus, the notice serves as a lead-in to the following account of a victory won, not directly by David, but by one of his commanders.

[437] In making "Abishai" the one through whom the victory is won, Josephus follows 1 Chr 18:12 as opposed to both 2 Sam 8:13 (David himself is the victor) and Ps 60:2 (Joab wins the battle).

[438] 1 Chr 18:12 calls Abishai "the son of Zeruiah," a designation used of him by Josephus in *Ant.* 6.311 and 7.11. He anticipates Joab's title from 2 Sam 8:16// 1 Chr 18:15, having previously related Joab's obtaining this by being the first to scale the walls of Jerusalem in 7.64.

[439] Josephus' designation of David's target as Idumea/ Idumeans (= Edom/ Edomites) corresponds to the readings of 1 Chr 18:12; LXX BL 2 Sam 8:13 (and Ps 60:2), whereas in MT 8:13 the enemy is "Aram."

battle.[440] The king then posted garrisons throughout all Idumea, and received taxes both from the country as a whole and each one of them individually.[441]

*David's offi-
cials*

110. David was also just by nature and pronounced judgment with an eye to the truth.[442] As the general of his entire army he had Joab.[443] He designated Josaphat,[444] son of Achil,[445] chief of the royal chancery,[446] and appointed Sadok, of the house of Phinees,[447] as high priest along with Abiathar,[448] for he was his friend.[449] He made Sisa[450] scribe,[451] while to Banai,[452] son of Ioad,[453] he handed over the command of his bodyguards.[454] His older sons were around his person and guarded this.[455]

*David seeks
Jonathan's sur-
vivors*

(5.5) 111. David likewise recalled his sworn agreements with Ionathes, the son of Saoul, and the former's friendship and solicitude for himself.[456] For in addition to all the other good qualities that he had, he was also mindful of the benefits he had received at other times.[457]

112. He therefore ordered that search be made whether anyone of Ionathes' line

---

[440] This is the enemy casualty figure given in 1 Chr 18:12// 2 Sam 8:13; Ps 60:2 reads 12,000. Josephus omits the location of the battle in "the Valley of Salt," common to all 3 biblical texts.

[441] In 2 Sam 8:14a// 1 Chr 18:13a the double sequel to Israel's victory is that David installs garrisons in Edom and the Edomites become his servants. Josephus spells out what it meant for the Edomites to become David's "servants," i.e. they had to pay taxes to him. David's double "imposition" on the defeated Idumeans here in 7.109 corresponds to his treatment of the vanquished Syrians in 7.104.

[442] See 2 Sam 8:15// 1 Chr 18:14. The word "just" (δίκαιος) is a key term in Josephus' characterization of David, see *Ant.* 6.165; 7.130, 391. The qualification of David as one who "pronounced judgment with an eye to truth" sets him in contrast with the sons of Samuel, who did precisely the opposite according to *Ant.* 6.34.

[443] See 2 Sam 8:16a// 1 Chr 18:15a and cf. 7.109.

[444] MT (2 Sam 8:16b// 1 Chr 18:15b) יהושפט (Eng.: "Jehoshaphat"); LXX Ἰωσαφάτ; Josephus Ἰωσάπατος.

[445] MT (2 Sam 8:16b// 1 Chr 18:15b) אחילוד (Eng.: "Ahilud"); LXX B (2 Sam 8:16b) Ἀχειτώβ; LXX L (2 Sam 8:16b) Ἀχιτώβ; LXX B (1 Chr 18:15b) Ἀχειά; LXX L (1 Chr 18:15b) Ἀχιλούδ; Josephus Ἄχιλος.

[446] The precise meaning of the various Hebrew and Greek terms used to designate Jehoshaphat's office in 2 Sam 8:16b// 1 Chr 18:15b is uncertain. In RSV's rendering he is called the "recorder."

[447] 2 Sam 8:17a// 1 Chr 18:16 call Zadok "son of Ahitub." Josephus derives his association of Zadok (already introduced by him as "high priest" in 7.56// 1 Chr 12:29) with Phineas, grandson of Aaron, from the genealogy of 1 Chr 5:30-34; 6:35-37. He will expatiate on Zadok's ancestry in *Ant.* 8.11-12.

[448] According to 2 Sam 8:17b// 1 Chr 18:16b David's other priest was Ahimelech son of Abiathar. Josephus' identification of him rather as Abiathar himself does, however, correspond to Abiathar's role both

earlier and later in David's reign in the Bible's own presentation, just as it matches the list given in 2 Sam 20:25b, where Zadok and Abiathar are cited as David's priests.

[449] This datum lacks a source counterpart, but does accord with Josephus' recurrent practice of introducing this Hellenistic court term into his biblical paraphrase.

[450] MT (2 Sam 8:17b) שריה (Eng.: "Seraiah"); MT (1 Chr 18:16b) שושא (Eng.: "Shavsha"); LXX B (2 Sam 8:17b) Ἀσά; LXX L (2 Sam 8:17b) Σαραίας; LXX B (1 Chr 18:16b) Ἰησοῦς; LXX L (1 Chr 18:16b) Σουσά; Josephus Σισάς.

[451] Josephus uses the same Greek word (γραμματεύς) for Sisa's office as does LXX.

[452] MT (2 Sam 8:18a// 1 Chr 18:17a) בניהו (Eng.: "Benaiah"); LXX B (2 Sam 8:18a) Βαναί; LXX L (2 Sam 8:18a); LXX BL 1 Chr 18:17a; and Josephus Βαναίας.

[453] MT (2 Sam 8:18a// 1 Chr 18:17a) יהוידה (Eng.: "Jehoiada"); LXX B (2 Sam 8:18a) Ἰανάκ; LXX L (2 Sam 8:18a and 1 Chr 18:17a) Ἰωάδ; LXX B (1 Chr 18:17a) Ἰωάδε; Josephus Ἰωάδης.

[454] This is Josephus' generalizing equivalent for the 2 groups ("Cherethites and Pelethites") that Benaiah commanded according to 2 Sam 8:18a// 1 Chr 18:17a.

[455] MT 2 Sam 8:18b calls (all) David's sons "priests." Josephus follows LXX 8:18b and MT LXX 1 Chr 18:17b in designating them in non-priestly terms, i.e. as royal officials/attendants. The specification that only his "older" sons served in this capacity is Josephus' own.

[456] The allusion here is to the exchange between David and Jonathan as related in *Ant.* 6.276.

[457] This editorial remark, preparing David's subsequent initiative and representing it as an expression of the king's habitual sense of gratitude, takes the place of the abrupt transition with which 2 Samuel 9 opens. On Josephus' version of this chapter (which has no parallel in Chronicles), see Begg 1998g: 166-71.

was safe, to whom he might give the recompense he owed to Ionathes for his companionship.[458] When therefore a certain freedman of Saoul,[459] who could provide information about the survivors of his family, was brought to him,[460] David asked him if he had something to report concerning any living relative of Ionathes on whom it would be possible to confer those beneficial favors that he himself had received from Ionathes.[461]

113. The freedman said that there remained a son of his, named Memphibosthos,[462] who was crippled in his feet, for his nurse, once it had been announced that the boy's father and grandfather had fallen in battle, had snatched him up and fled. He had, however, fallen off her shoulder, and his feet were injured.[463] When David learned where and by whom he was being brought up,[464] he sent to Macheir[465] in the city of Labatha[466]—for it was he who was rearing Ionathes' son[467]—and summoned him to himself.

Mephibosheth (Memphibosthos) comes before David

114. When Memphibosthos came to the king, he fell on his face and paid him homage.[468] David, however, urged him to take courage and expect better things.[469] He next awarded him both his father's house[470] and all the property that his grandfather[471] Saoul had possessed. He also directed that he be his guest at meals and table-companion, and that not a day should pass without his eating with him.[472]

115. After the boy had paid homage in response to these words and these gifts,[473] David called Siba[474] and told him that he had given the ancestral home and all the

David's instructions to Siba

---

[458] Josephus turns David's question (2 Sam 9:1) about whether any descendants of Saul survive into a command that such survivors be sought out.

[459] 2 Sam 9:2 designates "Ziba" as "a servant of the house of Saul." Josephus does not mention the man's name until a later point; see 7.115.

[460] Josephus omits as superfluous the king's question "Are you Ziba?" and the latter's response that he is of 2 Sam 9:2b.

[461] Josephus' formulation of David's question of 2 Sam 9:3a avoids its (presumptious) phrase "kindness of God" (RSV) in reference to David's intended benefactions, while also reiterating the idea that such benefactions will be a return for those received by him from Jonathan of 7.111.

[462] In 2 Samuel 9 the son's name is not mentioned by Ziba in his response of v.3b. Josephus anticipates the name, in the form Μεμφίβοσθος, from 9:6, where MT reads מפיבשת (Eng.: "Mephibosheth"); LXX B Μεμφιβόσθε; and LXX L Μεμφίβααλ. Josephus' form of the name thus corresponds to that of LXX B.

[463] Josephus here gives his delayed version of 2 Sam 4:4, which relates, in the form of a parenthesis, to which Ziba alludes in 9:3b, the origin of Mephibosheth's lameness. From his rendering of the former verse Josephus omits the detail that the prince was 5 years old at the time of the accident.

[464] This transitional phrase synthesizes the affirmative response by Ziba about the survival of a Saulide, David's further question about his whereabouts, and Ziba's reply to this of 2 Sam 9:3b-4.

[465] MT (2 Sam 9:4-5) מכיר (Eng.: "Machir"); LXX BL Μαξείρ; Josephus Μάχειρος. Josephus omits the name of his father, "Ammiel" (MT).

[466] MT (2 Sam 9:4-5) לו דבר (Eng.: "Lo-debar"); LXX Λαδαβάρ; Josephus Λάβαθα (which Schalit s.v. suggests could reflect the form בית ["house"] in MT 9:4-5).

[467] This inserted remark serves to explain what Mephibosheth is doing at Machir's house.

[468] See 2 Sam 9:6a. Josephus omits the parties' opening exchange of 9:6b, where David inquires about Mephibosheth's identity and the latter declares himself his servant. Compare his omission of the similar exchange between David and Ziba in 9:2b; see note to "him" at 7.112.

[469] Josephus transposes into positive terms David's urging Mephibosheth "not to fear" at the opening of 2 Sam 9:7. He leaves aside the king's attached general statement of his intention to show Mephibosheth kindness for the sake of his father Jonathan—a point already addressed in 7.111-112.

[470] Josephus goes beyond the Bible in having David explicitly award Mephibosheth the property, not only of Saul (so 2 Sam 9:7), but also of Jonathan himself.

[471] In designating Saul as Mephibosheth's "grandfather" Josephus aligns himself with LXX L 2 Sam 9:7 as opposed to MT LXX B, which call him his "father."

[472] See 2 Sam 9:7bβ.

[473] See 2 Sam 9:8a. Josephus leaves aside Mephibosheth's self-abasing reference to himself as a "dead dog" unworthy of David's attentions of 9:8b.

[474] MT (2 Sam 9:9) ציבא (Eng.: "Ziba"); LXX B

possessions of Saoul to the boy as a gift.[475] He further directed him to work his land and take care of it,[476] and to bring all the proceeds to Hierosolyma;[477] he was also to conduct Memphibosthos to his table each day.[478] David likewise bestowed Siba himself, his sons (of whom there were fifteen) and his servants, twenty in number, on the boy Memphibosthos.[479]

Mephibosheth at David's table

116. When the king had given these orders, Siba paid homage and said he would do them all.[480] He then departed, while Ionathes' son lived in Hierosolyma as the table-guest of the king and received every attention, as though he were his son.[481] He too had a son of his own, whom he called Michan.[482] **(6.1) 117.** These were the honors the survivors of Saoul and Ionathes' family received from David.[483]

David's overture to king Hanun (An-non)

At this time Naas,[484] the king of the Ammanites, who had been David's friend,[485]

Σειβά; LXX L Σιβά; Josephus Σιβᾶς. This is Josephus' first mention of the figure's name (see note to "Saoul" at 7.112), which appears rather abruptly at this point in his presentation.

[475] See 2 Sam 9:9, where David refers to Mephibosheth as "the son of your [Ziba's] lord." Josephus' designation of Mephibosheth as a "boy" (Greek: παῖς) at the time of David's favoring him goes beyond the Bible's own indications (cf. the reference to his having a son of his own in 9:12, which Josephus nonetheless will reproduce in 7.117).

[476] Josephus leaves to a later point in the paragraph the mention of Ziba's sons and servants, who are to assist him in cultivating Mephibosheth's land according to David's order in 2 Sam 9:10.

[477] For this portion of David's directive Josephus follows LXX L 2 Sam 9:10, where the king enjoins Ziba to bring food (literally "loaves") "to the house of your master," further specifying where that house is situated, i.e. in Jerusalem. MT reads simply "you [Ziba] shall bring," while LXX B has "you shall bring to the son of your master." Josephus leaves aside the additional source specification concerning the intended disposition of what Ziba is to bring, i.e. Mephibosheth (so MT LXX B)/ his household ("they," LXX L) will eat this.

[478] David's words to Ziba in 2 Sam 9:10a conclude with the statement that Mepibosheth is to always eat at his table (see 9:7). Josephus' turning this statement into a command that Ziba "bring" him has in view the handicap and age of Mephibosheth who, in his presentation, is only a "boy"; see note to "gift" at 7.115.

[479] With this mention of David's final award to Mephibosheth, Josephus combines the figures for Ziba's household given parenthetically in 2 Sam 9:10b with the statement of 9:12b about all who lived with Ziba becoming Mephibosheth's servants; cf. also David's injunction in 9:10a that Ziba's sons and servants are to cultivate Mephibosheth's land along with him.

[480] Josephus prefaces Ziba's statement of acquiescence to David's directives of 2 Sam 9:11a with men-

tion of his doing obeisance to the king. Thereby, he sets up a parallel between Ziba and Mephibosheth, who twice earlier prostrated himself before David (see 7.114// 9:6; 7.115// 9:8).

[481] Josephus combines into one the double notice on Mephibosheth's eating at David's table, 2 Sam 9:11b and 9:13a, of which the first mentions his being treated like one of David's own sons. He adds the opening remark about Ziba's departing, following his response to the king (// 9:lla).

[482] MT (2 Sam 9:12a) מיכא (Eng.: "Micah"); LXX B Μειχά; LXX L Μιχά; Josephus Μίχανος. Josephus' reproduction of this source mention of Mephiboseth's having a son of his own seems to stand in a certain tension with his earlier use of the term "boy" for the former himself; see note to "gift" at 7.115.

[483] This closing formula, rounding off the account of David's benefactions to the surviving Saulide in 7.111-116, underscores, once again, the king's magnanimity. It takes the place of the reiteration of the fact of Mephibosheth's lameness (see 2 Sam 9:3b) in 9:13b.

[484] MT (1 Chr 19:1 and 2 Sam 10:2) נחש (Eng.: "Nahash"); LXX 2 Sam 10:2/LXX L 1 Chr 19:1 Ναάς; LXX B 1 Chr 19:1 Ἀνάς; Josephus Ναάσης. Commentators generally suppose that the "Nahash, king of the Ammonites" of 1 Chr 19:1 (see 2 Sam 10:2) is the same figure as the opponent of Saul featured in 1 Samuel 11, with whom David would have formed an alliance at some point. This identification does not, however, hold for Josephus who, in his account of Saul's victory over Nahash, goes beyond the Bible in explicitly mentioning the killing of Nahash himself (see *Ant.* 6.70) and for whom, accordingly, the Nahash here in 7.117 must be another person. On Josephus' version of 2 Samuel 10// 1 Chronicles 19, see Begg 1998h.

[485] Nahash's "friendship" with David is nowhere mentioned in the Bible (although such a relationship is generally supposed to have existed between them by those scholars who identify Saul's opponent Nahash [see 1 Samuel 11] with the Nahash whose death is cited in 2 Sam 10:1// 1 Chr 19:1); see previous note. Jose-

died. When his son Annon[486] assumed the kingship,[487] David sent to console him, urging him to bear the death of his father with equanimity and to expect that the same friendship that he had with his father would continue [with him].[488]

118. But the Ammanite rulers took these things in a malicious spirit and not according to David's intent.[489] They incited the king, saying that David had sent men to spy on their country and force under pretext of humanity.[490] They advised him to be on guard and not credit his [David's] words, so that he would not be tricked and fall into irremediable misfortune.[491]

Overture rebuffed

119. Supposing then that the rulers' words to be more credible than they truly were,[492] Annon, the king of the Ammanites, grievously outraged the envoys sent by David.[493] For he shaved off half of their beards[494] and cut off half their clothes,[495] and then dismissed them to bring back an answer in deeds, rather than words.[496]

120. When he saw this, the Israelite king became indignant;[497] he made it clear that he would not ignore the outrage and their shameful treatment. Rather, he would go to war against the Ammanites and punish their transgression against his envoys by taking vengeance on their king.[498]

David resolves on vengeance

---

phus' insertion of the reference helps account for David's dispatching condolences to Nahash's successor in what follows.

[486] MT (2 Sam 10:1// 1 Chr 19:2) חָנוּן (Eng.: "Hanun"); LXX L (2 Sam 10:1// 1 Chr 19:2) Ἀννάν; LXX B (1 Chr 19:2) Ἀνάν; LXX B (2 Sam 10:1) Ἀννόν; Josephus Ἀννών.

[487] See 2 Sam 10:1b// 1 Chr 19:1b.

[488] See 2 Sam 10:2a// 1 Chr 19:2a. Josephus incorporates into the wording of the actual message what in the Bible itself is a prior remark by David about his intention of extending his friendly relations with Nahash also to his son. He leaves aside the sources' concluding mention of the envoys' coming before Hanun (10:2b// 19:2b).

[489] This inserted editorial comment explains the Ammonites' subsequent reaction, while also precluding reader suspicions about David's own motives in sending to Hanun.

[490] See 2 Sam 10:3// 1 Chr 19:3, whose opening rhetorical question by the leaders about whether the envoys have indeed been sent as a honor to Hanun's father Josephus converts into a (false) claim about the "pretext" of David's initiative. In having the leaders assert that David intends to spy out "the country" Josephus aligns himself with 1 Chr 19:3 against 2 Sam 10:3, which reads "the city." He adds the reference to the Ammonite "force" as a further object of David's (purported) spy venture.

[491] Josephus appends this "practical conclusion" to the leaders' accusation concerning David's purported spying of 2 Sam 10:3// 1 Chr 19:3.

[492] Josephus inserts this reference to the effect of the charges upon the king, this prompting him to act as he now does.

[493] Josephus prefaces the king's measures against the envoys with this evaluation, which, by highlighting their reprehensibility, prepares for the vehemence of David's response.

[494] In specifying that Hanun cut off (only) "half" of the envoys' beards, Josephus agrees with MT 2 Sam 10:4 against LXX, which lacks this specification (and 1 Chr 19:4, which speaks only of a "shaving").

[495] Josephus omits the sources' graphic specifications that the envoys' garments were cut "in the middle, at their hips" (2 Sam 10:4// 1 Chr 19:4, RSV).

[496] Josephus augments the closing mention of Hanun's dismissing the envoys in 2 Sam 10:4// 1 Chr 19:4 with this indication concerning the deliberately provocative intention behind his treatment of them. The concern to match words with deeds and seeming with being, evidenced by Josephus' formula here, was fundamental in both Greco-Roman and Judeo-Christian moral philosophy; see, e.g., Plato, *Resp.* 7.514A-517C; Sir 3:8; 3 Macc 3:17; 4 Macc 7:9; Luke 24:19; Acts 7:22. It likewise surfaces elsewhere in the Josephan corpus (see, e.g., *War* 1.110-112; *Ant.* 17.41; *Apion* 1.18). I owe this observation to Prof. Steve Mason.

[497] In 2 Sam 10:5// 1 Chr 19:5 David deals with the envoys through intermediaries since the former are too ashamed to appear before him. Josephus has him see their condition for himself, this provoking his anger.

[498] These statements concerning David's intentions in the face of what has happened, preparing readers for the subsequent conflict, take the place of David's enjoining the envoys to remain in Jericho until their beards grow back (2 Sam 10:5b// 1 Chr 19:5b). That injunction which would be out of place in his own presentation, where the envoys have already been seen by the king, presumably in Jerusalem; see previous note.

Ammonites hire
allies
121. Realizing that they had breached the treaty and were liable to judgment for these things,[499] [Annon's] relatives and the leaders made preparations for war.[500] They sent 1,000 talents[501] to Syros,[502] the king[503] of the Mesopotamians,[504] and appealed to him, along with Souba,[505] to become their ally in return for this remuneration.[506] These kings had 20,000 foot soldiers.[507] They likewise hired in advance the king from the country called Micha[508] and a fourth named Istob;[509] these had 12,000 troops.[510]

(6.2) 122. David, however, was not dismayed by the Ammanites' alliance or their army. Instead, he put his confidence in God and the justice of the war that he was about to make against them on account of those things by which he had been outraged.[511] He entrusted the best of his army to Joab, the commanding general, and sent this against them.[512]

Preparations
for battle at
Rabbah (Ara-
batha)
123. Joab made his camp at Arabatha, the capital of the Ammanites.[513] The enemy came out and drew themselves up, not together, but separately, with the auxiliary forces positioned by themselves in the plain and the Ammanite army at the gates over against the Hebrews.[514]

---

[499] In 2 Sam 10:6aα// 1 Chr 19:6aα the Ammonites "see" that they have made themselves "odious" (literally: stinking) to David.

[500] 2 Sam 10:6 attributes the subsequent military measures to the Ammonites as a whole, while 1 Chr 19:6 ascribes them to "Hanun and the Ammonites."

[501] This indication concerning the "hire price" corresponds to the plus of 4QSam^a 2 Sam 10:6 and 1 Chr 19:6 (both of which specify "silver" talents), lacking in MT LXX 10:6.

[502] This designation (Greek: Σύρον) for the name of the first of the Ammonites' "hires" reflects the gentilic τὸν σύρον ("the Syrian") of LXX 2 Sam 10:6, whereas the other textual witnesses for 10:6 and 1 Chr 19:6 speak rather of the country of Aram/Syria. See next note.

[503] This specification makes clear that Josephus understood "Syros" as a proper name, rather than the gentilic ("the Syrian") intended by the corresponding reading of LXX 2 Sam 10:6; see previous note.

[504] This designation for "Syros'" people has a counterpart in LXX BL 1 Chr 19:6, which mention "Syria of Mesopotamia" as the first of the Ammonites' "hires." Compare "Aram of Beth-rehob" (MT 2 Sam 10:6); "Syria and Roob" (LXX B 2 Sam 10:6); "the Syrian and Baithraam" (LXX L 2 Sam 10:6); "Aram-naharaim" (MT 1 Chr 19:6).

[505] This name for the 2nd of the Ammonite "hires" according to Josephus corresponds to the place name "Zobah," which appears in MT and 4QSam^a 2 Sam 10:6// MT 1 Chr 19:6; cf. "Souba" (LXX L 10:6) and "Sobal" (LXX BL 19:6). In a way similar to his preceding handling of LXX L 2 Sam 10:6's reading "the Syrian" (see note to "Syros" at 7.121), Josephus takes the sources' place name as that of a king, with whom the Ammonites contract an alliance.

[506] Josephus spells out the purpose of the Ammo-

nites' "hiring" as cited in 2 Sam 10:6// 1 Chr 19:6.

[507] Josephus derives this datum from the plus of 2 Sam 10:6.

[508] Compare "Maacah" (MT 4QSam^a 2 Sam 10:6// MT 1 Chr 19:7); "Amalek" (LXX B 2 Sam 10:6); "Maacha" (LXX L 2 Sam 10:6); "Syria of Moocha" (LXX B 1 Chr 19:7); "Syria of Maacha" (LXX L 1 Chr 19:7).

[509] Josephus follows 4QSam^a LXX B (Εἰστώβ) LXX L (Ἰστώβ) 2 Sam 10:6 in reading the MT's phrase אישטוב (RSV: "men of Tob") as a proper name, i.e. Ἴστοβος. 1 Chr 19:7 has no equivalent.

[510] 2 Sam 10:6 (MT) assigns "Maacah" 1,000 and the "men of Tob" 12,000 troops for a total of 13,000. Josephus' overall figure for the Ammonites' "hires" (32,000, i.e. 20,000 + 12,000) corresponds to that given in 1 Chr 19:7, where, however, the figure concerns, not hired men but "chariots." Josephus has no equivalent to the plus with which 1 Chr 19:7 concludes: "(the forces hired by the Ammonites) encamped before Medeba. And the Ammonites were mustered from their cities and came to battle."

[511] Josephus inserts this notice, highlighting the king's courage, piety, and justice, on David's state of mind in the face of the enemy initiatives.

[512] See 2 Sam 10:7// 1 Chr 19:8. Josephus inserts mention of Joab's status as commanding general on the basis of 7.110// 2 Sam 8:16a// 1 Chr 18:15a.

[513] Josephus inserts this reference to Joab's camping, drawing the name of the Ammonite capital city from 2 Sam 11:1// 1 Chr 20:1// 7.129.

[514] See 2 Sam 10:8// 1 Chr 19:9. Josephus' mention of the Ammonites' stationing themselves "at the gates" corresponds to the phrase "at the entrance of the gate" of MT LXX B 10:8, as opposed to "the entrance of the city" of LXX L 10:8 and 19:9. Like 19:9, which speaks

124. When he saw this, Joab devised counter-measures: selecting his bravest men, he drew these up for battle against Syros and the kings with him.[515] He handed over the remainder to Abessai his brother, whom he directed to draw them up for battle against the Ammanites,[516] saying that if he saw the Syrians pressing him and prevailing, he was to lead his division over to help him. He, for his part, would do the same, if he observed Abessai under pressure by the Ammanites.[517]

125. Having thus encouraged his brother and exhorted him to fight spiritedly and with an eagerness befitting men who feared shame,[518] Joab dismissed him to fight against the Ammanites, while he himself engaged the Syrians. **126.** Joab killed many of them after they had bravely stood their ground for a short time, and compelled them all to flee.[519] Seeing this and becoming anxious about Abessai and the army with him, the Ammanites did not remain in place; rather, imitating their allies, they fled into the city.[520] Having thus defeated the enemy, Joab returned splendidly to the king in Hierosolyma.[521]

Enemy coalition routed by Joab

(6.3) 127. This defeat did not, however, convince the Ammanites to remain quiet or to keep still, now that they had learned that [their enemies] were superior.[522] On the contrary, they sent to Chalam, the king of the Syrians[523] beyond the Euphrates, to hire him for an alliance.[524] He had as his commanding general Sebek,[525] along with 80,000 foot-soldiers and 10,000 horsemen.[526]

Ammonites hire new allies

128. When the king of the Hebrews found out that the Ammanites had again

David defeats enemy coalition

---

of "the kings who had come," Josephus has no equivalent to the list, replicating that of 10:6, of the 4 allied contingents given in 10:8.

[515] See 2 Sam 10:9// 1 Chr 19:10, which designate those against whom Joab arrays his elite forces globally as "Aram/Syria." Josephus' reference to "Syros" as the proper name of an allied king corresponds to his reading in 7.121.

[516] See 2 Sam 10:10// 1 Chr 19:11.

[517] See 2 Sam 10:11// 1 Chr 19:12.

[518] In 2 Sam 10:12a// 1 Chr 19:13a Joab urges the Israelite forces to "play the man for our people, and for the cities of our God." Josephus omits Joab's closing statement of 10:12b// 19:13b ("may the Lord do what seems good to him."). On this omission as part of Josephus' general downplaying of Joab's piety, see Feldman 1998a: 207-8.

[519] 2 Sam 10:13// 1 Chr 19:14 mention neither an initial resistance by the Syrians nor Joab's slaying of many of them. Josephus' insertion of these items makes Joab's victory appear more impressive.

[520] See 2 Sam 10:14a// 1 Chr 19:15a, into which Josephus inserts mention of the Ammanites' "fear" of Abishai and their "imitation" of the Syrians.

[521] See 2 Sam 10:14b// 1 Chr 19:15b, which Josephus amplifies, underscoring Joab's military success.

[522] In 2 Sam 10:15// 1 Chr 19:16 the reference is to measures taken, not by the Ammanites, but rather by the Syrians, their allies, in the face of their initial defeat. Josephus' formulation keeps attention focussed on

the former, given their role as the instigators of the whole affair, just as it directs attention, in first place, to their state of mind, i.e. their unbroken resolution to continue the conflict.

[523] The (Syrian) ruler to whom the Ammanites now turn is called "Hadadezer" in 2 Sam 10:16// 1 Chr 19:16, i.e. the king earlier defeated by David according to 2 Sam 8:3// 1 Chr 18:3// 7.99. Josephus' alternative designation (Greek: Χαλαμάς) seems inspired by the name (wrongly) given the "River" (i.e. the Euphrates) in LXX L 2 Sam 10:16, i.e. Χαλααμά (cf. B: Χαλαμάκ). Alternatively, or in addition, as Marcus (*ad loc.*) and Schalit (*s.v.*) suggest, Josephus' name for the king could reflect the site mentioned in MT 2 Sam 10:16-17 (though not in 1 Chr 19:16-17), i.e. חילם ("Helam"; LXX: Αἰλάμ).

[524] 2 Sam 10:16// 1 Chr 19:16 designate the Syrians' newly acquired allies as "the Syrians who were beyond the River," who are procured either by King Hadadezer (so 10:16) or by the Syrians collectively (so 19:16).

[525] MT (2 Sam 10:16) שׁובך (Eng.: "Shobach"); MT (1 Chr 19:16) שׁופך (Eng.: "Shophach"); LXX B 2 Sam 10:16 Σωβάκ; LXX L 2 Sam 10:16 Σαβεέ; LXX B 1 Chr 19:16 Σωφάρ; LXX L 1 Chr 19:16 Σωφάκ; Josephus Σέβεκος.

[526] As Marcus (*ad loc.*) points out, Josephus, in line with a tendency found elsewhere in *Antiquities*, simply "invents" these figures which, given their magnitude, serve to heighten David's subsequent victory over so large an enemy army.

levied so great a force against him, he resolved to no longer wage war on them through his generals.[527] Rather, he crossed the Jordan river with all his force, engaged those he met in battle, and was victorious.[528] He did away with about 40,000 of their infantry and about 7,000 of their calvary.[529] He also wounded Sebek, the general of Chalam, who died of his wound.[530] **129.** This being the outcome of the battle, the Mesopotamians[531] submitted to David and sent him gifts.[532] Since it was now winter, he returned to Hierosolyma,[533] but, at the beginning of spring,[534] he sent his commanding general Joab to make war on the Ammanites. Invading their entire country, Joab destroyed it; shutting them up in their capital Arabatha,[535] he besieged it.

Rabbah (Arabatha) besieged

(7.1) 130. Now, however, a terrible disaster befell David, even though he was a just and God-fearing[536] man by nature, and one who strictly kept the ancestral laws.[537] For late one afternoon he observed from the roof of the palace where he was walking—as was his custom at that hour—a woman bathing in cool water in her own house, who was of beautiful appearance and superior to all others,[538] named Beethsabe.[539] He was captivated by the woman's beauty; unable to restrain his de-

David's adultery with Bathsheba (Beethsabe)

---

[527] Josephus' reproduction of the notice of 2 Sam 10:17a// 1 Chr 19:17a calls attention to David's change of tactics at this point, i.e. he no longer (compare 10:7// 19:7// 7.122) entrusts the campaign to a general, but assumes command in person. Thereby, he both magnifies the extent of the new enemy threat and David's personal military prowess in overcoming it. Like 1 Chr 19:17, Josephus has no equivalent to the mention of David's proceeding "to Helam" of 2 Sam 10:17; see note on "Syrians" at 7.127.

[528] This notice, highlighting David's military success, takes the place of the sequence of 2 Sam 10:17b-18aα// 1 Chr 19:17b-18aα, in which the Arameans take their stand, fight with David, and eventually flee before Israel.

[529] Josephus' figures for the enemy casualties correspond to those given in 1 Chr 19:18aβ, whereas 2 Sam 10:18aβ reads 700 chariot(eer)s and 40,000 horsemen (MT LXX B; LXX L: 700 horsemen and 40,000 infantry).

[530] See 2 Sam 10:18b// 1 Chr 19:18b, where Shobach/Shopach is called "commander of their [the Syrian] army."

[531] 2 Sam 10:19a// 1 Chr 19:19a speak of "(the kings [so 10:19a, > 19:19a]), the servants of Hadadezer" who now submit; Josephus' substitution reflects the fact that the figure of Hadadezer is absent from his rendering of 2 Samuel 10// 1 Chronicles 19 (see note to "Syrians" at 7.127), just as it picks up on his reference to the Ammanites' hiring "Chalam, the king of the Syrians beyond the Euphrates" in 7.127.

[532] Josephus' mention of the "gifts" sent by those whom David has just defeated concretizes the reference to their "becoming subject to" him in 2 Sam 10:19a// 1 Chr 19:19a. He has no equivalent to the concluding

notice about the Syrians' "fearing to help the Ammonites any more" of 10:19b// 19:19b.

[533] This notice has no parallel in either biblical source. It serves to get David back from his foreign campaign to Jerusalem, where he "remains" during Joab's siege of Rabbah according to 2 Sam 11:1// 1 Chr 20:1.

[534] Josephus thus interprets the expression of 2 Sam 11:1// 1 Chr 20:1, which translates literally as "at the return of the year," while leaving aside the sources' further specification that this was the time "when kings go forth to battle."

[535] MT (2 Sam 11:1// 1 Chr 20:1) רבה (Eng.: "Rabbah"); LXX BL 2 Sam 11:1 Ῥαββάθ; LXX B 1 Chr 20:1 Ῥάββαν; LXX L 1 Chr 20:1 Ῥαββα; Josephus Ἀραβαθά (thus Niese; Marcus *ad loc.* and Schalit *s.v.*, both here and in 7.123, follow the conjecture of J. Hudson, i.e. Ῥαβαθά).

[536] Greek: Θεοσεβής. On this adjective (which Josephus will apply to David again in 7.153) and its noun cognate, see Spicq 1978 (II): 375-78.

[537] Josephus adds this foreshadowing of the following episode of David's sin with Bathsheba, at the same time underscoring how "out of character" David's behavior on this occasion was. In contrast to the Chronicler, however, he does not hesitate to reproduce the sordid episode related in 2 Sam 11:2-27.

[538] See 2 Sam 11:2. Josephus omits the source detail about David "arising from his couch," substituting the statement that the king's walking on the roof in the late afternoon was in accord with his regular practice, and accentuating the woman's attractiveness.

[539] MT (2 Sam 11:3) בת־שבע (Eng.: "Bathsheba"); LXX BL Βησάβεε; Josephus Βεεθσαβή. In 2 Sam 11:3 David learns her name in response to his inquiry about

sire,[540] he summoned her and had relations with her.[541]

Uriah's stay
with David

131. Having become pregnant, the woman sent to the king so that he might devise some way of concealing her offense, for she was liable to death as an adulteress according to the ancestral laws.[542] David then recalled from the siege the armor-bearer of Joab,[543] Urias[544] by name, who was the husband of the woman.[545] When he came, David asked him about the army and the siege.[546]

132. When Urias said that everything was going according to plan,[547] David took portions of his own supper and gave these to him.[548] He directed him to go off to his wife and relax with her.[549] Urias, however, did not do this, but rather kept watch beside the king, along with the other armor-bearers.[550]

133. When the king found this out, he asked him why he had not gone to his house and to his wife after so long a time, the way all men would naturally do when they came from a journey.[551] But Urias said that it was not just for him to relax with his wife and enjoy himself when his fellow-soldiers and general were lying on the ground in their camp in enemy territory.[552]

134. When he said this, David directed him to remain there that day so that on the next day be might dismiss him to his commanding general.[553] Having been invited to supper by the king, Urias continued drinking until he got drunk, since the

---

her. Josephus leaves aside the names of both her father ("Eliam") and—for the moment (but see 7.131)—her husband ("Uriah the Hittite").

[540] Josephus interjects this 2-part indication concerning the intensity of David's passion for Bathsheba.

[541] Josephus compresses the circumstantial account in 2 Sam 11:4 of the David-Bathsheba encounter. In particular, he passes over the incriminating detail that "Bathsheba was purifying herself from her uncleanness," which makes David a violator also of the prohibition of having sexual relations with a menstruating woman of Lev 18:19.

[542] Josephus expatiates on Bathsheba's laconic message to David in 2 Sam 11:5b ("I am with child"), having her recognize both the wrongfulness of her act and its potentially fatal implications for her. The reference to the "ancestral laws" ironically echoes the mention of David's "strictly keeping" these in 7.129.

[543] This qualification of "Uriah" has a counterpart in the plus of 4QSam^a 2 Sam 11:3, where it is attached to the initial mention of his name.

[544] MT (2 Sam 11:3, etc.) אוריה (Eng.: "Uriah"); LXX B Ὀρείας; LXX L and Josephus Οὐρίας.

[545] Cf. 2 Sam 11:6, where the wording of David's command to Joab is cited, as is the latter's execution of this.

[546] In 2 Sam 11:7 David asks Uriah about Joab, the people, and the war.

[547] In making explicit mention of a response by Uriah, Josephus follows the plus of LXX L 2 Sam 11:7 ("he said 'it is well'") against MT and LXX B, which lack this.

[548] This notice is perhaps inspired by (and anticipated from) 2 Sam 11:8b, where there is mention of "a present (Tg.: meal) from the king," which follows Uriah as he withdraws from David's presence.

[549] Josephus thus interprets David's ambiguous/euphemistic command in 2 Sam 11:8a ("[go down to your house] and wash your feet").

[550] See 2 Sam 11:9a, where those among whom Uriah sleeps are called "all the servants of his [Uriah's] lord."

[551] Josephus reverses the sequence of David's 2 questions to Uriah in 2 Sam 11:10b, attaching the first of these ("have you not come from a journey?") to his rendering of the 2nd ("why did you not go down to your house?") as its conclusion.

[552] Josephus re-arranges the sequence of Uriah's words in 2 Sam 11:11, where Uriah first evokes the situation of the Israelite forces and then asks rhetorically whether he should enjoy himself at home. From Uriah's reply Josephus omits his opening statement ("the ark and Israel and Judah dwell in booths [or at Succoth])," given that the ark's presence on the campaign has not been mentioned previously either by the Bible or himself. He further omits Uriah's concluding sworn affirmation that he will not do what David has been urging.

[553] See 2 Sam 11:12a. Josephus specifies the vague biblical indication ("tomorrow I will let you depart") concerning what David intends to do with Uriah the next day. He leaves aside the statement of 11:12b that Uriah did in fact remain in Jerusalem that and the following day.

David writes
Joab about
Uriah

king deliberately kept on toasting his health.[554] Nonetheless, he once again slept in front of the king's gates, having no desire for his wife.[555] **135.** David was displeased at these things[556] and wrote Joab, ordering him to punish Urias, for he disclosed to him that he had committed an offense and suggested the following mode of punishment, so that he himself should not appear to have wished this:[557] **136.** He directed Joab to station him [Urias] over against the most invincible division of the enemy, where, if left to fight alone, he would be in most danger, further directing that his fellow-combatants were to pull back once the battle was underway.[558] He wrote these things and, sealing the letter with his own seal, gave it to Urias to bring to Joab.[559]

Uriah killed in
battle

137. When Joab received the document and perceived the king's intention,[560] he set Urias in the place where he knew the enemy had caused difficulties to himself, likewise giving him some of the best men of his army. He said as well that he, together with the entire army, would rush to his aid, should they be able to overthrow any part of the wall and enter the city.[561] **138.** He also requested Urias, as one who was militarily distinguished and enjoyed a good reputation with the king and all his compatriots for courage, to rejoice in these great endeavors, rather than resent them.[562] Once Urias readily undertook the task, Joab privately told those drawn up with him to leave him by himself when they saw the enemy rushing out.[563]

139. When the Hebrews thus made a rush towards the city, the Ammanites were anxious that the enemy might rise up first and ascend to the spot where Urias was stationed. Having placed their bravest men in front, they suddenly opened the gate and went out against the enemy with great vigor and momentum.[564]

140. Seeing them, all those with Urias retreated, as Joab had told them in advance.[565] Urias, for his part, being ashamed to flee and leave the line of battle, held his ground against the enemy. Sustaining their assault, he did away with not a few

---

[554] Josephus' rendering of the notice of 2 Sam 11:13a about David's making Uriah drunk specifies how the king contrived to do this, likewise underscoring the calculation with which the king proceeds.

[555] To 2 Sam 11:13b Josephus adds the remark about Uriah's state of mind. The reference to his having no "desire" (Greek: ἐπιθυμία) for his wife echoes by contrast the statement of 7.130 that David was "unable to restrain his desire" (Greek: ἐπιθυμία) for Bethsheba.

[556] Josephus prefaces David's initiatives as related in 2 Sam 11:14-15 with this reference to his emotional response to Uriah's behavior.

[557] Josephus expands on David's message to Joab (2 Sam 11:14-15) with indications on why and how Uriah is to be disposed of.

[558] See 2 Sam 11:15. Josephus leaves aside the (self-evident) source indication concerning the purpose of the measures Joab is instructed to carry out, i.e. that "Uriah be struck down and die."

[559] See 2 Sam 11:14. Josephus adds the detail about the sealing of the letter. The sealing ensures that Uriah would not be able to read the letter himself and so discover what awaits him. The transmission of letters, the danger of their interception, and the precautionary measures that letter-writers might take regarding the

content of their messages are matters of considerable interest to Josephus, as appears especially from the *Life*; see 89-90, 177-181, 220-223, 228-229, 241, 245, 254-255, 260, 272, 285-287, etc. I owe this observation to Prof. Steve Mason.

[560] Josephus prefaces this transitional phrase to the account of Joab's measures given in 2 Sam 11:16.

[561] 2 Sam 11:16 simply notes Joab's positioning Uriah at a point where he knew the enemy forces were brave. Josephus has Joab go beyond his instructions in offering Uriah (false) assurances of support in his mission.

[562] This appeal by Joab to Uriah's concern for his good reputation is Josephus' further amplification of the measures taken by him as cited in 2 Sam 11:16.

[563] Uriah's (positive) reaction to Joab's appeal to him (see previous note) and the latter's instructions to Uriah's comrades are both Josephus' additions.

[564] 2 Sam 11:17a merely states that the Ammonites "came out and fought with Joab." Josephus dramatizes with his references to their psychology and preliminary measures.

[565] This retreat by Uriah's comrades in accordance with Joab's command (see 7.138) is not mentioned in 2 Samuel 11.

of them. Surrounded and caught in their midst, he died, some of his other comrades also falling together with him.[566]

141. After this happened, Joab sent messengers to the king, commanding them to say that, in his solicitude to storm the city quickly, he had made a rush upon the wall and, after losing many men, had been forced to withdraw.[567] He added that, once they saw David become wrathful with them, they should say that Urias was dead.[568]

Uriah's death reported to David

(7.2) 142. When the king heard these things from the messengers,[569] he was displeased,[570] and said that they had committed an offense by rushing upon the wall, whereas they ought to have tried to storm the city by means of tunnels and engines.[571] They had an instance of this in Abimelech, the son of Gedeon, who, in his desire to take the tower that was then in Thebes by force, was felled by a stone thrown by an old woman and who, although he was the bravest of men, died shamefully due to his reckless attack.[572] **143.** Remembering him, they should not have approached the enemy's wall, for it is best to keep in mind everything which has been done in war—whether successfully or not—so as to imitate the former, but guard against the latter in the same dangers.[573]

144. When, however, the messenger also disclosed to David, who was in this state, the death of Urias,[574] he ceased from wrath[575] and directed him to go off and

---

[566] Here too, Josephus elaborates on the summary notice of 2 Sam 11:17b that some among David's servants, including Uriah, fell. His embellishment accentuates Uriah's heroic stance and military prowess: he does not die before first slaying many of his attackers. He thereby proves himself worthy of the accolades that Joab had hypocritically bestowed on him in sending him to his unwitting death; see 7.138.

[567] 2 Sam 11:18 speaks of a single messenger, whom Joab instructs, in very general terms, to tell the king "all the news about the fighting."

[568] In having Joab simply allude to (the likelihood of) the king's anger at the messengers' report, which they in turn are to counter by mention of Uriah's death, Josephus conflates the data of 2 Sam 11:20aα, 21b. He thereby leaves aside the series of quite specific questions that Joab, rather implausibly, tells the messengers David will pose to them in his anger, 11:20aβb-21a.

[569] Having expatiated on the report Joab entrusts to the messenger(s) in 7.141 (compare 2 Sam 11:18), Josephus leaves aside the the content of their report to the king as cited in 11:23-24.

[570] The extended LXX plus following 2 Sam 11:24 mentions David's "anger" at the report made him.

[571] Josephus turns into a statement the reproachful question about why the Israelites approached so near the city, with which David's response opens in the LXX plus after 2 Sam 11:24. He adds mention of the appropriate alternative tactic that reflects the siege practice of his (Josephus') own time.

[572] Josephus continues to draw on the LXX plus

following 2 Sam 11:24, turning David's question about Abimelech and his death at the hands of a woman as cited there into a statement recalling that episode (related by him in *Ant.* 5.252// Judg 9:53-55). In fact, LXX has David recall this incident twice, i.e. in Joab's surmise about how the king will respond to the message brought him [11:21= MT] and here in his actual response (no MT parallel). Like MT then, Josephus has the case of Abimelech cited only once. Whereas, however, MT makes the case part of Joab's surmise about how David will react, Josephus incorporates it into the king's reply.

[573] This practical conclusion, drawn from David's foregoing allusion to Abimelech's fate, elaborates on the king's final question to the messenger in the LXX plus after 2 Sam 11:24, "why did you go close to the wall?," which itself reiterates his initial query to them. The military literature of Josephus' time (see, e.g., Frontinus [1. praef.]) emphasized, as David does here, that generals should learn from their predecessors. I owe this observation to Prof. Steve Mason.

[574] Like the LXX, Josephus reserves this final element of the messenger's report to after the king's initial, reproachful response, whereas in MT the messenger appends this as the conclusion to the single report he makes David in 2 Sam 11:23-24. At this point, Josephus speaks of a (single) messenger in accordance with the biblical account, whereas earlier (7.141-142) he referred to "messengers."

[575] Josephus inserts this reference to David's change of mood; compare the mention of his being "dis-

say to Joab that what had happened was [only] human and that such was the nature of war, namely that things go well now for one side, now for the other.[576] **145.** For the future, however, they were to give care to the siege and not suffer further defeats in this. Rather, having taken it by storm and subdued it by earthworks and engines, they were to raze the city and exterminate all those in it.[577] The messenger then hastened to bring the king's directives to Joab.[578]

Son born to David

146. When Beethsabe, the wife of Urias, found out about the death of her husband, she mourned him for several days.[579] Once she had ceased from her grief and her tears for Urias, the king immediately made her his wife and had a male child by her.[580]

Nathan's parable

(7.3) 147. God did not look favorably upon this marriage;[581] rather, in his wrath against David, he appeared in a dream to the prophet Nathas and denounced the king.[582] Nathas, who was a tactful and clever man, reasoning that when kings fall into passion, they are more affected by this than by what is just, resolved to keep silent about the threats made by God.[583] Instead, using other, kind words, he addressed him somewhat like this **148.** and appealed to him to tell him what he thought about the following matter:[584] "There were," he said, "two men living in the same city. The one was rich and had many herds of beasts of burden and cattle, while the poor man possessed only a single ewe lamb.[585] **149.** He raised it with his children, shared his food with it and showed it the tender love[586] one would give one's daughter. Now when a guest dropped in on the rich man, he was unwilling to slaughter any of his own beasts in order to provide for his friend. Instead, he sent and took

Judgment on David

away the poor man's lamb, which he prepared and used to entertain his guest."[587]

150. This story greatly grieved the king,[588] who asserted to Nathas that the man who had dared to do this deed was vile, and that it was just that he make fourfold[589] restitution for the lamb and, in addition to this, be punished with death.[590] Nathas

---

pleased" in 7.142 and Joab's telling the messengers what to do when they see David "becoming wrathful" with them in 7.141.

[576] Cf. 2 Sam 11:25a. Josephus expatiates on David's evocation of war's caprice there.

[577] Josephus expands on David's directives concerning the renewal of the siege as cited in 2 Sam 11:25b. In particular, he has him, echoing contemporary Roman military practice, again allude to the use of siege equipment (see 7.142), and spell out what is to be done with the city's population once it has been captured.

[578] Josephus supplies this notice on the (one) messenger's return; see note to "Urias" at 7.144.

[579] 2 Sam 11:26 does not specify the duration of Bathsheba's mourning.

[580] See 2 Sam 11:27a.

[581] See 2 Sam 11:27b, where God is "displeased" at "the thing that David had done."

[582] Josephus expatiates on the mention of God's "sending" Nathan to David of 2 Sam 12:1a with a variety of additional items: God's state of mind, his showing himself to the prophet (for this, see 7.92), and the content of the divine communication to him.

[583] This inserted preface to Nathan's "parable" (2

Sam 12:1b-4) serves to explain why it is that the prophet does not immediately and directly accuse David in accordance with what God has just told him.

[584] This further preface to Nathan's parable seems to reflect the LXX L plus in 2 Sam 12:1b, where Nathan begins his words to the king: "judge this case for me."

[585] See 2 Sam 12:1b-3aα.

[586] This reference to the man's emotional bond with the lamb takes the place of the further details concerning his care for it in 2 Sam 12:3aβb, i.e. its drinking from his cup and lying in his bosom.

[587] See 2 Sam 12:4.

[588] 2 Sam 12:5a speaks of David's "anger" against the rich man of the parable.

[589] Josephus' figure agrees with that of MT and LXX L* 2 Sam 12:6 (and with the law of Exod 21:27 [Eng. 22:1]// *Ant.* 4.272) against the "7-fold" of LXX B and some LXX L manuscripts (cf. Prov 6:31).

[590] Josephus reverses the order of the double sentence pronounced by David in 2 Sam 12:5bβ-6a, making the sequence more logical (the man is first to make restitution and then be executed). He omits both David's opening oath formula (12:5bα) and the appended motivation of his sentence in terms of the man's lack of pity (12:6b).

replied that he was the one who deserved to suffer these things, condemned by himself, who had dared to commit a grave and terrible act.[591]

151. He further revealed and manifested to him the wrath of God[592] who had made[593] him king over the whole force of the Hebrews and lord of all the many great nations round about,[594] just as he had previously delivered him from the hands of Saoul[595] and had given him wives, whom he had justly and lawfully married.[596] He [God], however, had been despised and treated impiously by him [David], who married the wife of another man and killed her husband, giving him over to the enemy.[597] **152.** He would, therefore, pay the penalty to God for these things: his wives would be violated by one of his sons;[598] he would also be conspired against by that one,[599] and would suffer public judgment for his outrageous secret offense.[600] "In addition, the son that she [Beethsabe] has borne to you will die shortly after his birth."[601]

153. The king, troubled and duly tormented by these things, said amid tears and grief that he had acted impiously (for it is generally acknowledged that he was a God-fearing man and in his whole life never offended, except in the matter of Urias' wife).[602] God then had pity and was reconciled to him, and announced the good news that he would preserve his life and kingship. He told David, who had changed his mind, that he was no longer resentful about what had happened.[603] Having

David pardoned by God

---

[591] Josephus embellishes Nathan's laconic statement of 2 Sam 12:7a: "you are the man," with allusion to the king's offense, self-condemnation, and impending punishment.

[592] This inserted reference picks up on the mention of God's "wrath" in 7.147. Josephus thus goes beyond the Bible in highlighting God's emotional response to David's deed.

[593] Josephus, here too, avoids the term "anointed" of 2 Sam 12:7b.

[594] Josephus adds this reference to God's subjugation of the nations to David to Nathan's mention of the divine appointment of him as king in 2 Sam 12:7bα. Both benefits appear together in Samuel's word to David at his anointing in *Ant.* 6.165.

[595] See 2 Sam 12:7bβ.

[596] According to Nathan's word in 2 Sam 12:8a, the wives whom the Lord has given David were those of Saul. Josephus' reformulation reflects the fact that the Bible does not elsewhere refer to David's obtaining his predecessor's wives. On David's "lawful wives," see 7.70.

[597] Josephus compresses Nathan's repetitious accusations against David as cited in 2 Sam 12:9, 10b into a single general charge of showing contempt for God (compare 12:9a, 10bα) coupled with a single specific charge of adultery and murder (compare 12:9b, 10bβ, where this charge is made twice).

[598] With the episode of Absalom's violation of David's concubines (2 Sam 16:21-22) in view, Josephus substitutes this designation of the culprit for the vaguer "your neighbor" of 2 Sam 12:11. In 7.214 he will intro-

duce a reference to the fulfillment of Nathan's announcement here.

[599] By inserting this prediction of Absalom's revolt into Nathan's announcement Josephus accentuates his prophetic powers.

[600] See 2 Sam 12:12, where more figurative language ("before the sun") is used in reference to the public character of David's punishment.

[601] Josephus makes this announcement the conclusion/climax to Nathan's judgment speech (7.151-152// 2 Sam 12:7-12), whereas in the Bible it comes (12:14b) only after the complex of notices recounting David's confession of sin (12:13a) and Nathan's declaration of divine pardon (12:13b), this coupled with a renewed mention of his offense (12:14a) as the ground for the child's fate.

[602] Josephus amplifies David's brief confession of 2 Sam 12:13a ("I have sinned against the Lord"), supplying mention of the king's emotional state and the outward manifestation of this ("tears") as well as a statement about David's normal godly manner of life reminiscent of his similar, exculpatory remarks in 7.130; note in particular the use of the term "God-fearing" (Greek: θεοσεβής) for David in both 7.130 and 153. The remark here in 7.153 seems inspired by 1 Kgs 15:5: "David did what was right in the eyes of the Lord, and did not turn aside from anything he commanded him all the days of his life, except in the matter of Uriah the Hittite."

[603] In 2 Sam 12:13b Nathan informs David that the Lord "has put away his sin" and that he will "not die."

David pleads for sick son

prophesied these things to the king, Nathas returned home.[604]

(7.4) 154. The Deity, for his part, sent a severe illness upon the child, whom the wife of Urias had borne to David.[605] Dismayed at this, the king took no food for seven days, even when pressed by his servants. Putting on a black garment, he fell on sackcloth and lay on the ground, begging God for the child's safety, for he greatly cherished its mother.[606]

Exchange between David and servants about son's death

155. When the child nonetheless died on the seventh day, his attendants did not dare to report this to the king. They were thinking that if he learned about it, in his dismay at his son's death, he would still more totally reject food and other needs, seeing that when the child was sick he had harmed himself due to his grief.[607]

156. Noticing the servants' dismay and their behaving like those who especially wish to keep something hidden, the king surmised that the child had died.[608] Summoning one of the servants, he learned that this was true.[609] He arose, bathed, donned a white garment,[610] and went to the tent of God.[611] **157.** He further directed that he be served his supper.[612] This unexpected turn of events caused much consternation to his relatives and servants given that, once the child was dead, he was suddenly doing all those things that he had not done while it was still sick.[613] After initially requesting permission to ask,[614] they appealed to him to tell them about what had happened.

158. Calling them ignorant,[615] he instructed them that when the child was still living and he had hope for its safety, he had done everything that was fitting, thinking by these things to render God benevolent.[616] When, however, the child died, there was no longer any need for vain grief.[617] When he said this, they extolled the wisdom and mind of the king.[618] He then had intercourse with his wife Beethsabe and

Solomon born

---

[604] See 2 Sam 12:15a. Josephus has anticipated Nathan's parting announcement of the child's death of 12:14 (see note to "his birth" at 7.152), from which he omits the motivation of this in terms of David's offense.

[605] See 2 Sam 12:15b.

[606] Josephus amplifies the notice of 2 Sam 12:16-17 on David's intercessory initiatives with a variety of items: the king's emotional state, the reason for his undertaking these measures (i.e. his attachment to Bathsheba), and the "black garment" donned by him. His explicit mention of David's placing himself "on sackcloth" reflects the LXX plus in 12:16. He replaces the designation "the elders of his [David's] house" of 12:17 with the more general term "servants" drawn from 12:18.

[607] See 2 Sam 12:18, where what the servants recall is their having spoken to David in vain (cf. 12:17).

[608] In 2 Sam 12:19a David sees the servants "whispering together."

[609] Compare 2 Sam 12:19b, where David asks and is answered by the servants as a group.

[610] 2 Sam 12:20aα has David simply changing his clothes. Josephus' inserted reference to the white garment donned by him sets up a contrast with the king's previous putting on a black garment; see 7.154.

[611] In 2 Sam 12:20aβ David goes "into the house of God," where he "worships." Josephus' substitution of a reference to "the tent of God" reflects the fact that a permanent "house" has not yet been built for God, and recalls the notice of 7.86 on David's setting up the tent for the ark.

[612] See 2 Sam 12:20b.

[613] Josephus prefaces the retainers' question to the king (2 Sam 12:21) with this notice on their inner reaction to his behavior, into which he incorporates an anticipated version of their words to him.

[614] The servants' initial asking permission to query David about his strange behavior is a Josephan amplification of 2 Sam 12:21, reflecting his concern with proper royal protocol.

[615] Josephus inserts this opening component of David's reply (2 Sam 12:22-23); it serves to accentuate the king's mental superiority vis-à-vis his questioners.

[616] This positive statement takes the place of David's reporting his asking himself about the possibility of the Lord's sparing the child in 2 Sam 12:22b.

[617] Josephus compresses David's triple affirmation concerning the futility of any further lamentation for the child of 2 Sam 12:23.

[618] The Bible reports no such reaction by the servants. It reminds one of the acclaim for Solomon's wis-

got her pregnant. She bore him a male child whom he named Solomon,[619] as the prophet Nathas had directed.[620]

(7.5) 159. Joab, for his part, severely harmed the Ammanites by his siege, cutting off their water and other supplies, so that they were in a very bad way, due to their lack of drink and food. For they were dependent on a little well and their sparing [use of] this, so that the spring would not fail them completely on account of more extensive use.[621]

Rabbah captured and plundered

160. Joab wrote to the king, disclosing these things and appealing to him to come for the capture of the city in order that the victory might be credited to him.[622] When Joab thus wrote, the king commended him for his loyalty and fidelity.[623] Taking the force along with him, he arrived for the destruction of Rabatha. Once he had taken it by storm,[624] he told the soldiers to plunder it.[625] **161.** He himself took the crown of the king of the Ammanites, the weight of which was that of a golden talent and in the center of which was some kind of precious stone, namely a sardonyx.[626] David always wore this on his own head.[627] He found many other splendid, costly vessels in the city,[628] whose males he destroyed after torturing them.[629] He did the same to the other Ammanite cities that he took by storm.[630]

(8.1) 162. When the king returned to Hierosolyma,[631] a disaster came upon his household on account of the following cause.[632] He had a daughter who was still a

Amnon's frustrated desire for Tamar

---

dom evoked by his judgment in the case of the 2 prostitutes in 1 Kgs 3:28 (// *Ant.* 8.34).

[619] In making David the one to name the child, Josephus follows the MT *ketiv* of 2 Sam 12:25 against the *qere*, which has Bathsheba name him. The LXX's verbal form could have either parent as its subject.

[620] 2 Sam 12:24-25 assigns 2 names to the newly born child: Solomon and "Jedidiah," of which the latter is connected with the Lord's "loving" the child and is given him in accordance with a divine message conveyed by the prophet Nathan. Josephus simplifies matters, eliminating all reference to a 2nd name for the child—in fact, "Jedidiah" is never used for him again in the Bible—and making "Solomon" the (single) name given him in line with Nathan's announcement in 7.93 that this was to be the name of the son who would succeed David.

[621] Josephus inserts these indications on the preliminaries to Joab's actual capture of Rabbah (2 Sam 12:26 // 1 Chr 20:1b) under the apparent inspiration of Joab's statement in 12:27 about his having taken the "city of waters."

[622] Josephus replaces the negative motivation for Joab's summons to David given in 2 Sam 12:28: (David is to come) lest Joab himself take credit for the city's capture with a positive one: David should come in order to get the credit due him.

[623] 2 Samuel 12 does not mention such a commendation of Joab by David. As Feldman (1998a: 295) notes, this is one of the few instances where Josephus goes beyond the Bible in portraying Joab positively.

[624] See 2 Sam 12:29 (in 1 Chr 20:1b the city's cap-

ture is attributed, not to David, but to Joab). Earlier (see 7.123, 129) the Ammonite capital is called "Arabatha."

[625] This "permission" is not mentioned in the biblical accounts of Rabbah's fall. It portrays David as a general who is solicitous for his men rather than only concerned to obtain plunder for himself—as he might appear to be in the source presentations.

[626] 2 Sam 12:30a// 1 Chr 20:2a do not identify the crown's precious stone.

[627] 2 Sam 12:30a// 1 Chr 20:2a seem to speak of a one-time placing of the crown on David's head, rather than of his constantly wearing this.

[628] 2 Sam 12:30b// 1 Chr 20:2b speak in more general terms of the vast spoil removed from the city by David.

[629] Josephus has David impose a still harsher penalty on the capital's inhabitants than do 2 Sam 12:31a // 1 Chr 20:3a, where he simply puts them to hard labor.

[630] In 2 Sam 12:31bα// 1 Chr 20:3bα the inhabitants of the other Ammonite cities, like those of Rabbah itself (see previous note), are put to hard labor.

[631] 2 Sam 12:31bβ// 1 Chr 20:3bβ note that the king was accompanied back to Jerusalem by "all the people."

[632] Josephus interjects this transitional notice with its ominous foreshadowing of the following "Tamar episode" (2 Samuel 13); on Josephus' version of this episode, see Begg 1996g. The wording of the notice echoes that used to introduce David's own sin with Bathsheba in 7.130.

virgin and of such beauty that she surpassed all lovely women.[633] Her name was Themar and she had the same mother as Apsalom.[634]

163. David's eldest[635] son Amnon fell in love with her. Unable to obtain his desire, given her virginity and her being [kept] under guard, he became sick.[636] His body, tormented by the pain, wasted away, and his color changed.[637]

Jonadab's (Ionathes') scheme

164. It was clear to a certain Ionathes,[638] a relative and friend of his,[639] that he was suffering these things, as he was a clever man and of especially sharp mind.[640] When therefore he saw each morning that Amnon's body was not in its natural condition,[641] he approached him and asked him to tell him the reason, while also saying that he guessed him to be suffering from erotic desire.[642] **165.** When Amnon declared his suffering, that he loved his sister by the same father,[643] Ionathes suggested a way and a scheme for attaining what he desired, namely he urged that he pretend to be ill. When his father came to him, he should appeal to him to direct that his sister be sent to wait upon him, for in this way he would recover and quickly be relieved of this illness.[644]

Tamar bakes for Amnon

166. Amnon therefore fell on his bed and feigned that he was ill, in line with Ionathes' suggestion.[645] When his father came and inquired how he was, he requested that he send him his sister.[646] David then immediately directed that she be brought. Once she came, he ordered her to personally bake bread for him, for he wanted to eat from her hands.[647]

---

[633] See 1 Sam 13:1b, whose reference to the woman's beauty Josephus embellishes, just as he did in the case of Bathsheba (see 7.130 and compare 2 Sam 11:2).

[634] 2 Sam 13:1a speaks of "Tamar" simply as Absalom's "sister"; Josephus has already mentioned her name and the pair's status as full siblings in 7.70; he cites the name of their common mother ("Machame") in 7.21. On Josephus' portrayal of Absalom, see Feldman 1998a: 215-29.

[635] This specification is lacking in 2 Sam 13:1b; Josephus derives it from 2 Sam 3:2// 7.21. See also 7.173 and note on "grief" at 7.173.

[636] 2 Sam 13:2 speaks vaguely of "it seeming impossible to Amnon to do anything to her [Tamar]"; Josephus spells out the reason for this, i.e. she was a virgin who was kept under guard.

[637] Josephus elaborates on the reference of 2 Sam 13:2 to Amnon's "making himself sick" because of Tamar, highlighting the effects of his passion upon him.

[638] MT (2 Sam 13:3) יונדב (Eng.: "Jonadab"); LXX B Ἰωνναδάμ; LXX L Ἰωναθάν; Josephus Ἰωάθης.

[639] In designating Jonadab as the son of David's brother "Shimeah" (MT) 2 Sam 13:3 makes him Amnon's cousin. Josephus will reproduce the source notices on Jonadab's parentage when this is repeated in 13:32; see 7.178. The Bible itself does not call Jonadab Amnon's "friend."

[640] 2 Sam 13:3 calls Jonadab "very wise" (Hebrew: חכם). *'Abot R. Nat.* 9 specifies "wise in evil." In Josephus' presentation Jonadab's "perceptiveness" is

evidenced first of all by his noticing Amnon's condition.

[641] Josephus incorporates into his account of what Jonadab perceives the content of his question to Amnon in 2 Sam 13:4: "... why are you so haggard morning after morning?"

[642] In 2 Sam 13:4 Jonadab simply asks Amnon to tell him what is wrong. Josephus highlights the latter's previously mentioned "perceptiveness" by having him inform Amnon that he has already divined the nature of his "ailment." The term "desire" (Greek: ἐπιθυμία) used of Amnon was previously applied to David (7.130), Uriah (7.134), and Amnon himself (7.163).

[643] In 2 Sam 13:4b Amnon refers to Tamar as "Absalom's sister." Josephus' Amnon uses a phrase which calls attention to the half-sibling relationship between himself and Tamar.

[644] Josephus modifies the conclusion of Jonadab's proposal according to 2 Sam 13:5, where Amnon is to ask David to have Tamar prepare food for him so that "I may see it, and eat it from her hand." Josephus' rendering sets out a more ultimate goal for the suggested procedure, i.e. Amnon's full recovery.

[645] See 2 Sam 13:6a; Josephus underscores the fact of Amnon's acting on Jonadab's advice.

[646] 2 Sam 13:6b does not mention an initial inquiry by David concerning Amnon's health. Josephus generalizes Amnon's request to the king, which in 13:6b recapitulates the wording of Jonadab's proposal to the former (13:5).

[647] 2 Sam 13:7 relates David's (single) sending to

167. As her brother looked on, she kneaded the flour and made small cakes, which she baked and brought to him.[648] He, however, did not taste them on the spot, but ordered the servants to clear everyone from in front of his bedroom, for he wanted relief from the uproar and trouble.[649]

168. Once it had happened as he directed, he asked his sister to bring the supper to him in the inner part of the house.[650] When the young woman did so, he took hold of her and attempted to get her to lie with him.[651] The girl cried out and said, "Do not do this violence[652] to me or act impiously, my brother, transgressing the laws[653] and involving yourself in terrible shame.[654] Desist from this unjust and filthy desire, from which our house will acquire shame and a bad reputation."[655] **169.** She further advised him to speak of the matter to their father, for he would give permission.[656] She spoke thus, wishing to evade his amorous assault for the present.[657] Amnon, however, was not persuaded; burning with erotic love and driven on by the spurs of passion, he did violence to his sister.[658]

Amnon rapes Tamar

170. Immediately following the rape,[659] however, hatred took hold of Amnon[660] who, insulting her further, directed her to get up and go away.[661] She called it some-

Tamar's lament

Tamar to direct her to go to Amnon's house to prepare food for him and her going there. Josephus substitutes 2 stages to David's instructions: Tamar is first conveyed to Amnon's residence at David's direction and then personally told by him what she is to do, the king's injunctions then concluding with an appended rationale, i.e. Amnon's readiness to "eat from her hands."

[648] See 2 Sam 13:8b-9aα, which lists a total of 6 actions performed by Tamar in Amnon's sight.

[649] See 2 Sam 13:9aββα. Josephus provides a motivation for Amnon's command that all are to withdraw.

[650] From 2 Sam 13:9bβ-10a Josephus leaves aside the (purported) rationale for Amnon's request of Tamar, i.e. "that I may eat from your hand."

[651] See 2 Sam 13:10b-11.

[652] Words of the βια-stem (here the verb βιάζομαι, "to do violence") permeate Josephus' version of 2 Samuel 13, occurring a total of 6 times. On the root in Josephus overall, see Moore 1974-1975.

[653] Tamar's initial attempt to dissuade Amnon as cited in 2 Sam 13:12 does not refer to the "laws," affirming rather "such a thing is not done in Israel." The "laws" in question are presumably those of Lev 18:9, 11; 20:17 (cf. Deut 27:22; Ezek 22:1), forbidding sexual relations with a half-sister. Josephus himself does not cite these laws in his version of the pentateuchal legislation.

[654] Compare Tamar's statement in 2 Sam 13:13aβ, "you would be one of the wanton fools in Israel," which itself follows her rhetorical question of 13:13aα: "as for me, where could I carry my shame?" Josephus thus omits Tamar's reference to the negative effects of Amnon's deed for herself in order to concentrate attention on a potentially more persuasive point, i.e. its deleterious consequences for himself.

[655] Whereas in 2 Sam 13:13a Tamar evokes the negative consequences of Amnon's intended action for herself and for him (see previous note), Josephus has her enlarge the perspective, reminding Amnon that their entire family stands to suffer, should he proceed with his intent. The addition recalls Josephus opening statement about a disaster befalling David's "house (hold)" in 7.162.

[656] See 2 Sam 13:13b.

[657] Commentators on 2 Sam 13:13b debate the intention behind Tamar's urging Amnon to speak to the king about her and her assurance that David will give her to him. Josephus, who has had Tamar previously allude to the "laws," i.e. those forbidding sexual relations with a half-sister (see note to "laws" at 7.168), clarifies the matter: Tamar knows that what Amnon desires is legally impossible, and is simply "playing for time" with her closing words to him.

[658] See 2 Sam 13:14, which Josephus amplifies with reference to the intensity of the lust that drives Amnon to consummate the rape.

[659] This is the reading (Greek: διακόρησις) of MP, which Marcus adopts; Niese reads κορεία ("virginity, maidenhood") with ROE. (Both Greek terms are quite rare in writers before Josephus). Reinach (*ad loc.*) conjectures μετὰ κόραν ("after surfeit").

[660] 2 Sam 13:15a specifies that Amnon's hatred for Tamar was greater than his previous love for her. *B. Sanh.* 21a quotes R. Isaac's dictum that Amnon's dramatic shift of feeling towards Tamar was to due to his having damaged his sexual organ while having intercourse with her.

[661] See 2 Sam 13:15b. Josephus adds the qualification of Amnon's command as an additional insult.

thing worse than the outrage itself[662] that, having done violence to her, he did not permit her to remain until night, but directed her to depart immediately in broad daylight such that those who met her would witness her shame.[663] He nevertheless ordered his servant to throw her out.[664]

171. Being very distressed at the outrage and the violence done her, she tore her tunic.[665] (Virgins[666] in ancient times[667] used to wear long-sleeved outfits that reached to the ankles[668] in order not to be exposed[669]). She poured ashes on her head and went off through the middle of the city, crying out and bewailing the violence done her.[670]

Absalom quiets Tamar

172. Her brother Apsalom met her and asked what terrible [thing] had happened to her that she was behaving thus.[671] When she disclosed the outrage to him,[672] he exhorted her to keep silent and to bear it with moderation, nor to think of her herself, though ravished by her brother, as having been outraged.[673] In obedience to him, she accordingly desisted from crying out and making the violence generally known.[674] She remained for a long time unmarried in the house of Apsalom her brother.[675]

David's and Absalom's re-action to rape

(8.2) 173. When he found out about these things, their father David was indignant at what had happened.[676] Because, however, he greatly loved Amnon—who was first-born son—he was compelled not to cause him grief.[677] Apsalom, on the

---

[662] See 2 Sam 13:16a, where Tamar's word to Amnon is cited in direct discourse.

[663] See 2 Sam 13:16a. Josephus' Tamar introduces the contrast between immediate and later, nocturnal expulsion and spells out what the former would entail for her. Josephus passes over the appended narrative (13:16b) statement that Amnon "would not listen to her."

[664] From Amnon's command to his servant concerning Tamar, 2 Sam 13:17, Josephus omits the concluding injunction that he is to "bolt the door after her." He likewise passes over the actual execution of Amnon's orders by the servant as related in 13:18b.

[665] Josephus anticipates this item from 2 Sam 13:19aβ, amplifying it with indications concerning Tamar's emotional state.

[666] Josephus generalizes the notice of 2 Sam 13:18a, where the reference is to the clothing worn by "the virgin daughters *of the king*."

[667] This phrase (Greek: τῶν ἀρχαίων) corresponds to an oft-proposed emendation, i.e. מעולם ("of old") for the MT form, i.e. מעילים ("garments") in 2 Sam 13:18a.

[668] Josephus' description of the item of clothing in question seems to represent a conflation of the terms used for it in LXX B ("a long-sleeved tunic") and LXX L 2 Sam 13:18a ("a tunic reaching to the ankles"). MT employs a phrase of uncertain meaning, i.e. כתנת פסים (RSV: "long robe with sleeves").

[669] Josephus adds this indication concerning the purpose of the garment in question.

[670] Josephus combines the 1st and 4th of the 4 actions attributed to Tamar in 2 Sam 13:19, expanding

the latter with mention of the "object" of her "crying." He has anticipated her 2nd source action (rending her garment) to an earlier point in the paragraph, while he leaves aside the 3rd, i.e. her laying her hand upon her head.

[671] Josephus substitutes this question for the one asked by Absalom in 2 Sam 13:20aα, i.e. "Has Amnon your brother been with you?," which leaves one wondering how Absalom surmised this.

[672] In 2 Sam 13:20aβ Absalom does not wait for an answer by Tamar to his initial question to her (see 13:20aα). Josephus inserts an allusion to the fact of her responding before Absalom resumes his speaking.

[673] In 2 Sam 13:20aβ Absalom urges Tamar to "hold her peace" and not "take this to heart," given Amnon's status as her "brother." Josephus' version at least acknowledges that a rape has occurred.

[674] Josephus interjects this notice on the effectiveness of Absalom's words to Tamar as cited in 2 Sam 13:20a.

[675] Josephus' word for Tamar's state (Greek: χηρεύουσα, literally "widowed") is the same as that used by LXX BL 2 Sam 13:20b. He adds the indication concerning the extended duration of her stay with her brother.

[676] See 2 Sam 13:21.

[677] This appended remark concerning David's non-activity in the face of Amnon's deed reflects the plus of LXX BL 2 Sam 13:21 (partially preserved also in 4QSam^a): "... but he did not grieve the spirit of Amnon his son because he loved him, because he was his first-born." Josephus earlier inserted a reference to Amnon's

other hand, hated him intensely. Concealing this, he kept watching for a suitable time to avenge his offense upon him.[678]

174. Two years had now already past since the disaster[679] of his sister. When about to set out for Belsephon,[680] a city situated in the inheritance of Ephraim,[681] for the shearing of his own sheep, Apsalom appealed to his father to come to him, along with his brothers, for a feast.[682]

Absalom has Amnon killed

175. Upon David's declining to go, so as not to be a burden to him,[683] he appealed to him to send his brothers.[684] Sending to his own men, Apsalom directed them, when they saw Amnon in a drunken state and sunk in a deep sleep, to murder him without fear of anyone, once he gave the signal.[685]

(8.3) 176. When they did as ordered, consternation and trouble took hold of his brothers. Anxious for themselves, they leapt on their horses and headed to their father.[686] Someone arrived before them and announced to their father that they had all been murdered by Apsalom.[687] **177.** At the loss of all these and a brother having done the deed—for his grief was made more bitter by the thought of who the purported killer was,[688]—he [David] was overwhelmed by his suffering. He did not inquire about the cause or pause to learn anything else—as might have been expected, given the enormity of the announced calamity, which was unbelievable on account of its excessiveness.[689] Instead, he tore his clothes and threw himself on the ground where he lay, mourning for all his sons, both those who had been disclosed as dead

Death of all David's sons reported

---

status as David's eldest son in 7.163, which serves to prepare his allusion to that status here in 7.173.

[678] Josephus expands the notice of 2 Sam 13:22 on Absalom's not speaking to Amnon because (or in spite of) his "hating" him for his violation of Tamar with a foreshadowing of his subsequent initiative against Amnon. The verb μισέω ("to hate") used of Absalom's stance towards Amnon here recalls Josephus' comment about the "hatred" (Greek: μῖσος) for Tamar that came over the satiated Amnon in 7.170.

[679] This same noun (Greek: πταῖσμα) occurs at the opening of the "Tamar interlude" in 7.162, which speaks of a "disaster" befalling David's household. Its presence there and here in 7.174 serves to frame Josephus' version of the Tamar story in 7.162-173.

[680] MT (2 Sam 13:23) בעל חצור (Eng.: "Baal-hazor"); LXX B Βαιλασώρ; LXX L Βασελλασώρ; Josephus Βελσεφών. Schlatter (1913, *s.v.*) suggests that Josephus' form has been influenced by the place name "Baal-zephon" in Exod 14:2.

[681] In locating "Belsephon" in "Ephraim," Josephus agrees with MT and LXX B 2 Sam 13:23 against LXX L, which places it in "Gophraim" (= Hebrew "Ophrah").

[682] 2 Sam 13:23b-24 appears to contain a double invitation by Absalom, i.e. first to the princes, seemingly made directly by him, and then a request to David that he and his "servants" attend the festival. Josephus has Absalom approach David at the outset to invite both him and his brothers. In specifying that the invitation is "for a feast," Josephus is perhaps inspired by the

LXX plus at the end of 13:27: "Absalom made a feast like the feast of the king."

[683] In 2 Sam 13:25a David declines to have "us all" go "lest we be burdensome to you." Josephus has the king specify that he is turning down the invitation for himself personally, thus opening the way for Absalom to renew his earlier invitation regarding his brothers.

[684] This 2nd, generalized request by Absalom takes the place of his specific appeal that Amnon be permitted to accompany them (2 Sam 13:26a), which itself so arouses the king's suspicions (13:26b) that Absalom must "press" David on the matter until he finally relents (13:27) Josephus further shortens the exchange between David and Absalom by omitting the latter's unsuccessful "pressing" of the king to attend in person and the latter's giving his "blessing" to the upcoming festival (13:25b).

[685] See 2 Sam 13:28.

[686] Josephus amplifies the princes' reaction in 2 Sam 13:29b with reference both to their emotional state and the "goal" of their flight. He further substitutes "horses" for "mules" as their mounts.

[687] See 2 Sam 13:30.

[688] Josephus interjects this notice on David's emotional response to the news.

[689] Josephus adds this remark on the impact of David's overwhelming grief upon him, i.e. it keeps him from checking into the veracity of the report. The addition serves to highlight by contrast the cool calculation that "Ionathes" will display in what follows; see 7.178.

and the one who had done away with them.[690]

178. But Ionathes, the son of his brother Sama,[691] appealed to him to desist somewhat from his grief and not believe that his other sons were dead—for he found no reason for supposing this.[692] He said too that he should investigate Amnon's case, for it was probable that Apsalom had ventured to do away with him because of his outraging of Themar.[693]

179. In the meantime, the noise of horses[694] and the uproar of those approaching attracted their attention; it was the king's sons, who had escaped from the feast.[695] Their father met them as they mourned, he too grieving at unexpectedly seeing those whom, a short time before, he heard had been destroyed. **180.** On all sides there were tears and wailing—on the sons' part for the brother who had been put to death,

on the king's for a son who had been butchered.[696] Apsalom, however, fled to Gessoura,[697] to his maternal grandfather who ruled the country there, and remained with him for three whole years.[698]

(8.4) 181. David's intention was to send for his son Apsalom, not in order that he should undergo punishment once he returned, but that he might be with him, for his wrath had ceased over time.[699] His commanding general Joab induced him to do this.[700] **182.** He caused a certain woman, who was already of advanced age, to approach David in the garments of a mourner.[701]

She said[702] that her sons, while quarreling in the countryside had recourse to acts

---

[690] Josephus' mention of David's lamenting and the object of this takes the place of the notice on 2 Sam 13:31b that has the king's "servants" rending their garments along with him. Josephus thereby keeps attention focussed on David personally and his manifestation of grief.

[691] MT (2 Sam 13:32) שמעה (Eng.: "Shimeah"); LXX B Σαμά; LXX L Σαμαά; Josephus Σαμᾶς. In his introduction of "Ionathes" in 7.164 Josephus left out the name of his father and the latter's relation to David as cited in 2 Sam 13:3; see note on "of his" at 7.164.

[692] Josephus provides a "supporting argument" for Jonadab's opening word in 2 Sam 13:32a, where he simply urges David not to suppose that all his sons have been killed.

[693] The Josephan Jonadab expresses his supposition about Amnon's death more tentatively and prudently than does his biblical counterpart, who asserts this as a fact in 2 Sam 13:32b. Josephus passes over Jonadab's repetition of his 2-part affirmation of 13:32 (the other sons are not dead, but only Amnon) in 13:33.

[694] Mention of these echoes Josephus' reference to the princes' mounting their "horses" in 7.176.

[695] In linking the princes' arrival (// 2 Sam 13:36aα) with Jonadab's statements about their fate (// 13:32-33), Josephus passes over the intervening 13:34-35, in which the watchman perceives the approach of many people and Jonadab reacts by identifying these as David's sons, whose safe return he has just predicted.

[696] Josephus expatiates on the summary mention of

the king and princes' grieving in 2 Sam 13:36aβb. As in his rendition of 13:31 in 7.177, he omits the participation of David's servants in the mourning.

[697] MT (2 Sam 13:37) גשור (Eng.: "Geshur"); LXX B Γεδσούρ; LXX L Γεσσείρ; Josephus Γεσσούρα. Like MT, Josephus has no equivalent to the varying geographical precisions appended to the name "Geshur" in LXX BL, as well as in 4QSamᵃ.

[698] See 2 Sam 13:37a, 38. Josephus has previously mentioned the name ("Thomomai") and kingdom of Absalom's maternal grandfather in 7.21 (// 2 Sam 3:3). He omits the intervening notice on David's morning for his son (Absalom) "day after day" of 13:37b.

[699] In 2 Sam 13:39a David "longs to go forth to Absalom." Josephus' rendering appends an indication of the king's plans regarding Absalom once they are reunited. His reference to the cessation of David's "wrath" against Absalom replaces the allusion to the king's being "comforted for" the deceased Amnon in 13:39b.

[700] This transitional notice takes the place of the mention of Joab's "perceiving that the king's heart went out to Absalom" of 2 Sam 14:1.

[701] Josephus drastically reduces the account of Joab's "instructing" the woman in 2 Sam 14:2-3, omitting, e.g., her status as a "wise woman" residing in Tekoa, the prohibition of her anointing herself, and Joab's supplying her with the words she is to say. The one item added by Josephus is his reference to the woman's age.

[702] Continuing to abridge the biblical account,

of violence, nobody appearing who was capable of putting a stop to this. One was struck by the other and died.[703] **183.** She asked those of her relatives who were rushing out after the one who had done away with him[704] to grant her the safety of her son and not deprive her of her remaining hopes for support in her old age.[705] This he [David] would do for her by preventing those who wished to kill her son.[706] For their solicitude would not be kept in check by anything other than their fear of him.[707]

184. When [David] assented to what the woman begged,[708] she replied to the king again: "I thank you," she said, "that in your kindness you have taken compassion on my old age and virtual childlessness.[709] In order, however, that your humanity to me be confirmed, first be reconciled to your own son and lay aside your wrath against him. **185.** For how can I be confident that you have truly given me this favor of yours, so long as you cherish hatred against your son for similar reasons? It is altogether foolish, now that one son has died contrary to your will, for you to willingly [kill] the other."[710]

186. David surmised that the imaginary case was the device of Joab in his solicitude for Apsalom.[711] By inquiring of the old woman, he found out that this was the truth.[712] Summoning Joab, he said that he had succeeded in his design and directed him to fetch Apsalom.[713] For he was no longer resentful towards him; rather, his wrath and rage had already left him.[714]

Absalom's return

Josephus passes over the woman's approach to David, her homage to him and request for help, the king's inquiry about her problem, and her introducing herself as a widow (2 Sam 14:4-5). In his version, she begins presenting her case immediately.

[703] See 2 Sam 14:6.

[704] In 2 Sam 14:7 the woman's "whole family" takes the initiative in demanding that she hand over the culprit. For Josephus' version of the law of blood vengeance (Exod 21:12-14; Num 35:19-21) to which the woman is alluding, see *Ant.* 4.277.

[705] Josephus reformulates in non-figurative terms the woman's statement of 2 Sam 14:7bα ("thus they [the family] will quench my coal that is left"). He passes over her concluding declaration about her husband being left without a "name" or "remnant" on earth (14:7bβ). He further omits the appended dialogue between David and the woman (14:8-10), in which the king twice reassures her (vv. 8, 10), with her offer to assume "guilt" in place of the king supervening (v. 9).

[706] Josephus here synthesizes the woman's various requests of the king regarding her surviving son as cited in 2 Sam 14:(7)11a, 15-16.

[707] These words, affirming the effectiveness of David's decisions, might be seen as Josephus' replacement for the woman's fulsome statement about the king's being "like the angel of God to discern good and evil" in 2 Sam 14:17.

[708] See 2 Sam 14:11b, from which Josephus leaves aside the king's oath formula and the figurative language of his declaration ("not one hair of your son shall fall to the ground"). He previously passed over the king's earlier, preliminary responses to the woman of vv. 8 and 10; see note to "age" at 7.183.

[709] This expression of thanks by the woman takes the place of her asking permission to speak further to the king and David's granting this (2 Sam 14:12), as well as her (obscure) reproachful question of 14:13a: "why then have you planned such a thing against the people of God?"

[710] With these statements by the woman, linking her own case with that of David and Absalom, and affirming the wrongfulness of the king's continued resentment towards his son, Josephus elucidates her rather obscure, figurative remarks on the matter in 2 Sam 14:13b-14. He mentioned the king's getting over his "wrath" towards Absalom in 7.181; here in 7.184 then, the woman is requesting David to do something that, in fact, he has done prior to her appeal. The juxtaposition of the 2 formulations points up the magnanimity of David, who has already laid aside his anger on his own.

[711] This statement, highlighting both David's insight and Joab's attachment to his son, takes the place of the king's calling on the woman to answer honestly whatever he may ask her and her reply, urging him to speak, in 2 Sam 14:18.

[712] Josephus drastically compresses the sequence of 2 Sam 14:19-20, where to the king's question about Joab's involvement (14:19a) the woman replies affirmatively with extended words of flattery for David (14:19b-20).

[713] See 2 Sam 14:21.

[714] Josephus appends this statement by David concerning his current stance towards Absalom to the

187. Joab, having paid homage to the king and welcomed his words,[715] immediately set out for Gessoura. Taking Apsalom, he came to Hierosolyma.[716] **(8.5) 188.** Once he heard that he had arrived, the king sent in advance to his son and directed him to go off to his own house. For he was not yet disposed to see him, immediately following his return.[717] Apsalom, upon his father's directing this, kept away from his presence, while continuing to be looked after by his servants.[718]

Absalom establishes himself in Jerusalem

189. He was not impaired in his good looks by grief or by his not receiving the concern due a king's son.[719] Rather, he still stood out and surpassed everyone in appearance and height, excelling those who lived in great luxury.[720] Now the weight of his hair was such that it could scarcely be cut within the course of a week;[721] it weighed 200 shekels,[722] that is five *minae*.[723] **190.** He stayed on for two years in Hierosolyma.[724] He was the father of three sons, and one daughter of outstanding beauty,[725] whom Solomon's son Roboam later married and by whom he had a son named Abias.[726]

David and Absalom reconciled

191. Apsalom himself then sent to Joab and requested him to finally conciliate his father and request him to permit him to come to see and speak to him.[727] When Joab neglected the matter,[728] Apsalom sent some of his men to burn down the field that adjoined his.[729] When Joab learned of what had been done,[730] he came to

---

king's directive that his son be brought back (2 Sam 14:21). The addition echoes the editorial remark in 7.181 that David's "wrath" towards Absalom had "ceased over time" as well as the woman's plea (7.185) that David lay aside his "wrath" against his son. See also note on "the other" at 7.185.

[715] See 2 Sam 14:22, from which Josephus omits the actual wording of Joab's response to the king.

[716] See 2 Sam 14:23.

[717] See 2 Sam 14:24a. Josephus provides a motivation for David's directive to his son.

[718] Cf. 2 Sam 14:24b, where Absalom is said to dwell in his own house and not enter the king's presence in accord with David's double directive in 14:24a. Josephus appends the notice about Absalom's being looked after by the servants.

[719] Josephus inserts this remark, highlighting the non-effect of Absalom's travails on his appearance, as a transition to the following parenthetical segment concerning Absalom's physique (// 2 Sam 14:25-27).

[720] See 2 Sam 14:25, which avers that Absalom was "without blemish" from head to crown.

[721] Josephus markedly embellishes the notice of 2 Sam 14:26 concerning the extraordinary weight of Absalom's hair when cut "at the end of every year," giving the same figure for the weight of the hair at its weekly cutting as does the Bible for the once-a-year cut. Rappaport (1930: 53, #219; 131, n. 232) calls attention to the comparable statement attributed to R. Joses in *b. Naz.* 5a according to which Absalom, in line with princely practice, used to have his hair cut each Sabbath eve.

[722] Josephus' figure agrees with that of MT, 4QSam[a]

and LXX B 2 Sam 14:26 against LXX L's 100.

[723] This equivalency replaces the specification of 2 Sam 14:26 according to which the 200 shekels that Absalom's hair weighed were "by the king's weight." On the problem of the relationship between the 2 units of weight cited by Josephus, see Marcus *ad loc.*

[724] Josephus anticipates this chronological indication from 2 Sam 14:28, which further specifies that throughout this time Absalom did not enter David's presence (see 14:24b).

[725] See 2 Sam 14:27. Josephus does not here reproduce the source's name(s) for Absalom's daughter; MT LXX B have "Thamar," LXX L rather "Maacha" (the name given her in 1 Kgs 15:2 as well). See next note.

[726] Josephus here follows the plus at the end of LXX BL 2 Sam 14:27, itself inspired by the subsequent reference to the later history of Absalom's daughter in 1 Kgs 15:2 (// *Ant.* 8.249). In designating the son of Tamar and Rehoboam as "Abias," Josephus goes together with LXX L 2 Sam 14:27 ("Abia") against the "Abiathar" of LXX B.

[727] Josephus expatiates considerably on Absalom's request to Joab as reported in 2 Sam 14:29aα, where he simply calls on the latter to "send him to the king."

[728] Josephus compresses the sequence of 2 Sam 14:29, where there is a double sending by Absalom and a double disregard of this by Joab.

[729] In 2 Sam 14:30a (see 14:31) it is Joab's own barley field, rather than an field adjacent to this, which the servants are instructed to burn. Josephus passes over the notice on their execution of Absalom's order, 14:30b.

[730] This transitional notice, with its mention of

Apsalom to complain and inquire about the reason for this.[731] **192.** Apsalom said: "I devised this stratagem so that I might bring you, who have disregarded the commands I made about conciliating my father, to me.[732] But now you are present, I beg you to reconcile me with the one who fathered me.[733] For my part, I consider my return more terrible than my flight itself, as long as my father remains wrathful towards me."[734]

193. Joab was persuaded and felt compassion for him in his necessity.[735] He mediated with the king, speaking of his son and making him so favorable towards him that David immediately called him.[736] When Apsalom threw himself on the ground and asked pardon for his offenses,[737] David raised him up and promised to forget what had happened.[738]

(9.1) 194. After matters with his father had turned out for Apsalom in this way, within a very short time,[739] he procured for himself many horses and chariots[740] and had fifty armor-bearers around him.[741]

Absalom ingratiates himself with people

195. Each day he used to go early in the morning to the palace[742] and speak obligingly to those who had come for judgments and gotten the worst of it.[743] He said that they had lost their cases[744] because his father had counselors around him who were not good and inclined to wrongdoing in judgment.[745] By saying that if he him-

---

Joab's learning of the field-burning, might reflect the extended plus of 4QSam[a] and LXX BL at the end of 2 Sam 14:30: "Joab's servants came to him with their clothes torn and said, 'The servants of Abishalom had set the property on fire'." (trans. McCarter 1984 *ad loc.*)

[731] See 2 Sam 14:31.

[732] In 2 Sam 14:32 Absalom begins by reminding Joab of why he had sent for him, i.e. that he might bring the king a message from himself, further asserting that he should have stayed in Geshur (a version of this assertion appears at the end of Josephus' version of Absalom's speech; see note to "towards me" at 7.192). Josephus' version of Absalom's reply incorporates a mention of Joab's previous disregard of Absalom's summons, while also echoing the wording of his original message to Joab (7.191).

[733] This appeal for Joab's mediation takes the place of Absalom's statement in 2 Sam 14:32b: "now therefore let me go into the presence of the king; and if there is guilt in me, let him kill me."

[734] This concluding affirmation by Absalom represents Josephus' version of the message that the prince had intended Joab to take to the king according to 2 Sam 14:32a: "Why have I come from Geshur? It would be better for me to be there still." The statement picks up the key word "wrath" used of David's feelings towards Absalom in 7.181, 185, 186.

[735] Josephus inserts this notice on the effect of Absalom's words upon Joab.

[736] See 2 Sam 14:33a. Josephus expatiates on the summary source reference to Joab's "telling" the king.

[737] 2 Sam 14:33bα mentions only Absalom's prostration, not his request for pardon.

[738] 2 Sam 14:33 concludes with David "kissing"

Absalom. Josephus supplies a preparatory action by the king (raising the prostrate Absalom) and replaces the royal kiss with an affirmative response to Absalom's—likewise added—request for pardon.

[739] Josephus interjects this indication about the brevity of the interval between Absalom's being pardoned by his father and his undertaking initiatives that will eventuate in his revolt against David. He thereby accentuates Absalom's heedlessness and ingratitude.

[740] 2 Sam 15:1 speaks merely of "a chariot and horses."

[741] In 2 Sam 15:1 Absalom's 50 attendants are called "those who run before him."

[742] Compare 2 Sam 15:2aα, where Absalom positions himself "at the way of the gate" (4QSam[a] lacks "of the gate").

[743] According to 2 Sam 15:2aβ Absalom addressed himself indiscriminately to all those who approached the king for judgment of their cases. Josephus has him focus on the group that would most likely be amenable to his subversive words, i.e. those who had lost their cases; see Feldman 1998a: 222.

[744] Josephus leaves aside the opening, introductory exchange (2 Sam 15:2b) between Absalom and those with cases in which the former asks the latter where they have come from and is informed by them of their tribal affiliation. He thereby has Absalom come immediately to the key issue.

[745] This is Josephus' intensified version of Absalom's assertion in 2 Sam 15:3 that, whereas his hearers had good cases, David had failed to provide anyone to hear them. For the Josephan Absalom, there are judges available, but these cannot be relied on to exercise their office appropriately.

self had that authority, he would have established a full and fair legal system,[746] he won the loyalty of everyone.

Absalom pro-claimed king in Hebron

196. In this way he curried favor with the crowd.[747] When he thought that the loyalty of the mobs was now secure,[748] four years after his reconciliation with his father having now already passed,[749] he asked that he be permitted to go to Hebron to offer a sacrifice to God, as he had vowed when a fugitive.[750] When David assented to his request, Apsalom went, and a great crowd assembled, many having been summoned by him.[751] **(9.2) 197.** There was also present David's counselor, Achitophel[752] the Gelmonite,[753] and some 200 from Hierosolyma itself, who, not knowing of the undertaking, [supposed] they had been summoned to a sacrifice.[754] He was appointed king by all, this being what he had contrived would happen.[755]

David flees Jerusalem

198. When these matters were reported to David and he heard of the unexpected things being done by his son against him, he was anxious and also marvelled at his impiety and daring, seeing that he [Apsalom] gave no thought to his having pardoned his offenses. Rather, he was [committing deeds] much worse and more lawless than those, by laying hands on the kingship which, first of all, had not been given him by God, and which, secondly, entailed the elimination of the one who had fathered him.[756] David then decided to flee to the regions across the Jordan.[757]

199. Calling together his most intimate friends and deliberating with them about

---

[746] Compare 2 Sam 15:4, where Absalom expresses the wish that he himself might be a "judge," so as to be able to give justice to those who come. Josephus' wording here echoes *Ant.* 6.32, where Samuel is said to do what Absalom here claims he would do if he had the authority, i.e. "establish a sound legal system." Josephus leaves aside the notice of 15:5 on Absalom's raising up and kissing those who pay him homage.

[747] See 2 Sam 15:6b: "so Absalom stole the hearts of the men of Israel." The word translated "curried favor" is the participle of the verb δημαγωγέω, a term used by Josephus also of his arch-rival, Justus of Tiberias; see *Life* 40 and cf. Feldman 1998a: 224; Mason: 2001: 45, n. 242.

[748] Josephus inserts this transitional phrase which suggests an explanation as to why Absalom waited so long (i.e. 4 years) before undertaking his revolt.

[749] Josephus gives the same figure for the amount of time elapsed as does LXX L 2 Sam 15:7 (and Syriac and Vulg.) against the improbable *40* years cited by MT (2 Hebrew MSS read 40 *days*) and LXX B. He adds the specification concerning the starting point of the period in question, having this commence with David's pardoning of Absalom (see 7.193); he thereby underscores the enormity of the latter's deed in rising up against his pardoner.

[750] Josephus compresses Absalom's extended address to the king concerning the vow he wishes to make at Hebron in 2 Sam 15:7-8.

[751] Josephus here seems to combine (and abridge) the data of 2 Sam 15:12b (the constant increase of Absalom's supporters) and 15:10 (Absalom's dispatch of messengers throughout Israel to urge people to acclaim

him king when they hear the sound of the trumpet).

[752] MT (2 Sam 15:12a) אחיתפל (Eng.: "Ahithophel"); LXX B Ἀχειτόφελ; LXX L Ἀχιτόφελ; Josephus Ἀχιτόφελος. According to 15:12a Absalom "sent/sent for" this figure.

[753] Josephus uses the same gentilic for Ahithophel as does LXX L 2 Sam 15:12a (MT calls him a "Gilonite," LXX B a "Tekonite"). At this point, he leaves aside the name of Ahithophel's city (MT: "Giloh"), which, however, he will insert into his account of Ahithophel's returning to die there in 7.228 (where in line with the gentilic "Gelmonite" used by him here in 7.197, he calls the site "Gelmon").

[754] See 2 Sam 15:11. In the sequence of 2 Samuel 15, Absalom's "sacrificing" is associated, not with the 200 Jerusalemites (v. 11), but rather with his summoning of Ahithophel (v. 12a).

[755] This closing notice on Absalom's launching his coup represents another (see note on "by him" at 7.196) echo of 2 Sam 15:10, where Absalom dispatches "secret messengers" throughout all the Israelite tribes to urge that, when the sound of the trumpet is heard, he be acclaimed king.

[756] Josephus elaborates on the notice concerning David's being informed of his son's initiatives (2 Sam 15:13), elucidating the king's interior response to this and highlighting, once again, the reprehensibility of Absalom's deeds; see note to "short time" at 7.194.

[757] Josephus turns into a narrative notice the opening words of David's address to his servants in 2 Sam 15:14: "Arise, and let us flee." He likewise introduces a specification concerning the king's intended destination, based on the subsequent course of the story.

his son's crazed act,⁷⁵⁸ he consigned everything to God, the judge.⁷⁵⁹ Leaving his ten concubines to guard the palace, he departed Hierosolyma,⁷⁶⁰ a part of the people accompanying him,⁷⁶¹ as well as the 600 soldiers who had shared his previous flight, when Saoul was alive.⁷⁶²

200. However, he persuaded the high priests⁷⁶³ Abiathar⁷⁶⁴ and Sadok⁷⁶⁵ who were intending to go with him, as well as all the Levites, to remain behind with the ark; God would, he said, rescue him, even though this were not carried along.⁷⁶⁶ He further enjoined them⁷⁶⁷ to secretly report to him everything that happened.⁷⁶⁸ (In all these matters he had reliable ministers⁷⁶⁹ in Achiman⁷⁷⁰ the son of Sadok and Ionathes⁷⁷¹ the son of Abiathar.)⁷⁷² **201.** Ethis⁷⁷³ the Gittite⁷⁷⁴ accompanied him as well, having prevailed over the will of David—who attempted to persuade him to remain—and in that way displayed his loyalty to him still further.⁷⁷⁵

Priests stay behind

Ethis (Ittai) accompanies David

---

⁷⁵⁸ 2 Sam 15:14a has David speaking to all his "servants" present in Jerusalem. Josephus makes him consult a more select body, made up of those whose loyalty could most be counted on.

⁷⁵⁹ Josephus gives this new, more pious, content to David's words to his retinue of 2 Sam 15:14, where the Deity is not mentioned, and it is rather the threat posed by Absalom which is in focus. He leaves aside the servants' response, pledging their continued loyalty, of 15:15.

⁷⁶⁰ See 2 Sam 15:16. Josephus mentioned David's "concubines" in 7.70 (// 2 Sam 5:13) without specifying their number.

⁷⁶¹ 2 Sam 15:17a has "all the people" (MT; LXX house[hold]) accompanying David. Josephus omits the detail about the party's "halting at the last house" of 15:17b.

⁷⁶² In 2 Sam 15:18 the 600 are qualified as "Gitittes who had followed him [David] from Gath." For Josephus' earlier references to the 600 as David's pre-kingship companions, see *Ant.* 6.299, 319, 351, 360. From the list of David's supporters in 15:18 Josephus omits the obscure groups of the "Cherethites" and the "Pelethites."

⁷⁶³ Josephus reverses the order of Samuel 15, where the fugitive David encounters first Ittai the Gittite (vv. 19-22) and then the cultic officers (vv. 24-29). The reversal could reflect the greater long-term significance of the latter meeting.

⁷⁶⁴ In speaking of "Abiathar" alongside Zadok, Josephus follows MT 2 Sam 15:24 (where he appears in 3rd place, after Zadok and the Levites, in the phrase "and Abiathar went up [or was sacrificing]") against LXX L, where the Levites carry the ark ἀπὸ Βαιθάρ ("from Baithar"). LXX B conflates the readings of MT and LXX L.

⁷⁶⁵ Josephus earlier mentioned Abiathar and Zadok (in reverse order) together as David's joint high priests in 7.110.

⁷⁶⁶ In 2 Sam 15:25a David addresses himself to

Zadok alone; Josephus has him speak to all the cultic officers previously enumerated in 15:24. His appended motivation for David's directive that the ark be brought back to Jerusalem (// 15:25a) picks up on the positive scenario cited by the king in 15:25b (God will restore him to Jerusalem), while leaving aside the more negative possibility (if God is not pleased with David, he may do what seems good to him with him) adduced by David in 15:26.

⁷⁶⁷ In 2 Sam 15:27-28 (compare 15:25) David addresses his word about being kept informed concerning events in Jerusalem to Zadok; Josephus, as in what precedes, has the king speak to all the cultic officers who have come out to him.

⁷⁶⁸ Cf. 2 Sam 15:28, where David announces that he will await a word from the priests "at the fords of the wilderness."

⁷⁶⁹ Greek: διάκονοι. On Josephus' use of this word and its cognates in light of biblical and extra-biblical Greek usage, see Collins 1990: 111-15, 120-21, 129-30, 131-44, 164.

⁷⁷⁰ MT (2 Sam 15:27) אֲחִימַעַץ (Eng.: "Achimaaz"); LXX B Ἀχειμαίας; LXX L Ἀχιμάας; Josephus Ἀχίμανος (this is the reading adopted by Niese, whereas Marcus *ad loc.* and Schalit *s.v.* read Ἀχίμας).

⁷⁷¹ MT (2 Sam 15:27) יְהוֹנָתָן (Eng.: "Jonathan"); LXX Ἰωναθάν; Josephus Ἰωνάθης.

⁷⁷² In 2 Sam 15:27 the 2 priestly sons are mentioned as part of David's address. Josephus transposes the mention into an editorial remark appended to David's words, which underscores the pair's reliability.

⁷⁷³ MT (2 Sam 15:19) אִתַּי (Eng.: "Ittai"); LXX B Γεθθί; LXX L Ἠθί; Josephus Ἔθις.

⁷⁷⁴ MT (2 Sam 15:19) הַגִּתִּי (Eng.: "the Gittite"); LXX τὸν Γεθθαῖον; Josephus ὁ Γιτταῖος.

⁷⁷⁵ Josephus drastically abridges the sequence of 2 Sam 15:19-22, where David urges Ittai to return (vv. 19-20), the latter demurs (v. 21), and David acquiesces in his coming with him (v. 22a). He likewise leaves aside the appended notices on Ittai's actual "passage" (v.

David's fear regarding Ahithophel

202. As he was ascending the Mount of Olives, barefoot and with all those with him weeping,[776] it was reported that Achitophel too had joined Apsalom and was supporting him.[777] His hearing of this increased David's grief, and he called upon God, asking him to cause Apsalom's mind to turn against Achitophel.[778] For he was anxious that he, in advising what was hostile, would persuade him, since he was an astute man and very keen in discerning what was advantageous.[779]

David sends Hushai (Chousis) to counteract Ahithophel

203. When he reached the summit of the mount,[780] David looked down on the city and with many tears prayed to God as one who had lost his kingship.[781] A man named Chousis,[782] who was his proven friend,[783] met him there. **204.** When David saw him with his clothes torn and his head full of ashes and mourning his change [of fortune],[784] he comforted him and appealed to him to cease his grieving.[785] Finally, he begged him to go off to Apsalom as if he were a supporter, and to find out the secret designs of his mind and to oppose the counsels of Achitophel.[786] For he would be of advantage to him, not so much by accompanying him, as by being with Apsalom.[787] Persuaded by David, Chousis left him and went to Hierosolyma. Apsalom himself arrived there not long afterwards.[788]

Ziba denounces Mephibosheth to David

(9.3) 205. When David had advanced a little further, Siba, the servant of Memphi-

---

22b) and the crossing of the Kidron by king and people (v. 23).

[776] See 2 Sam 15:30, which adds mention of David's own "weeping" and the (un)covered heads of king and people.

[777] See 2 Sam 15:31a.

[778] Josephus inserts the reference to the emotional effect of the report upon David. In 2 Sam 15:31b David prays that God will "turn Ahithophel's counsel "into foolishness" (MT LXX L; LXX B: "frustrate"). Josephus' rendition may have been inspired by the notice concerning the fulfillment of David's prayer in 2 Sam 17:14 (// 7.221), where Absalom decides that Hushai's plan is superior to that of Ahithophel, doing so in accordance with the divine decision of doom upon himself (17:15).

[779] Josephus appends this remark, underscoring the urgency of David's prayer, perhaps inspired by 2 Sam 16:23 (a passage not reproduced by Josephus in its biblical context), where the counsel of Ahithophel is said to be the equivalent of an "oracle of God" in the eyes of both David and Absalom.

[780] With his phrase "the summit" Josephus translates the MT form הראש of 2 Sam 15:32, which LXX BL transliterate as a proper place name, i.e. (τοῦ) Ῥοώς.

[781] Josephus intensifies the pathos of the source reference to David's (or the people's) "worshiping God" at the summit in 2 Sam 15:32a.

[782] MT (2 Sam 15:32) חושׁי (Eng.: "Hushai"); LXX Χουσεί; Josephus Χουσί. Josephus leaves aside Hushai's gentilic, i.e. "the Archite."

[783] In introducing Hushai as David's "friend," Josephus follows LXX BL 2 Sam 15:32, whereas in MT this title appears only at the very end of the exchange between him and David in 15:37.

[784] Josephus adds the reference to Hushai's lamenting and the reason for this to the description of his other mourning practices cited in 2 Sam 15:32b. He thereby accentuates both the pathos of the scene and Hushai's solidarity with the fugitive David.

[785] This reference to David's initial response to Hushai's mourning takes the place of the king's brusque opening declaration in 2 Sam 15:33 that Hushai will be a burden to him, should he accompany him (which Josephus does reproduce subsequently in the paragraph). Josephus thus portrays a king who, in his first response, appears more sympathetic to and appreciative of Hushai's grieving on his behalf.

[786] In his version of David's request of Hushai in 2 Sam 15:34, Josephus inserts a reference, inspired by 15:35-36, where David asks him to make use of the 2 priests' sons in sending him word about what he hears in the palace, to a further mission he has in mind for him, i.e. to ascertain Absalom's plans. His rendition of the former verse makes no use of its extended plus in LXX B (in LXX L this comes at the end of 15:36), according to which Hushai is to say to Absalom: "your brothers departed, O king, after the departure of your father and now I am your servant, O king. Spare my life" (trans. McCarter 1984: *ad loc.*).

[787] This is Josephus' delayed version of David's opening statement to Hushai in 2 Sam 15:33. See note to "grieving" at 7.204. Josephus omits—although see note to "Achitophel" at 7.204—David's extended remarks on the 2 priests' sons through whom Hushai may get word to him about developments in Jerusalem.

[788] See 2 Sam 15:37, the content of which Josephus prefaces with an allusion to the persuasive effect of David's speech on Hushai.

bosthos,[789] met him.[790] (David had sent him to take care of the possessions that he had given as a gift to the son of Saoul's son Ionathes.)[791] With him were a pair of donkeys loaded with provisions, from which he directed him to take what he and those with him needed.[792] **206.** When David, however, inquired where he had left Memphibosthos,[793] Siba said that he was in Hierosolyma, expecting that, due to the present confusion, he would be designated king, in memory of the things by which Saoul had benefitted them.[794] In his indignation against him, David granted to Siba everything that he had conferred upon Memphibosthos. For he now perceived that the former would possess these things much more justly than did the latter.[795] Siba, for his part, was overjoyed.[796]

David transfers Mephibosheth's property to Ziba

(9.4) **207.** When David was at a place called Choran,[797] he encountered a relative of Saoul named Samouis,[798] the son of Gera,[799] who came against him, throwing stones and insulting him. Even though David's friends stood round him and protected him, Samouis continued defaming David still more,[800] calling him an assassin and the source of many calamities. **208.** He also directed him to depart the country as one who was banned and accursed,[801] and thanked God who had removed the kingship from him and was taking vengeance on him through his own son for his offenses against his own master.[802]

Shimei (Samouis) verbally abuses David

All were stirred to wrath against him, and Abessai in particular wanted to put Samouis to death.[803] David, however, restrained his wrath.[804] **209.** "Let us not," he said, "add another calamity to the present ones, by generating a new one. For neither

David forbids killing of Shimei

---

[789] As in 7.111-116, Josephus uses this name for the Saulide, corresponding to that of MT LXX B 2 Sam 16:1, as against the "Memphibaal" of LXX L.

[790] See 2 Sam 16:1a.

[791] Josephus inserts this cross reference to his earlier presentation of the 2 figures in 7.111-116 (// 2 Samuel 9); see especially 7.115.

[792] Josephus markedly compresses the catalogue of supplies brought by Ziba as well as the exchange between David and him regarding these (2 Sam 16:1b-2), turning the latter into a "directive" by Ziba without a prior question by David.

[793] Josephus substitutes this proper name for the ambiguous phrase used by David in his question of 2 Sam 16:3a: "where is your master's son?"—who is the "master" (Jonathan? Mephibosheth?) and who the "son" (Mephibosheth?, Mica [2 Sam 9:12]?) here?

[794] Josephus appends a motivation for Mephibosheth's (purported) "expectation" about gaining the kingship that is keeping him in Jerusalem according to Ziba (2 Sam 16:3b).

[795] Josephus expands the notice (2 Sam 16:4a) concerning David's "donation" to Ziba with a reference to the king's emotional response to the latter's report as well as a motivation for his making the property award to him.

[796] This notice on Ziba's emotional state replaces his concluding statement to David in 2 Sam 16:4b: "I do obeisance; let me ever find favor in your sight,

my lord the king."

[797] MT (2 Sam 16:5) בחורים (Eng.: "Bahurim"); LXX B Βουρείμ; LXX L Χορράμ; Josephus Χώρανος (This is the reading adopted by Niese and Marcus *ad loc.*; Schalit *s.v.* proposes Βοκχόρης as the original form, i.e. the name found in 7.225, where Josephus is reproducing the reference to "Bahurim" of 2 Sam 17:18).

[798] MT (2 Sam 16:5) שמעי (Eng.: "Shimei"); LXX Σεμεεί; Josephus Σαμούις.

[799] MT (2 Sam 16:5) גרא (Eng.: "Gera"); LXX Γηρά; Josephus Γηρᾶ.

[800] See 2 Sam 16:5-6, where (v. 6) David's entourage consists of all his servants, all the people, and all the "mighty men."

[801] Josephus elaborates on Shimei's opening words to David according to 2 Sam 16:7: "begone, begone, you man of blood, you worthless fellow."

[802] Josephus reverses the order of 2 Sam 16:8, where Shimei speaks first of the Lord's vengeance on David for the blood of Saul's house and then of God's deposing David in favor of Absalom. He inserts the reference to Shimei's "thanking God" for these developments.

[803] 2 Sam 16:9 refers to the reaction of Abishai alone, who designates Shimei as a "dead dog" and asks David's permission to behead him.

[804] This editorial remark, prefacing David's response to Abishai, takes the place of the king's (obscure) opening question in 2 Sam 16:10a: "What have I to do with you, you sons of Zeruiah?"

shame nor worry affect me because of this dog that is raving against me.[805] I submit to God,[806] because of whom he is ranting against us.[807] It is no wonder that I am suffering these things from him, seeing what I have experienced from my impious son.[808] There will, however, be some pity for us from God, and we shall prevail over our enemies with him wishing this."[809]

David reaches Jordan

210. He then continued on his way, paying no attention to Samouis, who ran along the other side of the mountain, uttering many insults.[810] When he arrived at the Jordan,[811] he refreshed his tired men there.[812]

Hushai ingratiates himself with Absalom

(9.5) 211. When Apsalom and his counsellor Achitophel arrived in Hierosolyma with all the people, David's friend [Chousis] came to them.[813] He did Apsalom homage, expressing the wish that the kingship would remain his always and for all time.[814] Apsalom then asked him why, given that he had been a special friend of his father and had the reputation of being faithful in everything, he was not with him now, but rather, having deserted him, he had gone over to himself.[815] Chousis responded in a way that was both adroit and prudent.[816] **212.** For he said that one should follow both God and the whole crowd. "Since these are with you, O master, it is appropriate that I too follow you, for you have received the kingship from God.[817] I shall manifest that same fidelity and loyalty—should I be credited as a friend—that you know I bestowed on your father.[818] It is not fitting to be indignant

---

[805] These opening statements by David represent a elaboration of his injunction "let him [Shimei] alone, and let him curse" in 2 Sam 16:11bα. In having David himself qualify Shimei as a "dog," Josephus transfers to the king himself Abishai's reference to Shimei as a "dead dog" in 16:9.

[806] This declaration of resignation by David makes explicit what is implicit in his words in 2 Sam 16:10-12. It likewise echoes 7.199, where Josephus has David "consign everything to God, the judge."

[807] Compare David's double recognition of the divine prompting behind Shimei's cursing of him in 2 Sam 16:10b, 11bβ.

[808] Josephus elaborates on David's declaration in 2 Sam 16:11aβ: "Behold my own son seeks my life; how much more now may this Benjamite." His inserted negative qualification ("impious") of Absalom echoes the extended remarks on David's reaction to his son's revolt introduced by him in 7.198 (compare 2 Sam 15:14), highlighting its reprehensibility.

[809] Josephus has David voice a more definite hope than that attributed to him in 2 Sam 16:12, where he merely alludes to the possibility that the Lord will "look upon my iniquity" (so MT; LXX affliction) and "repay me with good."

[810] 2 Sam 16:13 also mentions Shimei's "throwing stones and flinging dust." Josephus inserts the reference to David's ignoring Shimei's provocations.

[811] In his mention of "the Jordan," Josephus agrees with the 2 LXX L manuscripts 19 and 108 in 2 Sam 16:14, whereas the other witnesses to that verse do not

[812] MT 2 Sam 16:14 has David "refreshing himself" upon his arrival, whereas LXX refers to the whole party doing so. Josephus' formulation highlights the king's solicitude for his supporters.

[813] 2 Sam 16:15-16a which mentions (v. 16a) the name of David's "friend," i.e. Hushai (see 7.203// 2 Sam 15:32). After the interlude featuring David's movements in 7.205-210, Josephus now returns to the scene in Jerusalem introduced at the end of 7.204.

[814] Compare 2 Sam 16:16b, where Hushai twice (MT; once, LXX) greets Absalom with the acclamation "Long live the king."

[815] Josephus expands Absalom's double question of 2 Sam 16:17 about Hushai's initiative (2 Sam 16:16) with a reference to the latter's "reputation," this underscoring how "out of character" his current move appears to be.

[816] Josephus prefaces the words of Hushai's response (2 Sam 16:18-19) with this editorial evaluation of them.

[817] See 2 Sam 16:18, where Hushai evokes the same 2 sources for Absalom's authority that he is now professing to recognize.

[818] See 2 Sam 16:19b, where Hushai declares his intention of "serving" Absalom as he had his father. Josephus' version has Hushai echo Absalom's challenge to him about his being David's "friend," with a particular reputation for "fidelity" in 7.211. The rhetoric Josephus attributes to Hushai here recalls Herod's argument before Augustus: his recent switch of sides is not,

over the present state of things, seeing that the kingship has not been transferred to another house, but has remained in the same one, now that the son has succeeded."[819]

At Ahithophel's urging, Absalom has intercourse with David's concubines

213. He persuaded in saying these things, for Apsalom had been suspicious of him.[820] When Apsalom then called Achitophel and took counsel with him about what he should do, he urged him to have intercourse with his father's concubines.[821] "For in that way," he said, "the people will come to believe that you are unreconcilable with him, and they will fight with great eagerness against your father.[822] For up to now, they had been anxious about assuming an open enmity, expecting that you will come to an agreement."[823] **214.** Persuaded by this counsel, Apsalom directed his servants to erect a tent for himself on top of the palace; entering this in the sight of the crowd, he had intercourse with his father's concubines.[824] These things happened in accordance with the prophecy of Nathas, which he had announced in advance, signifying to David his son's coming assault.[825]

Ahithophel urges immediate pursuit of David

(9.6) 215. Once Apsalom had done what Achitophel had urged him, he sought counsel from him a second time concerning the war against his father.[826] Achitophel then asked for 10,000 picked men,[827] promising both to kill his father and lead back alive those who were with him.[828] Then his kingship would, he said, be firmly established, with David no longer alive.[829]

Hushai's alternative proposal

216. Though pleased with this plan, Apsalom[830] also summoned Chousis, the chief friend of David (for thus he used to call him).[831] He disclosed Achitophel's plan to him, and inquired what he himself thought about it.[832]

---

the former tries to convince the latter, a matter of disloyalty to his previous patrons; rather he now intends to show Augustus the same loyalty he had previously displayed towards Antony (*War* 1.386-392). I owe this observation to Prof. Steve Mason.

[819] Josephus appends this closing statement of "satisfaction" by Hushai about how things have developed to his words as cited in 2 Sam 16:18-19.

[820] Together with the editorial comment at the end of 7.211 (see note to "prudent" at 7.211), this added remark about Hushai's persuasiveness frames Josephus' version of his answer in 7.212.

[821] See 2 Sam 16:20-21a. Cf. the notice on David's leaving his concubines behind in 7.199// 2 Sam 15:16.

[822] Josephus has Ahithophel spell out the meaning of his reference (2 Sam 16:21b) to Absalom's making himself "odious to" (MT; LXX shaming) his father with the proposed course of action: by so egregious a deed, he would render any rapprochement between himself and David impossible.

[823] Josephus appends this statement about the people's current stance to Ahithophel's proposal in 2 Sam 16:21.

[824] See 2 Sam 16:22, which Josephus prefaces with an allusion to the effect of Ahithophel's counsel.

[825] This fulfillment notice, alluding back to 7.152 (// 2 Sam 12:11-12), has no source equivalent. It takes the place of the parenthetical notice concerning Ahithophel's counsel being regarded as "the oracle of

God" by both David and Absalom of 16:23, which Josephus has anticipated in his remark about Ahithophel's astuteness in 7.202; see note to "advantageous" at 7.202.

[826] In 2 Sam 17:1 Ahithophel offers his 2nd suggestion unasked. Josephus' transitional phrase has Absalom take the initiative in requesting his further advice.

[827] Josephus' figure corresponds to that of LXX L 2 Sam 17:1b, whereas MT and LXX B read 12,000.

[828] Josephus focusses on these 2 core elements of Ahithophel's proposal in 2 Sam 17:1b-3a, leaving aside such additional details as David's present demoralized state (v. 2aα) and the image, used by Ahithophel in connection with his promise to bring all the people back to Absalom, of a bride coming to her husband's home (v. 3a).

[829] This affirmation replaces Ahithophel's statement of 2 Sam 17:3b that Absalom need eliminate only one man (David) in order for the entire people to be at peace.

[830] 2 Sam 17:4 mentions all the elders of Israel being pleased with Ahithophel's plan as well.

[831] See 2 Sam 17:5. Josephus' inserted reference to Hushai's title underscores the irony of the situation in which the latter, a supposed traitor to the king, will, in fact, prove himself David's "chief friend" by the fatal advice he gives Absalom.

[832] See 2 Sam 17:6.

Chousis, perceiving that if what Achitophel counseled were to happen, David would be in danger of being caught and killed, tried to propose an alternative plan.[833] **217.** "You are not ignorant," he said, "O king, of the courage of your father and of those with him, and that he has waged many wars and everywhere has come away triumphant over his foes. For the moment it is likely that he remains in camp—for he is a very capable general and will anticipate the designs of the enemies coming against him.[834] **218.** At evening, however, leaving his men, he will either hide himself in some valley or will lie in ambush at some rock.[835] When our men attack, his will fall back for a short time. But then, encouraged by the king's proximity to them, they will resist. As they are fighting, your father will suddenly appear and rouse their spirits for their dangers, while dismaying your men.[836]

219. Consider therefore my counsel and, realizing it to be the best, reject the plan of Achitophel.[837] Send then to the whole country of the Hebrews, calling them out for your campaign against your father.[838] Personally lead your force as its general against the enemy; do not entrust this to another.[839] **220.** For you might expect to easily be victorious, should you meet him with only a few men in the open country, while you yourself have many ten thousands, eager to display their solicitude and eagerness on your behalf.[840] But if your father lets himself be shut in by a siege, we shall raze that city by engines and subterranean devices."[841]

Hushai's plan adopted

221. In saying these things Chousis won more approval than Achitophel, for his plan was preferred by Apsalom to the latter's. It was God, however, who caused Chousis' counsel to seem better in Apsalom's mind.[842]

High priests dispatch their sons to David

(9.7) 222. Chousis then hurried to the high priests Sadok and Abiathar and told them of Achitophel's plan, as well as his own, and that it had been decided to do

---

[833] Josephus' remark about the realization that prompts Hushai's counter-proposal takes the place of his initial statement in 2 Sam 17:7, in which he calls Ahithophel's plan "not good"—an opening that might appear too blunt, especially after Absalom himself has been said to approve that plan in 17:4.

[834] See 2 Sam 17:8abα. Josephus leaves aside the biblical Hushai's image of David and his men as a bear bereft of her cubs (+ a sow snared in the wild, LXX B). His inserted reference to David's remaining in his camp "for the moment" sets up a contrast with what the king will do once evening comes (17:8bβ).

[835] See 2 Sam 17:8bβ-9a.

[836] Josephus recasts Hushai's words in 2 Sam 17:9b-10, where he speaks of the possibility that some of Absalom's men will be killed in combat, with the resultant reports of a rout generating panic even among his most courageous supporters. In so doing, he has Hushai highlight the threat posed by David himself.

[837] Josephus inserts this transitional exhortation within the 2 parts of Hushai's speech, i.e. his refutation of Ahithophel's proposal (7.217-218// 2 Sam 17:7-10) and the presentation of his own plan (7.219-220// 17:11-13). Whereas in 17:7 Hushai asserts that Ahithophel's advice is "not good," Josephus has him

declare that it is his own which is "best."

[838] Compare the figurative language of 2 Sam 17:11a, where Hushai urges that "all Israel from Dan to Beersheba" be assembled to Absalom like "the sand by the sea."

[839] Josephus accentuates Hushai's admonition of 2 Sam 17:11b that Absalom "go to battle in person."

[840] This assurance takes the place of Hushai's figurative language in 2 Sam 17:12, where he speaks of Absalom's forces lighting upon David "as the dew falls on the ground." Throughout his rendition of Hushai's speech in 7.217-220 (// 2 Sam 17:7-13), Josephus consistently either leaves aside or recasts its many images.

[841] In 2 Sam 17:13 Hushai refers to Absalom's forces using "ropes" to drag David's refuge city into the valley so that not even a pebble will remain. Josephus substitutes mention of the more elaborate siege procedures with which he was familiar from his own military experience.

[842] See 2 Sam 17:14. In reproducing the "theological commentary" of v. 14b, Josephus leaves aside its concluding indication of the purpose of the Lord's causing Ahithophel's plan to be rejected, i.e. "that he might bring evil upon Absalom." He thereby avoids attributing "evil" to God.

what he had urged.[843] He then directed that they send to David to report to him and to make clear the counsels [that had been given]. They were likewise to direct that he quickly cross the Jordan,[844] lest his son change his mind, decide to pursue and overtake, and catch him before he would be in security.[845]

223. The high priests had deliberately hidden their sons outside the city in order that they might report to David about what was being done.[846] They therefore sent a faithful female servant to them to relay what had been decided on by Apsalom and to order them to solicitously indicate these things to David.[847] **224.** They, for their part, did not delay or hesitate a moment, but received the commandments of their fathers as reverent and faithful ministers.[848] Judging speed and quickness to be the best kind of service, they hurried to join David.[849]

225. When they had gone two *stadia* from the city, some horsemen observed them and reported them to Apsalom.[850] He immediately sent men to arrest them. When they became aware of this, the high priests' sons right away turned aside from the road and headed to a certain village, not far from Hierosolyma, the name of which was Bocchores.[851] There they requested a certain woman to conceal them and provide for their security.[852]

Woman helps sons escape arrest

226. She lowered the youths down a well, on top of which she placed layers of wool.[853] Then, when their pursuers arrived and asked if she had observed them, she did not deny that she had seen them; once, however, they had taken a drink in her

---

[843] To Hushai's report in 2 Sam 17:15 Josephus adds the approval of his own proposal by Absalom. As in 7.216 (// 2 Sam 17:4), he leaves aside the role of the "elders of Israel" in the proceedings.

[844] Josephus omits Hushai's negative injunction of 2 Sam 17:16a that David not overnight at "the fords of the wilderness," while specifying that he is to cross "the Jordan." His version may be influenced by the LXX L plus, i.e. (David is to pass over) "the waters."

[845] In 2 Sam 17:16b Hushai warns David not to let himself and his people be "swallowed up," the subject of this action being left unspecified. Josephus inserts the reference to Absalom and the possibility of his reversing his endorsement of Hushai's own proposal, this making it imperative that David immediately put himself beyond his reach.

[846] 2 Sam 17:17a speaks of the priests' sons (on these see 7.200) waiting at "En-rogel." Josephus explains how they come to be in their current position.

[847] 2 Sam 17:17b speaks of the maidservant's general practice of coming and "telling" the priests' sons, given the impossibility of their own entering the city. Josephus has her come on this particular occasion to relay Hushai's message of 7.222.

[848] Josephus inserts this comment on the sons' reaction. Its positive qualification of the pair echoes his reference to them as David's "reliable ministers" in 7.200.

[849] Josephus elaborates the notice of 2 Sam 17:18aβ

about the sons' speedy departure with mention of their "judgment" that prompts this.

[850] Compare 2 Sam 17:18aα, where it is a "lad" who sees the pair and reports them to Absalom, this prompting their speedy departure. Josephus has their departure motivated, not by fear at having been reported, but rather, more loftily, by obedience to their fathers' commands; see 7.224.

[851] MT (2 Sam 17:18) בחורים (Eng.: "Bahurim") LXX B Βαορείμ; LXX L Βαιθχορρών; Josephus Βοκχόρος. Earlier (see 7.207), where 2 Sam 16:5 mentions "Bahurim" as a stopping place of the fugitive David, Josephus uses a different name for the site, i.e. "Choran"; see note to "Choran" at 7.207. Here in 7.225 he inserts the reference to the proximity of "Bocchores" to Jerusalem.

[852] This request has no counterpart in 2 Sam 17:18b-19, where, once the pair has descended into the well, the woman, on her own, conceals the opening. Here, as in what follows, Josephus goes beyond the Bible in accentuating the woman's stature as a "2nd Rahab"; see note to "them" at 7.226 and to "ways" at 7.227.

[853] In 2 Sam 17:18b the young men descend the well on their own. The witnesses for 17:19 offer various possibilities as to what substance (grain [MT], sand, dried fruit cakes [so LXX L]) was used by the woman to conceal their hiding place. Josephus' specification (wool) is unique to himself.

house, they went off again.[854] If, however, they made a quick pursuit, she predicted that they would overtake them.[855] When they then pursued for a long distance, but did not overtake them, they turned back.[856] **227.** Once the woman observed them setting off and that there was no longer any fear of the youths' arrest by them, she drew them up and appealed to them to proceed on the designated way.[857] They, employing much solicitude and speed in their journey, came to David and accurately disclosed to him everything planned by Apsalom.[858] He ordered those who were with him to cross the Jordan and, though it was already night, not to delay for that reason.[859]

David orders crossing of Jordan

Ahithophel commits suicide

(9.8) 228. Achitophel's plan having been rejected, he mounted his animal and set out for Gelmon, his native city.[860] Calling together all his servants, he told them what he had advised Apsalom and that, since he had not persuaded him, it was obvious that he would be annihilated within a short time. He further said that David would prevail and would recover his kingship.[861] **229.** He therefore said that it would be better that he remove himself from life, doing this freely and magnanimously, than to give himself up to David for punishment on account of his having supported Apsalom against him in everything.[862] When he had said these things, he went into the innermost part of his house and hanged himself.[863] Once Achitophel had sentenced himself to such a death,[864] his relations cut him down from the noose and buried him.[865]

---

[854] Josephus expatiates on the woman's answer as cited in 2 Sam 17:20bα, where she speaks of the pair's having "crossed the brook of water (MT)/ in haste (LXX L)." Her allusion to their having drunk in her house has a counterpart in OL.

[855] With this addition to the woman's response of 2 Sam 17:20bα Josephus establishes a parallel between her and Rahab, who in *Ant.* 5.9 (// Josh 2:6) avers that the Israelite spies can readily be apprehended if pursued.

[856] See 2 Sam 17:20bβ.

[857] Josephus continues to highlight the woman's role with this preface to 2 Sam 17:21, where she is not mentioned and where all attention goes to the initiatives of the priests' sons who, on their own, emerge from the well and go to David. Compare Josephus' presentation of Rahab in *Ant.* 5.11-12, where, once the pursuers have disappeared, she takes the initiative in bringing the spies down from the hiding place (the roof) where she had concealed them, and then urges them to return to their own place.

[858] See 2 Sam 17:21. Josephus underscores the pair's eagerness to fulfill their mission, while omitting their (presumptuous) "command" to David that he cross over quickly.

[859] Josephus recasts as a directive by David to those with him the notice of 2 Sam 17:22 that by daybreak the whole company had crossed the Jordan.

[860] Josephus, basing himself on his earlier reference in 7.197 (// 2 Sam 15:12 [where the place is called

"Gihon" in MT) to Ahithophel as the "Gelmonite," inserts the name of his hometown into the notice of 17:23aα on his departure thither.

[861] Josephus elaborates on the summary notice of 2 Sam 17:23aβ about Ahithophel's "setting his house in order." Specifically, he turns this into an address by him to his assembled household in which he first (accurately) predicts the outcome of Absalom's revolt, thereby demonstrating both the extent of his own wisdom (see 7.202) and Absalom's folly in rejecting this.

[862] With this conclusion to the speech he puts on Ahithophel's lips, Josephus has him prepare hearers and readers for his coming suicide and to spell out—as the Bible itself does not—his rationale for undertaking this.

[863] 2 Sam 17:23bα does not specify where Ahithophel hangs himself.

[864] This phrase lacks a biblical counterpart; it picks up on Ahithophel's previous speech to his servants announcing what he intends to do and the reason for this.

[865] Into the burial notice of 2 Sam 17:23bβ Josephus introduces a mention of those who perform the burial and their preliminary act of cutting him down. On the other hand, he passes over the source specification about Ahithophel's being buried "in the tomb of his father." Like the Bible, Josephus offers no evaluation of Ahithophel's suicide, just as he left Saul's similar deed without comment in *Ant.* 6.371.

230. Now David, having crossed the Jordan, as we said before,[866] came to The Camps,[867] a beautiful and very solid city.[868] All the leading men of the region received him most gladly, both out of compassion for his present flight and in honor of his previous success.[869] These were Berzelai[870] the Galadite, Seiphar[871] the dynastic ruler of Ammanitis,[872] and Macheir,[873] the chief of the Galadite area.[874]

Transjordanians welcome David

231. They bestowed on him and his [companions] a great abundance of necessities.[875] Neither covered beds[876] nor bread or wine were lacking. Likewise a large quantity of meats was supplied,[877] and a copious supply of things needed for the refreshment and nourishment of those already exhausted was provided.[878] **(10.1)**

232. This then was their situation.[879] Now Apsalom, having mustered a large army of the Hebrews against his father and crossed the Jordan river, encamped not far from The Camps in the Galadite country.[880] He appointed Amasa[881] general of his entire force in place of his relative Joab.[882] The former's father was Iethras,[883] and

Absalom crosses Jordan Amasa, Absalom's general

---

[866] See 7.227 // 2 Sam 17:22. After the "Ahithophel interlude" of 7.228-229 (// 2 Sam 17:23) Josephus now resumes his account of David's movements.

[867] Greek: Παρεμβολαί. Josephus shares this "translation" of the Hebrew place name "Mahanaim" of 2 Sam 17:24 (transliterated by LXX B as Μαναειμ) with LXX L. He mentioned the site previously as Ishbosheth's "capital" in 7.10 // 2 Sam 2:8.

[868] This qualification of the site lacks a counterpart in 2 Sam 17:24.

[869] Josephus appends his parallel to the account of David's reception in the Transjordan (2 Sam 17:27-29) directly to his mention of David's arrival at "The camps" (// 17:24a), reserving the sequence concerning Absalom's concurrent initiatives (// 17:24b-26) for a later moment; see 7.232. He likewise adds reference to the feelings of David's Transjordanian hosts.

[870] MT (2 Sam 17:27) ברזלי (Eng.: "Barzillai"); LXX BL Βερζελλεί; Josephus Βερζελαῖος. In the listing of 17:27 this figure is mentioned only in 3rd place; Josephus' "advancing" him to first position might reflect the fact that, of David's 3 Transjordanian hosts, only he will reappear in the subsequent course of the story. Josephus omits the name of his city, i.e. "Rogelim."

[871] MT (2 Sam 17:27) שבי (Eng.: "Shobi"); LXX B Ούεσβι; LXX L Σεφεεί; Josephus Σειφάρ. In 17:27 he is the first of the 3 figures to be mentioned.

[872] This designation takes the place of the more elaborate indications concerning "Shobi" given in 2 Sam 17:27, where he is called "son of Nahash from Rabbah of the Ammonites."

[873] MT (2 Sam 17:27) מכיר (Eng.: "Machir"); LXX BL Μαχείρ; Josephus Μάχειρος.

[874] This title for "Machir"—previously mentioned

by Josephus in 7.113 (// 2 Sam 9:4) as the guardian of Mephibosheth—substitutes for the name of his father ("Ammiel") and his city ("Lo-debar") given in 2 Sam 17:27.

[875] With this opening notice Josephus here sums up the long list of supplies brought David according to 2 Sam 17:28-29, underscoring the large quantities of everything provided.

[876] Like MT 2 Sam 17:28, Josephus lacks the LXX specification concerning the number, i.e. 10, of beds made available to David's forces.

[877] Josephus reduces the 13 items cited in 2 Sam 17:28 to 4, while adding a reference to "wine."

[878] This summary notice on the donated supplies takes the place of the realization attributed to David's hosts in 2 Sam 17:29b, i.e. that his men are "hungry, weary, and thirsty."

[879] Josephus rounds off his account of David's reception in the Transjordan (7.230-231) with this phrase.

[880] Josephus combines the data—previously passed over by him (see 7.230)—of 2 Sam 17:24b and 26 concerning Absalom's advance, appending to the latter verse the specification on the proximity of Absalom's camp to that of David.

[881] MT (2 Sam 17:25) עמשא (Eng.: "Amasa"); LXX B Ἀμεσσά; LXX L Ἀμεσσεί; Josephus Ἀμασᾶς.

[882] See 2 Sam 17:25a. Josephus appends the mention of Amasa being a relative of Joab. In what follows (// 2 Sam 17:25b), he will indicate that the men were cousins, sons of 2 sisters.

[883] MT (2 Sam 17:25) יתרא (Eng.: "Ithra"); LXX B Ἰοθόρ; LXX L Ἰεθέρ; Josephus Ἰέθρας. Josephus omits the gentilic of Amasa's father: the Israelite (MT)/ the Izreelite (LXX L)/ the Ishmaelite (LXX A and 1 Chr 2:17).

David divides up his army

his mother Abigaia[884] (she and Souria, the mother of Joab, were sisters of David).[885] **233.** When David mustered those who were with him, he found that they numbered about 4,000.[886] Deciding not to wait until Apsalom should come to him, he placed commanders of thousands and hundreds over these.[887] Dividing his army into three parts,[888] he entrusted one to the general Joab, the second to his brother Abessai, while he handed over the third division to his close associate and friend Esthai, who was from the city of Gitton.[889]

David restrained from going into battle

234. Although David wished to accompany them into battle,[890] his friends[891] did not permit him, restraining him in accordance with a very wise plan.[892] For if, they said, they were routed with him on hand, they would lose all good hope.[893] If one part of the force were defeated, however, they would flee to him with the remainder, and he would provide them with renewed strength.[894] The enemy too was likely to surmise that there was another army with him.[895]

David's words to army

235. Convinced by this advice, David decided to remain in The Camps.[896] Sending his friends and generals out against the enemy, he appealed to them to manifest their eagerness and fidelity, and, if they had ever obtained decent treatment from him, to remember this.[897] He also implored them, should they prevail, to spare his son Apsalom, so that he would not, with him dead, do himself some harm.[898] Then, after praying for their victory, he sent out the army.[899]

---

[884] MT (2 Sam 17:25) אֲבִיגַל (Eng.: "Abigail"); LXX and Josephus Ἀβιγαία.

[885] Josephus leaves aside the indication of 2 Sam 17:25b that Abigail was the daughter of "Nahash" (so MT LXX B; LXX L: Jesse), the sister of Zeruiah. In his presentation it is Abigail herself who is Zeruiah's sister. Josephus has already mentioned "Sarouia" as David's sister in *Ant.* 6.311.

[886] 2 Sam 18:1a does not specify the number of men "mustered" by David.

[887] See 2 Sam 18:1b, which Josephus prefaces with mention of David's "decision" that prompts him to organize his forces as he does.

[888] Josephus' explicit mention of this point reflects the opening plus of LXX L 2 Sam 18:2.

[889] See 2 Sam 18:2a. The 3rd of David's commanders was introduced by Josephus in 7.201 under the name of "Ethis (= MT 2 Sam 15:19 Ittai) the Gittite." Neither that earlier reference or the corresponding biblical passages designates him as David's "close associate and friend."

[890] See 2 Sam 18:2b, which quotes David's words to this effect.

[891] In 2 Sam 18:3 those responding to David are "the people."

[892] Josephus turns the people's opening words, forbidding David to go with them, of 2 Sam 18:3 into a (positive) editorial evaluation of the friends' response.

[893] This initial statement by the friends takes the place of the people's double affirmation in 2 Sam 18:3 that their flight or the loss of the lives of half of them

will be of no concern to the enemy.

[894] Josephus adapts the people's concluding words in 2 Sam 18:3, where they aver that David is worth 10,000 of themselves and that it is better that he send them help from (MT; LXX: to) the city.

[895] This final remark by the friends has no biblical counterpart. The meaning appears to be that the enemy, not finding David with the first detachment they engage, would conclude that there must be another such detachment with which he is present, and be intimidated by this realization. The tactical advice given David by Josephus' friends here has a counterpart in Josephus' approximate contemporary Onasander (*Strat.* 33), who counsels generals to stay back from the actual fighting. I owe this observation to Prof. Steve Mason.

[896] 2 Sam 18:4a quotes David's word resigning himself to what the people "think best."

[897] This exhortation by David to battlefield heroism lacks a counterpart in 2 Sam 18:4b, where David simply watches as his forces march forth. Josephus' insertion underscores David's concern, as the great general he is, to provide his men with the encouragement they need prior to battle. It likewise attenuates the impression left by the biblical presentation (see 18:5) that David's only concern at this critical moment is with the welfare of his rebel son Absalom.

[898] See 2 Sam 18:5a. Josephus intensifies the royal appeal by having David refer to the harm he might do himself should Absalom be killed.

[899] This inserted notice, highlighting the king's piety, takes the place of the mention of the whole army's

(10.2) 236. When Joab had drawn up his force opposite the enemy in a great plain hemmed in at the rear by an oak forest, Apsalom too led out his army against him.[900] When battle was joined, great deeds of might and daring were performed by both sides. The one side exposed itself to danger and employed the utmost eagerness in order that David might recover his kingship. The other side did not hesitate either to do or endure anything so that Apsalom would not be deprived of this [the kingship] and pay the penalty to his father, being punished for what he had dared to do. **237.** [They acted in this way also] so that, being in the majority, they would not be overcome by the few [men] and generals Joab had with him—for that would be a great shame for them. David's soldiers, on the other hand, were ambitious to defeat so many tens of thousands. The conflict was fierce, and David's men were victorious, being superior both in vigor and military expertise.[901]

Absalom defeated

238. Following those who fled through the oak-forests and ravines, they took and did away with many, so that more fell fleeing than they did fighting, for about 20,000 fell on that day.[902] All David's men made a rush against Apsalom, for he was obvious to them, given his handsomeness and height.[903]

Absalom's flight

239. Anxious that the enemy might capture him, he mounted the royal mule and fled.[904] He was carried along speedily and, being lifted up as a result of [the animal's] jerking motions, became entangled by his hair in a gnarled tree that extended far out with its great branches, and so was left unexpectedly suspended.[905] His animal, speeding along as though it were still bearing the master it had carried, proceeded further, while Apsalom, who was suspended from the branches, was captured [by the enemy].[906]

240. Seeing this, one of David's soldiers disclosed it to Joab.[907] When the general said that he would have given him fifty shekels had he struck and killed Apsalom,[908]

Joab kills Absalom

---

hearing David's injunction to his generals to spare Absalom in 2 Sam 18:5b (to which Josephus will allude in 7.240).

[900] 2 Sam 18:6 localizes the battle in the "forest of Ephraim" (MT LXX B; LXX L: Maainan) and does not mention Absalom's countermove.

[901] The above sequence, featuring the state of mind of the 2 armies, represents an elaboration of the rather jejune and anti-climactic notice (2 Sam 18:7a) on the outcome of the long-awaited battle: "the men of Israel were defeated by the servants of David."

[902] 2 Sam 18:7b-8 does not explicitly mention such a flight/pursuit, and speaks of the "forest devouring more than the sword."

[903] In 2 Sam 18:9aα it is Absalom who chances upon (MT; LXX L: was far ahead of) David's troops. Josephus' inserted reference to the rebel's appearance harks back to 7.189// 2 Sam 14:25.

[904] Josephus amplifies the mention of Absalom "riding upon his mule" of 2 Sam 18:9aβ with an allusion to the prince's anxiety and flight and the royal status of the mule.

[905] In 2 Sam 18:9bα it is Absalom's "head" that gets caught in the tree branches. Josephus' description echoes the mention of the prince's abundant hair in 7.189 // 2 Sam 14:26. Similarly, *b. Soṭah* 9b affirms that that which was the source of Absalom's pride, i.e. his hair, became the cause of his downfall during his flight.

[906] In the above reading, which follows the text printed by Niese, Josephus amplifies the notice about the mule's proceeding on its way of 2 Sam 18:9bβ with mention of Absalom's falling prey to David's men. The words "by the enemy" are, however, missing in Lat and omitted by Marcus who translates "(the branches) which held him up."

[907] See 2 Sam 18:10.

[908] In 2 Sam 18:11 Joab asks the man why he did not kill Absalom and affirms that he would have rewarded him with both money and a "girdle" had he done so. Josephus' figure for the reward money agrees with that given in 4QSam[a] and LXX L as against the 10 "pieces of silver" of MT and LXX B. His explicit mention of "shekels" has a counterpart in LXX L.

he replied: "Not even if you were willing to bestow a thousand on me, would I have done this to my master's son, particularly since all of us heard him asking us to spare the young man."[909]

241. Joab then directed him to show him where he had seen Apsalom hanging;[910] at that, he killed him, shooting him in the heart.[911] Joab's weapon-bearers, who stood in a circle around the tree, then cut the corpse down.[912] **242.** They tossed this into a deep, gaping chasm and covered it with stones, so that it was filled in and took on the appearance and dimensions of a tomb.[913] Sounding the signal for retreat, Joab restrained his own soldiers from pursuing the enemy force, thus sparing his compatriots.[914] **(10.3) 243.** Apsalom had erected a pillar of marble stone in the Royal Valley, two *stadia* distant from Hierosolyma.[915] He called this his own "hand,"[916] saying that, even if his children should be destroyed, his name would remain on the pillar.[917] For he had three sons, as well as one daughter, named Thomara, as we have said before.[918] **244.** Once she was married to Solomon's son Roboam, a son, Abias, was born who succeeded to the kingship. About these matters we shall speak later, at the appropriate point in our narrative.[919] Now after Apsalom's death, the people were dispersed to their homes.[920]

(10.4) 245. Achimas, the son of Sadok the high priest, approached Joab and asked

Absalom's burial and progeny

Ahimaaz (Achimas) and the Cushite (Chousis) dispatched to David

---

[909] See 2 Sam 18:12, which itself harks back to the notice—previously passed over by Josephus (see 7.235)—of 18:5b about the whole army's hearing David's command to his generals to spare Absalom. Josephus omits the man's further affirmation (18:13) that had he killed Absalom and gotten into trouble with David for this, Joab would not have intervened to protect him.

[910] In MT 2 Sam 18:14a Joab responds that he will "not waste time" with the man, whereas in LXX L he avers "I shall begin then with you." Josephus has him use the man to lead him to Absalom.

[911] Josephus' allusion to Joab's "shooting" Absalom seems to reflect the reading of LXX L in 2 Sam 18:14b, which speaks of his using 3 "darts" to dispatch him, whereas MT LXX B refer to 3 "sticks."

[912] According to 2 Sam 18:15, Joab's 10 "armor bearers" strike and kill Absalom. This initiative might appear otiose after the mention of Joab himself piecing him through the heart with 3 darts/sticks in 18:14 (see previous note). Josephus accordingly assigns them a different task, i.e. removing the already dead Absalom from the tree.

[913] See 2 Sam 18:17a, which Josephus amplifies with mention of the tomb-like appearance of the stone-heap. He "holds over" the attached (disruptive) notice on the Israelites' flight to their homes of 18:17b until the end of 7.244.

[914] See 2 Sam 18:16, to which Josephus appends the reference to the "sparing of his compatriots" by Joab—a rare positive touch in his portrayal of this figure. He reverses the sequence of 18:16-17a, where Joab's sounding of the retreat is mentioned prior to the

burial of Absalom.

[915] See 2 Sam 18:18a. On the "Royal Valley," see McCarter 1984: 408 *ad loc.* Josephus specifies the material of the "pillar" and the site's distance from Jerusalem.

[916] See the etiological notice of 2 Sam 18:18bβ: "it is called the hand (Tg.: place; RSV: monument) of Absalom to this day."

[917] Compare 2 Sam 18:18bα, where Absalom states that he erected the pillar, given that he had "no son to keep his name in remembrance." Josephus' rewording of this statement has in view the discrepancy between it and 2 Sam 14:27 (// 7.190), which affirms that Absalom had 3 sons. Jewish tradition resolves the "contradiction" on the supposition either that Absalom's sons had predeceased him (so Kimchi) or that "no son" in 18:18 means "no worthy son" (so *b. Soṭah* 11a); see Rappaport 1930: 131, #234.

[918] The reference is to 7.190, which, unlike the source parallel (2 Sam 14:27), does not name Absalom's daughter. Josephus draws the name here in 7.243 from that earlier biblical text.

[919] This appended notice on the future career of Absalom's daughter picks up on and echoes Josephus' statements concerning her in 7.190, themselves drawn from the LXX plus in 2 Sam 14:27. Compare *Ant.* 8.248, where, in line with 1 Kgs 15:2, he designates the wife of Rehoboam and mother of Abias, not as Tamar herself, but rather as her daughter "Machane," the grand-daughter of Absalom.

[920] This is Josephus' delayed equivalent to 2 Sam 18:17b; see note to "tomb" at 7.242.

him to allow him to go to David and report the victory and bring the good news that he had obtained the help and providential care of God.[921] **246.** Joab, however, said that it was not appropriate that he, who had always been a messenger of good news, should now go off and disclose to the king the death of his son.[922] Asking him to remain, he called Chousis, to whom he assigned the task of reporting to the king whatever he himself had seen.[923]

247. But when Achimas again asked him to confide the message to him, on the understanding that he would only report the victory, but would keep quiet about the death of Apsalom,[924] Joab permitted him to go to David.[925] Achimas then took the shorter route (of which only he knew) and got there before Chousis.[926]

248. Now David was sitting between the gates, waiting for someone to come to him from the battle and report about this.[927] One of the watchmen saw Achimas running, but was not yet able to recognize who it was. He told [David] that he saw someone coming towards him.[928] **249.** The king said that he was a messenger of good news;[929] when, shortly afterwards, the watchman disclosed to him that someone else was following, David said that he too was a messenger.[930] The watchman, seeing Achimas who was already near, indicated that it was the son of the high priest Sadok who was running towards him.[931] David, for his part, was overjoyed, saying that he was a messenger of good news who was bearing [a report of] successes from the battle.[932]

Achimas' report to David

(10.5) 250. As the king was saying these things, Achimas appeared and paid homage to the king.[933] When David inquired about the battle, Achimas announced the good news of victory and triumph.[934] Upon David's further asking if he had any-

---

[921] See 2 Sam 18:19. Josephus' specification that Ahimaaz addressed his word "to Joab" reflects the plus of LXX L. This figure was introduced by Josephus in 7.201.

[922] Josephus clarifies Joab's rationale for rebuffing Ahimaaz' request according to 2 Sam 18:20, where he is simply told that he cannot carry a message that day "because the king's son is dead." In Josephus' presentation, Ahimaaz is so identified with the bearing of good news that he would be the wrong man to bring the bad news of Absalom's death to David.

[923] See 2 Sam 18:21. Like LXX BL Josephus turns the ethnic designation of MT ("the Cushite") into a proper name, i.e. "Chousis," the friend of David (and purported traitor) introduced in 7.203.

[924] Josephus expands Ahimaaz' renewed request (2 Sam 18:22a) with a statement by him that picks up on Joab's earlier explanation (7.246) as to why it would be inappropriate for him to carry bad news to David. Ahimaaz now declares that he will only deliver the good news that is his trademark.

[925] Josephus compresses and simplifies the sequence of 2 Sam 18:22b-23a, where Joab first tries to dissuade Ahimaaz, warning him that he will get no reward for the news he wishes to bring (v. 22b), but then, in the face of Ahimaaz' continued insistence, tells him to "run" (v. 23a).

[926] 2 Sam 18:23b speaks of Ahimaaz' taking "the

circular route" and outrunning the Cushite. Josephus inserts an explanation as to why only Ahimaaz, and not also "Chousis," took the shorter route.

[927] Josephus expands 2 Sam 18:24a with mention of the purpose of David's "sitting" where he does.

[928] See 2 Sam 18:24b-25a. Josephus introduces the reference to the lookout's not recognizing Ahimaaz, this explaining why he does not identify him by name to the king. His specification that the lookout saw the man running "towards him" reflects the LXX BL plus at the end of v. 24b.

[929] From David's statement in 2 Sam 18:25bα Josephus omits its opening words, i.e. "if he is alone," whose connection with what follows ("there are tidings in his mouth") is not evident.

[930] See the (2nd) exchange between lookout and king reported in 2 Sam 18:26.

[931] See 2 Sam 18:27a.

[932] Compare David's reply in 2 Sam 18:27b, where he begins by designating Ahimaaz as "a good man." Josephus has the king focus not on the ("good") person of the messenger but rather on the good news he brings.

[933] See 2 Sam 18:28a. Josephus' reference to Ahimaaz' "appearing" stands closer to LXX L's opening verb ("he approached") than to the "he cried out" of MT LXX B.

[934] In 2 Sam 18:28b Ahimaaz takes the initiative in reporting his news; in Josephus he waits until asked by

thing to say about his son,[935] he said that he himself had rushed to him immediately, once the enemy was in flight. He had, however, heard a great noise from those pursuing Apsalom, but had not been able to learn more concerning it, due to his having been sent by Joab to hurry to disclose the victory.[936]

Chousis' report   **251.** When Chousis too arrived, paid homage, and indicated the victory,[937] David asked about his son. "May it happen to your enemies," he replied, "as it did to Apsalom."[938]

David's lament for Absalom   **252.** This word did not allow either David or his soldiers to rejoice in their victory—great though it was.[939] Going up to the highest point of the city,[940] David lamented for his son, beating his breast and tearing out his hair, and totally disfiguring himself.[941] He cried out, "My son, would that death had come upon me and that I had died along with you."[942] For by nature he was affectionate and quite sympathetic to Apsalom.[943]

Joab remonstrates with David   **253.** When the army and Joab heard that the king was mourning for his son in this way, they were ashamed to enter the city in the manner of victors. All, rather, were dejected and tearful, as though they were coming from a defeat.[944]

254. As the king was bemoaning his son with his face veiled,[945] Joab came into him and comforted him: "O master,"[946] he said, "in doing this, you are unconsciously slandering yourself, because you seem to hate those who love you and who are in danger for the sake of you and your family, while you cherish your greatest enemies and yearn for those who are no more, having died as a punishment.[947] **255.** For if Apsalom had prevailed and gotten secure hold of the kingship, none of us would be left surviving. Rather, all of us, beginning with you and your children, would have been annihilated in a horrible way. The enemy would not have lamented over us, but would have rejoiced and punished those who felt pity for our calamities.[948] You, however, are not ashamed of doing these things on behalf of one who

---

the king. From his report Josephus omits the reference to God as the author of the victory.

[935] See 2 Sam 18:29a.

[936] Josephus expatiates on Ahimaaz' answer (2 Sam 18:29b), likewise reversing its order, in which Joab's sending him is mentioned prior to his own being unable to investigate the uproar at the scene. Josephus' reference to Ahimaaz' "hearing" this uproar corresponds to LXX L, in contrast to MT and LXX B, where he speaks of "seeing" it. Josephus omits David's appended order that Ahimaaz take his place and the latter's doing so, 18:30.

[937] See 2 Sam 18:31. Josephus adds the reference to Chousis' paying homage, thereby paralleling him with Ahimaaz (see 7.250// 18:28a). As he did with Ahimaaz' report (7.250, cf. 18:28b), Josephus omits the invocation of the Deity from that of Chousis.

[938] See 2 Sam 18:32.

[939] Josephus adds this transitional formula, foreshadowing the emotional state of both king and army in what follows.

[940] 2 Sam 19:1a (MT; Eng. 18:33a) depicts David ascending to "the chamber over the gate."

[941] Josephus embellishes the summary reference to David's "weeping" in 2 Sam 19:1a (Eng. 18:33a). He thereby accentuates the intensity of the king's grief.

[942] See 2 Sam 19:1b (Eng: 18:33b).

[943] Josephus appends this remark explaining why David reacts as he does to the death of his rebel son.

[944] Josephus here compresses the circumstantial sequence of 2 Sam 19:2-4 (Eng: 19:1-3) with, e.g., its double mention of the king's grief becoming known.

[945] See 2 Sam 19:5 (Eng: 19:4), from which Josephus omits the repetition of David's words of 19:1 (Eng: 18:33), already reproduced by him in 7.252.

[946] In introducing Joab's intervention (// 2 Sam 19:6 [Eng. 19:5]), Josephus portrays him as acting more sympathetically and respectfully than does his biblical counterpart with his added reference to his "comforting" the king and his address to him as "master."

[947] Josephus compresses Joab's opening words as reported in 2 Sam 19:6-7a (Eng: 19:5-6a) with, e.g., its extended catalogue (19:6) of David's family members whose lives David's "servants" have saved, only to have David himself "cover their faces with shame." He likewise reverses the sequence of 19:7a, where Joab speaks first of those whom David "loves" (i.e. those who hate him) and then of those he "hates" (i.e. those who love him).

[948] For this part of Joab's discourse, Josephus elaborates on the general's evocation (2 Sam 19:7 [Eng. 19:6]bα) of the hypothetical case ("if...") of Absalom's

is all the more your enemy because, though he was your son, he was thus impious.[949]

256. Cease then from this wrongful grief.[950] Go out to be seen by your own soldiers and thank them for the victory and their eagerness for the struggle.[951] Otherwise, if you persist in what you are now doing, I shall this very day convince the people to revolt against you and hand the kingship over to someone else.[952] Then I shall truly make your mourning a most bitter one."[953]

257. By saying these things, Joab diverted the king from his grief and got him thinking about public affairs.[954] For David, having changed his clothes and made himself presentable to be seen by the crowd, sat at the gates[955] so that the whole people heard, rushed to him, and greeted him. This is how matters stood.[956]

David appears before army

(11.1) 258. Now when those of the Hebrews who had been with Apsalom returned from the battle and were back in their individual homes,[957] they sent round to their cities, recalling how David had benefitted them and the freedom he had conferred, rescuing them in many great wars.[958] **259.** They reproached themselves because they had expelled him from his kingship and handed this over to another,[959] and likewise because, now that the leader appointed by them was dead,[960] they were not appealing to David to desist from his wrath and be favorable towards them, and, having recovered his kingship, to take care of their affairs, as he had earlier.[961]

Israelites desire David's restoration

260. These matters were then continually being announced to David.[962] He,

David dispatches priests to Judahites and Amasa

---

being alive and all David's men dead at this moment. The elaboration, *inter alia*, reminds David that Absalom would not be mourning for him if he were in the former's position.

[949] This concluding charge replaces the final words of 2 Sam 19:7 (Eng. 19:6) where Joab avers that if Absalom were alive and all David's supporters dead, the king "would be pleased." Joab's characterization of Absalom's behavior as "impious" picks up on David's own references to his son's "impiety" in 7.198, 209.

[950] This exhortation has no direct counterpart in Joab's speech of 2 Sam 19:6-7 (Eng. 19:5-6).

[951] Josephus has Joab spell out what David should say to his soldiers when he goes out to address them—as the general calls on him to do in 2 Sam 19:8 (Eng. 19:7)aα.

[952] Josephus accentuates and personalizes Joab's conditional warning as compared with 2 Sam 19:8 (Eng. 19:7)aβ, where Joab simply avers that "not a man will stay with you this night," without any reference to his own role in the process of David's threatened abandonment.

[953] This concluding warning substitutes for Joab's assertion in 2 Sam 19:8 (Eng. 19:7)b that David's abandonment by his supporters would be the worst evil ever to befall him. Once again (see previous note), the Josephan Joab underscores his own part in bringing about the calamities with which he threatens David.

[954] Josephus adds this transitional notice on the salutary effect of Joab's speech upon David.

[955] See 2 Sam 19:9 (Eng. 19:8)a. Josephus inserts the reference to David's changing his clothes (or "ap-

pearance" as Marcus *ad loc.* translates)—something that would be necessary after the king's "self-disfigurement" as described in 7.252.

[956] In comparison with 2 Sam 19:9 (Eng.19:8)bα, Josephus accentuates the enthusiasm of the people's response to David's initiative. He appends the concluding notice about the outcome of the affair.

[957] See 2 Sam 19:9 (Eng. 19:8)bβ, which itself picks up on the reference to the Israelites' flight to their homes in 18:17b (// 7.244).

[958] Cf. 2 Sam 19:10 (Eng. 19:9)a, where the returnees send through "all the tribes of Israel," recalling David's past "delivering" of them, from the Philistines in particular.

[959] Josephus heightens the self-critical character of the Israelites' references to David's flight and their "anointing" of Absalom in 2 Sam 19:10 (Eng. 19:9)b-11 (Eng. 19:10)aα. In his presentation they confess that they expelled David and "reproach themselves" both for this and their appointment of Absalom. Here again, Josephus avoids a source reference to a royal "anointing."

[960] See 2 Sam 19:11 (Eng. 19:10)aβ.

[961] Josephus embellishes the Israelites' concluding words in 2 Sam 19:11 (Eng. 19:10)b, where they simply ask why "you" (i.e. their fellow Israelites) are "not saying anything" about bringing David back. In so doing, he accentuates their desire to see the king return to them and makes their failure to ask David to resume office an additional ground for communal self-reproach.

[962] Josephus' positioning of this notice at this point reflects its placement in LXX BL, i.e. at the end of 2

nevertheless, sent to Sadok and Abiathar, the high priests, so that they might say to the chiefs of the tribe of Iouda that it was to their shame that other tribes were designating David king before themselves, "particularly because you are his relatives and share a common blood with him."[963] **261.** He ordered them to say the same things to the general Amasa because he, although he was the son of his sister, was not persuading the crowd to give the kingship back to him.[964] Amasa, he said, might expect from him not only reconciliation—for this had already happened—but also that generalship of the entire people that Apsalom too had conferred upon him.[965]

Delegations to David

262. The high priests spoke both to the rulers of the tribe and to Amasa, whom, by telling him the king's words, they persuaded to undertake efforts on his behalf.[966] He, for his part, persuaded his tribe to immediately send messengers to David to urge him to return to his own kingship.[967] All the Israelites did the same, being urged on by Amasa.[968]

(11.2) 263. Once the messengers came to him, David went to Hierosolyma.[969] The tribe of Iouda went ahead of all the others to the Jordan river to meet the king.[970] Also [on hand were] Samouis, the son of Gera, along with 1,000 men whom he brought from the tribe of Benjamin and Siba, the freedman of Saoul, accompanied by his sons—who numbered fifteen—and twenty servants.[971]

Shimei pardoned by David

264. These, along with the tribe of Iouda, bridged the river so that the king might readily cross over together with his own men.[972] When David arrived at the Jordan, the tribe of Iouda greeted him.[973] As he was ascending the bridge, Samouis prostrated himself and grasped his feet.[974] He asked him to pardon his offenses against

---

Sam 19:11 (Eng. 19:10), whereas in MT it concludes 19:12 (Eng. 19:11).

[963] See 2 Sam 19:12-13 (Eng. 19:11-12). Josephus' rendition underscores the wrongfulness of Judah's lack of initiative and speaks of the kinship between David and the tribe in terms, not of common "bone and flesh," but rather of a shared "blood."

[964] 2 Samuel 19 says nothing of such a reproach, which the 2 priests are to convey to Amasa from David. Josephus' insertion on the matter picks up on his introductory presentation of Amasa and his receiving the command of the rebel Absalom's forces in 7.232 (// 2 Sam 17:25).

[965] Cf. 2 Sam 19:14 (Eng. 19:13). From David's words for Amasa there, Josephus eliminates the opening oath formula, while adding the assurance that David has already forgiven Amasa for his part in Absalom's rebellion and the reference to the former's appointment by the latter (see 7.232// 2 Sam 17:25).

[966] Josephus supplies this notice on the effect of the messengers' words on Amasa.

[967] 2 Sam 19:15 (Eng. 19:14) MT and LXX B state that "he (David?, Amasa [so LXX L]?) swayed the heart of all the men of Judah," with the result that they asked David and "all his servants" to return. Josephus follows the specification of LXX L about Amasa being the one whose "influence" with the Judeans prevailed.

[968] This notice has no equivalent in 2 Samuel 19 (where it is only in v. 42 (Eng. v. 41) that the Israelites

approach David). Here too (see previous note) Josephus goes beyond the Bible in highlighting Amasa's initiatives on David's behalf, as well as his persuasive abilities, which convince not only Judah but also (all) Israel.

[969] 2 Sam 19:16 (Eng. 19:15)aα represents David as returning "to the Jordan." Josephus' formulation has the king's ultimate goal in view.

[970] See 2 Sam 19:16 (Eng. 19:15)b. Josephus omits the specification that the Judeans stationed themselves "at Gilgal" for their meeting with the king.

[971] See 2 Sam 19:17-18 (Eng. 19:16-17). On "Samouis," see 7.207-210; on "Siba," see 7.111-116, 205-206.

[972] 2 Samuel 19 does not mention such a bridge-building activity by Shimei and Ziba in conjunction with the Judeans; compare 19:19 (Eng. 19:18)a, where the pair "crosses the ford to bring over David and his household." In *Ant.* 5.16 Josephus interjected a notice on the absence of bridges over the Jordan at the time of Joshua's invasion of the land. Apparently, the Jordan was, for Josephus, still without bridges in David's reign; this necessitated the building of one to facilitate David's passage, as related here in 7.264.

[973] This greeting of David by the Judeans lacks a biblical parallel.

[974] In 2 Sam 19:19 (Eng. 19:18)b Shimei "falls down before" David, who is about to cross the Jordan. Josephus' version of this event echoes the mention of

him and not be resentful towards him, nor, now that he was back in authority, to look to his punishment first of all.[975] Let him rather keep in mind that he, having changed his mind about the offenses he had committed, had hurried to be the first to come to him.[976]

265. As he was imploring and entreating David's mercy in this way, Abessai the brother of Joab said: "Shall you not die for having defamed him whom God appointed to rule as king?"[977] David, however, turning to him, said: "Will you not desist, O sons of Sarouia?[978] Do not stir up new troubles and revolts for us, in addition to the earlier ones.[979] **266.** For you ought not to be ignorant[980] that today I am inaugurating my kingship. Therefore, I swear that I shall forego the punishment of all those who have acted impiously and shall not requite any offender.[981] "And you," he said, "O Samouis, be of good cheer and do not be anxious that you will be killed."[982] Having paid him homage, Samouis went on ahead of him.[983]

(11.3) 267. Memphibosthos, the grandson of Saoul, also met him.[984] He was wearing soiled clothes and his hair was long and unkempt.[985] For, following David's flight, he had, in his grief, neither cut his hair, nor cleaned his clothes, condemning himself to this misfortune in response to David's change [of fortune].[986] He had also been wrongfully slandered to David by his overseer Siba.[987]

Mephibosheth's self-defense to David

268. When he had greeted David and paid him homage,[988] the king began to in-

---

the "bridging" of the Jordan at the start of 7.264.

[975] See 2 Sam 19:20 (Eng. 19:19) with its double appeal for pardon by Shimei, from which Josephus omits the allusion to the occasion of his offense, i.e. during David's flight from Jerusalem.

[976] See 2 Sam 19:21 (Eng. 19:20). Josephus generalizes Shimei's specific claim to have been the first "of all the house of Joseph" to approach the king on his return.

[977] See 2 Sam 19:22 (Eng. 19:21). Here too, Josephus takes care to reword the phrase "the Lord's anointed" used by Abishai in reference to David.

[978] As in the case of David's earlier, identical response to Abishai in 2 Sam 16:10a (// 7.209), Josephus here reformulates the king's obscure opening question of 19:23 (Eng. 19:22)a: "what have I to do with you, you sons of Zeruiah?"

[979] Josephus embellishes David's allusion to the sons of Zeruiah being "an adversary" to him (2 Sam 19:23 [Eng. 19:22]a), spelling out what their playing such a role involves.

[980] In making the sons of Zeruiah the subjects of this verb Josephus aligns himself with the "you (pl.) know" of LXX L 2 Sam 19:23 (Eng. 19:22)bβ as against MT and LXX B, where David refers to his own ("I") knowing that he is king of Israel.

[981] This statement by David corresponds to the king's rhetorical question in 2 Sam 19:23 (Eng. 19:22)bα ("shall any one be put to death in Israel this day?"), where it precedes his further rhetorical question about knowing that he is king over Israel this day in 19:23 (Eng. 19:22)bβ; see previous note. David's dec-

laration here is reminiscent of the victorious Saul's swearing not to permit the execution of those who had earlier opposed his kingship in *Ant.* 6.82.

[982] See 2 Sam 19:24 (Eng. 19:23)a, where David simply informs Shimei that he will not be put to death.

[983] This notice on Shimei's response to David's words takes the place of the king's "oath" to him in 2 Sam 19:24 (Eng. 19:23)b, confirming his promise that Shimei will not "die." See, however, 7.388, where Josephus, following 1 Kgs 2:8, does have the dying David allude to the "pledge" Shimei obtained from him that he would not be harmed "at that time"; cf. note to "vengeance" at 7.388.

[984] MT 2 Sam 19:25 (Eng. 19:24)a calls Mephibosheth simply "son of Saul"; in LXX BL he is "son of Jonathan, son of Saul." On the triangular exchange between David, Mephibosheth and Ziba in 7.267-271 (// 2 Sam 19:25-31[Eng. 19:24-30]), see Begg 1998g: 174-78.

[985] 2 Sam 19:25 (Eng. 19:24)b adds that Mephibosheth had "not dressed his feet" (+ and cared for his hands, LXX L), and refers to his not having trimmed his beard/mustache rather than his hair.

[986] With this added comment concerning Mephibosheth's actions, Josephus vouches for the sincerity of his subsequent protestations of attachment to David in a way the Bible itself does not.

[987] In 2 Sam 19:28 (Eng. 19:27)a (// 7.269), Mephibosheth claims to have been slandered by Ziba. Anticipating the claim, Josephus also invests it with his own authority as narrator: Mephibosheth had in fact been slandered to the king; see 7.206 (// 2 Sam 16:3b).

[988] 2 Sam 19:26(25)a does not mention Mephi-

quire why he had not accompanied him at that time and shared in his flight.[989] He then said that this was the wrong [done him] by Siba. For, when he had directed him to make ready for his departure, he had not obeyed, and disregarded him as though he were some slave.[990] **269.** "If, however, I had healthy legs and were able to use these for flight, I would not have been far from you.[991] Not only in this, however, did he do wrong to my piety towards you, master; he likewise maliciously denigrated me and told lies about me.[992] I know, however, that your just mind that loves the truth—which the Deity also wishes to be strong—will not approve of these things.[993] **270.** For although you were exposed to much suffering by my grandfather and our whole family was liable to destruction because of him,[994] you, on the contrary, were moderate and kind, particularly in making yourself forget all these things, when you could very well have remembered them and had the authority to punish them. Instead, you considered me your friend and had me daily at your table; I was in no way different from the most honored of your relatives."[995]

David divides up property between Mephibosheth and Ziba

271. When he said these things, David decided neither to punish Memphibosthos nor to condemn Siba as one who had lied about him.[996] Rather, he told the former that, because he had not come with Siba, he had awarded everything to the latter.[997] He promised, however, to pardon him and directed that half of the property be given back to him.[998] Memphibosthos, for his part, said: "Let Siba have everything, for I

---

bosheth's "paying homage" to David; Josephus has him do so, as had the suppliant Shimei before him (7.264// 2 Sam 19:19 [Eng. 19:18]b). He omits the problematic source indication that Mephibosheth came "to Jerusalem" for his meeting with the king, given that the latter will only arrive in Jerusalem at a much later point; see 2 Sam 20:3.

[989] See 2 Sam 19:26 (Eng. 19:25)b.

[990] In 2 Sam 19:27 (Eng. 19:26) Mephibosheth complains of being "deceived" by Ziba. Josephus' reference to his having "directed" Ziba to prepare for his departure corresponds to the LXX BL reading, whereas in MT Mephibosheth claims that he intended to saddle the ass himself. The allusion to Ziba's insolent treatment of his master takes the place of the biblical Mephibosheth's assertion about his planned accompaniment of David once his mount had been prepared.

[991] With this statement Josephus spells out the import of Mephibosheth's reminding David that he is "lame" at the end of 2 Sam 19:27 (Eng. 19:26): that condition precluded his accompanying David on foot—as he otherwise certainly would have done.

[992] See 2 Sam 19:28 (Eng. 19:27) and cf. note on "Siba" at 7.267. Josephus underscores the falsity of Ziba's charges by having Mephibosheth invoke his "piety" (Greek: εὐσέβεια) towards David.

[993] This statement of confidence by Mephibosheth replaces his designation of David as one "like an angel of God" in 2 Sam 19:28 (Eng. 19:27)b; Josephus earlier avoided the wise woman of Tekoa's use of such "angel language" for David in his version of 2 Sam 14:17 (cf. 14:20) in 7.183. The 2 terms applied to David by

Mephibosheth here ("just," "[loving] truth") occur together in Josephus' own remark about the king in 7.110.

[994] Josephus elaborates on Mephibosheth's allusion to his father's "house" all being "doomed to death" before David in 2 Sam 19:29 (Eng. 19:28)a.

[995] Josephus greatly embellishes Mephibosheth's summary mention of his having been given a place at David's table in 2 Sam 19:29 (Eng. 19:28)bα (even while passing over the rhetorical question about his not having any further right to appeal to the king of 19:29 [Eng. 19:28]bβ). He thereby underscores the contrast between what Mephibosheth deserved and what he actually received from the magnanimous David. The reference to David's treating him like an honored relative recalls 7.116.

[996] Josephus inserts this notice on David's (interior) decision, this involving the king's realization that Ziba had indeed spoken falsely of Mephibosheth—as both the latter (7.269) and Josephus himself (7.267) have affirmed.

[997] This report by David to Mephibosheth of his previous decision concerning the latter's property (see 7.206// 2 Sam 16:4a) takes the place of the curt question with which the king interrupts Mephibosheth's apology in 2 Sam 19:30 (Eng. 19:29)a: "Why speak any more of your affairs?"

[998] Compare 2 Sam 19:30 (Eng. 19:29)b, where David commands Mephibosheth and Ziba to "divide the land." Josephus makes the procedure more specific, just as he adds the assurance of pardon for Mephibosheth.

am content that you have recovered your kingship."[999]

(11.4) 272. Beerzel, the Galadite, a great and distinguished man, had supplied many things in The Camps.[1000] David appealed to him, who had escorted him to the Jordan, to accompany him to Hierosolyma. For he promised that he would tend to him in his old age[1001] with all honor and that he would provide and care for him as though he were his father.[1002] **273.** But he, out of home-sickness, declined to live with him.[1003] He said that he was so old that, having reached the age of eighty years, he did not enjoy pleasures, but already had death and the grave as his care.[1004] Therefore he asked David—if he wished to gratify his desires—to dismiss him.[1005] For, he had no taste for food or drink on account of age.[1006] **274.** Likewise his capacity to hear the sound and tones of flutes and other instruments, which give pleasure to those who live alongside kings, was already impaired.[1007]

When he had made this urgent request, David said, "I dismiss you.[1008] But leave with me your son Achiman,[1009] for I shall share every good thing with him."[1010] **275.** Beerzel, leaving his son behind and having paid homage to the king and prayed that everything would go according to his soul's wishes, returned home.[1011] David,

Barzillai (Beerzel) allowed to stay behind

---

[999] In 2 Sam 19:31 (Eng. 19:30) Mephibosheth expresses his satisfaction that David "has come safely home."

[1000] Josephus had introduced this figure—there called "Berzelai(os)"—as one of those welcoming the fugitive David in 7.230// 2 Sam 17:27. For his re-introduction of him here, he draws on 2 Sam 19:32 (Eng. 19:31), omitting its notice on his advanced age (80 years), which will be cited by Barzillai himself subsequently; see 7.273 (// 2 Sam 19:36 [Eng. 19:35]). Josephus turns the single source epithet (i.e. "great"; RSV: wealthy) for Barzillai into a double characterization of him as "great and distinguished."

[1001] The Josephan David's promise to tend to Barzillai "in his old age" reflects the wording of LXX BL 2 Sam 19:34 (Eng. 19:33), whereas in MT David simply promises to provide "for you" (Barzillai).

[1002] The promise of being treated "like a father" is Josephus' elaboration of the offer David makes Barzillai in 2 Sam 19:34 (Eng. 19:33).

[1003] This notice, with its mention of Barzillai's motivation for declining David's offer, replaces his opening rhetorical question in 2 Sam 19:35 (Eng. 19:34)a: "how many years have I still to live, that I should go up with the king to Jerusalem?"

[1004] See 2 Sam 19:36 (Eng. 19:35)aα. Josephus turns Barzillai's rhetorical question about his inability to enjoy pleasures into a statement. His appended reference to what "positively" the old man is awaiting at this point, i.e. death and the tomb, anticipate Barzillai's request that he be allowed to die near his parents' grave in 2 Sam 19:38 (Eng. 19:37)aβ.

[1005] From Barzillai's request to be allowed to return in 2 Sam 19:38 (Eng. 19:37)a, Josephus omits the motivation given by him for that request, i.e. "that I may

die in my own city, near the grave of my father and my mother." Rather, he has Barzillai point out that David's dismissal of him will be the true satisfaction of his desires. Josephus further places Barzillai's request at the center of his reply to David's offer, whereas in 2 Sam 19:35-38 (Eng. 19:34-37) this comes only after he has finished a series of complaints about his present state.

[1006] Here too (see note to "care" at 7.273), Josephus transposes Barzillai's rhetorical question of 2 Sam 19:36 (Eng. 19:35)aβ into a statement by him about what he can no longer do.

[1007] Compare 2 Sam 19:36 (Eng. 19:35)bα, where Barzillai asks rhetorically whether he can still listen to male and female singers. Josephus, who has already anticipated his request to be dismissed from 19:38 (Eng. 19:37)aα in 7.273, omits the remainder of Barzilai's discourse as cited in 19:36bβ-37 (Eng. 19:35bβ-36): his question about why he should be a burden to the king, proposal to accompany David to the Jordan, and further query about why the king should give him the proposed reward.

[1008] Josephus supplies this notice on David's agreeing to dismiss Barzillai.

[1009] MT (2 Sam 19:38) כמהם (Eng.: "Chimham"); LXX B Χαμαάμ; LXX L Ἀχιμαάμ; Josephus Ἀχίμανος. In designating this figure as Barzillai's "son," Josephus follows the plus of LXX L, where, after alluding to him as "your [David's] servant" (so MT and LXX B), Barzillai goes on to call him "my son."

[1010] In 2 Sam 19:38b-39 (Eng. 19:37b-38), it is Barzillai who requests David to show favor to "your [David's] servant Chimham," and David agrees to do so. Josephus accentuates the king's magnanimity by having him volunteer to provide for this figure.

[1011] Compare 2 Sam 19:40 (Eng. 19:39), where Bar-for his part, went to Galgala, already having half of the entire people around himself, as well as the tribe of Iouda.[1012]

Israelite–Judahite dispute

(11.5) 276. At Galgala the chiefs of every tribe came to him, together with a great crowd;[1013] they complained that the tribe of Iouda had come to him secretly, when all of them together ought to have met him simultaneously.[1014] But the rulers of the tribe of Iouda asked them not to be displeased that they had arrived before them,[1015] seeing that they were his relatives, and therefore, cherishing and caring for him more, they had been the first.[1016] They had not, however, received gifts on account of their arriving earlier, such that those coming to him later would have reason to be annoyed at this.[1017] 277. When the leaders of the tribe of Iouda said these things, the rulers of the other [tribes] did not keep quiet.[1018] "We are indeed," they said, "surprised, brothers, that you call yourselves alone relatives of the king. For the one who received authority from God over all ought to be considered the relative of all of us.[1019] And therefore the people have eleven shares [in him], but you only one, and we have a prior claim.[1020] You have not done what is just by coming secretly and stealthily to the king."[1021]

Sheba (Sabai) initiates revolt

(11.6) 278. While the leaders were saying these things to one another,[1022] a certain vile man who delighted in civil strife,[1023] Sabai,[1024] son of Bochori[1025] of the tribe of

---

zillai's return home is preceded by mention of the crossing of people and king, as well as of David's kissing and blessing of Barzillai.

[1012] See 2 Sam 19:41 (Eng. 19:40), from which Josephus omits the mention of "Chimham" accompanying David, which he has already anticipated in his notice on Barzillai's "leaving his son behind."

[1013] 2 Sam 19:42 (Eng. 19:41)a speaks globally of "all the men of Israel" coming to David at an unspecified location; Josephus derives his localization of the encounter from 19:41 (Eng. 19:40), where David's advance to "Gilgal" is mentioned.

[1014] Compare 2 Sam 19:42 (Eng. 19:41)a, where the Israelites complain about the Judeans' having "stolen David away" and escorted him and his entourage across the Jordan.

[1015] This "request" is Josephus' reformation of the Judeans' question to the Israelites in 2 Sam 19:43 (Eng. 19:42): "why then are you angry about this matter?"

[1016] Josephus elaborates on the Judeans' opening affirmation in 2 Sam 19:43 (Eng. 19:42) ("because the king is near kin to us"), spelling out the import of their status for their dealings with David.

[1017] In 2 Sam 19:44 (Eng. 19:43)b the Judeans ask—rhetorically—whether they have eaten at David's expense or been given gifts by him. In place of the first of these questions, Josephus appends an indication as to why—contrary to what would be expected—they had received no gifts from their relative the king.

[1018] Josephus supplies this transitional notice on the (non-) effect of the Judeans' reply on the Israelites.

[1019] This affirmation of kinship with David by the Israelites and their challenging of the Judeans' exclu-

sive claims in this regard has no counterpart in the Israelites' response as cited in 2 Sam 19:44 (Eng. 19:43).

[1020] This statement corresponds to the Israelites' opening words in MT 2 Sam 19:44 (Eng. 19:43) ("we have ten shares in the king, and in David also we have more than you"); Josephus, with his reference to the *11* non-Judean parts of the people, takes care to correct the mathematical problem of his source (*10* tribes plus Judah), which seems to leave one of the 12 tribes unaccounted for. The Israelites' further claim about "having a prior claim" (which might alternatively be rendered "we are older"—see Marcus *ad loc.*) seems to reflect the LXX BL plus ("and furthermore we, not you, are firstborn") that comes between the 2 parts of their MT affirmation in LXX.

[1021] This concluding declaration by the Israelites replaces their double closing question ("Why then do you despise us? Were we not the first to speak of bringing back our king?") as well as the notice about the Judeans' words being "fiercer" than those of the Israelites at the end of 2 Sam 19:44 (Eng. 19:43).

[1022] Josephus supplies this transitional phrase.

[1023] The above phrase (Greek: στάσει χαίρων) is used twice elsewhere by Josephus: *Ant.* 13.291 (Eleazar the Pharisee) and *Life* 87 (the inhabitants of Tiberias who opposed Josephus). Josephus expatiates on the single phrase (MT אישׁ בליעל, "a worthless fellow," RSV) used in 2 Sam 20:1 to characterize "Sheba."

[1024] MT (2 Sam 20:1) שׁבע (Eng.: "Sheba"); LXX BL Σαβεέ; Josephus Σαβαῖος. On Josephus' account of Sheba's revolt in 7.278-293 (// 2 Samuel 20), see Begg 1998i.

[1025] MT (2 Sam 20:1) בכרי (Eng.: "Bichri"); LXX B

Benjamin,[1026] standing in the middle of the crowd, cried out in a loud voice:[1027] "None of us has a portion in David or an inheritance in the son of Jesse."[1028]

279. After saying this, sounding the horn, he gave the signal for war against the king;[1029] at this, all left David and followed him [Sabai]. Only the tribe of Iouda stayed with him and escorted him to the palace in Hierosolyma.[1030] David transferred the concubines, with whom his son Apsalom had had relations,[1031] to another house and commanded his officials to supply all their needs. He himself, however, no longer approached them.[1032]

David sequesters his concubines

280. He likewise appointed Amasa general and gave him the rank which had been Joab's.[1033] He directed him to gather as large an army as he could from the tribe of Iouda and to come to him within three days, so that, once he handed the entire force over to him, he might send him out to make war on the son of Bochori.[1034]

Amasa appointed commander against Sheba

281. Amasa went out, but delayed in mustering the army.[1035] When he did not return on the third day,[1036] the king said to Joab[1037] that it was not advantageous to give Sabai a respite, in order that he not grow still greater and become the source of even worse calamities and affairs than Apsalom had brought upon them.[1038] **282.** "Do not then wait for anyone; rather, take the force that is available and the 600 men, and, along with your brother Abessai, pursue the enemy.[1039] Wherever you come upon him, make an effort to engage him. Make haste to anticipate him, so that he will not gain possession of fortified cities and cause us struggles and much strenuous exertion."[1040]

Amasa's command transferred to Joab

Βοχορεί; LXX L Βεδδαδί; Josephus Βοχορίας.

[1026] Josephus' designation of Sheba's tribal affiliation reflects MT (and LXX B) 2 Sam 20:1's calling him "a man of my right hand," an alternative designation for "Benjamin," the "son of the right hand." LXX L qualifies him as "a man of Arachi."

[1027] Josephus dramatizes the indications of 2 Sam 20:1a, which simply refers to Sheba's being "there" for the Israelite-Judean dispute (2 Sam 19:42-44 [Eng. 19:41-43]) and of his speaking in that context.

[1028] Josephus omits the concluding portion of Sheba's declaration according to 2 Sam 20:1b, i.e. "every man to his (MT LXX L; LXX B: your) tents, O Israel."

[1029] In 2 Sam 20:1 Sheba's blowing of the trumpet/ horn is mentioned prior to his words to Israel. Josephus appends a reason for the use of the horn by him.

[1030] See 2 Sam 20:2-3aα.

[1031] See 2 Sam 20:3aβ, where the reference is to David's having left the concubines "to care for the house" (see 2 Sam 15:16// 7.199). Josephus' alternative allusion to Absalom's intercourse with them as the ground for David's treating them as he now does recalls 7.214// 2 Sam 16:22.

[1032] See 2 Sam 20:3bα. Josephus omits the concluding source remark about the women being "shut up until the day of their death, living as if in widowhood."

[1033] This transfer of the high command from Joab to Amasa is not explicitly mentioned in 2 Samuel 20. It represents the fulfillment of David's promise to the lat-

ter as reported in 7.261// 2 Sam 19:14 (Eng. 19:13).

[1034] See 2 Sam 20:4. Josephus appends the notice on the purpose of the muster that David enjoins Amasa to undertake.

[1035] See 2 Sam 20:5.

[1036] Josephus supplies this transitional phrase.

[1037] In MT and LXX 2 Sam 20:6 David addresses rather Abishai. Josephus' mention of Joab as the addressee has a counterpart in the Syriac, and reflects the clearly dominant role assumed by Joab in what follows.

[1038] Josephus prefaces David's opening word in 2 Sam 20:6 about Sheba's potential to cause more harm than Absalom with the remark about the need to deal with him immediately, which the king's biblical statement then serves to motivate.

[1039] In 2 Sam 20:6 David refers more generally to "your servants," whom Abishai (the addressee of the king's words according to MT and LXX; see note to "Joab" at 7.281) is to take with him in pursuit of Sheba. The "600" have last been mentioned by Josephus in 7.199 (// 2 Sam 15:18), where they accompany David on his flight from Jerusalem.

[1040] Josephus expands David's concluding reference in 2 Sam 20:6 to the difficulties that Sheba's occupation of fortified sites will pose with the positive exhortation to Joab to engage him before he has the opportunity of doing this. In referring to the "exertion" that would be required to dislodge Sheba, once ensconced in a fortified location, Josephus clarifies the imagery used by David at the end of 20:6, where the

Joab murders
Amasa

(11.7) 283. Joab decided not to wait any longer. Rather, taking his brother and the 600 men and directing the rest of the force that was in Hierosolyma to follow, he marched out against Sabai.[1041] He was already at Gabaon[1042]—this village is forty *stadia* distant from Hierosolyma[1043]—when Amasa met him at the head of a large force.[1044] Joab was girded with a sword and wearing a breastplate.[1045] **284.** When Amasa approached to greet him,[1046] Joab caused the sword to fall, of itself, out of its sheath, and then lifted it up from the ground.[1047] With his other hand he grasped Amasa—who was close by—by the beard as if to kiss him.[1048] He struck him in the belly, unsuspecting as he was, and killed him.[1049] He committed an impious and altogether unholy act against a good youth and a relative[1050] who had done no wrong, because he was envious of his generalship and the equal honor of the king towards him.

Josephus' com-
mentary on Jo-
ab's deed

285. It was for the same cause that he [had] murdered Abenner. Whereas, however, that transgression seemed to have a decent pretext that made it pardonable, namely when considered as an avenging of his brother Asael, he lacked such an excuse for his murder of Amasa.[1051] **286.** Having killed his fellow general, he pursued Sabai,[1052] leaving one man behind by the corpse [and] commanding him to cry out to the army that Amasa had justly been killed and punished for a reason.[1053] "But if you support the king's cause, follow his general Joab and his brother Abessai."[1054]

MT has him speaking of Sheba's "snatching away our eyes" and LXX BL of his "casting a shadow over our eyes." The Targum ("cause us trouble") offers a similar elucidation of the MT reading.

[1041] Compare 2 Sam 20:7, where Joab follows Abishai, and 3 distinct groups of pursuing forces are mentioned, i.e. the Cherethites, the Pelethites, and the "mighty men." Josephus' mention of the 600 corresponds to his version of David's order to Joab in 7.282.

[1042] MT (2 Sam 20:8) גבעון (Eng.: "Gibeon"); LXX B and Josephus Γαβαών (LXX L translates: "on the hill"). Josephus omits the specification about the following episode transpiring "at the great stone which is in Gibeon."

[1043] Josephus supplies this distance (= *ca.* 5 miles); in *War* 5.216 he fixes the distance as 50 *stadia*.

[1044] 2 Sam 20:8a does not mention Amasa's retinue.

[1045] 2 Sam 20:8bα speaks of Joab's "soldier's garment" (RSV) and a "girdle" containing his sword.

[1046] Josephus supplies this transitional phrase.

[1047] Josephus clarifies what happens with Joab's sword. Compare the concluding words of 2 Sam 20:8, where the sword simply "falls out" as Joab advances. The source presentation thus leaves unspecified whether Joab himself deliberately caused the sword's "fall," and where it actually fell (on the ground? into the folds of his tunic?), just as it does not mention Joab's retrieval of the fallen sword. Conversely, Josephus omits Joab's inquiry about Amasa's welfare in 20:9a.

[1048] 2 Sam 20:9b speaks of Joab taking Amasa "by the beard with his right hand" in order to kiss him.

[1049] From the account of Joab's killing of Amasa in 2 Sam 20:10, Josephus omits the details of the latter's bowels being shed on the ground and the former's not striking a 2nd blow. His qualification of Amasa as "unsuspecting" picks up on the opening words of 20:10 ("but Amasa did not observe the sword that was in Joab's hand").

[1050] On Amasa's relationship to Joab, see *Ant.* 7.232 // 2 Sam 17:25b. Josephus' (added) reminiscence of the pair's kinship here highlights the reprehensibility of what Joab has just done.

[1051] The above sequence with its evaluation of Joab's deed and exposure of the motives behind it has no counterpart in the "neutral" account of Amasa's murder in 2 Sam 20:10a. The addition recalls Josephus'—likewise added—comments on Joab's killing of Abner in 7.35-36.

[1052] Continuing to minimalize the role of Abishai in the episode, Josephus leaves aside the mention of his accompanying Joab in his pursuit of Sheba from 2 Sam 20:10bβ.

[1053] In 2 Sam 20:11 one of Joab's men, on his own, positions himself by the body of Amasa and urges those coming behind to follow Joab. Josephus portrays Joab as taking the initiative in the matter, likewise having him provide the man with the statement he is to make concerning Amasa's death. Here too, then, Josephus accentuates Joab's all-dominant role in the proceedings.

[1054] The man's appeal to the soldiers in 2 Sam 20:11 is simply that they follow Joab. Josephus' (exceptional) addition of "Abishai" picks up on the mention of

287. Now the body was lying in the road;[1055] the whole crowd was flocking to-gether around it, and, as a mob loves to do, pushed forward, marveling and feeling pity.[1056] The attendant carried the body from there and brought it to a site a good distance from the road, where he deposited it, covering it with a garment.[1057] This done, the entire people followed Joab.[1058]

Disposal of Amasa's corpse

288. As Joab was pursuing him throughout the whole country of the Israelites, a certain man disclosed that Sabai was in the fortified city called Abelochea.[1059] Once he arrived there, Joab invested the city with his army, erected siegeworks around it, and directed his soldiers to dig under the walls and overthrow it.[1060] For he was resentful towards those in the city for not admitting him.[1061]

Joab besieges Sheba's place of refuge

(11.8) 289. Now a certain prudent and clever old woman,[1062] observing her native city already reduced to extremities, went up on the wall and, via the troops, called Joab to her.[1063] When he approached,[1064] she began to say that God had appointed kings and generals in order that they might expel the enemies of the Hebrews and give them peace from these. "You, however, are solicitous to overthrow and devastate a mother-city of the Israelites that has committed no offense."[1065]

Woman–Joab exchange

290. Praying that God would continue to remain merciful to him,[1066] Joab then said that he did not want to murder any of the people nor eradicate so great a city.[1067]

Joab's taking "his brother" along with him on his pursuit of Sheba in 7.283.

[1055] Josephus omits the graphic detail about Amasa "wallowing in his blood" from 2 Sam 20:12aα; see his omission of the similar items concerning Amasa's slaying of 20:10 in 7.284, cf. note on "killed him" at 7.284.

[1056] Josephus embellishes the "objective" reference to anyone who saw Amasa's body stopping (2 Sam 20:12bβ) with his remarks on "crowd psychology," these reflective of his characteristic disdain for crowds. At the same time he positions his rendition of this source notice—which in 20:12 appears only after the removal of the corpse—at a more logical point in the sequence of events.

[1057] These initiatives by the man each have their parallel in 2 Sam 20:12. Reversing the biblical sequence, Josephus cites them after his mention of the event that provokes them, i.e. the crowd's stopping; see previous note.

[1058] See 2 Sam 20:13.

[1059] MT (2 Sam 20:14) אבלה ובית מעכה (Eng.: "Abel of Beth-maacah"); LXX B Ἀβὲλ τὴν Βαιθμαχά; LXX L Ἀβηλὰ καὶ Βαιθμακκώ; Josephus Ἀβελωχέα (this is the reading adopted by Niese and Marcus; Schalit *s.v.* reads Ἀβελμαχέα with MSP Lat). In contrast to 2 Sam 20:14a, which focusses on Sheba's own movements, Josephus directs attention to those of his pursuer, Joab. In the same line, he inserts the reference to Joab's being informed of Sheba's whereabouts as the presupposition for his subsequent siege of the site. Conversely, he omits the (extraneous) notice of 20:14b that all the "Bichrites" (so LXX B; Berites, MT) followed Sheba

into his place of refuge.

[1060] In 2 Sam 20:15 the various initiatives against the city are attributed to Joab's forces as a whole. Josephus highlights the general's role as the initiator of these measures.

[1061] Josephus appends this reference to Joab's motivation for his measures against the city.

[1062] As he does with the "wise woman of Tekoa" (2 Sam 14:2) in 7.182, Josephus inserts the reference to the age of the wise woman introduced in 2 Sam 20:16.

[1063] Josephus supplies the reference to the city's desperate situation, which prompts the woman's initiative, as well as the mention of the "soldiers" as her intermediaries in his version of 2 Sam 20:16.

[1064] From the exchange between the woman and Joab in 2 Sam 20:17, Josephus omits the preliminaries of her initial question about his identity, his confirmatory response, her request that he listen to her, and his agreeing to do so. He likewise passes over the woman's invocation of her city's long-standing reputation as a place of wise counsel in 20:18.

[1065] The contrast drawn by the woman in 2 Sam 20:19 is between herself as a peace-loving person and Joab's aggressive action against an Israelite "mother city." Josephus substitutes a contrast between the God-given task of Israel's commanders and Joab's current initiative, which, as a general himself, Joab would likely find more compelling.

[1066] Josephus prefaces Joab's response to the woman (2 Sam 20:20-21) with reference to his first praying for God's continued support.

[1067] Compare 2 Sam 20:20, where Joab emphatically denies that he is looking to "swallow up or de-

Siege ends with execution of Sheba

If, however, he received from them the king's opponent, Sabai the son of Bochori, for punishment, he would terminate the siege and withdraw his army.[1068]

291. When the woman heard these things from Joab, she requested that he hold back a short while, for she would throw down the enemy's head to him right away.[1069] She then went down to the citizens and said: "do you want to be wretchedly destroyed as evildoers, along with your children and wives, for the sake of a vile man whom nobody knows and to have him in place of King David, who has done so much good to you and, as a single city, to oppose such a great force?"[1070]

292. She persuaded them to cut off the head of Sabai and to throw it to Joab's army.[1071] When this happened, the king's general sounded the retreat and raised the

David's officials

siege. He then returned to Hieroslyma and was once again appointed general of the people.[1072] **293.** The king likewise placed Banai over the bodyguards and the 600,[1073] just as he set Adoram[1074] over the forced labor and Iosaphat,[1075] the son of Achil,[1076] over the recorders. He designated Sousan[1077] as scribe and Sadok and Abiathar as priests.[1078]

Famine prompts David's appeal to God

(12.1) 294. After these things, when the country was being afflicted by a famine,[1079] David begged God to be merciful to the people and to make clear to him

---

stroy." The former term echoes the woman's question in 20:19 as to why he wants to "swallow up the heritage of the Lord." In both instances Josephus' rendition eliminates the Bible's metaphorical language.

[1068] See 2 Sam 20:21, from which Josephus omits Joab's reference to Sheba as a "man from the hill country of Ephraim." This omission may be inspired by the fact that in 7.278 Josephus has called Sheba a "Benjamite"; see note to "Benjamin" at 7.278.

[1069] Josephus inserts these preliminaries to the woman's approach to the townsfolk in 2 Sam 20:22. He thereby smooths the transition between this act of hers and her preceding exchange with Joab, which, in the biblical sequence, ends with her simply going off, having made no explicit reply to Joab's proposition to her in 20:21.

[1070] Josephus markedly accentuates the woman's role in the affair by attributing this extended speech to her. 2 Sam 20:22aα simply refers to her going to the people "in her wisdom," without citing any words by her to them. By means of the woman's speech Josephus highlights both the status of David as a beneficent king and the wrongfulness of Sheba's revolt against him. Rabbinic tradition as well provides the woman with a speech to the inhabitants; see, e.g., *Gen. Rab.* 94.9 and cf. Begg 1998i: 19, n. 129.

[1071] Josephus makes explicit that it was under the woman's influence that the inhabitants did as they did with Sheba; compare 2 Sam 20:22aβ.

[1072] See 2 Sam 20:22b. Josephus' appended notice on the returned Joab's reappointment anticipates the mention of him as commander in 20:23a; its wording recalls 7.110, where his initial appointment by David

is cited, and 7.280, where Joab loses his position to Amasa.

[1073] Compare 2 Sam 20:23b, where "Benaiah" appears as "commander of the Cherethites and the Pelethites." David's confiding the command of his "bodyguards" to Banai was mentioned in 7.110, while "the 600" figure among those pursuing Sheba in 7.282-283.

[1074] MT (2 Sam 20:24) אדרם (Eng.: "Adoram"); LXX B Ἀδωνειράμ; LXX L Ἰεζεδράν; Josephus Ἀδώραμος, a form reflecting the Hebrew name.

[1075] MT (2 Sam 20:24) יהושפט (Eng.: "Jehoshaphat"); LXX B Ἰωσαφάθ; LXX L Σαφάν; Josephus Ἰωσάφατος. This figure was previously mentioned in 7.110.

[1076] MT (2 Sam 20:24) אחילוד (Eng.: "Ahilud"); LXX B Ἀχειλούθ; LXX L Ἀχιθαλαά; Josephus Ἄχιλος. See 7.110, where this same name for Jehoshaphat's father occurs.

[1077] MT (2 Sam 20:25a) שיא (Eng.: "Sheva"); LXX Ἰησοῦς; LXX L Σουσά; Josephus Σουσάς (this is the reading adopted by Niese and Marcus; Schalit *s.v.* proposes Σισάς, i.e. the form of the name read by Niese in 7.110, where Marcus has Σεισάς).

[1078] See 2 Sam 20:25b. Josephus omits the name of David's 3rd priest as mentioned in 20:26, i.e. "Ira the Jairite."

[1079] Josephus' explicit mention of "the country" being afflicted by the famine corresponds to the LXX L plus in 2 Sam 21:1aα. He leaves aside the specification that the famine prevailed for 3 years. On Josephus' (highly abridged) version of the story of the execution of the Saulides (2 Sam 21:1-14) in 7.294-297, see Begg 1996h.

both the cause of and the cure for the illness.[1080] The prophets said[1081] that God
wished satisfaction to be given to the Gabaonites, against whom King Saoul had
acted impiously, killing and deceiving them, and not keeping the oaths the general
Iesous and the senate had sworn to them.[1082] **295.** If therefore David would allow
the Gabaonites to take what vengeance they wished on behalf of those who had
been done away with, he [God] promised that he would be reconciled and deliver
the mob from its calamities.[1083]

*God's direc-
tives about how
famine may be
ended*

296. When therefore David had learned from the prophets the things that God was
seeking, he summoned the Gabaonites[1084] and inquired what they wished to obtain.[1085] Upon their asking to take seven descendants of Saoul's family for punishment,[1086] the king had a search made and handed them over to them,[1087] while
sparing Iebosthos,[1088] the son of Ionathes.[1089] **297.** Taking the men, the Gabaonites
punished them as they wished.[1090] God immediately began to send rain[1091] and re-

*Saulides exe-
cuted*

*Land flourishes
again*

[1080] Josephus' account of David's initiative reads
like an elaboration of the LXX L text of 2 Sam 21:1aβ,
where David "seeks a word from the Lord" as opposed
to MT LXX B, which speak of his "seeking the face of
the Lord." Josephus' mention of David's appeal for divine "mercy" has a counterpart in Tg.'s rendering of the
MT phrase.

[1081] In 2 Sam 21:1b the Lord appears to communi-
cate directly with David; Josephus' inserted reference
to the prophets' role accords with his general tendency
to highlight their involvement throughout Israel's history. *B. Yebam.* 78b avers that the exchange between
God and king took place via the Urim and Thummim.

[1082] Josephus incorporates into the response he ascribes to the Deity elements both of the divine statement concerning the "blood-guilt" hanging over the
house of Saul for the king's killing of the Gibeonites (2
Sam 21:1b) and the parenthetical editorial notice (21:2)
concerning the Gibeonites as the beneficiaries of Israel's earlier oath to spare them (on this see *Ant.* 5.55//
Josh 9:15). He leaves aside the extenuating circumstances for Saul's deed alluded to in 21:2b, i.e. his "zeal
for the people of Israel and Judah." Neither in the Bible
nor in Josephus is there previous mention of a massacre
of the Gibeonites by Saul.

[1083] This conditional divine promise has no equivalent in the words of the Lord as cited in 2 Sam 21:1b.

[1084] Josephus supplies this transitional sequence between God's word (see 2 Sam 21:1b) to David and the
latter's query to the Gibeonites of 21:3, 4b.

[1085] Josephus here conflates David's double question to the Gibeonites of 2 Sam 21:3, 4b, likewise passing over their intervening statement (21:4a) about what
is not at issue (i.e. monetary recompense from the house
of Saul or their own taking the initiative in executing
any Israelite).

[1086] From the Gibeonites' reply in 2 Sam 21:5-6a
Josephus omits their charges against their would-be ex-
terminator Saul as well as their specification of the site

("at Gibeon on the mountain of the Lord") on which
they propose to carry out the execution of those given
them.

[1087] This narrative notice about what David did
combines the king's statement of intent to the
Gibeonites in 2 Sam 21:6b: ("I will give them") and the
statement of 21:9aα that he indeed "gave them [the
Saulides] into the hands of the Gibeonites."

[1088] This reading of the Greek codices is obviously
a mistake for the "Memphibosheth" cited in 2 Sam 21:7
(MT LXX B), given that "Ishbosheth" is already long
dead by this point (see 7.48// 2 Sam 4:7). Compare
"Memphiuos" in Lat and the emended form Μεμφιβόσ-
θου in the *Ed. pr.*

[1089] Josephus passes over David's motivation for
sparing Jonathan's son, namely, the oath between himself and Jonathan cited in 2 Sam 21:7b. He also leaves
aside the indications concerning the identity of the 7
Saulide victims furnished by David in 21:8-9, which
involve discrepancies with what one reads elsewhere in
the Bible regarding Saul's family members and their
relationships; see Begg 1996h: 10, n. 39.

[1090] The verb used in MT 2 Sam 21:9aβ (הוקיע)
leaves it unclear just what the Gibeonites did to their
victims—did they hang them, dismember them, or push
them down? Josephus here and in his formulation of the
Gibeonites' request in 7.296 // 21:6 (where the same
term occurs), substitutes generic punishment terminology. He further omits the precisions concerning the
where and when of the execution given in 21:9b.

[1091] Josephus draws his reference to the "rain" that
comes following the execution of the Saulides from 2
Sam 21:10aβ, expanding this with mention of the accompanying restoration of the earth's fertility. On the
other hand, he omits the whole surrounding context of
the source "rain notice," i.e. 21:10aαb, 11-14, which relates the watch over the bodies of the dead mounted by
Rizpah, Saul's concubine, and their eventual burial by
David. This large-scale omission might have to do with

store the earth's fertility, delivering it from drought. At this, the country of the Hebrews again flourished.[1092]

Ahishai rescues David

298. Not long afterwards, the king again campaigned against the Palestinoi.[1093] Having joined battle and routed them, he was left alone in his pursuit of them. Becoming weary,[1094] he was seen by a certain one of the enemy, named Akmon,[1095] the son of Araph,[1096] and also a descendant of the Giants.[1097] **299.** He had a spear whose hilt is said to have weighed 300 shekels,[1098] as well as a chainmail breastplate[1099] and a sword.[1100] He rushed forward, intent on killing the enemy king, who was weak from exertion.[1101] Suddenly, however, there appeared Abessai, the brother of Joab,[1102] who protected the king, placing himself alongside him as he lay, and

David agrees not to go into battle

killed the enemy.[1103]

300. The crowd was disturbed by how narrowly the king had escaped danger.[1104] The leaders made him swear that he would no longer march with them into battle, in order that, due to his courage and eagerness,[1105] he not suffer something terrible and so deprive the people of the good things [that came] through him, both those he had already bestowed on them and those in which they would yet share, should he live a long time.[1106]

---

the unflattering portrait of David conveyed by the biblical sequence, where he initially appears callous to the fate of the dead and only finally concerns himself with their burial under the influence of Rizpah's devotion.

[1092] Josephus' appended notice concerning the effect of the God-sent rain (see 2 Sam 21:10aβ) underscores that God did indeed fulfill the promise made by him in 7.295 about "delivering the mob from its calamities."

[1093] See 2 Sam 21:15a, which Josephus prefaces with a transitional chronological indication. On Josephus' version of the sequence concerning the exploits of David's heroes (2 Sam 21:15-22) in 7.298-304, see Begg 1997m: 140-51.

[1094] 2 Sam 21:15b speaks of David and his servants fighting against the Philistines and of the king's "growing weary." Josephus' added mention of David's isolation from his men during the pursuit better prepares for his subsequent endangerment.

[1095] MT (2 Sam 21:16) בנב [the *qere* reads ישבי] ישבו (Eng.: "Ishbibenob"); LXX B Ἰεσβί; LXX L Δαδού (cf. OL Dan); Josephus Ἄκμων. For more on Josephus' form of the name in relation to those of the biblical references, see Begg 1997m: 142, n. 22. Rabbinic tradition (see, e.g., *b. Sanh.* 95a; *Midr. Pss.* 18.30) identifies David's assailant, "Ishbibenob/Ishbi", as the brother of Goliath and son of a woman named "Orpah" (cf. הרפה [RSV: "... of the giants"] in MT 2 Sam 21:16), whom Abishai also kills on his way to rescue David.

[1096] For this name of the father of David's assailant, Josephus draws on the indication concerning the assailant's ancestry in MT and LXX B 2 Sam 21:16, where he is qualified, respectively, as "one of the descendants of הרפה" and "of the Rapha" (τοῦ Ῥαφά), taking this as a proper name. LXX L, Tg. and OL, as also RSV, "translate" the MT phrase with a common noun, i.e. "of the

giants." See next note.

[1097] With this specification concerning the ancestry of David's assailant, Josephus draws on the designation used of that figure in LXX L (and Tg. OL) 2 Sam 21:16, having previously cited his "proper name" under the influence of the MT and LXX B readings; see previous note.

[1098] Josephus omits the specification of 2 Sam 21:16b that the 300 shekels were "of bronze."

[1099] This item lacks an equivalent in the various witnesses for 2 Sam 21:16b, all of which mention only 2 pieces of equipment carried/worn by David's assailant, as compared with Josephus' 3.

[1100] Josephus' explicit mention of the assailant's "sword" has a parallel in the renderings of OL, Vulg., and Syriac 2 Sam 21:16. Compare "a new" (MT; RSV supplies "sword"), "club" (LXX B), "belt" (LXX L), "belt/sword" (Tg.). The 3 items that Josephus attributes to David's assailant each has an equivalent in his description of Goliath's accessories in *Ant.* 6.187, such that his "Akmon" appears as a 2nd Goliath.

[1101] These added indications highlight the danger facing David, due both to the determination of his assailant and his own weakness.

[1102] 2 Sam 21:17 calls him "son of Zeruiah."

[1103] Josephus embellishes and dramatizes the description of Abishai's intervention in 2 Sam 21:17a, where he simply attacks and kills David's assailant.

[1104] This reference to the emotional response of David's subjects to the danger he had run is supplied by Josephus.

[1105] Josephus inserts this mention of the (*per se* noble) motives that would prompt David's entering battle into the words he is made to swear in 2 Sam 21:17b.

[1106] Josephus elucidates the meaning of the figurative phrase "lest you quench the lamp of Israel," i.e. by

(12.2) 301. When the king heard that the Palestinoi were assembling at the city of Gazara,[1107] he sent his army against them.[1108] On that occasion Sabrech[1109] the Chettai,[1110] one of the heroes around David, distinguished himself and gained great glory.[1111] For he killed many[1112] of those who claimed to be descendants of the Giants[1113] and who thought much of their own bravery; thus, he was the cause of victory for the Hebrews.[1114]

302. Also after this defeat, the Palestinoi made war again.[1115] David sent out his army against them,[1116] and Ephan,[1117] his relative,[1118] distinguished himself. For, he singlehandedly killed the bravest man of all the Palestinoi[1119] and put the rest to flight, many of whom died as they fought.[1120]

David's heroes twice rout Philistines

---

being killed in battle, used by David's men in the oath they impose on him in 2 Sam 21:17b. Compare the Tg.'s rendition, where the image of the "lamp" is replaced by the non-figurative term "kingdom." Josephus' reformulation accentuates David's benefits for Israel over time.

[1107] MT (2 Sam 21:18) גוב (Eng.: "Gob"; some Hebrew MSS read נוב ["Nob"]); LXX B Γέθ; LXX L Γαζέθ; MT (1 Chr 20:4) גזר (Eng.: "Gezer"); LXX BL Γάζερ; Josephus Γάζαρα. 2 Sam 21:18-22 has its content parallel in 1 Chr 20:4-8. In his placement of his version of the segment in 7.301-304, Josephus aligns himself with the sequence of 2 Samuel, where 21:18-22 follows directly on the story of Abishai's rescue of David (21:15-17; no parallel in Chronicles) as opposed to 1 Chronicles, in which 20:4-8 represents the immediate sequel to Israel's subjugation of the Ammonites, 20:1-3 (// 2 Sam 11:1;12:26, 30-31).

[1108] 2 Sam 21:18a// 1 Chr 20:4a speak simply of a war with the Philistines without mentioning the movements of the 2 forces.

[1109] MT (2 Sam 21:18// 1 Chr 20:4) סבכי (Eng.: "Sibbecai"); LXX B 2 Sam 21:18 Ὀεβοχά; LXX L 2 Sam 21:18 Σοβοχαί; LXX B 1 Chr 20:4 Σοβοκχί; LXX L 1 Chr 20:4 Σοβακχεί; Josephus Σαβρήχης (Schlatter 1913 s.v. and Schalit s.v. propose reading Σαββήχης).

[1110] This same gentilic (Greek: ὁ Χετταῖος) appears in LXX L 2 Sam 21:18. Compare החשתי (MT 2 Sam 21:18// 1 Chr 20:4; Eng.: "the Hushathite"); ὁ Ἀστατωθεί (LXX B 2 Sam 21:18); Θωσασθεί (LXX B 1 Chr 20:4); Ἐσσαθεί (LXX L 1 Chr 20:4).

[1111] Josephus embellishes the source references to "Sabrech," who in 2 Sam 21:18// 1 Chr 20:4 is mentioned only by name and gentilic.

[1112] In attributing the slaying of multiple Philistines to "Sabrech," Josephus agrees with LXX L 2 Sam 21:18 (where the hero kills "those assembled of the descendants of the giants"). In the other textual witnesses to 2 Sam 21:18// 1 Chr 20:4 the Israelite's victim is a single individual named "Saph" (MT 21:18)/ "Sippai" (MT 20:4), etc.

[1113] Josephus' Greek term (Γίγαντες) for the ancestors of those killed by "Sabrech" is the same as that used in LXX L 2 Sam 21:18 and LXX 1 Chr 20:4; cf. הרפאים (RSV: "the giants") in MT 1 Chr 20:4. MT 2

Sam 21:18 has הרפה (RSV: "the giants") and LXX B τοῦ Ῥαφά, as in 2 Sam 21:16; see 7.298.

[1114] Josephus goes beyond his sources in magnifying "Sabrech's" exploit: this was accomplished against a group of enemies, who thought of themselves as very courageous, and it gave rise to a general Israelite victory.

[1115] Like 1 Chr 20:5, Josephus does not mention the site of the renewed hostilities. MT 2 Sam 21:19 places the conflict at "Gob" (many Hebrew MSS read "Nob," as they do in 21:18), LXX B at Ῥόμ, and LXX L at Ῥοβ.

[1116] Neither 2 Sam 21:19 nor 1 Chr 20:5 mentions this initiative by David. The insertion serves to make clear that, whereas David has ceased to accompany his armies (see 7.300), he continues to exercise military leadership.

[1117] Josephus' form of the hero's name (Ἐφάν) does not correspond to those used by any of the biblical witnesses—which differ markedly among themselves—compare: אלחנן (MT 2 Sam 21:19// 1 Chr 20:5 [Eng.: "Elhanan"); Ἐλεανάν (LXX BL 21:19 and LXX L 20:5); Ἐλλάν (LXX B 20:5); "Taman" (OL 21:19); "Adeodatus" (Vulg. 21:19 and 20:5); and "David" (Tg. 21:19 and 20:5). Schalit s.v. sees the above Josephan form as a corruption of an original Ἐλεχανάν.

[1118] This qualification of "Ephan" takes the place of the various names for the hero's father cited in the witnesses of 2 Sam 21:19// 1 Chr 20:5; see Begg 1997m: 147. Josephus was perhaps inspired to identify "Ephan" as David's kinsman, given the designation of "Elhanan" as "the Bethlehemite" in 2 Sam 21:19, Bethlehem being the hometown of David as well.

[1119] Josephus' leaving "Ephan's" victim(s) unnamed is his way of dealing with the problem posed by MT LXX OL and Vulg. 2 Sam 21:19, which identify the one killed by "Elhanan" (etc.) as "Goliath," whereas according to 1 Sam 17:50 (and *Ant.* 6.190) Goliath was slain earlier by David himself. Other biblical texts resolve the problem in different ways: Tg. 2 Sam 21:19 makes David rather than "Elhanan" the killer of Goliath; MT and LXX 1 Chr 20:5 designate the one slain by "Elhanan" (etc.) as Goliath's *brother* (called "Lahmi" in MT), while Tg. 1 Chr 20:5 states that *David* slew Goliath's brother Lahmi.

[1120] As he did in the case of "Sabrech" in 7.301 (see

Philistine champion killed

303. A short time having passed, they pitched camp at Gitta, a city not far from the border of the Hebrews' country.[1121] Among them was a man who was six cubits in height[1122] and who had one more toe on his feet and one more finger on his hands than is natural.[1123] **304.** From the army sent against them by David,[1124] Ionathes,[1125] son of Souma[1126] fought singlehandedly with him. He did away with him, becoming the decisive cause of a total victory, and carried off glory for his valor. For also this Palestinos claimed to be a descendant of the Giants.[1127] After this battle the Palestinoi no longer made war.[1128]

David's musical initiatives

(12.3) 305. Being now delivered from wars and dangers and enjoying profound peace for the future,[1129] David composed songs and hymns[1130] to God in varied meters. Some he made in trimeters, others in pentameters.[1131] He also produced musical instruments[1132] and taught the Levites to play hymns to God on these on the day

---

note to "Hebrews" at 7.301), Josephus magnifies "Ephan's" achievement: he kills the bravest of the Philistines and causes the others to flee, many of these in turn being killed. These indications take the place of the notice of 2 Sam 21:19// 1 Chr 20:5 that the slain Philistine had a spear shaft "like a weaver's beam."

[1121] This reading follows the conjecture (Γίττη) of Niese, which Marcus adopts for the articular form (τῇ) read by the codices. The conjecture is inspired by the mention of "Gath" (LXX: Γέθ) in 2 Sam 21:20// 1 Chr 20:6.

[1122] The reading/interpretation of the qualification used of the Philistine champion in Josephus' biblical sources is a matter of uncertainty. Josephus aligns himself with the designation of him as a "man of great size" (ὑπερμεγέθες) in LXX 1 Chr 20:6 (and possibly also in the qere of MT 2 Sam 21:20 [אִישׁ מדון] and the reading of MT 1 Chr 20:6 [אִישׁ מדה], both of which are rendered as "man of stature" by RSV); compare ἀνὴρ Μαδών (LXX B 2 Sam 21:20), ἀνὴρ ἐκ Ῥααζής (LXX L 2 Sam 21:20). Josephus goes beyond the sources in his specification that the Philistine's height was "6 cubits"; this particular figure was perhaps suggested to him by the reference to the champion's having 6 fingers and 6 toes in the source verses, see next note.

[1123] 2 Sam 21:20a// 1 Chr 20:6a specify that he had 6 fingers and 6 toes for a total of 24 extremities. Josephus leaves out the concluding notice of the source verses according to which also this Philistine was a descendant of הרפה (MT)/ "the giants" (LXX), as well as the opening reference to his "taunting Israel" in 2 Sam 21:21// 1 Chr 20:7.

[1124] As in 7.302 (see note on "against them" at 7.302), Josephus adds the reference to David's initiative in the face of a new military emergency.

[1125] MT (2 Sam 21:21// 1 Chr 20:7) יהונתן (Eng.: "Jonathan"); LXX (2 Sam 21:21// 1 Chr 20:7) Ἰωναθάν; Josephus Ἰωναθῆς.

[1126] This is the reading of the codices; cf. Lat "Sumae." Marcus follows the *Ed. prin.*, which reads

Σαμᾶ. Compare שמעי (Eng.: "Shimei," MT 2 Sam 21:21, *ketiv*); שׁמעה (Eng.: "Shimah," MT 21:21, *qere*); שׁמעא (Eng.: "Shimea," MT 1 Chr 20:7); Σεμεεί (LXX B 21:21); Σαμαά (LXX L 21:21; LXX BL 20:7). Josephus leaves aside the indication, common to both sources, that the father of "Jonathan" was David's "brother."

[1127] This indication concerning the ancestry of the final Philistine champion reflects the wording of LXX 1 Chr 20:7 (and Tg. 2 Sam 21:20// 1 Chr 20:7). In MT 2 Sam 21:20 and 1 Chr 20:7 he is called a descendant of הרפה, in LXX B 2 Sam 21:20 of "Rapha," and in LXX L 2 Sam 21:20 of "Titan."

[1128] This concluding notice for the sequence concerning David's heroes in 7.298-304 takes the place of the summary formula, rounding off the source parallels in 2 Sam 21:22// 1 Chr 20:7, which speaks of the 4 (21:22; 20:7 lacks this specification) Philistine champions brought down by David and his men.

[1129] This transition, leading into Josephus' account of David's musical initiatives, picks up on the introduction to the "Psalm of David" in 2 Samuel 22, which, according to its v. 1, was voiced by him "on the day when the Lord delivered him from the hand of all his enemies...."

[1130] With this phrase Josephus makes general reference to the 2 source poetic texts, i.e. the "Psalm of David" (2 Samuel 22) and the so-called "Last Words of David" (2 Sam 23:1-7). In accord with his standard practice, he does not reproduce the actual wording of these poetical compositions (to which Chronicles has no parallel either).

[1131] This reference to the "meters" used by David for his songs represents an obvious "Hellenization" of the biblical account, given that such meters are not a feature of Hebrew poetry. Similarly, in *Ant.* 2.346 and 4.303 Josephus states that Moses composed the "Song of the Sea" (Exod 15:1-18) and the "Song of Moses" (Deut 32:1-43), respectively, in hexameters.

[1132] This reference to David as maker of musical instruments has a biblical basis in the king's directive

called the Sabbath and on other feastdays.[1133] **306.** The form of these instruments is approximately as follows: the *kinyra* consisted of ten cords, which were plucked with a plectum. The *nabla* had twelve strings, which were plucked with the fingers, while the *kymbla* [was made of] heavy bronze plates.[1134] It suffices for us to have told this much about these matters, so that nobody should be completely ignorant concerning the nature of the above-mentioned instruments.[1135]

(12.4) 307. All those around the king were heroes; of these, there were thirty-eight who were outstanding and splendid in their actions.[1136] We shall, however, relate the deeds of only five of them, for these suffice to make clear the virtues of the others as well. For they were mighty, both in subjugating the country and defeating great nations.[1137]

David's five heroes

308. First then was Iseb,[1138] the son of Achemai.[1139] Many times dashing into the enemy's line of battle, he did not cease fighting until he had brought down 900 of them.[1140]

Iseb

After him was Eleazar,[1141] son of Dodei,[1142] who was with the king in Erasam.[1143]

Eleazar

---

cited in 1 Chr 23:4 that the 4,000 Levitical musicians are to praise God "with the instruments which I have made for praise."

[1133] For this reference to David's instructing the Levites in their duties as liturgical musicians, Josephus draws on such passages as 1 Chr 16:7-42; 23:4; and 25:1-8.

[1134] The 3 instruments listed by Josephus appear together in 1 Chr 25:1, where David directs the Levites to use them in their "prophesying." Of the 3 Hebrew terms cited there, Josephus follows LXX in his rendering of the first 2, i.e. כנרות (RSV: "lyres") and נבלים (RSV: "harps"), via transcription, likewise using LXX's "translation" ("cymbals") for the 3rd term. He elaborates the source's mention of the 3 instruments with indications concerning their appearance and use, likely on the basis of his personal familiarity with music in the temple.

[1135] With this formula Josephus provides a clear closure for the "musical interlude" of 7.305-306, prior to returning to his review of David's heroes in 7.307.

[1136] Josephus derives his overall figure for David's heroes from 2 Sam 23:39b, where, however, the number given is 37 (in fact, the preceding list of 23:8-39a mentions only 36 figures). Josephus' biblical text may have contained additional names or, alternatively, he might have miscounted the names before him.

[1137] Josephus' statement of the procedure he intends to use regarding the Davidic heroes and his rationale for following this is his own creation. On Josephus' treatment of the segment 2 Sam 23:8-39 with its presentation of additional Davidic heroes, see Begg 1997m: 151-65. In his placement of this sequence Josephus follows 2 Samuel, rather than the Chronicler's parallel (1 Chr 11:10-47), which is appended to the account of David's capture of Jerusalem (11:4-9// 2

Sam 5:6-10// 7.61-65).

[1138] MT 2 Sam 23:8 ישב בשבת (Eng.: "Josheb-basshebeth"); LXX B 2 Sam 23:8 Ιεβόσε; LXX L 2 Sam 23:8 Ιεσβαάλ; MT 1 Chr 11:11 ישבעם (Eng.: "Jashobeam"); LXX B 1 Chr 11:11 Ιεσεβαδά; LXX L 1 Chr 11:11 Ιεσσεβαάμ; Josephus Ιοεβος.

[1139] Josephus' proper name form for the hero's father (Αχεμαίος) stands closest to the reading of LXX 1 Chr 11:11, i.e. Αχαμανεί. Compare תחכמני (Eng.: "a Tahchemonite," MT 2 Sam 23:8); ὁ Χαναναῖος (LXX B 2 Sam 23:8); (υἱὸς) Θεκεμανεί (LXX L 2 Sam 23:8); בן־חכמני (Eng: "a Hachmonite," MT 1 Chr 11:11). Josephus' qualification of "Iseb" as "the first" replaces the sources' designation of him as "the chief of the three/captains."

[1140] Josephus' figure for the enemy casualties agrees with LXX L 2 Sam 23:8 and 1 Chr 11:11 (as well as OL 23:8). MT and LXX B 2 Sam 23:8 have 800, MT and LXX B 1 Chr 11:11 300.

[1141] MT (2 Sam 23:9// 1 Chr 11:12) אלעזר (Eng: "Eleazar"); LXX B 2 Sam 23:9 Ελεανάν; LXX L 2 Sam 23:9// LXX BL 1 Chr 11:12 Ελεαζαρ; Josephus Ελεάζαρος.

[1142] MT (2 Sam 23:9) דדי (Eng.: "Dodo"); LXX B υἱὸς πατραδελφοῦ (taking the Hebrew form, not as a proper name, but rather as a common noun, i.e. "his paternal uncle"); LXX L Δουδί; MT (1 Chr 11:12) דודי (Eng.: "Dodo"); LXX BL 1 Chr 11:12 Δωδαί; Josephus Δώδειος.

[1143] Josephus' mention of this site, unparalleled in 2 Sam 23:9, seems inspired by the place name of 1 Chr 11:13: בפס דמים (MT; Eng.: "at Pasdammim"); LXX B Φασαδομή; LXX L Σεφφάν. Marcus (*ad loc.*) opines that Josephus' form (Greek: Ερασαμός) is a corruption of L's reading, whereas Mez (1895: 51) maintains the reverse.

309. Once, when the Israelites were dismayed before the crowd of Palestinoi and were fleeing, he alone remained and, falling upon the enemy, killed many of them.[1144] When his sword was sticking to his right hand from their blood, and the Israelites saw the Palestinoi had been put to flight by him, they resumed the fight; pursuing, they won a marvelous and brilliant victory. The crowd followed Eleazar as he killed, stripping those who had been done away with.[1145]

Sabai

310. The third was named Sabai,[1146] the son of Elos.[1147] In struggles with the Palestinoi, who were drawn up at a place called Siagon,[1148] when the Hebrews, once again fearing their force, did not stand firm, he alone resisted, as though he were himself an army and a battle line. He brought down some of them, and pursued the others, who, unable to prevail over his strength and violence, took to flight.[1149] **311.** "The Three" performed such deeds in their conflicts and battles.[1150]

David brought water from Bethlehem

During this time when the king was in Hierosolyma, the Palestinoi's force went out to make war.[1151] David went up to the citadel, of which we spoke previously,[1152] inquiring of God concerning the war.[1153] **312.** Now the enemy camp was situated in the valley which extends to the city of Bethleem, twenty *stadia* distant from Hierosolyma.[1154] David said to his companions: "We have good water in my ancestral city," especially extolling the water in the cistern by the gate. If anyone were to bring him a drink from this cistern, he would prefer that to one's giving him a lot of money.[1155]

[1144] This sequence corresponds to the notice on the Israelites' flight and Eleazar's successful resistance in LXX BL 1 Chr 11:13b-14aα (MT 11:14aα speaks of a collectivity ["they"] who resist and slay the Philistines). It also has a counterpart in 2 Sam 23:11bβ-12a, where, however, the victorious champion is not Eleazar (as in Chronicles and Josephus), but rather a new figure, i.e. "Shammah" (see 2 Sam 23:11aα).

[1145] With this sequence Josephus makes delayed use of 2 Sam 23:10 (cf. 1 Chr 11:14), which relates Eleazar's hand sticking to his sword, the Lord's victory, the return of the fugitive Israelites to Eleazar, and their stripping of the dead. Josephus eliminates the source reference to God as the source of the victory.

[1146] MT (2 Sam 23:11) שַׁמָּא (Eng.: "Shammah"); LXX B Σαμαιά; LXX L Σαμαίας; Josephus Σαβαίας. This figure is not mentioned by the Chronicler, who appears to conflate the accounts of Eleazar and Shammah in 2 Sam 23:9-10 and 11-12, respectively.

[1147] MT (2 Sam 23:11) אָגֵא (Eng.: "Agee"); LXX B Ἀσά; LXX L Ἠλά; Josephus Ἠλός. Josephus has no equivalent to the gentilic (MT "the Hararite") used of the hero in 23:11.

[1148] Josephus' designation of the battle site with the Greek term Σιαγών ("jawbone") corresponds to the reading of LXX L 2 Sam 23:11 (as well as to those of OL and Tg.). MT and LXX B read "to the wild beast," while Vulg. offers *in statione*. Josephus omits the appended biblical qualification of the site as containing a "plot of ground full of lentils."

[1149] See 2 Sam 23:11b-12. Josephus accentuates

Sabai's exploit both positively (e.g, with his designation of him as the equivalent of an army and a battle line on his own), and negatively (by omitting the concluding reference to the Lord as the source of his victory of 23:12).

[1150] Josephus anticipates this concluding formula for his individual presentations of the first 3 heroes in 7.308-310 from 2 Sam 23:17bβ// 1 Chr 11:19bβ ("these things did the three mighty men").

[1151] Compare 2 Sam 23:13// 1 Chr 11:15, which place David at "the cave of Adullam" and the Philistines "in the valley of Rephaim" at the start of the following episode (23:13-17// 11:15-19) featuring a joint exploit by "The Three."

[1152] David's presence in the "citadel" is cited in 2 Sam 23:14a// 1 Chr 11:16a. Josephus' appended cross reference reminds readers of his account of David's capture of the Jerusalem "citadel" in 7.63-64.

[1153] Neither source mentions such a "consultation"; Josephus' reference to it accentuates David's piety and reminds readers of the king's previous inquiries of God in the face of Philistine assaults; see 7.71, 76.

[1154] Josephus elaborates on the source reference (2 Sam 23:14b// 1 Chr 11:16b) to the Philistine garrison being "in Bethlehem" with his characteristic specification of the distance between Bethlehem and Jerusalem. Marcus (*ad loc.*) points out that Josephus' distance indication (= *ca.* 2.5 miles) is inaccurate; the actual distance is *ca.* 5 miles.

[1155] Josephus' version of David's words as cited in 2 Sam 23:15// 1 Chr 11:17 accentuates both the quality

313. When they heard this, these three men immediately ran out and, rushing through the middle of the enemy camp, came to Bethleem. Having drawn the water, they again returned to the king through the camp, since the Palestinoi, overwhelmed by their daring and high spirits, kept quiet [and made no war upon them],[1156] after having despised their meager number.[1157]

314. When the water was brought, the king did not drink, saying that it had been brought by the danger and blood of his men, and therefore it was inappropriate for him to drink it.[1158] Instead, he poured out a libation from it to God and gave thanks to him for the safety of his men.[1159]

After these was Abessai, the brother of Joab.[1160] **315.** For he killed 600[1161] of the enemy on a single day.[1162] The fifth was Nabai,[1163] a priest by birth.[1164] When challenged by some well-known brothers in the country of the Moabites, he crushed them by his valor.[1165] Likewise being challenged by a man of the Egyptian race and of extraordinary size,[1166] and being himself unarmed,[1167] he killed his armed opponent, throwing the latter's own spear at him.[1168] For he took away his javelin and, while he was still alive and fighting, stripped him and slew him with his own weapons.[1169] **316.** To his above-mentioned actions let there be added also this one, which

Abessai
Nabai's exploits

---

of the Bethlehem water and the king's desire for this.

[1156] This phrase, bracketed by Niese, but not by Marcus, is absent from the codices RO.

[1157] Josephus appends this explanation as to why the Philistines did not attempt to block the movements of "The Three" as described in 2 Sam 23:16aba// 1 Chr 11:18aba.

[1158] See 2 Sam 23:16bβ-17abα// 1 Chr 11:18bβ-19abα. Josephus' omits the self-curse with which David begins his words in 23:17// 11:19.

[1159] See 2 Sam 23:16bβ// 1 Chr 11:18bβ. Josephus appends mention of David's accompanying "thanks."

[1160] Josephus omits the further characterizations of Abishai as "son of Zeruiah" and "chief of the 30" of 2 Sam 23:18// 1 Chr 11:20 (in both instances RSV follows the Syriac in reading "of the 3").

[1161] Josephus' figure for Abishai's victims agrees with that cited in LXX L (and OL) 2 Sam 23:18 against the 300 of the other witnesses.

[1162] Josephus omits the source indications (2 Sam 23:18-19// Chr 11:20-21) concerning Abishai's status vis-à-vis "The Three."

[1163] This is reading (Greek: Ναβαῖος) adopted by Niese; Marcus *ad loc.* prefers the Βαναίας of codex M, which accords with the hero's name given in LXX BL 2 Sam 23:20 and LXX L 1 Chr 11:22. Compare בניהו (Eng.: "Benaiah," MT 2 Sam 23:20); בניה (Eng.: "Benaiah," MT 1 Chr 11:22); Βαναιά (LXX B 1 Chr 11:22).

[1164] This phrase takes the place of the various data concerning "Benaiah" found in 2 Sam 23:20// 1 Chr 11:22: his father ("Ishbai," MT 23:20/ "Jehoiada," MT 11:22), his hometown ("Kabzeel"), and his status as a doer of mighty deeds. Niese, and following him Mez

(1895: 52), view Josephus' reference to "Nabai's" priestly ancestry as likely "corrupt." Marcus, who reads the hero's name rather as "Banai" (see previous note), points out that 1 Chr 27:5 mentions "Benaiah the son of Jehoiada [see the same pairing in 1 Chr 11:22] *the priest.*"

[1165] Josephus' reference to "Nabai's" rout of "brothers" in Moab is in the line of the renditions by LXX 2 Sam 23:20a and LXX L 1 Chr 11:22a ("two sons of Ariel of Moab") and Tg. 2 Sam 23:20a// 1 Chr 11:22a ("two princes of Moab") of the mysterious entities "two ariels," whom Benaiah slays according to MT 2 Sam 23:20a// 1 Chr 11:22a. In 2 Sam 23:20b// 1 Chr 11:22b there follows as Benaiah's 2nd exploit his killing of a lion. Josephus makes this the 3rd, climatic deed of the hero; see 7.316-317.

[1166] Josephus follows 1 Chr 11:23a in highlighting the Egyptian's height as against the reference to his (handsome) appearance in 2 Sam 23:21a. On the other hand, he omits the Chronicler's specification that the Egyptian was "5 cubits" tall.

[1167] Josephus accentuates the disparity between the 2 parties in portraying the Israelite hero as "unarmed," whereas according to 2 Sam 23:21// 1 Chr 11:23 he was carrying a "staff."

[1168] Like 2 Sam 23:21, Josephus has no equivalent to the qualification of the Egyptian's spear as "like a weaver's beam" of 1 Chr 11:23.

[1169] 2 Sam 23:21bβ// 1 Chr 11:23bβ speak only of the "spear," which Benaiah seizes from the Egyptian and uses to kill him. Josephus embellishes both the latter's threat and the former's triumph with his reference to the Egyptian's having, not just one, but several weapons at his disposal.

manifests either greater, or in any case, no less high spirits than these.[1170] For when God sent down snow, a lion slipped and fell into a certain cistern. Since the entrance was narrow, it was clear that the lion was about to perish, being trapped by the snow. Seeing no way of exit or safety, it roared.[1171] **317.** When Nabai heard the animal— for he was passing by at that time—he came to the place where the noise was. Going down to the entrance, he struck the lion as it fought with the stick in his hands, and immediately killed it.[1172] The rest of these men were of equal valor.[1173]

David decides on census

(13.1) 318. Now King David, wishing to know how many ten thousands there were among his people,[1174] ignored the commandments of Moyses, who had previously prescribed that, if the crowd were counted, a half-shekel per head was to be paid to God.[1175] He ordered his general Joab[1176] to go and count the entire people.[1177]

Joab conducts census

319. Although Joab said that there was no need to do this,[1178] David was not convinced. Rather, he ordered him to go without delay for the census of the Hebrews.[1179] Joab, taking the rulers of the tribes[1180] and the scribes,[1181] marched through the Isra-

---

[1170] This added transition underscores the remarkable character of the exploit that is now to be related (and which Josephus has reserved to last place in his account of "Nabai"; see note to "valor" at 7.315). It takes the place of the closing notice for Benaiah given in 2 Sam 23:23// 1 Chr 11:24-25 concerning his (non-)standing among "The Three."

[1171] Josephus embellishes the circumstances of the lion's entrapment; compare 2 Sam 23:20b// 1 Chr 11:22b, which merely mention the beast's presence "in the middle of a pit on a snowy day."

[1172] Josephus dramatizes the simple mention of Benaiah's "slaying" the lion in 2 Sam 23:20b// 1 Chr 11:22b.

[1173] This statement echoes Josephus' announcement in 7.307 that he intends to provide an account of only 5 of David's 38 heroes. Having done this in 7.308-317, he leaves aside the list of the remaining champions given in 2 Sam 23:24-39a// 1 Chr 11:26-47 in accordance with his usual tendency to abridge or omit extended biblical name lists.

[1174] This motivation for David's census-taking draws on the reason the king gives for commanding Joab to undertake the census in 2 Sam 24:2// 1 Chr 21:2b ("that I may know the number [of the people]"). Josephus passes over the "supernatural explanations" of the king's initiative put forward in 2 Sam 24:1 (in his—not further motivated—anger against Israel the Lord prompts David to number the people) and 1 Chr 21:1 (Satan incites David to undertake the census; on Josephus' non-mention of "Satan" in *Antiquities*, see Schlatter 1932: 36-37). In Josephus' presentation then, the census results exclusively from David's own wishes, no higher agency being involved. On Josephus' version of the story of David's census, see Begg 1994.

[1175] With this added statement Josephus spells out—as his biblical sources do not—in what the wrongfulness of David's census consisted. The reference is to

the law requiring the payment of a "head tax" for those counted in a census in Exod 30:11-13; 38:25-26// *Ant.* 3.194-196; see Feldman 2000: 283, n. 508. Compare *b. Ber.* 62b, which avers that God, through the agency of Satan (see 1 Chr 21:1), caused David to "stumble over" the Mosaic ordinance of Exod 30:12.

[1176] Like MT LXX B 2 Sam 24:2a, Josephus has David address his order to Joab alone, whereas in 1 Chr 21:2a (and LXX L 24:2a) he speaks to the army commanders as well.

[1177] Josephus abbreviates David's order as cited in 2 Sam 24:2b// 1 Chr 21:2b, omitting, e.g., the specification concerning the extent of the territory to be traversed by Joab ("from Dan to Beersheba") as well as the motivation for David's project (which he has already anticipated when introducing the census story; see note on "people" at 7.318).

[1178] Here too, Josephus compresses the biblical exchange between king and general. Compare 2 Sam 24:3// 1 Chr 21:3, where Joab first expresses a wish for the increase of David's people and then asks why the king should want to number them, thereby bringing guilt on Israel (this final element of Joab's reply is absent from 24:3).

[1179] Josephus elaborates on the summary statement of 2 Sam 24:4a// 1 Chr 21:4a: "but the king's word prevailed against Joab (+ and the commanders of the army, 24:4a)."

[1180] Josephus' reference to these figures reflects the plus of 2 Sam 24:4b with its mention of the "commanders of the army" accompanying Joab. In 1 Chr 21:4b Joab alone goes forth to conduct the census.

[1181] Neither biblical source mentions this group as accompanying Joab. Josephus' insertion of them reflects the obvious need for their services during a census-taking. Cf. his likewise added reference to "scribes" in *Ant.* 6.120.

elites' country.[1182] Having ascertained what the amount was, he returned to the king in Hierosolyma,[1183] nine months and twenty days later.[1184] He reported to the king the number of the people, the tribe of the Benjamites excepted.[1185] **320.** For he did not have the time to count either this or the tribe of the Levites,[1186] since the king changed his mind about having offended against God.[1187] The number of the other Israelites was 900,000[1188] men capable of bearing arms and going on campaign, while that of the tribe of Iouda by itself was 400,000[1189] men.

(13.2) 321. When the prophets disclosed to David that God was wrathful with him,[1190] he began to beg and appeal to God to be benevolent and to pardon his offense.[1191] God sent the prophet[1192] Gad[1193] to him, bringing three choices in order that he might choose whichever of these seemed good to him:[1194] first, if he so wished, there would be a famine throughout the country for seven[1195] years; or for

Joab reports results to David

David offered three choices of punishment

[1182] This generalized reference to Joab's "tour" as encompassing the entire land of Israel corresponds to 1 Chr 21:4bα// 2 Sam 21:8a. Like the Chronicler, Josephus has no equivalent to the listing of the various regions and sites visited by Joab and his party in 2 Sam 24:5-7.

[1183] See 2 Sam 24:8b// 1 Chr 21:4b; Josephus supplies the transitional phrase concerning the conclusion of the census.

[1184] This figure for the duration of Joab's mission corresponds to the plus of 2 Sam 24:8b. The Chronicler (see 1 Chr 21:4b) has no equivalent.

[1185] Josephus here combines mention of Joab's report (2 Sam 24:9a// 1 Chr 21:5a) with the Chronicler's "afterthought" plus concerning the non-numbering of the Benjamites (21:6, where they are mentioned after the other non-counted tribe, i.e. the Levites).

[1186] The plus of MT 1 Chr 21:6 attributes Joab's non-numbering of the Levites and Benjamites to his "abhorrence" of David's command; LXX L ascribes that "failure" to the king's "hurrying" of Joab (Marcus *ad loc.* suggests that Josephus' wording reflects this reading).

[1187] With this statement Josephus provides an explanation concerning Joab's not having the time to complete the census as previously mentioned by him in apparent dependence on LXX L 1 Chr 21:6; see previous note. The statement is likewise an anticipation of the notice of 2 Sam 24:10a that "David's heart smote him *after* he had numbered the people." By having David repent of his misdeed even while the census is being conducted, Josephus accentuates the king's piety/ sensitivity of conscience.

[1188] Josephus' figure for the Israelites agrees with that given in LXX L 2 Sam 24:9// 1 Chr 21:5. MT and LXX B 2 Sam 24:9 have 800,000, MT and LXX B 1 Chr 21:5 1,100,000. On Rabbinic attempts to resolve the discrepancy between (MT) 24:9 and 21:5, see Begg 1994: 206, n. 19.

[1189] This figure for the Judeans agrees with that given in LXX L 2 Sam 24:9. MT and LXX B 24:9 speak of 500,000, MT LXX L 1 Chr 21:5 of 470,000 (LXX B does not provide a total for the Judeans counted).

[1190] In both sources (see 2 Sam 24:13// 1 Chr 21:11) a single prophet, Gad, addresses David only after the latter has expressed repentance for his deed (see 24:10 // 21:8). Josephus' added reference to a nameless group of prophets who speak for God to the king is reminiscent of 7.294 where—without biblical basis (compare 2 Sam 21:1b)—he has "prophets" inform David of the divine will concerning the famine. Here in 7.321 the prophets' announcement of God's anger likewise provides a rationale for David's addressing God with his words of appeal/confession, which in the sources are left without explicit motivation.

[1191] See 2 Sam 24:10// 1 Chr 21:8.

[1192] Josephus leaves aside the other designation used of Gad in 2 Sam 24:11// 1 Chr 21:9, i.e. "David's seer." He draws his identification of Gad as "the prophet" from 24:11 (MT LXX L, > LXX B).

[1193] MT (2 Sam 24:11// 1 Chr 21:9) גד (Eng.: "Gad"); LXX Γάδ; Josephus Γάδος. Josephus, like Chronicles, has no counterpart to the mention of David's "arising in the morning," which precedes God's commissioning of Gad in 2 Sam 24:11.

[1194] See the divine word to Gad cited in 2 Sam 24:12// 1 Chr 21:10. Josephus conflates the presentation of his sources where, between God's commissioning Gad to inform the king of his 3 choices (24:12// 21:10) and the prophet's spelling out those choices to the king (24:13b// 21:12), there intervenes mention of Gad's approach to David (24:13a// 21:11). Passing over this last element, Josephus combines the 2 preceding ones into a continuous sequence, in which God instructs Gad about both the number and content of the choices he is to offer David.

[1195] Josephus' figure for the duration of the famine agrees with that given in MT 2 Sam 24:13 as against the "3 years" of LXX 24:13 and 1 Chr 21:12.

three months he would be defeated by his enemies when fighting against them; or a pestilent disease would be sent upon the Hebrews for three days.[1196]

David chooses plague

322. David, confronted with the difficult choice among these great calamities,[1197] grieved and was thrown into great consternation.[1198] But the prophet said that this would happen of necessity, and directed him to answer quickly, so that he might announce his choice to God.[1199] The king thought that if he requested famine, it would seem to the others that he had done so without risk to himself, because he had much grain stored up, while to them it would bring harm. **323.** And if he opted to have them defeated for three months [they would say][1200] he had opted for war because he had heroes around himself as well as fortresses, and so had nothing to fear. He therefore requested a suffering common to both kings and subjects, in which the anxiety would be equal for all,[1201] having previously declared that it was much better to fall into the hands of God than into those of the enemy.[1202]

Effects of plague

(13.3) 324. When he heard this, the prophet announced it to God who sent a devastating plague upon the Hebrews.[1203] They did not die all in the same way, that the disease might easily be recognized. For though the calamity was a single one, it eliminated them for countless real or supposed causes, which they could not differentiate. **325.** For they were destroyed by turn; the terror came unexpectedly upon them and brought quick death. Some breathed out their souls suddenly to the accompaniment of severe pains and bitter distress. Others were so diminished by their sufferings that nothing remained for burial, but everything was eaten up by the illness itself. **326.** There were those whose eyes were struck by sudden darkness and who suffocated even as they moaned; still others passed away while burying a family member so that the burial rites remained unfinished.[1204] From the onset in the

---

[1196] Like 2 Sam 24:13, Josephus speaks of the 3rd proposed punishment simply as a "pestilent illness." In 1 Chr 21:12 the reference is amplified with mentions of the "sword of the Lord" and "the angel of the Lord destroying throughout all the territory of Israel."

[1197] This added phrase highlights the magnitude of David's dilemma.

[1198] Josephus transposes David's opening word to Gad in 2 Sam 24:14a// 1 Chr 21:13a: "I am in great distress" into this editorial remark about the king's emotional state.

[1199] Gad's demand for an answer here might be seen as Josephus' delayed utilization of the injunction with which the prophet concludes his earlier address to the king in 2 Sam 24:13// 1 Chr 21:12: "Now decide what answer I shall bring to him who sent me."

[1200] This conjectured reading (Greek: ἐροῦσιν) fills in an apparent lacuna in the text; see Marcus *ad loc.*

[1201] The sources have no equivalent to the above "process of elimination" whereby David reached his decision among the choices offered him. The insertion depicts David as a prudent man who, even in a moment of intense pressure, thinks through the ramifications of his choices for the public perception of himself. It also has noteworthy similarities with the Tg.'s amplified

version of 1 Chr 21:13 and a range of rabbinic texts; see Begg 1994: 209, n. 26.

[1202] From David's response to Gad in 2 Sam 24:14b // 1 Chr 21:13b Josephus leaves aside the king's appended explanation of his choice of falling into the hand of the Lord rather than into those of men, i.e. the fact that the Lord's mercy is "very great."

[1203] Josephus prefaces the notice of God's unleashing the pestilence (2 Sam 24:15a// 1 Chr 24:14a) with mention of Gad's reporting David's answer. Conversely, he has no parallel to the LXX plus at the opening of 2 Sam 24:15: "So David chose the plague. And in the days of the wheat harvest..." (trans. McCarter 1984 *ad loc.*).

[1204] The entire above sequence of 2.5 paragraphs is Josephus' dramatic embellishment of the summary source notices on the plague's casualty figures (2 Sam 24:15b// 1 Chr 21:14b). Marcus (*ad loc.*) calls attention to the segment's similarities with Thucydides' account (2, 47-54) of the plague that devastated Athens, while Mach (1992: 328) alludes to its reminiscence of Josephus' own narrative of the afflictions of besieged Jerusalem in *War* 5.512-518 (in both passages, e.g., persons die even while burying others; see *Ant.* 7.326; *War* 5.514).

morning of the pestilent disease that wasted them until noon,[1205] 70,000 persons perished.[1206]

327. The angel then stretched out his hand also towards Hierosolyma, sending the terror there.[1207] The king put on sackcloth and lay on the ground,[1208] begging and asking God to be cease and desist, being satisfied with those already dead.[1209] When the king looked up into the air, he observed the angel, who was borne aloft by it, opposite Hierosolyma with his sword drawn.[1210] **328.** He said to God that it was just that he, the shepherd,[1211] be punished, but the flock should be saved, for they had committed no offense. He implored him to vent all his wrath against him and his family, but to spare the people.[1212]

David's appeal to God

(13.4) 329. God listened to his begging and stopped the pestilence.[1213] Sending the prophet Gad,[1214] he directed him to go up immediately to the threshing floor of the Jebusite Oronnas[1215] and, having built an altar, to offer sacrifice to God.[1216] When David heard this, he did not ignore it, but immediately hurried to the place

Gad sends David to Or-nan (Oronnas)

[1205] Josephus' indication concerning the duration of the plague parallels that found in LXX 2 Sam 24:15b (MT: "from morning until the appointed time"). Like Chronicles, Josephus has no equivalent to the specification of 2 Sam 24:15b that the pestilence raged from "Dan to Beersheba."

[1206] Josephus' figure for the plague's victims agrees with that given in all witnesses of 2 Sam 24:15b// 1 Chr 21:14b.

[1207] This notice corresponds to the opening words of 2 Sam 24:16; 1 Chr 21:15 does not mention the angel's "hand." Josephus leaves aside the remainder of 24:16// 21:15, in which the Lord "repents of the evil," and commands the angel—who is himself present at the threshing floor of Araunah/Ornan—to desist. Josephus' omission of this source sequence is understandable given that the Lord's "repentance," already at this juncture, would seem to render pointless David's following urgent appeal, just as the reference to the angel's presence on earth would be at odds with Josephus' subsequent mention of the angel's being carried along on the air current.

[1208] This is Josephus' anticipated version of the plus of 1 Chr 21:16b, where David and the elders respond to the vision of the angel and his drawn sword (21:16a) by donning sackcloth and prostrating themselves (this plus also appears in the 4QSam[a] text of 2 Sam 24:16, where the initiatives of David and the elders are cited in reverse order). Josephus has the king alone undertake these penitential practices.

[1209] This initial appeal by the king—already before his vision of the destroying angel—is Josephus' own creation. By having David address God at this point, prior to the angelic apparition, Josephus accentuates the king's piety/penitence. Subsequently, he will have David also use the words attributed to him in response to his angelic vision in 2 Sam 24:17// 1 Chr 21:17. See 7.328.

[1210] Josephus reverses the sequence of his sources, where David's seeing of the destroying angel (2 Sam 24:17a// 1 Chr 21:16) precedes his appeal to the Lord (24:17b// 21:17). His specifications concerning the airborne angel and his "drawn sword" correspond to the wording of 1 Chr 21:16, whereas in 2 Sam 24:17a the king simply sees the angel, "who was smiting the people."

[1211] David's designation of himself as a "shepherd" corresponds to the 4QSam[a] LXX L and OL plus in 2 Sam 24:17, lacking in MT LXX B and 1 Chr 21:17.

[1212] See 2 Sam 24:17b// 1 Chr 21:17, whose content Josephus utilizes at this point, having earlier cited an initial "pre-vision" entreaty by David of his own creation in 7.327. The concluding appeal that God "spare the people" is Josephus' positive rendering of David's closing words in 1 Chr 21:17: "... let not the plague be upon thy [God's] people."

[1213] This notice on the effect of David's appeal has no counterpart in the sources, where God's "repenting of the evil" is mentioned already prior to the king's prayer; see 2 Sam 24:16// 1 Chr 21:15 and cf. note to "there" at 7.327.

[1214] In making God himself dispatch Gad to David, Josephus differs from both 2 Sam 24:18 (where the prophet appears to approach David on his own initiative) and 1 Chr 21:18 (where it is "the angel of the Lord" who instructs him to go to the king).

[1215] MT 2 Sam 24:18 אֲרַנְיָה (Eng.: "Araunah"); MT 1 Chr 21:18 אָרְנָן (Eng.: "Ornan"); LXX Ὀρνά; Josephus Ὀροννᾶς.

[1216] Josephus amplifies God's command that David build an altar in 2 Sam 24:18// 1 Chr 21:18 with the additional directive about offering sacrifices. He thereby makes David's subsequent sacrificing (24:25// 21:26) a matter of obedience to a divine injunction, rather than something that he (apparently) undertakes on his own initiative.

David buys threshing floor from Ornan

that had been mentioned to him.[1217]

330. Oronnas, who was threshing grain there,[1218] observed the king approaching, along with all his servants.[1219] He ran forward and paid him homage.[1220] He was indeed a Jebusite by race, but a special friend of David and because of this the king had not harmed him when he conquered the city, as we mentioned a short while ago.[1221]

331. When Oronnas inquired why he, the master, had come to him, the slave,[1222] David said that it was in order to buy the threshing floor from him, so that he might erect an altar to God on it and make a sacrifice.[1223] Oronnas said that he would make a present of the threshing floor, as well as the ploughs and the oxen for a holocaust,[1224] and prayed that God would willingly accept the sacrifice.[1225] **332.** The king said that he appreciated his liberality and magnanimity and accepted the favor,[1226] but asked him to take payment for all these things, for it would not be just to offer a sacrifice without cost.[1227] When Oronnas said that he might do what he wished,[1228] he brought the threshing floor[1229] from him for fifty shekels.[1230]

David's sacrifice placates God

333. Having built an altar, he consecrated it, and offered sacrifices and holocausts and presented peace offerings.[1231] The Deity was appeased by these things and became benevolent once again.[1232] Now it happened that Abram had brought his son

[1217] See 2 Sam 24:19// 1 Chr 21:19, whose reference to the (prophetic) "word" Josephus, in line with his usual practice, eliminates.

[1218] This reference to what Oronnas is doing at the moment of David's approach corresponds to the plus of 1 Chr 21:19 and 4QSam^a 2 Sam 24:20. Josephus has no equivalent to the (variable) additional material of these witnesses, which reads in the version of MT 1 Chr 21:19: "... he (Ornan) turned and saw the angel [so also 4QSam^a; LXX 1 Chr 21:19: the king], and his four sons hid themselves [4QSam^a: and his servants coming towards him clothed in sackcloth—cf. note on "servants" at 7.330]."

[1219] See 2 Sam 24:21a (no equivalent in 1 Chronicles 21). The term rendered "servants" above (Greek: παῖδες) is the same used in LXX 24:21. It might also be translated "sons," as it is by Weill *ad loc.*; see Begg 1994: 215, n. 47. 4QSam^a 24:21a specifies that the servants were "clad in sackcloth"; see note to "there" at 7.330.

[1220] See 2 Sam 24:20b// 1 Chr 21:21b.

[1221] This appended notice concerning "Oronnas" recalls Josephus' (also added) introduction of him in connection with David's seizure of Jerusalem in 7.69.

[1222] In having Oronnas initiate the exchange with his question about David's coming to him, Josephus follows 2 Sam 24:21a; in 1 Chr 21:22a, by contrast, David immediately calls on Ornan to hand over his threshing floor to him.

[1223] See 2 Sam 24:21b// 1 Chr 21:22. The Josephan David's mention of his intended sacrifice picks up on Gad's command that he sacrifice on the altar he is to build (7.329). It takes the place of the sources' own in-

dication concerning the purpose of David's altar-building, i.e. "that the plague may be averted from the people." Josephus likewise leaves aside the plus of 21:22, in which David asks Ornan to give him the threshing floor "at its full price."

[1224] See 2 Sam 24:22// 1 Chr 21:23. Josephus' mention of the "ploughs" as one of the objects offered by Oronnas has a counterpart in LXX L 24:22 and LXX B 1 Chr 21:23. He omits the various additional/alternative items that Aranuah/Ornan offers to David in several of the biblical textual witnesses (e.g. "the wheat for a cereal offering," MT 21:23); see Marcus *ad loc.* and Begg 1994: 217.

[1225] This allusion to Oronnas' "prayer" draws on the plus of 2 Sam 24:23b, where he expresses the wish that "the Lord your God accept you [David]."

[1226] Josephus prefaces David's brusque rejection of Ornan's offer (2 Sam 24:24a// 1 Chr 21:24) with this polite acknowledgment of the spirit in which the offer is made.

[1227] See 2 Sam 24:24a// 1 Chr 21:24. Josephus omits the plus of 21:24, in which, speaking to Ornan, David refers to "taking for the Lord what is yours."

[1228] Josephus interjects this response by Oronnas to David's proposal.

[1229] 2 Sam 24:24b mentions also David's purchase of the oxen.

[1230] Josephus' figure for the price paid by David corresponds to that cited in 2 Sam 24:24b (which further specifies that the 50 shekels were "of silver"). 1 Chr 21:25 reads a much higher figure: 600 shekels of gold.

[1231] See 2 Sam 24:25a// 1 Chr 21:26a.

[1232] Josephus' notice on the outcome of David's

Isak to this very spot to offer him as a holocaust. When he was about to slaughter the boy, a ram suddenly appeared, standing beside the altar, which Abram sacrificed in place of his son, as we have said earlier.[1233] **334.** When David saw that his prayer had been heard by God and his sacrifice willingly accepted, he decided to designate that whole site as an altar[1234] for the entire people and to build a sanctuary for God.[1235] With this word he was not far off from what was to happen, for God sent the prophet to him who said that his son, who would assume the kingship after him, would build the sanctuary there.[1236]

(14.1) 335. After this prophecy, the king directed that the aliens be counted, and they were found to be 180,000.[1237] From these, he appointed 80,000 stone-cutters, while the rest of the crowd were to carry the stones.[1238] Of these, he set 3,500 over the workmen.[1239] He likewise prepared much iron and bronze for the works,[1240] as well as many gigantic cedar timbers. The Tyrians and Sidonians sent these things to him, for he ordered a supply of timber from them.[1241]

336. To his friends[1242] he said that he was preparing these things now, in order

David prepares workers and material for temple-building

---

sacrifice follows 2 Sam 24:25b ("so the Lord heeded supplications for the land, and the plague was averted from the land") as against the more elaborate account of 1 Chr 21:26b-27, where David calls upon the Lord, who answers him with fire from heaven upon the altar, and who further commands the angel to sheath his sword, as he does.

[1233] Josephus appends this cross reference to his account of the *Aqedah* in *Ant.* 1.222-236. His connecting of David's sacrifice with that of Abraham is likely inspired by 2 Chr 3:1 (Solomon builds the temple "on Mount Moriah... on the threshing floor of Ornan") taken in conjunction with Gen 22:1-2 (Abraham is told to go to "the land of Moriah," where he will be shown a "mountain" on which he is to sacrifice Isaac). The Targum's rendering of 1 Chr 21:15 likewise makes an explicit connection between the account of David's census and Genesis 22 with its reference to the angel who is about to destroy Jerusalem seeing the "ashes of the binding of Isaac which were at the base of the altar" and "remembering his covenant with Abraham which he had set up with him on the mountain of worship."

[1234] Niese *ad loc.* conjectures ἅλων ("threshing floor") on the basis of Lat for the βωμόν ("altar") of the Greek witnesses followed in the above translation. On Niese's conjecture, see the critique of Marcus *ad loc.*

[1235] Josephus derives the content of this notice from 1 Chr 21:28 (David's seeing that the Lord had answered him at Ornan's threshing floor) and 22:1 (David declares "here shall be the house of the Lord God and here the altar of burnt offering for Israel"). He leaves aside the intervening parenthesis of 21:29-30, which states that David was unable to go to Gibeon to inquire there of the Lord at the Mosaic tabernacle and altar of burnt offering on account of his fear of the sword of the Lord's angel. Such "fear" on David's part would seem out of place at this point, given the reference to God's

being "appeased" and "benevolent once again" in 7.333.

[1236] Neither source speaks of a further prophetic intervention at this point. Marcus *ad loc.* suggests that the content of the prophet's message according to Josephus with its allusion to Solomon was inspired by the LXX plus at the end of 2 Sam 24:25: "And Solomon added to the altar later, for it was small at first" (trans. McCarter 1984 *ad loc.*). In any case, the anonymous prophet's announcement here is also reminiscent of Josephus' version of Nathan's word to David (2 Sam 7:13// 1 Chr 17:12) in 7.93: "...the sanctuary would be built by his son, who would receive the kingship after him and who would be called Solomon."

[1237] See 1 Chr 22:2a, which does not a mention a total for the "aliens" assembled by David. Having followed the sequence of 2 Samuel through its chap. 24, Josephus now switches over to the special material of 1 Chronicles 22 in 7.335-342.

[1238] 1 Chr 22:2b mentions David's appointment of stone-cutters, but gives no figure for these. Josephus also supplies the notice on the task assigned the remaining 100,000 foreigners.

[1239] 1 Chronicles 22 does not mention David's overseers. Josephus derives his reference to them from 1 Kgs 5:30 (RSV 5:16), where LXX A has the same figure as his, i.e. 3,500 (MT 3,300; LXX B 3,600; LXX L 3,700).

[1240] See 1 Chr 22:3. Josephus omits the source indications concerning the intended uses of the collected iron.

[1241] See 1 Chr 22:4. Josephus appends the reference to David's "order," this explaining why the Phoenicians should have brought him the timber.

[1242] 1 Chr 22:5a does not specify to whom David addresses his words concerning the measures undertaken by him.

that he might leave the material for the building[1243] ready for the son who would rule as king after him so that he, being young and inexperienced in these matters due to his age, would not have to collect it, but having it prepared, might complete the work.[1244]

David addresses Solomon

(14.2) 337. Calling his son Solomon, he directed him, once he had assumed the kingship, to construct a sanctuary for God.[1245] He said that he himself had wished to do this, but had been prevented by God, since he had been defiled by blood and wars.[1246] At the same time he had, however, announced that his youngest son Solomon, who was to be called by this name, would build it for him.[1247] He [God] promised that he would take care of him like a father.[1248] He would make the country of the Hebrews happy under him with other good things, and indeed the greatest of all of these, namely peace and deliverance from war and civil disturbances.[1249]

338. "Since, therefore, you have been appointed king by God before your birth, try to be worthy of his providential care by being pious, just, and courageous.[1250] Keep his commandments and the laws that he gave us through Moyses, and do not allow others to transgress them.[1251] **339.** Make haste to complete for God the sanctuary that he has decided is to be [built] for him during your reign.[1252] Do not be dismayed by the magnitude of the task, nor lose heart in the face of it.[1253] For I shall prepare everything for you prior to my death.[1254] **340.** Know that already

---

[1243] MSP, followed by Marcus *ad loc.*, adds the specification τοῦ ναοῦ ("of the sanctuary"), which Niese omits with RO Lat.

[1244] See 1 Chr 22:5a. From David's speech concerning his project Josephus leaves aside the reference to the requisite magnificence of the house that is to be built for the Lord. He likewise omits the parenthetical narrative remark of 22:5b about David's accumulating large quantities of material before his death.

[1245] See 1 Chr 22:6.

[1246] Josephus compresses David's address to Solomon about his plan and God's veto of this (1 Chr 22:7-8), eliminating, e.g., the phrase "the word of the Lord came to me" of v. 8a. The wording of David's speech here recalls Nathan's message to him as cited in 7.92.

[1247] Josephus combines elements of David's discourse from 1 Chr 22:9bα (the name of David's son) and 10aα (Solomon's building of the temple). He reserves until the end of the paragraph his version of the source's wordplay (see v. 9) on the name "Solomon" and the term שלום ("peace"), while adding the reference to Solomon's being David's "youngest son." David now begins recapitulating Nathan's word of promise to him as cited in 7.93.

[1248] Compare 1 Chr 22:10bα: "He shall be my son, and I [God] will be his father," and cf. 7.93, where Nathan assures David that God "would protect and take care of him [Solomon] as a father does his son." Josephus omits the further divine promise of 22:10bβ: "I will establish his royal throne in Israel for ever" with its Messianic connotations.

[1249] Josephus elaborates on David's earlier (see 1

Chr 22:9; cf. note to "him" at 7.337) double mention of the "peace" God promises to give in Solomon's day with, e.g., a characteristic allusion to intra-Jewish conflict as something especially undesirable.

[1250] Compare 1 Chr 22:13b, where Solomon is called on to "be strong and of good courage." Josephus has David exhorting his successor to the practice of 3 cardinal virtues.

[1251] See 1 Chr 22:12bβ-13a. The injunction that Solomon is to prevent others from violating the Mosaic code is without source parallel. Conversely, Josephus omits the opening conditional assurance of 22:13a, i.e. "then you will prosper if...."

[1252] Compare 1 Chr 22:11, where David prays "... may the Lord be with you [Solomon], so that you may succeed in building the house of the Lord your God, as he has spoken concerning you." Josephus turns David's expression of hope for Solomon into a directive by him to his son.

[1253] This exhortation that Solomon begin work on the temple immediately and without hesitation replaces David's more general call to strength, courage, and fearlessness on his part in 1 Chr 22:13b—anticipated by Josephus in 7.338 (see note to "courageous" at 7.338)—, which does not explicitly relate these qualities to the temple-building task.

[1254] Josephus inserts this general assurance by David as a motivation for his preceding exhortation that Solomon not be intimidated by his temple-building task—he need not be, given that David will have made the necessary preparations—and as an introduc-

10,000[1255] golden talents have been collected, as well as 100,000[1256] silver talents. I have assembled bronze and iron beyond counting, along with a innumerable amount of stones and timber.[1257] In addition, you have many ten thousands of masons and carpenters.[1258] If you have need of anything beyond this, supply it yourself.[1259] So be brave, having God as your protector."[1260]

341. He also exhorted the rulers of the people to help his son in the building and, without fear of any misfortune, to occupy themselves with the worship of God.[1261] For in recompense for this, they would enjoy that peace and loyalty with which God rewards pious and just persons.[1262] **342.** He ordered that, once the sanctuary had been built, they should deposit within it the ark and the sacred vessels[1263] to which a sanctuary was long since owed, had not our ancestors disregarded the commandments of God that once they occupied this land, they were to build him a sanctuary.[1264] This is what David said to the leaders and to his son.[1265]

David's directives to leaders

(14.3) 343. David was now already quite old[1266] and his body was growing frigid; over time, he became so sensitive to cold that he could not be warmed, even when covered by many garments.[1267] When the physicians[1268] convened, they advised that a pretty virgin be selected from the entire country to lie with the king. For the young woman's warming him would be a help to him against the cold.[1269]

Abishag (Abisake) brought to warm David

344. Now there was found in a city...[1270] a woman named Abisake,[1271] who excelled all women in appearance; she was brought to the king solely to warm him,

---

tion to the list of items David has previously assembled, as cited in 1 Chr 22:14abα.

[1255] The figure given in 1 Chr 22:14 is 100,000. In his later allusion (see 7.371) to his statement here, David will speak simply of the "large amount" of gold collected by him.

[1256] The total cited in 1 Chr 22:14 is 1,000,000. Josephus' David will repeat the same figure for the silver collected by him in 7.371.

[1257] The above 4 items appear in David's catalogue of the objects collected by him in 1 Chr 22:14bα.

[1258] Josephus reduces the 4 categories of available workers cited by David in 1 Chr 22:15-16a to 2.

[1259] Compare 1 Chr 22:15bβ, where David calls Solomon to "add to" what he himself has already collected.

[1260] Compare 1 Chr 22:16b: "arise and be doing! The Lord is with you."

[1261] Josephus combines elements of David's address to the leaders (1 Chr 22:17-19): the call to assist Solomon (22:17) and the positive exhortation to wholehearted seeking of the Lord (22:19aα). The negative command that the leaders "fear no misfortune" has no equivalent in the biblical David's words to the leaders.

[1262] This statement turns David's reference to Israel's current divinely blessed situation of 1 Chr 22:18 into a conditional promise for the leaders' future.

[1263] See David's concluding directive to the leaders in 1 Chr 22:19b.

[1264] This reminder of the long-standing, but as yet unrealized divine command about building a temple

has no counterpart in David's words to the leaders in 1 Chr 22:17-19. It harks back to the Mosaic ordinance about the building of a temple in the land cited by Josephus in *Ant.* 4.199-200, which, in turn, has no precise biblical parallel.

[1265] Josephus appends this concluding formula to his rendition (7.337-342) of David's double speech in 1 Chr 22:6-19, first to Solomon personally (22:6-16) and then to the leaders (22:17-19).

[1266] In 1 Chr 23:1 mention of David's advanced age is followed by a summary reference to his making Solomon king. Josephus at this point turns to the much more elaborate account of 1 Kings 1 in relating the difficult circumstances surrounding David's designation of Solomon.

[1267] See 1 Kgs 1:1.

[1268] In 1 Kgs 1:2 it is David's "servants" who advise him. See the similar substitution of "physicians" for the source's "servants" in Josephus' account of Saul's mental illness in *Ant.* 6.166 (// 1 Sam 16:15).

[1269] See 1 Kgs 1:2, from which Josephus omits the mention of the woman's waiting upon the king and functioning as his nurse. He makes part of the physicians' own proposal the narrative notice of 1 Kgs 1:3a that the search was conducted "throughout all the territory of Israel."

[1270] 1 Kgs 1:3 calls Abishag a "Shunamite." Niese and Marcus posit that the name of the woman's hometown has fallen out of the text of Josephus.

[1271] MT (1 Kgs 1:3) אֲבִישַׁג (Eng.: "Abishag"); LXX B Ἀβεισά; LXX L Ἀβισάκ; Josephus Ἀβισάκη.

since due to age he was too feeble for sexual pleasure and intercourse with a woman.[1272] About this virgin we shall speak shortly.[1273]

(14.4) 345. The fourth[1274] son of David, a tall and handsome youth,[1275] born to him by his wife Aigisthes,[1276] named Adonias[1277] who was similar in mind to Apsalom.[1278] He boasted that he would rule as king and said to his friends that he ought to receive the rule.[1279] He acquired many chariots and horsemen and fifty men who ran before him.[1280]

346. Although he saw this, his father did not censure him or restrain his intention, nor did he ever allow himself to inquire why he was doing these things.[1281] As his collaborators Adonias had the general Joab and the high priest Abiathar.[1282] His only opponents were the high priest Sadok and the prophet Nathas, as well as Banai, who was over the bodyguards,[1283] and Simoueis,[1284] the friend of David,[1285] and all the heroes.

347. Adonias prepared a supper[1286] outside the city[1287] beside the fountain[1288] in the royal park[1289] and invited all his brothers, except Solomon.[1290] He also took along the general Joab, Abiathar, and the rulers of the tribe of Iouda.[1291] He did not invite

---

[1272] Josephus provides an explanation for the concluding statement of 1 Kgs 1:4 ("but the king knew her not").

[1273] See *Ant.* 8.5 (// 1 Kgs 2:17), where Adonijah asks Bathsheba's help in obtaining her as his wife.

[1274] 1 Kgs 1:6β speaks more generally about Adonijah's being born "next after Absalom." Josephus recapitulates the specification about his being the 4th-born son from 7.21// 2 Sam 3:4.

[1275] Josephus anticipates this reference to Adonijah's appearance from 1 Kgs 1:6bα.

[1276] See 1 Kgs 1:5 (MT LXX B; LXX L calls him "son of David"). Josephus has mentioned the mother of Adonijah previously in 7.21.

[1277] MT (1 Kgs 1:5) אדניה (Eng.: "Adonijah"); LXX B Ἀδωνείας; LXX L Ὀρνιά; Josephus Ἀδωνίας.

[1278] Josephus appends this remark about Adonijah's similarity to Absalom; it serves to prepare for the former's recapitulation of the latter's revolt against his father and his ultimate bad end in what follows.

[1279] See 1 Kgs 1:5a, which does not specify to whom Adonijah makes his statement "I will be king."

[1280] Josephus embellishes the notice of 1 Kgs 1:5b on Adonijah's retinue with his specification that the prince had "many" chariots and horsemen. Compare 7.194, where Absalom—with whom Josephus has just compared Adonijah here in 7.345—is described as having "many horses and chariots," as well "50 armed men" around himself.

[1281] See 1 Kgs 1:6a; Josephus' opening reference to David's "seeing this" makes clear that the king's failure to rebuke his son was not due to ignorance of his doings. Josephus has anticipated the notice of 1:6bα on Adonijah's good looks in 7.345.

[1282] See 1 Kgs 1:7.

[1283] In 1 Kgs 1:8 "Benaiah" is identified rather as "son of Jehoiada." Josephus has previously mentioned this figure and his office in 7.110, 293.

[1284] MT (1 Kgs 1:8) שמעי (Eng.: "Shimei"); LXX B Σεμεεί; LXX L Σαμαίας; Josephus Σιμούεις.

[1285] MT 1 Kgs 1:9 mentions רעי (Eng.: "Rei"; see LXX B Ῥησεί) as another of David's "mighty men," alongside the previously cited "Shimei." Josephus apparently (mis-) read this form as the common noun רע ("friend"); cf. LXX L's οἱ ἑταῖροι αὐτοῦ. See Rappaport 1930: #229.

[1286] Compare 1 Kgs 1:9a: "Adonijah sacrificed sheep, oxen, and fatlings [LXX L lacks this last term]."

[1287] This general localization takes the place of the specification "by the Serpent Stone" (RSV) in 1 Kgs 1:9a.

[1288] Josephus' Greek term (πηγή) corresponds to that used by LXX L to render the first part (omitted by LXX B) of the composite expression of MT 1 Kgs 1:9a, i.e. "En-rogel." Conversely, he has no equivalent to the 2nd part of the MT place name.

[1289] This localization of the "spring" has no equivalent in 1 Kgs 1:9a. Josephus designates the site with a Greek word, i.e. παράδεισος that is ultimately of Persian origin and that eventually came to denote "Paradise," the place of protological and/or eschatological bliss.

[1290] Josephus combines the statements of 1 Kgs 1:9b and 10 concerning which of his brothers Adonijah did (not) invite. Like LXX B 1 Kgs 1:9a, he has no equivalent to the MT and LXX L specification that the brothers were "the king's sons."

[1291] 1 Kgs 1:9b mentions Adonijah's inviting "all the royal officials of Judah," but not specifically Joab and Abiathar.

the high priest Sadok, the prophet Nathas, Banai, the head of the bodyguards, nor those belonging to the opposing party to the banquet.[1292]

348. The prophet Nathas reported to Bersabe, the mother of Solomon, that Adonias wished to be king and that David was ignorant of this.[1293] He advised her to save herself and her son Solomon, and, seeing that Adonias was already taking over the rule,[1294] to inquire of the king concerning this.[1295] **349.** The prophet said that, while she was saying these things to the king, he would enter and second her words.[1296]

Nathan warns Bathsheba

Persuaded by Nathas, Bersabe presented herself before the king. Having paid him homage and asked for a word with him,[1297] **350.** she reported everything to him as the prophet had suggested,[1298] mentioning Adonias' supper[1299] and informing him of those who had been invited by him [Adonias], namely Abiathar the high priest, and Joab the ruler, and David's sons, except for Solomon and his closest friends.[1300] She further said that all the people were looking to whom he would designate king,[1301] and appealed to him to keep in mind that if after his departure Adonias ruled as king, he would do away with her and her son Solomon.[1302]

Bathsheba and Nathan report Adonijah's initiatives to David

(14.5) 351. While the woman was still speaking, the chamberlains announced that Nathas wished to see him. When the king directed that he be admitted,[1303] he came in and inquired whether he had today appointed Adonias king and handed the rule over to him.[1304] **352.** "For he made a splendid supper and invited all David's sons—

[1292] Josephus expands the list of those not invited of 1 Kgs 1:10 with the name of Zadok, having already anticipated its mention of "Solomon" to an earlier point in 7.347. His expression "those belonging to the opposing party" takes the place of "the mighty men" cited in the list of 1:10 (cf. 1:5).

[1293] In 1 Kgs 1:11 Nathan asks Bathsheba: "have you not heard that Adonijah... has become king and David does not know it?"

[1294] This translation follows the text of Niese; Marcus (*ad loc.*), basing himself on a somewhat different text, renders "... Adonias was king and David does not know this."

[1295] See 1 Kgs 1:12-13. From Nathan's proposal as to what Bathsheba is to say to the king in 1:13 Josephus leaves aside—in the above rendering (but see note on "words" at 7.349)—the invocation of David's (purported) previous "oath" that Solomon would succeed him. His omission of this element likely reflects the concern that the prophet Nathan not appear to be fabricating the oath in question, given that there has been no previous mention of such an oath in the biblical (or Josephus' own) account.

[1296] See 1 Kgs 1:14. Marcus (*ad loc.*) follows a longer, variant Greek text: "(he advised her)... to go alone to David and tell him, although he had sworn that Solomon should be king after his death, Adonias had meanwhile taken over the royal power." On the problem of David's (alleged) oath, see previous note.

[1297] Josephus modifies the sequence 1 Kgs 1:15-16 in several respects: He adds the opening reference to the persuasive effect of Nathan's words, omits the par-

enthetical allusion to David's age and Abishag's waiting on him (1:15b), and has Bathsheba, rather than David (so 1:16), open the exchange between them with her request to speak to him.

[1298] This generalized formulation takes the place of Bathsheba's initial invocation of David's (purported) oath to her in 1 Kgs 1:17, made in accordance with Nathan's instructions in 1:13, which Josephus previously left aside; see note to "this" at 7.348 and to "words" at 7.349.

[1299] As in the case of 1 Kgs 1:9 (see 7.347), Josephus uses this term in place of the reference to Adonijah's sacrifice of "oxen, fatlings (> LXX L) and sheep" of 1:19.

[1300] In having Bathsheba mention Adonijah's non-inviting Solomon, Josephus goes together with MT LXX B 1 Kgs 1:19 against LXX L. The reference to Solomon's "closest friends" also not being invited is his own.

[1301] See 1 Kgs 1:20.

[1302] Josephus has Bathsheba make more explicit the nature of the threat facing herself and her son. In 1 Kgs 1:21 she simply avers that after David's death the 2 of them will be "counted as offenders."

[1303] In 1 Kgs 1:22-23a Nathan first "comes in," at which an unspecified "they" informs David that the prophet is on hand, and finally Nathan, without being given explicit permission to do so, "comes in before the king." Josephus reworks this sequence to bring it more into conformity with the requirements of royal protocol.

[1304] See 1 Kgs 1:24. Josephus omits the notice on Nathan's prostration before the king of 1:23b.

except Solomon—as well as the general Joab.[1305] These were feasting with much clapping and joyful noise and wishing him an everlasting leadership.[1306] However, he invited neither me nor the high priest Sadok, nor Banai, who is over the bodyguards.[1307] Everyone ought to know whether these things are happening in accordance with your intentions."[1308]

353. When Nathas said this, the king directed that Bersabe be called to him (for she had exited the bedroom once the prophet arrived).[1309] Once the woman came,[1310] he said, "I swear to you by the greatest God[1311] that your son Solomon will indeed rule as king, just as I swore earlier, and will sit on my throne. And this will happen today."[1312]

David issues directives about Solomon's succession

354. When the woman paid him homage and prayed that he might live long,[1313] David summoned Sadok the high priest and Banai, who was over the bodyguards.[1314] **355.** Upon their arrival, he directed them to take Nathas the prophet and the soldiers stationed around the court.[1315] They were to set Solomon his son on the royal mule and bring him outside the city to the spring called Geion[1316] and appoint him king, anointing[1317] him with holy oil. He ordered the high priest Sadok and the prophet Nathas to do this.[1318] **356.** He further ordered those following [them] through the middle of the city to blow the trumpets and cry out "may Solomon sit for ever on the royal throne," in order that the entire people might know that he had been appointed king by his father.[1319] To Solomon himself he gave instructions concerning the rule in order that he might piously and righteously govern the whole nation of the Hebrews and the tribe of Iouda.[1320]

[1305] From Nathan's list of those invited (1 Kgs 1:25a) Josephus omits "Abiathar the priest" (earlier cited by him as among the guests in 7.347). His reference to "the general Joab" corresponds to the LXX L reading in 1:25a, whereas MT and LXX B have Nathan allude to "the commanders of the army." He anticipates the non-invitation of Solomon from 1:26.

[1306] In 1 Kgs 1:25b Nathan "quotes" the assembly's acclamation "Long live King Adonijah." Josephus adds the reference to the "clapping and joyful noise."

[1307] See the list in 1 Kgs 1:26, whose mention of Solomon Josephus has anticipated earlier in 7.352.

[1308] Josephus transposes into a pointed statement Nathan's question (1 Kgs 1:27) as to whether the king had prompted Adonijah's current initiative, without bothering to inform his own entourage.

[1309] See 1 Kgs 1:28a. Josephus appends the clarification concerning Bathsheba's whereabouts during Nathan's address to the king (1:24-27).

[1310] Josephus omits the reference to Bethsheba's "standing before the king" after her entry of 1 Kgs 1:28b.

[1311] Compare 1 Kgs 1:29, where David swears "as the Lord lives, who has redeemed my soul out of every adversity."

[1312] See 1 Kgs 1:30. In Josephus' presentation David alone cites his previous oath to Bathsheba (compare 1 Kgs 1:13, 17). Thereby, any suspicion that this was something fabricated and "put over on" the senile king

by Nathan and Bathsheba is eliminated; see note to "this" at 7.348.

[1313] See 1 Kgs 1:31.

[1314] David's directive about who is to be summoned in 1 Kgs 1:32a includes mention also of Nathan who—one might suppose—is still present before him, nothing having been said about his exiting prior to Bathsheba's 2nd interview with the king. Accordingly, Josephus has David summon Zadok and Benaiah alone.

[1315] In 1 Kgs 1:33 David commands the trio Zadok, Nathan and Benaiah (see v. 32) to take "the servants of your lord (LXX BL, MT lords)."

[1316] MT (1 Kgs 1:33) גִּחוֹן (Eng.: "Gihon"); LXX and Josephus Γειών. Josephus adds the specification about the localization of the spring.

[1317] Greek: περιχρίω. This compound form occurs only here in Josephus.

[1318] See 1 Kgs 1:34a (where LXX L has the sg. imperative "anoint" together with a pl. subject, i.e. Zadok and Nathan). Josephus adds the reference to the "holy oil" as the "matter" of the anointing, anticipating mention of the oil from the "anointing scene" of 1 Kgs 1:39.

[1319] See 1 Kgs 1:34b. Josephus appends David's remark concerning the purpose of the initiatives in question.

[1320] This admonition addressed *to* Solomon takes the place of 1 Kgs 1:35, where David speaks *about* Solomon as his successor whom he has appointed ruler

357. Once Banai had prayed that God would be benevolent to Solomon,[1321] they lost no time in setting Solomon on the royal mule and conducting him outside the city to the spring.[1322] After anointing him with the oil,[1323] they entered the city,[1324] showing their assent by applause and praying that his kingship would last a long time.[1325] **358.** When they arrived at the palace, they seated him on the throne.[1326] The entire people immediately turned to feasting and entertainment,[1327] rejoicing with dancing and flute-playing,[1328] so that the whole earth and air was filled with sound, due to the number of the instruments.[1329]

Solomon acclaimed king

(14.6) 359. When Adonias and those present at his supper heard the shouting, they were troubled,[1330] while the general Joab said that he was uneasy about the noise and the trumpet.[1331] While supper was being served—though no one tasted anything due to their apprehension—[1332] Ionathes, the son of the high priest Abiathar, came running to them.[1333] **360.** Adonias was pleased to see the young man and addressed him as a messenger of good things.[1334] He, however, disclosed everything to them concerning Solomon and the plan of King David.[1335] At that, Adonias and all the guests leapt up from the banquet and each one fled to his own home.[1336]

Adonijah's supporters scattered

"over Israel and over Judah." Josephus' rewording highlights Solomon's own role in the proceedings.

[1321] Josephus compresses the more extended hope expressed by Benaiah in 1 Kgs 1:36-37, omitting, e.g., its (potentially offensive) wish that God might make Solomon's throne "greater" than David's own.

[1322] See 1 Kgs 1:38. Josephus passes over the source catalogue of those accompanying Solomon, including "the Cherethites and the Pelethites," who were not specifically cited in David's preceding order (see 1:32-33) concerning the makeup of Solomon's entourage.

[1323] Josephus' participle, attributing Solomon's "anointing" (Greek: χρίσαντες; compare the compound περιχρίω used in David's order in 7.355) to a plural "they," corresponds to his rendering of David's order in 7.355 (// 1 Kgs 1:34), where Nathan and Zadok are instructed to do this. In 1 Kgs 1:39a, by contrast, Zadok alone anoints David. Josephus does not reproduce the source specification that the (horn of) oil was brought "from the Tent" by Zadok for the anointing.

[1324] This "entry" is not explicitly mentioned in 1 Kgs 1:39bα, which speaks rather of the blowing of the trumpet (cf. David's order to this effect in 1:34b) following Solomon's anointing. Josephus will make use of the source reference to trumpet-blowing in the word he attributes to Joab in 7.359 (// 1 Kgs 1:41).

[1325] See 1 Kgs 1:39b. Josephus adds the reference to the "applause" of Solomon's entourage.

[1326] 1 Kings 1 makes no explicit mention of such a post-anointing "enthronement" of Solomon (although cf. 1:35a, where David states that Solomon is to "sit upon my throne").

[1327] In 1 Kgs 1:40a the people are said rather to "go up after" Solomon.

[1328] See 1 Kgs 1:40bα. In speaking of both "danc-

ing" and "flute-playing," Josephus conflates the readings of LXX B (which has the former) and MT LXX L (which mention the latter).

[1329] Josephus wording here reflects LXX L 1 Kgs 1:40bβ, which speaks of the earth's "resounding," as opposed to its being "split" (so MT LXX B). Josephus goes beyond the former reading in having also "the air" affected by the noise.

[1330] 1 Kgs 1:41a does not mention the party's emotional response to what they hear.

[1331] Josephus turns Joab's question of 1 Kgs 1:41b ("what does this uproar in the city mean?") into a ominous statement of foreboding on his part. His mention of the "trumpet" picks up on the notice, previously passed over by him, about the trumpet being blown following Solomon's anointing in 1:39b; see note to "city" at 7.357.

[1332] Compare 1 Kgs 1:42a, where Jonathan's arrival coincides with Joab's query (1:41b) that he makes as the supper is ending (1:41a).

[1333] See 1 Kgs 1:42a (where "Jonathan" simply "comes" [MT LXX B; > LXX L]). Josephus last mentioned "Ionathes" by name in 7.201.

[1334] See 1 Kgs 1:42b. Josephus adds the reference to Adonijah's emotional response to Jonathan's arrival. From the former's words to the latter, he omits Adonijah's calling Jonathan a "worthy/strong man."

[1335] Josephus drastically compresses Jonathan's elaborate and repetitious recapitulation (1 Kgs 1:43-48) of what has already been reported in detail earlier in the chapter.

[1336] See 1 Kgs 1:49. Josephus leaves aside the source mention of the guests' "trembling," while introducing a reference to Adonijah's personal response to Jonathan's report.

Solomon spares Adonijah

361. Adonias, fearing the king because of what had happened, became God's suppliant and took hold of the protruding horns of the altar.[1337] What he had done was disclosed to Solomon, as was his asking that he receive pledges from him that he would neither hold a grudge nor do anything terrible to him.[1338] **362.** He, in a quite humane and prudent way, let him off unpunished for his offense this time,[1339] saying, however, that if he were caught again attempting to rebel, he would be the cause of his own punishment.[1340] Then he sent and removed him from the place of suppliants.[1341] When Adonias came and paid him homage, Solomon directed him to depart to his own house and not be apprehensive about anything. For the future, he requested him to behave well, since this would be to his advantage.[1342]

David organizes Levites and priests

(14.7) 363. David, wishing to appoint his son king over all the people, assembled the rulers and the priests and Levites at Hierosolyma.[1343]

First taking a count of the Levites, he found that there were 38,000 between the ages of thirty and fifty.[1344] **364.** Of these, he appointed 24,000 as overseers of the construction of the sanctuary,[1345] 6,000 of them as judges of the people and scribes,[1346] 4,000 as gatekeepers, and the same number as singers of God's praises on the instruments that David had made, as we previously mentioned.[1347]

365. He likewise divided them [the Levites] up according to their ancestral houses.[1348] When he separated out the priests of the tribe, he found that among these there were twenty-four ancestral houses.[1349] Sixteen were from the house of Eleazar, eight from the house of Ithamar.[1350] He appointed one ancestral [house] to minister to God for an eight-day period from sabbath to sabbath.[1351] **366.** Thus all the ances-

---

[1337] See 1 Kgs 1:50; Josephus' reference to Adonijah's becoming a "suppliant" spells out the sense of his altar gesture. Like MT and LXX B, Josephus lacks an equivalent to LXX L's mention of Adonijah's going "to the tent of the Lord."

[1338] Compare 1 Kgs 1:51, where Adonijah asks that Solomon swear "not to slay his servant with the sword."

[1339] Josephus renders more definite the pardon of Adonijah that is expressed hypothetically by Solomon in 1 Kgs 1:52a: "If he prove to be a worthy man, not one of his hairs will fall to the earth." He likewise introduces the initial (positive) evaluation of the king's response as "humane and prudent."

[1340] Compare Solomon's (alternative) hypothetical statement concerning Adonijah's case in 1 Kgs 1:52b: "If wickedness is found in him, he shall die."

[1341] See 1 Kgs 1:53a.

[1342] See 1 Kgs 1:53b. Josephus expands considerably on Solomon's curt source directive to the prostrate Adonijah: "go to your house." He thereby, once again (see note to "time" at 7.362), underscores the "humaneness" of the king's dealings with his brother.

[1343] At this point, Josephus returns to the presentation of the Chronicler (see 1 Chr 23:1-2) that he interrupted after 7.342 in order to incorporate the material peculiar to 1 Kings 1 in 7.343-362.

[1344] In 1 Chr 23:3 the 38,000 Levites counted are "thirty years old and upward." Josephus derives his more precise 2nd figure (i.e. 50) from Num 4:3 (cf. Num

8:24-25), where this is specified as the age of retirement for the Levites.

[1345] According to 1 Chr 23:4a the task of the 24,000 was "to have charge of the work in the house of the Lord."

[1346] In assigning the 6,000 the roles of "judges" and "scribes," Josephus agrees with LXX BL 1 Chr 23:4b against MT, which mentions "officers" (Hebrew: שֹׁטְרִים) alongside the "judges."

[1347] See 1 Chr 23:5. The appended cross reference to David's making of musical instruments points back to 7.305.

[1348] With this formula Josephus' introduces the topic of the Levitical divisions treated at length in 1 Chr 23:6-24(25-32). Immediately thereafter, however, reversing the sequence of 1 Chronicles 23-24, he speaks in the remainder of 7.365 and 366 about the priestly divisions and the lot-assigned sequence in which they are to undertake their liturgical service (// 1 Chr 24:1-19), before returning to the divisions of the (non-priestly) Levites in 7.367.

[1349] Josephus bases this figure on the list in 1 Chr 24:7-18, where 24 ancestral priestly houses and their assignment by lot are enumerated.

[1350] See 1 Chr 24:4.

[1351] Cf. 1 Chr 24:19, which refers to the priestly houses having as their "appointed duty to come into the house of the Lord." Josephus appends the specification concerning the duration of their "shifts."

tral houses were chosen by lot in the presence of David and of the high priests Sadok and Abiathar and all the rulers.[1352] The first ancestral house to come up in the lot-casting procedure was inscribed first, the second in turn, down to the twenty-fourth. And this division has continued down till today.[1353]

367. He also established twenty-four divisions of the tribe of Levi.[1354] According to the order in which the lots appeared when they were drawn, [they were selected] for eight-day periods, in the same way as were the priestly courses.[1355] He likewise honored the descendants of Moyses. For he made them keepers of the treasuries of God and of the devoted things that the kings used to dedicate.[1356] He appointed all those of the tribe of Levi and the priests to serve God night and day, as Moyses had commanded them.[1357]

(14.8) 368. After this, he divided up the army into twelve divisions with their leaders, along with commanders of hundreds and subordinate officers. Each division comprised 24,000 men.[1358] These he directed to be continuously in attendance on King Solomon, for thirty days from the first to the last day, along with the commanders of thousands and hundreds.[1359] **369.** He also appointed as ruler of each division one whom he knew to be good and just.[1360] Others, whose names we do not think it necessary to mention, were to be overseers of the treasuries, and villages, and fields and livestock.[1361]

David appoints secular officials

(14.9) 370. When he had taken care of each of these matters in the way described above, David assembled the rulers of the Hebrews, the tribal rulers and the leaders of the military divisions, and those placed over all the king's works or possessions.[1362] Standing on a lofty platform, the king said to the crowd:[1363]

David addresses people

[1352] See 1 Chr 24:5-6, where the selection of the priestly houses by lot is also witnessed by the Levite "Shemaiah," who records the outcome of the process.

[1353] Cf. the listing of the 24 priestly houses by name in 1 Chr 24:7-18; Josephus typically refrains from reproducing this catalogue of obscure names. In place of this he appends a notice on the duration of the arrangement. In *Life* 1-3 Josephus situates his own priestly lineage in the first of the 24 courses.

[1354] After the interlude concerning the priests of 7.365-366 (// 1 Chr 24:1-19) Josephus now returns to the subject of the non-priestly Levites, their divisions and the sequence in which these perform their liturgical duties (// 1 Chr 23:6-32; 24:20-31), introduced by him at the start of 7.365; see note on "houses" at 7.365. He derives his figure for the divisions of the latter group from the listing given in 1 Chr 25:1-4, which cites the 4 sons of Asaph, 6 sons of Jeduthun, and 14 sons of Heman for a total of 24 Levitical families. Here, as with the priests (see 7.366), he avoids reproducing the source's lengthy catalogues of Levitical names.

[1355] See 1 Chr 25:8, which mentions the casting of lots for the duties of the Levitical divisions. Josephus appends the cross reference, assimilating the procedure used for determining the order in which the Levitical "courses" perform their service and the duration of that service, to his notice on the arrangements for the priestly houses in 7.366.

[1356] Josephus anticipates this item from 1 Chr 26:24-28, which mentions various descendants of Moses as overseers of the temple treasuries and their contents.

[1357] This concluding remark rounds off Josephus' summary reproduction of the extended account given in 1 Chronicles 23-26 concerning David's organization of the 2 categories of the clergy. Josephus highlights the status of these arrangements by citing Moses as the ultimate authority behind them.

[1358] Josephus derives his figures for the number of the military divisions and their complements from the listing in 1 Chr 27:1-15.

[1359] Cf. 1 Chr 27:1, where there is reference to the "divisions that came and went, month after month throughout the year." Josephus inserts the mention of Solomon as the one whom the military divisions are to watch over.

[1360] The names of the division commanders are given in 1 Chr 27:2-15. Josephus adds the remark about the requisite moral qualities of these figures.

[1361] Josephus here alludes to the names of these various officials given in 1 Chr 27:25-31. He leaves aside the enumeration of the tribal heads of 27:16-24 and of David's "cabinet"—already cited by him in 7.110 and 293—of 27:32-34.

[1362] Josephus compresses the more detailed listing of those convened by David found in 1 Chr 28:1.

371. "Brothers and fellow-nationals, I want you to know that, planning to build a sanctuary for God, I prepared much gold and 100,000 talents of silver.[1364] God, however, via the prophet Nathas, prevented me, since my right hand was soiled by the wars I waged on your behalf and the slaughter of the enemy.[1365] Instead, he directed the son who would assume my kingship to build the sanctuary for him.[1366]

372. Now therefore, whereas our ancestor Jacob had twelve sons, you know that it was Iouda who was appointed king.[1367] Likewise when I was preferred over my six brothers and received leadership from God, none of them resented [this].[1368] I ask too that my own sons not rebel against each other, now that Solomon has received the kingship, but rather, recognizing that God chose him, submit willingly to him as their master.[1369] **373.** For it is not something terrible to serve even a foreign overlord if God wills this. When, however, it is a brother who has obtained this honor, it is appropriate to rejoice in it as something in which they too have a share.[1370] I pray that the promises of God will reach fulfillment and that this well-being that he promised to bestow during Solomon's reign may extend throughout the entire country and endure along with it for all time.[1371] **374.** These things will be established and have a good outcome if, my son, you show yourself pious and just by keeping the ancestral laws; if, on the contrary, you transgress them, you may expect worse things."[1372]

David gives Solomon plan of temple

(14.10) 375. When the king had ceased speaking these words, in the presence of everyone, he gave to Solomon the sketch and layout for the building of the sanctuary, for its foundation, rooms, and upper stories, what was to be their number and

---

[1363] In 1 Chr 28:2aα David "rises to his feet" for his following speech.

[1364] David's opening words in 1 Chr 28:2 refer more generally to his having "made preparations for building." With his mention of the precious metals amassed by him, the Josephan David harks back to his statement on the matter in 7.340 (// 1 Chr 22:14), which gives the same figure for the amount of silver collected by him, while specifying that the golden talents assembled amounted to 10,000.

[1365] David's reference to the divine prohibition of his temple-building in 1 Chr 28:3 does not mention Nathan's role as conveyer of God's message to him, which Josephus has already cited twice previously now; see 7.92, 337.

[1366] See 1 Chr 28:6a, where the divine word quoted by David mentions Solomon by name.

[1367] Cf. 1 Chr 28:4aβ, where David recalls God's choice of "Judah as leader" without mention of Jacob and his 12 sons.

[1368] Josephus expatiates on David's allusion to God's choice of himself from among his father's house in 1 Chr 28:4aαb with mention of his brothers' non-resentment of that choice. He likewise specifies the number of those brothers, recalling the figure given by him in *Ant.* 6.161.

[1369] This appeal by David that his sons follow the example of his brothers towards himself in accepting

Solomon's God-given kingship has no counterpart in David's address to the assembly in 1 Chr 28:2-8. The addition reflects the historian's recurrent concern with intra-Jewish harmony.

[1370] This continuation of and motivation for David's appeal to his (other) sons to accept Solomon's rule (see previous note) has no biblical parallel. Its reference to foreign rulership as tolerable when this is something willed by God clearly has in view the contemporary situation of Josephus' compatriots whom, through the mouth of David, he is calling to adopt a like outlook on Roman domination. The reference recalls the sentiments voiced by Agrippa in his speech to the Jews at the outbreak of the revolt in *War* 2.350-391, as well as Josephus' own words to the insurgents as cited by him in *Life* 17-22. I owe this observation to Prof. Steve Mason.

[1371] This "prayer" with its reference to God's earlier promises for Solomon's reign has no counterpart in David's address to the assembly in 1 Chr 28:2-8.

[1372] See David's words to Solomon personally in 1 Chr 28:7, 9; cf. the intervening v. 8, whose similar exhortation to observance of the Law is directed to the people as a whole. Josephus passes over David's concluding admonition of 28:10, in which Solomon is called on to undertake the building of the temple, given its duplication of 28:20 (which he will reproduce in 7.376).

how high and wide they were to be. He likewise fixed the weight of the golden and silver vessels.[1373]

David's exhortations regarding temple-building

376. He further exhorted him by his words to apply the utmost eagerness to the work,[1374] at the same time urging the rulers and the tribe of Levi[1375] to support him, given his age and God's having selected him as patron both of the building of the sanctuary and of the kingdom.[1376]

377. He declared that the construction would be practicable for them and not very laborious,[1377] given that he had already prepared many talents of gold and more of silver as well as timber and a crowd of carpenters and masons, in addition to emeralds and every kind of precious stone.[1378] **378.** He now said that he was giving an additional 3,000 talents of pure gold as his personal contribution to the service; this was for the inner sanctuary and the chariot of God, the Cherubim, which were to be placed upon the ark, veiling it.[1379]

Contributions for temple-building project

When David fell silent, the eagerness of the assembled rulers, priests and the Levitical tribe was great; they made splendid and generous promises.[1380] **379.** For they undertook to donate 5,000 talents and 10,000 *staters*,[1381] 10,000 silver talents, and many ten thousands of iron talents.[1382] And if anyone had a precious stone, he brought it and handed it over to the treasuries of which Ial, a descendant of Moyses, was in charge.[1383]

Praise of God by David and people

(14.11) 380. The whole people was pleased by these things, and David, seeing the solicitude and readiness of the rulers, the priests and all the rest,[1384] began to praise God in a loud voice, calling him the father and origin of all,[1385] the creator[1386]

[1373] Josephus compresses the lengthy enumeration of the various items featured in the "plan" given Solomon by David in 1 Chr 28:11-19.

[1374] Josephus abridges David's extended final admonition to Solomon about his temple-building task cited in 1 Chr 28:20, leaving aside, e.g., its assurance about God's supporting him in the enterprise; see note to "things" at 7.374.

[1375] Josephus modifies David's words in 1 Chr 28:21, where, speaking to Solomon, David calls his attention to the availability of the priestly and Levitical groupings, as well of "the officers and all the people." Josephus highlights the status of the leadership groups he mentions by having David speak not of them, but to them.

[1376] For this motivation of David's appeal to the leaders, Josephus draws on the king's word to the assembly in 1 Chr 29:1a, where he calls attention to Solomon's being "young and inexperienced."

[1377] Contrast David's statement in 1 Chr 29:1b: "the work is great; for the palace will not be for man but for the Lord God." The Josephan David aims to encourage, not intimidate, his hearers regarding their task.

[1378] See David's listing of the temple-building supplies amassed by him in 1 Chr 29:2, which Josephus generally abridges but into which he inserts mention of the 2 groups of workers in reminiscence of David's earlier reference to them in 7.340 (// 1 Chr 22:15).

[1379] To the mention of David's personal donation of

gold in 1 Chr 29:4a Josephus appends the specification concerning the use to which this will be put. His apposition of the "Cherubim" with the "chariot of God" has an approximate biblical counterpart in Ps 18:10, which speaks of the Lord "riding on a cherub." Josephus leaves aside David's subsequent words about his further personal gifts (29:4b-5a) and his appeal that others "consecrate themselves" as well (29:5b).

[1380] The list of donors in 1 Chr 29:6 does not mention the priests and Levites. Josephus highlights the generosity displayed by the various leadership groups.

[1381] MT 1 Chr 29:7 uses the Persian loan word "darics." Josephus' term reflects the standard Greek rendering of this term, i.e. στατὴρ δαρφεικός; see Marcus *ad loc.*

[1382] 1 Chr 29:7 specifies 100,000 talents of iron; it also mentions 18,000 talents of bronze.

[1383] MT (1 Chr 29:8) יְחִיאֵל (Eng.: "Jehiel"); LXX B Βεσιήλ; LXX L Ἰειήλ; Josephus Ἴαλος. The source verse calls him "the Gershonite." Josephus' linking of him with Moses seems inspired by this identification taken in combination with 1 Chr 26:24, where there is reference to "Gershom, son of Moses." On Moses' descendants as treasurers, see 7.367.

[1384] In 1 Chr 29:9 there is separate mention of people and king "rejoicing." Josephus makes what David "sees" the occasion for his following benediction (cf. 29:10).

[1385] In his "eulogy" of God in 1 Chr 29:10 David

of things human and divine,[1387] with which he adorned himself, the patron and protector[1388] of the Hebrew race, as well as of its well-being and of the kingship he had given to himself [David].[1389]

381. He prayed as well for good things for the whole people,[1390] and for an upright and just mind, one made strong by all the components of virtue, for his son Solomon;[1391] he then directed the crowd as well to praise God.[1392] Falling on the ground, they paid homage; they also gave thanks to David for everything they had enjoyed since he had received the kingship.[1393]

Sacrifices and feasting

382. On the following day they offered to God as a holocaust 1,000 calves, as many rams, and 1,000 lambs.[1394] They also sacrificed many peace offerings, having slaughtered many ten thousands of victims.[1395] Throughout the day the king feasted

Solomon's rule confirmed

with the entire people.[1396] They anointed Solomon a second time with oil, appointing him king,[1397] and Sadok high priest of the whole people.[1398] They brought Solomon to the palace and seated him on the throne of his father, and were subject to him from that day on.[1399]

David informs Solomon of his imminent death

(15.1) 383. Shortly afterwards David fell sick, due to age. Realizing that he was about to die, he summoned his son Solomon and spoke to him in this way:[1400] "I am now, my son, departing to my fate[1401] and to my ancestors; I am going the way that is common to all who now exist and who will be, from which no one has been known to return so as to find out what is being done among the living.[1402]

---

calls him "the Lord, the God of Israel our father." Josephus' formulation highlights God's own paternity, while also underscoring the Deity's universal solicitude.

[1386] Josephus here uses the term "Demiurge" (Greek: δημιουργός) of Platonic philosophy. As a designation for God the word is used by him also in *Ant.* 1.155, 172; on the term, see Feldman 2000: 45, n. 500.

[1387] On this merism, see *Ant.* 6.264.

[1388] In *Ant.* 3.98 this same combination of terms (Greek: προστάτης καὶ κηδεμών) is applied to Moses by the people.

[1389] Josephus compresses David's extended praise of God's universal power cited in 1 Chr 29:11-13.

[1390] This transitional phrase is Josephus' drastically reduced version of David's extended appeal for his people in 1 Chr 29:14-18.

[1391] Compare 1 Chr 29:19, where David prays that Solomon be given "a whole heart," which will enable him to keep the Law and build the temple.

[1392] See 1 Chr 29:20a for this command by David.

[1393] See 1 Chr 29:20b; Josephus expands the source reference to the assembly's (wordless) "obeisance" to the king with a verbal expression of their thanks for his services.

[1394] See 1 Chr 29:21a; Josephus omits the accompanying "drink offerings."

[1395] 1 Chr 29:21b speaks of "sacrifices in abundance for all Israel."

[1396] 1 Chr 29:22a does not mention the king's own participation in the people's "eating and drinking before the Lord on that day with great gladness."

[1397] See 1 Chr 29:22bα, which Josephus follows in having Solomon anointed by an indeterminate "they." Like LXX, he speaks of Solomon being anointed "king" rather than as "prince (Hebrew: נגיד) for the Lord," as in MT. He inserts an explicit mention of the "oil" used in reminiscence of his mention of Solomon's initial anointing in 7.357 (cf. 7.355).

[1398] See 1 Chr 29:22bβ, which has the same "they" who anoint Solomon as prince in 29:22bα likewise anoint Zadok "as priest." Josephus will return to the subject of Zadok's high priesthood and the removal of his earlier colleague Abiathar from this position in *Ant.* 8.10-12 (// 1 Kgs 2:26-27, 35b).

[1399] See 1 Chr 29:23, where Solomon "sits himself" upon the throne. As in 7.358, Josephus has an indeterminate "they" seat him on the throne. His reference to the general "obedience" given to Solomon following his enthronement compresses the more detailed indications on the matter found in 29:24-25.

[1400] With this phrase, corresponding to 1 Kgs 2:1, Josephus makes the transition back to the presentation of his other biblical source, i.e. 1 Kgs 2:1-9 (David's final words to Solomon) after the sequence of 7.363-382 drawn, in highly abbreviated fashion, from 1 Chronicles 23-29.

[1401] Greek: χρεών. On Josephus' use of this and other terms for "fate," see Schlatter 1932: 32; Stählin 1974; Feldman 1998: 194-97.

[1402] Josephus embellishes David's opening declaration to Solomon ("I am about to go the way of all the earth") of 1 Kgs 2:2a.

384. Therefore, while I am still alive but about to die, I commend to you those *David urges* things of which I spoke earlier, advising you to be just towards your subjects and *Solomon to* pious towards God who has given you the kingship,[1403] keeping his commandments *keep law* and laws, which he sent down to us through Moyses; do not fail to be attached to these on account of favor, flattery, desire or any other passion.[1404] **385.** For you will forfeit the Deity's loyalty towards you if you transgress any of his laws and will totally turn away his good providential care.[1405] If, on the other hand, you prove yourself to be the kind of person you should (and which I appeal to you to be), you will secure the kingship for our family, and no other house will rule the Hebrews except ourselves, through all ages.[1406]

386. Remember also the transgressions of the general Joab, who, out of envy, *Punishment of* killed two just and good generals, namely Abenner, the son of Ner[1407] and Amasa, *Joab enjoined* the son of Iethras.[1408] Requite their deaths as seems good to you,[1409] since Joab, being mightier and more powerful than I, has escaped punishment until now.[1410]

387. I entrust to you as well the sons of Berzel the Galadite, whom, as a favor to *Barzillai's* me, you are to hold in all honor and care, for we are not the ones initiating the ben- *(Berzel's) sons* efits here, but are rather repaying the debt for what their father granted me during *to be provided* my flight.[1411] **388.** As for Soumouis, the son of Gera, of the tribe of the Benjamites, *for* who defamed me greatly during my flight, when I was going to The Camps, and *Shimei (Sou-* who then met me at the Jordan and received pledges that he would suffer nothing at *mouis) to be* that time—seek out a justified cause and take vengeance on him.[1412] *punished*

(15.2) 389. After he had urged his son concerning political affairs as well as about *David dies* his friends and those whom he knew to be worthy of punishment, David died.[1413] He had lived seventy years,[1414] having reigned seven years and six months in

---

[1403] Compare 1 Kgs 2:2b, where David's initial exhortation to Solomon is "be strong and show yourself a man." The (added) cross reference to David's earlier admonitions to his son has in view 7.338, 356, 374, where, each time (as here in 7.384), Solomon is urged to be "just" and "pious."

[1404] See 1 Kgs 2:3, whose conclusion Josephus modifies, substituting reference to what might divert Solomon from obeying the Law for the source's allusion to the (positive) outcome of such obedience.

[1405] This warning (which Marcus *ad loc.* renders "and you will turn His kind watchfulness into a hostile attitude") has no explicit equivalent in David's opening admonition in 1 Kgs 2:2-4. It serves to prepare for Solomon's eventual defection and the consequences this will have for his kingdom.

[1406] This is Josephus' rendering of David's (modified) quotation (1 Kgs 2:3-4) of the divine promise of 2 Sam 7:13-16, in which that promise is recast in conditional terms.

[1407] On Joab's killing of Abner, see 7.31-38.

[1408] On Joab's murder of Amasa, see 7.284-285. From the source verse, 1 Kgs 2:5, Josephus leaves aside the obscure reference to Joab's "putting innocent blood on the girdle of his loins and the sandals of his feet."

[1409] Compare 1 Kgs 2:6, where David urges Solomon to use his wisdom to insure that Joab's "grey head

not go down to Sheol in peace."

[1410] This "confession" on David's part has no counterpart in his words concerning Joab in 1 Kgs 2:5-6. On the other hand, it echoes the king's admission about his powerlessness to requite Joab (and Abishai) in 7.45// 2 Sam 3:39.

[1411] Josephus expatiates on David's instructions concerning the good treatment Solomon is to give the sons of Barzillai in 1 Kgs 2:7. On "Berzel," see 7.230, 272-275 (where there is reference, as in 2 Sam 19:37-38, to a single son of his, i.e. the biblical "Chimham").

[1412] Compare 1 Kgs 2:8-9. Josephus compresses David's directives concerning how Solomon is to deal with "Shimei" of v. 9. On the interactions between this figure and David, to which the king alludes here, see 7.207-210, 264-266 (where Josephus, in 7.266, avoids reproducing the reference to David's "swearing" to Shimei of 2 Sam 19:23b; here in 7.388, however, following 1 Kgs 2:8, he does have the king allude to that earlier oath of his, see note to "him" at 7.266).

[1413] See 1 Kgs 2:10a// 1 Chr 29:28a. Josephus prefaces the source notices on David's demise with a long transitional phrase linking this with his preceding farewell discourse to Solomon (// 1 Kgs 2:2-9).

[1414] The biblical sources do not specify David's total life-span; 1 Chr 29:28a has him dying "in a good old age."

Hebron[1415] over the tribe of Iouda, and thirty-three in Hierosolyma over the entire country.

Eulogy for David

390. In addition to his being an excellent man,[1416] possessing every virtue and being entrusted with the safety of so many nations, he ought also to be praised on account of his vigorous strength and prudential understanding.[1417] For he was more courageous than anyone else; in his struggles on behalf of his subjects, he was the first to rush into danger, appealing to his soldiers to [move] against the [enemy] battlelines by exerting himself and fighting, rather than issuing orders like a master. **391.** He was very competent in thinking and in perceiving both the future and present matters. He was prudent, gentle, kind towards those in misfortune, just, and humane—qualities that are suitable only for [outstanding] kings. Moreover, with such great authority, he never once offended, the case of the wife of Urias excepted.[1418] He left behind as well wealth such as no other king, whether of the Hebrews or of other nations, ever did.[1419]

David buried

(15.3) 392. His son Solomon buried him magnificently in Hierosolyma,[1420] along with everything else that is customary at royal funerals. He interred with him much, uncountable wealth, the abundance of which any one may easily perceive from what we shall now relate:[1421]

David's tomb plundered twice

393. For 1,300 years later,[1422] the high priest Hyrcanus, when he was being besieged by Antiochus called the Pious, the son of Demetrius,[1423] wished to give him money so that he would raise the siege and withdraw his army. There being nothing else available, he opened up one of the structures in the tomb of David and removed 3,000 talents, part of which he gave to Antiochus. By doing this, he brought the siege to an end, as we have related elsewhere.[1424] **394.** Many years later King Herod

---

[1415] Both 1 Kgs 2:11 and 1 Chr 29:27 give the round figure of 7 years for David's reign in Hebron. Josephus' mention of an additional 6 months corresponds to the more precise figure given by him in 7.65 (// 2 Sam 2:11; 5:4). Josephus does not reproduce the sources' figure of 40 years for David's entire reign.

[1416] Josephus' eulogy of David in 7.390-391 elaborates on the reference to his dying "full of honor" in 1 Chr 29:28a. The terms of the eulogy echo those used in his own earlier evaluations of the king; see *Ant.* 6.160; 7.110, 130.

[1417] The above translation is based on the text of Niese, which itself follows RO. Marcus, calling the RO text "undoubtedly corrupt," offers an emendation, which he translates as follows: "He [David] was a most excellent man and possessed of every virtue which should be found in a king entrusted with the safety of so many nations."

[1418] On Josephus' version of the Bathsheba episode (2 Sam 11:2-12:25), see 7.130-158. The qualification concerning David's overall rectitude echoes that made by Josephus in 7.153 (cf. 1 Kgs 15:5).

[1419] Josephus embellishes the summary reference to David's dying "full of wealth" in 1 Chr 29:28a, thereby preparing his subsequent remarks on the rich plunder subsequently yielded by his grave; see 7.393-394.

[1420] In 1 Kgs 2:10b David "is buried in Jerusalem" (MT; LXX: in the city of David), the subject being left unspecified; 1 Chronicles 29 does not mention David's burial.

[1421] Josephus' notice on the opulence of David's burial has no biblical counterpart. It serves to counteract charges that the Jews were an impecunious people, on which see Feldman 1998: 93.

[1422] Josephus' figure for the period between the death of David and the reign of John Hyrcanus is considerably higher than that of modern chronological estimates, where David's death is placed *ca.* 960 BCE and Hyrcanus' rule dated 134-104, this yielding a total interval of *ca.* 825 years.

[1423] The reference is to the Seleucid king Antiochus VII, who ruled 139(138)-129(128) BCE. The title "Pious" (Greek: εὐσεβής) used for him by Josephus here (and in *Ant.* 13.244) is not attested in other sources, where he is called rather "Soter" (as in *Ant.* 13.222) and "Sidetes" (from the city of Side, where he was raised). See Marcus 1933: 338-39, n. b.

[1424] Josephus here alludes to his account in *War* 1.61, where he specifies that Hyrcanus gave Antiochus 300 of the 3,000 talents taken by him from David's tomb and used the remainder to pay his own mercenary forces. His retelling of the same event in *Ant.* 13.249

again opened another structure and removed a good deal of money.[1425] Neither of them, however, came upon the kings' coffins, for these had been skillfully buried beneath the ground, so as not to be visible to those entering the tombs. It is sufficient, however, for us to have said this much about these matters.[1426]

---

states that Hyrcanus, in his use of the 3,000 talents, became the first Jewish king to make payments to foreign troops.

[1425] Josephus relates this incident in *Ant.* 16.179-183(188), where he refers to Nicolas of Damascus as his authority.

[1426] Josephus' lengthy appendix concerning David's tomb takes the place of the reference to the "Chronicles" of Samuel, Nathan, and Gad as a source for David's reign of 1 Chr 29:29-30. Josephus invariably leaves aside such biblical source references in his account of the kings, presumably because he is basing himself directly on the Bible rather than its (no longer extant) sources.

Alexander, Patrick H. et al., eds. 1999. *The* JBL *Handbook of Style for Ancient Near Eastern, Biblical, and Early Christian Studies*. Peabody, Mass.: Hendrickson.

Amaru, Betsy H. 1980-81. Land Theology in Josephus' *Jewish Antiquities. JQR* 71:201-29.

———. 1994. *Rewriting the Bible: Land and Covenant in Post-Biblical Jewish Literature*. Valley Forge: Trinity International Press.

Attridge, Harold W. 1976. *The Interpretation of Biblical History in the* Antiquitates Judaicae *of Flavius Josephus*. Missoula: Scholars.

Aune, David E. 1982. The Use of προφήτης in Josephus. *JBL* 101: 419-21.

Barthélemy, Dominique. 1982. *Critique textuelle de l'Ancien Testament*. 1. *Josué, Juges, Ruth, Samuel, Rois, Chroniques, Esdras, Néhémie, Esther*. Fribourg: Presses universitaires; Göttingen: Vandenhoeck & Ruprecht.

Beattie, D.R.G., tr. 1994. *The Targum of Ruth*. Collegeville: The Liturgical Press.

Begg, Christopher. 1993. *Josephus' Account of the Early Divided Monarchy (AJ 8,212-420): Rewriting the Bible*. Leuven: Leuven University Press.

———. 1994. Josephus' Version of David's Census. *Hen* 16:199-226.

———. 1996. Abimelech, King of Shechem according to Josephus. *ETL* 72:146-64.

———. 1996a. The Loss of the Ark according to Josephus. *LASBF* 46:167-86.

———. 1996b. The Ark in Philistia according to Josephus. *ETL* 72:385-97.

———. 1996c. The Royal Lottery according to Josephus. *RCT* 21:273-88.

———. 1996d. Saul's War with Amalek according to Josephus. *Laur* 37:387-415.

———. 1996e. Samuel's Anointing of David in Josephus and Pseudo-Philo. *Rivista di Storia e Letteratura Religiosa* 32:492-529.

———. 1996f. The Abigail Story (1 Samuel 25) according to Josephus. *EstBíb* 54:5-34.

———. 1996g. The Rape of Tamar (2 Samuel 13) according to Josephus. *EstBíb* 54:465-500.

———. 1996h. The Execution of the Saulides according to Josephus. *Sef* 56:3-18.

———. 1997. Israel's Treaty with Gibeon according to Josephus. *OLP* 28:123-45.

———. 1997a. The Cisjordanian Altar(s) and their Associated Rites according to Josephus. *BZ* 41:192-211.

———. 1997b. The Ceremonies at Gilgal/Ebal according to Pseudo-Philo. *ETL* 73:72-83.

———. 1997c. The Transjordanian Altar (Josh 22:10-34) according to Josephus (*Ant.* 5.100-114) and Pseudo-Philo (*LAB* 22:1-8). *Andrews University Seminary Studies* 35:5-18.

———. 1997d. Samuel Leader of Israel according to Josephus. *Ant* 72:199-216.

———. 1997e. Israel's Demand for a King according to Josephus. *Mus* 110:329-48.

———. 1997f. Saul's Royal Start according to Josephus. *SacEr* 37:5-32.

———. 1997g. Samuel's Farewell Discourse according to Josephus. *SJOT* 11:56-77.

———. 1997h. The Massacre of the Priests of Nob in Josephus and Pseudo-Philo. *EstBíb* 55:171-98.

———. 1997i. David's Second Sparing of Saul according to Josephus. *TynBul* 48:93-117.

———. 1997j. David's Philistine Service according to Josephus. *Jian Dao* 7:1-16.

———. 1997k. The Ziklag Interlude according to Josephus. *Teresianum* 48:713-36.

———. 1997l. David's Transfer of the Ark according to Josephus. *BBR* 7:11-36.

———. 1997m. The Exploits of David's Heroes according to Josephus. *LASBF* 47:139-69.

———. 1997n. Israel's Battle with Amalek according to Josephus. *JSQ* 4:201-16.

———. 1998. Josephus' Account of the Benjamite War. *LASBF* 48:273-304.

———. 1998a. The Return of the Ark according to Josephus. *BBR* 8:15-37.

———. 1998b. David's Double Escape according to Josephus. *JPJ* 10:28-45.

———. 1998c. David's First Sparing of Saul according to Josephus. *Laur* 39:455-71.

———. 1998d. David's Dismissal by the Philistines according to Josephus. *TZ* 54:111-19.

———. 1998e. The Assassination of Ishbosheth according to Josephus. *Ant* 73:241-53.

———. 1998f. David's Capture of Jebus and its Sequels according to Josephus. *ETL* 74:93-108.

———. 1998g. David and Mephibosheth according to Josephus. *Andrews University Seminary Studies* 36:165-82.

————. 1998h. David's Double Victory according to Josephus. *Emerita* 66:27-48.

————. 1998i. The Revolt of Sheba according to Josephus. *Jian Dao* 9:1-26.

————. 1999. King Saul's First Sin according to Josephus. *Ant* 74:685-96.

————. 1999a. The David and Goliath Story according to Josephus. *Mus* 112:3-25.

————. 1999b. The Death of King Saul according to Josephus. *Annali di storia dell'esegesi* 18:485-505.

————. 1999c. David's Reaction to the Death of Saul according to Josephus. *Jian Dao* 11:1-13.

————. 1999d. David's Initial Philistine Victories according to Josephus. *Skrif en Kerk* 20:1-14.

————. 1999e. David's Conquests and Officials according to Josephus. *Athenaeum* 87:169-90.

————. 2000. *Josephus' Story of the Later Monarchy (AJ 9,1-10,185)*. Leuven: Leuven University Press.

————. 2000a. The Retellings of the Story of Judges 19 by Pseudo-Philo and Josephus: A Comparison. *EstBíb* 58:33-49.

————. 2000b. The Dynastic Promise according to Josephus. *SacEr* 39:5-19.

————. 2001. The Ai-Achan Story (Joshua 7-8) according to Josephus. *Jian Dao* 16:1-20.

Best, Ernst. 1959. The Use and Non-Use of Pneuma by Josephus. *NovT* 3:218-25.

Betz, Otto. 1987. Miracles in the Writings of Flavius Josephus. In *Jesus, Judaism and Christianity*, ed. L.H. Feldman and G. Hata. Detroit: Wayne State University. 212-35.

Bilde, Per. 1988. *Flavius Josephus Between Jerusalem and Rome: His Life, his Works and their Importance*. Sheffield: JSOT.

Blenkinsopp, Joseph. 1974. Prophecy and Priesthood in Josephus. *JJS* 25:239-62.

Bloch, Heinrich. 1879. *Die Quellen des Josephus in seiner Archäologie*. Leipzig: Teubner.

Bowley, James E. 1994. Josephus's Use of Greek Sources for Biblical History. In *Pursuing the Text: Studies in Honor of Ben Zion Wacholder on the Occasion of his Seventieth Birthday*, ed. John C. Reeves and John Kampen. Sheffield: JSOT. 202-15.

Braude, William G. and Kapstein, Israel J., tr. 1981. *Tanna děbe Eliyyahu: The Lore of the School of Elijah*. Philadelphia: Jewish Publication Society of America.

Brooke, Alan England and Mᶜlean, Norman. 1917. *The Old Testament in Greek*, vol. 1, pt. 4: *Joshua, Judges and Ruth*. Cambridge: Cambridge University Press.

————and Thackeray, Henry St. John. 1927. *The Old Testament in Greek*, vol. 2, pt. 1: *I and II Samuel*. Cambridge: Cambridge University Press.

————. 1930. *The Old Testament in Greek*, vol. 2, pt. 2: *I and II Kings*. Cambridge: Cambridge University Press.

————. 1932. *The Old Testament in Greek*, vol. 2, pt. 3: *I and II Chronicles*. Cambridge: Cambridge University Press.

Brown, Cheryl Anne. 1992. *No Longer Be Silent: First Century Jewish Portraits of Biblical Women*. Louisville: Westminster/John Knox.

Brüne, B. 1913. *Flavius Josephus und seine Schriften in ihrem Verhältnis zum Judentume, zur griechisch-römischen Welt und zum Christentume*. Gütersloh: Bertelsmann.

Cohen, Shaye D. 1979. *Josephus in Galilee and Jerusalem: His Vita and Development as a Historian*. Leiden: Brill.

Collins, J.N. 1990. *Diakonia: Reinterpreting the Ancient Sources*. Oxford/New York: Oxford University Press.

Daube, David. 1980. Typology in Josephus. *JJS* 31:18-36.

Deines, Roland. 2003. Josephus, Salomo und die von Gott verliehene τέχνη gegen die Dämonen. In *Die Dämonen: Die Dämonologie der israelitischen-jüdischen und frühchristlichen Literatur im Kontext ihrer Umwelt*, ed. Armin Lange, Hermann Lichtenberger and K.F. Diethard Römheld. Tübingen: Mohr Siebeck. 365-94.

Delling, Gerhard. 1958. Josephus und das Wunderbare. *NovT* 2:291-308.

————. 1974. Die biblische Prophetie bei Josephus. In *Josephus-Studien: Festschrift Otto Michel*, ed. Otto Betz et al. Göttingen: Vandenhoeck & Ruprecht. 109-21.

Dietrich, E.K. 1936. *Die Umkehr (Bekehrung und Busse) im Alten Testament und im Judentum*. Stuttgart: Kohlhammer.

Endres, John C., Millar, William R., and Burns, John Barclay. 1998. *Chronicles and its Synoptic Parallels in Samuel, Kings, and Related Biblical Texts*. Collegeville: The Liturgical Press.

Epstein, I., ed. 1935-48. *The Babylonian Talmud*. London: Soncino.

Fallon, F., tr. 1985. Eupolemus. OTP 2. Garden City, New York: Doubleday and Co. 861-72.

Feldman, Louis H. 1984-85. Josephus as a Biblical Interpreter: the 'Aqedah. *JQR* 75:212-52.

————. 1990. Prophets and Prophecy in Josephus. *JTS* 41:386-422.

————. 1991. Reflections on John R. Levison's 'Josephus' Version of Ruth'. *JSP* 8:45-52.

———. 1998. *Josephus' Interpretation of the Bible*. Berkeley: University of California Press.

———. 1998a. *Studies in Josephus' Rewritten Bible*. Leiden: Brill.

———. tr. 2000. *Judean Antiquities 1-4*. Leiden: Brill.

———. 2000a. Josephus' Portrayal (*Antiquities* 5.136-174) of the Benjamite Affair of the Concubine and its Repercussions (Judges 19-21). *JQR* 90:255-92.

———. 2001. On Professor Mark Roncace's Portraits of Deborah and Gideon in Josephus. *JSJ* 32:193-220.

———. 2001a. Josephus' Liberties in Interpreting the Bible in the *Jewish War* and in the *Antiquities*. *JSQ* 8:309-25.

———. 2002. The Portrayal of Phineas by Philo, Pseudo-Philo, and Josephus. *JQR* 92:315-45.

———. 2003. The Command, according to Philo, Pseudo-Philo, and Josephus, to Annihilate the Nations of Canaan. *Andrews University Seminary Studies* 41:13-29.

Fernández Marcos, Natalio and Busto Saiz, José Ramón. 1989. *El texto antioqueno de la Biblia griega*, vol. 1: *1-2 Samuel*. Madrid: Instituto de Filología del C.S.I.C.

———. 1992. *El texto antioqueno de la Biblia griega*, vol. 2: *1-2 Reyes*. Madrid: Instituto de Filología del C.S.I.C.

———. 1996. *El texto antioqueno de la Biblia griega*, vol. 3: *1-2 Crónicas*. Madrid: Instituto de Filología del C.S.I.C.

Fincke, Andrew. 2001. *The Samuel Scroll from Qumran: 4QSam^a restored and compared to the Septuagint and 4QSam^c*. Leiden: Brill.

Fischer, J.B. 1958-59. The Term ΔΕΣΠΟΤΗΣ in Josephus. *JQR* 49:132-38.

Freedman, H. and Simon, Maurice, ed. 1983. *Midrash Rabbah*. 7 vols. London: Soncino.

Gibbs, John G. and Feldman, Louis H. 1985-86. Josephus' Vocabulary for Slavery. *JQR* 76:281-310.

Ginzberg, Louis. 1913. *The Legends of the Jews*. Vol. 4. Philadelphia: Jewish Publication Society.

———. 1928. *The Legends of the Jews*. Vol. 6. Philadelphia: Jewish Publication Society.

Girón Blanc, Luis-Fernando, tr. 1996. *Seder 'Olam Rabbah El Gran Orden del Universo: Una cronologia judía*. Estella (Navarra): Verbo Divino.

Glessmer, U. 1994. Leviten in spät-nachexilischen Zeit. Darstellungsinteressen in den Chronikbüchern und bei Josephus. In *Gottes Ehre erzählen. Festschrift für Hans Seidel zum 65. Geburtstag*, ed. M. Albani and T. Arndt. Leipzig: Thomas Verlag. 127-51.

Gnuse, Robert K. 1996. *Dreams and Dream Reports in the Writings of Josephus: A Traditio-Historical Analysis*. Leiden: Brill.

Goodblatt, D. 1994. *The Monarchic Principle: Studies in Jewish Self-Government in Antiquity*. Tübingen: Mohr Siebeck.

Grillet, B. and Lestienne, M., tr. 1997. *Premier Livre des Règnes*. Paris: Cerf.

Harding, M. 1994. Making Old Things New: Prayer Texts in Josephus' *Antiquities* 1-11: A Study in the Transmission of Tradition. In *The Lord's Prayer and Other Prayer Texts from the Greco-Roman Era*, ed. J.H. Charlesworth et al. Valley Forge: Trinity Press International. 54-72.

Harlé, Paul, tr. 1999. *Les Juges*. Paris: Cerf.

Harrington, Daniel J. and Saldarini, Anthony J., tr. 1987. *Targum Jonathan of the Former Prophets*. Collegeville: The Liturgical Press.

Harvey, Graham. 1996. *The True Israel: Uses of the Names Jew, Hebrew, and Israel in Ancient Jewish and Early Christian Literature*. Leiden: Brill.

Heiligenthal, R. 1983. Freiheit II.1 Frühjudentum. TRE 11:498-502.

Höffken, Peter. 2001. Bekehrung von Nichtjuden als (Nicht-) Thema bei Josephus Flavius. *TZ* 57:391-401.

Jacobson, Howard. 1996. *A Commentary on Pseudo-Philo's* Liber Antiquitatum Biblicarum. 2 vols. Leiden: Brill.

Jaubert, A. 1963. *La notion d'alliance dans le Judaïsme aux abords de l'ère chrétienne*. Paris: Seuil.

Jones, F.S. 1992. Freedom. ABD 2:855-59.

Krenkel, Max. 1894. *Josephus und Lukas*. Leipzig: Haessel.

Krieger, K.S. 1994. *Geschichtsschreibung als Apologetik bei Flavius Josephus*. Tübingen: Franke.

Legasse, S. 2000. Exégèse juive ancienne et exégèse patristique. Le cycle biblique de Gédéon. *LASBF* 50:181-261.

Levine, Daniel B. 1993. *Hubris* in Josephus' *Jewish Antiquities*. *HUCA* 64:51-87.

Levison, John R. 1991. Josephus' Version of Ruth. *JSP* 8:31-44.

———. 1994. The Debut of the Divine Spirit in Josephus' *Antiquities*. *HTR* 87:123-38.

———. 1996. Josephus' Interpretation of the Divine Spirit. *JJS* 47:234-55.

Levy, J. 1881. *Chaldäisches Wörterbuch über die Targumim*. Leipzig: Baumgärtner's Buchhandlung.

Liddell, Henry G., Scott, Robert, Jones, Henry S. 1940. *A Greek-English Lexicon*. Oxford: Clarendon.

Lindsey, Dennis R. 1996. *Josephus and Faith:* Πίστις *and* Πιστεύειν *as Faith Terminology in the Writings of Flavius Josephus and in the New Testament*. Leiden: Brill.

Lührmann, D. 1971. Epiphaneia. Zur Bedeutungsgeschichte eines griechischen Wortes. In *Tradition und Glaube: Festschrift K.G. Kuhn*, ed. G. Jeremias et al. Göttingen: Vandenhoeck & Ruprecht. 185-99.

McCarter, P. Kyle. 1980. *1 Samuel*. New York: Doubleday.

———. 1984. *II Samuel*. New York: Doubleday.

Mach, Michael. 1992. *Entwicklungsstadien des jüdischen Engelsglaubens in vorrabinischer Zeit*. Tübingen: Mohr Siebeck.

McIvor, J. Stanley, tr. 1994. *The Targum of Chronicles*. Collegeville: The Liturgical Press.

Macrae, George W. 1965. Miracle in The Antiquities of Josephus. In *Miracles: Cambridge Studies in Their Philosophy and History*, ed. Charles F.D. Moule. London: Mowbray. 127-47.

Maier, Johann, 1994. Amalek in the Writings of Josephus. In *Josephus and the History of the Greco-Roman Period: Essays in Memory of Morton Smith*, ed. Fausto Parente and Joseph Sievers. Leiden: Brill. 109-26.

Marcus, Ralph. 1933. *Josephus*, vol. 7: *Jewish Antiquities*. Books XII-XIV. Loeb Classical Library. Cambridge, Mass: Harvard University Press.

———. 1934. *Josephus*, vol. 5: *Jewish Antiquities*. Books V-VIII. Loeb Classical Library. Cambridge, Mass.: Harvard University Press.

———. 1937. *Josephus*, vol. 6: *Jewish Antiquities*, Books IX-XI. Loeb Classical Library. Cambridge, Mass: Harvard University Press.

Mason, Steve. 1991. *Flavius Josephus on the Pharisees: A Composition-Critical Study*. Leiden: Brill.

———. 2000. Introduction. In *Judean Antiquities 1-4*, tr. Louis H. Feldman. Leiden: Brill. xiii-xxxvi.

———. 2001. *Life of Josephus*. Leiden: Brill.

———. 2003. Flavius Josephus in Flavian Rome: Reading on and Between the Lines. In *Flavian Rome: Culture, Image, Text*, ed. A.J. Boyle and W.J. Dominik. Leiden: Brill. 559-90.

———. *Josephus and the New Testament*. 2003a. 2nd ed.; Peabody, Mass: Hendrickson.

Mayer-Schärtel, Bärbel. 1995. *Das Frauenbild des Josephus: Eine sozialgeschichtliche und kulturanthropologische Untersuchung*. Stuttgart: Kohlhammer.

Metzler, Karin. 1991. *Der griechische Begriff des Verzeihens untersucht am Wortstamm* συγγώμη *von den ersten Belegen bis zum vierten Jahrhundert n. Christus*. Tübingen: Mohr Siebeck.

Mez, A. 1895. *Die Bibel des Josephus untersucht für Buch V-VII der Archäologie*. Basel: Jaeger & Kober.

Moatti-Fine, Jacqueline, tr. 1996. *Jésus (Josué)*. Paris: Cerf.

Moehring, Horst R. 1957. Novellistic Elements in the Writings of Flavius Josephus. Diss, Ph.D., University of Chicago.

———. 1973. Rationalization of Miracles in the Writings of Flavius Josephus. *TU* 112:376-83.

Montgomery, James A. 1920-21. The Religion of Flavius Josephus. *JQR* 11:277-305.

Moore, E. 1974-75. ΒΙΑΖΩ, ΑΡΠΑΖΩ and Cognates in Josephus. *NTS* 21:519-43.

Naber, S.A. 1888-96. *Flavii Josephi Opera omnia*. 6 vols. Leipzig: Teubner.

Nestle, D. 1972. Freiheit. RAC 7:269-306.

Niese, Benedict. 1885-95. *Flavii Josephi Opera*. 7 vols. Berlin: Weidmann.

Nodet, Étienne. 1995-2001. *Flavius Josèphe, Les Antiquités Juives*, Vol. 2: Livres IV et V; Vol. III: Livres VI et VII. Paris: Cerf.

Noort, Ed. 1998. 4QJosh[a] and the History of Tradition in the Book of Joshua. *JNWSL* 24:127-44.

Pax, E. 1955. ΕΠΙΦΑΝΕΙΑ: *Ein religionsgeschichtlicher Beitrag zur biblischen Theologie*. Munich: Zink.

Pérez Fernández, Miguel, tr. 1984. *Los capítulos de Rabbí Eliezer*. Valencia: Institución San Jerónimo.

Price, Jonathan J. 1992. *Jerusalem under Siege: The Collapse of the Jewish State 66-70 C.E.* Leiden: Brill.

Rappaport, Salomo. 1930. *Agada und Exegese bei Flavius Josephus*. Vienna: Alexander Kohut Memorial Foundation.

Remus, Harold. 1982. Does Terminology Distinguish Early Christian from Pagan Miracles? *JBL* 101:531-35.

Rengstorf, Karl H. 1973-83. *A Complete Concordance to Flavius Josephus*. 4 Vols. Leiden: Brill.

Roncace, M. 2000. Josephus' (Real) Portraits of Deborah and Gideon: A Reading of *Antiquities* 5.198-232. *JSJ* 31:247-74.

Schalit, Abraham, ed. 1944-63. *Josephus. Antiquities of the Jews* [Hebrew]. 3 vols. Jerusalem: Mosad Bialik.

———. 1968. *Namenwörterbuch zu Flavius Josephus* (A Complete Concordance to Flavius Josephus, ed. Karl H. Rengstorf, Supplement 1). Leiden: Brill.

Schlatter, Adolf. 1910. *Wie Sprach Josephus von Gott?* Gütersloh: Bertelsmann.

———. 1913. *Die hebräischen Namen bei Josephus.* Gütersloh: Bertelsmann.

———. 1932. *Die Theologie des Judentums nach dem Bericht des Josephus.* Gütersloh: Bertelsmann.

Schröder, Bernd. 1996. *Die 'väterlichen Gesetze': Flavius Josephus als Vermittler von Halachah an Griechen und Römer.* Tübingen: Mohr Siebeck.

Schutt, Robert J.H. 1961. *Studies in Josephus.* London: SPCK.

———. 1980. The Concept of God in the Works of Flavius Josephus. *JJS* 31:171-89.

Schwartz, Daniel R. 1983-84. Josephus on Jewish Constitutions and Community. *SCI* 7:30-52.

Schwartz, Seth. 1990. *Josephus and Judaean Politics.* Leiden: Brill.

Siker, Jeffrey S. 1987. Abraham in Graeco-Roman Paganism. *JSJ* 18:188-208.

Skehan, Patrick W. 1976. Turning or Burning? 1Sam 17:53 LXX. *CBQ* 38:193-95.

Spicq, Ceslas. 1958. La philanthropie hellénistique, vertu divine et royale. *ST* 12:161-91.

———. 1978. *Notes de Lexiocographie néo-testamentaire.* Vol. 1. Fribourg: Editions universitaires; Göttingen: Vandenhoeck & Ruprecht.

———. 1978. *Notes de lexiocographie néo-testamentaire.* Vol. 2. Fribourg: Editions universitaires; Göttingen: Vandenhoeck & Ruprecht.

———. 1982. *Notes de lexiocographie néo-testamentaire.* Supplément. Fribourg: Editions universitaires; Göttingen: Vandenhoeck & Ruprecht.

Spilsbury, Paul. 1998. *The Image of the Jew in Flavius Josephus' Paraphrase of the Bible.* Tübingen: Mohr Siebeck.

Stählin, Gustav. 1974. Das Schicksal im NT und bei Josephus. In *Josephus-Studien: Festschrift Otto Michel,* ed. Otto Betz et al. Göttingen: Vandenhoeck & Ruprecht. 319-43.

Sterling, Gregory E. 1992. *Historiography and Self-Definition: Josephos, Luke-Acts and Apologetic Historiography.* Leiden: Brill.

———. 1998. The Invisible Presence: Josephus' Retelling of Ruth. In *Understanding Josephus: Seven Perspectives,* ed. Steve Mason. Sheffield: Sheffield Academic Press. 104-71.

Strotmann, Angelika. 1991. *"Mein Vater bist Du!" (Sir 51,10): Zur Bedeutung der Vaterschaft Gottes in kanonischen und nichtkanonischen frühjudischen Schriften.* Frankfurt am Main: Knecht.

Thackeray, Henry St. John. 1929. *Josephus the Man and the Historian.* New York: Jewish Institute of Religion.

Troiani, Lucio, 1994. The πολιτεία of Israel in the Graeco-Roman Age. In *Josephus and the History of the Greco-Roman Period,* ed. F. Parente and J. Sievers. Leiden: Brill. 11-22.

Ulrich, Eugene C. 1978. *The Qumran Text of Samuel and Josephus.* Missoula: Scholars.

———. 1989. Josephus' Biblical Text for the Books of Samuel. In *Josephus, the Bible and History,* ed. Louis H. Feldman and G. Hata. Detroit: Wayne State University Press. 81-96.

van Unnik, Willem C. 1973. An Attack on the Epicureans by Flavius Josephus. In *Romanitas et Christianitas, Studia Iano Henrico Waszink... VI Kal. Nov. a MCMLXXIII XIII Lustra Complenti Oblata,* ed. W. den Boer et al. Amsterdam: North Holland Publishing. 341-55.

Villaba i Varneda, Pere. 1986. *The Historical Method of Flavius Josephus.* Leiden: Brill.

Wacholder, Ben Zion. 1962. *Nicolaus of Damascus.* Berkeley: University of California Press.

———. 1989. Josephus and Nicolaus of Damascus. In *Josephus, the Bible and History,* ed. Louis H. Feldman and G. Hata. Detroit: Wayne State University Press. 147-72.

Weill, Julien et al., tr. 1900-1932. *Oeuvres complètes de Flavius Josèphe,* ed. Thédore Reinach. Paris: Leroux.

Weiss, H.F. 1979. Pharisäismus und Hellenismus. Zur Darstellung des Judentums im Geschichtswerk des jüdischen Historikers Flavius Josephus. *OLZ* 74:421-33.

Wilkens, M.J. 1988. *The Concept of Disciple in Matthew's Gospel.* Leiden: Brill.

INDEX OF MODERN SCHOLARS

INDEX OF ANCIENT AUTHORS

PSEUDO-PHILO

Polybius
  10.165: 6n1322

Thucydides
  2.47-54: 7n1205

CLASSICAL LATIN AUTHORS

Cicero
  Pro Caelio
    11.25: 6n124
    12.28-29: 6n124
  De republica
    1.40.62: 6n135
    2.30.52: 6n135

Frontinus
  1. praef.   7n573

Livy
  Preface, 12: 5n356
  1.9: 5n450
  2.5: 6n471
Nepos, Cornelius
  Chabrias
    3: 6n228
Virgil
  Aeneid
    6.32 6n120

BIBLICAL PASSAGES

10:17-27	6n229
10:17-25	6n259
10:17	6n229
10:18	6n230, 6n231
10:19	6n232, 6n236, 6n237
10:20-21	6n239
10:21-22	6n243
10:21	6n238, 6n240, 6n241, 6n244
10:22	6n242, 6n245, 6n246, 6n247
10:23	6n248, 6n249, 6n250, 6n251
10:24	6n251, 6n252, 6n253
10:25	6n254, 6n255, 6n256, 6n257, 6n258
10:26	6n260, 6n261, 6n408
10:27	5n399, 6n262, 6n310
11	6n265, 6n270, 6n281, 6n353, 7n485
11:1-11	6n1352
11:1	6n263, 6n264, 6n271, 6n272, 6n273
11:2	6n269, 6n273, 6n274, 6n280
11:3	6n277, 6n278, 6n279
11:4	6n280, 6n281, 6n283, 6n284, 6n408
11:5	6n285, 6n286
11:6	6n287
11:7-8	6n288
11:7	6n290, 6n291, 6n292, 6n293, 6n294, 6n295, 6n296, 6n297
11:8	6n298, 6n299, 6n300
11:9	6n288, 6n289
11:11	6n303, 6n304, 6n307
11:12	6n308, 6n309, 6n310, 6n311, 6n312
11:13	6n312, 6n313, 6n314
11:14-15	6n218, 6n315, 6n325
11:14	6n369
11:15	6n316
12	6n325, 6n336
12:1	6n325, 6n326
12:1-2	6n326
12:2	6n326
12:3-4	6n336
12:3	6n326, 6n329, 6n330, 6n331, 6n332, 6n333, 6n334
12:4	6n336
12:5	6n336
12:6-25	6n338
12:6-7	6n338
12:6	6n329, 6n337, 6n338
12:7	6n338
12:8	6n329, 6n339, 6n340, 6n341, 6n342, 6n344
12:9	6n345, 6n346, 6n347, 6n348, 6n349, 6n350
12:10	6n351
12:11	6n351, 6n352, 6n353
12:12	6n353
12:13	6n354, 6n355
12:14-15	6n355
12:14	6n367
12:15	6n368
12:16-17	6n355, 6n357
12:17	6n355, 6n356
12:18-19	6n362
12:18	6n358
12:19	6n364
12:20-25	6n364
12:20-22	6n367
12:23-24	6n367
12:23	6n364
12:25	6n368, 6n369
13-14	6n485
13	6n389, 6n413
13:1	6n370
13:2	6n371, 6n372, 6n373, 6n374, 6n486
13:3-4	6n381
13:3,5	6n381
13:3	6n375, 6n376, 6n377, 6n380, 6n387, 6n388
13:4	6n381, 6n386, 6n388, 6n389
13:5	6n381, 6n382, 6n383, 6n384, 6n385, 6n386, 6n387, 6n388, 6n617
13:6-7	6n392
13:6	6n390, 6n391, 6n425, 6n440
13:7	6n386, 6n392
13:8-15	6n393
13:8	6n218, 6n393, 6n394, 6n397, 6n398
13:9	6n400
13:10	6n401
13:11-12	6n404
13:11	6n403
13:13	6n403, 6n405, 6n406
13:14	6n403, 6n405, 6n406
13:15-16	6n409
13:15	6n408, 6n413, 6n487
13:16-18 (+ 23)	6n412
13:16	6n409
13:19-21	6n411
13:19	6n378
13:20	6n379
13:21	6n379
13:22	6n410
14	6n421
14:1	6n417
14:2	6n416
14:3	6n414, 6n415, 6n435, 6n456
14:4-5	6n420
14:4	6n420
14:5	6n420
14:6	6n417
14:7	6n418
14:8	6n422
14:9-10	6n423
14:10	6n423
14:11	6n424, 6n425
14:12	6n426, 6n427
14:13-14	6n430
14:13	6n428, 6n429
14:14	6n430
14:15	6n432
14:16-17	6n433
14:17	6n434
14:18	6n435, 6n436, 6n437, 6n457
14:19	6n438
14:20	6n439
14:21	6n440

INDEX OF PERSONAL NAMES

7n1126

Soumouis: *see* Samouis, son of Gera

Souri, father of Joab, 7.11

Souria: *see* Sarouia

Souron, king of Tyre and Phoenicia, 7n381

Susak, king of Egypt (Shishak, Susakeim), 7.105, 7n414-15

Susakeim: *see* Susak, king of Egypt

Sousan (Sheva), 7.293, 7n1077

Syros, 7.121, 7.124, 7n503-5, 7n515

Taliab, son of Iesse, 6.161, 6n651

Talmai: *see* Tholomai

Tamar: *see* Thamara, daughter of David; *see* Thamar, daughter of Apsalom

Tarquin, 6n135

Thaenos (Rechab), 7.46, 7n168

Thain, king of Amathe (Toi), 7.108

Thamar, daughter of Apsalom (Maacha, Tamar, Thomara), 7.243, 7n725-26, 7n919

Thamara, daughter of David (Tamar, Themar), 7.70, 7.162, 7.178, 7n265-67 *passim*, 7n632-79 *passim*

Themar: *see* Thamara, daughter of David

Tholomai, father of Machame (Talmai, Thomomai), 7.21, 7n84, 7n698

Thomomai: *see* Tholomai

Thomara: *see* Thamar, daughter of Apsalom

Titus, 6n1088, 7n280

Toi: *see* Thain, king of Amathe

Tola, 5n685

Uriah the Hittite: *see* Urias

Urias (Uriah the Hittite), 7.131-41, 7.144, 7.146, 7.153-54,

7n539, 7n543-44, 7n546-48, 7n550-59, 7n561-63, 7n565-66, 7n568, 7n578, 7n602, 7n642

Uzza: *see* Ozas

Uzzah: *see* Ozas

Uzzi: *see* Ozi

Vaphres, king of Egypt, 7n381

Vespasian, 6n213, 7n280

Xerxes, king of Persia, 6n416

Zabdi: *see* Zebedai

Zaboul (Zebul/ Zeboul), 5.243-46, 5n482-57, 5n659, 5n661, 5n663-64, 5n666-67

Zadok: *see* Sadok

Zalmuna: *see* Zarmoune

Zarmoune (Zalmuna/ Salmana/ Selmana), 5.228, 5n603

Zeb (Zeeb), 5.227, 5n598, 5n610

Zebah: *see* Zebe

Zebe (Zebah/ Zebee), 5.228, 5n602

Zebee: *see* Zebe

Zebedai (Zabdi), 5.33, 5n97

Zeboul: *see* Zaboul

Zebul: *see* Zaboul

Zeeb: *see* Zeb

Zerah: *see* Ezeleos

Zerahiiah, 5n1070

Zerubbabel, 5n111

Zeruel, 6n673, 6n692, 6n699

Zeruiah: *see* Sarouia

Ziba: *see* Siba

INDEX OF GEOGRAPHICAL NAMES

Bethsan: *see* Bethesan
Beth-Shan: *see* Bethesan
Bethshean: *see* Bethesan
Bethshemesh: *see* Bethes
Bethor (Bethoron), 5.60, 5n167
Bethoron: *see* Bethor
Bezek: *see* Zebeke
Bocchores (Bahurim), 7.225, 7n851, 7n979
Bochim: *see* Weepers, the

Camps, The (Manalis/ Madaim/ Mahanaim), 7.10, 7.18, 7.230, 7.232, 7.235, 7.272, 7.388, 7n38, 7n72, 7n867
Canaan: *see* Chananaia
Carmel, Mount: *see* Karmel, Mount
Carmel (in Judah), 6n1049, 7n81
Chalaama (Chalamak), 7n523
Chananaia, 5.56, 5.128, 5n62, 5n148, 5n512
Chananaian plains, 5.63
Chephirah, 5n142
Choice oak, the: *see* Tabor, Oak of
Choran (Bocchores, Bahurim), 7.207, 7n797, 7n851
City of Palms, the: *see* Jericho
Cun: *see* Machon

Damascus, 5.86, 5n231, 7.100, 7.101, 7.104, 7n395, 7n396, 7n402, 7n1426
Dan (Laish), 5.178, 5n454, 5n459, 5n460, 7n1178, 7n1206
David, City of, the, 7.65, 7n227
Debir, 5n336, 5n468
Deborah, Palm of, 5n521
Dor (Endor), 5.83, 5.87, 5n226, 6.330, 6n1185, 6n1186, 6n1199, 6n1252, 6n1266

Ebal, Mount: *see* Hebel, Mount
Ebenezer: *see* "Strong One"
Edkeipa (Ekdippa, Achzib), 5.85, 5n230
Edom: *see* Idumea
Effrata: *see* Pharath
Egypt, 5.72, 5.82, 5.261, 5n101, 5n315, 5n352, 5n398, 5n707, 6.38, 6.89, 6.132, 6.140, 6n231, 6n329, 6n338, 6n339, 6n340, 6n508, 6n512, 7.102, 7.105, 7n381, 7n415
Ekdippa: *see* Edkeipa
Ekron: *see* Akkaron
Elah, 6n620
El-berith, stronghold of the house of, the, 5n671
Emman: *see* Simon, Desert of
Endor: *see* Dor
Engedi: *see* Engedon
Engedon (Engedi/ Paran, Wilderness of/ Ziph, Wilderness of), 6.274, 6.282, 6n978, 6n992, 6n1004, 6n1047, 6n1115
En-rogel, 7n846, 7n1289
Ephesdammim, 6n619
Ephra (Ophrah/ Ephrata), 5.229, 5.232, 5n606, 5n625
Ephraim, forest of, the (Maainan), 7n900
Ephrata: *see* Ephra
Erasam (Pasdammim) 7.308, 7n1144
Escape, Rock of, 6n1002
Estaol, 5n895
Etam: *see* Aita
Euphrates, River, 5.183, 7.99, 7.100, 7.101, 7.127, 7n390, 7n398, 7n403, 7n523, 7n524, 7n531
Ezel, 6n825

Gaash, the mountain of, the, 5n315
Gaba/ Gabaa: *see* Gabatha
Gaba/Gabaa of Benjamin: *see* Gebal

Gabao(n) (Gibeon, Gablon), 5n140, 5n142, 5n162, 6.105, 6n409, 7.11, 7.283, 7n40, 7n49, 7n65, 7n140, 7n292, 7n1042, 7n1086, 7n1236
Gabatha (Gaba/ /Gabaa/ Gibeah/ Gibeah-elohim/ Gibeah of Saul, Saul, Hill of), 5.119, 5.140, 5.141, 5.157, 5.164, 5n316, 5n317, 5n357, 5n370, 5n372, 5n373, 5n374, 5n402, 5n407, 5n411, 5n419, 5n433, 5n451, 6.56, 6.67, 6.156, 6n211, 6n260, 6n280, 6n283, 6n556, 6n896, 6n1113, 7.292; *see also* Gebal
Gablon: *see* Gabao(n)
Gai: *see* Gitta
Galaad: *see* Galadene
Galadene (Gilead/ Galaad/ Galaditis), 5.254, 5.257, 5.269, 5.270, 5n685, 5n688, 5n690, 5n695, 5n701, 5n742, 6n217, 6n392, 7.8; *see also* Peraia
Galaditis: *see* Galadene
Galatidis (Tob, land of), 5.260, 5n702, 7n509, 7n510
Galbouath (Naioth), 6.221, 6n785
Galgala (Gilgal), 5.34, 5.48, 5.62, 5.68, 5n63, 5n101, 5n137, 5n190, 5n247, 5n351, 5n373, 5n492, 6.57, 6.83, 6.98, 6.103, 6.134, 6.145, 6.155, 6n116, 6n217, 6n218, 6n219, 6n325, 6n386, 6n388, 6n392, 6n393, 6n394, 6n404, 6n408, 6n493, 6n513, 6n523, 7.275, 7.276, 7n970, 7n1013
Galilee, 5.63, 5.86, 5.91, 5n178
Galilee, Sea of: *see* Genesar, Lake of
Gallim: *see* Gethla
Garizeis, Mount (Garizin, Mount/ Gerizim, Mount) 5.69, 5.235, 5n139, 5n194, 5n196, 5n629
Garizin, Mount: *see* Garizeis, Mount
Gath: *see* Gitta
Gath-rimmon: *see* Gitta
Gaza, 5.81, 5.128, 5.304, 5n218, 5n342, 5n547, 5n860, 5n861, 6.8
Gazara (Gazera, Gezera, Gezer), 5.83, 5n225, 7.77, 7.301, 7n292, 7n1107
Gazera: *see* Gazara
Geba: *see* Gebal
Gebal (Gibeah of Benjamin/ Geba/ Gabaa of Benjamin), 6.95, 6n374, 6n376, 6n408, 6n409, 6n416, 6n420, 7n292; *see also* Gabatha
Geion (Gihon), 7.355, 7n1317
Gelboue (Gilboa), 6.328, 6.372, 6n1190, 6n1268, 6n1342, 7n1
Gelmon (Giloh), 7.197, 7n753, 7n860
Genesar, Lake of (Galilee, Sea of), 5.84, 5n228
Gerizim, Mount *see* Garizeis, Mount
Geseir: *see* Gessoura
Geshur: *see* Gessoura
Gessir: *see* Gessoura
Gessoura (Geshur/ Geseir, Gessir), 7.180, 7.187, 7n85, 7n697
Geth: *see* Gitta
Gethla (Gallim), 6.309, 6n1112
Geththaim, 6n452
Gezer: *see* Gazara
Gezera: *see* Gazara
Giah, 7n65
Giants, Valley called that of, the (Rephaim, Valley of, the, Titans, Valley of, the), 7.71, 7n270, 7n287, 7n1152
Gibeah: *see* Gabatha
Gibeah of Benjamin: *see* Gebal
Gibeon: *see* Gabao(n)
Gihon: *see* Geion
Gilboa: *see* Gelboue
Gilead: *see* Galadene
Gilgal: *see* Galgala
Giloh: *see* Gelmon
Gitta (Gai/ Gath-rimmon/ Geth/ Gath/ Gitton), 5.87, 5n232,

INDEX OF GREEK, LATIN, HEBREW, ARAMAIC, ARABIC, AND COPTIC-EGYPTIAN WORDS AND PHRASES

GREEK WORDS AND PHRASES

ἀγαθοὶ καὶ δίκαιοι, 6n528
τοὺς ἀγαθούς, 6n328
τὸ ἅγιον ἔλαιον, 6n200
τὸ ἀγγεῖον, ἔλαιον, 6n200
ἄγγελλος, 5n767
ἅγιος θεοῦ, 5n770
ἄγνοια, 6n442
ᾅδης, 6n1214
ἀκοσμία, 5n477
ἡ ἀκοσμία ἡ κατὰ τὴν πολιτείαν, 5n476
ἀλείφω, 6n592
τοῖς ἄλεσει τοῖς... Κλαυθμῶσι, 7n286
ἀλήθεια, 6n359
ἀλλότριος, 5n405
ἀλλόφυλοι, 5n690, 6n1155
τὰ ἄλση, 6n79
τοῦ ἄλσους τοῦ κλαυθμῶνος, 7n286
ἁμαρτίαν, 6n361
ἁμαρτίας, 6n361
ἀναβάς, 6n1154
ἀναρχία, 5n474, 6n321
ἀνὴρ ἐκ Ῥααζῆς, 7n1122
ἀνὴρ Μαδών, 7n1122
ἀοίδιμος, 6n595
ἀπανθρώπως, 6n1088
ἀπείχετο, 6n1175
ἀρετή, 5n609 (bis)
ἀριστοκοκρατούμενοι, 6n323
ἀριστοκρατέομαι, 6n320
ἀριστοκρατία, 5n354
ἄριστος, 6n306, 6n323
ἄρματα, 7n394
ἄρουρα, 6n1358
τῶν ἀρχαιων, 7n667
ἄρχων, 6n202
Ἀσιανός, 5n585
ἀσκήσεως, 6n1054
ἀσπίς, 6n632
Ἀστάρτειον, 6n1349
ἀστεῖος, 5n491
ἀτίμως, 5n125 (bis)
Ἀυαθ ἐν Ῥαμά, 6n785
αὐτοκράτωρ ἡγεμών, 5n754
ταύτην ἀφεῖναι τὴν ἁμαρτίαν, 6n361
ἄφες ἡμῖν τὰς ἁμαρτίας ἡμῶν, 6n361
Βαμά, 6n298
ὁ τῶν Ἰουδαίων Βασιλεύς, 7n273
βια-, 7n652
βιάζομαι, 7n652
βωμόν, 7n1234
βουλ-, 5n273
τὸ τοῦ θεοῦ βουλητὸν, 5n273
Γαλβουάθ, 6n785

γενόμενος ἔνθεος, 6n213
γερουσία, 5n52, 5n947
Γίγαντες, 7n1113
τῶν Γιγάντων, 7n270
γίνεται, 6n793
γηροκομία, 5n961
γνώσται, 6n1186
γραμματεύς, 7n451
γυμνός, 6n101
γυνή πόρνη, 5n700
δαιμονία, 6n602
δεινὸν ὄντα συνιδεῖν πράγματα, 7n126
δεσπότης, 5n115 (bis), 5n249
δημαγωγέω, 7n747
δημιουργός, 7n1386
διαβολαί, 6n960
οἱ διαβάλλοντες, 6n960
διαβάλλω, 6n960
διαθήκη, 5n147, 6n813, 6n905, 7n102
διάκονοι, 7n769
διακόρησις, 7n659
διαλλάττω / διαλλάττεται, 5n539
δίατια, 5n795, 5n865, 5n999
διαυγασθείς/ διαυγάζω, 5n1024
διευπραγέω, 6n710
δίκαιοι, 6n78, 6n528
δίκαιος, 5n251, 6n69 (bis), 7n442
δικαιοσύνη, 6n69
δικαιοσύνη καὶ θρησκεία, 6n67
δικαίως, 6n335
διυπνισθείς/ διυπνίζω, 5n1024
δοῦλος, 5n111
δυναστεία, 6n941
τῶν δυνατωτάτων, 7n209
δυστυχία, 5n1059
δῶρα, 5n486
δωρεά, 5n148
οἱ ἐγγαστρίμυθοι καὶ γνῶσται, 6n1186
ἐγγαστρίμυθος, 6n1186
ἑδραί, 6n13, 6n29
ἔθεος γενόμενος, 6n287
εἷς θεός, 5n259
ἑκάστοις, 6n114
ἔκφρων, 6n878
ἔκφρων γίνεται, 6n793
ἔλαιον, 6n200
ἐλευθερία, 5n101, 5n499
ἐλευθερόω, 5n499
ἐμφανίζω, 5n138
ἕνδεκα, 7n252
ἔνθεος/ ἔνθ(ε)ος, 6n213 (ter)
ἐξᾴδω, 6n605
τὴν Ἐπήκοον, 6n1047

ἐπίβουλος, 6n 1276
ἐπιγείοι, 6n680
ἐπιεικής, 6n360
ἐπιείκια, 6n360
ἐπιείκεια καὶ χρηστότης, 6n520
ἐπιθυμία, 7n555
ἐπιτυχής, 6n783
ὃς ἔργον . . . αὐτοῦ, 6n234
οὐχ . . . ἴδιον ἔργον, 6n234
ἐροῦσιν, 7n1200
ἑταιριζομένης/ ἑταιρίζω, 5n867
οἱ ἑταῖροι αὐτοῦ, 7n1285
εὐαγγελίζομαι, 5n81
εὐδαιμονία, 5n452, 5n463
εὐεργεσία, 5n304
εὐεργέτης, 5n675
εὐγενής, 6n470
εὐγενῶς καὶ μεγαλοφρόνως, 6n470
εὐθανάτως, 6n12
εὐμένεια, 5n558, 6n75
εὐμενής, 5n558, 6n75, 6n96, 6n1090
εὐμενής καὶ σύμμαχος, 6n96
εὐμενής... καὶ φίλος, 6n75
εὐνομια, 5n253, 5n264, 5n876, 6n117
εὔνους, 5n264
εὐσέβεια, 5n306, 5n930, 6n345, 7n992
εὐσεβής, 7n1423
εὐτυχία, 5n920
εὐψυχία, 6n1260
εὔψυχος, 6n1260
ἡγεμονία, 6n489
ζηλόω, 6n1251
τοῦ θείου πνεῦμα, 6n600
θεόπεμπτος, 6n59
θεοπρεπής, 6n1215
θεός, 6n327
θεός εἷς, 5n259
Θεοσεβής, 7n536, 7n602
τοῦ θεου, 6n782
τοῦ θεοῦ προφητεία, 6n496
θεοφιλής, 6n997
θρησκεία, 5n261, 6n67, 6n73
θρησκεία καὶ εὐσέβεια, 6n345
[τοῦ] θυμοῦ, 6n782
ἱερον . . . (τὰ) Σόλυμα, 7n244
ἱερός, 5n1016
τὸ... ἱεροῦ, 7n244
ἱλάσκομαι, 6n461
οἱ Ἰουδαῖοι, 6n99
ὁ τῶν Ἰουδαίων Βασιλεύς, 7n273
ἰσχύς/ ἰσχυρός, 5n794, 5n855, 5n872
καταβάς, 6n1154
κατακληρόω, 6n239
καταπηδάω, 6n1077
κατασοφίζομαι, 6n776

LATIN WORDS AND PHRASES

HEBREW WORDS AND PHRASES

ואבות ואת־הידענים, 6n1186
אחרי, 6n698
אין הקורא, 5n859
איש בליעל, 7n1027
איש מדה, 7n1122
איש מדון, 7n1122
אשם, 6n31
אשה זונה, 5n700
אשפר, 7n345
בהדשה: see הדשה
בור הסרה, 7n135
בית, 7n455
(ה)בכאים, 7n286
בצנור: see צנור
ברית, 5n147
גאל, 5n943
בגיות, 6n785
דודי / דדי, 7n1142
בהדשה, 6n780
החתי: see חתי
החשתי: see חשתי
הוקיע, 7n1090
היוצא, 5n715
עזים: see העזים
ראש: see הראש
רפה see: הרפאים / הרפה

השרי: see שרי
השן, 6n104
התרפים: see תרפים
חלצה, 7n60
החשתי, 7n1110
החתי, 6n1124
הידענים, 6n1186
יריב, 5n564
כבוד, 5n1064
כביר העזים, 6n770
כידון, 6n632
כלבו, 6n1054
כלבי, 6n1054
כליל, 6n93
כנור, 6n606
כנרות, 7n1134
כתנת פסים, 7n668
מנחה, 5n486
מדלק אחרי, 6n698
מעילים, 7n667
עולם, see מעולם
מרא, 5n916
משיחו, 6n570
משפט המלך / משפט המלכה, 6n255
נבלים, 7n1134
נגיד, 6n202, 7n1397

(ב)ניות / (ב)נוית, 6n785
נזיר אלהים, 5n770
(ב)ניות, 6n785
נציב, 6n375
נצבים, 5n211
מעולם, 7n667
העזים, 6n770
עפלים, 6n13, 6n29
פסים, 7n668
בצנור, 7n228
הראש, 7n780
רכב, 5n343, 7n394
רע / רעי, 7n1285
הרפאים, 7n1113
הרפה, 7n1096, 7n1123, 7n1127
שטן, 6n1276
השרי, 6n1173
שרים, 6n1271
שטרים, 7n1346
שלום, 7n244, 7n1247
שלטים, 7n411
שלשים, 6n703
שן: see השן
התרפים, 6n769

ARAMAIC WORDS

פונרקיתא, 5n18, 5n700

Flavius Josephus
Translation and Commentary

3. Feldman, L.H.; Mason, S.N. (ed.) Flavius Josephus. Judean Antiquities 1-4.
   ISBN: 9004106790

4. Begg, C.T.; Mason, S.N. (ed.) Flavius Josephus. Judean Antiquities Books 5-7.
   ISBN: 9004117857

5. Begg, C.T.; Spilsbury, P. (ed.) Flavius Josephus. Judean Antiquities Books 8-10.
   ISBN: 9004117865

9. Mason, S.N.; Mason, S.N. (ed.) Flavius Josephus. Life of Josephus. ISBN: 9004117938